In Memoriam

CORNELIUS WALWORTH MIDDLETON

1893-1966

Effective Advocate
Generous Benefactor
of Education

Trustee

VIRGINIA FOUNDATION
FOR INDEPENDENT COLLEGES

1959-1966

Political and Social Thought in the Contemporary Middle East

Political and Social Thought in the Contemporary Middle East

EDITED BY
KEMAL H. KARPAT

FREDERICK A. PRAEGER, *Publishers*
New York • Washington • London

FREDERICK A. PRAEGER, PUBLISHERS
111 Fourth Avenue, New York, N.Y. 10003, U.S.A.
77-79 Charlotte Street, London W.1, England

Published in the United States of America in 1968
by Frederick A. Praeger, Inc., Publishers

Library of Congress Catalog Card Number: 67-20484

Printed in the United States of America

Preface

This book is intended basically to provide students of Middle Eastern affairs with direct access to contemporary political and social thought in the area. A correct understanding of the Middle East requires close familiarity with the ideas that prepare the ground for political action and that justify it. The study of writings by Arab, Turkish, and Iranian intellectuals that appear in reviews and books is the best means to gain this familiarity. These writings, in addition, help the outside observer to gain a better understanding of how Middle Eastern intellectuals view events and issues in their own countries and in the world at large. Understanding is a two-way communication. Westerners need to know the thoughts and aspirations of other peoples at the same time that people in the rest of the world must know the thoughts and aspirations of the West.

Although some books and articles by Middle Eastern intellectuals have been translated into Western languages, mainly since World War II, they have not provided the means for a comprehensive, comparative study of major contemporary currents of thought in the Middle East. Consequently, this book attempts to present a broad, comparative view of Middle Eastern thought through a selection of appropriate writings. With few exceptions, none of the extracts have previously been published in English. A few have appeared in French, in various issues of *Orient,* which has pioneered the translation of Middle Eastern writings.

In preparing a book of this kind, an editor is faced with various methodological possibilities. He may, for example, classify the currents of thought into various categories with well-determined characteristics and select texts accordingly. Or he may follow a historical approach and choose material to indicate, step by step, the evolution of a particular current of thought. Both approaches, however, are guided by the compiler's understanding and interpretation of what he regards as the main current of thought at a given time. Moreover, an editor may be persuaded to accept a text as important because of its clarity and comprehensiveness rather than because of its actual place and impact in the society from which it derives. Contemporary writing in the Middle East cannot be classified in well-determined categories because there is much overlapping of ideas of nationalism, socialism, modernism, cultural reformation, and other subjects. Some writings are so comprehensive that they can be fitted into almost any category, while others require a special category of their own. Although the historical approach is relatively sound, the tendency in the Middle East to ignore many writings of the past renders the element of thought continuity rather tenuous. The Middle Eastern intellectual reveres history but rarely reads it.

I have followed an entirely empirical method in selecting the material for this book. First, from various sources, I accumulated a list of authors and texts related to Middle Eastern political and social thought. My courses at New York University and a preliminary reader compiled for a summer seminar at Columbia University served as preparatory steps. Subsequently, I spent the summers of 1964 and 1965 in the Middle East interviewing newspaper and magazine publishers, politicians, writers, scholars, and students. I asked these people to define the main political and social issues of public interest and to name the most influential writers and, if possible, some of their principal works. My ultimate choice of texts was determined primarily by issues and only secondarily by the personality or style of the authors. My purpose was to accumulate texts that would give a broad picture not only of the major political and social currents in the area but also of various social groups, self-interpretive opinions, causes of change, and the like. Texts by a few important writers associated with Middle Eastern thought were omitted either because their writings had lost their current appeal or were too didactic. Yet, writings by several men no longer alive, such as Hasan al-Banna and Antun Saadeh, were included mainly because their ideas continue to exert an influence. Articles by relatively unknown writers were selected either because they were by dissenters from generally accepted views or because they expressed a viewpoint that may become significant in the near future. Moreover, since public opinion in the Middle East, as elsewhere in the world, is formed by a mixture of propagandistic writings and carefully formulated thoughts, I did not hesitate to include examples of both. A few of the authors casually paraphrase or quote passages, often from memory, from Western writers. It is tradition, in Islam, to back a statement by referring to, or quoting from, an authority. But by not giving full references, some contemporary authors make it virtually impossible to locate their sources. Consequently, such quotations should be regarded as part of the writer's ideological argument rather than as accurately representing the thought of the original author.

The texts have been arranged for convenience according to topics that correspond approximately to what may be considered as the principal currents of thought in the Middle East today. The arrangement, however, is not based on, nor does it establish, well-defined categories, since the contemporary ideology of transition in the Middle East defies precise classification.

The book consists of a general introduction and three major sections. Each of these sections—Arab, Turkish, and Iranian—is preceded by an introductory survey of thought development, and each selection by a brief biography of the author and, if his ideology is at all influential, by an analysis of it and suggestions for further reading. Thus, there are relatively long analyses—and annotations—of the Muslim Brotherhood, the Ba'ath, and various other important issues or groups. Although the translations of the texts have been somewhat simplified and adapted to English usage, the original style has been preserved as much as possible. The titles of some of the extracts have been changed. The Arabic transliterations are adapted from the system used by the *Middle East Journal;* the Turkish and Iranian transliterations are the compiler's.

Iran has not been treated extensively, first, because political thought in that country pertains basically to the establishment of a truly constitutional monarchy and, second, because I was unable to undertake field research in Iran and so gain personal insight into the problems of that country as I did elsewhere in the Middle East. Although originally, in order to point out similarities and differences, I had hoped to compare contemporary thought in Israel with that in the Arab world, I was not able to do so, partially because of lack of space and partially because I found it difficult to fit Israel organically into the general historical introduction. Fortunately, this omission is compensated for by the fact that there are several excellent anthologies of Israeli or Zionist thought.

Although the military events of June, 1967, in the Middle East occurred after much of this book had been typeset, those events will presumably affect few of the basic views expressed herein. In all likelihood, however, the Arab-Israeli conflict of 1967 will exacerbate the ideological debate in the Arab world, and the leftward trend will continue, with an increasing emphasis on the virtues of organization, science, and indoctrination.

Compiling a work of this kind requires the cooperation of a great number of people and entails many years of tedious toil and frustrations that are well known to those who have worked on similar projects without the aid of sophisticated bibliographical tools. (The main one available in this case was Fahim I. Qubain's very useful *Inside the Arab Mind* [Arlington, Va.: Universal Printers and Lithographers of America, 1960].) I have striven to do my best in such a situation, and I hope that others, perhaps with greater financial and other assistance, will produce works that are more complete.

My thanks go to the many people who contributed to this book in various ways. Drs. Don Peretz and Ward Morehouse of the Area Studies Program of the University of the State of New York sponsored the project and provided its main support. Mr. Tarif Khalidi, of the American University of Beirut (AUB), rendered invaluable assistance in translating Arabic materials; Professor Frank Tachau of Rutgers University and Dr. Sakina Berenjian helped to translate the Turkish and Persian texts. The advice of Professors Nicola Ziadeh, Nabih Faris, and Constantin Zurayk of AUB and the work of Mr. Adnan Bakhit greatly facilitated my selection of Arabic texts. Professors Yusuf Ibish and Walid Khalidi of AUB kindly contacted many leading politicians and writers in Beirut, allowed me extract passages from their valuable source book *Arab Political Documents 1963*, and put at my disposal the secretarial facilities of their office. For their advice and time, I am grateful to the editors and staff of *al-Akhbar, al-Amal, al-Ba'th, al-Hayat, Hivar, al-Jumhuriyya, al-Nahar, al-Yawm, Ruz al-Yusuf,* and others; to many leaders of political groups and to writers too numerous to mention; and to various Arab information offices. Thanks also are due to the librarians of AUB, Mr. Bekhazi and Miss Linda Sadaka, and to the librarians of the Turkish National Library. For information and advice, I extend my thanks to Mr. Sina Akşin of Robert College of Istanbul, Dr. Kenan Bulutoğlu of the University of Istanbul, Mr. Yaşar Nabi, the editors of *Yön,* and various newspaper editors in Turkey. The editors of *Middle East Journal* and *Middle Eastern Affairs* graciously permitted me to reproduce texts. Dr. Barbara Stowasser skillfully transliterated and clarified Arabic terms and nomenclature and established the basis for an index. The editors at Frederick A. Praeger, Inc., rendered various gallant services. Whatever errors occur—despite all this competent assistance—are entirely my own.

K. H. K.

December, 1967

Contents

Political and Social Thought
in the Contemporary Middle East

INTRODUCTION

Sources and Functions of Ideology

The Middle East, like other developing areas, is in ideological ferment. The political and social ideas expressed in the various nations of the Middle East are an inseparable part of the general process of modernization. Primarily action-oriented, they are, in fact, the intellectual justification for material developments as well as an attempt to incorporate empirical acts in an intellectual framework. Ideology in the Middle East thus embodies the values associated with modernization and is as important in understanding it as the material forces that triggered modernization.[1]

Middle Eastern political thought comprises, in varying degrees, the four elements accepted as general characteristics of ideology: a philosophy of history, an analysis of man's present stage of development, a projection into the future, and a plan of action.[2] Each characteristic assumes peculiar forms according to the historic cultural, social, and political conditions specific to the area. A brief analysis of the rise of modernist thought in the Middle East may explain the political and social functions of ideology in the area.

The principal source of ideological upsurge in the contemporary Middle East is the social dislocation caused by the breakdown of the traditional social and political order. Traditional society was divided basically into four social groups or estates: men of the pen, men of the sword, merchants and craftsmen, and food producers. Each social group had its assigned role, status, and function, and developed a philosophy of life, manners, expectations, modes of expression, and general attitudes according to its place and function in society. The traditional organization thus produced a division of labor each of which had a specific culture. The functions of government were determined by the needs of the community and the religious principles underlying the social structure. Government and religion—that is to say, authority and legitimization—in the traditional Muslim society of the Middle East had developed in intimate association with each other. Islam came to accept this social arrangement, despite contradictions with some of its basic monolithic principles and the fact that the social system originated in Greek thought and Persian practices. In other words, Islam incorporated in its social and political system elements of other cultures which it reinterpreted and adopted to its own dogma.

1. Since we consider ideology primarily within the framework of political action, we have used the terms "ideology" and "currents of thought" as synonymous. It is impossible to speak of philosophy in the Middle East in the Western sense of the word. Speculative, pure philosophy has enjoyed limited popularity in the Middle East since thought has been predominantly concerned with the organization and behavior of society.

2. L. H. Garstin, *Each Age Is a Dream: A Study in Ideologies* (New York: Bouregy & Curl, 1954), p. 3.

Government maintained this social arrangement by keeping each group in its assigned place. Numerous social conflicts, appearing in the form of heretical religious movements, created divisions within the existing order, but did not alter its basic structure and philosophy.

Since the social and political order was considered divinely prescribed, it was natural that the laws governing the order were also immutable. Consequently, man gained a certain sense of emotional security, inner contentment, and serenity in the belief that his place in society and the government that ruled him were determined by divine will. The disintegration of the traditional social order in the Ottoman Empire shook man's view of his role in society and his relation to the government, and eventually compelled him to create a new social and political order. The roots of modern ideology lie in this search for a new social and political order—that is, the modern state.

The economic and social basis of the old Ottoman system was the land system, which was organized to provide obedient support for the upper levels of the social structure. The *sipahi* (cavalryman) administered the *timar* (land unit), supervised its cultivation, and maintained its legal status and that of the peasant, thus indirectly assuring social stability in the rural areas of the empire. The disintegration of the timar system—that is, of the government's military and bureaucratic organization supervising a large segment of the rural economy—created the conditions for a new social mobility.[3]

The emergence of the *ayan* (notables) in the Ottoman provinces, chiefly after the seventeenth century, marked the beginning of class differentiation based on wealth and communal authority. The ayan were originally communal leaders, who gradually acquired tax collecting privileges, and in some areas replaced the sipahis as administrators of state lands. Eventually, in the eighteenth and nineteenth centuries, they challenged the power of the central government. In that period, the increase of trade with Europe, the introduction of manufactured goods from the West, and the government's need for revenue and its consequent search for new sources of income created patterns of social and economic relations unknown in the past. These relations intensified in the second half of the nineteenth and the beginning of the twentieth century and irrevocably disrupted the traditional concepts of social organization and government and their legitimizations based on Islam.

The disruption of the old social organization created a crisis of identity and political purpose, which first manifested itself among the ruling groups in the form of dissatisfaction with, and criticism of, the government system. The so-called modernization reforms in the Ottoman Empire, Egypt, and Iran in the nineteenth century aimed to re-establish political and social cohesion by simply reorganizing government institutions. The reforms failed to achieve the desired results, not only because of foreign interference, but also because the theory and practice of the reforms did not adequately take into account the

3. Discussed in Kemal H. Karpat, "Social Structure, Land Regime and Modernization in the Ottoman Empire," in William R. Polk (ed.), *Social Structure, Land Regime and Modernization in the Ottoman Empire,* to be published by the University of Chicago Press. For background information, see Charles Issawi, *Economic History of the Middle East, 1800–1914* (Chicago: University of Chicago Press, 1966).

causes of the changes. The new ruling elite (bureaucracy, military, and intelligentsia) monopolized power within the "modernized" government structure, justifying it largely on the basis of political tradition, as in the past. They disregarded the essential fact that the lower social groups supporting the new political edifice were undergoing a process of political and social awakening similiar in the long run to that of the "modernized" ruling groups. In due time, the wealthy agrarian, commercial, and other elite groups capitalized on the social discontent among the masses and used them to further their own ambitions. Thus, the forces that caused the disintegration of the old order also determined the nature of the emerging currents of thought.

The sources of ideology in the Middle East are, as stated, on the one hand in social dislocation and the crisis of identity—a new pattern of social differentiation and stratification—and on the other in the need to establish a new cohesive social and political order with an identity of its own, capable of reaching the material and intellectual standards of contemporary civilization and of solving the conflicts in the social body. Modern ideology began to develop in the Middle East as a search first for a collective identity and then for modernist goals. The search was conditioned by the society's own historical sense of identity and by the political goals of the modern states in which the new social arrangement took place. Each ethnic group glorified its own national characteristics. Turks, Arabs, and Iranians reinterpreted history to prove that they preserved their national identity and creative genius, which were not destroyed by alien influences, but only prevented from keeping abreast of modern civilization. Turks and Iranians did not hesitate to blame religion for the backwardness of their society. Arabs, being intimately identified with Islam, accused the Iranians and Turks of imprinting on Islam their authoritarian concepts of government and rigid class differentiation. In reality, less than a century ago, Turks and Arabs shared a common Islamic affiliation under the Ottoman Empire.

Ideology strove to reinterpret history, to create pride in the past and confidence in the future, and to identify an ethnic group with a geographic region. It also operated in the field of social reconstruction, attempting to redefine the relations among social groups, to establish new divisions of labor, and to assign responsibilities, with the ultimate purpose of achieving social cohesion and national solidarity. Moreover, ideology sought to relieve social tension by introducing the idea of social justice, which became, in fact, the most powerful motive for political action.

Ideology in the Middle East also performed an intellectual function within the general framework of modernization. It introduced new ideas by adapting them to indigenous forms of expression and values, and eventually claimed to have created a new—albeit eclectic—national ideology. The claim to possess a national ideology strengthened newly acquired political identities and facilitated further borrowing of ideas and values from other cultures without risking internal opposition. Ideology broke the limitations imposed by the old culture on the freedom and scope of thought. It added new dimensions to thought by introducing to it economic, social, and political elements. Thus, it helped achieve a sort of intellectual liberation, a renaissance (as it is often referred to in the Middle East), and a recognition of man's empiricism, on which the humanist edifices of modern culture and science could more easily be built. The idea that change, progress, better living—in a word, modernity—were induced scientifically by man was popularized through ideology.

All currents of thought in the Middle East had a common background and, as different aspects of the same continuous process of change, they remained related to each other. The successful execution of the course of action advocated by the ideology required some sort of directing authority. This authority turned out to be the government. Consequently, state intervention in economic, social, and cultural activities was advocated in one form or another by all major ideologies and became a common characteristic of Middle Eastern political thought. In this respect, all Middle Eastern ideologies may be considered statist. The state thus became the "source of inspiration and of authority for action . . . [and] built up [its image] as a source of power, knowledge, wisdom, [and] resourcefulness."[4] When the state espoused radical methods, it was able to justify them as necessary for the creation of the new life.[5]

In summary, ideology in the Middle East performed at least three basic functions. First, it strove to create a political identity, which served as the foundation of modern nationhood. In this capacity, ideology was nationalistic. Second, ideology attempted to consolidate the social content of the political state through a series of economic and educational measures. In this function, it was socialistic. Third, ideology attempted to enlarge the cultural and intellectual horizon of Middle Eastern society in conjunction with nationalism and socialism. The modernizing functions of ideology are embodied in nationalism and socialism.

Modes of Expression

The emotional, subjective, and unsystematic writing emanating from the contemporary Middle East has baffled Western observers. Some Westerners have, in fact, been insultingly critical, without bothering to seek the significance of this writing. Current Middle Eastern writing is, indeed, far inferior to the accomplished style and crisp expression of traditional Arab, Persian, and Turkish poetry. One must, however, place this writing in its proper context. It has caused revolutions, affected government policies, and produced mass movements. It is, in the last analysis, a powerful factor for political change, and it must be studied as such.

An Arab, a Turk, or an Iranian writes for a domestic audience and must

4. Yusif A. Sayigh, "Development: The Visible or the Invisible Hand," *World Politics*, XIII (July, 1961), 573. See also Malcolm H. Kerr, "Political and Ideological Aspects of Economic Development in the U.A.R.," paper presented to the Princeton University Program in Near Eastern Studies, May 14–16, 1964.

5. On this point, see Malcolm H. Kerr, "Arab Radical Notions of Democracy," in Albert Hourani (ed.), *Middle Eastern Affairs Number Three* (St. Antony's Papers, No. 16) (London: Chatto & Windus; Carbondale, Ill.: Southern Illinois University Press, 1964), pp. 9–40; see also Munif al-Razzaz, *Ma'alim al-hayat al-'arabiyya al-jadida* (*Foundations of New Arab Life*) (Cairo: Dar Misir, 1953).

convey his thoughts intelligibly and effectively to that particular audience. The writer must conform to native patterns of communication, using words and symbols with specific psychological effect, to persuade his readers. The most frequent form of persuasion in the Middle East is an appeal to the emotional and the personal, rather than to logical reasoning. Societies such as that of the Middle East—with a strong literary tradition and historic attachment to mysticism and religion, but forced to accept the changes imposed by progress—develop their own intricate processes of persuasion, through which they assimilate changes without acknowledging them. This process of assimilation is deeply rooted in the literature of the area. Many Middle Eastern political writers have been poets and novelists. The most successful modernizing poets and writers were those who could articulate modern ideas through the traditional forms of expression. Ahmet Mithat Efendi's educational novels in the Ottoman Empire were popular because he used the folk story genre. Political writing makes use of many literary techniques, such as metaphors, analogy, and allegory. The poet thus performs the function of social philosopher by using the traditional methods of persuasion to root new ideas. In fact, during this stage of intellectual development in the Middle East, any political writing was ineffective if the author disregarded the traditional forms of expression and that subtle mixture of myth and emotion with reality.

The writing of the Middle East is, nevertheless, changing rapidly. Rational, logical, and consistent thought and expression are a matter of intellectual training as much as the result of environmental influences. A transitional society, with all its traditional forms of organization disrupted and perverted, can produce only a fragmented, organically unrelated thought process. Many of the forms of contemporary ideology in the Middle East do not stem from the direct social experience of society, but are borrowed from abroad. Middle Eastern intellectuals agonize over the application to their own society of ideas and concepts developed in the West through centuries of consistent intellectual development. Arab intellectuals refer continually to a crisis of thought and spirit caused by the struggle between the past and the future, between materialism and spiritualism. The crisis will be resolved, many feel, through the discovery of an ideology that will galvanize all the dormant virtues of the Arab soul.

The stabilization of social and political life and the advent of a regular process of change may produce in the Middle East intellectual responses similar to those of the West. This admittedly deterministic view may be tempered with the observation that the Middle East is experiencing a literary revolution, especially in novel and short story writing. Prose is largely a modern import. Through prose, the Middle Eastern intellectual learns to organize his thoughts and relate them in an organic fashion to life around him. The present relatively advanced level of political writing in Turkey occurred only after one generation of writers developed through literature an organic, consistent thought process, capable of conceptualizing and expressing the intricacies of modern life. The same development will undoubtedly occur shortly in the Arab world. The modern short story and the novel, which are presently developing rapidly, will give Arabic prose the flexibility and precision it needs to describe social phenomena.

The Middle East swept in less than a century from a predominantly oral system of communication to the mass media of the twentieth century—the newspaper, radio, and television. Governments used these media to mobilize the masses politically and inadvertently, perhaps, to imbue them with the idea of change. The effect of the communications media and of the audience on the content of communications cannot be ignored. Contemporary Middle Eastern writing can be better understood if judged in the perspective of the above conditions—that is, the need of a cohesive political and social doctrine and the availability of modern mass media.

The Rise and Evolution of Nationalism

The development of nationalism in the Middle East was intimately associated with efforts to create a modern political system, the national state. Through the idea of the national state, the concept of the territorial state revolutionized traditional Middle Eastern thought. The true political modernization in the Middle East occurred within the framework of national statehood.[6] Thus, it resembled the process of national formation in Eastern Europe in the nineteenth century. It emphasized language, history, and culture. On the other hand, the struggle for liberation from Western domination made the process of nation formation in Arab countries resemble in some respects that of the African countries after World War II.

The Arab nationalist movement for separation and independence from the Ottoman Empire in 1908–16 was not identical in motivation and ideology with the anti-Western nationalist movement in Egypt after 1882 and in the Fertile Crescent after 1920. The Arab provinces of the Ottoman Empire did not have colony or mandate status. All provinces were equal within the framework of the Empire until the central government, failing to produce a successful, modern organization based on the universalist ideas of Islam, resorted to a nationalist, secularist political organization based on the supremacy of the Turkic ethnic group.

The early advocates of modernization, the Young Ottomans (1865–76), attempted to lay the theoretical foundations for a political organization that would preserve the basic Islamic characteristics of the Empire and incorporate into it the ideas of Western liberalism. They reached larger audiences with the press and literature in their attempt to create a new Ottoman identity and attachment to the fatherland.

Ottomanism, however, was essentially a legal concept. It ignored economic interest, ethnic and social origin, and language. It could not forgo the reliance on Islam, since religion was still the only force capable of achieving social cohesion and loyalty to the state. The ideology of the Young Ottomans thus became an Ottoman nationalism rooted psychologically in Islam. It had no ap-

6. Bernard Lewis, *The Emergence of Modern Turkey* (London and New York: Oxford University Press, 1961), and Bernard Lewis, *The Middle East and the West* (Bloomington, Ind.: Indiana University Press; London: Weidenfeld & Nicolson, 1964).

peal, therefore, to the various Christian groups in the Empire, such as the Greeks, Bulgarians, and Maronite Arabs, whose commercial middle classes and Western-educated intellectuals had laid the ideological foundations for their independence and nationhood.

Though temporarily successful among the Muslims, Ottomanism eventually proved to be powerless. New solutions were needed. Some thirty years later, Yusuf Akçura (Akçoraoğlu) accurately analyzed the dilemma of political modernization in the Ottoman Empire. In his classic *Üç Tarz-i Siyaset (Three Political Ways)*, first published in Cairo in 1904, he pointed out that Pan-Islamism and Ottomanism were no longer suitable as bases of a modern political organization. Ottomanism rejected the idea of an ethnic nation—or a true nation, as he described it—and Islamism could not appeal to Christians. Akçura advocated Turkish nationalism, since this ideology could bring together all Turks and make them the foundation of the new state. This became the policy of the Young Turks (1908–18). It is understandable that the political ideas of the Young Ottomans, developed to correspond to social realities in 1865–76, did not appeal to the twentieth-century Young Turk movement. The Young Turks adopted from the Young Ottomans only those precepts—such as loyalty to fatherland and nation—that had lasting practical value.

The Young Turks, stressing Turkish national characteristics, departed radically from the Islamic universalism and expressly anti-Turkist policy of Ottomanism. The divisive impact among Muslims of this nationalist policy was dramatically illustrated in the poems of Mehmet Akif (d. 1936), the author of the text of the Turkish national anthem. In his "From the Rostrum of Suleymaniye," he cried in 1912: "Is it the devil that put into your mind the idea of nationalism? Nationalism shall destroy from its foundations Islam which keeps under one nationality so many different national groups."[7] Obviously, if ethnic origin, language, and territory were given priority, and the state was reshaped accordingly, religious ties and a sociopolitical system based on religion lost their importance. The Young Turks' glorification of Turkish national history and character, their attempt to introduce Turkish in all schools, and the secularist thought implicit in all these attempts were the initial factors in the undermining of Islamic unity in the Middle East. They carried out their ideas by instituting practical measures intended to establish a central administration and to bring under its control the various areas and groups that had preserved semiautonomous administrative status, e.g., the Muslim holy lands in the Hijaz.

The economic and social changes in the Ottoman Empire at the beginning of the twentieth century created new social and economic aspirations which were eventually included in the general term populism. Indeed, populism emerged at the turn of the century as a new dimension of modernization and included nascent economic and social aspirations in the form of a unique egalitarianism. It proposed to bridge the gap between the elite and the masses, spread education, establish a national economy, and reform government in-

7. Cevdet Kudret, "Mehmet Akif," *Yön (Direction)*, Istanbul, No. 196 (December, 1966), 8.

stitutions to serve society's needs. Thus, nationalism began to derive part of its force from social demand. (Many studies of the Middle Eastern nationalism, however, tend to overlook the social foundations of this ideology.)

The Young Turks' nationalism, with its secular orientation, threatened to reduce the Muslim Arabs to the status of a secondary ethnic group. Consequently, the nationalist ideas of the Ottoman Empire's Christian Arab subjects, expressed in various forms toward the end of the nineteenth century, began to appeal to the Empire's Muslim Arab subjects. The Arab students' convention in Paris in 1913, often cited as the first formal expression of Arab nationalism, claimed allegiance to the Ottoman Empire, but demanded decentralization and local government. Those reforms, if granted, would have jeopardized the integration the Young Turks rightly considered a prime condition of nationhood.[8] Foreseeing the downfall of the Ottoman Empire in World War I and aware that the Young Turks, if victorious, would pursue their nationalist policy, the Arab nationalists eventually decided to support the British. The exchange of letters between Sharif Husayn of Mecca with the British, in which the British agreed to independence for the Arabs, was followed by the Arab Rebellion of 1916, which cut Arab links with the Ottomans.[9]

The results of the Arab and Turkish nationalist efforts were thus determined by World War I. The defeat and disintegration of the Ottoman Empire in 1918 was not only an international event, but the beginning of an important transformation of the area internally. The Middle East as a whole, after existing for thirteen centuries under imperial forms of government, finally entered the age of modern nationhood.

The modern unitary (national) state in the Middle East began to emerge after the religiously legitimized sociopolitical organization of the Ottoman Empire broke down. This "emergence" was, in fact, a continuous process, operating at several levels. Politically, it called for integration around a new political authority exercising effective control over the people and territory that comprised the nation. At this stage, however, there was no nation in the cultural and historical sense of the word. The state consequently assumed the responsibility for creating a nation with an identity and national consciousness of its own, as other empires did when they broke up into nations. It developed a nationalist ideology and used it to define its own future goals. These goals became a unifying factor among the various social groups and a form of legitimization for the state authority. The state strove to identify itself with the nation by describing its actions in terms of their benefits to the nation. At the social and cultural levels, the modern state attempted to integrate all social groups

8. See C. Ernest Dawn, "From Ottomanism to Arabism: The Origin of an Ideology," *The Review of Politics,* III (1961), 378–400; and H. Z. Nuseibeh, *The Ideas of Arab Nationalism* (Ithaca, N.Y.: Cornell University Press, 1956), pp. 49 ff. The classic book on Arab nationalism—George Antonius, *The Arab Awakening: The Story of the Arab National Movement* (London: Hamish Hamilton, 1938; Philadelphia: Lippincott, 1939)—overemphasizes the role of the Lebanese Christians in the development of Arab nationalism.

9. Zeine N. Zeine, *Arab-Turkish Relations and the Emergence of Arab Nationalism* (Beirut: Khayat's, 1960), pp. 137–38.

into the new system by developing a national identity and a new sense of community, not necessarily by destroying the traditional values and loyalties, but by incorporating them, when feasible, into the value system of the new political structure. It stressed the cultural and linguistic characteristics of the dominant majority group, and claimed a geographic area to which it could be historically related.[10]

After 1918, one cannot speak of a commonly shared Middle Eastern ideology or political aspiration. Henceforth, one must deal separately with Arabs, Turks, and Iranians, as each country or group of countries tried to fashion its own nation-state. Iran had preserved its national boundaries, which had begun to be formed in the sixteenth century, but it, too, strove to create a modern, integrated national state. After achieving independence in a bitter struggle with the occupying Allied powers in 1919–22, Turkey embarked under an authoritarian regime onto a vast program of nation-building. The Arabs, exchanging Ottoman rule for the French and English mandate, fought for national independence. After World War II, the Arabs finally gained their independence and began to build a modern Arab national state. Whether this would be unitary or federal, socialist or democratic, was secondary to the creation of Arab national consciousness. Constantin Zurayk pointed out as early as 1938 that no Arab national renaissance was possible without a national philosophy that would establish goals and methods of achieving those goals. A national revival could succeed only by

> considering carefully the means and the ends involved, by defining the meaning of nationhood and nationalism, establishing the special traits and characteristics of the Arab nation and making manifest its special place among the nations and the role it has fulfilled in the past . . . and [will] fulfill in the future . . . through the creation of a comprehensive, clear and systematic national philosophy.[11]

This still remains a central problem.

The foreign policy of the Middle Eastern countries had a profound effect on the course of nationalism and on the very concept of modernism. After World War II, Arab nationalism adopted an anti-Western stand. It stood for nonalignment and neutralism and often rejected Western civilization, even

10. I am aware of the fact that many scholars may not share my viewpoint. For instance, Gustave E. von Grunebaum, *Modern Islam: The Search for Cultural Identity* (Berkeley, Calif.: University of California Press, 1962), p. 221, rejects the idea that the Arab Middle East is engaged in nation-building. In support of his view, he quotes a work by Rashid Rida (1865–1935) to prove that the Arabs placed religious above national allegiance. I believe that the conflict between national and religious allegiance is bound to continue for some time but that the victory belongs to the nation. See also Gustave E. von Grunebaum, "Problems of Muslim Nationalism," in Richard N. Frye (ed.), *Islam and the West* (The Hague: Mouton & Co., 1957), pp. 7–40. At the time this Introduction was written, I had not been able to consult E. I. J. Rosenthal, *Islam in the Modern National State* (Cambridge: Cambridge University Press, 1966).

11. Constantin Zurayk (Qustantin Zuraiq), *al-Wa'y al-qawmi* (*National Consciousness*) (Beirut: n.p., 1940), pp. 19–22. Quoted in Shimon Shamir, "The Question of a National Philosophy in Contemporary Arab Thought," *Asian and African Studies* (Jerusalem: Israel Oriental Society, 1965), p. 1. See also Hasan Sa'b, *al-Wa'y al-'aqidi* (*Ideological Awareness*) (Beirut: Dar al-'ilm lil-malayin, 1959).

though in practice it continued to emulate its achievements. The creation of Israel, with the support of the West and on the Western model of political organization, exacerbated Arab opposition to the West and its culture.

In Turkey, after 1923, there was little question that modernization necessitated a wholesale adaptation of and identification with Western values. However, the Cyprus dispute chilled Turkey's relations with the West after 1963 and stimulated an anti-Western cultural reaction. The socialists and Marxists led the anti-Western drive, using, in a new social context, many of the ideas originally put forth by the Islamists and conservative nationalists. Iran falls into the same category as Turkey; the anti-Western feeling among some members of the intelligentsia is fueled by Western oil concessions.

Nationalism and Secularism

Nationalism must have an emotional content in order to generate enthusiasm and loyalty on behalf of its goals. In other words, nationalism must also be viewed as a system of values. In the Middle East, Islam is considered the mainstay of culture and the binding force among all social values. One must, however, distinguish between the original values and culture stemming from Islam proper and those that were already in existence and were gradually incorporated into the belief system of Islamic society. The physical environment, the family, the community, historical experience, and tradition formed the bases of subcultures, which in turn created value systems of their own. The Islamic belief system, however, superseded them in terms of scope and loyalty, although without fully assimilating them. The coexistence of a purely religious culture with a nonreligious subculture is possible only to the extent that the prevailing system of thought does not recognize their separate sources or functions. In practice, the religious and nonreligious cultures follow their own pattern of development. Thus, in the Middle East the subcultures developed under the impact of geographic, economic, and social forces not related to religion. Religious culture answered spiritual needs, and nonreligious cultures responded to worldly needs, although the distinction was never formally made. In the case of the Arabs, whose cultural identification with Islam was greater than that of the Turks and Iranians, the distinction was almost impossible.

Nationalism relied essentially on various nonreligious subcultures within a specific region, and eventually tried to integrate these subcultures into one dominant national culture. The religious culture in turn became a subculture —although, in some places, a major one in the new national political system.

In practice, however, this cultural operation was neither clear nor easy. The Muslim's only loyalty was to his religion. Consequently, modern Middle Eastern statesmen had to find the means to transfer to the national culture the various loyalties previously perpetuated by Islam, without destroying the social cohesion and solidarity built by the religious culture. The conflict for loyalty between politics and Islam was actually a matter of separating the subcultures from the purely religious culture and of creating a new secular loyalty to the modern state. The formal institutional separation of religion from politics could be accomplished only by a similar success in the field of culture.

The policies adopted by Middle Eastern statesmen toward this difficult social-psychological problem have differed in method but not in substance. A comparison between the policies of Atatürk in Turkey and Gamal Abdel Nasser in Egypt may illustrate the point. Although both adopted a secularist approach to the consolidation of the state, they accepted the importance of religion. Both came to power partly through the support of religious groups: Atatürk made wide use of the religious leaders of Anatolia in 1919-22; the Muslim Brotherhood supported the officers' revolution in 1952 that brought Nasser to power in Egypt. Both leaders turned against their former religious supporters because the religious hierarchy posed a challenge to the establishment of the modern national state. Both blamed the religious leaders for opposing the "true" spirit of Islam, which Atatürk and Nasser reinterpreted according to nationalist ideas.

Atatürk and Nasser differed, however, in their methods of action. Aware of the symbolic power of organized institutions, Atatürk methodically destroyed the political-educational institutions of Islam. He tried gradually to incorporate into the fabric of nationalism the political values, loyalties, and sense of identity promoted by Islam. Turkish nationalism had from the very beginning substituted itself for all feelings, values, and loyalties expressed through religion in the past. The years between 1930 and 1960 in Turkey may be considered a period of nationalist assimilation of subcultures and of Islam as well. A certain separation also occurred. The religious system began to acquire certain spiritual characteristics that conformed, to some extent, to the Western understanding of religion, and some now claimed independence from state control because religion had acquired these spiritual features and could no longer impair the government's worldly tasks. Nasser, on the other hand, maintained Islamic institutions almost intact in Egypt and gradually incorporated them into his modernist state. Without challenging the existence of the religious establishments, he tried to invest them with some modern functions on behalf of Arab nationalism, which came to be synonymous with the religious definition of Arabism. Islam in Egypt was formally affiliated with, although subordinated to, the state. Coexistence between state and religion, however, was possible only to the extent that the religious hierarchy believed state actions conformed basically to Islamic precepts. Modern national statehood—that is, nationalism, whether Turkish or Arab—cannot act forever in consensus with organized religion, especially in view of the political system's need to justify its deeds sooner or later in secular terms. Nationalism inevitably made secularism a condition for its own survival.

The conflict between the state and Islam is taking shape in Egypt (U.A.R.). Some members of the faculty of al-Azhar University in Cairo have timidly rejected the separation of state from religion as an artificial concept borrowed from the West. They have advocated a state policy that would attempt to fulfill the commandments of Islam. Consequently, some Arab intellectuals with a predominantly religious viewpoint have rejected the idea of Arab nationalism as formulated by Nabih Faris, Fayez Sayegh, Hazem Z. Nuseibeh, and other nationalists, who have claimed that Arabism, as it is understood by the Islamists, is not nationalism. In their view, nationalism is an ideology exclusive of religious affiliation while Arabism is an integral part of Islam.[12]

Socialism in the Middle East

In its politically meaningful phase, socialism developed in the Middle East almost entirely after World War I and, especially, World War II. Its birth was preceded and conditioned by the rise of nationalism and statehood, usually after monarchy or foreign rule were toppled by political revolution.[13] The beginnings of socialism may be traced to the nineteenth century, when all nationalist thinkers and movements had social purposes. The Young Ottomans, the 'Urabi revolt of 1882 in Egypt, the Young Turks, the workers' strike of 1908-9 in Turkey's Balkan provinces and of the socialist parties of the Ottoman Empire in 1908-11, and a series of scattered writings expressed social discontent of some sort.[14] But these lacked a rationally formulated, comprehensive scheme of social organization, possessed little understanding of the forces causing social unrest, had limited popular following, and ignored economic development and political action as means for attaining social goals.

Socialism in the Middle East is an extension of nationalism. It aims to consolidate the power of the modern state through an internal reorganization of the productive forces and a reassignment of roles and responsibilities, with the idea of creating a participant society. It proposes to create social consciousness, responsibility, and dedication to ideas above individual interests and loyalties. It strives to arouse mass enthusiasm on behalf of its goals by appealing to the social ethics rooted in the native culture and by creating desires and expectations. Socialism in the Middle East has two facets. It may appear as a rejection of the Western economic system (capitalism), of excesses of individual economic power, and of class differentiation. Socialism may also appear as an egalitarian movement to eradicate differences of wealth and position and thus pave the way for the social integration necessary for the survival of the modern state.

12. See Isma'il Ragi A. al-Faruqi, *On Arabism: 'Urubah and Religion—A Study of the Fundamental Ideas of Arabism and Islam at its Highest Moment of Consciousness* (Amsterdam: Djambatan, 1962). The following bibliographical articles provide an excellent view of currents of thought in the Arab world until the ealy 1950's: Nicola A. Ziadeh, "Recent Books on the Interpretation of Islam," *Middle East Journal,* V (1951), 505–10, and "Recent Arabic Literature on Arabism," *Middle East Journal,* VI (1952), 468–73; Nabih Amin Faris, "The Arabs and Their History," *Middle East Journal,* VIII (1954), 155–62; Nissim Rejwan, "Arab Nationalism in Search of an Ideology," in Walter Z. Laqueur (ed.), *The Middle East in Transition: Studies in Contemporary History* (London: Routledge & Kegan Paul; New York: Frederick A. Praeger, 1958), pp. 145–65.

13. See *President Gamal Abdel Nasser's Speeches and Press Interviews* (Cairo: Information Department, 1962), p. 177.

14. For the history of socialism in the Arab world, see Nicola Haddad, *al-Ishtirakiyya* (*Socialism*) (Cairo: Dar al-hilal, 1920); Kamel S. Abu Jaber, *The Arab Ba'th Socialist Party* (Syracuse, N.Y.: Syracuse University Press, 1966), pp. 1–7, and his *Judhur al-Ishtirakiyya* (*Roots of Socialism*) (Beirut: Dar al-tali'a, 1963). For Turkey, see Huseyin Avni (Sanda), *Bir Yarı Müstemleke Olus Tarihi* (*The History of Semicolonialism*) (Istanbul: Sinan Matbaası, 1932); L. Erisçi, *Türkiye'de Isçi Sınıfının Tarihi* (*History of the Workers' Class in Turkey*) (Istanbul: Kutulmuş Basımevı, 1951); and Mete Tunçay, *Türkiye'de Sol Akımlar* (*Leftist Currents in Turkey*) (Ankara: Sevinç Matbaası, 1967).

Socialism is also a kind of a modern moral system. It draws much of its ethical-moral strength from both Islam and the West. The Islamic ideas of charity, social justice and responsibility, mutual assistance, and communal solidarity, reinterpreted in the light of contemporary needs, provide powerful bases for socialist action. Even some conservatives in the Muslim Brotherhood, such as Mustafa al-Siba'i, used the teaching of Islam to develop an Islamic brand of socialism. Other social-minded Muslim scholars, such as Mahmud Shaltut, the former head of al-Azhar, relied on Islamic ideas to justify the social and economic policies of his government. In Turkey, too, many contemporary socialists strive to prove that there is no conflict between modern socialism and the social purposes of Islam.[15]

The other source of socialism was the West. Indeed, the secular understanding of man and justice, of man's enlightenment achieved through education and science, which occupies such a central position in Middle Eastern socialism, came from the West. Middle Eastern intellectuals became acquainted with various versions of Western socialism after the turn of the century. They borrowed social ideas rather indiscriminately from Fabianism, Darwinism, Bergsonism, welfare socialism, and Marxism. Western socialism appeared at this stage as a condemnation of the unjust aspects of Western civilization, while simultaneously demonstrating that the same civilization had preserved humanitarian and altruistic ideals. Some early Middle Eastern socialists, such as Salama Musa, admired Western intellectual achievements and advocated emulating them, at the same time that they condemned Western imperialism. Although they occasionally had roots in Islamic belief, socialist arguments in favor of social justice, egalitarianism, and elimination of class differences were based primarily on the writings of Western socialists.

Participation in the production of wealth became the outstanding feature of socialism after World War II. The basic purpose of this approach was to create national economic self-sufficiency, which appeared to be the principal condition for progress in all areas. After World War I, Atatürk expressed the idea in the form of a call for all social groups to create wealth; Nasser strove constantly to convince the masses that the chief benefits of socialism would come only if they applied themselves to its tasks.[16] At present, the overwhelming majority of socialists in the Middle East have accepted the idea that economic development is essential to the success of their doctrine. The idea of building a just social system on the material foundation of economic efficiency was socialism's major contribution to Middle Eastern thought.

The acceptance of economic development as the vehicle of social progress transformed socialism into a method of action and returned to the government primary responsibility for drawing up and enforcing plans for economic devel-

15. Mehmet Emin Bozarslan, *Islamiyet Açısından Şeyhlik-Ağalik* (*Sheyhs and Agas from the Viewpoint of Islam*) (Ankara: Joplum Yayınevi, 1964); and A. Cerrahoğlu, *Islamiyet ve Sosyalizm Bagdaşabilir mi?* (*Can Islam and Socialism Be Reconciled?*) (Istanbul: B. Kervan, n.d.).

16. Fayez Sayegh, "The Theoretical Structure of Nasser's Socialism," in Albert Hourani (ed.), *Middle Eastern Affairs Number Four* (St. Antony's Papers, No. 17) (London and New York: Oxford University Press, 1965), pp. 20 ff.

opment. Thus, the government became the ideological-organizational nucleus around which postwar Middle Eastern socialism developed. Statism would, in fact, be a more appropriate name for this kind of socialism.[17]

Middle Eastern socialism rejects class struggle, even though it does not hesitate to condemn the former regimes for having been dominated by feudalists, capitalists, and agents of the West. Socialism stresses unity at all costs and condemns any opposition—regardless of whether it is led by Communists or ordinary dissatisfied citizens—as divisive and subversive. Middle Eastern socialism is promoted mainly by intellectual elites who are supposed, as Nasser expressed it, "to build a mighty structure for their homeland . . . direct their country toward a specific goal . . . and gain insight into the people's hopes and aspirations."[18] This is the socialism of the elites, which has not yet faced squarely the challenge of populism.

In terms of political action and economic reorganization, Middle Eastern socialism has turned its back on the West. It has borrowed planning, administration, and industrialization techniques from the socialist countries of Eastern Europe. While firmly anti-Communist and pro-Western in its internal and external policies, even Turkey in the 1930's adopted many ideas on economic development and organization from the Russians. Yugoslavia served as a model for Egyptian socialism after 1956, and enjoys considerable popularity among Middle Eastern socialists for its successful combination of nationalism and Marxism, measured in practical terms as the ability to achieve national independence and economic development.[19] Some Marxist ideas on history and social classes and Leninist views on imperialism have entered into the stream of Middle Eastern socialism, chiefly since World War II. But Arab socialists have firmly rejected Communism. Middle Eastern socialism is also anti-Western, anti-imperialist, and anticapitalist. National independence is its major foreign policy goal. Consequently, it is only as friendly to the Soviet Union as is necessary to safeguard national independence. It rejects alignment with Soviet foreign policy and has lately developed considerable interest in Communist China, primarily as a means to offset any danger from possible Soviet-American collusion.

Middle Eastern socialism belongs in a special category. Use of the term socialism is inaccurate, since the socialism of the Middle East describes chiefly the social goals of modernization. One may divide socialism in the Middle East first according to the country and second according to its ideological characteristics. Egypt advocates Nasserite or Arab socialism; Syria, Ba'th socialism; Algeria, Algerian socialism; various groups in Lebanon promote progressive

17. The extensive authority acquired by governments, first on behalf of nationalism and then of socialism, conforms, according to some scholars, to the traditional concepts of the state in the Middle East.

18. *President Gamal Abdel Nasser's Speeches and Press Interviews*, p. 178.

19. Malcolm H. Kerr, "The Emergence of Socialist Ideology in Egypt," *Middle East Journal*, XVI (Spring, 1962), 127–44. See also Hisham Sharabi, "The Transformation of Ideology in the Arab World," *Middle East Journal* (Autumn, 1965), pp. 471–86. An excellent survey of Arab political development is Charles F. Gallagher, "Language, Culture and Ideology: The Arab World," in K. H. Silvert (ed.), *Expectant Peoples: Nationalism and Development* (New York: Random House, 1963), pp. 199–231.

socialism; while Islamic and Marxist socialism are found among small groups throughout the Middle East. Only Islamic and Marxist socialism have international goals or look beyond their own national boundaries. Although it was for a brief period victorious in Iraq and enjoys some popularity among intellectuals in Jordan and Lebanon, Ba'th socialism seems to be limited to Syria.[20] The Arab nationalist movement, advocating Arab socialism, follows Nasser's social and political views on unity. It is active in several Arab countries, but its success has thus far been only moderate. It accepts class struggle to the extent necessary to defeat the Arab monarchies, which are allegedly supported by feudalists, capitalists, or the middle classes, created through association with the West and largely supported by the oil industry.

Of the various Arab socialist schools of thought, only the Ba'thist possesses a fairly broad doctrine. The Ba'thists have a Marxist view of social classes, rely on a political party to achieve revolution, accept secularism, and court social reconstruction and economic development as essential conditions for development. The Ba'th philosophers Michel 'Aflaq, Salah Bitar, and Nureddin Atasi claim that their ideology is original and corresponds to the social and spiritual characteristics of the Arabs. In reality, however, the core of their doctrine rests on Marxist materialism, while the remainder of their teachings are syncretic and oratorical additions to this base. Recent developments in Syria indicate that the Ba'th has deviated to the extreme left, following the logic of its basically Marxist beliefs.

Nasser's socialism rejects class struggle, accepts the petty bourgeoisie as "national capitalists," and strives to associate itself with peasants and workers through the Socialist Union, a loose organization dominated by Nasser himself. Nasser's Arab socialism emerged fully in 1961, well after the military took power in 1952, while the Ba'th developed its doctrine and organization simultaneously in the early 1940's, and then tried to acquire power. The Ba'th claims that Nasser borrowed many of its socialist and nationalist ideas in his bid to assume the leadership of the Arab world. Nasser won the race for this leadership, primarily because he had behind him a relatively well organized government and because he succeeded in winning over the Arab masses through modern communications media. Both types of socialism are becoming inadequate to meet the sophisticated demands of a modernized, complex Arab society. Both are challenged on the one hand by extreme Marxist socialism and on the other by the timid requests of some intellectuals for a more liberal democratic regime.[21]

There are striking similarities between the social and economic measures adopted by Turkey in the 1930's and the so-called socialist measures adopted

20. George Lenczowski, "Radical Regimes in Egypt, Syria and Iraq: Some Comparative Observations on Ideologies and Practices," *Journal of Politics,* XXVIII (1966), 29–56; Charles Issawi, "The Arab World's Heavy Legacy," *Foreign Affairs,* XLIII (1965), 501–12.

21. A perceptive discussion of currents of thought in the Arab world is Morroe Berger, "Ideology and Democracy in the Arab World," a paper submitted to the Princeton Conference on the Middle East, 1962. See also Leonard Binder, *The Ideological Revolution in the Middle East* (New York: John Wiley & Sons, 1964).

by some Arab countries after 1956. Despite marked differences in style, justification, and scope, Turkey and the Arab countries followed a common course in industrialization, economic planning, the nationalization of foreign enterprises, the replacement of minority middle classes with native ones, rejection of the class struggle, and bureaucratization of the economy. The present differences between the Turkish and Arab brands of socialism or statism have been determined by their different levels of cultural and economic development, foreign policy alignment, and the degree to which each country consolidated modern statehood.

The development of a pluralist social order in Turkey has brought about a marked change in the ideological role of the government. Socialist ideas in Turkey are now promoted by private groups, while in some Arab countries socialism is the official government ideology.

Despite the upsurge of the leftist Tudeh Party in Iran after World War II, socialist ideas in that country are still in their infancy.

Conclusion

Nationalism and socialism in the Middle East are ideologies of transition. Their basic functions are to establish a modern political organization and rejuvenate society, thus completing the transition to a new phase of life.[22] The ideologies of transition in the Middle East enabled society to acquire a modern identity and to adapt itself to new forms of modern organization. These ideologies are bound to disappear or to change in form and content once the main phase of the transition is completed. Subsequently, after the emergence of differentiated social, political, and economic systems, one may expect Middle Eastern ideologies to reflect more accurately the views of various social groups, rather than those of the government elites.[23] Further structural differentiation in the Arab world coupled with freedom of thought may stabilize the ideologies.

22. Albert Hourani, "Near Eastern Nationalism Yesterday and Today," *Foreign Affairs*, XLII (1963), 123–36.

23. See, on this point, Charles Issawi, "Social Structure and Ideology in Iraq, Lebanon, Syria, and the UAR," in J. H. Thompson and R. D. Reischauer (eds.), *Modernization of the Arab World* (Princeton, N.J.: Princeton University Press, 1966), pp. 141–49.

PART ONE

Political and Social Thought in the Arab Countries of the Middle East

I. *Introduction to Political and Social Thought in the Arab Countries of the Middle East*

Virtually no independent school of Arab political thought existed until nationalism emerged as an ideological force toward the end of the nineteenth century. In the past, practically every Muslim intellectual in the Middle East, regardless of his ethnic origin, had tried to interpret changing social and political conditions according to Islamic notions of government and authority. It was mainly the Christian Arabs of Lebanon and Syria—notably the Maronites and, to a lesser extent, the members of other Eastern churches—who had developed an interest in their local history and language as early as the eighteenth century.[1] Muslim Arabs, however, did not experience a truly nationalist awakening until the end of the nineteenth and the beginning of the twentieth century. (A large proportion of the educated Arab elite, "particularly in Syria and Iraq, received their education not so much from French and American schools and colleges, the importance of which has perhaps been overstressed, as from the educational institutions set up in the successive phases of the Ottoman reform. Consequently, many developments can only be fully appreciated in this larger context.")[2] The Wahhabi Movement, founded by Muhammad ibn 'Abd al-Wahhab (1703–87), was not a nationalist but a religious movement. Even the early nationalist writings, such as the manifesto of Faris Nimr and the poem of Ibrahim al-Yaziji addressed to the Arabs (c. 1879), were not so much nationalist appeals as exhortations to reject fanaticism and embrace a new outlook on life. The secret society established (c. 1882) in Beirut to evict the Ottomans attracted no support among the Muslims and dissolved itself.[3]

The nationalist endeavors of the Christian Arabs had a major handicap that Christian groups in the Ottoman Empire's Balkan possessions were spared: The overwhelming majority of the Arabs were Muslims. The language and culture used as bases for nationalism by the Christian Arabs had developed in intimate association with Islam and were consolidated under Ottoman rule. The Ottomans had masterfully used the Islamic concepts of government and social organization to build and justify their own political system, which in turn became an inseparable part of Islam itself. Even though the separation of government and religion was greatly accelerated in the nineteenth century, the religious justification of the political system did not change. The Empire continued to guarantee in theory the fundamentals of

1. Albert Hourani, *Arabic Thought in the Liberal Age, 1798–1939* (London and New York: Oxford University Press, 1962), pp. 55 ff.

2. Bernard Lewis and P. M. Holt (eds.), *Historians of the Middle East* (London and New York: Oxford University Press, 1962), p. 17.

3. Sylvia G. Haim (ed.), *Arab Nationalism: An Anthology* (Berkeley, Calif.: University of California Press, 1962), p. 5.

the *umma* (Islamic community)—its universality, faith, and integrity—against outsiders. Consequently, "modernist" political thought in the nineteenth century developed mainly in Istanbul, the Ottoman capital, and concerned itself chiefly with the adaptability of Islamic political concepts to Western representative institutions. The Young Ottoman school of political thought (1865), represented chiefly by Ibrahim Shinasi, Ziya Pasha, Ali Suavi, and Namik Kemal, along with nineteenth-century statesmen such as Hayreddin Pasha,[4] attempted unsuccessfully to reconcile modern and traditional concepts of government within the framework of the imperial-religious state.

Beneath the entire process of political and ideological transformation lay the basic changes that had gradually shattered the economic and social foundations of traditional Muslim society and its universalist government. A mere change in Ottoman political institutions could not solve the social and economic problems resulting from the disintegration of the traditional sociopolitical order. Broader measures were necessary. The eventual solutions were centralization (introduced after 1839) and nationalism, which provided administrative and ideological bases for a new sociopolitical reorganization. Turkish nationalism and secularism—promoted by the Young Turks in 1908–18 as principles of reorganization—undermined the political foundations of Islamic universalism and stimulated the rise of nationalism among the Muslims of the Empire. Albanian nationalism, which resulted in the creation of an independent Albanian state in 1912, is an excellent measure—better than Arab nationalism—of the impact of the Young Turks' nationalist policies.

The efforts of the Turkish political elite to improve the economic and social situation of its own ethnic group could only strengthen the determination of the Arabs and other ethnic minorities to establish their own states. The social transformation in the Arab lands was propitious for such a political endeavor. Although this transformation occurred much later, it was not essentially different from the social transformation in the Western sections of the Empire that led to the establishment of independent states in the Balkans. The Arabs had their own derebeys, ayan, middle classes, ulama, and governors—such as the Shihabs and Jumblats in Lebanon, Zahir al-'Umar in Galilee, and Baban in Kurdistan—who extended their hold over surrounding areas and aspired to national independence.[5]

Although they provide some social basis for the eventual evolution of Arab nationalism, these developments cannot be separated from the transformation of the Middle East as a whole that occurred within the Ottoman Empire. The rise of Egypt as a separate political system in open defiance of the Sultan at the beginning of the nineteenth century had far-reaching effects on the Ottoman Government and eventually on the Arab world. It is important to note that

4. Hayreddin Pasha (Khayr al-Din Pasha), prime minister of Tunisia, wrote a treatise on government in 1867.

5. Leading families, such as Tannus al-Shidyaq, claimed that Lebanon should be a separate independent nation. On the other hand, a new middle class, emerging in the market towns of Syria, Lebanon, and even Palestine, fought against the old feudal structure and in some cases even caused civil war (e.g., the civil war in Lebanon in 1960). Hourani, *op. cit.*, p. 235. See also Malcolm H. Kerr, *Lebanon in the Last Years of Feudalism, 1840–1864* (Beirut: Catholic Press, 1959), pp. 3 ff.

Egypt, despite occasional appeals to the Arabs, developed essentially as a national state. It took up the banner of Arab nationalism mainly after World War I. New currents of thought, occasionally stressing Arab nationalism, developed within the context of Egyptian nationhood and the slowly emerging Egyptian political system. Current works by Arab nationalists, however, aimed at preparing the ground for Arab unity, tend to stress the more universal Arab character of Egyptian nationalism rather than its particularist aspects.

Mehmet Ali (Muhammad 'Ali) (d. 1849), the founder of modern Egypt, was of either Albanian or Turkish origin. He came to Egypt at the time the Ottoman armies were fighting the French, who had invaded the country in 1798. Mehmet Ali remained there as a governor, seized power, and was recognized as a viceroy by the Sultan in 1805. He eventually embarked on an ambitious military, administrative, and economic program designed to establish a strong state and thus to ensure his position against possible attack by the Sultan. Mehmet Ali probably could not have risen to power without the defeat inflicted by the French on the Ottomans. One may ask whether Mehmet Ali could have established relatively modern political and military structures if his efforts had not been preceded by a series of internal social changes that prepared the ground for his reforms. A study of Egypt before 1800 could furnish rather edifying answers to this basic problem. Mehmet Ali was, after all, an ayan,[6] without a popular following. He defeated the ruling Mamluks by taking advantage of increasing popular dissatisfaction with them, liquidated the old feudal order, and established his own state in which a new landowning class and a small bourgeoisie became the dominant social forces. He was able to carry out these reforms because Egypt was prepared internally to move to a higher level of political organization. The French invasion was meaningful not because it demonstrated the inability of the Sultan to defend a Muslim territory—the Sultan had already lost many territories considered Muslim, including the Crimea and sections of the Balkan Peninsula, without impairing his religious authority—but because it facilitated the liquidation of a disintegrating social order and the subsequent establishment of a new political system.

The Ottoman Government imitated some of Mehmet Ali's most successful reforms and used Egypt, an orthodox Muslim country, as an example to prove that innovation and change did not undermine Islamic faith. The Egyptians, in turn—still recognizing formally the suzerainty of the Sultan and regarding him as the representative of the Islamic community—borrowed freely the ideas developed by the Young Ottomans. Indeed, the modernizing influences exerted on each other by the Ottoman and Egyptian intellectuals could provide new insights into the process of change in the Middle East and place the Western impact on the area in its proper perspective. The most important contribution of Egypt to ideological development in the Middle East was its political system, which conditioned a new pattern of socio-economic and cultural relations. These relations, developing in a relatively rational and secular spirit and amidst increasing social differentiation, provided the material bases

6. A notable, or a man of influence. *Ayan* (Arabic *a'yan,* the plural of *'ain*) is the form of the word generally used in English for both the singular and the plural.

for future ideological development. Consequently, Egypt provided the most fertile soil for the emergence of a new type of thinker.

The first thinker of renown, Rifa'a Badawi Rafi' al-Tahtawi (1801–73), belonged to an ancient landowning family that lost its fortune because of Mehmet Ali's tax policies.[7] Al-Tahtawi was inspired by classical Islamic ideas, but he also adopted a rational view of reality, possibly because of ideas acquired during his stay in Paris (1826–31). He pondered the idea of geographically limited communities and the theory that the "rise and fall of states was due to causes," and he related them to Egyptian society. Several of his writings deal specifically with Egyptian history and society and the type of economic activity necessary to restore Egypt's lost power. By stressing any given section of the body of ideas he developed, al-Tahtawi may be described as the precursor of nationalism or even of socialism.[8] While adhering closely to Islamic views, al-Tahtawi implied that changing conditions had altered both the nature of society and the function of government.[9]

Al-Tahtawi's philosophy was comprehensive enough to provide sound foundations for intellectual development, but modern Egyptian and Arab thought was not able to mature along these lines, largely because of European involvement in Egypt. The British occupation of Egypt in 1882 stimulated the rise of anti-Western nationalism and distorted the positive aspects of al-Tahtawi's philosophy. It eventually compelled nationalism to revert to Islam as the only ideological force capable of preserving the integrity and identity of Egyptian society. Hence, any effort by the British to modernize Egypt's social or political structure could easily have been interpreted as likely to undermine the society's culture and identity. This situation affected the entire process of change and modernization in the Arab world.

The independent states of Iran and Turkey had the illusion that they decided freely what to take from the West. Assured of political sovereignty and a corresponding national identity, they could play down the Islamic heritage and forestall the objections of Muslim theologians to imitation of institutions from the non-Islamic world.[10] Egypt, deprived of such assurance, had to

7. Anouar Abdel Malek (Anwar 'Abd al-Malik), *Anthologie de la littérature arabe contemporaine* (Paris: Éditions du Seuil, 1965), p. 34, describes al-Tahtawi as an humble *kuttab* (secretary) in order to show that rational thought and socialism arose among the lower classes. Hourani, however, points out that al-Tahtawi had a conventional Islamic view and stressed the supremacy of the Shari'a (Islamic law) over the ruler. Hourani, *op. cit.*, pp. 73–74. See also Ibrahim Abu-Lughod, *Arab Rediscovery of Europe* (Princeton, N.J.: Princeton University Press, 1963), pp. 49–62, 166–67.

8. This seems to be the case of Abdel Malek, who opens his anthology with an excerpt from al-Tahtawi's writings on the value of labor.

9. Hourani, *op. cit.*, p. 76.

10. The involvement or noninvolvement of Islam in nationalist movements among Muslim peoples was determined largely by the political status of those peoples. Iran and the Ottoman Empire (and later Turkey), enjoying independence, could adopt secularist policies, since their national identities were determined essentially by the political considerations of a national territorial state. The Turkic peoples in Czarist Russia, however, had no independence and had to rely on Islam to develop a sense of national identity, while trying to reform and enlighten their respective communities from inside. This question of political independence goes a long way to explain the rise

use Islam to mobilize popular support. It is quite understandable, therefore, that the Islamic Reformation—which had profound political consequences in the Middle East—found fertile ground for development in Egypt. The revolt of al-'Urabi precipitated the British occupation of Egypt in 1882 and strengthened the rise of an anti-Western nationalism.

British policy in Egypt, although far less motivated by considerations of cultural domination than, for example, French policy in Algeria and elsewhere, still seemed to pose a threat to Egypt's cultural identity. The profound impact on Egyptian development of Jamal al-Din al-Afghani (1839–97) can be explained chiefly by the potentiality of his ideas on Islamic reform to awaken the Muslim community and to strengthen its political opposition to the British. Al-Afghani's Pan-Islamism, constitutionalism, and opposition to the ruling Khedive (who was ready to give in to foreign demands) stemmed from his religious convictions. Muhammad 'Abduh (1849–1905), a close friend and follower of al-Afghani, while firmly dedicated to safeguarding the integrity of his community, tried to visualize the threatening West not in terms of material power but as a "challenge of the intellectual, social, and ethical dynamism underlying that power to an Islamic superstructure no longer suitable to the present age."[11] Later in his life, 'Abduh, who was already known to disapprove of violent action, including Urabi's methods, dealt with philosophical questions and detached himself from politics.

The ideas of al-Afghani, 'Abduh, and the latter's pupil Rashid Rida (1886–1935), Qasim Amin (1849–1905), and several other thinkers are usually referred to as forming the core of the movement of Islamic Reformation.[12] They stressed in various degrees the necessity of free inquiry and reasoning (opening the gates of Ijtihad), free will, reinterpretation of Islamic teachings in the light of new conditions, and they debated the questions of faith and science, always upholding Islam's ability to adapt to modern conditions. Their efforts were directed toward delivering Muslim countries from backwardness and toward restoring them to moral and material vitality through positive effort. The movement of Islamic Reformation opened the door to serious thinking among small groups of intellectuals, but without visibly penetrating the masses. It remained relatively without effect among Turks and Iranians, chiefly because, in the case of the former, reformations were secured by political action and open acceptance of positivist scientific ways of Western thought.

In the Arab world, 'Abduh's ideas created continuous interest and debate. Rashid Rida left his native Syria and came to Cairo, in 1897, where he published the review *al-Manar* (*The Beacon*) until his death, in 1935. In addition to expanding 'Abduh's ideas, Rida wrote numerous articles and books and be-

---

of Muslim reformist movements (which did not appear in Iran and Turkey) in the Islamic world. Serge A. Zenkovsky, *Pan-Turkism and Islam in Russia* (Cambridge, Mass.: Harvard University Press, 1960), p. 9, writes that "the Turkic national revival was preceded by a Moslem cultural revival."

11. Nadav Safran, *Egypt in Search of Political Community* (Cambridge, Mass.: Harvard University Press, 1961), p. 63.

12. Malcolm H. Kerr, *Islamic Reform: The Political and Legal Theories of Muhammad 'Abduh and Rashid Rida* (Berkeley, Calif.: University of California Press, 1966).

came involved in a variety of religious organizational activities. 'Abd al-Rahman al-Kawakibi (1849–1903), a Kurd from Syria who opposed the despotism of Sultan Abdulhamid, contributed to *al-Manar* and also wrote two books—one on the future of Islam and the other on despotism. His major political contribution was his demand that the power in the Islamic community be taken by Arabs, whom he considered to be better people than the Turks, and that a caliph be chosen from among them, possibly the ruler of Egypt.[13] The reformist ideas of 'Abduh found positive support among some religious men; 'Ali 'Abd al-Raziq, for example, claimed in 1925 that Islam was free of political and social preoccupations and pointed out the nonreligious basis of the caliphate, and in 1950, Khalid Muhammad Khalid directed a bitter attack on religious dogmatism and conservatism.

The counterpart of the Islamic Reformation, the Muslim Brotherhood (*Ikhwan al-Muslimun*), demanded a return to the original form and spirit of Islam, while initiating practical programs of economic and social development. Spokesmen for the Muslim Brotherhood included Hasan al-Banna, the founder, Muhammad al-Ghazzali, Sayyid Kotb (Qutb), and Mustafa al-Siba'i.

Guided by Muhammad 'Abduh's fundamentalist philosophical views, the Islamic Reformation lost its active interest in practical politics. A new militant generation turned nationalism into a vehicle for mobilizing public support in the struggle for independence from the British. The leaders of this movement were the 'Urabi group, 'Abdallah al-Nadim (1843–93), the journalist Mustafa Kamil (1874–1908), and Sa'd Zaghlul, the leader of the Wafd Party. Members of the lower class intelligentsia, they were interested primarily in political action. Their polemically oriented writings lack depth and do not have much intellectual value. Yet, this kind of militant nationalism—represented so well by Mustafa Kamil—later became generalized.

At the end of the nineteenth and the beginning of the twentieth century, Egypt witnessed the rise of another group of intellectuals that formed the backbone of the liberal nationalist and humanist school of thought. The best-known members of this group are Ahmad Lutfi al-Sayyid (1872–1964), Taha Husayn (b. 1889), Muhammad Husayn Haykal (1889–1956), Ibrahim al-Mazni (1889–1949), Tawfiq al-Hakim (b. 1889), and the "socialist" Salama Musa (1887–1959). It may be said that the intellectual aspects of modernization found their way into Egypt and eventually into the Arab world through the publications of this group.[14] Members of the group debated basic issues such as constitutionalism, liberalism, secularism, modernization, and Islamic reform, largely within the framework of Egyptian culture, history, and identity. They viewed Egyptian nationalism not in a limiting political light, but in a broad philosophical and human context, and strove in many cases to identify Egypt with Western civilization. This group, however, represented the views of a minority. Many of its members belonged to the upper wealthy

13. Haim, *op. cit.*, pp. 26–29; Hourani, *op. cit.*, pp. 271–72.

14. The works of Safran (*op. cit.*) and Hourani (*op. cit.*) and Jamal M. Ahmed, *The Intellectual Origins of Egyptian Nationalism* (London and New York: Oxford University Press, 1960), deal mostly with these writers and thinkers.

groups. In some cases, they supported the monarchy and, by implication, the British.

The formal independence granted to Egypt in 1922 and the constitution promulgated in 1923 did not change the dual character of Egyptian thought. The Wafd nationalist movement lost many of its progressive features in the struggle with the British, but it increased its militancy. The liberals, in turn, became less influential, and were gradually estranged from the mainstream of political life.

Paradoxically, the British occupation stimulated modernization of the Egyptian economy and administrative system by establishing a communications network and reorganizing the civil service and education. All these reforms later gave Egypt an organized power base from which to advance claims to the leadership of the Arab world. Until World War I, ideological developments in the Arab world were thus concentrated chiefly in Egypt and centered on Egyptian nationalism.

Well formulated ideologies did not appear in the Fertile Crescent until the end of World War I. Despite its appeal to an Arab consciousness, Arab nationalism—promoted by Christian Arabs such as Butrus al-Bustani, Khalil Ghanim, Jurji Zaydan, and Nagib 'Azuri—found relatively little response among Muslims. As early as 1904–5, the Christian Arabs demanded independence for a Muslim-Christian Arab nation, and blamed the Turks for having caused the backwardness of the Arab lands. The Christian Arabs eventually came to think more in terms of an independent Syria and, especially, Lebanon, with ties to the West, rather than a single large Arab state with its center at Damascus. With the exception of a few, such as al-Kawakibi, operating out of Cairo, Muslim Arabs in the Fertile Crescent had shown little interest in disengaging themselves from the Ottoman Empire until the Young Turks' policies—designed to transform the Empire into a centralist, nationalist, and secularist Turkish state—became evident in 1908. The Arab reaction manifested itself in the form of a series of societies founded after 1908 to defend Arab interests.[15] Eventually, an Arab congress was held in Paris in 1913 to demand a degree of autonomy and decentralization for the Arab provinces. Secret societies, such as al-Qahtaniyya and al-Fatat, formed mostly by army officers after 1908, seemed to be oriented toward Arab independence, although even in these cases some officers still wanted to preserve Muslim unity within the Ottoman Empire.[16]

These activities led to Sharif Husayn's agreement with the British and subsequently to the revolt of 1916, which severed the Arabs' ties with the Ottoman Empire and supposedly paved the way for the independence of the Arab lands after the downfall of the Ottoman state. The Fertile Crescent did not win its independence, however, and was not united under one Arab state

15. Zeine N. Zeine, *Arab-Turkish Relations and the Emergence of Arab Nationalism* (Beirut: Khayat's, 1958), p. 80.

16. Majid Khadduri, "'Aziz 'Ali Misri and the Arab Nationalist Movement," in Albert Hourani (ed.), *Middle Eastern Affairs Number Four* (St. Antony's Papers No. 17) (London and New York: Oxford University Press, 1965), pp. 140–63.

except for a very short time in 1920–21. The area was divided between the French and the British: The French established a mandate over Syria and Lebanon; the British gained full control of Egypt and established mandates over Palestine, Transjordan, and Iraq. The British promised to facilitate Jewish migration into Palestine and to establish a Jewish National Home. Only Hijaz, the desert heartland of the Arabian Peninsula, was free. Thus "betrayed" by the West, the Arabs in the Fertile Crescent were placed politically in the same subordinate position as Egypt and eventually forced to shape their ideologies in the light of the struggle for independence and opposition to Jewish immigration to Arab lands, rather than in terms of internal conditions. The Arab leadership in the East was in the hands of a small group of officers and bureaucrats educated in Ottoman schools, who often borrowed the Young Turks' ideas on nationalism. This tendency is particularly evident in the writings of Sati' al-Husri.

The present ideological features of Arab nationalism began to appear after 1919. The basic idea of the nationalist movement was that Arabs constituted one single nation, a political entity with a common culture and language that prevailed in an area stretching from the Atlantic Ocean to the Indian Ocean. Islam, in turn, had an Arab character, and, in fact, was an inseparable part of the Arab national identity. The reliance on history, the glorification of the past and of everything even slightly related to Arabs, and the wholesale Arabization of the Muslim heritage, were the inevitable results of this nationalism. Among the better known exponents of Arab nationalism were Sati' al-Husri and 'Abdallah al-'Alayli, who even engaged in polemics with Egyptian intellectuals in their efforts to downgrade local and regional nationalism in favor of the emerging broader concept of Arabism. They stressed the political role of Islam in the formation of the Arab nation but defended also the reformist principles necessary to modernize Arab society. The Muslim Brotherhood, on the other hand, accepted Islam and the return to its original principles as its cardinal doctrine and rejected the idea of an Arab nation with a nationalist and functionally differentiated political system. Secularism, which formed an indivisible part of Turkish nationalism, was dismissed by Muslim Arabs as incompatible with their nationalism, although it was enforced in practice. A secular, regional nationalism, represented chiefly by Antun Saadeh (Sa'da) (1904–49), developed in Syria and Lebanon parallel to the development of Arab nationalism in the other Arab lands. Saadeh's nationalism emphasized the common culture and history of the ethnic groups that had inhabited Syria and Lebanon for thousands of years, and proposed to establish an independent country based on an indigenous culture.

In comparison with nationalism, the socialist and Communist movements, promoted by small urban groups, were relatively unimportant in the Arab world in 1918–52.

Most of the Arab lands won their independence after World War II. The boundaries of the new states were determined chiefly on the basis of the administrative divisions that had been imposed by the mandatory powers. The new though feeble local identities (such as Iraqi and Jordanian) fostered by the occupying powers were reinforced by group alignments and by the national, educational, and bureaucratic systems that had developed in 1920–45. These tended to strengthen separatist tendencies in the Arab world. The West, according to the Arabs, had calculatedly thwarted the aims of Arab nationalism. It had left the Arabs disunited and weak so that, at the first opportunity, it could re-establish its domination. The British-French-Israeli attack on Egypt in 1956 reinforced that belief.

The establishment of Israel as a national state in the former mandate of Palestine and the Arab defeat in the war of 1948–49, followed by Western efforts to drag the Arabs into military pacts (such as the Middle East Defense Organization and the Baghdad Pact, which later became CENTO), increased Arab suspicion of the West. The Arabs believed that a strong, unified Arab state, capable of preserving its independence and of forging a modern society, could not only oppose foreign encroachment but also play a leading role in world affairs.

The failure of the Arab League (1945) to achieve lasting unity increased the insecurity and sense of frustration felt by the rapidly growing Arab intelligentsia. The revolution that resulted in the overthrow of the Egyptian monarchy in 1952 was one of the most dramatic results of these political and psychological frustrations. At the beginning, the revolution was not very different from other Arab military coups. It entered a new phase after the withdrawal of the British, the nationalization of the Suez Canal, and the abortive British-French-Israeli expedition in 1956. Overnight, Gamal Abdel Nasser (Jamal 'Abd al-Nasir) was transformed into an Arab hero capable of avenging all past humiliations and of restoring Arab national self-confidence and pride. All other Arab leaders rapidly lost their stature, especially after Nasser asserted his position as one of the three leaders of the neutralist bloc.

The rise to power of Nasser and his associates was also a social change of great magnitude. The sons of government clerks and small merchants, they represented the lower social level of the intelligentsia and displayed religious attitudes similar to the pietism of the masses. Reinforced with ideas on social, economic, and educational development, this pietism could mobilize the masses to share the leaders' political ideas and condemn their opponents.[17] The social and political changes wrought by the Egyptian Revolution gave a new orientation to Arab nationalism (which was aimed at independence), transforming it into Arabism (oriented toward internal modernization and unity) and making Egypt its spokesman.

Arabism stresses the similarities of culture, history, and ideals among Arabs and minimizes their differences. It draws heavily on Islam as the emotional link among Arabs, but without using it as a principle of political organization. As it was defined by a variety of groups in Egypt, Arabism gradually

17. For instance, in a speech attacking the Ba'thists as atheists, Nasser declared: "The Revolution is of the people. The Revolution leaders are from the people. Religion forms the frame which limits the action of everyone. This particular thing can be done because

absorbed or replaced Islamism and the various forms of regional and local nationalism.

Egypt adopted national economic plans and launched a completely socialist development program in 1961–63. Consequently, Arabism, without losing its nationalist features, broadened its scope to include socialism. Arab socialism was essentially a radical form of statism, relying mostly on the bureaucracy and the intelligentsia, rather than the workers or peasants, to enforce its program. It opposed Communism and remained a tool of its goal of establishing an advanced society unified in one Arab state. Socialism is thus being used by Nasser to achieve throughout the Arab world the uniform social structure and political regime considered prerequisites of unification.

The nationalist socialist doctrines of Arabism as it is promoted by the United Arab Republic (Egypt) have their counterpart in the doctrine of the Syrian Ba'th Party. The Ba'th strives on the one hand to maintain Syria as the leader of the Arab world, and on the other to preserve a degree of secularism in its nationalist and socialist ideology. Ba'thism is the doctrine of an intellectual group rather than of the masses, and it relies on a formally established political organization, the Ba'th Party, to maintain its supremacy. The victory of the Ba'th Party in Syria and Iraq failed to wrest the leadership of the Arab world from Nasser.

The influence of the United Arab Republic is chiefly a result of Nasser's charisma and the nation's relatively well-organized government, internal cohesion, and integration, achieved during the 150-year effort to develop a modern state. Indeed, modern nationhood gave to Egypt the material basis to launch its ideological drive for unification and, incidentally, domination of the other Arab lands.

The overabundance of ideologies in the Arab world today results largely from lack of consensus on a commonly acceptable political system. Some fundamental developments, however, may soon give a new direction to Arab political thought. Tensions, created by the emergence and continuous secularization of a large bureaucracy as the dominant social class, restrictions on political freedom, and Nasser's growing militancy toward his royalist opponents and his direct involvement in Yemen, may soon reach the breaking point.

The ideational limitations of Arabism in its present form will probably affect the future of ideology in the Arab world. Arabism is a conglomerate of ideas

---

it is right, while that other thing cannot be done because it is sinful. Piety is the basis of religion. On these bases, the Revolution has made its way bringing together the hearts of the people and working for the elimination of exploitation, for the elimination of tyranny, for the removal of class differences and in order to render everyone free, with a free will forging along his own way and finding honest and honourable work. . . . If those who dominate Syria today believe that religious ideas are rotten, we tell them that it is the atheist ideas that are rotten. It is by no means possible that a religious people would respond to atheist leaders." *President Gamal Abdel Nasser's Speeches and Press Interviews, January–December,* 1963 (Cairo: Information Department, [1964]), pp. 187–88.

fashioned in accordance with and designed to serve an immediate political goal. It does not and, in its present form, could not express the endless conflicts in Arab society, because such conflicts have been temporarily eclipsed by the pressing need to establish a modern political system. The Marxists have pinned their greatest hopes for their own success on the insufficiency of Arabism. They feel that Arabism is essentially a bourgeois doctrine, able to resuscitate hopes and awaken society, but ideologically and organizationally incapable of meeting the expectations of the masss. When the masses realize the inadequacies of Arabism, the Marxists expect that it will be their turn to take power. It may be more accurate to say that Arabism, whatever its faults, prepares the ground for the transition of Arab society to a truly modern political system in which ideology can freely express the diversified views of groups and interests.

The major internal problems faced by the Arabs in their transition from universalism to nationalist particularism and the politics of a modern state can thus be summarized as follows:

1. The definition of Arab national identity was particularly difficult because of the Arabs' intimate association with Islam and their pride in their language (the language of the Qur'an). The secular nationalism of the Arab Christians, which had been useful in supporting Arab claims to independence from the Ottoman Empire, proved difficult after independence to reconcile with Arabism, which was firmly rooted in the Islamic identity of the masses. Arabism, in fact, eventually led to the redefinition of Islam as a national Arab religion.

2. The modernizing and social and political reconstructing of Arab society occurred mainly within units corresponding roughly to some of the historical areas. The mandates established by England and France after World War I divided the Arabs still further and stimulated independent social and economic growth, thus consolidating regional differences. Henceforth, independence from foreign rule and then unification became the major ideological themes of Arab nationalism.

3. The European powers encouraged the development of local and regional nationalism, which was enhanced by objective historical heritages, such as the Egyptian and the Syrian, and produced corresponding local political cultures and strong commitments to them.

4. The emergence of various political regimes from absolute monarchy (Arabia) to republicanism and democracy (Lebanon) and socialism and economic development (U.A.R.), carried out independently by each Arab political unit, further consolidated the political and social differences among the various Arab territorial units.

5. The above conditions created great difficulties in arriving at a general consensus on the political and social structures to be adopted in a unified Arab state, the present goal of the Arab intelligentsia.

6. Until very recently, the Arab countries, with the exception of Egypt, lacked the administrative apparatus and the elites capable of pro-

viding effective leadership to create a modern political system. Consequently, the society remained divided into groups, each leading its own independent but traditional way of life.

7. Arab nationalism has thus been unable to arrive at a general consensus on the exact content and scope of the unified Arab motherland and its relation to the component social and political units. Moreover, there has not been a clear definition of the modern political system and its functions and its differences from its predecessor. Indiscriminate glorification of the Arab past may often obscure its shortcomings.

8. Contemporary Arab ideology deals essentially with the above points. It tries to clarify the issues, to define its goals, and to mobilize society accordingly. It may eventually succeed in creating a modern political system, the basic condition for twentieth-century modernization, and then —if the society's social structure and political climate permit—enter the era of true ideological development. Until then, Arab ideology, despite its numerous forms and denominations, is bound to remain confined to the task of creating a modern state, unified or otherwise. Because such a state does not yet fully exist (Egypt and Lebanon excepted), ideology often confuses the issues and prevents an objective appraisal of the social and political realities, past and present, but it does ease the strains arising from those realities.

The extracts presented here give an idea of some of the major currents of thought in the Arab world. They are not chosen to support a given viewpoint, but merely to acquaint the reader with the complexity of problems faced by Arab society in its struggle to modernize and at the same time to preserve as much as possible of its rich culture and identity.

II. *The Background of Arab Nationalism*

1. THE HISTORICAL ROOTS OF ARAB NATIONALISM*

'Abd al-'Aziz al-Duri

After studying at the University of London's School of Oriental Studies, al-Duri returned to Baghdad and taught at the Higher Training College there. He served as dean of the University College (1949–60) and as professor of Islamic history at Baghdad University. In 1963, after the revolution, he became dean of the University. He had published several serious books on the early history of Islam. In the book from which these excerpts have been taken, al-Duri traces the origin of Arab nationalism to its pre-Islamic roots "in the move toward formulating a unified literary language" and finds a continuity in Arab nationalism after the emergence of Islam.

If we examine the beginnings of Arab consciousness, we find that the first vague stirrings occurred prior to the rise of Islam. During that pre-Islamic period, the Arabian Peninsula was threatened by two powers, the Sassanians in the east and Byzantium in the west, each of which tried to dominate the civilized borders of the Peninsula.

The civilized principates and other states collapsed one after another and either came under direct foreign domination (as in Iraq, Syria, and the Yemen) or relapsed into tribal chaos. This wave of tribalism spread into the more civilized regions. The Peninsula suffered from internal conflicts and fragmentation and passed through a period of religious anarchy.

Amid this total chaos, Arab consciousness first appeared. It made its presence felt in politics, society, and culture and prepared the way for a total renaissance. Here, we are concerned with only a few of these aspects.

Arab consciousness began with the move toward replacing the many dialects with a unified literary language—a language that appeared first in poetry and crystallized in the Qur'an. Historically, therefore, the Arabic language was the first common denominator.

Arab consciousness also coincided with a kind of political renaissance, which originated when tribes living on the edges of the Peninsula began individually

* Extract from 'Abd al-'Aziz al-Duri, *al-Judhur al-tarikhiyya lil-qawmiyya al-'arabiyya* (*The Historical Roots of Arab Nationalism*) (Beirut: Dar al-'ilm lil-malayin, 1960), pp. 10–14, 41–42, 85, 91–92.

to fight with the Eastern and Western powers. (The Battle of Dhu Qar[1] and its consequences in the northern part of the Peninsula are an example.) This renaissance was further manifested in attempts to create a limited political sovereignty—as, for instance, in the principality of Kinda.[2]

Commercial activities, which involved a certain measure of independence, enhanced the development of this social [i.e., national] consciousness. This in turn produced a certain degree of unity and the diffusion of common social norms and conventions. This consciousness was also apparent in a religious tension, religion being an important social and ideological substructure. The Arab worship of individual tribal gods was transformed into the worship of more universal gods and into communal prayers at holy sites. With the development in the Yemen and Hijaz of a form of early monotheism, there also arose a type of monotheism that was connected neither with Byzantine-supported Christianity nor with Judaism, which enjoyed some protection from the Sassanians. The believers in this creed looked toward a sublime God transcending the local deities and called Allah in the western Peninsula. They considered the various deities as intermediaries between the people and Allah, and regarded the Kaʿba, to which pilgrimage was made from all parts of the Peninsula, as the House of Allah. Thus, the pilgrimage was another unifying factor among the Arabs.

Hence, we observe a renaissance, not devoid of anxiety, but containing a common consciousness and a new self-awareness—an awareness that lacked clarity, organization, and guidance.

With the appearance of the Prophet and Islam, the Arab spirit burst forth and the common consciousness reached its climax. The Prophet provided the leadership and the total framework for this consciousness, and Islam furnished Arab consciousness with a clear content and a well-defined direction. The movement was therefore Arabic in language, habitat, and message-bearers. In essence, it expressed a comprehensive Arab spirit. It rejected tribalism and all its attendant values and ideals, and it provided a barrier against social and ideological anarchy. It sought political unity, rejected fragmentation and servility, tended to evolve unified values and ideals, and adopted a secular attitude toward life.

The Qur'an was revealed in Arabic. It struck a blow at all other dialects and provided the Arabs with one language, the language of the Qur'an. This important foundation of the nation was fixed. We can go even further and say that this new movement guaranteed the perpetuation of linguistic unity when it added a new and common dimension to the Arabic language. Arabic became the greatest common denominator and [those who spoke it had] the

1. The Battle of Dhu Qar took place near Kufa in 610 and resulted in a decisive Persian defeat. Despite the small number of troops involved, the victory by the Arabs is seen as the beginning of a new era, since it gave the Arab tribes a new confidence and enthusiasm.

2. One may take issue with the statement that the principality of Kinda truthfully reflected an attempt to express Arab consciousness. Kinda was one of the many examples of a tribal leader's briefly establishing his personal supremacy without any clear political aim.

proof of belonging to the Arab race. The Arabs did entertain certain vague notions about a common stock and descent, and this feeling of a unified origin crystallized in the well-known distinction between Bedouin Arabs, genuine Arabs, and naturalized Arabs. But the new movement did not encourage the perpetuation of vague lineage to old ancestors. It emphasized the language, considering it as a total framework within which people might truly belong. Thus, the Arab came to be distinguished from the non-Arab, and the most Arab of all peoples were regarded as those whose language most closely resembled that of the Qur'an. Coming out into the world [i.e., out of the Peninsula], the Arabs carried this distinction with them.

The Arabs were unified through the Islamic movement and became "one nation." Although the term "nation" in this context may possess a religious connotation, in fact it included only Arabs. Thus, we can say that in that period the nation was an Arab nation. Islam provided this Arab nation with a humanistic message that it carried throughout the world, and it gave the Arabs a comprehensive foundation for the creation of a new society and a new civilization.

Thus, Arab consciousness and the Arab renaissance acquired significance through Islam: one nation, one language, a historic message, and a common destiny. For the first time, the Arabs emerged united onto the stage of history out of chaos, fragmentation, and the conflict between the Sassanian East and the Byzantine West. . . .

We are concerned here with understanding how the Arabs met the challenge to Arab consciousness and the Arab idea.

The attacks [of the Shu'ubiyya] against the Arab heritage caused the Arabs all the more tenaciously to embrace this heritage of wisdom in prose and poetry.[3] They took care to collect this heritage and to base Arabic culture upon it. Gone was the old attempt to divide Arab history into Islamic and pre-Islamic periods, to ignore all pre-Islamic culture, and to regard Islam as the starting point that superseded the dark ages. Thus, both al-Jahiz (d. 869) in his *al-Bayan wal-tabyin* [*Book of Eloquence and Exposition,* a treatise on rhetoric] and Ibn Qutayba (d. 889) in his *'Uyun al-akhbar* [*Choice Histories,* a medley of citations and reminiscences from poetry, history, and traditions] presented a vivid picture of pre-Islamic Arabic culture in the form of elegant and attractive selections. They did so in order to refute the anti-Arab charge

3. At least two major movements in ancient Islam were known as *Shu'ubiyya.* The word, derived from *shu'ub,* meaning "peoples" or "nations," and referring mostly to non-Arabs, is derived from the Qur'an, XLIX, 13 ("Men, We have created you from a male and a female and divided you into nations [*shu'uban*] and tribes that you might get to know one another"). The purpose of this passage from the Qur'an was to create brotherhood among Muslims. The first Shu'ubiyya movement arose among the Kharijites (about A.D. 657), who claimed that no race or tribe was inherently superior to others, and therefore rejected the claim of the Quraysh (the Prophet's tribe) to the caliphate. The second Shu'ubiyya, a sociopolitical-literary movement of the second half of the eighth century, represented the efforts of the urban middle classes, especially in Iraq and Persia, to achieve political and social equality with the Arabs. The Shu'ubiyya in this sense was an egalitarian movement. Ignaz Goldziher, *Muhammedanische*

that the Arabs did not possess a literature and a heritage to compare with those of the Persians. The two verse anthologies *Diwan al-hamasa* [*Anthology of Fortitude,* by Habib ibn Aus al Ta'i Abu Tammam (d. 845)] and *al-Mufaddaliyat*[4] offered easy access to the grandeur of Arabic poetry (including pre-Islamic poetry) for the benefit of the younger generation and the educated classes.

For the first time, the idea of the cultural continuity of Arabic before and after Islam made itself clearly felt in the life of the Arabs. We can feel that at that period they came to realize that they possessed a rich pre-Islamic heritage, contrary to the charges of the anti-Arabs. This outlook was not confined merely to men of letters but appeared also among historians. In his *Kitab al-ma'arif* [*Book of Knowledge*], Ibn Qutayba dealt at length with pre- and post-Islamic Arab cultural history. This book was in fact a short literary, historical, and Islamic encyclopedia, in which he intended to provide the writer or literate gentleman with brief information on these topics. . . .

In our study of the historical roots of nationalism, we must distinguish between Arabism and Islam. Although Islam appeared as an Arab revolt, and although the Islamic and Arab movements were identical in the heyday of Islam, the two movements diverged when Islam began to expand, when it was used as a weapon to attack the Arabs, and when the Arabs were led, in the name of religion, to accept a foreign domination, against which they later rose. The pride we take in our heritage and the proper attention we pay to its values do not mean that we must forge a political union out of Islam or base our Arab state upon it.

Studien (Halle, 1888–90), Part I, pp. 147 ff. Sir Hamilton Gibb has stressed the special role played by secretaries (*kuttab*) at the 'Abbasid court, who were involved in the Shu'ubiyya. They used the Persian language and tried to frame Islamic political and social institutions according to Sassanian forms. Representatives of the Shu'ubiyya rejected the view that the Arabs were pure of race and descent (Abu Ubayda) and resented the Arabs' emphasis on the close relation between the Arabic language and the Qur'an. The Shu'ubiyya's development of certain anti-Islamic tendencies led to repressive measures by the state and prepared the ground for the emergence of the *Mu'tazila,* a movement of rationalists who defended the orthodoxy of Islam. The other important reaction to the Shu'ubiyya referred to by al-Duri was a literary movement that sought the primacy of the Arabic language. Al-Jahiz (Abu 'Uthman 'Amr ibn Bahr, d. 869) and Ibn Qutayba (Muhammad ibn Muslim al-Dinawari, d. 889) borrowed some Persian forms, adopted a more common language and expressions, and thus widened the range of Arabic literature to cover most aspects of life. Thus, the Shu'ubiyya ended with a compromise by which Arabs borrowed forms, expressions, ideas, and approaches, mainly from Persian, and in exchange assured respect for Arabic as the language of the Qur'an. In later days, the term implied divisive tendencies. See H. A. R. Gibb, *Studies on the Civilization of Islam,* ed. William R. Polk and Stanford Shaw (Boston: Beacon Press, 1962), pp. 12-13, 66-72; and R. A. Nicholson, *A Literary History of the Arabs* (Cambridge: Cambridge University Press, 1962). For other forms of the Shu'ubiyya, see Sami A. Hanna and George H. Gardner, "Al-Shu'ubiyyah Up-Dated," *Middle East Journal,* XX (Summer, 1966), 335–51. See also 'Abd al-'Aziz al-Duri, *al-Judhur al-tarikhiyya fi al-shu'ubiyya* (*The Historical Roots of the Shu'ubiyya Movement*) (Beirut: Dar al-tali'a, 1962), and pp. 80–86, below.

4. The title bears the name of the compiler, Mufaddal al-Dabbi (d. 786). The original title was *al-Mukhtarat* (*Selections*).

The Arab contact with the West, first as a culture and then as an imperialist power, was very important in clarifying the historical roots of Arab nationalism, in consolidating these roots, and in establishing their true import. The Arabs welcomed the implications of freedom and tried to imitate the West in bettering their way of life and their economy. But they were not prepared to forsake their heritage or deny their identity. In their anxiety that this heritage and identity should not disappear, they took great pains to emphasize these [national] characteristics. . . .

The study of the historical roots of Arab nationalism is valuable in helping us to establish and clarify the content of nationalism on a firmer level than that of the emotions. It also enables us to lay down the philosophical foundations for Arab nationalism.

We have seen that Arab nationalism is essentially cultural. It is not based on a racial concept, since the conception of the Arab nation was drawn from the language, the process of Arabization, the cultural heritage, and the historic role of the Arabs.

The Arab nationalist idea is neither ephemeral nor borrowed. It is the result of the development of Arab consciousness, which blazed forth 1400 years ago, was gradually unraveled and defined through the course of Arab history, and finally emerged in modern times in a self-awareness which is manifested in a new vitality that seeks to reactivate the Arab nation and build up its own state. This is the modern Arab nationalist consciousness.

We have seen that Arab consciousness began by being comprehensive and popular but, because of certain ideological and political factors, was somewhat weakened in the course of history. The Arab intellectuals stoutly defended Arab consciousness when it came under attack during the 'Abbasid period; it again became comprehensive and popular when other peoples overran the Arabs. Finally, in modern times, it reappeared among the intellectuals but has developed until now it is again popular and comprehensive.

We have also seen that Arab consciousness was [universally] humanistic in character, since it carried its message of religion and civilization throughout the world. When it reappeared in the guise of nationalist consciousness, it stood up against tyranny and foreign domination, and sought to liberate the Arabs and create a new Arab society. Thus, this movement is essentially peaceable and constructive in its aims. It emphasized the revival of the Arab cultural heritage and the proper understanding of the path of the Arab nation in history. It views this as a means of understanding the Arab character.

2. THE QUR'AN AND ARAB NATIONALISM*

'Ali Husni al-Kharbutli

'Ali Husni al-Kharbutli is a professor of Islamic history at the University of 'Ain Shams in Egypt. In al-Quawmiyya al-'arabiyya min al-fajr ila al-zuhr (Arab Nationalism from Its Dawn to Its Fulfillment) *(Cairo: Mu'assasat al-matba'a al-haditha, 1960), al-Kharbutli claimed that religious and national unity are distinct questions. Another book of some interest by al-Kharbutli is* al-Mujtama' al-'arabi (The Arab Society) *(Cairo: Mu'assasat al-matba'a al-haditha, 1960). In the following extract, al-Kharbutli emphasizes the religious sources of Arab nationalism.*

The Qur'an is a holy book that was revealed to Muhammad. It is an Arab Qur'an, revealed to an Arab prophet on Arab soil and transmitted by the Prophet to the Arabs, who have conformed to it and preserved it. Not surprisingly, therefore, the Qur'an is considered a factor in the manifestation of Arab nationalism. . . .

The Qur'an was revealed in the language of the Arabs, according to the Arab manner. The words it contains are Arab words, except for a few rare words that were borrowed from foreign languages and Arabized. The Arabs made them their own and applied their grammatical rules to them. The Qur'anic expressions are the expressions of spoken Arabic. We find in the Qur'an the etymological sounds, as well as the metaphor and metonymy, of the everyday language of the Arabs. That is quite normal, for the Qur'an existed first of all to call the Arabs to Islam and it therefore had to be written in a language they could understand. "Each apostle We have sent spoke in the language of his own people, so that he might make plain to them his message" (Qur'an, XIV, 4).

God chose Muhammad from among the Arabs in order that he might set seal to the succession of the prophets. The miracle concerning Muhammad necessitated two conditions: first, that he possess the qualities most admired and appreciated by the Arabs, for the miracle of any particular people is the miracle in which they most excel; second, that this miracle remain eternal and that it last as long as the Law by which God wished to close the series of all other laws, since God desired that all laws be brought to an end by the Prophet chosen to transmit the Law. These two conditions have made the Qur'an the miracle of the Prophet.

* Extract from 'Ali Husni al-Kharbutli, *Muhammad wa-al-qawmiyya al-'arabiyya* (*Muhammad and Arab Nationalism*) (Cairo: Mu'assasat al-matba'a al-haditha, 1959), pp. 67–75. Here and elsewhere, the translations from the Qur'an follow the version of N. J. Dawood (trans.), *The Koran* (Harmondsworth and Baltimore, Md.: Penguin, 1956).

The words and style of the Qur'an were widespread among all the Arab tribes, and the Arabs used them when they made speeches or wrote poems. The Qur'an therefore became a common language for the Arabs, unifying their tastes and forming among them a power of imagination with common affinities and a common ideal.

The Qur'an was revealed in a style comparable to no other. It is written neither in verse, nor in free prose, nor in measured rhyming lines. It is a composition that pleases, whose words have an agreeable ring and that express lofty thoughts. All the literary figures of speech and all styles of rhetoric are encompassed there. The Arabs found in the language of the Qur'an and in its beauty and style an object of admiration and wonder. They began to imitate it. Their admiration for the Qur'an and the wonder it inspired led certain of them to abandon poetry, as was the case with Labid ibn Rabi'a, one of the authors of the *Mu'allaqat*.[1] Each time he was asked to recite one of his poems, he would reply, "God has given me something better instead," and he would recite a sura of the Qur'an.

The Qur'an is considered the most literary book the Arabs have ever possessed. Without it, they would have neither the arts and humanities nor law: It is "a Book of revelations well-expounded, an Arabic Koran for men of understanding" (Qur'an, XLI, 3).

Although famous for their literary debates, and although literature was always honored among them, Arab literary men have been incapable of producing a book equal to the Qur'an. After long discussions, they had to admit that by its composition and the diversity of its methods, the Qur'an differs from all other compositions conceived up to now, treads a different path, and possesses a style of its own that distinguishes it, in its expressions, from other styles that are generally used. . . .

The Arab Qur'an was the miracle of the Arab Prophet. It is through him that God has challenged the Arabs. Muhammad himself stated that the Qur'an was an exceptional work and that it was impossible to produce anything like it. And that is why the believers turn to him so faithfully.

In their eyes, the different elements of which it is composed are not differentiated in value. The Arabs consider the Qur'an in its entirety as a divine miracle achieved by the Prophet; they even see it as the greatest of all miracles that prove the sincerity of the Prophet's divine mission.

The Qur'an launched its challenge to the Arabs in this verse: "Bring down from Allah a scripture that is a better guide than these [the Qur'an and the Torah] and I will follow it" (XXVIII, 49). We find in the Qur'an a clear and precise challenge: "If men and Jinn combined to write the like of this

1. "The *Mu'allaqat* are prize-winning poems which traditionally date back to the period just preceding the Qur'an, and are generally supposed to have been written in the language spoken in Mecca. The common belief is that these poems were all written in the dialect of Mecca because poetical competitions were held there during the pilgrimage season, and the winning poems were attached to the walls of the Ka'bah; hence the name *mu'allaqat,* i.e., things that are hung, or attached to something." E. Shouby, "The Influence of the Arabic Language on the Psychology of the Arabs," *Middle East Journal,* V (Summer, 1951), 284–302.

Koran, they would surely fail to compose one like it, though they helped one another" (XVII, 88). These two verses constitute the last challenge contained in the Qur'an. It finishes as it began, by demonstrating clearly to the Arabs their inability to produce a comparable work. The reason for their inability is contained in two factors: first, that the Qur'an is a book of direction and guidance; second, that it was composed in an Arab manner. These two factors cannot help forming a part of any challenge to produce anything comparable to the Qur'an.

The inability of the people of Quraysh to take up the challenge considerably influenced their attitude toward the Prophet. They were the most cultivated of the Arabs in science and knowledge, and the most able in literature and rhetoric, to the point that poets allowed them to judge their recitals. They gave up opposing the Qur'an by speech and finally took up opposition by arms. The Prophet was obliged to confront them armed, but he had recourse to the sword only thirteen years later.[2] During the time he spent among them at Mecca, he had called them to Islam by persuasion, then had challenged them by a divine miracle in order not to close the door to reflection but to lead them gently and with indulgence toward faith.

They refused, and left it to arms to judge between him and them. There was then a succession of wars, through which the infidels aimed to distract attention from the miracle that they had been challenged to accomplish, and to camouflage their own weakness in the eyes of the public.

The Qur'an is a mirror that reflects certain images of the life of the Arabs and of the call that was addressed to them to come to Islam. There also exist archives in which may be found writings about the events that occurred at Mecca and Medina during the time of the Prophet.

Goldziher says that among the 114 suras of the Qur'an, one can clearly distinguish those of Mecca and those of Medina. This chronological distinction is absolutely justified by a critical and esthetic examination of the Qur'an. Dating from the Meccan period are the sermons in which Muhammad presents in a fantastic, impetuous, and spontaneous form the images suggested to him during his passionate exaltation. There is no clanking of swords; he addresses himself neither to warriors nor to subjects. He reveals rather to those who contradicted him the conviction that dominates his soul, the infinite omnipotence of God—creator of the world and his sovereign—and of the approach of the terrible Day of Judgment. He tells of the punishment of peoples and tyrants who paid no heed to the warnings of God that were sent to them by His Messengers and His Prophets. . . .

We know that the sole aim of this miracle was not the Arabic language itself; it aims at political unity, even if this unity is based on language. In effect, the Qur'an represents for Arabs the very essence of the language, for

2. Presumably this indicates the period between 610—the date of the first divine call (*laylat al-qadr*, or Night of Power)—and the attack on a Meccan caravan that resulted in the Battle of Badr in 624. In 628 and 630, the conquest of Mecca was completed. The "thirteen years" may also apply to the period between the first revelation (610) and Muhammad's flight from Mecca to Medina (Yathrib) in 622 (the Hijra or Hejira).

by its style and perfection it has torn down the barriers and wiped out the language differences among the Arabs.

Such was the policy of the Qur'an about uniting the Arabs; there was a realization that their language influenced their spirit. They were led, therefore, by means of their language. That is why it [the language] became second nature for them, the victorious nature that prevails in all people and endows them with intelligence and makes them derive from this intelligence the key [knowledge] to open the door to their destiny.

It is the Qur'an that purified the instincts of the Arabs and softened the asperity of the Arab spirit, to the point that the sense of the divine manifested itself therein as if they themselves had produced it.

Why, then, have the Arabs emerged so stormily from their history after Islam, as though coming out of their skin, although Islam offered them tranquillity and the inherited moral qualities of their earlier times, traditions to which they were naturally drawn, and practices that were known to them?

By impressing its miraculous aspect on the Arab nature, the Qur'an has left its imprint on the Arabs as time does. He who revealed it by His knowledge, and who in His wisdom gave it this power, is the creator of all Time. What He destroyed in the hearts of the Arabs, He built anew. That is the difference between the human and the divine, between what is possible and what is impossible.

One of the impossibilities that the Qur'an achieved was to unite those who over the centuries had remained divided, by a racial bond in which there was no sectarianism except that of the spirit. The Qur'an touched the intimate side of their nature and brought together their hearts to establish equality between them. It made of them a nation ready and capable of embracing all other nations from wherever they might come, for this nation looked only toward God. Between it and God there was everything under the sky. It is this aptitude that led to the blossoming of the Arab race. The Qur'an began this work by fusing the various primitive dialects. It then united their hearts in a single religion, and finally gave to Arabs the chance to understand the languages and feelings of other peoples, by a good and wise method which no science or education could improve.

If nations do not have a linguistic bond to unite them, religion or anything else will unite them, except an artificial union of the kind made in business while buying and selling.

The fact that the Qur'an has preserved its Arabic aspect means that, as regards society and in their own eyes, all Muslims—no matter what race they belong to, red or black—become one single body expressing themselves in the language of history, in one single language, and all racial particularities disappear.

3. THE FOUNDATIONS AND OBJECTIVES OF ARAB NATIONALISM*

Darwish al-Jundi

Since literary Arabic is used by intellectuals throughout the Arab world, whereas the vernacular, in a variety of dialects, is spoken by the lower classes, there are profound barriers of communication between the upper and lower strata in all the Arab countries. Arguing that the literary language is "the ideal self of the Arabs" and that colloquial Arabic is "the monopoly of the practical functions of the real self," E. Shouby, a noted student of Arabic, has claimed that the differences between the "ideal" and "real" language also create deep repercussions in the Arab personality structure. (See E. Shouby, "The Influence of the Arabic Language on the Psychology of the Arabs," Middle East Journal, *V (Summer, 1951), 284–302.) Darwish al-Jundi, however, like Sati' al-Husri, stresses the importance of language in creating a bond of unity. Al-Jundi is an Egyptian with a Ph.D. degree in Arabic literature. Despite his gross errors of history and interpretation, al-Jundi gives a fair picture of the ideas and spirit of the current understanding of nationalism. His argumentation is typical.*

The Foundations

Arab nationalism possesses all the foundations and constituents that appear in the various definitions of a nation. Perhaps no other nation can compare with the Arabs in the numerous, deep-rooted, and continuous links that bind its various groups to each other. We shall first mention the constituent features of the Arab nation . . . :

(1) *A common land.* The lands inhabited by the Arab nation span two continents, Asia and Africa. But these lands are by nature very closely tied to each other. Indeed, they constitute a region by themselves, independent of the two continents. This region stretches from Persia, the Arabian Gulf [Persian Gulf], and the Indian Ocean in the east to the Atlantic Ocean in the west, and from the Taurus Mountains and the Mediterranean Sea in the north to Central Africa in the south. The region is bounded by such natural frontiers as oceans, plateaus, and mountains. For the sake of accuracy, we ought to mention that two natural barriers separate the Arab land mass. They are: (a) *the Red Sea,* but this sea is a narrow inlet of little importance as a barrier,

* Extract from Darwish al-Jundi, *al-Qawmiyya al-'arabiyya fi al-adab al-hadith* (*Arab Nationalism in Modern Arab Literature*) (Cairo: Maktabat nahdat misr, 1962), pp. 36–43, 141.

since it ends with Sinai in the north, where land communications exist, and with Bab al-Mandab in the south, where the straits are very narrow; (b) *the Western Egyptian Desert,* which, although constituting a natural barrier, does not prevent communication and the movements of peoples from that region to another.

This means that the fragmentation of Arab lands at the hands of imperialists following World War I goes against the natural features of this land mass and that the frontiers erected thereafter are all artificial. It also means that the creation of Israel in the midst of Arab lands is equally unnatural. Israel, however, cannot prevent Arab unity since the Arabs encircle it on all sides. Israel exists amid an Arab world that has vast potentialities, and the day will come when Arab nationalism will wipe out this foreign body from the Arab map.

Certain enemies of Arab nationalism attempted to create geographical entities that are non-Arab in character, such as an Eastern or Mediterranean league of nations, basing themselves on mere proximity and neglecting the national bonds. But proximity alone is not enough. If there exists a certain measure of sympathy among the group of Arab nations called "Eastern," this is because they fought imperialism in a common front and not because the national links binding them together are stronger than elsewhere.

France attempted to keep Syria and Lebanon under its tutelage and so championed a Mediterranean league, aiming thereby to convince the Syrians and Lebanese that they were nearer to France than to the Arab world. The French argument was that the shores of the Mediterranean had been, at one stage in human history, the only center of world civilization. But the world has changed. Civilization has spread and the Mediterranean Sea no longer possesses a unique advantage in this respect.

Arab sentiment is what binds together the inhabitants of this region where the Arab nation first appeared. This nation first arose in the Arabian Peninsula, then in Syria, Lebanon, Palestine, and Iraq. From the earliest times, the nation spread westward across the Red Sea and the Sinai Peninsula and mingled with the races that inhabited North Africa. A racial mixture occurred, and the result was a nation that was patently Arab in its descent, customs, way of life, language, and general outlook on life.

(2) *A common economy*. The wealth of the Arab lands is complementary. If the Arab nations were freely allowed to draw up a single economic policy, the ensuing economic self-sufficiency would be unparalleled. We all await the day when this Arab region finally rids itself of the imperialism that has exploited its riches and prevented the Arabs from having a unified economic policy capable of ensuring prosperity to the Arabs.

(3) *A common race*. Although . . . racial unity exists nowhere among the peoples of the world, yet the Arab nation is the most racially homogeneous group of all. The story of the Arab race goes back to the days when the inhabitants of the Arabian Peninsula spread out in search of water and pastures. When the Peninsula could no longer contain them, they moved out into neighboring regions. It is well known that the first Semitic race was the Arab race and that this stock was originally located in Najd, Hijaz, 'Arud, and Yemen. From

there, the first Semitic advance was made into the northern Peninsula, where the Jewish Arabs lived. Thereafter, the Arabs advanced into Palestine, Syria, Iraq, Ethiopia, and the Nile Valley. The Arab exodus from the Peninsula increased with Islam. The Arabs came to live and mix with their neighbors until the Arab stock spread as far east as Central Asia and as far west as Spain. Racial purity varied. It became more pronounced as one moved closer to the [Arabian] Peninsula. . . . Thus the central region of the Islamic world was stamped with the Arab conquest, which has now come to form the Arab nation.

The Arab man, despite the various types appearing in the various countries, can be easily recognized through his spiritual make-up. He undoubtedly differs from both Europeans and Far Easterners, since, historically his life has given him certain traditions and a particular view of virtue and goodness.

The Arab is courageous, but despite his great courage in war, he is very humane. He is generous, enlightened, tolerant, faithful to his promise, averse to all illusions and superstition, and protects the weak. He is eloquent and is enchanted by sublime literature.

(4) *Religion.* Religion is a factor in Arab national sentiment. God has favored this spot by making it the origin of divine revelation and of messages that are similar in doctrine and essence. These religions teach men to be tolerant and to reject fanaticism, which breeds injustice and tyranny. Although Muslims are a majority in the Arab world, their religion enjoins them to be tolerant and to live in peace and good will with non-Muslims, as appears from the following verse in the Qur'an: "There is to be no compulsion in religion." Muslims in many periods of their history gave us noble examples of their treatment of the People of the Book [*ahl al-kitab;* or the Protected People, *ahl al-dhimma*], which helped to strengthen the bonds between Arabs of various religions. The sporadic outbreaks of sectarian fanaticism have been caused either by ignorance or by the malice of the enemies of the Arabs. Perhaps the most notable example of this is Ottoman fanaticism.

European imperialism also helped to create sectarian feuds in certain regions of the Arab world, but the Arabs of all religions have finally come to live together in mutual understanding and affection, recognizing in this their path to dignity and prosperity, and regarding sectarian feuds as serving the interests solely of their enemies.

Our Arab nationalism does not disown religion but at the same time does not tolerate its exploitation. It believes that genuine and sincere Muslims and Christians serve not merely their own good but the good of society and of humanity.

(5) *Language.* The Arabic language is the strongest foundation of Arab nationalism. It has drawn together the Arabs of the various countries and has been the means of communication of both their mind and spirit since the emergence of Islam. The Arabic language is a record of Arab creativity, a symbol of their unity, and the expression of their intellectual and technical achievements. The Arabic language has displayed a tremendous vitality in its

meticulous structure, its wide extension, and its flexibility, which has rendered it a fitting vehicle for the transmission of the arts and sciences.

The imperialists were aware of the influence of the Arabic language in drawing the Arabs together, in binding their past to their present, and in consolidating Arab nationalism. They fought it and tried to replace it with their own languages. They also attempted to develop colloquial and regional dialects, hoping thereby to stamp out classical Arabic, tear the links between Arabs, and weaken Arab sentiment, which is everywhere nourished by the language.

In fact, the history of classical and colloquial Arabic is closely linked with the imperialist policies of France and Britain. In the beginning, these two powers encouraged adherence to classical Arabic, since they wanted to stamp out the influence of Turkey. When the Arabs were no longer in the British, French, or Italian spheres of influence, the imperialists everywhere fought classical Arabic and helped to strengthen the colloquial dialects, in order to sever the common Arab link for the communication of sentiments, ideas, and opinions. In a speech, for example, delivered at the Uzbakiyya Club in Cairo in 1893 and entitled "Why Is the Power of Creativity Absent Among Egyptians?" Sir William Wilcox maintained that the most important reason was the use of classical Arabic for reading and writing. He urged the adoption of the colloquial language as a means of literary expression, in imitation of other nations. He cited the example of Britain and added that it "profited a great deal when it abandoned Latin which was once the language of writing and education."

This view is echoed by Salama Musa, who was the most prominent champion of colloquial Arabic. . . .

> The ideal language is one whose words are not forced, whose meanings are neither blurred nor closely similar but are sharply differentiated as five is from six. It must be a rich and fertile language that can supply the multitude of words needed by civilized men and can absorb the new words coined to suit the increasing requirements of modern life. . . . In Egypt, a class of writers has been trying to use the Arabic language as a literary means to recapture the past. Indeed, we have certain linguists who speak about Arabic in much the same way as European Orientalists discuss Sanskrit, but with this basic difference, namely, that the latter are not trying to revive dead Sanskrit words, whereas the former are trying to revive ancient Arabic words. Had they been in touch with the modern age they would have been well advised to bury such words. Most of this class is found among teachers of Arabic in our schools. . . .
>
> Nothing in the world is more valuable than a good language. Our feelings and actions are determined by words. Our behavior at home, in the street, in the fields, and in factories is above all a linguistic behavior, since the words of the language determine our ideas and reactions and dictate our behavior. We can even say that the British domination of India and civilized domination over barbarians is, to a certain extent, linguistic, i.e., a rich and comprehensive vocabulary of knowledge and morals, artistically creative and ethically oriented, which leads to domination and, sometimes, to aggression. . . .
>
> Since our language lacks the vocabulary of modern culture, our nation is

> denied the benefits of modern life. We still use the language of agriculture and have not yet acquired an industrial vocabulary. Therefore, our mentality is stagnant and anachronistic and looks always to the past. We occupy ourselves with writing about Mu'awiya ibn Abi Sufyan while we should be writing about Henry Ford, or the significance of industry in our age, or Karl Marx and the meaning of futuristic thought.
>
> The call for a modern language is in effect a call for a modern life, since the writer who adopts foreign words as they are, without attempting to translate them, is in fact adopting the civilization of science, logic, and industrial progress instead of the civilization of literature, dogmas, and agriculture.

The imperialists worked to introduce their languages on a large scale and to impose them on the Arabs as the languages of education in order to stifle Arab national sentiment. We saw how Turkey tried to make Turkish the language of instruction in government schools and to confine Arabic education to the *kuttab* where the Qur'an was taught. Turkish was made the language of the law courts and of government administration. France in Syria and Lebanon and Britain in Egypt followed an identical policy.

Sati' al-Husri[1] in one of his articles has described the imperialist conspiracies against education in the Arab world and the attempts made to eradicate Arabic. He wrote:

> In Libya, Italian imperialism was one of the worst, since it was coupled with a policy of Italian colonization. The object was to turn Libya into a home for vast numbers of Italians, and education, in general, was conducted in Italian.
>
> In Tunis, French policy aimed at making the country French by all possible means, and the schools were one of the means to that end. Thus, France made French the language of instruction in all French and Arab schools. At the beginning of this century, Tunisian schools followed the same curriculums prescribed for schools in France itself. Arabic was an optional language to be learnt by students outside school hours. The French authorities did not agree to include Arabic among the compulsory subjects of instruction in regular school periods until toward the end of the thirties of this century.
>
> In Algeria, France pursued a much more rigorous policy in this respect. French was the only language of instruction, Arabic being confined to Arab schools only. Great efforts were made to turn Berber into a literary language and to teach it in Berber areas so as to curtail the influence of Arabic. There was one student per 102 of the population. Again, in Morocco the same policy was pursued. Egypt was exposed to the well-known Dunlop policy for eradicating Arabic. There, English triumphed over French.
>
> In Syria and the Fertile Crescent, Turkish was the language of instruction in all schools at the beginning of this century. As for Arabic, only the grammatical rules also used in Turkish and which were indispensable to the understanding of Ottoman literature were taught. Identical rules were taught in the Arab vilayets [provinces] as in the rest of the Turkish vilayets.

Arab nationalism, however, resisted the languages of the imperialists since World War I and strove to increase the influence of Arabic until it had come to dominate the Arab world. Arabic vigorously survived this test and regained

1. See pp. 55–58.

its beauty and vitality. Today, it is everywhere at its most attractive and most splendid.

(6) *A common history*. From its earliest times, this Arab nation has lived through common historical experiences. We in the Arab world have all faced the invasion of Alexander the Great, and been subjected to Roman injustice, Mongol barbarity, Crusader violence, and Turkish ferocity.

Today, we face various forms of imperialism and we all suffer from the tragedy caused by Zionism. We are all equally exposed to the machination of our common enemy who lies in waiting for us.

A common history gives rise to common sentiments and aspirations, a common memory of past glories and tribulations, and similar hopes for a renaissance and a bright future. A common history does not involve a mere outlook on the past but expands to the future and embraces a common destiny. Thus interpreted, a common history and a common destiny are both included in the definition of Arab nationalism.

The Objectives

Since Arab nationalism embraces the common destiny of the Arab nation, common objectives and a common pursuit of these objectives follow of necessity.

Every nation desires what is in conformity with its basic structure and with the conditions of its own existence amid current world events. Hence, the objectives of Arab nationalism are confined to the achievement of our political and social revolution, to laying the foundations of an Arab society which is free from all foreign influence of every description, and to internal stability, through the destruction of feudalism, reaction, opportunism, and the predominance of capitalism. Our nationalism seeks complete and total liberation, where the Arabs would be sovereign in their own land and sole beneficiaries of its wealth and riches. It also seeks to destroy Israel, which is an imperialist bridgehead erected on Arab soil. It seeks to achieve a better and more dignified social life for all Arabs.

President Nasser has sketched the broad outlines of nationalist objectives under the following heads:

1. Arab nationalism means dignity and construction.
2. It spells the end of foreign occupation and exploitation.
3. It casts out all agents of foreign powers.
4. It implies unity, strength, and stability. . . .

Dealing with the characteristics of Arab nationalism, Dr. Taha Husayn writes:

> . . . This then, is Arab nationalism. At first, it was expressed in poetry but was finally consummated in the Qur'an. It then began to assert itself peacefully throughout the ancient world until it came to occupy the place of the Roman and Persian empires. Even now, after all the disasters it has met with, all the persecutions it has undergone, especially at the hands of the Turks, all the centuries of weakness and stagnation, Arab nationalism still retains its language and its own distinctive mentality and emotions. Despite all the divisions, and

despite the creation of states within the Arab world, our nationalism has preserved its common sentiments, common outlook, common Islamic religion, and common aspirations.

4. THE IDEOLOGY OF ARAB NATIONALISM: THE AUTHENTICITY OF ARAB THOUGHT*

Ibrahim Jum'a

Dr. Ibrahim Jum'a was formerly professor on the faculty of arts at the University of Cairo. At one time, he strongly favored an Egyptian Islamic nationalism by stressing the special characteristics of religion in that country. See al-Qawmiyya al-misriyya al-islamiyya (Egyptian Islamic Nationalism) (*Cairo: Matba'at Kustsa Tsumas, 1944*). *In the work from which the extracts are taken, Jum'a embraced the cause of Arab nationalism and regarded Islam as an outgrowth of Arabism.*

Arab nationalism is not an imitation of the nationalist movements that appeared in Europe toward the end of the nineteenth century. It is much older than they are: it is as old as the Arabs. Indeed, it is even older than the Arab state that emerged with Islam. Nationalism as a sentiment and a common history and interest preceded its emergence in the form of a state. It is true that the nationalist objectives are usually defined when a single state is created for members of the same nation. But nationalism remains a meeting ground of common sentiments, thought, history, and interests until these potentialities are translated into a common actuality in the form of a unified state or federal union.

In this sense, then, Arab nationalism was an existing reality before the emergence of Islam. This nationalism forcefully manifested itself through a common Arab sentiment and a defensive movement opposing the invasion of the Arabian Peninsula by the Ethiopians under "Abraha," fifteen years before the rise of Islam. This sentiment and movement again reappeared in the "Dhu Qar" battle against the Persians A.D. 610. On both occasions, through a feeling of national sentiment and unity, the Arabs defended their land against invaders.

Arab nationalism achieved its completed form with the creation of the Arab state by Islam. In this state, Arab society grew, its political characteristics were acquired, tribal prejudice disappeared, and the Arabs were molded into one

* Extract from Ibrahim Jum'a, *Idiolojiyya al-qawmiyya al-'arabiyya bi-shakuha min al-damir al-'arabi* (*The Ideology of Arab Nationalism in Emergence from the Consciousness of Arabs*) (Cairo: Dar al-fikr al-'arabi, 1960), pp. 41–44, 92–97, 107–8.

Arab nation with one national state. The Arab spirit then invaded all the lands occupied by the Persians and Byzantines, Arabizing their peoples and engulfing their national spirit within its own. Thus, Arab nationalism came to comprise all the distinctive national constituents of the groups who inhabited this wide region, and was later to form [the base of] the national Arab state known to history.

The Arabs undertook a moral invasion of these lands at a time when Arab military power was inferior to that of the Persians and Byzantines. But the invasion of ideals proved stronger than that of armies. The Arabs had left their homeland armed with a religious message and a body of doctrines centering around justice, truth, brotherhood, freedom, and peace. The peoples at that time had lost all hope of a decent life under the shadow of Persian or Byzantine regimes, in which virtue and the noble values of humanity had degenerated into nothingness. Everywhere, there was unjust materialism, corruption, subjugation, the worship of riches, stark divisions between masters and slaves, and a sword dangling over the heads of suffering humanity. The world awaited a divine act of justice that would liberate men from the injustice of their fellow men.

The Arabs as Guides and Liberators of Mankind

Amid this hopeless human community, the genuine Arab code of morality, graced and systematized by a divine message, restored dignity to mankind. It converted injustice into justice, fear into tranquility, war into peace, and slavery into freedom. It reconciled the followers of Muhammad to the followers of Christ, declared all men free and equal, and established democracy, socialism, and a cooperative spirit long before these systems of life had been regulated and codified.

This is the ethical and cultural content of the human Arab message which emanated as a spontaneous philosophy from the depths of the Arab conscience. No one taught this message to the Arabs. To quote Ibn al-Muqaffa': "Their own spirit refined them, their own courage sustained them, and their own hearts and tongue exalted them."[1] They were self-taught and knew of no other experiences and mode of life from which to draw inspiration, morality, and values except their own.

In this respect, the Arabs were the first to define national conduct and the first to originate a human ideology which they then implemented and made into a code of ethics for mankind, to be followed by whoever wished to do so.

The Arab world endured long and peacefully until the Battle of Marj Dabiq in 1516 between the guardians of Arab values and the Turks.[2] This

1. 'Abdallah ibn al-Muqaffa' was put to death *ca.* 757 because his orthodoxy was suspected. (Before his conversion from Zoroastrianism, his name had been Ruzbih.) He is best known for his translation from Persian into Arabic of *Kalila wa-Dimna* (*Kalila and Dimna*), a book of animal fables that originated in India and that had as its purpose the teaching to princes of the laws of polity.

2. The "guardians of Arab values" referred to by Jum'a were those Mamluk rulers of Egypt and Syria who defeated the Crusaders, checked the Mongols, and ruled much of the Middle East for two and a half centuries. At the Battle of Marj Dabiq (August 24,

battle spelled the end of prosperity for Arab society and of domination for Arab ideals.

The whole world was thereafter swept by a wave of confusion and perplexity which overwhelmed the understanding of men and perverted their morality and conduct. Humanity lapsed into its former state—that which had preceded the emergence of the Arabs as guides and counselors of mankind.

The Characteristics of Arab Nationalism

Arab nationalism derives its existence from the very depths of the Arab spirit and the nature of Arab life. It is, furthermore, a body of truths that transcend all discussion and argument. It is neither an importation nor an imitation of mechanistic philosophies. It is not a system of dialectics that relies for its origin and development upon logical argument and its ability, or lack of ability, to convince others.

Arab nationalism is a comprehensive, deeply ingrained faith which manifested itself in a past that the Arabs once lived through and want to relive, thus harking back to their true origin.

The fact that Arab nationalism harks back to its past and to its genuine character proves that this nationalism has a historic continuity which lacks neither a program nor a plan. The ideals of Arab nationalism have been established ever since the Almighty shaped the national character of the Arabs and endowed them with the most sublime of characteristics.

Thus authenticity is the first characteristic of Arab nationalism.

This nationalism is in all respects a purely Arab growth. It represents Arab morality as dictated by the Arab conscience and manner of life as shaped by the early Beduin existence, long before the Arabs had a state and established their dominion. It is thus a fact of history that preceded the emergence of the Arab state.

This nationalism was embodied, first, in certain values and ideals that the Arabs recognized before civilized man formulated the principles of national conduct in the form of theories, laws, and ideals. Second, it was embodied in the principles of individual, tribal, and social freedom, prior to Islam. Third, it was embodied in the unity of clan, tribe, and national group—a unity that manifested itself against the Persians and Ethiopians, prior to Islam. Fourth, it was embodied in the freedom and unity that endured throughout the period of the national state created by the Arabs and immortalized in history. Fifth, it was embodied in the principle of open deliberation [*shawra*], which the Arabs adopted ever since their Beduin days, believing in freedom of opinion, courageously declaring their views, defending justice, and ready either to persuade or to be persuaded. Sixth, it was embodied in Arab views on equality, for the Arab had always been self-respecting and had felt his own value to the

---

1516), north of Aleppo in Syria, the Ottoman army under the command of Selim I defeated the Mamluks, and at a battle outside Cairo, on January 22, 1517, the Mamluks were further, and decisively, defeated. As a consequence, Selim assumed the title of caliph and succession to the caliphate, which thereafter remained with the Ottoman sultans.

social group. No regard was ever paid to social status, riches, or power, and, throughout their wide empire, the Arabs never discriminated against color or race. Seventh, Arab nationalism was embodied in brotherhood, chivalry, love, and sympathy, ever since the earliest days of Arab history, when the actions of the Arabs resulted from their subconscious nature and their inherited customs. These reappeared thereafter in their unwritten moral code; which lasted throughout their long period of foreign domination.

Eighth, it was embodied in democracy, socialism, and the cooperative spirit, as understood by the early Arabs, who relied on public deliberation, the common enjoyment of riches, and cooperation in philanthropic deeds long before democracy, socialism, and the cooperative movement were systematized and codified. Ninth, it was embodied in the capacity of the Arabs to learn, digest, and reconcile various cultures and civilizations from the moment that the Arabs left their homeland to preach a human message and to establish the foundations for ideological cooperation among the nations. Tenth, it was embodied in the spiritual values of the Arabs, which prevented them from becoming worshipers and slaves of material life. They much preferred dignity with a hard life than comfort in slavery, refusing to barter their honor for riches. Eleventh, Arab nationalism was embodied in their liberation of mankind from injustice and poverty, in their support of the weak and the downtrodden, from the time that the Arabs became the messengers of political and social justice, bestowing dignity on medieval man. Twelfth, it was embodied in a characteristically Arab spirit of charity when they offered the world all that the Almighty had bequeathed to them by way of science, art, literature, and ethics. As guides and counselors, they were neither selfish nor closed in upon themselves but freely made available the fruits of their civilization.

Thirteenth, Arab nationalism was embodied in their gentleness, love of peace, and hatred of violence, coupled with a proper self-respect, aversion to injustice, and refusal to tolerate any insult or injury to Arab dignity.

Fourteenth, it was embodied in their firm belief in what is right, in their unswerving sense of duty, and in their complete antipathy to vassalage and dependence on others.

These were the noble values that emanated from the conscience of the Arabs. They were unique in their firmness and moderation. God Himself so disposed them that light may be distinguished from darkness, the true from the false, and the good from the evil, and that humanity may abide by such values in order to escape from perplexity and confusion.

Arab Nationalism: Assumptions and Contents

The Arab revolution constitutes a body of assumptions complemented by another coherent body of contents and facts. It also includes planning and a course of action that transforms these assumptions and contents into realities of everyday life which the Arabs come to live by, in freedom, unity, and power, and in a society that is democratic, socialist, and cooperative according to the traditional Arab interpretation of these concepts. The Arab revolution is thus a national urge that is intimately connected with human values, giving freely of its spiritual power and believing that a nationalism which is closed in upon itself is nothing more than prejudice and that a genuine nationalism is one which grows in peace, brings happiness to mankind, and protects men from the evils of exploitation.

It is, at once, a political, social, and human revolt. Politically, it implies democracy, freedom, unity, and adherence to a policy of positive neutrality.

Socially, it implies the creation of a democratic, socialist, and cooperative society, where harmony prevails between material and spiritual factors, where there is no trace of monopolies, opportunism, and exploitation, where production develops according to scientific methods, where equality of opportunities is provided, and where a just distribution of income is guaranteed.

In terms of its humanity, it implies the tendency of the Arabs to support the weak against their powerful oppressors, to achieve justice and establish peace, to substitute a brotherly cooperation in place of weapons of destruction, and peaceful coexistence in place of conflict and war, and, finally, to contribute to the progress and prosperity of civilization.

5. A SUMMARY OF THE CHARACTERISTICS OF ARAB NATIONALISM*

'Abd al-Rahman al-Bazzaz

'Abd al-Rahman al-Bazzaz, a former Iraqi teacher and Iraqi ambassador to Egypt, became his country's Prime Minister in 1962. He was known first for a lecture given in 1952 in Baghdad, in which he expressed the view that there was no contradiction between Islam and Arab nationalism. This talk, al-Islam wa-al-qawmiyya al-'arabiyya (Islam and Arab Nationalism), *was translated by Sylvia G. Haim,* Die Welt des Islams, *III (Leiden, 1954), pp. 201–19, and is reproduced in her* Arab Nationalism *(Berkeley, Calif.: University of California Press, 1962), pp. 172–88. Al-Bazzaz asserted in his lecture that those who considered nationalism as essentially secular had adopted the Western view of nationalism. Arab nationalism and Islam, according to al-Bazzaz, were intimately connected. Islam was a kind of national religion; its inner core was truly Arabic, but its Arabic purity was destroyed by other nations who came into its fold. The Prophet was an Arab, the language of the revelation, the Qur'an, was Arabic, and Islam retained many of the customs of the Arabs. Therefore, notwithstanding its universality, Islam had an inner appeal to the Arabs and, through its language, formed the core of Arab nationalism.*

* Extract from 'Abd al-Rahman al-Bazzaz, *Buhuth fi al-qawmiyya al-'arabiyya* (*Studies in Arab Nationalism*) (Cairo: Ma'had al-dirasat al-'arabiyya al'aliyya, Ja'miyyat al du'wal al-'arabiyya, 1962), pp. 320–23.

Al-Bazzaz' views on the relation between Islam and Arabism are not new. Rashid Rida (1886–1935), another famous exponent of Arab nationalism, had similar ideas, but he placed priority on Islamic solidarity, condemning racism and local or regional nationalism. This partiality shown to the Arab origins of Islam and the sense of superiority with which it was expressed caused adverse reactions among the non-Arab Muslims. Since the turn of the century, Turkish nationalists and secularists have contended that, with its Arab characteristics, Islam jeopardized the development of Turkish national culture and identity. Both Arabs and Turks had thus come to view religion, though for different purposes, in purely particularist, nationalist terms. Consequently, they had overlooked the historical fact that Islam became a truly universal religion after it renounced its Arabic racism in the 'Abbasid period (750–1258). Thereafter, it was possible for Arabs, Turks, Iranians, and other nationalities to live together for centuries by giving their allegiance to the universally binding precepts of Islam. In the age of nationalism, however, the Middle Eastern Muslims were committing an error that Western nationalists were able partially to avoid, namely, using religion to further nationalist claims.

It may be useful to summarize in a few paragraphs the salient features of Arab nationalism, some of which we have already discussed at greater length elsewhere. Our nationalism is "comprehensive," in the sense that it believes in the whole of the Arab nation and embraces the entire Arab homeland and all concepts connected with Arab life. At the same time, it is not a fossilized dogma that dispenses with man's humanity or denies his individuality.

It is also "fixed," in the sense that it is neither a temporary nor a transitory phase that nations pass through on their way to a wider internationalism. Nevertheless, and despite its fixed foundations, our nationalism is neither stagnant nor reactionary nor hostile to the noble ideals of humanity.

It is also "democratic," in the sense that it believes in the right of the Arab nation to decide its destiny and to govern itself, for the benefit of all its sons. Its democracy is based on open deliberation [*shawra*], which is averse to tyranny and dictatorship. At the same time, it does not feel obliged to cling obstinately to certain types of democratic practice. It is concerned, above all else, with the democratic spirit, as it understands it and as guided by its own democratic experience and development.

Furthermore, it is "socialist," in the sense that it is socially oriented, serving the public interest before individual freedom and seeking to achieve social justice and cohesion and fruitful cooperation among all citizens. It works to develop the Arab economy on the basis of planning that aims to create a just and healthy economy and to achieve prosperity for all. But its socialism is not Marxist and its economic beliefs are based solely neither on the material things of life nor on the domination of one class by another.

Our Arab nationalism is "cooperative," in the sense that it propagates a spirit of cooperation, not of conflict and hostility among the citizens in all sectors of life. But its cooperative character does not entail the total subjection of the economy to a system of cooperatives, of which it makes only a limited use. It regards cooperation, with its wide horizons, as extending beyond the realm of the merely economic.

It is "progressive" and forward-looking, and believes in renewal and creativity. But it pursues its clearly defined objectives with perspicacity. Its progressive character does not make it deny its past, and it moves forward, not for movement's sake, but in order to achieve its unalterable nationalist objectives.

It is "revolutionary"; it believes in, propagates, and adheres to the demands of the revolution. But it distinguishes between constructive revolt and negative destruction that leads to chaos and fails to achieve reform.

It is "positive," for it cooperates with all nations, exchanging its ideas with all modern ideas consonant with its philosophy. But despite its positive character, it does not aim at dissolving itself into internationalism or at losing its distinctive character by attaching itself to leagues and treaties. At the present juncture in particular, it prefers to adhere to a policy of positive neutrality and nonalignment.

It is "mobile," in the sense that it actively pursues its objectives. But its constant advance does not blind it to its ideals. It does not wish to lose sight of its path by indulging the wishes of one group or another who attempt to pull it in various directions.

In addition to all this, our nationalism, despite its belief in the importance and necessity of the material things of life, places its faith in the spiritual aspect of life, holding that the souls of men are in need of high ideals and creeds, and that noble spirits cannot be satisfied by bread alone but require a certain nourishment which exemplifies the genuine dignity of existence.

To sum up, then, Arab nationalism is an eternal message emanating from the character of the Arab nation and is inspired by Arab history. Historical inevitability calls upon it to achieve its material and spiritual purposes, both present and future.

It is the mission and the rallying point of Arab nationalists who have faith in its requirements, believing it to be the only road to salvation, dignity, peace, justice, and stability.

III. *Modern Arab Nationalism*

6. THE HISTORICAL FACTOR IN THE FORMATION OF NATIONALISM*

Sati' al-Husri

Since the mid-1950's, Abu Khaldun Sati' al-Husri (b. 1879) has been the most influential contemporary writer on Arab nationalism. Born in Aleppo, al-Husri studied in Istanbul before World War I and became an official in the Turkish Ministry of Education. After the war, he associated himself with the Arab nationalist movement, as represented by King Faysal, whom he followed from Damascus to Baghdad, where al-Husri became the head of general education. Banished from Iraq because of his involvement in Rashid Ali's pro-Nazi coup of 1941, al-Husri went to Beirut, then to Cairo. In 1947, he became the head of the cultural section of the Arab League, a position he held until his retirement.

*Al-Husri believed that nationalism is a question of belonging to and identifying with a group, and that history and especially language create such conditions. Departing from his early views, he increasingly advocated the fusion of the individual into the nation, even if this meant sacrificing the individual's freedom. It is interesting that al-Husri's friend, Ziya Gökalp, a prominent Turkish nationalist, arrived at more or less the same conclusion, following not the logic of free thought but the rise and evolution of the political state capable of acting on behalf, and fulfilling the ideals, of a nation. (Al-Husri differed from Gökalp on the purposes of education.) This identification of the individual with his political group has a religious mystical significance that is rooted, as Sylvia G. Haim remarked, in the "union of the worshiper with the Godhead" of the Islamic mystics. (*Arab Nationalism: An Anthology *[Berkeley, Calif.: University of California Press, 1962], p. 44.) Haim claims that using a religious concept for a secular purpose is al-Husri's great innovation. Actually, Ziya Gökalp, a mystic in his own right, had stated this even earlier, and far more explicitly, than al-Husri. Gökalp discussed the obligations stemming from life in a community and stated that "one must develop a will powerful enough to overcome individual ambitions. In short, the individual must 'negate' himself in the community before he may 'survive' in it. . . . In this way a self-seeking being becomes a sacrificing citizen." (See translation in Niyazi*

* Extract from Sati' al-Husri, *Hawla al-qawmiyya al-'arabiyya* (*Concerning Arab Nationalism*) (Beirut: Dar al-'ilm lil-malayin, 1961), pp. 104–5, 108–10.

Berkes, Turkish Nationalism and Western Civilization *[New York: Columbia University Press, 1959], p. 188.)*

Both al-Husri and Gökalp present similar arguments about the differences between their respective nationalisms and Islamic universalism and about the place of language in nationalism. With his convincing style and argumentation, al-Husri has continually and successfully argued against the views of those Arab writers who excluded Egypt from the proposed Arab state or did not consider it Arabic. The emergence of Egypt as the center of Arab nationalism and her advocacy of the union of all Arabs have greatly facilitated the popularization of al-Husri's ideas. Their popularization was also possible because of al-Husri's sense of political realism and his ability to distinguish between the practical and the utopian. These characteristics resulted not only from al-Husri's being "marginal to the process he was describing" (as Albert Hourani puts it) but also from his knowledge of the history of European nationalism and his keen understanding of the Turkish experience in building a national state.

On al-Husri, see L. M. Kenny, "Sati' al-Husri's Views on Arab Nationalism," Middle East Journal, *XVII (Summer, 1963), 231–56, and Albert Hourani,* Arab Thought in the Liberal Age, 1798–1939 *(London and New York: Oxford University Press, 1962), pp. 311–17. Unfortunately, the scanty Western writings on al-Husri ignore his intellectual activity in Istanbul and the Rumelian provinces and his many publications in Turkish, including his basic articles on education published in the review* Muallim (Teacher) *in 1915. For al-Husri's activities in Turkey, see Hilmi Ziya Ülken,* Türkiye'de Çağdaş Düşünce Tarihi (History of Contemporary Thought in Turkey), *I (Konya: Selçuk yayinlari, 1966), 269–92.*

Al-Husri's writings on nationalism have been reprinted several times. Mention should be made of Ara' wa-ahadith fi al-wataniyya wa-al-qawmiyya (Views and Speeches on Patriotism and Nationalism) *(Cairo: Matba'at al-risala, 1944), and* Muhadarat fi nushu' al-fikra al-qawmiyya (Lectures on the Origins of the Nationalist Idea) *(3d ed.; Beirut: Dar al-'ilm lil-malayin, 1956). In* Ma hiya al-qawmiyya (What Is Nationalism?) *(Beirut: Dar al-'ilm lil-malayin, 1959), and in the following extract based on his prior writings, al-Husri restates his views on the foundations of Arab nationalism and on who is an Arab.*

A young man once relayed to me a criticism he had heard over the radio of my book *What is Nationalism?* The critic apparently said that, in the concluding sentence of my book, I wrote that "The basic factor in the formation of the nation and nationalism is the unity of the nation and of its history." The critic added that, in a book of 250 pages, I had not touched upon the unity of history prior to this phrase.

I was astonished. I opened the book and read the following sentences. . . .

> A common descent cannot by any means be considered as among the distinguishing characteristics of a nation. . . .
>
> In fact, the sons of a single nation consider themselves as kinsmen and brothers, as though they descended from a common stock. In general, they call

> their ancestors 'grandfathers' [*ajdad*]. But the relationship that they feel toward their ancestors is spiritual. It is a relationship that is born of various social bonds, especially a common language and history, but that in no way denotes a relationship of blood or descent (p. 45).

It may be noted that I have here mentioned history together with language. Furthermore, having explained this spiritual relationship, I wrote: "In any case, a common descent must form no part of any definition of the nation. It would be more appropriate to substitute a common history instead. The importance of a common history in the formation of this spiritual relationship and in the creation of the widespread myth of a common descent is paramount" (p. 46). Here again I wrote about history, citing it as one of the most important constituents of this spiritual relationship, and urging that it should occupy a special place in the definition of a nation, instead of a common descent and blood, which must be discarded from such a definition.

Thus, it is patently false to claim that I did not discuss the question of a common history until the concluding sentence of my book. As a matter of fact, I did not revert to a discussion of the two passages quoted above, because this problem was never a subject for debate among scholars. My book *What is Nationalism?* was devoted to a critical review of the various theories. Furthermore, in my other works—especially in my *Patriotism and Nationalism* [*al-Wataniyya wa-al-qawmiyya*]—I have explained the role of history in the formation of nationalism.

Who Is an Arab?: A Reappraisal

In my book *Views and Speeches on Arab Nationalism* [i.e., *Views and Speeches on Patriotism and Nationalism*], I described an argument that took place in the lecture hall of the Society for Arab Unity concerning the question, "Who Is an Arab?"

The lecturer who opened the discussion said, "An Arab is a man who speaks Arabic and wants to be an Arab." I objected to the latter part of his statement. "Suppose," I said, "a fellow is an Arab but ignores this fact—what then?" The lecturer replied, "If he does not want to be an Arab, how can you consider him as one? Would it not be better to make the will a condition for being an Arab?"

This is how I answered: "When we find a man who disowns, and takes no pride, in the fact that he is an Arab, even though he is Arabic-speaking and belongs to an Arab nation, we must discover the reasons for his attitude. It may be out of ignorance, in which case we should tell him the truth. It may be that he is deluded, in which case we should direct him to the true path. It may be that he is too selfish, in which case we must work to curtail his egoism. Whatever the reason, we must not say he is not an Arab as long as he does not wish to be an Arab but disowns and despises his Arabism. He is an Arab, whether he likes it or not, whether he accepts it or not—at the present time. He may be ignorant, stupid, ungrateful, or treacherous, but he is an Arab all the same—an Arab who has lost his sensibility, his emotions, and maybe even his conscience" (pp. 65–66).

It appears that the view I briefly outlined above escaped the notice of some and did not alter the opinions of others. Some writers and scholars still claim that an Arab is "a man who speaks Arabic and wants to be an Arab." This has led me, on several occasions, to reopen the controversy and to express my views on the matter in greater detail. A man once put forward the following objection: "I say very frankly that I cannot consider a person to be an Arab when I see him disowning his Arabism and unwilling to be an Arab." I decided to adopt a new approach in the hope of convincing him, so I said, "I would like to know what our attitude would be toward someone who, having previously disowned his Arabism, says 'I am an Arab.' Should we say, 'He was not an Arab but then became one' or should we not rather say, 'He was not conscious of his Arabism, but when he discovered his true Arab identity, he recognized this fact'?" Having put this question to him, I followed it up with references to factual examples: "Two years ago," I said, "I read an article by Ahmad Bahaeddin [Baha' al-Din], in which he admitted that he was once very far from Arabism. He then related the particular circumstances and events that made him change his mind and become conscious of his Arab identity. Last year, I read an article by Salah 'Abd al-Sabur in which he eloquently and candidly described the development of his inner self and the change that came upon his views and emotions and restored him to Arabism.

"Here then," I continued, "we have frank confessions from two of our ablest younger writers. Given these circumstances, should we say about them that they were not Arabs but then became Arab at the moment when they published their confessions and explained the change that had come over them? It is obvious that this would be absurd. Faced with such circumstances, we are, logically speaking, obliged to say that the fellow was unconscious of his Arabism but then came to discover his Arab identity."

I noticed that the objecter was impressed by this argument. Nevertheless, not wishing to abandon his former position, he added: "But these are exceptional cases. Should we base our judgment on exceptions?" "No," I said, "they are not exceptions. I mentioned these two confessions because they appeared in print. But I assure you that I heard similar confessions in conversations with many writers and thinkers. Furthermore, if we closely examine these articles by 'Abd al-Sabur and Bahaeddin we shall find that they mirror, not only the writer's own feelings, but the feelings and sentiments of a whole generation."

7. WHO IS AN ARAB? ARAB NATIONALISM AND THE PROBLEM OF MINORITIES*

Clovis Maqsud

Clovis Maqsud (b. 1925), a Maronite Lebanese, is one of the most original thinkers in the Arab intellectual community. After attending the American University of Beirut, he studied for an advanced degree at Oxford, and, after many years of activity in Lebanese politics, he served for a time as the Arab League's representative in India. For additional information about Maqsud, see pp. 166–75 of this book.

Although Maqsud is known as an ideologue of Arab nationalism, his ideas in this field are usually subordinate to his socialist doctrine. In the following extract, Maqsud attempts to define Arabness on the basis not of race and religion but of direct affiliation with a country through citizenship, acquired either by conscious decision or by force of circumstance. Thus, Maqsud's allowance for will in determining one's Arabness contrasts sharply with Sati' al-Husri's view that one should be made aware, through indoctrination, of his identity as an Arab. Maqsud uses the term nationalism in the sense of loyalty to and political identification with one's country of citizenship.

Who is an Arab? This may, at first sight, appear to be a simple question, but it is in fact of momentous importance to the Arab nationalist movement.

An Arab is one whose "destiny" is, either by force of circumstances or intentionally, bound to the Arab world as a whole. This definition may lead to further questions, so we shall attempt to clarify it. If we establish this bond of destiny to the Arab world as the criterion for judging whether a man is or is not an Arab, it follows that historical connections to the Arab race do not necessarily imply that one's destiny is bound up with that of the Arab world. For example, an American or Brazilian descended from Arab stock is not an Arab, according to our definition, since his destiny, both by circumstance and by free will, is bound up with that of the USA or Brazil. He has become an American or Brazilian citizen, owing allegiance to the state to whose destiny he has linked his own. This affiliation gains in strength with the second and third generation of emigrants descended from Arab stock.

This holds true of the Arab world as well. Whoever is descended from Kurdish, Negro, or Armenian stock but has inhabited an Arab country becomes an Arab by force of circumstances and by reason of the free association of his own destiny with that of the Arab world.

But at this point, some may claim that this definition implies that Arab

* Extract from Clovis Maqsud, *Azmat al-yasar al-'arabi* (*Crisis of the Arab Left*) (Beirut: Dar al-'ilm lil-malayin, 1960), pp. 113–21.

nationalism wishes to dissolve those ethnic groups and that it, in turn, means a violation of their rights and of the principle of self-determination. The answer to this is that the acceptance of various ethnic groups within a national society does not entail the dissolution of the groups but, on the contrary, offers the national society the chance to benefit to the full from ethnic diversity. In India, for example, there are various nationalities, regional languages, and religious sects, but this diversity has not prevented the emergence of an Indian society capable of absorbing these ethnic and religious groups and of molding them into one Indian nationalism, without violating their rights.

There is no doubt that various groups of non-Arab origin have settled in the Arab world, not temporarily but freely and permanently. A considerable number have acquired Arab nationality and are now enjoying all the rights and obligations of Arab citizenship. With the passage of years, the new generations have been absorbed into their new nationalism [derived from citizenship].

That the process of absorption did not happen as speedily as was expected is due to the attempts by imperialist powers to use these minorities as an integral part of their policy and as a tool with which to attack nationalism. Although the process has been slow, the nationalist movement must not tolerate the reluctance of some minority groups to be absorbed. However, it must be fully aware of its responsibilities toward those groups and must realize that their reluctance has been caused by two basic motives, which must be radically dealt with along socialist lines that emanate from and complement the national movement. These two motives are: (1) The first generation of emigrants who have settled in other countries are characteristically aloof from the nationalist movements of countries in which they have settled. This was the case, for example, with the first generation of Italian, Irish, and Greek emigrants to the United States. But in subsequent generations, the process of absorption becomes automatic. It appears that absorption happens quickly in national societies which are themselves capable of accepting new ethnic groups. Unified educational curriculums, common habits of economic consumption, and continuous opportunities for interaction created by industrialization, the economy, the general political scene, and a common culture—all these factors ensure a more thorough process of absorption.

It may be maintained that emigration to independent countries differs from emigration to countries under foreign domination, where the new emigrants, because of their aloofness, become tools in the hands of imperialists to be used against nationalism. It may also be said that many Englishmen and Frenchmen have settled in Kenya and Algeria and, as a result, deprived the original inhabitants of their rights. But does our definition take such cases into account? Obviously, the answer is no, since those groups do not emigrate for the purpose of linking their destiny to that of the original inhabitants but they emigrate as a result of aggression and with the object of exploiting and controlling the new lands for their own benefit. They remain aloof from the national societies not because they are reluctant to be absorbed but, rather, because they are intent upon gaining mastery. They may be compared with armies of occupation rather than settlers. Settlement presupposes the existence of a homeland and the will to belong to that homeland, whereas those groups deny the existence of a homeland and link their destiny to that of the imperialist power, which gave them their authority in the first place.

It is obvious, therefore, that we must distinguish between the settlers and the occupiers. In concrete terms, there is a difference, therefore, between the Armenian who has settled in Lebanon and the Frenchman who came to live in Algeria. The latter considered himself to be indissolubly linked to the future of France in Algeria and worked to prevent Algeria's self-determination. Therefore, aloofness among new emigrants is not a sign of vestigial passivity but may become so if the emigrants keep to themselves and do not interact fruitfully with the society to which they belong. Doubtless there are some elements among those groups who exploit this original aloofness for their own purposes in the hope of attaining leadership among them. This opportunistic attitude, however, is not dominant. The mood dominant among them is one of doing things by stages. Inevitably, this process of evolution will lead to a natural merger.

In Iraq, for example, certain elements (i.e., among the Kurds) encourage secessionist sentiments and call for independent nationalism. Since the international situation does not permit this, those elements exert pressure on the Communist Party in order to keep Iraq away from healthy interaction with the rest of the Arab world. But the noise that they succeed in making does not mean that they represent the group in whose name they claim to speak and whose aspirations they pretend to express. Even if, for the sake of argument, we admit that they do represent the majority opinion of those groups, this can only last for a certain time but cannot continue indefinitely. . . .

The reluctance of some minority groups to be absorbed . . . is due to two reasons:

1. The first generation of emigrants are characteristically aloof from the general nationalist current in the society where they have settled. Succeeding generations, however, are soon absorbed.

2. Frequently, the majority itself is reluctant to allow the minorities to be absorbed into Arab society, owing to the cultural and social differences between them. This mutual reluctance and the consequent aloofness engendered is, however, soon abated, since it is caused by purely psychological motives that tend to lose their importance in relation to the cultural, economic, and political factors making for a common destiny for both the majority and the minority. But such unification depends on the opinion of the majority about the creation of the state. If the Arab majority fancies that descent from an Arab stock is a necessary prerequisite for acquiring Arab citizenship, its attitude will lead to fragmentation and secession. But if it realizes that the modern state is based upon foundations that are quite distinct from racialism, then its mental readiness to absorb racial diversity becomes clearer and more forceful. . . .

The majority's readiness to absorb minorities must be accompanied by a basic guarantee—namely, that such absorption will not mean the dissipation of the nationalist character of the nation to which the majority belongs. The minority, therefore, must be prepared to accept the nationalism of the majority.

The large-scale exodus that creates minorities happens only under abnormal international circumstances or as a result of massive persecutions or in the search for a livelihood. Therefore, domination by a minority over a majority of another race is not usual except in cases where the minority intends to take over the homeland of the majority and deny them their basic rights. In such cases, the right to defend national existence becomes legitimate even if it leads to some racial discrimination. That is the case with the Arabs and the Zionists in Palestine, the French in Algeria, and the national struggle in Kenya and South Africa against the aggression of foreign colonizers.

The acceptance by the majority of the principle of absorbing and merging minorities into one national mold depends upon the motives and circumstances of the exodus of the minorities. Usurpation clearly signifies the refusal of the minorities to belong to the nationality of the majority and the presence of a narrow racialist outlook which urges the minorities to exploit and dominate. Such minorities are obviously not ready to be absorbed into the larger national whole.

However, in the case of minorities that have settled in a homeland as a result of persecution (e.g., the Armenians) or of other historical circumstances, and which have not merged into Arab society to any desirable extent, the motives for their presence among us do not justify any reluctance on our part (i.e., the Arab majority) to accept their absorption into Arab nationalism. It may be claimed that some of these groups possess a certain secessionist outlook and a racialist nationalism militating against absorption. In such cases, we must not tolerate the spokesmen for such opinions, since they deliberately set out to falsify the issue. We must work to isolate them from their popular support.

When minorities bind their destiny to that of the nation, of their own free will and by force of circumstances, they cannot possibly be allowed to harbor racialist sentiments within our homeland. To belong wholly to one nation presupposes loyalty, and loyalty cannot be temporary. Thus, if certain racial minorities consider themselves to be temporary refugees, their loyalty cannot be always for the nation. In this case, such groups would not constitute a part of the national entity which we advocate and which, according to our definition, is nonracial. Among racial groups which believe that their stay in the Arab world is temporary there is the Armenian Tashnak Party which asks Armenians to consider their stay in Lebanon to be temporary and calls for a return to an independent Armenia. But the political importance of such groups decreases with time and with the increasing readiness of Arab society to absorb minorities.

Zionism, similarly, asks the Jews to consider themselves temporary citizens of the countries where they have settled and to owe full allegiance to the Jewish State. Such calls among racial and religious minorities throw doubt on their loyalty to the nations where they have settled and are detrimental to the minorities themselves. Furthermore, they impede the mental readiness of the majority to accept the minority. The mutual antipathy between majority and minority distorts the progressive image of Arab nationalism and hinders the nation's struggle for unity and liberation.

Hence, we maintain that we must not acquiesce in the principle of self-determination for these minorities because this would imply our recognition of the creation of racial and religious "enclaves" within our homeland and would turn Arab nationalism itself into a racialist and religious call. It may be claimed that since some minorities inhabit exclusive geographical regions, they are entitled to self-determination and secession from the Arab homeland. This claim, at first sight, appears to be just but is, in essence, unjust, since it implies that these calls for secession enjoy the full support of racialist minorities. That is clearly not so. Furthermore, secessionist notions expose these groups to grave setbacks when they venture outside areas where they are in control. In addition, international impediments militate against this kind of self-determination.

Finally, these groups have not found that their presence in certain areas has prevented their leaving those areas. The conduct of these minorities, their efforts to learn Arabic in addition to their mother tongue, the expansion of their economic interests into regions of the state to which they legally belong, and their association with the public and political life of the country—all these factors indicate that a considerable number among the minorities do not believe in secession and that they are prepared to be absorbed into the nation to which they belong. Therefore, to admit their right to secede, several generations after their settlement, is to encourage a hopeful trend of fanaticism among racial and religious minorities.

The socialist standpoint, then, as regards this problem is to make racial diversity in the national society a source of cultural benefit. This means that socialism encourages the revitalization of the various cultures and considers their organization and interaction to be a source of vitality and creativity to the new Arab society we are advocating.

8. ARAB NATIONALISM ON BALANCE*

George Hanna

George Hanna, a physician practicing in Beirut, was born a Christian but apparently has no religious affiliation at this time. He is considered a materialist, and some regard him as an extreme Marxist. He has read Marx, but in

* Extract from George Hanna, *Ma'na al-qawmiyya al-'arabiyya* (*The Meaning of Arab Nationalism*) (Beirut: Dar al-thakafa, 1959), pp. 33–34, 60–63.

interviewing him one gets the impression that he tries to remain nondogmatic. Hanna's nationalism has economic foundations but also a certain mystical, revolutionary tendency. His influence seems to be rising, and his writings continue to be published frequently.

Is Arab nationalism a reality or an illusion? In order to answer this question, we must revert to what we have termed the nationalist characteristics, consider them one by one, and then see whether they are present among the ethnic group inhabiting this part of what we call the Arab world and whether such characteristics are sufficiently in evidence to constitute one nationalism, namely Arab nationalism. Let us begin with the first of these characteristics: a common language. Does the Arab world possess a common language? In the pre-Islamic age, the Arabic language was confined to the region called the Arabian Peninsula. The rest of the world spoke different languages, such as Hebrew, Aramaic, Syriac, Chaldean, etc. In that age, there was no such thing as nationalism. The peoples led a tribal existence, bound by no social, historical, or economic ties.

But the emergence of the Islamic message and the expansion of Arab conquest changed Arab life from a tribal to a social one, dominated by Islam. This manner of life was the seed from which nationalism sprang.

It is true that Arabism was then more Islamic than it was nationalist. But the constant and deep interaction in that period between Christian and Muslim Arabs—whether it was in their common stand against a non-Arab enemy, in their common life together, in their cooperation and mutual interests, or in their common customs—this interaction provided the basis for the creation of a common nationalism, even though the genuine nationalist idea had not yet crystallized.

Because of this interaction and the spread of Islamic conquests, the Arabic language overran all the other languages then in use. Arabic became the language of both Muslims and Christians and was written and used by both. Furthermore, Arabic became the language of literature, poetry, and publication in general, even of the published literature which was non-Arabic in origin and of whatever was translated from foreign literature and sciences. . . .

[Two obstacles stand] in the way of the development of Arab nationalism: the economic and political obstacles. From these two spring all other obstacles, which would also disappear if they disappeared. What exactly are these obstacles?

They are poverty, disease, ignorance, dependence on others, the absence of a sense of responsibility, the adoption of corrupt and corrupting political and economic governmental systems, acquiescence to tyranny, the all-too-easy idolatry practiced toward rulers, kings, and so-called leaders, strongmen, and prominent personalities, before one has had time to test them, review their achievements, and get to know the extent of their loyalty to their country, their peoples, and their nationalism.

Poverty and disease must of necessity result from an economic system that tolerates exploitation, monopolies, and the trading with the souls of men and their means of subsistence.

Ignorance, dependence on others, the lack of a sense of responsibility, and the idolization of rulers, kings, and leaders—these qualities result from a political system that makes gods of kings, saints of leaders, and gives the "governmental cells" the authority to decide upon legislation and the implementation of the law.

To talk about the necessity for combatting poverty, disease, ignorance, and all the other ills of the Arab world before one has taken positive, effective steps to reform the political and economic system in the Arab world is, indeed, neither more nor less than an attempt at camouflage.

The obstacles to the development of Arab nationalism are not only internal. Certain external obstacles are no less, if not more, important. The two types of obstacles, external and internal, are closely linked and mutually interdependent. What are the foreign obstacles to the growth of Arab nationalism? They are nothing more nor less than imperialism. Arab nationalism can never develop nor be based on firm, progressive, and humanistic foundations as long as imperialism or imperialist influence is still active in the Arab world.

Throughout the centuries when the Arab world was a plaything in the hands of the imperialists, nationalist consciousness fluctuated between regional, religious, sectarian, and anti-Arab nationalisms (if one may use this term). Amid this chaos, imperialism was the effective force and always held the winning card. Throughout this period, the Arabs did not learn their lesson from the blows that imperialism was dealing to their nationalism. Whatever one may say, catastrophes are instructive. But the Arabs were like the prodigal son who was not willing either to learn or to wake up. The greatest catastrophe of all, Palestine, befell them, but they did not learn a single lesson from it. The Arab rulers who were in power during the catastrophe and who helped to bring it about remained in power afterward. Imperialism, which planted this thorn in the heart of the Arab world and dispersed 1 million Palestinians, did not lose any of its standing with the Arab countries. Indeed, in some countries, it increased its influence, especially with the rulers.

Owing to these rulers, the catastrophe of Palestine was transformed from a national and human tragedy into a human tragedy only, whose remedy lay with "relief agencies," "supervisory committees" over the shameful situation, and the useless debates of the U.N. and that abortive body called the Arab League.

Arab nationalism needed something more than complaints, compromises, empty boasts, and congresses. It needed a new drive, a revolution that would succeed both at home and abroad. This new revolution materialized in Egypt on July 22, 1952. Let those who attempt to deny, resist, or belittle that revolution be silenced.

9. THE NATIONALISTS' WAR AGAINST COMMUNISM*

Fayez Sayegh

Fayez Sayegh (Fayiz Sayigh), born in Syria in 1922 and brought up in Palestine, has taught in the United States and is professor of international studies at the American Uinversity of Beirut. He was formerly counselor to the Arab League. His best known book is Arab Unity: Hope and Fulfillment *(New York: Devin Adair, 1958).*

The course of a battle always depends on the combatants and on the issue over which the battle is fought. Our battles against Zionism, imperialism, and reactionary Arab regimes all differ from each other and from our battle against Communism, depending upon the enemy. If Communism had been nothing more than a destructive movement intent on destroying the state that embodies the liberated Arab nationalism, on fragmenting its unity and undermining the sovereignty of other Arab states in order to establish a fully Communist-inspired regime, and if Communism had no other aim, then the responsibility of combating it would have fallen upon the particular government or governments concerned. The method of fighting it would have been limited to such methods as are normally resorted to by governments that face the conspiracies of dissident groups and threaten the state security, such as dissolving conspiratorial parties, banning their activities, and controlling, prosecuting, and arresting their members.

Since Communism's challenge to liberated Arab nationalism is not confined solely to conspiracy and destructive activity, this challenge cannot be effectively met if it is limited only to government counteraction and public warnings against conspiracies.

Communism possesses another nature, in addition to its conspiratorial character. Communism is itself a message. Communism's attempts at destruction are not an end in themselves but are only a means to achieve a Communist society. Thus, to fight Communism solely by repression does not guarantee the protection of Arab society from its dangerous appeal as a message.

To the extent, therefore, that Communism depends in propagating its message on actual injustices born of corrupt conditions—exploitation, monopolies, cruelty, absence of social justice, poverty, a low standard of life, and other such manifestations of regression and backwardness in Arab society—by that

* Extract from Fayez Sayegh, "Ma'rakatuna ma'a al-shuyu'iyya" ("Our Battle Against Communism"), *al-Adab (Literature)*, Beirut, June, 1959, pp. 1–3.

much will resistance to it by Arab nationalism have to depend on concentrated, serious endeavor to build a healthy, progressive society.

The suppression of feudalism and exploitation, the struggle against destitution by providing equality of opportunities for all so that they can contribute to their nation's progress and enjoy its prosperity, the establishment of social justice, and the eradication of all other causes of bitterness among the citizens —all these actions, in harmony with the national ideals, hasten the removal of injustice and rancor, through which Communism attempts to infiltrate into the hearts of men.

The methods of repression used by governments against Communism as a destructive movement may be compared to therapeutic medicine, employed against disease when it has spread, while economic reconstruction and social reform may be compared to preventive medicine, used in order to forestall the spread of the disease, not solely through inoculation and the creation of body resistance but also by improving health and physical exercise. There is yet another aspect to Communism that is perhaps more dangerous than the first two. It is the fact that responsibility for fighting Communism is handed over to individuals, public societies, national parties, and, perhaps most of all, to intellectuals, not to the governments. Communism as a destructive movement and as a movement that exploits injustices and the greed for a better life is in fact an extension of Communism as a comprehensive dogma. Dogmas cannot be fought except by other dogmas. Therefore, Communism cannot be fought effectively and in the long term unless and until Arab nationalism presents to the millions of Arab masses, who yearn to place their faith in a sublime ideal, a clear social dogma that can win their faith, call forth sense of sacrifice, and dominate their hearts.

Slogans alone cannot satisfy this yearning, for slogans can be easily counterfeited by impostors, and it is often difficult to distinguish the false from the true when there is no specific content according to which this distinction is to be made.

I firmly believe that liberated Arab nationalism can furnish a dogma of a sufficiently positive content that can forestall the Communist attempt to infiltrate the masses through the twin paths of coining slogans and claiming to be what it is not, on the one hand, and breaking into the ideological vacuum with the purpose of filling it, on the other.

The advocates of liberated Arab nationalism among men of thought are called upon to draw up this dogma, define it, and make it clear-cut and profound. This article does not propose to offer such a creed. It is merely a call to follow what can be the only path if we want to succeed permanently in our struggle against Communism and to achieve a victory that is worthy of our beliefs. We can now outline, in a preliminary manner, certain major differences between liberated Arab nationalism and Communism.

Communism differs from Arab nationalism in its premises and its final objectives, in the interests each is seeking to realize, and in the higher values influencing each. Our premise is not that of Communism. Nationalism is born of love: the love of the citizen for his fellow-citizens and his hopes for their prosperity and dignity. Communism, however, is born of a deep-rooted grudge, of hatred, and of rancor against exploiters and exploitation, whoever they are.

We, as nationalists, seek to liberate every citizen from exploitation, poverty, and indignity, out of love for him as a human being and a citizen. Communism, however, emphasizes the object of its hatred more than the object of its love and loyalty.

Liberated nationalism seeks to free all citizens and all classes in the nation of whatever deprives them of their humanity and degrades them as human beings. Communism, however, has a limited allegiance. It seeks to turn the deprived into a depriving class and to degrade those who are degrading it at present.

Thus we see that nationalism differs from Communism in its premise. The first is born of love and charity and comprehends all the citizens of the nation.

Again, there is a difference in the ideal system that each pursues. The difference may be seen if one compares a system that takes its form from the existing conditions of each society with one that is ossified and whose advocates are seeking to implement an identical system in every society, without taking into account particular circumstances, distinctive traditions, and national entities.

The Communist system revolves around economic organization, inspired, as it is, by Marxism, which places economic considerations above all others and views every human activity as a mere extension or result of economics. The dominating principle in this system is one whose end is to suppress free individual and public initiative in the economy and in all other walks of life. Nationalism, however, does not merge all humanity into the economic mold, nor does it deny free individual initiative except in so far as this creates or propagates exploitation.

Liberated nationalism works for the sovereignty of the nation and the best interests of the people. But Communism works, first and last, to serve the interests of an international movement that may conflict with the interests of a particular nation. National interest will then be sacrificed for the sake of the movement. Furthermore, Communism requires subservience and lays down its policies and its strategy in accordance with orders received from abroad. National sovereignty would be forsaken and effective control handed over to foreign powers.

Finally, Communism is in reality a comprehensive outlook that sets itself up as a reference point for all other beliefs, as a judge of all action and a standard for all values. No truth and no virtue can exist outside of itself. It is a comprehensive faith that embraces the whole of human existence, leaving nothing unaccounted for. It is a religion that seeks to deny all others and to outlaw all other forms of worship! The society it seeks to erect, the dictatorship of the proletariat, is the idol compared to which the human personality is erased and which commands man's total allegiance without recognizing his genuine individuality.

Upon this level of comprehensive dogma, Communism is revealed in all its terror: It is found to be a creed that begins by claiming to be a champion of man against injustice and exploitation and ends by robbing man of all his values and degrading him until it can later satisfy his bodily needs.

Nationalism neither pursues nor claims such a comprehensive outlook. It admits the sanctity of such areas of human life that fall outside the scope of social reorganization. Nationalism does not claim the right to judge questions pertaining to art, science, philosophy, or religion. It does not set itself up as an arbiter of truth, virtue, or beauty. It realizes that man's pursuit of such ideals can become creative only if it is coupled with absolute freedom. The standards of such ideals spring from the ideals themselves and are not borrowed from the outside. Loyalty to these values is not limited by loyalty to others. Any dogma, therefore, that lays claim to what it does not own is deceptive and tyrannical, however much it pretends to safeguard human freedom.

Both the danger and the error of Communism lie in the fact that it is comprehensive, whereas nationalism's point of pride is that it is not so.

In facing Communism, nationalism must undertake a process of ideological clarification whose end is to define the nationalist content and to make it substantive.

Nevertheless, the present ideological vacuum is no more dangerous to nationalism than the attempts currently undertaken by certain nationalists to fill it with a comprehensive nationalist creed. Success against Communism can only be attained if we work to substitute a clear nationalist ideal for this vacuum, being constantly on our guard against formulating a dogma that claims to be total and comprehensive.

It is by means of a clearly defined nationalist ideal that one will come plainly to distinguish between the negative contribution of Communism in certain directions (e.g., the struggle against imperialism, reaction, and regression) and the positive contribution of nationalism. One will also be able to distinguish between the motives that lead Communism and nationalism to make these contributions and between their other objectives where no common ground can be found.

10. THE CRISIS OF ARAB NATIONALISM*

Arkan Abadi

The question of defining a modern Arab ideology that would combine the major ideas of the Arab world—nationalism, social reform, and democracy—has been a preoccupation of the liberal-minded intellectuals in the Arab world. A democratic-nationalist group, they are striving to preserve within the new

* Extract from Arkan Abadi, *Mihnat al-qawmiyya al-'arabiyya* (*The Crisis of Arab Nationalism*) (Beirut: Matabi' jaridat al-hayat, 1962), pp. 137–42.

context of nationalism some of the liberal values they regard as inherent in any modern humanist system. Despite great difficulties, they are trying to maintain a balance between the extremes of left and right. Moderately and objectively, Arkan Abadi, a Lebanese intellectual, expresses the need for an Arab ideology to be defined by learned men, conscious of the traditions and values of Arab society and determined to preserve them instead of permitting their destruction by military revolutions.

We call on all Arab men of thought and on the whole Arab nation to join hands in serious common endeavor and to sacrifice themselves for the sake of our sublime ideals. Our scholars who have grasped both the spirit of the past and the problems of the present must define anew the foundations of this nation's intellectual renaissance in order to revive the nation's institutions, customs, and mission for the sake of a better future and before it is too late.

The National Charter

Its general bearing. A national charter would be promulgated, having been previously ratified at a general congress which would include a group of leading thinkers, political leaders, journalists, authors, educators, and jurists in the Arab world. This congress would be under the general supervision of a leading thinker or Arab leader, who can then support this charter with all his moral authority and present it to the Arab peoples, rulers, Arab League, and cultural institutions for their ratification and support. The congress would aim at:

1. The firm establishment of facts, principles, and essential objectives that are indisputable, in order that they may constitute a comprehensive review of Arab ideology.
2. The definition of ideals, reforms, and the path to political unity. The ways and means shall also be determined.
3. Repeated annual or periodic sessions of the congress shall be held until the objectives are achieved. The political parties of the Arab world must then adopt these principles in order to progress.
4. The formation of a permanent secretariat, with branches in all Arab countries, whose aim would be to enlighten public opinion, through various educational publications, in a manner that transcends the affairs of parties and internal Arab politics.

Axiomatic facts and objectives. We do not need to invent a new society. The Arab society, with all its essential components and foundations, is in existence. We do not destroy in order to build. We merely repair and revitalize. It would be easy to destroy since destruction is negative and, I fear, may be sought for its own sake. Construction, however, is positive, difficult, and takes a long time in preparation and execution.

Therefore,

1. We must protect our heritage against dissolution or subversion. We must

build on the firm foundations of stable institutions and customs that are adaptable [to new conditions].

2. Our constitutions and legislation must emanate from the essential features of our civilization.

3. We must realize that true reform can be effected only on the basis of a comprehensive, scientific study that aims at raising our economic, social, and moral standards, within a general ideological framework.

4. We must promote and exalt our noble ethical heritage for the benefit of the present generation. Traditional Arab virtues like chivalry, loyalty, generosity, and love of truth must be instilled.

5. We must encourage a tolerant human spirit and fortify religious beliefs so that the spiritual forces can be released to help us lessen the effects of materialism and the anguish pervading the world.

6. We must rebel against social corruption and injustice, by enacting the proper legislation and by preparing an honest generation that would implement the law.

7. Reform must be based upon a thorough study and natural evolution. It must not come by surprise, in the name of armed revolutions.

The reform movement. In the economic field, we must work to obliterate inequalities left over from regimes of corruption, exploitation, and foreign domination. This must be done legally and in an enlightened manner. Poverty must be ended, not by robbing the rich of their legal property but by economic development, by providing sufficient means of livelihood, by affording opportunities to all through compulsory education, by establishing technical teaching centers, and by instituting a system of graduated taxation. The Arab nation must industrialize to a considerable extent in order to provide employment and to create productive labor to meet the increase in population. Preparations must be made for emergency situations, like disruption of transport or war. The income of the Arab countries from oil and other sources is sufficient for this purpose.

In the political field. Politics are an accurate reflection of the values that a given society is seeking to implement in its system of government. Politics grow and acquire polish through experience. Politics is the science of what is required and what is possible.

The principles of the revolution. Some members of the present Arab generation call for armed revolutions in order to change the systems of government or to usurp power by one means or another. We must strictly warn against such views.

The revolutions we have witnessed in history, both old and new, have failed to achieve the purpose for which they originally arose. They have left behind them problems and difficulties exceeding in their complexity the original problem that the revolution had set out to solve. The armed revolutions that have succeeded each other in the Latin American countries from the beginning to the present day are, we believe, the most important cause for the relative backwardness of those countries compared with the USA.

From another point of view, the leadership of revolutions may fall into the hands of men who most often are not part of the elite. That is always dangerous. Revolutions break out in the same way as natural disasters, i.e., when a fault occurs in the general system. The only way to prevent revolutions is to make law and justice prevail in society.

The armed revolutions erupting in the various Arab countries and elsewhere, especially those bloody revolts that aim to destroy a whole system by attempting to implement imported theories, have taught us a lesson. We must discard revolution from our minds as an unhealthy means to achieve the desired progress and reform.

If we interpret revolution in the sense of serious revitalization of one aspect of our social or economic life—e.g., a cultural and literary renaissance, like the European Renaissance, or the 'Ukaz market place in pre-Islamic Arabia, or the industrial revolution of the West—then revolution would be acceptable. But if we adopt the principle of armed revolution against the government or the subversion of civilian government by one group or another, then it can lead only to backwardness and regression.

11. GENUINE AND FALSE ARABISM*

Antun Saadeh

Antun Saadeh (Sa'da) (1904–49) was the founder of the Syrian regional nationalist movement. For details of his career, see pp. 87–88. In the extract below, Saadeh attempts to refute the idea that religion is a basis for Arab nationalism and that the Qur'an calls for spreading Islam beyond the boundaries necessary to consolidate the Prophet's authority.

In the previous chapter, we refuted the arguments put forth by the advocates of religious nationality and the religious Muhammadan state. These men interpreted the Qur'an to suit their purposes. We maintained that their interpretations are false, since they are based on some passages of the Qur'an, taken out of context. Thus, the very unity of the Qur'an and the religion is undermined, the genuine religious message is perverted, and an attempt is made to

* Extract from Antun Saadeh, *al-Islam fi risalatayhi al-masihiyya wa-al-muhammadiyya* (*Islam in its Christian and Muhammadan Messages*) (3d ed.; Beirut: n.p., 1958), pp. 207–16, 243–45.

deceive the faithful and to prevent them from distinguishing between the secular and the sacred, which is, indeed, the height of iniquity.

We also cited many passages in the Qur'an in order to counter the false argument of the owners [Jamal al-Din al-Afghani and Muhammad 'Abduh] of *al-'Urwa al-wuthqa*[1] about religion. We maintained that the doctrine of "the growth of the sect" [*tanmiyat al-milla*] was an obligation upon the faithful for purposes of establishing their religion in pagan lands and of eradicating the danger of paganism. We proved that the obligation to fight was aimed against those who fought the faithful on grounds of religion. We may here add to what we have already proved elsewhere that the following verse in the Qur'an (IX, 28-30) must not be used as a pretext in this connection:[2] "Fight those who do not believe in God and the Day of Judgment, those who do not forbid what God and his Prophet have forbidden, and those who do not believe in the religion of truth among the People of the Book until they have paid the *jizya* [tax paid by free non-Muslims, which became a kind of poll-tax] in subjection to you" (*Surat al-tawba* [Chapter on Repentance, IX]). This verse occurs in a passage that calls for war against the polytheists [*Mushrikun*] and others among the People of the Book who joined them in fighting Muhammad and his message. It is, therefore, a part of the *Surat al-anfal* [The Spoils, VIII], which justifies the breaking of faith with polytheists and explicitly calls for war against them. The verse therefore serves a purely temporary purpose, namely, the war between Muhammad and his enemies. In specifying that the People of the Book should pay the *jizya* rather than be compelled to change their beliefs, a conclusive proof is given that the war between them and the Muhammadans was not to be waged on account of their faith or their belief in God. Indeed, the Qur'an came as "a confirmation of their beliefs." Thus, they are to be fought if they reject Muhammad and help the polytheists against him. The verse also is directed against the Arab Christians who worshipped three gods instead of one, made the Virgin divine, and perverted the teachings of Christianity. The conclusion is that the verse cited is peculiar to a certain time and place. The proof of this is that there are many Meccan and Medinan verses that should not be literally interpreted as they stand—e.g., "You must then hate mankind until they embrace the faith"; "Say:

1. The expression *al-'Urwa al-wuthqa,* which can be translated as *The Firm* (or *Indissoluble*) *Link* (or *Bond*) (Ilse Lichtenstadter, *Islam and the Modern Age: An Analysis and an Appraisal* [New York: Bookman Associates, 1958], p. 183), was taken from the Qur'an and used by al-Afghani and 'Abduh as the name for the journal they published in Paris in 1884. Although only eighteen issues were published, *al-'Urwa al-wuthqa* set the tone for other journals with similar ideas, such as Rashid Rida's *al-Manar* (*The Beacon*), which was published in Cairo.

2. Below is the translation of this passage from the Qur'an as it appears in N. J. Dawood's version (which is used throughout this work). The "Chapter on Repentance" (IX, 28–30) reads: "Fight against such of those to whom the Scriptures were given as believe neither in Allah nor the Last Day, who do not forbid what Allah and His apostle have forbidden, and do not embrace the true faith until they pay tribute out of hand and are utterly subdued." *The Koran* (tr. N. J. Dawood) (Harmondsworth and Baltimore, Md.: Penguin, 1956), p. 313.

we believe in Him who had revealed Himself to us and to you. Your God and ours is one and we submit to Him"; "Religion must not be forced upon men since virtue is now clearly distinct from vice"; "Neither your wishes nor the wishes of the People of the Book"; "God shall judge your conflicts at the Last Day"; and many others. Consider the difference between the verse about the acceptance of the *jizya* and the following, "Those among the People of the Book who do not believe in the religion of truth."[3] The reference here is to some, but not all, the People of the Book. The verse about the war to be waged against the polytheists until they embrace the faith occurs in the same sura, as follows: "When the sacred months are over, kill the polytheists wherever you find them; seize them, besiege them, and ambush them; then if they repent and observe prayer and pay the alms, let them go their way, for God is Merciful and Compassionate" (*Surat al-tawba,* IX, 5). Hence, the war against "those among the People of the Book who do not believe in the religion of truth" is not to include all the People of the Book but only those among the Arabs who have misunderstood their religion, as we have already made plain.

It follows that to specify "those who do not believe in the religion of truth" means that there are those who do so believe, in accordance with their books. To interpret the meaning in any other way would be very far-fetched. In any case, no one is obliged to act upon the interpretations of the *mujtahid* [authoritative interpreter of the Law], since the *mujtahid* is limited by his own understanding and his motives.[4] His interpretation expresses only a personal opinion, since he is neither a prophet nor divinely inspired. Whenever some men thought of this *ijtihad* [interpretation] as prophetic and divinely inspired, and attempted to get the faithful to ignore the text in favor of their own *ijtihad,* calamity always followed.

Those among the *mujtahidun* who advocate religious nationality and the religious state are in fact avid seekers of power who are misusing religion. They cannot see beyond their noses and know nothing of human societies and states. What is even more astonishing is that they did not bother to study the rise and fall of the Muhammadan state nor the rise and fall of the Christian state. Thus, they [al-Afghani and 'Abduh] ascribe the fragmentation of the Muhammadan state to the "quarrels among princes and seekers of power." The leaders of this allegedly modern school of thought[5] wrote in their article "Islamic Unity" [in *al-'Urwa al-wuthqa*]:

> Among the most important reasons for the present weakness in their state of knowledge and their power is the conflict among seekers of power in their ranks

3. The verses are taken out of context.

4. Saadeh seems to use the term *mujtahid* purposely in order to bring out its original meaning, "one who by his own exertions formed his own opinions." The orthodox doctrine held the view that the individual interpreter could err, while the *ijtihad* of the Muslim community—the ijma', or agreement—was free of error. See "Idjma," in H. A. R. Gibb and J. H. Kramers (eds.), *Shorter Encyclopaedia of Islam* (Leiden: E. J. Brill; Ithaca, N.Y.: Cornell University Press, 1953), pp. 157–58.

5. The reference is to Jamal al-Din al-Afghani and Muhammad 'Abduh, especially to the former, who advocated unity among Muslims.

> [i.e., the Muhammadans]. We have already proved that Muslims can acquire nationality only through their religion. Thus, the many rulers they have are like many leaders within a single tribe and many sultans of a single nation, each going his own way contrary to the others. They occupied the people's time by showing off, each in front of his opponent, and by preparing the means to combat each other. Such conflicts, or internal dissensions, made them forget their culture and their achievements and neglect the pursuit of knowledge. The weakness we witness today is the result of these dissensions, which also brought about a disorganization in their way of life. The quarrels of leaders led to disunity (p. 150).

Another passage in the same article is as follows: "Responsible Muslims are full of grief for the present disunity and fragmentation of Islam. Had it not been for some power-loving princes, Muslims everywhere would have been united." An objective examination of the view expressed here—namely, that the breakup of the Muhammadan state was due to the activities of seekers for power—reveals the utter falsity of the above. The author apparently believes that religion forms the only link that binds human societies together, although it is well known that the formation of societies began in the earliest stages of human history. History records the exploits and achievements of great states that came into being before the advent of divine revelation and the rise of monotheism, as, for example, the Syrian states, which lasted from the Phoenician Age down to the Age of the Seleucids. The Eastern Syrian Empire, which began in Tyre, later in Sidon, lasted until the end of the Seleucid state, while the Western Syrian Empire, with its capital at Carthage, lasted longer than any other state or religious empire and enjoyed greater unity and harmony than anything achieved by a religious state. Thus, the conflicts of princes and ambitious men may be the major cause for the failure of a secular, but certainly not of a religious, state. The formation of societies is something different from either religion or belief. The body of the faithful of every religion are brothers in spirit only, but in the socio-economic sense the brothers are only those who live within the same society and who have come together in one community to pursue their life together, not to worship together.

In the Muhammadan state, conflict among leaders was there from the beginning. The quarrels of the *sahaba* [the Companions of the Prophet] and their wars were not over a religious text or for religious ends, but for the acquisition of power and influence. The nature of Arab life and traditions and the customs and requirements of the tribes caused the quarrels among the *sahaba* which spread with the Arab conquests. Those conflicts were not, strictly speaking, within the Muhammadan state but within the Arab environment and, hence, must not be held as solely responsible for the break-up of the Muhammadan state. The reasons for the conflicts that led to the break-up are precisely the same as those that led to the break-up of the Christian state, namely, national reasons. Nationalism triumphed over the religious state. The Syrians could not bear to be subject, in the name of religion, to Persia or to any other foreign religious state; the Persians could not bear the Arab yoke; Syria and the other Arab countries did not submit to the rule of Turkey. The differences in national traits and traditions cannot be effaced by unity of religion or of law since these differences are social in character. It is precisely an ignorance of this social substratum that made the owners of *al-'Urwa al-wuthqa* claim that the major cause for Muslim disunity is "the quarrels among princes and seekers of power" and that "Muslims (Muhammadans) can only acquire nationality through their religion." Their arguments reveal their lack of understanding of the rise and fall of the Muhammadan state. Was the great ethnic conflict between the Arabs and the anti-Arabs [*Shu'ubiyyun*][6] merely a conflict of princes and power-seekers? Do the advocates of a Muhammadan religious nationality seriously believe that if Muhammadanism were to sweep the world, a single unitary state to include the whole earth would be created? They entertain and preach such illusory notions without paying heed either to science or to history. The differences in the temperament, habits, and aspirations of the peoples of the earth are not caused by "the presence of princes greedy for power," but by climatic, ethnic, environmental, and geographical differences. Thus, only ignorance or vanity can lead one to suppose that men of the same religion scattered all over the globe should be united in one state. But Muhammadans might object by saying that it is only their cultural shortcomings that prevent such a unity. In point of fact, their cultural shortcomings prevent them from seeing the falsity of such a view. Thus, the Christian nations that have achieved the highest degree of civilization are still unable to unite, although Christians consider themselves as brothers, and although their own religion enjoined them to be brothers. Religious brotherhood cannot possibly replace national brotherhood or national needs and aspirations. Thus, the idea of an absolute religious state has faded away from all religions, and any call to restore such a state would be deceptive and unrealistic. To have recourse to the principle of a substitute [*badal*] for the creation of a limited instead of a general religious state is a mere trick, since this substitute is itself a proof of the inefficacy and impracticability of the original idea, which is to found a state upon religion. If the original idea had been valid, the religious state would never have fallen.

We have thus far revealed the falsity of the call for the creation of a limited, instead of a general, religious state. We have also shown that no firm foundations exist or can be found for the conception of an Arab state that would embrace, as its advocates imagine, all Arabic-speaking and Muhammadan nations. We have also shown that this concept is nebulous and open to many interpretations. It is indeed nothing but a substitute for a doctrine that was itself discredited. Thus, its advocates were unable to generate a single comprehensive movement in the countries that are both Arabic-speaking and Muhammadan.

An Arabism that takes no account of geographical, regional, ancestral, historical, social, economic, and psychological principles, i.e., all the factors that constitute the social reality; an Arabism that is based merely on religion and language—such an Arabism is false and sterile, breeding nothing but obstacles in the way of the true Social Nationalist principles and their progress in Syria

6. For *Shu'ubiyya,* see p. 35, fn. 3, and p. 80.

and the Arab countries in general. Such an Arabism gives foreign powers an opportunity to dominate and deceive the Arab nations. It is false because it does not aim to exalt the Arab nations but aims rather to stir up sectarian conflicts and civil war in every nation where other, non-Muhammadan sects are living.

The advocates of this Arabism are the real enemies of the Arabs, since they oppose the growth of genuine nationalism in the Arab nations and the unified upsurge of these nations in their struggle to win their independence and to fulfill their true aspirations, which are rooted in the spirit and temperament of each nation. In their ignorance of all sciences and arts, of politics, economics, sociology, and psychology, they imagine that a sectarian majority could impose their view by disregarding the true social situation and comprehensive national unity.

Those so-called Arabists have prostituted nationalism, which is the feeling that each nation possesses regarding its own inner character, its rights, and its aspirations. Just as those with no expert knowledge of currency are unable to distinguish the true from the forged, so those with no expert knowledge of the social and political sciences are unable to distinguish true from false nationalism. These men have equated nationalism with the religious bond, which they then proceeded to paint in nationalist colors, merely to increase their deception.

We have said that nationalism is the feeling that each nation possesses regarding its own inner character, its rights, and its aspirations. Indeed, nationalism constitutes the character and spirit of a given society and can be found only in a society that is fused both physically and spiritually. Therefore, since the Arab world does not constitute one country, one environment, and one society, we cannot say that it has one nationalism, common aspirations, and a common outlook on life and art. The Arab world is made up of scattered regions, great parts of which are uninhabitable desert. Although a slight admixture of Arab blood has occurred in these countries, their geographical position, the density of their population, and their economic potentialities have not provided them with the means for creating a single society joined together by social and economic links or ties of common blood. A common civilized spirit and outlook upon the world has not arisen in these countries, which constitute neither a single environment nor a single nation. In fact, calling the peoples of the Arab world a "nation" is a misnomer.

The Arab world is made up of diverse societies and environments whose needs, aspirations, and views on life are divergent. Hence, the Arab world is a group of nations, not a single nation. These nations possess certain linguistic and religious links that impel them to reach a close understanding and to cooperate in certain political, cultural, and economic matters. The only way to reach such understanding and cooperation would be if each nation were to improve itself, to understand its condition and its sublime ideals, and to train its own citizens in the exercise of their civic and political rights. In this way, each nation would come to know the extent to which it can usefully cooperate with the other Arab countries in accordance with its needs and desires. This is the genuine Arabism, since it combines the preservation of the identity, liberty, and rights of each Arab nation, with free cooperation in matters of mutual interest. This is the genuine Arabism whose firm foundations were laid down by the Syrian Social Nationalist Party. While working for the Syrian renaissance, our Party has not neglected Syria's position in the Arab world and what Syria can do in that field.

Unity, in order to be effective and to be able to withstand political *coups d'état,* must be natural, not artificial. The Muhammadan-Arab Empire was a political and religious unity which was socially artificial, since it grew through conquest and not through the willing acceptance of those who joined it. As soon as the momentum of conquests abated, anti-Arab conflicts appeared. Each nation became aware of its own peculiar needs and wishes, this artificial unity broke up, and the empire collapsed. It cannot be recreated except by the ancient means—namely, by conquest, since a social, economic, spiritual, and geographical union cannot come about, for the reasons stated above. The question of conquest depends on the conqueror. It is, in any case, a political and international rather than a national question. It is a matter of deciding the fate of whole nations and countries, not simply the renaissance of one nation through a common will.

Concerning this problem, the Syrian Social Nationalist theory states: first a Social Nationalist renaissance in Syria, then a policy of cooperation for the good of the Arab world. This renaissance of the Syrian nation would liberate Syrian potentiality from foreign domination and transform it into an effective force aimed at helping the remaining Arab nations to progress.

This Arab Syrian Social Nationalism is the only genuine Arabism. It is the only practical Arabism that can help the Arab world in the most effective manner. It is an Arabism that is neither religious nor capitalistic nor pseudo-political: it is the ideal good for the whole Arab world. . . .

Conclusion

This brief discussion has shown that the reactionary advocacy of a Muhammadan or a Christian state is corrupt and reveals an ignorance of matters sacred and secular. It has become clear that religious and sectarian fanaticism is the greatest misfortune of the Syrian nation and that it can only be avoided by embracing Syrian nationalism, which our Party has made into the religion of life for Syrians. There are many theoretical and practical proofs for the validity of this national religion which unites all Syrians in one indissoluble bond and makes no distinctions among them except insofar as they labor for the good of the nation as a whole.

The palpable results of the growth and progress of Syrian nationalism and the National Syrian movement have demonstrated that what is needed is simply the general diffusion of our principles so that one nation can rise up, holding fast to one doctrine and one faith and proving that it can take its proper place in the general struggle for human progress. This happy state of affairs, which no enemy of Syria can bear to think about, requires a rapid and large-scale reaction from those elements and groups who have become convinced that our message is true. Money must be provided for our movement so that it can disseminate its theories and explain its teachings to the masses who yearn for the truth. This blessed movement must be supported both morally and materially against the advocates of perverted and reactionary doctrines. The result will be that the nation's divisions, weaknesses, and discords shall be transformed into harmony, cooperation, power, and glory.

True knowledge must be disseminated in all quarters if deception is to be overcome and the people are to be guided to the path of righteousness. This in itself requires great efforts and plenty of written and oral instruction. If we merely contemplate this task and its requirements we can see how necessary it is to support the Syrian Social Nationalist movement, both morally and materially. If an effective response to our call had rapidly spread both in the homeland and among Syrian communities abroad, if our movement had obtained enough funds to launch an extensive propaganda campaign, including speech-making, pamphlets, broadcasting, publication of newspapers, and printing of books, then it is most probable that Syria's paralyzed attitude toward the present war would have been vastly different. This inertia is caused by the multiplicity of false injunctions and propaganda spread by reactionary and opportunistic politicians and encouraged by various foreign powers who do not wish to see a united Syrian nation, bound by a common doctrine and will, and capable of frustrating their machinations.

Every Syrian man and woman who sincerely cares for the honor of his nationalism and who has the interests and prosperity of his people at heart, must realize that his aspirations cannot be fulfilled by laziness, indifference, or good intentions. The path lies through a careful examination of the sacred doctrine of Social Nationalism. He must then act in accordance with the dictates of duty and combat all false patriots, artists, and men of letters. In this manner, true national consciousness would be attained and the Syrian nation would rid itself of all sectarian feuds and feudal injustice. Syria would then close its ranks and step forward to take its rightful place in the very forefront of the civilized nations of the world.

The genuine foundations for a great Syrian Social Nationalist renaissance have been laid down. Indeed, this great upsurge began ten years ago [1932?], and all that is needed is a widespread and effective response to our call. The path of glory lies before us.

Syrians in the homeland and abroad, be merciful toward yourselves, your progeny, and your descendants, and God shall show you His mercy. Spurn from your ranks all those who work to divide you. Rally around those who desire your good, and let us all rally to the principle that shall unite us and restore to us our homeland, our glory, our dignity, and our rights: to Syrian Social Nationalism which binds all Syrians one to another and links the Syrian generations, past, present, and future.

Syrians, uphold your nationalism, since it is your principle and your livelihood, which shall make you triumph and achieve glory.

IV. *Regional and Local Nationalism*

12. THE *SHU'UBIYYA* AND ARAB NATIONALISM*

'Abd al-Hadi al-Fikayki

'Abd al-Hadi al-Fikayki, a Shi'ite from Baghdad, was closely associated with the Ba'th Party in Iraq. Representing current thought among the extreme nationalists, his writing expresses resentment against liberal nationalists, Fabian socialists, and Westernists. Al-Fikayki finds it difficult to explain the conflict between Egypt's attachment to her own past and her leadership role in the drive for unity based on an Islamic interpretation of Arabism. Consequently, he adopts the expedient viewpoint of the polemicists—that Egyptians were Arabs who came out of the Arabian Peninsula thousands of years ago and established the Pharaonic civilization. The racial implications of this view are too evident to warrant further discussion. It is also interesting to note that al-Fikayki refers to the Shu'ubiyya *(discussed above, p. 35, fn. 3) as a disruptive movement as it was understood by the orthodox in the past. The* Shu'ubiyya *is considered an attack on the Arab aspect of Islam and on Arab nationalism.*

Local Communism: The Climax of Anti-Arabism and Its Extension

No sooner had the Arabs cast off Turkish domination and the danger of Pan-Turanism than they fell victim to the great imperialist powers, following the Sykes-Picot Treaty of 1916 which divided the Arab world into several weak states.

At that time, Communism was still new in the Arab world. The anti-Arabs wanted to use it for their own intrigues as they saw in it the best cover for their malice against the Arabs. Communism was encouraged and supported by them. In support of our view, we notice that the leaders of the Arab Communist parties were, for the most part, non-Arabs who bore a bitter grudge against Arab nationalism and unity.

Local Communism proved, in effect, to be more than a continuation of the anti-Arab movements that had plagued the Arabs ever since the emergence of

* Extract from 'Abd al-Hadi al-Fikayki, *al-Shu'ubiyya wa-al-qawmiyya al-'arabiyya* (*The Shu'ubiyya and Arab Nationalism*) (Beirut: Dar al-Adab, 1961), pp. 97–98, 100, 102–11. (The titles of subdivisions in the extract have been added.—ED.)

the Arab state. The attitude of the local Communists to problems like Alexandretta, Palestine, Arabistan, and in particular the idea of Arab unity, is the best proof of their treachery to the Arab cause, the Arab liberation movement, and all that relates to Arab nationalism. We must bear in mind that anyone who has fought the Arab liberation movement and Pan-Arab unity is an anti-Arab conspirator and traitor who must be destroyed, whatever his nationality.

Much documented evidence indicates that local Arab Communism is the climax and extension of anti-Arabism. The local Communist parties have been, and will always be, hostile to Arab nationalism and Arab unity, working hand in hand with imperialism for their ultimate destruction.

On many occasions, and especially in Iraq and Syria, those anti-Arabs found themselves in league with imperialism at a certain level. It is worth while to re-emphasize the hostility of Communist leaders to Arabism; most of them are non-Arabs, and some are even Zionist Jews. It would be unnecessary to enumerate all the documented proofs that indict Communism as treacherous, anti-Arab, and an ally of imperialism. This is not the place for such details. Suffice it to say that the anti-Arab used Communism as a weapon with which to attack the Arab nation and the Arab liberation movement.

Regional Nationalism

In addition to the various anti-Arab movements and currents like the "Turkification" movement and local Communism, there also appeared the Syrian Social Nationalist Party, founded in 1936 [*sic*] by Antun Saadeh.[1] What is most important in the teaching of this new anti-Arab party is its active hostility to Arab nationalism, its denial of the Arab character of Syria, Jordan, Palestine, and Iraq, its advocacy of "Syrian," or "Phoenician" nationalism and "Greater Syria," its rejection of the essential features of Arab nationalism, and its view that the Arabs are foreign conquerors and that Syria is not a part of the Arab nation but is an independent nation. On this false anti-Arab propaganda they based their policy of "Syria for the Syrians." In attacking Arab nationalism, Arab unity, and everything else that stood in its path, the Party adopted a policy of vicious gangsterism. In its hostility to Arab nationalism, this Party did not differ from other anti-Arab movements that had preceded it. It worked closely with imperialism and with all other enemies of the Arab liberation movement. The most recent manifestation of their anti-Arab sentiment appeared in a document captured by the Lebanese police following [the Syrian Social Nationalists'] unsuccessful *coup d'état* [in Lebanon] in 1961. The document reads, "He who believes in Islam is a heretic [*kafir*]; he who believes in Christianity is even more heretical; he who believes in Lebanon is not of our number!"

The Pharaonic Movement and Salama Musa

There also appeared a new anti-Arab movement in Egypt, prior to its Arab revolution, represented by the Pharaonic movement, which denied Egypt's Arab character and called for a severance of its Arab links, a revival of the

1. Antun Saadeh's nationalist ideas are discussed on pp. 72–79, 87–98.

Pharaonic language, and an "Egyptian nationalism" divorced from Arab Egypt and its struggle for Arab nationalism. Thus we see Salama Musa calling upon the Arabs of Egypt to substitute Latin in place of Arabic characters in the Arabic language.[2]

He went so far as to advocate, quite openly, the abandonment of Arab society, when he wrote, "Let us turn our faces toward Europe." Either because he was ignorant of, or (what is more likely) because he ignored Egypt's Arab character, he considered Egypt a part of Europe, justifying this astonishing claim on the basis that Egypt is situated on the shores of the Mediterranean Sea. In his book *Today and Tomorrow* [*al-Yawm wa-al-ghad* (Cairo: al-Matba'a al-'asriyya, 1928)], we find him, in the chapter entitled "The Search for the Egyptian Nation," casting doubts on Egypt's Arab character and mounting an exaggerated attack on Arab civilization, preparatory to his advocating closer ties with the West. To those who call Salama Musa's thinking "progressive," we answer that it is precisely the theories of Musa and like-minded writers which have retarded the progress of Arab consciousness in Egypt, helped to keep the Arab youth of Egypt away from their Arab society, and erected a cultural barrier between them and Arab culture and revolutionary movements elsewhere in the Arab countries.

The theories of Salama Musa and other writers of his school concerning Arabism are indeed reactionary. They obstinately propagate error and give currency to ideas that are dangerous to the Arab revolutionary movement. We do not deny Musa's deep influence on youth and on the intelligentsia. But we cannot also deny that his call, for example, to replace the tarboosh [or fez] with the European hat is an absurd mimicry of inessentials. Can we really believe that Musa was unaware of the strong nationalist bond between Egypt and the rest of the Arab countries? Is it possible that such a prominent writer never came across those nationalist bonds, those spiritual, literary, historical, and social links that bind Egypt to the Arab world? Did he ever stop to think why Egypt was called the sheath [literally, quiver of the Arabs (*kinanat al-'arab*)]? He and his followers should have championed an Arab, not a European, league. He should rather have taught the Egyptians about their genuine

2. Salama Musa (1887–1959), a Christian Copt, is well known for his advocacy of anti-imperialist socialism and of Egyptian nationalism inspired by the Fabians as well as by liberal thinkers. Salama argued in favor of reforms that would accompany independence. His autobiography, *Tarbiyat Salama Musa* (*The Education of Salama Musa*) (Cairo: Mu'assasat al-Khanji, 1949), which has been translated into French and English (see L. O. Schuman, *The Education of Salama Musa* [Leiden: E. J. Brill, 1961]), gives an excellent picture of educational and cultural conditions in Egypt at the end of the nineteenth century and at the beginning of the twentieth century. Salama repeatedly criticized the "purist" attitude of Arab intellectuals, the difficulty in writing Arabic, and the obsession with the linguistic past. He advocated the introduction of Latin characters as the possible avenue for a basic change in the Arab outlook. See his article "Arab Language Problems," translated in *Middle Eastern Affairs*, VI (February, 1955), and reproduced in Benjamin Rivlin and J. S. Szyliowicz (eds.), *The Contemporary Middle East* (New York: Random House, 1965), pp. 325–28. See also K. S. Abu Jaber (Jabir), "Salamah Musa: Precursor of Arab Socialism," *Middle East Journal* XX (Spring, 1966), 196–206, and Mohamed-Saleh Sfia, "Egypte: Impacte de l'idéologie socialiste sur l'intelligentsia arabe," in Georges Haupt and Madeleine Reberioux (eds.), *La Deuxième Internationale et l'Orient* (Paris: Editions Cujas, 1967), pp. 409–38.

Arab character and about the close national link that binds them to their Arab brethren, instead of waving the European hat in place of the Turkish tarboosh. Had this school of writers that talked about "Egyptian" and "Pharaonic" nationalism not included some of Egypt's leading men of thought, we might have found excuses for them, such as their misunderstanding of Arabism or perhaps their lack of culture or knowledge of Arab history. Those champions of "Egyptian" nationalism, those enemies of Egypt's Arab character, went so far as to hold a conference in Asyut and Cairo in 1911, in order to clarify their theories and propagate their teaching. Their message was an anti-Arabist movement in disguise. Thus 'Abd al-'Aziz Jawish . . . made a distinction between the Arab and Egyptian nations, . . . [and] Muhammad Magdi . . . regarded the Egyptian nation as comprising Egypt's Pharaonic population only.[3]

Had these scholars merely been ignorant of Arabism and upholders of a narrow regionalism, the harm engendered would have been mild. Not content with this, they proceeded, like other anti-Arabs, to attack the Arab national liberation movement. Muhammad Farid, in an article published in the magazine *The Sciences* [*al-'Ulum*], describes Arab nationalism as "trivial" and "the work of devils."[4] In another article, Ahmad Lutfi al-Sayyid, in his usual argumentative, conservative style, denied both the merits and the future of Arab endeavor.[5] He even denied the existence of an Arab problem. He

3. These authors belong to an earlier period, almost at the beginning of the twentieth century, when local liberal and Western-oriented nationalism was on the rise. The fact that they are still remembered indicates that their influence persists.

4. Possibly Muhammad Tal'a Farid, who was Minister of Education in the Sudan in 1962.

5. Ahmad Lutfi al-Sayyid (1872–1963), member of a rich landowning family in Egypt, began his political career as a nationalist but soon adopted a moderate nationalism opposed to Pan-Islamism. He was founder and editor of *al-Jarida* (*The Daily*), 1907–16, which expressed the viewpoint of the Umma (Nation) Party. It was the party of the upper social groups who wanted to stay on good terms with the British, as opposed to Mustafa Kamil's extreme nationalists, who fought the British. Al-Sayyid was, with the exception of short periods, the head of the state university in Cairo from 1924 to 1941. He was instrumental in shaping the Egyptian intellectuals' viewpoint through books and especially through newspaper articles. Al-Sayyid believed that freedom—meaning chiefly freedom from state control—was the natural condition of man. He regarded utility as the foundation of all sentiments, actions, and human society. His main purpose in gaining freedom was to free reason from imposed authority and to liberate the individual from uncritical acceptance of thoughts and ideas on authority. Al-Sayyid rejected Pan-Islamism as well as attempts to deprive the Egyptians of their national identity. Since this identity had a Pharaonic core on which were grafted various influences, Egyptians would not lose their national personality by borrowing from the West. These ideas were expressed by al-Sayyid as early as 1913–14. See *al-Muntakhabat* (*Selections*) (2 vols.; Cairo: Maktabat al-Anglo-Misriya, 1937–45). As late as 1950, as al-Fikayki resentfully states, Lutfi al-Sayyid still defended the Egyptians' own national personality.

Taha Husayn (b. 1889), a leading Egyptian novelist, essayist, literary historian, and educator, as well as defender of the Pharaonic past, was brought up under al-Sayyid's influence and shared his views. In fact, in 1926, when Husayn published a book on pre-Islamic poetry in which he upset some Islamic dogma, al-Sayyid, as head of the university, defended Husayn against the attacks of conservatives and religious leaders. Taha Husayn's abandonment of Egyptian nationalism in favor of a broader Arab nationalism seemed to have escaped al-Fikayki's attention. For background developments, see Marcel Colombe, *L'Evolution de l'Egypte, 1924–1950* (Paris: Maisonneuve, 1951).

protested against the concern some Egyptians had shown regarding the Italian attack on Arab Libya and took them to task when they collected donations for the benefit of the Arab victims. On May 5, 1950, *The Illustrated Magazine* [*al-Musawwar*] published an interview with Lutfi al-Sayyid, in which he said:

> I was always a firm upholder of the Egyptian character of Egyptians. Some of them claimed that they were Arabs, others that they were Turks of Circassians. . . . We Egyptians must hold fast to our Egyptian character and must belong to no other nation save the Egyptian, irrespective of our Hijazi, Syrian, Circassian, or other origin. We must preserve our nationalism, honor ourselves and our fatherland, and belong to no other nation. . . .

'Abdallah al-Nadim in the magazine *The Teacher* [*al-Ustadh*] once described the fighters for the Arab cause as "stupid."[6] Among other writers who held similar views in their writings were Dr. Taha Husayn and Fathi Radwan, who championed a revival of the Phoenician language in *The Journal* [*al-Majalla*].

I may add here that I do not personally object to pride being taken in Pharaonic civilization, nor would I attempt to denigrate it. What is truly regrettable is that the enemies of the Arab liberation movement have hit upon this current as a means for disseminating their evil propaganda and justifying their anti-Arab views. Indeed, I personally consider the Pharaonic to be a part of Arab culture.

In answer to those who strive to conceal their anti-Arabism under the false pretense of preserving the Pharaonic heritage, let me quote the words of Sati' al-Husri:[7]

> Egypt has forsaken the Pharaonic religion without destroying the Sphinx. It has abandoned the Pharaonic language without destroying the Pyramids. . . . These Pyramids, along with all other Pharaonic monuments, have not prevented Egypt from achieving a total linguistic union with the rest of the Arab countries. . . . The deep nationalist currents that have swept over Egypt during the past centuries, creating new movements in their path, have effaced its old religion and language—despite the Pyramids and the Sphinx. Egypt does not need either to destroy or to conceal any of its old monuments prior to adopting the policy believed in by supporters of Arab unity.

6. 'Abdallah al-Nadim (1844–96), born in Alexandria, joined revolutionary movements in his early life. He published several reviews supporting the nationalists and promoted programs of social and educational development. After the revolution of 1882, al-Nadim eluded the authorities for nine years by hiding in villages and towns; he thus acquired first-hand information about the life of the lower classes. Beginning in 1892, his writings were often published as social satire, especially in the review *al-Ustadh* (*The Teacher*). Later, he was invited to Istanbul and left Egyptian politics.

Al-Nadim was both an Egyptian nationalist and a populist intellectual. He wanted Egyptians to understand Europeans but also to appreciate their own values, rights, language, and religion. Whether Muslim or Christian, Egyptians were tied together by national bonds superior to religious allegiance. "Preserve Egypt for Egyptians" was his motto. His chief writings are collected in *Sulafat al-Nadim* (*The Choicest Wine* [or, *The Drinking Companion*] *of al-Nadim*) (2 vols.; Cairo: Amin Hindiyya, 1897–1901).

7. For a discussion of Sati' al-Husri, see pp. 55–58.

> The champions of Arab unity have not called upon the Egyptians, either implicitly or explicitly, to abandon their Egyptian character. They have merely required them to add a comprehensive Arab sentiment to their own peculiar Egyptian one. They ask them to work for the Arab cause in addition to working for the Egyptian one. They have not and will not tell Egypt, "Forget yourself," but rather, "Enrich yourself by working to unite those who speak your own language."

This anti-Arab current will never be able to efface the Arab character of Egypt or to shake the faith in Arabism that has swept the hearts of the Arabs of the United Arab Republic.

Despite the anti-Arab inclinations and campaigns of certain writers against Arab nationalism and unity, Egypt (the U.A.R.) has now become the standard bearer of Arab nationalism and of the struggle to achieve freedom, unity, and socialism for the Arabs. This is the best proof of Egypt's Arab character and the secret of its progress.

Those regionalists who do not wish to look beyond Egypt's frontiers to the wider Arab world and who, in their dogmatism and their ignorance of Arabism, declared that "Egypt is for the Egyptians" and "Egypt comes first"—those men must now admit, if they are sincere, that Egypt is for the Arab cause and that Arabism comes first. They must come to recognize that the Egyptians are Arabs by language, culture, history, religion, and common nationalist sentiment and will. Furthermore, there is abundant historical evidence for the Arab origin of the Pharaohs, which can silence all dissent and deception. The Arabs of ancient Egypt, the Pharaohs, belonged to an Arab-Semitic stock whose original home was the Arabian Peninsula. There is evidence to prove that they settled in Egypt after a migratory wave stretching from Chaldea to the Nile Delta. Indeed, the majority of the Arab peoples living in the Arab world are descended from a single stock, the Semitic or ancient Arab. In this context, the famous French Egyptologist Maspero has written, "The ethnic ties linking the ancient Egyptians, Arabs, Phoenicians, and Chaldeans are very close. The ancient Egyptians were Semites who moved away from their original home before the others."

Lebanese Nationalism, the West, and Charles Malik[8]

In Lebanon, the imperialists chose an anti-Arab idol, whom they called a philosopher, and trained him to be hostile to Arab nationalism, Arab history, culture, and civilization. This was the man [Charles H. Malik] about whom Dr. Muhammad Majdhub wrote, "The West picked upon a mouthpiece who would serve their purposes. He was chosen as a purveyor of poisonous ideological and political views and an agent for their designs upon the free na-

8. Charles Habib Malik (b. 1906) is a well-known Lebanese teacher, statesman, diplomat, and liberal thinker whose generally pro-Western attitude has earned him the enmity of extreme Arab nationalists. Malik's rather liberal recognition of Islam's place in present-day Arab nationalism was short of the total surrender desired by Islamist Arab nationalists.

tions. The West loaded him with gifts, conferred titles and decorations upon him, and exalted him."

When the imperialists had made him a cabinet minister, he issued a statement that is replete with malice against Arabism, Arab history, thought, and culture. He wrote:

> Our ideal is to enter seriously into the positive Western heritage of thought. In this heritage we find the complete truth. . . . This heritage is the sole historical arbiter of existence. . . . It represents the living, active, and ultimate entity and every entity outside it inclines either to nothingness or to being connected with it in a master-slave relationship. To enter upon this heritage means to adopt it without qualification so that we can become parts of it and vice versa. . . . One of our noblest ideals, then, is to arrive at a time when Arab thought will be perfectly at home in Oxford, Freiburg, the Sorbonne, and Harvard.

We do not object to the Arab intellectual's acquaintance with the honest intellectual heritage of the West or to his adoption of knowledge useful to the Arab nation. Indeed, we call upon all Arab intellectuals to acquaint themselves with Western thought, on condition that they embrace only what is essential and useful to the Arab peoples, whose culture and outlook would thereby be broadened and would contribute to the Arab intellectual renaissance.

But we cannot possibly tolerate the boasts of an anti-Arab, who uses this cultural exchange as a means of attacking Arab thought and culture and of making the Western heritage of thought the sole origin for the culture of the Arab man.

This new anti-Arab movement aims not so much to serve the Arabs as to create a generation who would disown their Arab character and Arab civilization, and deny the splendid Arab intellectual heritage, which was itself a rich source of inspiration for the Western culture that Malik raves about in Lebanon today.

It may be noticed, in conclusion, how all anti-Arab movements, both ancient and modern, have adopted a common policy in attacking Arabism—a policy which differs only in methods, in accordance with the circumstances and the degree of Arab consciousness.

If we were to summarize the objectives of anti-Arabism we would find that it concentrates upon attacking Arab nationalism, perverting Arab history, emphasizing Arab regression, denying Arab culture, being hostile to everything Arab, and being in league with all the enemies of Arab nationalism. In all its various roles, anti-Arabism has adopted a policy of intellectual conquest as a means of penetrating Arab society and combatting Arab nationalism. At the same time, these anti-Arab movements, at all stages of their existence, unwittingly helped Arab consciousness to appear. The Arabs rallied around their Arabism, defended and took pride in their civilized heritage, and obstinately withstood the attacks of anti-Arabism and imperialism. Anti-Arabism produced a reaction among the Arabs and was partly responsible for their literary and intellectual renaissance.

13. THE PRINCIPLES OF SYRIAN NATIONALISM AND ITS PARTY*

Antun Saadeh

Antun Saadeh (Sa'da) (1904-49), the founder of Syrian regional nationalism, was the son of a physician of Greek Orthodox faith who migrated to South America. Saadeh returned to Lebanon in 1929, and for a time tutored German at the American University of Beirut. He developed the idea that the Syrian nation differed from the Arab nation and consisted of a unique historical synthesis of Arabs, Phoenicians, and other groups who lived in Syria, Lebanon, Iraq, Jordan, and part of Palestine and who therefore must be united under the flag of a Greater Syria. This nation would form a homogeneous society in which traditional group loyalties, feudal land relations, and capitalism would be abolished and religion separated from the state. These ideas, which Saadeh regarded as a scientific national philosophy and made mandatory learning for his disciples, were embodied in a program (reproduced here) that formed the ideological basis of the Syrian Social Nationalist Party† (SSNP) and had a lasting impact on the thinking of some Arab intellectuals. The party began as a secret organization in 1932 and was discovered by the authorities in November, 1935. Saadeh and his lieutenants were arrested, charged with plotting against the state, and sentenced to prison. The SSNP attracted both Muslim and Christian Arab intellectuals, for its prime purpose was independence and the assertion of national identity.

Saadeh left for America in 1938, but came back to Lebanon in 1947 and engaged in politics. In 1949, after attempting an unsuccessful coup in Lebanon, he fled to Syria. The Syrian dictator Husni Za'im received him well at first, but then handed him over to the Lebanese authorities, who, within a twenty-four–hour period in July, 1949, tried and executed him. (The Lebanese Government tried to justify its hasty and much criticized action in Qadiyat al-hizb al-qawmi [The Case of the Nationalist Party] *[Beirut: Ministry of Information, 1949].)*

After 1945, the idea of a Greater Syria, which was the backbone of Saadeh's nationalism, no longer appealed to the Christians of Lebanon, who rightly feared that they would be lost in the Muslim majority. Nor did the idea appeal to Muslim Arab nationalists, who had begun to think in terms of a union of the entire Arab-speaking world. Thus, Saadeh's brand of totalitarian, corporative, antireligious nationalism was overwhelmed by the rising tide of Arabism. Unlike the Egyptian nationalism defended for long and then abandoned

* Extract from *The Syrian Social Nationalist Doctrine: The Principles and Aims of the Syrian Social Nationalist Party* (Beirut: n.p., 1949), pp. 21–33.

† Also known as the Syrian National Party.

(e.g., by Taha Husayn) in favor of Arabism, Saadeh's Syrian nationalism is still effective. It appeals to those groups who are interested in maintaining Syria's national existence and making it the center of a large Arab political entity. It also appeals to extremist secularists, including some Christian Arabs, who feel that neither Islam nor any other religion should be made the basis of nationalism, since they consider national bonds, such as language and history, stronger than religion.

It may rightly be said that Saadeh's condemnation of feudalism and his call for economic progress and social justice formulated within the context of secular nationalism and corporatism have been preserved and reshaped under the new ideology of Arab socialism. There is a striking similarity between the principles of the Syrian party and the writings of some contemporary socialists. Finally, in his paradoxical manner, Saadeh's missionary appeal on behalf of independence left its imprint on all subsequent Arab revolutionary movements. Many of Saadeh's followers joined the Ba'th; and then, after Arab nationalism began to lose its secular character, supported President Nasser or joined other socialist parties.

Saadeh's continuing influence is well illustrated by the repeated publication of his writings and the continuation of political activities inspired by his writings. SSNP was active in Syria until 1955, when it was banned and its rank and file driven underground. Many of its leaders came to Lebanon and continued to work as the Parti Populaire Syrien. The well-organized and trained groups of this party provided vital armed assistance to the Lebanese Government in preventing a takeover by Pan-Arabists in 1958, and the party was allowed to act freely. But its almost successful coup on December 31, 1961, led to its being banned. The prosecution's case presented to the military tribunal in 1963 showed clearly that the party had preserved its original Greater Syria ideology. See al-Hayat, *October 8, 1963; sections translated in Walid Khalidi and Yusuf Ibish (eds.),* Arab Political Documents, 1963 *(Beirut: Slim Press, 1964), pp. 415–20.*

A fairly complete list of Saadeh's writings may be found in Fahim I. Qubain, Inside the Arab Mind *(Arlington, Va.: Universal Printers and Lithographers of America, 1960), pp. 45–48. For background, see Stephen Hemsley Longrigg,* Syria and Lebanon Under French Mandate *(London and New York: Oxford University Press, 1958), and Albert H. Hourani,* Syria and Lebanon: A Political Essay *(London: Oxford University Press, 1946). The best and most comprehensive treatment is Labib Zuwiyya Yamak,* The Syrian Social Nationalist Party: An Ideological Analysis *(Cambridge, Mass.: Harvard University Press, 1966).*

The principles of the party reproduced here were written by Saadeh and published in 1932; they were translated into English in 1943 and revised and enlarged in 1949.

Syria represents to us our character, our talents, and our ideal life; it signifies for us an outlook on life, art, and the universe; it is the symbol of our honor, glory, and final destiny. This is why to us Syria is above every individual consideration, above every partial interest.

The Reform Principles

The First Principle: *Separation between religion and state.*

The greatest obstacle in the way of our national unity and our national welfare is the attachment of our religious institutions to temporal authority, and their claim that there is sufficient justification for the religious centers of influence to exercise sovereignty within the state and to dominate, wholly or at least partly, the functions of political authority. But the truth is that the great struggles for human liberation have always arisen between the interests of nations on the one side and the interests of religious institutions on the other, the latter claiming the divine right to rule and to exercise the judiciary functions. This principle of divine right is a dangerous one and has enslaved many peoples to the point of exhaustion. It was used not only by the religious institutions but also by the sacred royalty, which claimed to derive its authority from the will of God and the sanction of the religious institutions, but not from the people.

In the state where there is no separation between the state and the church, we find the government ruling in the place of God, and not of the people; but wherever the excessive dominance of the state by religious institutions is diminished, we find the latter always trying to preserve themselves as civil authorities within the state.

Theocracy, or the religious state, is opposed to the principle of nationhood, because it stands for the dominance over the whole community of believers by the religious institutions, as do the papacy and the caliphate. The pope, for example, is the prince of all the believers wherever they may happen to be, and the same is true of the caliph. Religion as such recognizes no nation and no national interests because it is concerned with a community of belief dominated by a central religious institution. It is only from such a point of view that religion can become a temporal, political, and administrative affair, monopolized by the sacred religious institution. This is the temporal aspect of religion, and religion was suited for it when mankind was still in his savage stage or close to it, but not in our modern civilization.

It is against this aspect of religion that the Syrian Social Nationalist Party fights, not against religious or theological thoughts and philosophies which deal with the mysteries of the soul and immortality, the Creator and the supernatural.

The concept of pan-religious political community is opposed to nationalism in general and to Syrian Social Nationalism in particular, because the adherence of the Syrian Christians to a pan-Christian political movement makes of them a group with special interests discordant with the interests of other religious groups within the country and, on the other hand, exposes their own interests to the danger of dissolution in the interests of other peoples to whom they are tied by religious bonds. In the same way, the adherence of the Syrian Muslims to a pan-Islamic movement exposes their interests to coming in conflict with the interests of their countrymen of other faiths and to becoming lost in the interests of the greater community, over which they have no control, and which is always in danger of disintegration in the struggle for political power on the part of the constitutive nations, as has happened in the 'Abbasid period and in the Turkish period. The call for pan-religious movements can lead only to the disintegration of national unity and to failure in the struggle for national existence.

Neither nationalism nor the national state is based on religion. This is why we find that the two greatest religious communities in the world, Christianity and Islam, did not succeed in being temporal or political communities as they did in being spiritual and cultural communities. A religious spiritual community is not a danger nor need have any fear; as for the religious temporal-political community, it is a great danger to the existence of nations and to the interests of their peoples. This was clearly demonstrated by the last Turkish regime.

National unity cannot be attained by making the national state a religious state, because in such a state the rights and interests are religious rights and interests, enjoyed exclusively by the dominant religious community. Where rights and interests are the rights and interests of a religious group, there can be no realization for those national rights and interests which are common to all the children of the one nation. And without the unity of interests and of rights there can be no unity of duties and no unified national will.

With this legal national philosophy the Syrian Social Nationalist Party has succeeded in laying down the foundations for national unity and in bringing about its actual realization.

The Second Principle: *Prohibition of the clergy from interference in political and judicial matters of national concern.*

This principle is implied by the previous one, the only reason for stating it explicitly being due to what we have already stated concerning the surreptitious ways by which religious institutions attempt the attainment or preservation of temporal authority even where the separation between church and state is admitted in principle. It is meant to put an end to the indirect interference by religious institutions in the course of temporal and political affairs with the hope of directing matters in favor of their interests.

This principle specifies what is meant by separation of church from state, so that the meaning of that principle may not remain ambiguous and subject to false interpretations; because the reform must not be restricted to the political sphere alone but must extend to the legal-judiciary sphere as well.

It is not possible to have well founded national civil status and common rights when a varied and discordant judiciary is based on, and divided among, the different religious sects. This is an evil which stands in the way of unifying the laws that are necessary for the following of one national order.

It is necessary, therefore, that the Social Nationalist state have a unified judiciary and one system of laws. For this unity makes the citizens feel and know that they are all equal before the law.

We cannot possibly have one and the same mentality and at the same time act according to different and conflicting conceptions which are incompatible with the oneness of our social community.

The Third Principle: *Removal of the barriers among the different sects.*

Undoubtedly there are, among the different sects and denominations of our nation, traditional barriers not necessitated by religion. These discordant traditions derive from the organizations of our religious and denominational institutions and they have exercised a tremendous influence in weakening the social and economic unity of the people and delaying our national revival. As long as these traditional barriers remain, our calls for freedom and for independence will continue to be cries of pain and sighs of ineptitude. It is not proper that we should know the illness and continue to ignore the cure. We the Syrian Social Nationalists are not like the quacks who call for union while ignoring the true ties of union and who shout for unity while concealing a different purpose in their hearts.

Every nation which wills to live a free and independent life in which it can realize its ideals must be a nation with a strong spiritual unity. And a strong spiritual unity cannot develop while every one of the religious groups of the nation leads a secluded existence within a separate social-legal circle making of it a mentality independent from the mentalities of the other groups, hence leading to variance in purposes and aims.

National unity cannot be realized except by the removal of all causes of dissension. And the social-legal barriers between the sects and denominations of the same nation obstruct the realization of a material-spiritual national unity.

Unity is something real, not fictitious, so replace not reality with a fiction.

As a nation we must stand one and united under the sun, and not as separate groups and heterogeneous factions of discordant mentalities. The existence of the present social and legal barriers among our different sects means the persistence of this incurable sectarian cancer in the body of the nation. We must break down these barriers in order to render social unity a deep-rooted fact, and to set up the Social Nationalist order which will bestow health and power upon the nation.

The Fourth Principle: *The abolition of feudalism, the organization of national economy on the basis of production, the security of the rights of labour, and the protection of the interests of the nation and of the state.*

Is there in Syria a feudal order? In one sense one could say that there is no feudalism in Syria, because feudalism is not legally recognized; but in another sense we find that there exists in different parts of Syria a feudalistic state, both from an economic and from a social point of view. There are in Syria real feudal estates which involve a considerable part of the national wealth and which cannot be considered as private property in any sense of the word. These estates are under the disposal of Beks, or feudal lords, who manage these properties or neglect them as they choose, without any consideration for the national interests. Some of them neglect their feudal properties and go to such excesses in their mismanagement as to lead to financial difficulties which end by reducing the land to the possession of foreign banks, foreign capital, and foreign plutocracy. The Syrian Social Nationalist Party considers it very necessary to put an end to this state of affairs, which threatens national sovereignty.

On some of these feudal lands live hundreds and even thousands of peasants in a miserable state of slavery. Such a state of affairs is not only inhuman, but also endangers the safety of the state, because it leaves a large section of the laboring and fighting people in a state of weakness, and a considerable part of the national wealth in a state of underdevelopment. The Syrian Social Nationalist Party cannot keep silent with regard to these matters.

As for the organization of national economy on the basis of production, it is the only way for the attainment of normal balance between the distribution of labour and the distribution of wealth. Every member in the state must be productive in some way or other. Production and the producers must be classified in such a way as to insure cooperation and the participation in labour to the widest possible extent and the attainment of a just share in the produced goods, and to insure the right of labour and the right to its proportionate share. This principle puts an end to absolute individualism in labour and production, which entails great social damage, because every form of labour and production in society is a form of common cooperative labour or production; hence if absolute freedom were left to the capitalist in his dealings with labour and production, it is inevitable that great injustice would fall upon labour and upon individual workers. The common wealth of the nation must be subject to the common interests of the nation and to the control of the national state. It is impossible to develop all the resources of power and progress in the state to the highest possible level except by this principle and this way.

The Syrian Social Nationalist Party wants to realize a strong national unity in which the Syrian nation may be enabled to persist in the struggle for life and progress. This national unity cannot be realized within a bad economic order, just as it cannot be realized within a bad social order. Therefore, the realization of social-legal justice and economic-legal justice are two necessary prerequisites for the success of the Syrian Social Nationalist Movement.

Social production is a common and not a private right. Capital, which is the resultant of production and the guarantee of its continuity and increase is, in principle, a common national property despite the fact that individuals acting as trustees utilize it for the sake of production; and active participation in the process of production is a condition sine qua non for the participation in the common right.

On the basis of this economic organization we will insure our economic revival, better the lot of millions of workers and farmers, increase the national wealth, and strengthen our Social Nationalist state.

The Fifth Principle: *Preparation of a strong army, which will have an effective role in defending the country and in determining national destiny.*

The competition for the resources of life and supremacy among nations is a question of a struggle between national interests. The vital interests of a nation cannot be protected in the struggle except by force in its two manifestations, the material and the spiritual. Now, spiritual power, no matter how perfect it may be, is always in need of material power. In fact, material power is itself an index and manifestation of an advanced spiritual power. Hence, it follows that an army and the military virtues are essential bases for the state.

National rights are not asserted in the struggle of nations except to the extent to which they are supported by power in the nation. For force is the decisive factor in the assertion or denial of national right.

By the armed forces we understand the Army, the Navy, and the Air Force. The art of war has reached such an advanced stage of development that it becomes incumbent upon us to be in perfect military readiness. Indeed, the Syrian nation in its totality must be powerful and well armed.

It is our own power that we trust in attaining our rights and in defending our interests. We intend to persevere in the struggle for existence and for supremacy in life, and life and supremacy shall be our reward.

The Aim and Program of the Party

The aim of the Syrian Social Nationalist Party is the creation of a movement which will realize its principles and revivify the nation, and the establishment of an organization which will lead to the complete independence of the Syrian nation, to the affirmation of its sovereignty, the setting up of a new order capable of protecting its interests and raising its standard of living, and the endeavor for the formation of an Arab front.

It is plainly manifest from the wording of this article that national revival is the center of attention for the Syrian Social Nationalist Party. The rise of the Social Nationalist Movement involves the realization of nationhood in Syria, the protection of the life and interests and means of progress of the Syrian nation, and equipping it with the power of strong union and true national cooperation. Thus, the Party seeks a distant aim of the highest order of importance because it does not restrict itself to dealings with some political form but rather involves the foundations of nationhood and the basic trends of national life. The purpose of the Party is to orient the life of the Syrian nation toward progress and success and to activate the elements of national power in Syria. This national power, once developed, will crush the force of tradition, liberate the nation from the chains of sluggishness and acquiescence to antiquated beliefs, and place an impregnable obstacle in the way of foreign ambitions threatening the interests of the millions of Syrians and their very existence.

The aim of the Syrian Social Nationalist Party is a comprehensive view which involves national life from its very foundations and from all its aspects; it includes all the basic issues of the social community—social, economic, political, spiritual, moral—and the final aims of life. It involves the national ideals, the purpose of independence, and the establishment of a true national society. This implies the founding of a new moral mentality and the establishment of a new basis of ethics. Consequently, the fundamental and reform principles of the Party reveal a new and a complete philosophy of life.

A complementary part to the foreign policy of the Party is the realization of an Arab front from the Arab nations. This front will become a strong barrier in the way of foreign imperialistic ambitions and a power of considerable weight in deciding the major political questions.

Syria is one of the Arab nations, and indeed it is the nation qualified to lead the Arab world, as is proved decisively by the Syrian Social Nationalist revival. It is obvious that a nation with no internal cohesiveness to insure its own unity and progress is not the one that can help revive other nations and lead them in the way of progress and success. Syrian nationalism is the only true and practical way and the first prerequisite for the awakening of the Syrian nation and for enabling it to work for the Arab cause.

Those who believe that the Syrian Social Nationalist Party proclaims Syria's withdrawal from the Arab world, because they do not distinguish between the Syrian national awakening and the Arab world, are in great error.

We shall never relinquish our position in the Arab world nor our mission to the Arab world. But we want, before everything else, to be strong in ourselves in order to convey our mission. Syria must be strong in its own national revival before it can undertake the realization of its greater task.

The comprehensive idea which was conceived by the Syrian Social Nationalist Party constitutes an idealistic mission in national life. The Party does not intend to restrict this fine concept and its great effects to Syria alone, but it intends to carry it to our sister Arab nations by way of cultural activities, exchange of opinions, and mutual understanding, not by way of the destruction of the nationalities of these Arab nations and the imposition of these principles on them.

As to the political aspect of the Party's aim, the Party, from the interior point of view, considers that the Lebanese question has arisen because of justifications which were acceptable when the concept of the state was still a religious concept. But the principles of the Syrian Social Nationalist Party have established the national social-legal basis for statehood. By the realization of the principles of the Syrian Social Nationalist Party, those justifications for the separation of Lebanon are removed.

As to what concerns the Arab world, the Party is in favor of following the road of conferences and alliances, as being the only practical way of leading to the cooperation of Arab nations and to the formation of an Arab front of considerable weight in international politics.

14. THE TEACHING BOOK OF THE SYRIAN SOCIAL NATIONALIST PARTY*

Antun Saadeh

Antun Saadeh's execution in 1949 by the Lebanese Government did not prevent his followers from perpetuating their leader's ideas and engaging in political activity. The Syrian Social Nationalist Party (SSNP), founded by Saadeh in 1932, continued to fight underground or to work openly for the ideal of a Greater Syria. Postwar developments, however, forced the SSNP to think in terms of Arab unity and devise a role for Syria accordingly. Consequently, Saadeh's original ideas were emphasized in those aspects that advocated a greater role for Syria among the Arab nations. Moreover, based again on Saadeh's writings, his followers tried to reconcile local differences in favor of the ideal, a single unified Arab nation and social progress. This extract is taken from a relatively new edition of Saadeh's writings, issued on behalf of the party.

The Syrian nation represents the unity of the Syrian people with a long historical past stretching back to prehistoric times.

This principle evolves from the theory of progression. It defines the nation as mentioned in previous articles, and requires, from the ethnic point of view, a closer examination. The principle is not meant to assign the Syrian nation to one common stock, Aryan or Semitic, but aims to describe the reality. This latter constitutes the final outcome of a long history comprising all nations that have settled in these countries and mingled therein, from the Late Stone Age, prior to the Chaldeans and Canaanites, down to the Amorites, Arameans, Assyrians, Hittites, and Akkadians, all of whom eventually became one nation. Thus, we see that the principle of Syrian nationality is not based upon common descent but upon the social and natural unity of a mixture of stock [i.e., of various stocks]. This is the only principle that embraces the interests of the Syrian people, unifies their aims and sublime ideals, and safeguards the national ideal from bloody and barbaric conflicts and national fragmentation.

Those who know nothing about sociology or their nation's history challenge these facts, claiming purity of blood and common descent and refusing to admit the mingling of blood. These people are commiting both a philosophical

* Extract from al-Hizb al-suri al-qawmi al-ijtima'i (Syrian Social Nationalist Party), *Kitab al-ta'alim al-suriyya al-ijtima'iyya. Mabadi' al-hizb mashruha bi-qalam al-za'im* (*Teaching Book of Socialist Syria. The Principles of the Party Interpreted by the Leader*) (n.p., 1955), pp. 17–20, 77–82.

and a scientific mistake. To ignore the reality, which is the basis of our temperament and our psychic make-up, and to erect an illusion in its place is a sterile philosophy, akin to saying that it would be preferable for a body revolving around an axis to leave it because this would improve its motion! As for the claim of purity of stock or blood, it is a myth that obtains nowhere among the civilized nations and is rare even among savages.

All nations at present are a mixture of species of flat-heads, round-heads, and long-heads, and of several historic peoples. The Syrian nation is a mixture of Canaanites, Arameans, Assyrians, Chaldeans, Hittites, and Akkadians, while the French nation, for example, is a mixture of Ligurians, Franks, etc., and the Italian nation a mixture of Romans, Latins, Samnians, Etruscans, etc., and so on for other nations. "Saxons, Danes and Normans, that is what we are," says Tennyson about the English.

As for the superiority of the pure stock and descent over the mixed stock (especially among homogeneous and civilized stocks), this myth, too, has been exploded. The genius and mental superiority of the Syrians over their neighbors and others is a self-evident truth. It was they who civilized the Greeks and laid the foundations of Mediterranean civilization in which the Greeks joined them later. Greek genius flowered in Athens, a city of mixed stock, not in Sparta, which was proud of its descent and preserved its purity of blood.

Nevertheless, we must accept the fact that differences among stocks do exist. Some stocks are civilized and others are degenerate. We must also recognize the principle of homogeneity and diversity, both of blood and of stock. This principle will enable us to understand the reasons for the psychological superiority of the Syrians, which is not the result of unconstrained mixture but of the superb quality of homogeneous mixing, perfectly in harmony with the type of environment. . . .

The Objectives and Plan of the Party

The aim of the Syrian Social Nationalist Party is to effect a Syrian national social renaissance capable of achieving its ideals and restoring to the Syrian nation its vitality and power. The party also aims to organize a movement that would lead to the complete independence of the Syrian nation, the consolidation of its sovereignty, the creation of a new system to safeguard its interests and raise its standard of life, and the formation of an Arab front. This article makes it perfectly plain that national resurgence is the party's main concern. National social renaissance embraces the establishment of the concept of the nation, the preservation of the life of the Syrian nation, and the means for its progress, furnishing it with the power of unity and proper national cooperation and creating a new national social system.

The party's objectives are long-term and of paramount importance. They are not limited to the treatment of political questions but deal with the very roots of nationalism and the trend of national life. The party's aim is to guide the life of the Syrian nation toward progress and virtue. The party desires to activate the various elements of national strength in order to destroy the hold of outdated customs, to liberate the nation from lethargy and submission to antiquated beliefs, to stand firmly opposed to foreign rapacity which threatens the interests and the sovereignty of millions of Syrians, and, finally, to establish new traditions that would institute our new attitude to life and our national social dogma.

Thus, the objectives of our party embrace a comprehensive view of the roots of national life in all its aspects. They include all the social, economic, political, spiritual, and methodological questions of national society, together with the larger problems of life. They incorporate the sublime national ideals, the objectives of independence, and the creation of a just national society. Implied in these objectives is the formation of a new ethical outlook and a new ideology, which is to be found in the basic principles and reforms of the party, constituting, as they do, a comprehensive outlook on life and a complete philosophy.

The formation of a front of Arab nations in order to stand as a barrier against imperialist designs and as a force of considerable importance in deciding major political issues is indeed a complementary part of the party's foreign policy. Syria is one of the nations of the Arab world and is fitted for the leadership thereof. In fact, the Syrian national social renaissance is the conclusive proof of its fitness to lead. It is obvious that a nation that does not possess a spirit of unity (*'asabiyya*) capable of self-regeneration, is not one that can be expected to lead other nations into the path of virtue. Syrian nationalism is the only practical method and the basic prerequisite for Syrian regeneration and the consequent participation of Syria in Arab affairs.

Those who believe that our party teaches the abandonment by Syria of Arab questions plainly do not understand the difference between the Syrian national social renaissance and the Arab question, and are greatly mistaken.

We shall not abandon either our position in the Arab world or our mission to it. But we must, first of all, strengthen ourselves so that we can fulfill our mission. Syria's national social renaissance must itself be powerful before it can achieve its major tasks.

The comprehensive outlook of our party raises a problem of ideals in national life. The party does not wish to restrict this noble ideal and its momentous consequences to Syria but wishes to carry it forth to sister Arab states, by means of cultural activity and the exchange of opinions. We do not advocate the dissolution of the various Arab nationalities or the imposition of theories upon them by force.

From the internal political point of view, the party considers that the Lebanese question [i.e., the existence of a separate Lebanese state] originated from side-issues that were justifiable when the conception of the state was a religious one. But our party's principles have created a social, legal, and national foundation. When our principles are put into effect, the isolation of Lebanon would no longer be justifiable.

As for the Arab world, the party considers that alliances and conferences are the only practical method for achieving cooperation among Arab nations and for creating an Arab front that can wield international authority.

But national sovereignty is a principle that must be safeguarded in all agreements and alliances.

15. THE GENESIS OF THE SYRIAN SOCIAL NATIONALIST PARTY*

Jamil Sawaya

Jamil Sawaya, a close friend of Antun Saadeh, was a founding member of the Syrian Social Nationalist Party, but later broke away from the movement. This excerpt provides insight into the background conditions and intellectual state of mind that led to Saadeh's initial success and later failure.

I met Antun Saadeh for the first time in the summer of 1930, on the tennis court of the Shuwayr High School (in Beirut). Saadeh was a native of that town, a strong-willed, intelligent person. Our meetings continued and our discussions expanded until Saadeh broached the subject for whose sake he had returned to Lebanon: the Syrian problem and Syrian nationalism.

This took place when the French mandate was at the height of its power. It was very common for French officials, even the lowest of them, to use the phrase *"sal Syrien"* [dirty Syrian] to describe us.

That summer, we hardly ever missed a game of tennis, and it was rare not to find Saadeh seated under an oak tree nearby, reading a book or talking to a group of young men.

Summer passed, and I returned to the American University of Beirut to complete my studies, firmly convinced that everyone, whether weak or strong, must serve his homeland and his society to the best of his ability.

During the academic year, I told fellow-students about the discussions I had had with Saadeh during the summer. Some of them wanted to arrange a meeting in which to discuss these ideas; the most enthusiastic was George 'Abd al-Masih, whose drive was apparent in everything he did. After a long discussion with me, during the course of which I had convinced him that action along the Communist pattern was undesirable, he had decided not to join the Communist Party. Further contacts were established with the late Raja' Khawli, Fakhri Ma'luf, Zaha' al-Din al-Hammud (a Jordanian), Wadi Tal-

* Extract from Jamil Sawaya, "Nash'at al-hizb al-qawmi al-suri" ("Formation of the Syrian National Party"), in Kamal Jumblat (ed.), *Adwa' 'ala haqiqat al-qadiyya al-qawmiyya al-ijtima'iyya al-suriyya* (*Light on the Real Issue of Syrian Social Nationalism*) (Beirut: n.p., 1962), pp. 142–49.

huk, Fu'ad Khuri, Anis Sawaya, and George 'Abd al-Masih. After a couple of meetings, 'Abd al-Masih and I felt that Talhuk and al-Hammud wanted to dominate the movement before they had even been converted, so we decided not to cooperate with them. We communicated our decision to the rest of the group and the activity was interrupted until these two had been ejected.

In the summer of 1931, Saadeh had started to work for a newspaper in Damascus, but he came to Dhur al-Shuwayr, where we met and I told him the news. We agreed to hold a preliminary meeting with the rest of the group in Beirut.

In the autumn of 1932, and before leaving Damascus for good, Saadeh came over to Beirut and, after certain preparatory meetings with the group named above and with Ni'ma Thabit, Jubran Jurayj, Ma'mun Ayas, 'Aziz Thabit, and 'Abdallah Kubursi, Saadeh decided to draw up the statutes of the party and to make it a secret organization. The authorities would not have allowed a political party to operate without the approval of the mandatory power. Thus, in 1932, the Syrian National Party was founded officially, after two years of consultations, preparation, and a very careful selection of members. The founders were a group of well-educated and enthusiastic persons. This fact helped the party to remain secret for four years and to work energetically. The membership figure had reached almost a thousand before its existence was revealed, and the first prosecutions followed.

Saadeh had enough time to devote to party activity. He was aware of every small detail. With the help of a few members, including Ni'ma Thabit, 'Abd al-Masih, and myself, the party's constitution was drafted and its articles were initially ratified, except for those concerning the administration of the party. Saadeh thought in terms of a party council, two-thirds of whose members would be permanent (the founding members) and who would not relinquish their position except through death or expulsion (at that time, withdrawal was not recognized—membership was regarded as permanent). The other third of the party council would be elected. 'Abd al-Masih did not like this idea at all and insisted upon dictatorial control. Thus we met Saadeh. 'Abd al-Masih stood up, closed the door and announced: "No one will leave this place until we have finalized the party's administration." In fact, this was what happened. 'Abd al-Masih's ideas won the day, and the party's administration became not consultative but dictatorial. It remained thus until I left the party temporarily in 1937 and finally in 1947.

The party's affairs progressed slowly. But the party was like a smoldering fire under a haystack; the French mandate became more rigid and the Syrian and Lebanese peoples more conscious of their true interests. Thus, we were easily able to attract the intelligentsia into the party by appealing to them to fight the mandate and to reconstruct a homeland laid waste by an unjust and duplicitous Turkish regime and by a French mandate of exploitation that encouraged sectarian conflict and feudalism.

In its propaganda, the Syrian National Party stressed the following principles: first, the separation of church and state; second, the dissolution of feudalism; and, third, the destruction of differences between religious sects, etc., etc.

Like every political party wishing to focalize its message, the leaders of the party took up Saadeh's idea that Syria is for the Syrians and that the Syrians are a complete nation, and made it the alpha and the omega of their teachings. These teachings were then crystallized through lectures, meetings, and contacts. Special care was taken to keep the party secret since it could not yet emerge into the open. At that time, the party overreached itself and Sa'id 'Aql wrote an anthem for the party set to the tune of *"Deutschland, Deutschland, über alles."* This is what I remember of it: "Is it the roar of the sea or a surging army? It is the land that fills the earth with its thundering cry. Syria is the hope awakening for all, is the smiling hope of the Spring. Syria, Syria above all . . ."

In this anthem, we defined the borders of natural Syria as we then believed them to be, for the anthem continues: "You stretch from the Taurus Mountains to the Sinai Desert and from the Mediterranean Sea to the Tigris River. You are a flame, a nation that ascends until the horizon is covered in glory. The roar of the sea or a surging army," etc. etc.

In 1935, membership increased, and it was difficult to keep the party's existence secret, although we could still not obtain a permit, for we were certain that we would not succeed. It was preferable to work in a party that was not licensed than in one whose request for a permit had been denied.

In September of the same year, there were rumors that the French authorities were spying on the party and that they had discovered its activities. In November, prosecutions commenced, and rumors multiplied. In December, arrests were made, the party was indicted at open sessions in court, and sentences were passed. The party received its first shock and its strength was tested. At that time, the party derived its strength from the steadfast courage of the party members, led by Saadeh himself. Despite arrests, the officials who got out of prison continued to work for the party, reorganized the ranks, and put it back into shape. But this first crisis landed the party in financial difficulties. In 1937, the elections came around and the bargaining started. The government was then headed by Khayr al-Din Ahdab. The party was asked to back Ahdab if the French would free its prisoners, turn a blind eye on its activities, and help to obtain a permit for the party. Some party leaders secretly accepted this bargain, and thus the party became guilty of its first act of dishonesty. At that very time, the party wanted to replenish its treasury. It therefore contacted certain parliamentary candidates and agreed to support some of them in return for money. They thus obtained money from the late Emile Lahoud and instructed party members to vote for him against the late Rawkaz Abu Nadir. The night before the elections, however, they secretly ordered members to vote for Abu Nadir instead of Lahoud. This turnabout was made in return for a very small sum.

Honest members then felt it their duty to ask why this line of activity was pursued. Unconvincing excuses were offered. As a result, some members neglected their party responsibilities, and others began to doubt the party line. But since the party statutes did not allow withdrawal, and since they had taken an oath to obey the party principles and the leader, they remained in the party. Nevertheless, their enthusiasm was dampened and a spirit of despair set in.

This was the situation until the outbreak of war and Saadeh's departure for South America. The party was then led by Ni'ma Thabit. It sided with Germany at the beginning of the war. When the British and the Gaullists gained the upper hand and the British Army entered Lebanon, most party officials were incarcerated in the Miyye-Miyye prison near Sidon. The British also made sure that no party officials still at large would be employed.

Soon, however, and following certain agreements, the prisoners were released and party activity was resumed, the party being still led by Thabit. At that time, many founder-members—among them Thabit, Ayas, Asad al-Ashqar, and I—began to feel that Lebanese independence, the departure of the French, and the development of the idea of Syrian nationalism itself necessitated a reappraisal of party policy and the adoption of a new party line. The party then became the Social Nationalist Party, as a result of the growth of national Lebanese sentiment. Each branch of the party was to be autonomous in its own country, but the principles were to be unchanged. If all the branches could get their peoples to accept the same principles, then there would have been no objection to unifying all these peoples into one nation. Otherwise, each branch was to be independent and linked to the other only through the same principles. This was in fact the idea that some of us had proposed when we founded the party. The conservative members then got in touch with Saadeh and told him about this new development. He wrote back, saying he would be arriving soon, and declared from Argentina that Iraq was to be joined to the Syrian nation.

The first thing that Saadeh did after his return was to make a speech declaring his adherence to the old party line and condemning the conduct of the officials during his absence. Having read the text of his speech, I went to see him in Dhur al-Shuwayr, where he was in hiding, a summons having been issued against him.

He did not meet me in his old friendly manner but criticized me because I had supported a line that, according to him, would destroy all the achievements of the party. He asked me by what right I did so. I replied that a party leader who adds new countries to his own conception of the region, thereby contradicting what he had previously explained to his party members, cannot forbid those members to take him to account and to consider his conduct contrary to agreements they had helped to formulate. If the leader's theories have developed, this does not mean that the members' theories should be prevented from developing. We had allowed ourselves what he had arrogated to himself. If his own emendations of party theory could be considered as developments, then our emendations must be regarded equally as so. I pointed out that in the seven years during which he had been away the country had changed, ideas had changed, and independence had brought about new nationalist concepts which must be carefully taken into account. After a long, fruitless debate, I felt that I had finally been absolved of my oath to the party and its leader. I told him this and I pointed out that I was going to start a new line of political activity in accordance with what I had come to believe, socially, politically, and nationally. I promised that I would not indulge in any counter-propaganda among my former party colleagues.

Thus it came about that I was one of the first who answered the call, fifteen years ago, to found the Progressive Socialist Party. I did not break the promise made to Saadeh, although the party was later to disavow me and the others who were also convinced that they must liberate themselves from the party and its worship of idols.

16. SPIRITUAL MATERIALITY IS A FALSE THEORY THAT EXISTS NEITHER IN MAN NOR IN THE UNIVERSE*

Kamal Jumblat

Kamal Jumblat, an influential Lebanese politician who has held ministerial positions, is a writer and thinker and a chief of the Druzes. He is the founder and leader of the Social Progress Party (Progressive Socialist Party), which has attracted many former members of the SSNP. He is a humanist and a democratic socialist, and he is familiar with the West; he was educated in France. Jumblat has often been associated with men who represented a liberal viewpoint in Lebanon, such as former President Camille Chamoun (Sham-'un), the late Emile Bustani, and Ghassan Tuwayni, the editor of al-Nahar (The Day). *Beginning in 1952, Jumblat cooperated with these men in the Socialist and National Front, which achieved a bloodless, reformist revolution, and then eventually faded away. These passages criticizing Antun Saadeh's social nationalists represent Jumblat's general views on ideology, religion, nationalism, and Arab socialism.*

"Spiritual materiality" [*Madrahiyya*] is a term that Saadeh coined from spirit and matter, attempting with this new theory to put an end to the traditional dispute between the philosophers of matter and the philosophers of spirit.

The latter maintain that the absolute eternal spirit is itself the whole of existence and that the world of appearances is transitory and nonessential, and exists only in as much as it participates in spirit which creates all matter. We

* Extract from Kamal Jumblat, *Adwa' 'ala haqiqat al-qadiyya al-qawmiyya al-ijtima-'iyya al-suriyya* (*Light on the Real Issue of Syrian Social Nationalism*) (Beirut: n.p., 1962), pp. 9–12, 43–48.

believe that the oldest prototype of this philosophy can be found in Plato's theory of ideas.

The former maintain that the eternal absolute spirit does not exist, that matter is itself the whole of existence, and that spirit is the reflection of matter upon itself, as is claimed for instance by Marx and the Marxists.

We suppose that Saadeh intended that his theory of spiritual materiality would reconcile these two theories of existence. That intention is apparent in the following extract from [an article by Antun Saadeh] in *al-Nizam al-jadid* [*The New System*]:

> The world has now realized, after World War II, the extent of the damage wrought by the emergence of fragmentary philosophies—the selfish philosophies that thrive on destruction, such as suffocating capitalism and violent Marxism, which have finally united in their denial of spirit; and other philosophies like fascism and National Socialism, which appropriate spirit to themselves and aim to dominate the whole world thereby. This world of ours stands today in need of a new philosophy that would rescue it from the falsity and confusion of such philosophies. This new philosophy—the philosophy of the unifying interaction of all the human forces—is the one represented by your renaissance." (*al-Nizam al-Jadid,* March, 1948, p. 5.)

Instead of turning to science and to the empirical method for a foundation on which to build the philosophy of his party (even though science would not be able to clarify everything), Saadeh turned to the German social thinkers and to Durkheim and his followers and modeled his theory of spiritual materiality after them—a theory that is nonempirical and has roots in neither Greek nor any European cultural tradition. Saadeh's theory was incomplete, confused, false, and out of date, since Durkheim and his school had neglected to base their theories on modern science. Thus, his theory may have suited men of the late nineteenth or early twentieth centuries, but it is of no use to us today. It is a theory rejected by both science and history. Those who make of this theory their object in life are like students who fail in a modern medical school and revert to the study of Galen, Hippocrates, Avicenna, and others and content themselves with ancient knowledge and satisfy themselves that these ancient books contain all that is to be known about medicine. They may then prescribe remedies that would prove fatal to patients. Furthermore, Saadeh in his spiritual materiality confuses "spirit" as defined by the traditional idealist philosophies with "social consciousness" as defined by the German social school and Durkheim, a consciousness that is a mere perpetuation of the "mana" of primitive African tribes.

Spirit, according to Saadeh, is sometimes the spirit of society—every society, whether German or Syrian, possesses a spirit, so how can he speak, as he does earlier, of "appropriating the spirit"?—and that is all he means when he says that "justice, virtue, and beauty, inasmuch as they are absolute values, are the values of society." Saadeh confesses that such values as justice, virtue, and beauty may be absolute—i.e., fixed, final, and comprehensive—for all societies at the same time, for all individuals in the same society, and for the whole of humanity as well. He does not realize that these values cannot, at the same time, be absolute for every single society without also being absolute for all societies. If the values of justice, virtue, and beauty were at the same time absolute in the German, British, and Syrian societies, absolute chaos would ensue.

Every nation and every state would rise and struggle for what they consider absolute relative to themselves but what would not be absolute relative to the others. Might, rather than correct belief, would then make right. This theory of "absolute international chaos" entails the extinction of the human race or at least their dispersion into various societies which cannot agree upon any value and which hold their own peculiar opinion concerning justice, virtue, and beauty. It would in effect mean the end of the world, the end of civilization, and the end of men as human beings.

At other times, we find Saadeh using the word "spirit" to mean the individual soul of each human being. He says, for instance, "The values of justice, truth, virtue, and beauty are not material. They are human and personal" (meaning the values of the human being and his personality which form the essence of all creatures that belong to the human race). But he corrects himself later by writing, "They are social values."

Saadeh, then, is either contradicting himself or mixing man's social and human attributes. If the latter is what he means, then we may rightly conclude that, as certain species of insects (e.g., ants and bees) possess social instincts, then they must also be human. Saadeh does not realize that man's human rather than social attributes make him man. His social attributes he shares with many animal species.

Saadeh also means by "spirit" the individual soul of each human, the basic essence in us as used by the idealist philosophies. Thus he claims, for example, that justice, truth, virtue, and beauty are "the values of the soul's triumph, the triumph of the strong and beautiful personality." Saadeh is at his most confused stage when he illustrates to us this conflict in his thinking between the concepts of the individual and the social spirit. Thus he says, "We should not believe that justice, virtue, and beauty require us to relinquish our genuine soul [*sic*]. What would it profit us if we gain the whole world and lose ourselves?" (This last sentence he has taken from the Bible.)

In this passage, the contradictions in Saadeh's thought become evident. He attempts therein to reconcile the individual human spirit with the social spirit. He believes that the social values of justice, virtue, and beauty need not entail relinquishing our genuine soul and that it would not profit us to gain the whole world but lose ourselves. This means that the social values of justice, virtue, and beauty conform with our genuine personal desires for justice, virtue, and beauty. They are, indeed, identical. If the essence of the individual soul differs in various persons, we would not be able to talk about the human race. Thus, Saadeh implies that the absolute values of justice, virtue, and beauty are themselves the values of the private soul which are called by the common people the values of the conscience. Saadeh should have reached this conclusion by himself, especially since he had already declared that we need not "relinquish our views of life, the universe, and art or abandon the ideals entrenched in our soul." He means here that this view of life, the universe, and art (our own personal view) conforms to and joins with the social values of justice, virtue, and beauty. Similarly, our own private ideals are identical with the ideals of society, just as the private conscience is reflected in social relations.

Surely, no one can argue that man can possess two sets of ideal views (one social and the other individual) or two views of life, the universe, and art (one social and spiritual-materialist and the other individual). Such ideals and such views are themselves comprehensive and absolute. Man cannot harbor within himself two theories both of which are absolute and comprehensive. Saadeh's mistake—and it is also the basic error in his theory of spiritual materiality—is that he relied in constructing this theory upon a purely rational *a priori* hypothesis, namely that "Throughout the world, there exists no unanimity concerning the interpretation and the absolute understanding of these values except where the variety and conflict of opinion and interests in human societies are negated."

In Saadeh's language, this means that the values of justice, virtue, and beauty are subject to the division of mankind into groups and societies, since the interests of the group, in his view, do not conflict within a single society but do conflict between one society and another.

Herein lies Saadeh's misunderstanding of man's true social existence, which does not involve the whole of man and his essence but provides only a field for man's activities and is the product of such activities. Saadeh also displays here his ignorance of the true foundation for the values of justice, virtue, and beauty and his misunderstanding of the function of these values in society.

These values, which are to a certain extent abstract, have been formulated and have become manifest because of the diversity of opinion and interests and the conflict between individuals and societies. These values are the fixed criteria to which people resort when they clash or quarrel. Without a diversity in views and interests, and without conflict between varying societies, these values would not have emerged among societies and individuals.

These values emerge from the conflict of individuals belonging to the same society, and thus is born the science of personal ethics, of constitutional, civil, and criminal rights, all of which regulate the relations among the citizens. In the field of international justice, these values reappear in common definitions of concepts like science, thought, philosophy, and civilization in general. In private and public international law, which regulates the relations of states and citizens with other states and citizens, these values are also felt. Just as the citizens of one society have observed in the course of history the growth of public institutions that provide greater guarantees for their rights, so, for the last twenty-five years or so, we have all witnessed the growth of public international institutions and laws that protect the rights of private and public societies. . . .

Egocentricity and Other Political Cheaters

The cheating social nationalists, the "worshippers of the state"—this new idol—have failed everywhere, having filled the world with malice, wars, ruin, ignorance, and sorrow. They shall inevitably fail in the East as they have failed in the West, since they tell mankind things that are not consonant with human nature. They have produced their magic lantern and told mankind, "You are only a potentiality, you have no real existence." This selfish nationalism with its malicious and disruptive spirit makes distinctions between one race and another, between one human being and another, and treats men not according to the dictates of justice and fair-dealing but in accordance with the private, selfish interests of the people and in accordance with personal whims and the thirst for power. Machiavellism remains unchanged; in the past, the justification offered was the interest of the Prince; now it is the interest of "society." But the ignorant nation soon perceives, behind this new idol of society, the men who hold the reins of power as they manipulate man, who, according to them, has become a social animal, an ape. Thereafter, the nation rejects those cheaters who had for long screamed in its face, "You are social animals. We want to liberate you from every trace of humanity."

These national social theories are in origin drawn from the writings of Hegel about the state and society and from Durkheim, Lévy-Bruhl, Bougle, Halbwachs, and other social thinkers of the German and French school in the last half of the last century.

The other sort of cheaters are those who tell mankind, "Economics is the basis of everything, of society, the family, the fatherland, philosophy, public morality, and religion. Man is nothing but the reflection of matter upon itself" —as if matter can, by itself, reflect itself upon itself and at the same time be conscious of such reflection! Economics implies the exploitation of a country's resources by a certain class of people. Salvation lies in changing the economy by handing over the means of production from the owning classes to the non-owning ones. All men would then become employees and workers in a state that is administered on a class basis by a new class of people, even if such administration were to be achieved by force for a certain period of time.

These cheaters also claim that both reform and salvation lie in adopting and casting upon the world a materialist and socialist outlook—an outlook that takes no account of spiritual morality—as if a change of systems would suffice to reform mankind or as if justice, virtue, and love were confined only to one class of people who, once in power, would bring about the Golden Age which has been the dream of mankind since the world began!

All these theories misapprehend the truth. It is not enough to substitute one class for another, one system for another, and one law for another, in order that justice, virtue, and love may prevail.

Justice and love are aspects of the reflection of self as revealed in the apparent dualism in man. Reform must come from both within and without the human being. A virtuous socialism that believes in man's influence on social systems and their implementation is alone capable of guiding us to the true way. Otherwise, we would be like machines without fuel and bodies without soul.

Indeed, if mankind is able to reform itself, to eradicate its egocentricity, and to allow its true self to appear, it would have no need to reform its social systems and enact legislation.

17. LEBANESE NATIONALISM AND ITS FOUNDATIONS: THE PHALANGIST VIEWPOINT*

Pierre Gemayel

Pierre Gemayel (Jumayyil), a Maronite Lebanese who has served in several national cabinets, is the leader of the Lebanese Phalanx (al-Kata'ib al-lubnaniyya), *or Lebanese Social Democratic Party, founded in 1936. It publishes the daily* al-'Amal (Action). *The party was organized to foster Lebanese nationalism, but, as it turned out, it relied chiefly on the support of the Maronite community for the purpose of maintaining the supremacy of that community. The census of 1932, according to which the Christians formed a majority, serves as the basis for Lebanon's present constitutional regime, the President being a Maronite, the Premier a Sunni Muslim, etc. Gemayel's party (about 60,000 members) is determined to preserve the system, which is based on the assumption that Christians still constitute a majority of Lebanon's population, and the party therefore considers all Lebanese living abroad (mostly Christians) as permanent citizens of Lebanon. In 1953, the restive Muslim groups published in English a pamphlet—which was later banned—*Muslim Lebanon Today, *written by Mustafa Khalidi. In it, Khalidi proposed that a census be held and criticized the priority given to Christians in government jobs. The speech reproduced here, addressed to President Chamoun, constituted an answer to Khalidi's pamphlet. It was preceded by a memorandum. Both the memorandum and the speech were published in English in a party pamphlet as indicated.*

The Lebanese nationalism defended by Gemayel's party differs radically from Antun Saadeh's Syrian nationalism—first, in that it is limited to Lebanon; second, by its recognition of democratic freedoms and by its representation of the political views of the Maronites (Saadeh rejected all local interests).

Memorandum

Lebanon, small as it is, constitutes an irreducible entity. None can question its tradition of independence. If it were absorbed by a larger neighbor, it would create insurmountable difficulties for this neighbor, so great is its capacity for resistance and its faith in its own mission.

* Extract from *Al-Kataeb Al-Loubnaniat* [i.e., *al-Kata'ib al-lubnaniyya*]: *"Phalanges Libanaises"* (*The Lebanese Phalanx*) (Beirut: Parti democrate social libanais, 1956), pp. 22–25, 26–36, *passim*.

Lebanon is "a soul, a spiritual principle." It would be materially possible to absorb it into a Syrian or Arab empire temporarily; it is spiritually impossible to unite it to a world which does not share its state of soul, its spiritual principles.

Lebanon is a "mission." And this mission is incompatible with that which the Arabs aspire generally to realize. A Syrian or Arab empire in which Lebanon would be swallowed would not be on a human level. From the start, it would find itself divided against itself, in its view of life, in its intelligence, in its soul, and in its being.

Undermined by diversity and by antagonism, it would be unable to realize the common good and it would not be long before it would give birth to troubles, to discord, to havoc.

Since far antiquity, Lebanon has marched with giant's feet on the road of civilization. Even while they were only Phoenicians, the Lebanese already showed their sense of the universe, their attachment to liberal traditions, and a generosity of spirit and heart so great that it enabled them to love and understand even the most distant peoples.

It is thus that they have contributed to the blossoming of Mediterranean civilization in the domain of art, science, religion, and material progress. Western humanism, a tributary of Rome and Athens, owes to them its first foundations.

The faithfulness of Lebanon to its mission and to its heritage had never been denied over the last six thousand years of history. A small land, ten thousand square kilometers in size, it remains at the crossroads of human civilizations which it always seeks to know and to assimilate.

Traditionally, Lebanon is both of the Orient and of the Occident. This explains why it is periodically the object of attacks; these attacks are made by those who have been unable to follow the royal path of universal humanism, who have not shared its vision of the world, and who are, in fact, permanently against the idea it embodies and wish its liquidation.

In the Middle Ages, Lebanon affirmed its personality with even more marked vigor with the adhesion of a part of the population to Christianity. Thus, the physical, social, and political geography of this country have naturally placed it in the heart of the Eastern Question.

Heirs of Byzantine and Sassanian caesaropapism, the Muslim caliphs imposed on their lands a theocratic regime involving a state of discrimination against non-Muslim religious minorities. Class distinctions and inequalities were established. The Christians, called dhimmis or the protected, were not equal to the Muslims in regard to rights.

This situation continued into the period of the Ottoman Empire until after the 1914–18 war. If it has generally disappeared in the documents, it has persisted in customs. Moreover, the constitutions of seven members out of eight of the Arab League provide that Islam is the religion of the state or that the head of state must be a Muslim.

It is against this theocratic system that Lebanon (Islamo-Christian by its social structure) has always stood with firmness.

Settled in their inaccessible mountains, the Lebanese first won a *de facto* autonomy, which extended itself under the government of the quasi-independent dynasties of the Ma'an and of the Shihab. This autonomy received legal consecration in 1864, with the promulgation of the organic stature guaranteed by the seven powers of the European Concert, and in 1920, with the establishment of Greater Lebanon. In 1943, Lebanon became fully independent; finally, in 1945, it was admitted to the United Nations Organization and it participated in the establishment of the Arab League.

It is because it was constituted in protest against imperialism of all sorts that Lebanon has served, in the course of the centuries, as an asylum and a refuge for ethnic minorities and those persecuted because of their religion. It is thus that it has given hospitality successively to Mardaites, Maronites, Druzes, Shi'ites, Armenians, Kurds, Assyrians, Syriacs, and Chaldeans. Today still, it often provides an asylum for political personalities of the Arab world who are harassed by their compatriots.

Thus, while still remaining in the center of the Arab world with which it shares language and certain elements of cultural heritage, Lebanon maintains a character to which it remains fiercely attached, because its instinct for survival dictates this to be categorically imperative.

Lebanon is of the Orient and of the Occident. It intends to continue to serve as a link between the two worlds without being absorbed by either, for then it would fail its mission.

Lebanon is liberal and humanistic. It is the only Arab country where all citizens without distinction as to religion enjoy real equality and public liberties of the sort intended by modern constitutionalists. It is more particularly the only Arab country that applies the provisions of the Universal Declaration of the Rights of Man especially in matters of personal status and liberty of conscience, the latter being understood in its broadest sense and including the right to change religion. Indubitably, it is to its liberalism that Lebanon owes its spiritual and material impetus.

Lebanon considers itself to be a modern and secular state. It repudiates any theocracy that produces discrimination and inequality. As it is the fatherland of all cultures, it is also that of all religions and does not hold any cult as official to the exclusion of the others. Secular authority is distinct from religious authority without the two being in conflict. No opposition, but rather separation and cooperation. Lebanon is the only Arab state in the Arab League which practices the maxim "A free religion in a free state."

Lebanon is necessary to the West. It is the interpreter of its culture, of its ideas, and of its spiritual values, to the Arabs. It provides full guarantees to Western material interests. Nowhere else is foreign capital so safe.

Lebanon is culturally necessary to the Arab East. The latter owes to the former its intellectual renaissance in the nineteenth century. It was the Lebanese, and the monks in particular, who, in their convents, according to the Muslims themselves, protected the literary heritage of the Arabs. The greatest journalistic enterprises in the Arab world are still, in Egypt and elsewhere, directed by Lebanese.

Lebanon is politically necessary to the East. It is a factor for balance and reason. It is listened to by Christian nations with which it has long had friendly relations. For the Arabs, it is an incomparable lawyer in the West. For the West, it is an irreplaceable interpreter to the Orient. For both, it is a center of meeting and exchange.

Thus, national and international considerations militate strongly in favor of maintaining Lebanon free and independent.

Conscious of these needs, the Lebanese are determined to spare no effort to repulse any attack that would constitute a formidable peril for both this little country and the civilized world. If Lebanon disappears someday, it is not Lebanon, but the West, and secondly the Arab world, that will bear the stamp of defeat.

Lebanon refuses to consider such a possibility. It will never resign itself to it. It will mobilize all of its resources against any combination of evil forces united against it.

Beirut, February 25, 1955

PIERRE GEMAYEL
President of the Lebanese Phalanx

We Want Lebanon To Be a State, Neither a Church nor a Mosque

Mr. President,

It would have been my desire to avoid this discussion of a complex and boundless problem, but I feel forced to deal with it because of a tendency which, if it finds free expression and is followed to its logical conclusion, threatens to confront our country with an imminent catastrophe. . . .

In spite of the declaration of the "Preparatory Committee for a General Muslim Conference," with all its surprising foolishness—and in spite of the pamphlet *Muslim Lebanon Today* with all its false accusations and preparatory intrigues, all of it constituting an instigation to open troublemaking—we have always believed that these opinions and actions were no more than the passing fancies and boastfulness of ignorant men imbued with an odious fanaticism, which deserves no attention.

Today, however, when we see people and organizations who bear the burden of leadership, and who comprise doctors, lawyers, journalists, politicians, intellectuals, and notables, associating themselves with these ideas, it becomes clear that this question is more profound and of wider scope than it would have been if it had been created only by ignorant troublemakers. It is obvious that silence concerning this bitter fact will bring about a grave and general danger.

It might have been possible for us to say nothing about this problem, as some Pharisees, both Christians and Muslims, would have wanted us to. . . .

But silence at this time and in these circumstances, now that this problem of Muslim-Christian relations in Lebanon has taken such an evil turn, would be synonymous to crime. And it would indeed be nothing but crime, and treasonable crime at that. . . .

Al-Kata'ib, which was founded as a national patriotic organization and the aim of which has been the establishment of Lebanon as a secular state founded on freedom—an aim testified to by its actions even more than by the mere statements of its supporters—is happy to be the only organization to warn against the grave dangers constituted by these fanatical sectarian movements which are supported by some groups in Lebanon. *Al-Kata'ib* is happy to be the one organization to assume this national patriotic duty, for no one can accuse *al-Kata'ib* of being a bargainer among the bargainers, or an appeaser among the appeasers, or of acting with hypocrisy and deceit.

And I, Pierre Gemayel, a Christian proud of my Christianity and a dutiful observer of its doctrines, am happy to interpret the thoughts of the majority of the Lebanese and the basic ideas we are now presenting.

I am happy to be such an interpreter because of the general recognition that in national politics I have never acted as a religious "doctrinaire," and that in all my activities I have endeavored to be guided by the most general principles of humanity and exclusively by the interests of the country as a whole. . . .

All of us are acquainted with the difficult problem of the Christian minorities in the Muslim states of the East, including the Arab states.

All of us know that these states, in another era, used to pervert the Muslim religion—a noble, generous and idealistic religion—into a narrowly fanatical doctrine which caused some Muslim majorities to persecute non-Muslims in a way that conscience and honor can never have condoned. . . .

The state of affairs described above lasted until the dawn of the blessed Arab National Renaissance. Christians were the first to support this progressive movement, and they did so with all their strength. Their sacrifices on behalf of this movement and their services, in the East and in the West, cannot be denied even by the most extremist of the ignorant fanatics.

In Lebanon, the seeds of this movement fell on good soil, and we, of *al-Kata'ib,* were the first to proclaim it and to fling away the conception of majority and minority. We were the first to demand that the policy of Lebanon be national and patriotic, that is, nonsectarian. We were the first to make the people of Lebanon accept the belief that Lebanon must be a nation and a fatherland, and not a church or a mosque.

We, of *al-Kata'ib,* fought for this idea. We struggled against the foreigners with all our strength, not like so many others whose struggling was done around cocktails in drawing-rooms.

In our struggle, we opposed many Christian groups who were suspicious and hostile to our ideas, many sincere people with good intentions, because they were afraid of a new movement and of new catastrophes which might have made the old catastrophes seem less dangerous, if this new movement were to fail. . . .

The Muslim organizations claim to desire "the realization of social justice, and the distribution of offices on a basis of equality. . . ."

And we, too, want this demand fulfilled, and that within the next 24 hours; on condition that it be based on justice and truth, which means that offices must be allocated according to character, training, and productivity, regardless of sectarian origins. This means that equality implies obligation as well as rights.

Accordingly, Christians would not be compelled to pay 80% of the taxes, while non-Christians pay only 20%.

It also means that the national treasury would not give money to one sect and take it away from other sects. . . .

The Muslim organizations demand a "general census and the application of Lebanese laws to all those who apply for Lebanese citizenship. . . ."

We are happy to see eye to eye with these organizations. We, too, insist on a general census—on condition that we do not consider the Lebanese immigrants unclean, who should be excluded from our Lebanese community.

And on condition that the government makes good its shortcomings by registering the hundreds of thousands of immigrants in an appropriate period of time. . . .

Are those fighting the registration of the immigrants spokesmen for these immigrants? Why are they acting against the immigrants instead of supporting their rights, when they know that the immigrants are the shields of our Lebanon, its staunch defenders, and the guarantors of our happy life? . . .

The Muslim organizations want "the realization of economic union with Syria."

In plain language, this means that Lebanon should show the white flag and surrender unconditionally to a Syrian union that would destroy its freedom and sovereignty, and reduce it to a mere satellite of Syria, whose ambitions with respect to Lebanon are a matter of notoriety.

How can the Muslim organizations reconcile these two opposites: union with Syria, and the preservation of Lebanon as a free and independent state?

If the Muslim organizations are really sincere in their desire for the economic recovery of Lebanon on behalf of Arabism, why do they not join with us in demanding an economic union with all the Arab states together, and not Syria alone? . . .

The Muslim organizations wish "to abolish sectarianism."

This is exactly what we long for, and what we are striving to achieve in a practical way. The total abolition of religious sectarianism, or at least of some of it, can be achieved only through the liquidation of the legal personal courts and by making the Lebanese Republic a secular state in toto. Thus, all Lebanese citizens would have to submit to a civil legal code that would apply uniformly to everyone in Lebanon.

Here we ask: Are the Muslim organizations really prepared to go along with us toward total secularism, or do they have a hidden objective in demanding the abolition of sectarianism? Are they aiming at putting a certain definite group of people into power? . . .

The Muslim organizations wish to "amend the constitution."

The aim of this is clear. It is either to put a stop to the power of the President of the Republic, or to distribute the power between him and the Prime Minister equally. It is obvious that the only reason for this is that the President is a Christian and the Prime Minister is a Muslim.

This is the real objective, and as for what they say by way of argument, it is all a fraud and an attempt to hide the truth.

This demand, with its accompanying agitation, has increased the suspicion of all Christians and put them on their guard. They are afraid that this demand for an amendment to the constitution may turn out to be a step imperiling the existence and future of the country. . . .

All sincere Lebanese view this problem as one of their personal security, menaced and compromised by a destructive emergence of fanaticism. It is a problem that must be solved if Lebanon can fulfill its mission and help in the solution of the problems confronting all Arabs. This can only be done in an atmosphere free of suspicion and the threats arising from an upsurge of ignorant dictatorial egotism.

If these Muslim organizations were sincerely devoted to Arabism, as they pretend, they would have exerted every effort to preserve the special quality for which Lebanon is celebrated. Lebanon, impregnated with Christian civilization, is regarded as holy, and is dedicated to the human values, though it is not ourselves who regard this as "Christian," but these Muslim organizations themselves. Hence, Lebanon can only serve Arabism if it remains national, and not religious, and it would fail altogether if it were transformed into one more Muslim theocracy which is what these deluded and short-sighted dreamers want it to become.

But if Arabism is Islam, and the religion of Islam has a lofty, spiritual source and is not based on vulgar egotism, how can we ask Christians to be Arabs when they know the sinister designs of these ignorant fanatics?

And if the ultimate goal of all this agitation is to make Lebanon part of a Syrian, Arab, or Muslim state, then we say firmly and unequivocally to these Muslim organizations: In that direction we will not go with you one single step.

We, of *al-Kata'ib,* want Lebanon to be a country of freedom, untainted by any sectarianism, independent of the East and of the West, and cooperating fully with the Arab states; but we do not want Lebanon to be a "province" in some other unit, and we will never allow it to become a "district" of a union with anyone else. . . .

At a time when civilized nations are laboring ceaselessly to raise the living standards of their people through the exploitation of all their natural resources, while they are struggling to wipe out ignorance, disease, and poverty, and while Lebanon urgently needs to exploit its potential capital of water and electricity on the model of the TVA in the United States and the Volga project in the Soviet Union, it pains us to see our people diverting themselves with delusions and planting a wind to harvest the tempest, and seeds of strife to reap the evil of destruction. . . .

If these evil movements, which aim at the destruction of sovereign Lebanon, call for a strike in support of what they call "some demands," we, of *al-Kata'ib,* can only oppose such a strike by another one of our own, in the interests of our country.

And if demonstrations are made, we will make our own, in order to prevent our house from crumbling according to the wish of the sinister forces opposing us.

If the Government fails to do its duty in safeguarding our laws and our security, then the youth of Lebanon [the *al-Kata'ib* youth branches] will do its duty by providing security and tranquility on its own terms.

And if the state fails to rule according to civilized standards, then the Lebanese people will have to reconsider its option of this state! We feel compelled to do this, in order to preserve our beloved country, Lebanon. . . .

Let us assume for a moment that the sectarian struggle for which some egotists are carrying the banner has achieved a Muslim victory over the Christians.

Let us suppose that the road was made easy for the demented sectarianism of the mob, as we saw at the end of July, 1954.

Let us suppose that Lebanon has succumbed to such a catastrophe, sinking to the status of other countries backward in civilization and culture.

Let us suppose that all this has happened.

Do those who wish this to happen to the Christians imagine that the Christians will fall asleep over their grievances, and humbly and obediently submit without conjuring up a flame that will enable the "foreigners" to enter Lebanon at will and harm Lebanon itself and every other Arab state?

Would this be a service to Lebanon or the Arab states, to lean backward so violently while the nations of the world are gradually awakening to progress. . . .

To the Muslims in Lebanon particularly, and to the Arabs in general, we say: You must never forget one thing, and that is that the paramount interest of the nation demands that you never make the Christians suspicious of your aims. Never let them lose the feeling of security and tranquility, even if you, the Muslims, must sacrifice something of your own rights and interests. The Christians will rise to defend their interests and those of the Arabs only insofar as they have confidence in you. And, on the other hand, just as far as you make the Christians suspicious, and disgusted with you, just so far will this lead to calamity for the cause of Lebanon and the cause of the Arabs together. . . .

V. *Islam, Modernism, and Socialism*

18. NEW RENAISSANCE: THE VIEWPOINT OF THE MUSLIM BROTHERHOOD*

Hasan al-Banna

Hasan al-Banna (1906–49), the founder of the Muslim Brotherhood (or Muslim Brethren), was born in the village of Mahmudiyya in the Nile Delta province of Beheira, Egypt. His father, a respected scholar and a follower of the fundamentalist Hanbalite Sunni school, greatly influenced his son. Al-Banna received a religious education and teacher training, the latter at Dar al-'Ulum in Cairo. Early in life, he became a member of various orthodox religious organizations and took part in anti-British activities; and his dedication to Islam, to teaching, and to missionary work was evident. His nationalist feelings were probably aroused by the British occupation of Egypt. While teaching in Isma'iliyya, the administrative center of the Suez Canal, he was constantly aware of the relatively easy life enjoyed by British troops and French officials, whose standard of living was far better than that of the average Egyptian. He was also opposed to the missionaries' evangelical activities. Al-Banna founded the first nucleus of the Brotherhood in Isma'iliyya in 1928.

Officially established in 1929, the Jam'iyyat al-ikhwan al-muslimin *(Society of Muslim Brethren) became the most powerful Islamic organization since the heyday of the Wahhabi movement. Al-Banna came eventually to Cairo, where he taught from 1934 to 1946 while leading the organization. Endowed with a prodigious memory, inexhaustible energy, oratorical skill, and personal charm, he was a born leader. He had a keen knowledge of various Sufi, heretical, and subversive movements in Islam, as well as of their techniques, which he combined with modern notions of organization and propaganda.*

The secret organization soon spread throughout the towns of Egypt, and then to Sudan, Syria, Lebanon, Jordan, Palestine, and North Africa, and al-Banna became known as Murshid al-'amm *(the Supreme Guide). The organization advocated a return to orthodox Islam but also devoted attention to education, community development, training in industrial skills, and social welfare, and it even owned commercial companies. In 1948, it was estimated*

* Reprinted, with a new title, from Hasan al-Banna, "Min al-qadim: Ittijah al-nahda al-jadida fi al-'alam al-islami" ("Of Old: The Direction of the New Renaissance in the Islamic World"), *al-Muslimun (The Muslim)*, Damascus, February, 1958, pp. 55–60.

that the membership amounted to 2 million, most of whom were from the lower classes. Al-Banna reportedly defined the Brotherhood as a Salafi movement, an orthodox way, a Sufi reality, a political body, an athletic group, a scientific and cultural society, an economic company, and a social idea.

Beginning in 1939 and during the war years, the Brotherhood came into conflict with the government. The Brethren advocated independence for Egypt, unity of the Nile Valley, and eventually a government with a caliph at its head, but also reforms, which, if not forthcoming, they argued might cause revolution. Later, they urged a jihad (holy war) against the Jews, and pressed for full return to the laws of Islam. The Brethren were implicated in the assassination of two Egyptian Prime Ministers, and consequently many members were arrested and persecuted. Al-Banna made futile attempts to extricate the movement from politics, but he was assassinated on February 12, 1949, probably by order of King Faruq, and the Brethren were outlawed. In 1950, however, their freedom was partially restored, and the Brethren again engaged in politics under a director general. Hasan al-Hudaybi, a former judge attached to King Faruq, assumed this position in 1950, after the position had been filled by several people, including Ahmad Hasan al-Baquri, who became Minister of Waqfs (Foundations) from 1952 through 1953.

The Brotherhood supported all independence movements. It was one of the principal forces that contributed to the success of the officers' revolution of July, 1952, and immediately afterward enjoyed full freedom. Even before 1952, in fact, the officers' secret organization had established relations with the Brotherhood through Anwar al-Sa'dat, and even Nasser (Jamal 'Abd al-Nasir) was thought to have been a member for a short time. But after the revolution, the Brotherhood's ideal of a theocratic state based on Islamic principles clashed with the more practical aims of the officers, who, although faithful to Islam, believed that the renewal of the social, political, and economic systems called for a secular approach. The Brethren tried to impose their viewpoint on the Egyptian Government and even interfered in the negotiations with the British. Finally regarded as a political party, they were dissolved on January 12, 1954, briefly restored, and then abolished again. The military found it necessary to explain at great length their repressive action. See "Dissolution of the Muslim Brotherhood—Statement of the Council of the Revolutionary Command," Middle East Affairs, *V (March, 1954), 94–100 (a translation of the original statement, which appeared in* al-Ahram, *January 15, 1954: "Mu'amarat kubra li-iqsa' al-'ahd al-hadir yudabbiruha al-ikhwan al-muslimun ma'a rijal al-safara al-baritaniyya fi al-Qahira. Hajama'at al-ikhwan al-muslimin wa-ghalq markazaha wa-furu'iha fi anha' misr" ["Great Plot for Overturning the Present Regime Prepared by the Muslim Brethren and the Men of the British Embassy in Cairo. Dissolution of the Muslim Brethren Group and Closing of its General Headquarters and Branches in Egypt"].*

The dismissal of Muhammad Neguib (Nagib), the nominal head of the Egyptian Revolution, brought Nasser to power and sealed the doom of the Brethren. The final rift with the Revolutionary Council, which had wanted to retain friendly relations with the Brethren, came after the evacuation agreement was signed with the United Kingdom on October 19, 1954. The evacua-

tion was to take place in 1956. The Brethren opposed the terms of the agreements and accused Nasser of collaborating with the British, but also criticized the fact that all these decisions were made by the government without the consent of a freely elected parliament and without freedom of expression. An abortive attempt to assassinate Nasser on October 26, 1954, led to the trial and execution of six Brethren and the imprisonment of many others.

The Egyptian ouster of the Brethren dealt a deadly blow to the organization. Many of its followers were won over by Nasser's economic and social policy as well as by his ability to gain the support of al-Azhar, the citadel of Muslim orthodoxy. The movement, however, remained active for some time in Syria, Iraq, Jordan, Lebanon, and Sudan. Mustafa al-Siba'i, the head of the Syrian organization, reportedly was elected director general. The Brethren's publication Majallat al-ikhwan (Magazine of the Brethren)*—generally known as* al-Muslimun (The Muslim)*—continued its publication in Damascus in 1955, under al-Siba'i's editorship, and was transferred to Lebanon in 1958, after the emergence of the United Arab Republic. Later, the organization moved to Geneva, which apparently became its propaganda center. It continued its underground activities. As late as the summer of 1965, the organization planned to assassinate President Nasser and take power. It was a rather massive plot involving university students, upper class intellectuals, and engineers, who provided the explosives. More than 400 plotters were arrested. For the official view of this plot, see* Arab Observer *(an English weekly published in Cairo), September 13, 1965, pp. 7–12.*

Aided by special temporary conditions, the Brotherhood for a time spread into practically every Arab country. Its importance as a truly international movement with genuine popular support cannot be summarily dismissed. Appealing to their common religious feelings, the organization mobilized the Arab masses against foreign domination. It emphasized the primacy of Islam while stressing in theory and practice the need for economic, social, and educational progress. It also successfully organized the masses for political purposes. Thus, in all these fields, it prepared the psychological and organizational ground on which the later regimes established their own power and were forced to abide by some of the ideas of the Brethren. However, it failed politically for it was unable to remold the classical Muslim idea of government and state and to adapt it to modern requirements. In fact, it became a partisan movement by competing with the government. It also adopted an unrealistic view of international relations and was utterly inflexible on matters of law.

Al-Banna was certainly aware of the threat to Islamic values posed by modernization and by identification with the West, especially in matters of economic and social organization, and he therefore tried to incorporate them into Islam or at least to redefine them according to the Muslim ethos.

Sayyid Qutb, an influential member of the Brotherhood and first editor of some of its journals, tried to interpret social justice, a dynamic idea in the present drive for socialism in the Middle East, from an Islamic viewpoint. See his al-'Adala al-ijtima'iyya fi al-islam *(Cairo: Lajnat al-nashr lil-jami'iyyin, 1954); in a translation by John B. Hardie, it was published as* Social Justice in Islam *(Washington, D.C.: American Council of Learned Societies, 1953).*

Many publications in Arabic about the Brotherhood represent both positive and negative points of view. The best book in English is Ishaq Musa al-Husayni, The Moslem Brethren: The Greatest of Modern Islamic Movements, *translated by John F. Brown and John Raey (Beirut: Khayat's, 1956). The original appeared as* al-Ikhwan al-muslimun: kubra al-haraka al-islamiyya al-haditha *(Beirut: Dar Bairut, 1952). Christina Phelps Harris,* Nationalism and Revolution in Egypt: The Role of the Muslim Brotherhood *(The Hague: Mouton & Co., 1964) is based largely on Husayni's book. A good article summarizing the basic principles of the movement as expressed in al-Banna's pamphlet* Da'watuna (Teachings) *is Franz Rosenthal, "The 'Muslim Brethren' in Egypt,"* The Muslim World, *XXXVII (October, 1947), 278–91. See also Francis Bertier, "L'Idéologie politique des frères musulmans,"* Orient, *No. 8 (1958), 43–57; and Kenneth Cragg,* Islamic Surveys: Counsels in Contemporary Islam *(Edinburgh: Edinburgh University Press, 1965), pp. 110–21. Cragg (pp. 120 ff.) discusses a similar movement in Pakistan, the Jama'at-i Islami-Muslim community, under the leadership of Lawlana Abu al-Mawdudi (b. 1904).*

Al-Banna's writings and speeches have been repeatedly issued in various editions. The article reproduced here extolls perfection in Islam and points out that the Brotherhood arose because of the West's failure to provide spiritual nourishment.

When we observe the evolution in the political, social, and moral spheres of the lives of nations and peoples, we note that the Islamic world—and, naturally, in the forefront, the Arab world—gives to its rebirth an Islamic flavor. This trend is ever-increasing. Until recently, writers, intellectuals, scholars, and governments glorified the principles of European civilization, gave themselves a Western tint, and adopted a European style and manner; today, on the contrary, the wind has changed, and reserve and distrust have taken their place. Voices are raised proclaiming the necessity for a return to the principles, teachings, and ways of Islam, and, taking into account the situation, for initiating the reconciliation of modern life with these principles, as a prelude to a final "Islamization."

Causes

This development worries a good number of governments and Arab powers, which, having lived during the past generations in a state of mind that had retained from Islam only lessons of fanaticism and inertia, regarded the Muslims only as weak drudges or as nations easily exploitable by colonialism. In trying to understand the new movement [the Brotherhood], these governments have produced all sorts of possible interpretations: "It is the result," said some, "of the growth of extremist organizations and fanatical groups." Others explained that it was a reaction to present-day political and economic pressures, of which the Islamic nations had become aware. Finally, others said, "It is only a means whereby those seeking government or other honors may achieve renown and position."

Now all these reasons are, in our opinion, as far as possible from the truth; for this new movement can only be the result of the following three factors, which we will now examine.

The Failure of the West

The first of the three is the failure of the social principles on which the civilization of the Western nations has been built. The Western way of life—founded in effect on practical and technical knowledge, discovery, invention, and the flooding of world markets with mechanical products—has remained incapable of offering to men's minds a flicker of light, a ray of hope, a grain of faith, or of providing anxious persons the smallest path toward rest and tranquillity. Man is not simply an instrument among others. Naturally, he has become tired of purely materialistic conditions and desires some spiritual comfort. But the materialistic life of the West could only offer him as reassurance a new materialism of sin, passion, drink, women, noisy gatherings, and showy attractions which he had come to enjoy. Man's hunger grows from day to day; he wants to free his spirit, to destroy this materialistic prison and find space to breathe the air of faith and consolation.[1]

Perfection of Islam

The second factor—the decisive factor in the circumstances—is the discovery by Islamic thinkers of the noble, honorable, moral, and perfect content of the principles and rules of this religion, which is infinitely more accomplished, more pure, more glorious, more complete, and more beautiful than all that has been discovered up till now by social theorists and reformers. For a long time, Muslims neglected all this, but once God had enlightened their thinkers and they had compared the social rules of their religion with what they had been told by the greatest sociologists and the cleverest leading theorists, they noted the wide gap and the great distance between a heritage of immense value on one side and the conditions experienced on the other. Then, Muslims could not but do justice to the spirit and the history of their people, proclaiming the value of this heritage and inviting all peoples—nonpracticing Muslims or non-Muslims—to follow the sacred path that God had traced for them and to hold to a straight course.

Type of Development

The third factor is the development of social conditions between the two murderous world wars (which involved all the world powers and monopolized the minds of regimes, nations, and individuals) which resulted in a set of principles of reform and social organization that certain powers, in deciding to put them into practice, have taken as an instructional basis. These principles have become the prey of change and transformation, in fact subject to disappearance and ruin. Muslim thinkers looked on, observed, and returned to

1. This argument has been put forth in various forms by Muslim writers since the end of the nineteenth century, and it is continually stressed by various other writers included in this anthology.

what they already possessed in their own right—the great Book of God, the brilliant manifest example of their Prophet and their glorious history. There was nothing of value they could accredit to any existing regime that could not be already found inspiring their thought and conduct and already inscribed in Islamic social organization. There was no blemish against which the social organization of a watchful Islam could not guard [its people] by showing them its fearful consequences.

The world has long been ruled by democratic systems, and man has everywhere glorified and honored the conquests of democracy: freedom of the individual, freedom of nations, justice and freedom of thought, justice for the human soul with freedom of action and will, justice for the peoples who became the source of power. Victory at the end of World War I reinforced these thoughts, but men were not slow to realize that their collective liberty had not come intact out of the chaos, that their individual liberty was not safe from anarchy, and that the government of the people had not in many cases freed society from camouflaged dictatorship that destroyed responsibility without limiting jurisdiction. Quite the contrary, vice and violence led to the breaking loose of nations and peoples, to the overthrow of collective organization and family structure, and to the setting up of dictatorial regimes.

Thus, German Nazism and Italian Fascism rose to the fore; Mussolini and Hitler led their two peoples to unity, order, recovery, power, and glory. In record time, they ensured internal order at home and, through force, made themselves feared abroad. Their regimes gave real hope, and also gave rise to thoughts of steadfastness and perseverance and the reuniting of different, divided men around the words "chief" and "order." In their resolutions and speeches, the Führer and the Duce began to frighten the world and to upset their epoch.

What happened then? It became evident that in a powerful and well-knit regime, where the wishes of the individual were based on those of their chiefs, the mistakes of the chiefs became those of the regime, which shared also in their acts of violence, their decline, and their fall; then, everything was at an end, all had been cut down as in a single day, but not until the world had lost in a second war thousands of men, the flower of her youth, and masses of wealth and material.

The star of socialism and Communism, symbol of success and victory, shone with an increasing brilliance; Soviet Russia was at the head of the collectivist camp. She launched her message and, in the eyes of the world, demonstrated a system which had been modified several times in thirty years. The democratic powers—or, to use a more precise expression, the colonialist powers, the old ones worn out, the new ones full of greed—took up a position to stem the current. The struggle intensified, in some places openly, in others under cover, and nations and peoples, perplexed, hesitated at the crossroads, not knowing which way was best; among them were the nations of Islam and the peoples of the Qur'an; the future, whatever the circumstances, is in the hands of God, the decision with history, and immortality with the most worthy.

This social evolution and violent, hard struggle stirred the minds of Muslim thinkers; the parallels and the prescribed comparisons led to a healthy conclusion: to free themselves from the existing state of affairs, to allow the necessary return of the nations and peoples to Islam.

The Three Regimes and Prayer

In a whimsical moment, I happened to say to my audience at a meeting—which, thanks to God, was a complete success—that this Islamic prayer which we perform five times a day is nothing but a daily training in practical social organization uniting the features of the Communist regime with those of the dictatorial and democratic regimes. Astonished, my questioners demanded an explanation. "The greatest value of the Communist regime," I said, "is the reinforcement of the notion of equality, the condemnation of class distinction, and the struggle against the claim to property, source of these differences." Now this lesson is present in the mind of the Muslim; he is perfectly conscious of it and his spirit is filled with it the moment he enters the mosque; yes, the moment he enters, he realizes that the mosque belongs to God and not to anyone of his creatures; he knows himself to be the equal of all those who are there, whoever they may be; here there are no great, no small, no high, no low, no more groups or classes. And when the muezzin calls, "Now is the hour of prayer," they form an equal mass, a compact block, behind the imam.[2] None bows unless the imam bows, none prostrates himself unless the imam prostrates himself; none moves or remains motionless unless following the imam's example. That is the principal merit of the dictatorial regime: unity and order in the will under the appearance of equality. The imam himself is in any case limited by the teachings and rules of the prayer, and if he stumbles or makes a mistake in his reading or in his actions, all those behind him—young boys, old men, or women at prayer—have the imperative duty to tell him of his error in order to put him back on the right road during the prayer, and the imam himself is bound absolutely to accept this good advice and, forsaking his error, return to reason and truth. That is what is most appealing in democracy.

How, therefore, can these regimes be superior to Islam, which astonishingly unites all their merits and avoids all their sins? "If this message came from some other than God, many contradictions would be found in it" (Qur'an).

No Incentive for Trouble

As I have said, [the people of] the West—and with them those who are blind—are worried by this development, which they consider serious, since they see themselves forced to combat it by every means, being less accustomed to finding themselves facing such a situation than to seeing the success of their reactionary principles on the less developed nations, in contempt of all the rules of civilization followed by cultivated and orderly peoples; judgment steeped in error and the flagrant suppression of rights can be seen as clearly as daylight.

2. The imam referred to here is a leader of prayer, and should not be confused with the Shi'ite imam, who is the supreme head of the community.

Here, our intention is to demonstrate to the West two points:

(1) Demonstration of the excellence of Islamic principles of collective organization, and their superiority over everything known to man until now, these principles being:

(*a*) Brotherly love: condemnation of hatred and fanaticism.

(*b*) Peace. Error is committed by the misguided thinking on the legitimacy of the Holy War.

(*c*) Liberty. Error is committed by those who suspect Islam of tolerating slavery and interfering with liberty.

(*d*) Social justice: obvious character of the Islamic theory of power and class structure.

(*e*) Happiness: manifest error in the appreciation of the reality of abstinence.

(*f*) Family: matters concerning the rights of women, number of wives, and repudiation.

(*g*) Work and profit: matters concerning the different kinds of profit, and error in the appreciation of the fact of relying on God.

(*h*) Knowledge. Error is committed by those who accuse Islam of encouraging ignorance and apathy.

(*i*) Organization and determination of duties. Error is committed by those who see in the nature of Islam a source of imperfection and indolence.

(*j*) Piety: the reality of faith, and the merit and reward attached to it.

(2) Demonstration of the following facts:

(*a*) For the good of man in general, Muslims must move toward a return to their religion.

(*b*) Islam will find in this return her principal strength on earth.

(*c*) Far from receiving impetus from a blind fanaticism, this movement will be inspired by a strong regard for the values of Islam which correspond fully to what modern thought has discovered as most noble, sound, and tested in society. It is God who says what is true and who shows the way.

19. ISLAMIC SOCIALISM*

Mustafa al-Siba'i

Mustafa al-Siba'i (b. 1910 in Homs, Syria) is one of the best known leaders and writers of the Muslim Brotherhood. He occupied several high positions in the

* Extract from Mustafa al-Siba'i, *al-Wahda al-kubra* (*The Great Union*), Damascus, October 29, 1961. A French translation, "À propos du socialisme de l'Islam," appeared in *Orient,* No. 20 (1961), 175–78.

Brotherhood—as controller general, head of the Syrian branch, and then, reportedly, as director general. Al-Siba'i began publishing al-Manar (The Beacon) *in Damascus in 1946. He became the editor of* al-Muslimun (The Muslim) *after it began publication in Damascus in 1955, and he gave intellectual tone to the Brotherhood. Al-Siba'i is definitely more socially and politically oriented and farther to the left than was al-Banna. He considers himself a Muslim socialist and a republican. In the Constituent Assembly of 1949, al-Siba'i had made common cause with Akram Hawrani, the leader of the Syrian Arab Socialist Party, in support of a republican regime. The Muslim Socialist Front (al-Jabha al-ishtirakkiya), headed by al-Siba'i and representing essentially the views of the Muslim Brotherhood, had four seats, and the Ba'th Party had three. During debates in the Assembly, al-Siba'i proposed a social program on behalf of the Front. He declared that he would work for a true Islamic socialism. Al-Siba'i claims that some of the socialist principles of his movement—in particular, the limitation of land property—were introduced in the constitution of 1950 (Art. 22) as measures of social reform. He clashed with the Syrian Social Nationalist Party (followers of Antun Saadeh) and later with the Ba'th Party. His group was so powerful in Syria that it forced the Egyptian Government to ask the Syrian authorities for written guarantees that the Brotherhood's actions would be brought under control. After 1955, however, al-Siba'i and his group associated with forces trying to oppose the leftists and thus indirectly pushed the Ba'th Party into a coalition with the Communists.*

Al-Siba'i wrote articles for reviews and published several books, among which is al-Ahzab al-siyasiyya fi suriyya (The Political Parties of Syria) *(Damascus; Dar al-rawwad, 1954). An article proposing Islam as the state religion of Syria ("Islam as the State Religion: A Muslim Brotherhood View in Syria," translated by R. Bayly Winder) appeared in* The Muslim World, *XLIV (July–October, 1954), 215–26; the original had appeared in* al-Ayyam, *March 9, 1950, and in* al-Samir, *a New York daily, March 9–14, 1950. Al-Siba'i's views on socialism are expressed in* al-Ishtirakiyya al-islam (Islamic Socialism) *(Cairo: Dar al-qawmiyya lil-tiba'a wal-nashr, 1960), in which he suggested that practically all major economic and social problems could be solved by the socialism of Islam. Reprinted several times, the book met with the approval of some of the 'ulama' but, since al-Siba'i had opposed nationalization and the type of socialism enforced in Egypt, the Voice of Arabs and Cairo radios, both controlled by Nasser, attacked it as having distorted Islam and socialism. Al-Siba'i rejected Egyptian accusations in a series of speeches and articles. The following article summarizes al-Siba'i's book on socialism; the pages cited refer to the book.*

Islamic socialism rests on five fundamental rights that must be guaranteed to all its citizens:

1. The right to live and, as its corollary, the safeguarding and protection of health and illness (p. 59).

2. The right to liberty in all its forms, and particularly to political liberty (p. 75).

3. The right to knowledge: This right extends to all the knowledge the nation needs, both spiritual and material (p. 59).

4. The right to dignity, in all its aspects (p. 113).

5. The right to property, subject to certain conditions (p. 124).

I have also mentioned in my book the most important principles on which property is based in Islam:

1. Work—the most important way of acquiring property. All work leads to possession; it is legal if it involves neither fraud nor injustice (p. 132).

2. Private property is an indefeasible right. The state guarantees it and punishes those who interfere with it (pp. 133–35).

3. Property is a social function; the state forbids its utilization as a means of oppression and exploitation (p. 134).

4. Wealth involves social duties: legitimate charity, pensions for relatives, mutual social aid (p. 136).[1]

5. Inheritance is a legitimate right protected by the state (p. 136).

Nationalization can be applied to goods and articles necessary to society only if their possession by one or several individuals involves the exploitation of society, on condition also that economic experts agree that it is in the obvious interest of the nation (p. 163).[2]

Henceforth, when the state has recourse to nationalization in cases of social or economic necessity, it is obliged to afford adequate compensation to the dispossessed proprietors (p. 164).

The principles of Islam, our social situation, and the obligation placed upon us by our religion to wipe out oppression and give human dignity to the peasants—all this renders the limitation of landed property legal in the eyes of the law and makes it one of the duties of the state (p. 170). Nevertheless, it must be applied in all fairness and in conformity to the general interest, and not merely to satisfy rancor and vengeance.

Moreover, the seizure of private goods should be carried out only under certain conditions, especially in cases of extreme danger, invasion, public disaster, famine, flood, or earthquake. Only if the state treasury and the funds held by the authorities are inadequate to guard against any danger is it lawful to deduct from people's wealth what is strictly necessary to meet such necessity, as proclaimed by the 'ulama' of Islam, such as al-Nawawi,[3] al-Ghazzali,[4] etc. (pp. 194–96).

I have then cited the rules of mutual social aid. Numbering twenty-nine,

1. This principle forms the key difference between the voluntary personal concepts of social aid or charity defended by al-Siba'i and the institutionalized, state-controlled social welfare system enforced by Egypt.

2. According to al-Siba'i and the doctrine of the Muslim Brotherhood, nationalization is limited to movable goods and items—that is, to the products of labor. This provision applies more to handicrafts and to small plants than to industry as a whole.

3. A Shafi'i jurist known for his high erudition, al-Nawawi Muhyi al-Din Abu Zakariya Yahya al-Hizami al-Dimashqi (1233–77), was also famous for his opposition to Sultan Baybars' confiscatory policies and tax exactions.

4. The greatest Sufi theologian of Islam, Abu Hamid al-Ghazzali (1058–1111) was also a great jurist who dealt extensively with questions of property. Works on al-Ghazzali are extensive; see *Encyclopaedia of Islam*, new edition.

they guarantee the fulfillment by the state of this obligation vis-à-vis its subjects, thus assuring them as well as their children a decent life in case of incapacity, illness, or unemployment.

Briefly summarized, such is the conception of Islamic socialism that I have set out in my book. I have then compared it with the socialism of the extreme left.

1. In recognizing the lawful character of private property, Islamic socialism allows those with talent to participate in constructive competition, an essential conditions for the expansion of civilization and the development of production (p. 259).

2. This socialism encourages and leads to cooperation and friendship, not to class struggle (p. 260).

3. It is a moral socialism based on sound morals, of which it makes a foundation in its doctrine (p. 261).

4. All that concerns man comes under the care of this socialism: religion, morals, education, clothing, food, and not only the material aspects of life (p. 264).

5. It is an integral part of the credo of the Muslim, who can but apply it. It constitutes a more rapid and more effectual method than any other socialism for the reform of our society (p. 266).

As for the socialism of extreme left, this is what I wrote: "Its roots are not in the depths of the human soul; it is not based upon religion or human nature or conviction. It cannot therefore be applied except by force and in an atmosphere of terror" (p. 267).

Such are the aspects and characteristics of socialism in Islam. Without doubt, it is totally different from the type of socialism that attaches no importance to religious values, relies on the class struggle in society, seizes private property without good reason, nationalizes industry and economic concerns that contribute to the national economic prosperity, paralyzes initiative and competition in the individual as well as the community, impoverishes the rich without enriching the poor, originates from hate and not from love, claims to work for the people while it terrorizes them, impoverishes them, and humiliates them. A socialism of this kind is as far removed as possible from Islam and has nothing in common with it. Moreover, Islam foresees in it the inevitable ruin of any society where it reigns and exercises influence.

Finally, since our revolutionary order [the Syrian revolution] and our government have agreed on socialism as a social regime, and since they have published a detailed program which is in no way contrary to Islam,[5] it is good —and I say this in all sincerity and frankness—that the cause of Islamic social-

5. These views were put forth in October, 1961, apparently just before Syria decided to pull out of the union with Egypt. The decision was prompted by the Syrian reaction to the overwhelming domination by Egyptians of Syrian life as well as by the nationalization decrees of July and August, 1961, which threatened to liquidate the upper- and middle-class enterprises in Syria. The government that was established after the revolution considerably softened the socialist measures, but in 1963 the Ba'thists and the military introduced their own brand of socialism, which led almost to the annihilation of private enterprise.

ism should be encouraged, because of its profound influence on the minds of the masses and its facility for building a worth-while society, unique and advanced in its economy and its social relations. It is also desirable that this socialism should be embraced by every zealous defender of our nation who is anxious to avert the danger of extreme left-wing socialism.

In fact, Islamic socialism conforms to human nature. It satisfies the dignity of all citizens as well as their interests. To the workers, it grants a decent standard of living and an assured future; to the holder of capital, it opens up wide horizons as regards production under state control. Finally, it applies to all citizens without discrimination, and is not the prerogative of the followers of one religion to the exclusion of those of another.

20. SOCIALISM AND ISLAM*

Mahmud Shaltut

Long known for his reformist views, Shaykh Mahmud Shaltut was dismissed as a member of the faculty of al-Azhar in the 1930's, but he was appointed wakil *(rector) of al-Azhar in 1958. In 1961, when religious and administrative authority in al-Azhar were separated, Shaltut retained his office as religious head and Dr. Muhammad al-Bahi became the head of the administration. Although it has often been described as the citadel of resistance to oppression and strong government, al-Azhar actually has associated itself more often than not with the policies of the ruling governments. In the 1930's and the 1940's, al-Azhar had a progressive group of teachers, who eventually (in the 1950's and 1960's) came to support President Nasser's social and economic policies. These teachers, representing the weight of religious sanction, provided one of the main channels for winning over the population to these policies. In this article, which is also an indirect rebuttal to Mustafa al-Siba'i's work, Shaltut invokes various Qur'anic citations to prove, in effect, that Egyptian socialism conforms to Islamic laws. In many respects, his views about the universality of Islam; are similar to those put forth by the Muslim Brotherhood; Shaltut, however, suggests that the state's extensive role is implicit in the idea that all the social obligations of Islam can be met by increased production or wealth. He insists on the need for increasing wealth and gives the government a unique role in achieving it.*

Social solidarity proceeds from men's feelings of responsibility toward one another. Each individual bears the faults of his brother; if he does ill, he does

* Extract from Mahmud Shaltut, "al-Ishtirakiyya wa-al-islam" ("Socialism and Islam"), *al-Jumhuriyya,* Cairo, December 22, 1961. A French translation, "Le Socialisme et l'Islam," appeared in *Orient,* No. 20 (1961), 163–74.

it both for himself and for his brother; if he does good, he does it for himself and for his brother.

Islam and Society

Islam is not only a spiritual religion, as some wrongly imagine, thinking that it limits itself to establishing relations between the servant and his Lord, without being concerned with organizing the affairs of the community and establishing its rules of conduct. On the contrary, Islam is universal in character. Not only does it determine the relations between man and his Lord, but it also lays down the rules that regulate human relations and public affairs, with the aim of ensuring the welfare of society.

Islam's sole desire has been that men shall accept this organization, that their attitude in this regard should stem from the fear they feel for the One who created Islam, from the veneration they have for His power, and from their conviction that He knows the secrets of their hearts; so that there may be ingrained in their minds the principles of clemency, love, cooperation, mutual help, and unanimity. Each man then considers himself as a stone in the structure of society, and becomes an integral part of society, paying for it with his person and his property.

Mutual Social Aid Among Muslims

Members of human society cannot be considered independent of one another. On the contrary, as a result of their existence in this world and the very conditions of their lives, they render each other mutual service and cooperate to satisfy their needs.[1]

Nevertheless, as regards relations between individuals who constitute human society, Islam has not limited itself to the necessities and conditions of life. Above all, it has taken upon itself the task of strengthening the very nature of social life, of preventing deterioration, breaking up, and the consequences of the psychological factors and personal tendencies that often make

1. The idea that human society originated in man's practical need for help has been the cornerstone of Islamic social thought. The idea may be traced to Aristotle's view that "every polis (or state) is a species of association and . . . [that] all associations are instituted for the purpose of attaining some good." *The Politics of Aristotle,* trans. Ernest Barker (London: Oxford University Press, 1958), p. 1. Muhammad ibn Muhammad ibn Tarkhan Abu Nasr al-Farabi (*ca.* 870–950) states in his work *al-Siyasat al-madaniyya* (*Political Economy*) (Hyderabad text; 1346 [1930]) that "man belongs to the species that cannot accomplish their necessary affairs or achieve their best state, except through the association of many groups of them in a single dwelling place." Quoted from an edition in preparation by Fawzi M. Najjar, in Ralph Lerner and Muhsin Mahdi (eds.), *Medieval Political Philosophy* (New York: Collier–Macmillan–Free Press of Glencoe, 1963), p. 32. Finally, in his *Muqaddima* (*Prolegomena*), 'Abd al-Rahman ibn Khaldun (1332–1406), states that "Human society is necessary. Philosophers express the truth by saying that man is social by nature, i.e., he needs society or a city as they call it. The reason for this is that . . . it becomes necessary for him to unite his efforts with his fellow men." (Charles Issawi ['Isawi], *An Arab Philosophy of History: Selections from the Prolegomena of Ibn Khaldun of Tunis [1332–1406]* [London: John Murray, 1958], p. 99.) There are, however, basic differences between Aristotle and Muslim thinkers about the nature and source of laws that govern human society.

men exceed the limits of moderation necessary to tranquility, happiness, security, and stability. That is the reason why Islam wants to establish emotional bonds that unite men in their orientation and in their aims, and that make of them a strong, united force, soundly organized, with love as the thread, the common good as the chain, and as their aim happiness in this life and in the life hereafter. This bond is one of faith and belief, which are linked to the source of all good—that is, to God.

This bond is, in Islam, the "religious brotherhood" among Muslims. It is in the "brotherhood" that rights and social duties are expressed in the most sincere fashion. It is this that constitutes the most powerful factor leading toward clemency, sympathy, and cooperation, and giving a sense of the idea; it leads society toward good and banishes evil.

Islam has established this "brotherhood" among Muslims. "The believers are a band of brothers" (Qur'an, XLIX, 10), and the Prophet said, "Muslim is brother to Muslim." Moreover, Islam has raised the religious brotherhood over and above the blood relationship.[2]

Muslims have attained social solidarity to a unique degree in their Islamic society, which God has immortalized in His Book, which says, "Prize them above themselves, though they are in want" (LIX, 9).

Although the word of today may proclaim social solidarity between its members and society, it nevertheless assigns it only a limited objective—simply to ensure the material needs of those who are in need of food, clothing, housing, etc. For fourteen centuries, Islam, for its part, has not contented itself with these objectives. It has given to man five rights, the loss of a single one of which means the loss of all happiness and dignity. Then turning to the fate of those whom circumstances have prevented from enjoying these rights, it has called on society to make these rights available to them.

Social solidarity in Islam, therefore, is conceived in the widest and most complete sense. In effect, it is not limited to the needs of food, housing, and clothing; it stretches still further to the five rights of man:

To preserve his religion
To preserve his life
To preserve his children
To preserve his possessions
To preserve his reason

Thus, the Muslim conception of mutual social aid extends to all the aspects of life, both material and religious.

Mutual social aid in Islam exists in various forms, each of which must be achieved. These are:

1. Moral mutual aid: Desire for another man what you desire for yourself.
2. Mutual aid regarding knowledge: "When our guidance is revealed, those who accept it shall have nothing to fear or to regret; but those that deny and reject Our revelations shall be the heirs of Hell, and there they shall abide forever" (Qur'an, II, 154-55).

2. Elsewhere, the author defines in detail the features of this brotherhood.

3. Political mutual aid: Muslims are equal in blood; the most humble of them will give his word. They form a solid block in the face of others.
4. Mutual aid regarding defense: "Whether unarmed or well-equipped, march on and fight for the cause of Allah with your wealth and your persons" (Qur'an, IX, 41).
5. Mutual aid with regard to crime: In Islam, blood cannot be shed with impunity. It will be paid for, either by retaliation ("Believers, retaliation is decreed for you in bloodshed" [Qur'an, II, 173]) or by payment by kinsmen of the author of the crime, by those who refuse to swear the oath [*qasam*] five hundred times, or by the public treasury. The price of the blood will be sent to the family of the victim.
6. Collective mutual aid: This is fixed by legal provisions that define "collective obligation"; individual mutual aid corresponds to this; it is fixed by the provision of individual duties, such as prayer and fasting.
7. Economic mutual aid: Do not squander your possessions. "Do not give to the feeble-minded the property with which Allah has entrusted you for their support" (Qur'an, IV, 4).
8. Moral mutual aid: Let him among you who witnesses a reprobate act change it by his hand; if he is incapable of this, let him do so by his tongue; if he cannot, with his heart; that is the minimum of faith. Those who revolt against the sanctions of God and those who apply them are like the people who share a ship—some have the top, others the bottom. When they need water, the latter must cross the territory of the former. They decide to make a hole in their part, without harming their neighbors up above; if the others prevent them, all are saved.
9. Mutual aid as a product of civilization: "Help one another in what is good and pious, not in what is wicked and sinful" (Qur'an, V, 3). . . .

[*In the following sections, Shaltut discusses the benefits and conditions of mutual assistance and the sources necessary to finance the assistance. Among the latter, he cites the alms* (zakat) *which can be collected by force; the religious foundations* (awqaf)[3]; *the voluntary help of the rich; the voluntary distribution of property in case of inheritance; booty; mines; and a variety of other sources.*]

Social Solidarity Among Muslims

Social solidarity among Muslims is of two kinds—the moral and the material. Moral solidarity derives from two factors. The first is recognizing good and virtue and inviting one's neighbor to conform to it with sincerity and fidelity. "You are the noblest nation that has ever been raised up for mankind. You enjoin justice and forbid evil. You believe in Allah" (Qur'an, III, 106).

The second allows one to hear the Word of God and receive it with gratitude and acknowledgment. "Give good news to My servants, who listen to My precepts and follow what is best in them. These are they whom Allah

3. Generally given in the anglicized plural form *waqfs*.

has guided. These are they who are endued with understanding" (Qur'an, XXXIX, 19–20).

The interaction of these two forces makes cooperation between members of a Muslim society more sound.

Material solidarity consists of meeting the needs of society, of consoling the unfortunate, of helping to achieve what is in the general interest, i.e., whatever increases the standard of living and serves all individuals in a beneficial manner.

It is not to be doubted that all those foundations on which life rests, such as perfection, happiness, and grandeur, matters of science, health, greatness, dignity, civilization, power, and strength, cannot be attained without wealth.

In its attitude toward allowing man to assure his needs, Islam considers wealth realistically. Islam has made wealth an "ornament" of this life (Qur'an, XVIII, 44). It also qualified it as the "support of man." Wealth is not an end in itself. It is only one of the means of rendering mutual service and procuring what one needs. Used thus, it is a good thing, both for the one who possesses it and for society. Considered as an end in itself, and with the sole aim of being enjoyed, wealth becomes for its owner the cause of great harm, and at the same time sows corruption among men. . . .

That is why the Qur'an regards wealth as a good thing, on condition that it is acquired legally and spent for the good of others, and that it remains not an end in itself but simply a means.

Agriculture, industry, and commerce, on which the material life of society depends, are the sources of wealth. Society needs agriculture for the foodstuffs that are produced by the soil. It also needs the various industries that are necessary to man. Clothing, housing, agriculture, machinery, roads, waterways, and railways are also necessary for the protection and defense of the state. All these can be acquired only through industry.

Agriculture, industry, and commerce must therefore be developed as much as possible. That is why the men of Islamic religious learning [*'ulama'*] teach that it is a collective obligation to learn to make all that one cannot do without, and that if this obligation is not fulfilled the sin that falls back on the whole nation can be effaced only if a part of the nation discharges the obligation.

There is no doubt that this obligation consists in working for the achievement of the principle that Islam imposes on its followers, i.e., the autarky [or establishment of self-sufficiency] that allows the Muslim community itself to meet all its needs. Henceforth, the other industrial and mercantile nations have no means of interfering in the affairs of this community, which thus safeguards its existence, its glory, its internal order, its traditions, and its natural wealth. This interference has, in fact, often been utilized to introduce foreign states into our countries, culminating in the occupation and exploitation of the industry and commercial wealth of the country.

It cannot be doubted that agriculture, commerce, and industry are the pillars of the national economy in all nations that wish to live an independent, enlightened, and worthy life. These three realms of activity must be coordinated so that the nation can reach the aim which Islam has assigned to it with the sole aim of preserving its existence and its governmental and administrative independence.

Now history teaches that a nation's lack of the means for self-sufficiency in agricultural, commercial, and industrial matters constitutes the first cause of colonialism.

Whoever holds authority in the Muslim community and influences its interests must therefore take steps to see to it that the nation draws the greatest profit possible from agriculture, commerce, and industry by coordinating the three sectors of activity so that, in the matter of investment, one does not develop at the expense of the others—even if this means transforming agricultural land into capital or industrial concerns, according to the country's needs as dictated by its interests. The country is therefore organized in such a way as to be self-sufficient. Foreign countries can then no longer interfere in its affairs, except in the course of the usual general exchanges between states. The government is therefore an organization that benefits the country and preserves it from all foreign interference. . . .

[*After citing instances of limitation of land property in Islamic history, Shaltut continues:*]

Muslim jurists are unanimous in recognizing the right of authorities to expropriate [land] in order to enlarge the place of prayer [i.e., the jurisdiction of Islam] until the whole world becomes a mosque. They also have the right to act likewise to enlarge a street or any other public service, in the interests of both individuals and the community. . . .

[*Continuing, Shaltut claims that to be rich is a social function and to be poor is a social ill.*]

Worldly possessions are the possessions of God, given by Him to His servants for the benefit of the universe. God sometimes claims possession of these goods: "Allah gives without measure to whom he wills" (Qur'an, XXIV, 38). At other times, He attributes them to their previous owners: "Do not give to the feeble-minded the property with which Allah has entrusted you for their support" (Qur'an, IV, 4).

God has clearly established that the possessors of goods, who are the holders after Him, must preserve, increase, and spend them in a manner laid down by Him: "Give in alms of that which He had made your inheritance" (Qur'an, LVII, 7). God also has put his wealth at the disposal of all men equally: "Allah created the heavens and the earth to reveal the truth and to reward each soul according to its deeds. None shall be wronged" (Qur'an, XLV, 12).

If worldly possessions are the possessions of God, if all men are the servants of God, and if the life in which they toil and do honor to the possessions of God belongs to God, then wealth, although it may be attributed to a private person, should also belong to all the servants of God, should be placed in the safekeeping of all, and all should profit from it. "Men, serve your Lord, who has created you and those who have gone before you, so that you may guard yourselves against evil; who has made the earth a bed for you and the sky a dome, and has sent down water from heaven to bring forth fruits for your sustenance" (Qur'an, II, 19–21).

Thus, to be rich is a social function whose aim is to ensure the happiness of society and satisfy its needs and interests.

So that all men may profit from worldly goods and their souls be free from all greed in this regard, Islam has opposed all who hoard and jealously watch over their wealth. . . . "Proclaim a woeful punishment to those who hoard up gold and silver and do not spend it in Allah's cause. The day will surely come when their treasures shall be heated in the fire of Hell, and their foreheads, sides, and backs branded with them. Their tormentors will say to them: 'These are the riches which you hoarded. Taste then the punishment which is your due' " (Qur'an, IX, 36).

Similarly, Islam has fought the stupidity that leads to the squandering of goods uselessly: "The wasteful are Satan's brothers" (Qur'an, XVII, 29).

Islam has fought luxury, which has created hatred among the social classes, which menaces a peaceful and stable life, not to mention corruption and anarchy. . . .

Islam has traced the straight path of the ideal society; it is a path of solidarity by which the nation lives and which ensures the strength of society. With this end in view, Islam has abolished from the minds of owners [of property] and capitalists such vices as meanness, the taste for squandering the luxury. It has employed all means to encourage men to give generously and to be afraid of appearing miserly and of neglecting the right of the people and of society, to such a point that it has raised liberality to the rank of faith. . . .

"The true servants of the Merciful are those who walk humbly on the earth and say 'Peace!' to the ignorant who accost them; . . . who are neither extravagant nor niggardly but keep the golden mean; who invoke no other God besides Allah . . ." (Qur'an, XXV, 64–66).

For Islam, avarice similarly is one of the traits that condemn the infidel: " 'What has brought you into Hell?' They will reply: 'We never prayed or fed the hungry . . .' " (Qur'an, LXXIV, 43–44).

Islam has maintained this view for so long that it considers it a denial of the Judgment not to encourage giving to the needy: "Have you thought of him that denies the Last Judgement? It is he who turns away the orphan and does not urge others to feed the poor" (Qur'an, CVII).

Briefly summarized, such is the doctrine of Islam regarding the relations among men from the point of view of the solidarity of members of society. It contains in detail all the solid foundations necessary to make our nation a magnificent stronghold, a haven of happiness for those who shelter there.

The doctrine also contains a clear statement of what the socialism of Islam is, for adoption by those who wish to adopt it. Can man find a more perfect, more complete, more useful, and more profound socialism than that decreed by Islam? It is founded on the basis of faith and belief, and all that is decreed on that basis participates in the perpetuation of life and doctrine.

VI. *Arab Socialism and Its Relation to Social Structure: Nationalism, Communism, and Capitalism*

21. THE END OF FEUDALISM IN IRAQ AND THE LAND REFORM LAW*

Muhammad Tawfiq Husayn

Iraq depends on irrigation possibly more than any other country in the Middle East except Egypt. Its fluctuations between prosperity and regression can be measured according to its ability to make use of its land and water. Consequently, political and social changes in Iraq have invariably been bound to changes in the system of ownership. Thus, at the beginning of the nineteenth century, when the Ottoman Government's need for revenue became acute, Iraq was one of the areas that acquired a new system of land administration. By 1831, the Ottoman Government had established firm control by defeating the local ruling Mamluks. It later tried to apply the Land Code of 1858, which resulted from the need to modernize agriculture. Inadvertently, perhaps, its effect was to accelerate the establishment of a system of private land ownership, together with a new arrangement of social classes. In the following excerpt, an Iraqi intellectual looks at Iraq's problems of social organization and uses them to justify the revolution and socialism. He indicates how the change in economic organization forced on society a new group differentiation. Muhammad Tawfiq Husayn received his M.A. degree at the American University of Beirut and taught history there.

About Iraq's land problems, see Charles Issawi, The Economic History of the Middle East, 1800–1914 *(Chicago: University of Chicago Press, 1966), pp. 129–97,* passim; *Salih Haydar,* Land Problems of Iraq *(unpublished thesis, London University, 1942), cited and quoted by Issawi,* op. cit., *pp. 164–78; and Albertine Jwaideh (Zuwayda), "Mithat Pasha and the Land System of Lower Iraq," in Albert Hourani (ed.),* Middle Eastern Affairs Number Three *(St. Antony's Papers No. 16) (London: Chatto & Windus; Carbondale, Ill.: Southern Illinois University Press, 1964), pp. 106–36. For general background,*

* Extract from Muhammad Tawfiq Husayn, *Nihayat al-iqta' fi al-'iraq, bahth fi ahwal al-fallah al-'iraqi wa-qanun al-islah al-zira'i (The End of Feudalism in Iraq, Research into the Situation of the Iraqi Peasant, and the Law of Agricultural Reform)* (Beirut: Dar al-'ilm lil-malayin, 1958), pp. 21–39, 117–26.

see Gabriel Baer, Population and Society in the Arab East *(New York: Frederick A. Praeger, 1964).*

The Shaykh

Even when they settle on the land, the tribes abide by the laws and customs that they followed when they were still Bedouin. They are divided into tribes, clans, and families of paternal or maternal descent. Every clan has its shaykh, or leader, whom it obeys. In the past, the shaykh fulfilled an important social function and occupied a basic position in the tribe or clan. He ran the affairs of individuals, was in charge of the tribe's defense, solved all quarrels and rivalries, guided the tribe when it settled or was on the move, and led it in its forays. He was also in charge of guests. In other words, the shaykh was a sort of government when the state authority did not extend over the desert or the countryside. When the tribes settled down to an agricultural life, agricultural land and pastures were considered the common property of the whole tribe. The shaykh would assign to each man a plot of land, and would arbitrate the disputes arising because of land ownership and irrigation rights. The shaykh himself owned extensive lands. The tribesmen would present him with a certain share of the produce as a payment for his duties as the highest authority within the tribe.

The shaykh's relations with the tribesmen were well-knit. He lived among them and knew all their problems. His mode of life was similar to their own, although more "luxurious." His habitation was extensive and his food varied; his clothes were sumptuous and his home furnishings relatively comfortable.

This manner of life changed radically around the middle of the nineteenth century. Iraq was opened to the outside world through extensive commercial connections with Europe, especially England, when the Suez Canal was opened in 1869. In the mid-nineteenth century, Iraq's exports of grains and other foodstuffs did not exceed ID 100,000.[1] By 1920, this figure had reached ID 3,000,000. Internal trade flourished as the various Iraqi cities became connected to each other through roads, railroads, and steamships. Agricultural products were more in demand both for home consumption and for export. The shaykhs thus became aware of the importance of agriculture and of the need for proper exploitation of land. Where previously their agricultural economy was directed toward satisfying their own needs, they now began to produce for sale and tried to obtain the maximum profit. Their contacts with cities increased, and they tasted the luxury of modern life. Consequently they needed more money, and so they began to appropriate rich agricultural lands and register them in their own names, until some of them came to own as much as 1 million dunums.[2] They exacted harsh terms of rent from the peasants, took as much of their produce as they could, and left them only what

1. The Iraqi dinar was equivalent to one pound sterling.
2. The Iraqi *dunum,* or *mi'shara,* is equivalent to 0.25 of a hectare, or 0.613 of an acre. Elsewhere the dunum is equivalent to 919 square meters.

was sufficient for bare subsistence. Even this was not given out of kindness but only in order that the peasants might continue to work and support them.

Most shaykhs abandoned their tribal tents and habitations and built modern palaces for themselves, complete with electricity and all modern comforts. The shaykhs would receive there their friends, senior officials, and other shaykhs and offer them the best of food and the choicest of European beverages, in an atmosphere far different from the tribal one. The contrast between the stately mansions of the shaykhs and the sordid dwellings of the peasants became glaring. Most of the feudal shaykhs took to city life, to gambling, drinking, and dancing. Many built palaces for themselves in Baghdad and became absentee landlords. Many of them used to spend the summer outside Iraq where they would spend vast sums of money on entertainment. The developments in the Iraqi economy toward the end of the nineteenth century produced a great change in the position of the shaykh. The shaykhs became feudal landlord, no longer guarding the interests of their fellow tribesmen.

Their influence increased with the British occupation of Iraq. The Law of the Rights and Obligations of the Farmers consolidated their ownership of the land and increased their hold over the peasants. The Law of Tribal Litigation consolidated their power and privileges. These were further strengthened when most of the shaykhs became members of parliament and therefore were close to the government and the royal family. They thus became absolute overlords in their estates and villages.

The governments of the *ancien régime* would do their bidding, either because they were afraid of them or because they were bribed by them. Every shaykh surrounded himself with a body of armed ruffians from his own tribe, called *hushiyya* in Southern Iraq. These gangs acted as his bodyguard and ruthlessly kept the peasants in subjection. Supported by these armed forces, the official police force, and the government machinery, the shaykhs were able to control the peasants. No one dared to complain or tried to prevent the shaykh from stealing the fruits of his labor or refused to work on his land. The punishment would have been prison, torture, or exile. In fact, some shaykhs in the south had dreary, insect-infected prisons, into which their victims would be thrown, flogged, and tortured by the shaykh's ruffians until they promised again to obey the master.

The shaykhs would visit their estates from time to time. A shaykh once visited his estate and stayed at the house of one of his peasants. It happened that the two quarreled over some question related to the land. The peasant dared to raise his voice in speaking to the shaykh, who thereupon departed in a rage. Afraid of the consequences, the peasant sought refuge with a friend of the shaykh and asked this friend to mediate. After much bargaining, the shaykh agreed to pardon his peasant if he would pay him ID 7½—a sum that amounted, in fact, to double the peasant's yearly income.

It was not surprising, therefore, that thousands of peasants left the estates of the shaykhs and drifted to the big cities, where they would work for very low wages.

The Serkal[3]

The conditions of business of the shaykhs and landowners and their expanding estates required them to hire agents to act as intermediaries between them and the peasants. These agents would lease the land to the peasants, hire villagers for work, and supervise their labor. The agents were called *sarakil* [singular, *serkal*], or bailiffs. The influence of the sarakil grew and their authority increased in recent years, when the shaykhs began to absent themselves from their lands and it became common for influential city-dwellers to own land in the countryside. Both the absentee shaykh and the townsman-landowner needed someone to manage their estates and supervise their peasants. The serkal, like the shaykh, did not usually work the land himself. In return for his services, he received a share of the produce from both the peasant and the landowner. But he took more from the peasants than from the landowner. His share of the produce varied between one-sixth and one-tenth of the crop. In some regions, and in lieu of his share of the produce, the serkal often was given a piece of land, called *al-tali'a,* by the landowner and was provided with seeds. Thereafter, it was the peasant's duty to farm it and give him its produce without anything in return for himself. The office of bailiff had its own rights and services, defined by the Law of the Rights and Obligations of the Farmers. Although of peasant origin, the serkal was far better off than his fellow villagers. His standard of living was nearer the standard of shaykhs than that of the peasants. He owned a more extensive dwelling, had better food, and enjoyed greater comfort than the peasant. The serkal replaced the office of the shaykh and enjoyed a comparable measure of authority in a village where no shaykh resided.

The Peasant

In addition to these two, numerically few, and comfortable classes in the countryside, there was a third and extensive class, the peasantry, who constituted the bulk of dwellers in the countryside and formed the majority of the people of Iraq. The situation of peasants in northern Iraq, differed from that in the center and south. In northern Iraq, small individual landholdings were common, and some peasants owned small plots of land which they cultivated. In the other parts of the country, the peasants were deprived of land ownership. They could rent land from the shaykhs, landowners, and sarakil, for which they paid half or more of its produce or worked as laborers, receiving either a share of the produce or a sum of money. Peasants might also work in partnership with the shaykhs and landowners; the latter provided the land, seeds, and animals, while the villager provided the labor and got the worse part of the bargain.

The Iraqi peasant is a wretched creature, leading a primitive existence, deprived of the simplest comforts, and far removed from the benefits of modern civilization. Most farmers in central and southern Iraq live in dark huts made

3. From the Persian *sarkar,* agent. Also pronounced, in various Arab dialects, *sarkal* or *sirkal.*

of reeds or palm leaves and called *sara'if* (singular, *sarifa*). The area of the average sarifa is about 6 to 7 meters by 2 to 3 meters. The sarifa has a small, narrow door in front; one has to bend in order to enter the hut. It has no windows and is perpetually dark. To protect themselves from the floods, the peasants build their huts on elevated ground, which they pile up from earth they excavate. After the floods, the ditches become malarial swamps.

In northern Iraq, and in some central regions where there are little or no reeds or palm trees, the peasants live in dried mud huts. These huts either are windowless or have small slits which provide scant ventilation. The animals often live with the peasants in the huts.

The peasant's food is simple and lacks nutrients. It consists in the main of bread made from barley, corn, or rice, which is cooked without oil, and some dates and milk. Coffee and black tea are his favorite drinks. "Those who can add to this diet a plate of rice with no fats, or sometimes some yoghurt or onions, would consider this a sumptuous meal. . . . Peasants do not eat any meat or sweets cooked in milk except when the shaykh's guesthouse receives a visiting shaykh or official or when one of them dies. The spectacle of the peasants at these banquets is indeed a miserable and sorry one."[4]

The peasant's clothing is very simple. During both winter and summer, he wears . . . a woolen *'abaya* and the traditional head-dress, the *kuffiyya* and *'iqal*. These clothes are discarded only when they are in tatters and become unwearable. It is rare to find a peasant wearing shoes either in winter or in summer. His utensils are equally simple. In most cases, they include a pot for boiling rice, a cauldron for tea, a few copper plates, a few tea cups, a thick mat woven locally, and a wooden box for clothes.

Most shaykhs and sarakil have either guesthouses, built of reeds or palm leaves, or tents, which differ in size according to the wealth of the owners and the number of peasants employed. The guesthouses are built on high ground. In the extensive yard in front—*the dakka*—peasants and guests congregate in the summer. The guesthouse is a kind of club for the farmers. They meet there in the evening or during the break from work, when they converse, tell stories, and discuss the affairs of their narrowly circumscribed society. "The seating arrangements in the guesthouse follow certain rules. The peasants sit in the lower part of the guesthouse, close to the coffee pot, which is placed in the center. The upper part is occupied by the sarakil of the lower rank and by religious preachers. At the other end, seats are provided for government officials, shaykhs, and notables."

Certain seminomadic Arab tribes inhabit the interior of Iraq and the edges of the southern lakes [*al-ahwar;* singular, *hor*]. Their houses are simple sara'if built of reeds or palm leaves. These sara'if are located on the sand islands of the lakes. If there are no islands, and these people are forced to settle on the land, they build themselves artificial islands made of layers of mud interwoven with mats and reeds for reinforcement. Sometimes, they also erect their sara'if on poles imbedded in the water. They move from one island to another in long boats called *mashahif* [singular, *mashhuf*]. They grow rice and keep cattle

4. No source is indicated.

and buffaloes. But most of them live on fish and water birds. These latter people, called the *Ma'dan,* are the poorest, most ignorant, least hygenic, and most underdeveloped social group in Iraq. It would be no exaggeration to say that their social, mental, and economic condition is no better than that of their ancestors, the *hor* dwellers, before the time of Hammurabi.

In essence, the life of the Kurdish peasants is similar to that of the Arabs. Every tribe or tribal group has a leader whom the tribesmen obey and who enjoys the fruits of their labor. Every village has a leader called either *katkhuda* or *tashmal* or *kukha,* according to the region. These are like the sarakil, for they act as intermediaries between landowners and peasants and the government. They are the village elders, and they receive their share directly from the landowners. They rent land from the landowners and farm it at their own expense. They thus have the authority of both a serkal and a landowner. Their authority over the village is supreme. They manage its affairs and exact complete obedience from the villagers.

The Bedouin Tribes

The Bedouin tribal population of Iraq [is estimated at] between 300,000 and 450,000. The best-known Bedouin tribes in Iraq are the Shammar, 'Arza, and Dhafir. Several tribes whose original home is the Najd roam southwestern Iraq at certain seasons only. Certain Syrian tribes also roam about Iraq.

The Bedouin live in tents woven of camel hair and keep cattle and sheep, which they carefully tend. Cattle and sheep constitute their entire wealth and are the backbone of their economy. They move from place to place seeking water and grassland, in accordance with the seasons and the weather. Their mode of life is very simple. Their food consists mainly of bread, dates, and yoghurt, and, occasionally, rice and meat. The Bedouin have recently taken to coffee and tea, which have now become a basic factor in their daily diet.

The Bedouin are one of Iraq's fundamental problems, since they constitute an obstacle to the country's economic growth. Their role as producers in the national economy is minimal. Even their livestock does not fulfill the present requirements as regards quality and quantity, since they do not follow scientific methods in feeding and growing them. Their value to the economy as consumers also is minimal, since their income is scanty and the requirements of their simple life can be provided very cheaply.

The Bedouin lives in total obedience to the laws of nature. However hard he tries, he is unable to change the primitive economic system in which he lives. Hence his submission to fate and his apathy. "The Bedouin knows nothing about the morrow and does not think of the future or prepare himself for it. He is deeply influenced by the experience of centuries which has made him to believe that God would always provide the necessities of life. His world does not allow for individual opinions as regards duties and labor. Undoubtedly, this life of constant search, which has no parallel anywhere, is a basic condition of the system in which he lives. We cannot expect this mode of existence to produce anything of permanence or any work that requires initiative and conscious creativity."

The bleak and wretched existence of the Bedouin and the primitive economy which circumscribes it have produced a strange mentality, which is unsuited to the modern life that the country aims to realize. The Bedouin feels loyalty only to his family or clan. However wide his social horizon, it cannot extend beyond his own environment. He has learned to obey and respect his shaykh. The notion of fatherland or of state is alien to him, if not hateful and contrary to his nature. The Bedouin wishes to live and move in total freedom, appropriating whatever he can lay his hands on, whether this belongs to other tribes or to the state. He aims to ignore as much as he can whatever is connected with the authority of the state, such as, for instance, recognizing the central administration, paying taxes, and obeying the law.

The problem of the Bedouin is not confined to them alone. A large number of the country's population are in a similar situation. Their narrow mentality, their rough life, and their lack of responsibility toward the state make them regard with hostility all those who are not of their tribe. Forays have come to an end, and the Bedouin can no longer exact their forced tax [*khawa*] from peasants or from caravans of traders and travelers. The growing power of the state and the police have put an end to such practices. But conflicts and rivalries between the Bedouin and the townsmen still are rife. Such conflicts usually revolve around pasturage and water. The Bedouin regard pastures as the property of God and, thus, available for use by their sheep whenever they feel like it. The peasants rightly claim that such pastures are within the boundaries of their own villages and so belong to them alone. They maintain that if their pastures are denuded of grass, they cannot move, like the Bedouin, to other pastures. In the Introduction to *The Desert,* by 'Abd al-Jabbar Rawi, 'Ali al-Sharqi writes:

> Some scholars investigating the ancient history of Iraq have discovered a historical conflict, which is still with us, taking place on the borders of Iraq and the desert between the peasant and the shepherd, concerning the waters of the Euphrates and the agricultural needs of each. The Iraqi peasant wants to organize and arrange for irrigation, whereas the Arab shepherd wants all dams to be broken so that water will inundate the desert and increase pastures.

The resettlement of the Bedouin is an urgent national necessity, required by both the Bedouin's interests and the interests of the peasants who desire to be rid of constant attacks on their farms and pastures. The country's developing economy requires this resettlement to an agricultural mode of life. Forays and forced taxes are ended, so the Bedouin have lost their two most important sources of livelihood. With the introduction of the motor car and railways, they have also lost another source of income, i.e., the transportation of cargo, which they formerly carried on their camels. Pastures, upon which they depend for tending their sheep, are now shrinking gradually as farmlands grow. The presence of the Bedouin is a threat to the state and to any national or social renaissance.

The Bedouin, as indicated above, feel no loyalty to the fatherland, and regard the state as an evil and a restriction on their liberty. They obey only their own leaders and shaykhs, and many of the latter are prepared to offer their allegiance and service to the highest bidder. Many tribal leaders thus supported the ex-royal family and British Imperialism in Iraq. The British Government befriended the Shamar tribe and strengthened their influence so that they could protect the British Petroleum Company's installations and the Iraq Petroleum Company's pipelines and be of help to the British in establishing their influence over the land. . . .

The *ancien régime* resettled some Bedouin on the land, gave them fertile land, and encouraged them to farm and settle down. But it practiced a wrong policy in implementing this resettlement, as was the case with other reforms that the regime claimed to have achieved. The result was contrary to the interests of the Bedouin and the country generally, and contrary to the views of the reformers. The government gave land to the Bedouin shaykhs and thus increased their power by giving them a new source of authority—land-ownership—and by adding to their wealth from agricultural products. The free Bedouin became a slave peasant or a poor tenant. The new peasant preserved his Bedouin traditions and his blind loyalty to his shaykh. The best example of this wrong policy of the *ancien régime* was the resettlement of part of the Shammar Jarba tribe on the outskirts of Mosul. The shaykhs appropriated the fertile lands and exploited the tribesmen, who did not benefit from this resettlement. . . .

'Abd al-Razzaq Tahir wrote:

> A recent feudal phenomenon, invented by the British and implemented by a perplexed and inexperienced national regime, has appeared in the Mosul Governorate. Policy required, logically enough, that the government should care for the Shammar tribes living near Mosul. It was decided to give them vast tracts of land for this purpose. The Shammar tribe is an old and important Arab tribe. But this noble project was perverted. It turned out that the shaykhly families of that tribe were made into feudal landlords. The tribe itself "was well off, without either food or clothing," as the saying goes. Those who know say that the area of these feudal estates was vast, exceeding half a million dunums. Thus, projects for public welfare are turned into personal enrichment and gain.

The correct method for resettling the Bedouin would be to apportion the land and register the plots in the name of the tribesmen themselves and curtail the influence of the shaykhs and other leaders. This can be done by establishing peace in the new villages, providing education for the peasants, and nurturing proper civic spirit among them. The Bedouin, who are highly individualistic and hostile toward the state, toward discipline, and toward the townsmen, would become valuable citizens, loyal to the fatherland, and would recognize no authority but that of the state and the law. They would then join in the national drive for liberation, progress, and a decent life. This is what the Iraqi Republic aimed to do when it promulgated its Agrarian Reform Law. . . .

The Agrarian Reform Law

For centuries, the Iraqi peasant, a tool in the hands of feudal landowners, toiled away to provide them with the luxuries of life. He lacked character and was despised and neglected. The feudal landowners and their allies formed a parliamentary majority and so controlled the government and enacted legislation that protected their own private interests. Most government officials did their bidding and guaranteed their plundering the labor of others. The people revolted several times against imperialism and its feudal allies, but the royalist regime proved itself to be stronger and more organized. All the revolts failed, the prisons were full of freedom lovers, and spies were everywhere. This policy of repression and violence did not silence the complaints of the people. It was inevitable, therefore, that, when all peaceful solutions had failed, a violent revolutionary act was needed. This was the Revolution of July 14 [1958]. The revolutionary government then began to revitalize Iraq and to rectify the corruption of centuries of injustice. One of its noblest and most important enactments was the Agrarian Reform Law No. 30 of 1958, which outlawed feudalism. The leader of the Revolution, 'Abd al-Karim Qasim[5] says: "In announcing this Agrarian Reform Law, I proudly and joyfully declare the end of feudalism in Iraq and the beginning of a new era of great prosperity for the whole nation. I ask my fellow-citizens to join hands in order to implement it sincerely and correctly."

What are the aims of the law? The law aims at many things the most important of which are: the liberation of the peasant and the improvement of his social and economic status, the development of agriculture, and the abrogation of feudalism, which is considered to be an outdated mode of production, an ally of imperialism, and an obstacle in the way of democratic government. Hudayb Hajj Mahmud, the minister of agriculture, says:

> The aims of agrarian reform are, first, to put an end to feudalism both as a means of production and as a political and imperialist force, to destroy the influence of the feudal landowners which they derived from their extensive estates and which they manipulated in order to serve their own interests and the interests of the imperialists and to obstruct the machinery of government. We have promulgated this law in order to facilitate the proper functioning of the government administration in accordance with the public interest. We want, in the second place, to raise the living standard of a large class of the population, the peasants, and to provide them with the opportunity to improve themselves in general. We want, in the third place, to raise the level of agricultural production in the country in such a way that it would effectively contribute to increasing the national income and strengthening the economy.

I shall attempt, in what follows, to summarize the most essential features of this law.

1. The limitation of land ownership. The law prescribed a limit to agricultural land ownership. The first article states: "The area of agricultural land that is owned or granted by official concession to an individual must not exceed either 1,000 dunums irrigated by flowing water or by artificial means, or 2,000 dunums irrigated by rainfall [i.e., dry farming]. When both are combined, one dunum of the first variety is to be counted as equivalent two dun-

5. Qasim was overthrown and executed in the revolution of 1963 that was led by his former colleague 'Abd al-'Arif.

ums of the second." The government is considered as the owner of the land sequestered (Art. 24). Within five years of the date in which the law becomes operative, the government shall seize all lands whose area exceeds the maximum limit (Art. 4). This seizure of land shall be effected in return for a compensation equal to the value of the land seized, in addition to compensation equal to the value of buildings, trees, pumps, and agricultural machinery. A sum equal to the government's share in lands that are consigned in the land office or others granted by official concession shall also be paid (Art. 6). Compensation shall be in the form of government bonds at a 3 per cent rate of interest, to be redeemed within twenty years. These bonds shall be personal (Art. 8).

The land that the law has allowed for the individual ownership of the feudalists is indeed vast: either 1,000 dunums, i.e., 2.5 million square meters, of land irrigated by flowing water or pumps, or 2,000 dunums, i.e., 5.5 million square meters, of land irrigated by rainfall. If they tend their lands carefully and follow government instructions, the old landowners will continue to live in luxury. Their compensation is a just one and is, if anything, excessive. Previously, I have shown how most of these feudal landowners obtained their land and how they plundered the state's property and the property of their tribesmen, to the detriment of the poor peasant. The Revolutionary Government has behaved very kindly and generously toward them. The law does not aim at persecuting a certain class or at destroying the feudal landowners as farmers and productive citizens. It aims merely at ending their mode of production, which retards the development of agriculture, at stopping the exploitation of the peasantry, and at terminating their political influence, which impedes the country's national progress. In truth, this law leaves no room for complaint or obstruction by the feudal landowners. The minister of agriculture says:

> The old landowner and the new proprietor of the maximum amount of land has two courses open to him. He can either cooperate with the revolution and respond to support its objectives for achieving social justice and for combating exploitation, in which case he would be considered a worthy citizen whose rights, work, and future are protected. Or he can defy the people and so expose himself to the people's anger and be liable to severe prosecution. . . .
>
> I sincerely hope that no citizen will choose this second fatal alternative. With the end of feudalism, exploitation, and injustice, there is no longer any justification for conflict or hatred among the agricultural producers and, indeed, among all classes of the noble people of Iraq.

2. The law recognized the peasant's rights of total ownership of a plot of land which he can farm and whose fruits he alone can enjoy. This individual possession of the land by the peasants would increase their attachment to the soil. They will then exert themselves to farm it and to increase its produce. Their rights shall be fully guaranteed and this shall restore to them a sense of dignity and make them feel that they are protected by the fatherland and are partners in its prosperity. The law also prescribed a minimum allotment

of land to the peasant. Article 11 states: "The land that is either seized or is state property or is without owner shall be redistributed. . . . Distribution among the peasants shall be carried out in such a way as to permit each one to own either a plot, not less than 30 dunums and not more than 60 dunums, of land irrigated by flowing water or by artificial means, or a plot, not less than 60 dunums and not more than 120 dunums, of land irrigated by rainfall [i.e., dry farming], depending on the quality of the land." Article 12 specified the conditions to be met by the beneficiaries of this redistribution of land: "He must be an Iraqi of full legal age, must be a farmer by profession, and must own less than 60 dunums of land irrigated by flowing water or by artificial means, or 120 dunums irrigated by rainfall. Priority shall be given to those who were actually farming the land, either as tenants or partners [share croppers] or workers. Thereafter, priority shall be given first to those with the highest numbers of dependents, then to the poorest inhabitants of the region, and, finally, to others who do not inhabit the region." The farmer would pay for the land allotted to him regardless of whether the land is seized, or is government property, or is without owner. In addition to the value of the land, he shall pay for the buildings, trees, and agricultural machinery at a 3 per cent rate of interest, plus a sum equivalent to 20 per cent of the total cost to defray the expenses of distribution and administration. The total sum is to be repaid in equal annual installments within twenty years (Art. 12).

The distribution of land is to be completed within five years of the date in which the law becomes operative (Art. 25). The land distributed to peasants shall be free of all debts and of all former tenants' rights, and it shall be registered free of charge as the outright possession of its owner (Art. 26).

3. In a previous chapter, I have outlined some of the problems facing the growth of agriculture in Iraq. The republican leaders have devoted much care to these problems and have decided to solve them through the establishment of agricultural cooperative societies. The Republic hopes that this land redistribution will bring prosperity, not encumberment, to the peasants.

According to the law, one or more cooperative societies are to be formed in every county [*nahiya*] where land has been redistributed. The society may accept as members persons whose lands do not exceed the maximum limit, if these persons apply for membership (Art. 31). Various cooperative societies shall join together to form a general cooperative union (Art. 34). The cooperative society shall perform its functions under the guidance of a supervisor appointed by the minister of agriculture (Art. 33). "The Cooperative Society shall perform the following functions: to obtain agricultural loans depending upon the area of land owned by its members; to provide the farmer with the necessary seeds, fertilizers, sheep, pumps, agricultural machinery, and other means necessary for the preservation and storage of the harvest; to organize the farming of land in the best possible manner, including the selection of seeds, the classification of the produce, the combating of pests, and the digging of canals and wells: to sell its members' chief products, deducting from their value the cash installments being paid for land, agricultural loans, and other loans from the government and the cooperative society; to undertake all agricultural services required by members; and to provide them with various social services" (Art. 32).

4. The law annulled the previous feudal relations, which were vague and undefined and which had nullified the rights of the peasants, as, for example, the Law of the Rights and Obligations of the Farmers, and the Decree Determining the Division of Agricultural Produce Between the Landowner and the Peasant, and other laws and decrees that violated the provisions of this law (Art. 49).

In addition, the law created new and just agricultural relations that would protect the peasant as a working man and as a citizen of a free country. The relations between the landowner and the one possessing the means of irrigation were regulated as follows by the law: The period of agricultural contracts must not be less than three years. A peasant cannot be evicted from the land against his will unless he has failed to abide by a basic committment stemming from contract, law, or custom (Art. 37). The contract of an agricultural relation must be in writing (Art. 43). The law has rescued the peasants from the unjust domination of feudal landowners, who often evicted the peasants on the most negligible pretexts. Article 39 clearly defined the obligations of both landowner and peasant, while Article 40 defined the duties of the farm superintendent.

Article 41 specified the distribution of the income derived from the produce of the fields as follows:

	Irrigation		
	by flowing water	by artificial means	by rainfall
Land	10%	10%	10%
Water (irrigation)	10%	20%	—
Peasant's labor and seeds	50%	40%	50%
Ploughing	7.5%	7.5%	12.5%
Harvesting	12.5%	12.5%	17.5%
Administration	10%	10%	10%

The peasant's share may be increased by agreement.

5. The law took care to protect the rights and interests of the agricultural worker, in order to encourage financial transactions. The wages of the agricultural worker were no longer determined by the landlord but vary according to the worker's poverty or need. Wages would henceforth be determined by committees in which workers themselves took part. Article 47 stated:

> Wages of agricultural workers in the various agricultural regions are determined annually by a [five-man] committee organized by the Minister of Agriculture to be headed by a senior ministry official, aided by four other members chosen by the Minister. Of the latter, two shall represent landowners, while the other two shall represent the agricultural workers. The decisions of this committee shall be considered binding when ratified by the Minister. Agricultural workers shall not be employed at wages below what is specified for each district.

The law scored another democratic achievement toward the protection of the workers' rights by allowing them to form unions, which would defend their common interests (Art. 48).

6. Agrarian reform shall be put into effect by the Higher Committee for Agrarian Reform. Article 15 states: "The government shall be represented by a committee called the Higher Committee for Agrarian Reform which undertakes all transactions connected with the seizure, redistribution, and administration of land until redistribution is complete. The Committee shall also guide and supervise the Agricultural Cooperative Societies within the limits of the law and shall be attached to the Council of Ministers. The Committee shall be presided over by the Prime Minister, while the Ministers of Agriculture, Home Affairs, Finance, Social Affairs, Reconstruction, and Economy shall act as members. Not more than five other members shall be appointed by decision of the Council of Ministers, one of whom must be a prominent jurist while two others must be agricultural experts." The Committee has in fact been formed and has commenced its implementation of the Agrarian Reform Law.

22. THE ERA OF MILITARY COUPS*

Ahmad Baha' al-Din

Ahmad Baha' al-Din, a well-known Egyptian intellectual, belongs to a group that strives to define a democratic cooperative socialism as the ideology of the unified Arab world. He writes for Ruz al-Yusuf (Rose of Joseph), Sabah al-Qahira (Cairo Morning), *and* Akhbar al-Yawm (Daily News) *on cultural, political, and ideological problems of the Arab world. See his book,* al-Thawra al-ishtirakiyya (The Socialist Revolution) (*Cairo: al-Maktaba al-Thaqafiyya, 1962*). *The following article deals with military revolutions and regards as legitimate those that aim changing the old, corrupt form of society.*

A military coup is now a frequent phenomenon in many countries of Asia and Africa. The recurrence of this pattern is not a mere accident, nor can one explain it away as simple imitation. Some of these repeated military coups may be genuine, others not. Indeed, the very occurrence of spurious coups complements the moral contained in genuine ones.

The military coups of Asia and Africa have all occurred in countries where the following objective circumstances obtained:

1. They were all countries that were recently rid of imperialism. The point

* Extract from Ahmad Baha' al-Din, "Marhalat al-inqilabat al-'askariyyat" ("The Era of Military Coups"), *Ruz al-Yusuf (Rose of Joseph)*, Cairo, November 24, 1958, p. 10.

is that imperialism leaves subject countries in ruins. Corruption is rife, social injustice predominates, and the governmental machine is rotten. Political values are fictitious: the parliament, democracy, and the political parties are sham. This situation breeds popular odium against all these institutions, and their destruction becomes easy and even welcome.

2. These countries are economically backward. There are more workers than work, more mouths to feed than there are hands to feed them, and more hopes than realities. These countries bitterly resent their backwardness in a world that is progressing by leaps and bounds. They refuse to accept the slow and gradual evolution that was responsible for the progress of the developed nations, since they feel that they have a lot of ground to make up for and that they must catch up soon. Thus, they are anxious to leap forward, through a coup, in order that they may shorten the road ahead.

3. They are countries encumbered by many legacies of the Middle Ages. Such traditions, whether they be corrupt monarchies, feudalism, or fictitious authorities that serve particular interests, hold powerful sway and cannot be dislodged peacefully.

4. They are countries where imperialism, although no longer in a direct position of power or occupation, still retains considerable influence through its agents, interests, or financial commitments. This vestigial influence casts a calamitous shadow over these countries and again threatens them with loss of independence. Imperialism attempts to distort the genuine popular trend by wasting the countries' energies in, for example, military pacts rather than reconstruction. It formulates a plan for their economic progress that differs from the one sought by the people.

5. They are countries where no powerful, progressive popular movement is to be found that can at least force progress along. The popular movements in these countries are usually engaged in indecisive struggle with the regime—a ding-dong struggle that is in reality a vicious circle.

These circumstances, then, are present in countries where a military coup has taken place. These factors add up and are intensified until explosion point is reached. The army forsakes the old regime and goes to the aid of the people. The old regime is robbed of its weapons and collapses with astonishing ease. People thereafter are amazed at the hollow weakness of the former regime.

Nevertheless, we must beware of passing identical judgment upon all military coups or of treating them all similarly. History teaches us about revolutions and counterrevolutions. Thus, before we assess any military coup, we must analyze its course and its trend so that we can decide whether it is a genuine revolution or a counterrevolution.

A revolution is a violent action that completely destroys the old order bitterly resented by the people and that fulfills the basic requirements of the people at the particular stage through which they are passing.

A counterrevolution, on the other hand, is a violent action that assumes the form of a revolution. It may fulfill certain superficial popular requirements, but its real purpose is to forestall the occurrence of a genuine revolution and to direct the people's attention to certain unrealistic issues.

There are plenty of examples that prompt us to make this distinction, foremost among which are the recent military coups in Burma and Thailand and the abortive military coup in Indonesia.

The various revolutionaries concerned all bandied the same slogans, chief among which were the abolition of corruption and bribery, the termination of political feuds of a personal or opportunistic nature, and the purging of the administration. All these slogans are appropriate, for corruption, bribery, and opportunistic political wrangling are diseases that do actually exist and plague the people. But to stop at this is to achieve nothing, since these are the symptoms of the disease, not its causes. Its real causes may be found in imperialist influence, class exploitation, absence of economic planning, feudal or fictitious authority, and in the danger of being trapped by the imperialists into accepting spurious aid or joining military pacts or needlessly antagonizing foreign powers.

A military coup that preserves all the foundations of the old order and rests content with mere polish and superficial purging cannot be called a revolution, but rather a counterrevolution.

This, then, is the real criterion for distinguishing a revolution from something else: Does it come from within or from without?

Nevertheless, we must not expect every military coup to lay its cards on the table from the very first moment. By so doing, it would be merely helping its enemies to close their ranks against it and fight it along a common front while it is still in its infancy. Therefore, we must always wait for some time before we are able clearly to distinguish the black of night from the light of day.

23. NATIONALISM AND UNITY IN THE MODERN ARAB NATIONAL MOVEMENT*

'Abdallah al-Rimawi

'Abdallah al-Rimawi, a former Minister of Foreign Affairs in Jordan and the enfant terrible *of the Ba'th Party, was secretary general of its branch in Jordan. After he was expelled from the main Ba'th in 1959, he established his own Ba'th Party in Jordan, and then became a supporter of President Nasser of the U.A.R. Al-Rimawi's confusing thought is akin to nihilism, but paradoxically it also has a missionary aspect as concerns action. Al-Rimawi assumes that the human will is the source of all action. Thus, following the traditional way of thinking, al-Rimawi ignores the influences of environment on individ-*

* Extract from 'Abdallah al-Rimawi, *al-Qawmiyya wa-al wahda fi al-harakat al-qawmiyya al-'arabiyya al-haditha (Nationalism and Unity in the Modern Arab National Movements)* (Cairo: Dar al-ma'arif, 1961), pp. 21–25, 431–33, 462–64.

ual and society. He favors Arab unity through revolution, if possible: see al-Mantiq al-thawri lil-haraka al-qawmiyya al-ʿarabiyya (Revolutionary Logic of the Arab Nationalist Movement) (*Cairo: Dar al-maʿarif, 1961*).

The conflicts raging in man's modern existence revolve around certain basic axes and encompass man's life in its various fields: theoretical-ideological, practical, economic, social, and political. Perhaps the most important of these great axes, from which evolve other secondary axes, are three: the axis of "nationalism versus nonnationalism," of "socialism versus nonsocialism," and of "freedom and democracy."

In thus formulating the problem and subject matter of each axis on the theoretical and practical levels, we do not pretend that this is the only possible formulation of such problems, nor do we imply that our own formulation of these questions and problems will guarantee a detailed definition of each axis. In the first axis—namely, nationalism versus nonnationalism—such a formulation does not imply that the problem is as simple as might appear. Our own phrasing of this question does not mean that the depth, vitality, and scope of the problem are thereby defined within the choice between nationalism and nonnationalism. For within the framework of nationalism there exist diverse schools of thought and diverse national movements. Whether on ideological or practical levels, the conflicts concerning the interpretation of the role of nationalism, its genesis, development, and destiny—such conflicts go wide and deep, and have a long history behind them—are still acute at the present day.

Similarly, within the framework of nonnationalism, as we formulated the problem, there are many schools of thought, and various nonnational movements and doctrines, such as internationalism, cosmopolitanism, and transcendentalism (metaphysics). These schools of thought and these doctrines are also divided by differences and conflicts that are wide and deep. By designating them all as nonnational movements and doctrines, we are simply generalizing their common negative attitude toward nationalism, whatever the causes, motives, and contents of such attitudes. Equally, we do not imply that their positive content is common to them all. It may be objected that this particular formulation of the problem—namely, nationalism versus nonnationalism—is in itself an indication of a preconceived notion and that it reveals a foreordained method of inquiry. It may also be objected that such a formulation betrays a predisposition to accept and emphasize the principle of nationalism, both in theory and in practice, in such a way that nationalism appears as the positive aspect and all else as the negative aspect of the problem. Some, for example, might maintain that it would be more accurate to phrase the question included in the first axis as "class versus classlessness," where class and class warfare would appear as the original and positive aspect and all else as negative and secondary. It may be that by phrasing any question properly half the battle is already won. However, we do not intend to discuss the objections against our own formulation of the problem, since our discussion of them, sufficient and responsible, is part of the discussion of the essence of the problem itself, which forms the major theme dealt with in this book. Let us content ourselves by saying that the formulation and presentation of the problem must assume a certain form. If there are any objections to the form we have chosen, then they will be answered in the course of our discussion. What is important is our attitude toward this problem as a whole, around which revolve the life and conflicts of modern man. We shall deal not only with the objections to our formulation of the question but expound our own ideological and practical attitude toward it.

Similarly, our phrasing of the problem of socialism versus nonsocialism, which is the second axis around which revolve the conflicts of modern man, does not imply the simplification of a complicated and animated problem. Under the name "socialist," many movements and schools of thought preach different doctrines concerning such questions as the ideological definition of socialism, the values to be achieved in a socialist society, the regulation of socio-economic relations in such society, the programs for the realization of socialism in one particular society or in the world, problems of production, distribution, and profits, the question of private property and its limits, the ownership of the means of production (whether by the state or by public, nongovernmental institutions), the question of class warfare and whether this is the only path to socialism or whether a modified version is acceptable, scientific and nonscientific socialism, and the problem of national versus international socialism. Such deep-rooted conflicts are embodied in movements and schools of thought, known throughout history, but especially in modern times, where they still thrive today. Within the framework of "nonsocialist" are also found diverse ideologies, practices, and movements varying from the capitalist-imperialist, which stubbornly reject the logic of history and life, to other reform-minded capitalisms, which try to prevent the emergence of socialism by various means and whose aim is to limit the degree of exploitation of the workers and peasants by capitalists and feudalists. They attempt to provide the exploited with certain living conditions that would, for a certain time, obviate the risk of socialist revolutions and the revolt of exploited against the exploiters. Such movements claim that they are socialist, although they still cling to and justify exploitation under the pretext of "free enterprise as an incentive to profit," which, they claim, is only human. Within this framework, also, may be found various parties, movements, ideologies, and practices, especially in the colonialist states, which claim to be socialist and may even in theory uphold the principle of the nationalization of the means of production or forbid exploitation within their own countries. But despite this, such movements . . . support exploitation and colonization in their colonies, thereby rendering their socialism a farce.

If anyone objects to this particular formulation of the problem, we can refer him to the answers given to similar objections against our previous formulation of the question of nationalism.

As for the problem of freedom and democracy, which is the third axis around which revolve the conflicts of modern man, it may be noted that we have not formulated the question in the same way as the previous two. We have not presented the matter in the form of freedom and democracy versus nonfreedom and nondemocracy. We have done so deliberately, not because the phrasing of the problem is complicated but because no school of thought, no ideology, no movement, and no state openly declares that it rejects freedom and democracy. It is therefore ironical that the imperialist powers style themselves as the "free world" and claim that only they are free democracies. At the same time, the Communist countries also style themselves as "popular democracies" and the Communist parties describe themselves as "democratic."

Undoubtedly, the real meaning of freedom and democracy, in theory and practice, is a bone of contention among movements and ideologies. We feel that it would be both difficult and wrong to phrase and present this problem in the manner of the previous two. We believe that our own phrasing of it is more correct.

The Nationalist Attitude—Its Ideological Bases . . .

Where do we start in our definition of man, his history, and his civilization? Where do we start in our definition of the nation, of nationalism, of the national movement, and of the role and destiny of each in history? How do we begin to define other basic concepts that are closely linked to the above, and to elucidate such terms as "state," "sovereignty," "nationality," and "patriotism"? How and where do we begin to explain our ideology on the individual level—i.e., our understanding of man, his society, his history, and his culture?

Should we begin by accepting the general presuppositions of our ideology and say that when these are "applied" to man, his society, history, and civilization, such and such "results" will ensue which we can then consider as our ideology with respect to the individual? This is the method employed by Marxism, which describes historical materialism as its doctrine with respect to "man, his society, and culture." The bases of historical materialism, it is claimed, are the "results" of the "application" of dialectical materialism to man.

We shall not adopt this method, whose false philosophical supposition we have already demonstrated. Our general ideological presuppositions themselves reject this particular approach. Although movement [action] is regarded as the essence of all existence and of all existing things, it has been shown that according to the dialetic, this movement differs in essence, in logic, and in content from one level of existence to the other. It is useless—since we have already accepted movement as the essence and the logic of the growth of all existence and of existing things—to expand this principle of movement, its content and logic as it applies to one particular level of development in order to embrace other levels. It is futile to arrive at an understanding of the essence and logic of action at one particular level by way of deduction by using our understanding of it as it applied to another level of existence and to existing things. The logic of action at one level may differ qualitatively from that of another level.

The only way to arrive at an understanding of movement at every level, and especially at the three basic levels of organic, inorganic, and "conscious, rational organisms," is to study separately the phenomena, the facts, the changes, and the development of each of them. This is the only way to understand existence and the existing things, and the essence and logic of movement at every level. We do not imply at all that our study of the results at one particular level has no bearing on the study of a higher level, but we maintain that:

1. The results obtained by science in, say, the inorganic field may be true at a higher level, where they may be applied to the study of higher substances, although they still, as constituents, belong to a lower level; but they cannot be held to apply to all substances at a higher level, where such substances are taken as a whole and thus regarded as "on a higher level."

When one, for example, studies the substances [i.e., their movement] at the inorganic level—say, calcium in chemistry—the results obtained about calcium still hold true whether calcium is found in a rabbit or in man. If one studies the living cell in a dog or the genes in guinea pigs, the results obtained will hold true of human cells or genes. But this does not mean at all that by studying all elements such as calcium and phosphorus in the rabbit, and then the results obtained by biology and physiology, that one can then understand man, his society, history, and culture. Such studies are undoubtedly useful and important and help us to understand man, but they do not add up, as in arithmetic, to a total and comprehensive understanding of man, who is in reality higher than the sum total of all phenomena that constitute the subjects of research at a level lower than his own.

2. The presuppositions constituting the outline of our general ideology are very clear in the negative sense, since they reject all other presuppositions such as idealism, transcendentalism (metaphysics), entropy, and infinity in beings and substances and on the three levels described above. At the same time, they reject dialectical materialism as a philosophical presupposition, again on the three levels mentioned above. Thus they reject:

(*a*) The results obtained by the compulsory and abstract application of general ideological presuppositions, as embodied at the inorganic, organic but nonrational, and human levels.

(*b*) The results following from the acceptance of such general ideological presuppositions, especially transcendentalism (metaphysics), entropy, and infinity, in so far as they constitute a method of enquiry into man, his society, culture, and history.

The Factors of Historical Change

1. All these factors, from beginning to end, emanate from "man in society." They are neither external to, nor independent of, his life. "Man as he really lives in society" is the origin, axis, and decisive impulse of his historical development.

2. The basic and ultimate impulses that arise from "man in society" are:

(*a*) Man's needs as a living and productive creature. The biological-economic factor follows from this.

> (*b*) Man's curiosity and his thirst for knowledge as a rational creature. The rational factor follows from this.
>
> (*c*) Man's will and freedom, as a rational creature possessing a will, which implies that he is active and that his actions flow from his free choice. Man has to bear the responsibility for his choice.
>
> (*d*) Man's urge toward equality. As a rational creature possessing will, freedom, and responsibility, he strives to achieve equality with other human beings.

These factors must be properly understood. The relationship between them as living forces that causes the continuation of man's life and movement in man's history must also be thoroughly grasped.

Despite the existing relationship between the forces, it must not be assumed that some factors are basic while others are secondary. However, some of these factors could be more important at certain stages of human history than at others.

3. The basic contradictions known to history and the movement in history itself were determined by the struggle to resolve these contradictions, which, in essence, emanate from the factors enumerated above. These contradictions concerned the relations involving each of these factors. Man's struggles and endeavor to respond to the pressure of these forces and to solve the contradictions resulting from them constitute the most important phase of human activity in history.

Thus we discover:

> (*a*) Human activity that aims at satisfying man's needs and a struggle that embodies the contradictions originating in the "production and productive relations of these needs." These form the essence of class struggle.
>
> (*b*) Human activity that aims at satisfying man's curiosity and the pursuits of his mind, plus a struggle that embodies the contradictions originating in "the process of question and answer," and their relations. These are the ideological and mental struggles.
>
> (*c*) Human activity that aims at achieving the conditions and circumstances necessary for human freedom and equality and a struggle that embodies the contradictions originating in the "attempt to achieve these conditions and circumstances." Most often, such struggles represent both class and ideological conflicts, since freedom and equality ultimately develop within a set of objective, productive, and mental conditions.
>
> (*d*) Activities, relations, and conflicts between one human society and another. The activities, conflicts, and contradictions in sections (*a*), (*b*), and (*c*) above concern, even in an abstract sense, man facing problems within his own society.
>
> Activities, relations, and conflicts in section (*d*) concern a human society facing another, within humanity as a whole.

Since human society, as we have explained, embodies the sum total of relations originating in the constituent features of man's humanity, we find that the activities, relations, and contradictions among human societies are decided in accordance with the productive, mental, and cultural contents of these societies. These activities, relations, and contradictions that have crystallized in the course of human history are national in character.

4. In addition to these factors and to what originates from them by way of relations, contradictions, and conflicts that, as a whole, constitute the life of "man in society," we also find that man's view of the life beyond, and man's urge to attain immortality, is a factor that has had great influence on the progress of human history. Although the influence of this factor is on the decline as man progresses, it has undoubtedly been embodied in certain ideas and doctrines, certain activities and relations, and has given rise to contradictions and conflicts, without an understanding of which many historical events of great moment, and man himself in the course of history, are unintelligible.

Man's views—even such as have originated from his inability, at certain periods of history, to face certain problems or answer certain questions—have been important factors in the movement of history. It may even have been that some or all such views and opinions were exploited by certain ruling classes in order to bolster their class interests, and that some originated in reality from class interests and were a reflection of such interests.

24. COOPERATIVE SOCIALISM*

Ramadan Lawand

Ramadan Lawand, a young Lebanese writer, discusses cooperative socialism in a book dealing with various problems encountered by Arab nationalism. His objective viewpoint was rather uncommon in the early 1960's. The implicit demands in this extract refer to free exchange of ideas, less reliance on leadership from the top, and participation in the decision-making processes.

The Arab intellectuals who carried back with them to their homeland the socialist theories of the West brought with them also the interests of the ruling classes.

Whatever the opinion each group entertains of the other, it cannot be doubted that Arab socialists are a copy of socialists in the West. Thus, the Arab socialist movement has lost its genuine and distinctive character.

Nevertheless, some socialists still attempt to ascribe certain peculiar charac-

* Extract from Ramadan Lawand, *Masir al-qawmiyya al-'arabiyya* (*The Future of Arab Nationalism*) (Beirut: Munsharat dar maktabat al-hayat, n.d.), pp. 120–21, 136, 140, 85–86.

teristics to Arab socialism. The most recent example of such attempts is a book by Dr. Muhammad Majdhub entitled *The United Arab Republic*. Discussing the theoretical and practical differences between Communism and Arab socialism, he writes:

> 1. Marxism maintains that an idea is nothing but the reflection of matter in the human brain. This cannot be accepted by the Arab socialism.
> 2. Marxism states that atheism is an essential prerequisite for accepting Marxist theory. But Arab socialism rejects atheism and considers itself the guardian of a spiritual heritage.
> 3. Marxism does not recognize the nationalist spirit, whereas Arab socialism is not prepared to forsake its nationalism.
> 4. Marxism was born from European thought and in circumstances peculiar to Europe in the last two centuries.

But Arab socialism affirms that "Marxism cannot strike roots in Arab soil because Arab history differs from European, etc. . . ." Then Dr. Majdhub adds that most of these differences are literary and historical and that the views of Marx did not prove accurate in all respects.

I was quite prepared to agree with the author's views regarding these differences, but, on p. 143 of his book, he wrote "Socialism today does not concern itself merely with the economic but with all walks of life, all principles, all foundations, etc."

Socialism, in his opinion, is a comprehensive outlook on man, life, and existence. If, for the sake of argument, we agree that Arab socialism is a nationalistic socialism and is a guardian of a religious heritage that believes in a Creator and in the dualism of spirit and matter, and emanates from Arab history, then we are entitled to ask about the program of Arab socialism. Is it dialectical, historical, and material, or is it something else, and, if so, what?

If we try to answer this question in the light of his own negative definition of Arab socialism, we would have to say that Arab socialism, in his view, is nonscientific in method. Why? Because faith in a Creator, in a religion, and in a special spiritual Arab heritage constitutes one of its foundations, and science, he knows well, does not accept transcendental causation.

If, on the other hand, he tells us that Arab socialism is an organization of economy and human relations, and safeguards human dignity, then it is no longer the comprehensive outlook which, he explicitly states, is one of its distinguishing features. The astonishing thing in Dr. Majdhub's socialism is that it enjoins upon all Arab socialists "a thorough study of all states that practice socialism and of the methods used for its development and adaptation." He says this although the non-Communist socialist systems are all forged copies of Marxism and of some of its doctrines and methods which various countries try to implement by way of a compromise with the working classes.

Socialism and Religion

When Arab cooperative socialism places man midway between absolute freedom in work and creativity and absolute subjection to the machine and to the economy, this is because it respects man and because it considers that the great reform movements of history as preached by prophets and reformers are beneficent and fruitful human phenomena. These movements, in its opinion, are not warning signals but manifestations of faith. The response of the people, over the ages, to these movements have demonstrated man's struggle for sublime ideals. Religion is an embodiment of this manifestation of faith; it is not "the opium of the people," even though many religious movements have been perverted and have degenerated into becoming identified with the interests of a clerical class. Religion is a positive, genuine, and uninterrupted endeavor, which links man to the sublime and the ideal. It is not a pagan rite where the relationship of the worshipper to the worshipped is rigidly defined by ceremonial and where man becomes the stupid slave of meaningless symbols and slogans. Religion, according to cooperative socialism, is a process of revitalizing human freedom which can then create anew through the contemplation of the ideal it worships.

Conclusion

In the light of the above, it appears to us that the sort of socialism that suits Arab nationalism is one that provides a meeting point between the inevitability of matter and free human creativity. It is a constant interaction between the mechanical law of matter and the flexible and creative will. Herein lies the perversion of Marxism and of the other counterfeit socialist systems which were meant to be a series of compromises formulated in order to avoid the conflict of employers and workers. We have also discovered the reality of the religious mission and its true content. The relationship between religion and the clerical class, on the one hand, and between dictatorship of various kinds and religion, on the other, has also been clarified.

In calling this socialism "cooperative," we wish to convey our faith in cooperation, which is the practical expression of the values of love, goodness, and sincerity linking man to his great Creator.

Cooperative socialism, then, is a revolutionary and optimistic movement which places its faith in man's will and man's ability to surpass himself and rid himself of all malice and all indifference.

Our revolutionary Arab nationalism is the force that finds in cooperative socialism its social and economic expression and its proper plan for the reconstruction of the Arab society. . . .

Arab nationalists can now reinterpret their nationalism. Only in this context they can hark back to our historical roots and revitalize our moribund traditions and values. In this manner, the Arabs would finally and decisively rid themselves of the spiritual roots that have so far bound them to Western values and ideals, ethical and human. They can abandon this nihilism that until quite recently rendered a pale reflection of the genuine Arab personality.

The Arab renaissance today is not merely political, although it seems to have become arrested at the stage of political liberation. . . . The revolutions breaking out in the Arab homeland do not merely aim at liberation from foreign domination. This is a meager objective, easy to achieve, and it is also negative in character, since it involves the rejection of an evil but brings no benefit according to our understanding of Arab nation's mission. The Arab national renaissance is a comprehensive movement that bids us to re-examine our very existence and the nature of our life. It aims in reality at placing us in the forefront of world progress as leaders and guides to human faith, love, and a happier future. It follows that this renaissance involves not merely a rational spirit, optimism, and trained technical specialization but something nobler and more consequential. It demands simple faith, selfless heroism, a powerful spirit, optimism, piety, and a view of life that transcends man and nature, elevating man above his vanities, his instincts, and his greed.

This renaissance ushers in a new beginning, a new examination of man. It involves a recasting of an old Arab national heritage in such a way that only its creativity and its wonderful simplicity are preserved. In the light of this, we today look forward to a new leadership which can finally end this crisis in leadership that has long plagued us and perverted our values. We want this leadership to steer us back to the path laid down by life's youthful urge. We desire a dignified nation whose humanism is apparent in all its policies, thought, and feelings.

25. COMMUNISM AND OURSELVES: SEVEN DIFFERENCES BETWEEN COMMUNISM AND ARAB SOCIALISM*

Muhammad Hasanayn Haykal

Muhammad Hasanayn Haykal (b. 1924), the editor of al-Ahram, *is a close friend of President Nasser of the U.A.R. Covering a wide range of topics, his articles in* al-Ahram *have expressed the government's viewpoint on current problems and have varied according to changes of opinion or policy in the ruling circles. His views have regularly been reproduced by other Egyptian newspapers, as well as by Nasserite publications throughout the Arab world. The article reproduced here appeared during the first major phase of socialism in Egypt. After the decrees of July, 1961, which nationalized more than 80 percent of the economy, the country seemed to move to the extreme left. Haykal's purpose was to assure both the moderate Egyptians and the Western world that Nasser's socialism was not Communism. Moreover, the ruling circles were concerned with the growing ideological tension between the intel-*

* Reprinted, in a slightly abbreviated form, from Muhammad Hasanayn Haykal, "Nahnu wa-al-shuyu'iyyah: 7 fawariq bayn al-shuyu'iyyah wa bayn al-ishtirakiyya al-'arabiyya. Al-Tarikh la yasir fi tariq masdud" ("Communism and Ourselves: 7 Differences Between Communism and Arab Socialism. History Does Not Unfold on a Closed Path"), *al-Ahram,* Cairo, August 4, 1961.

lectuals with Marxist tendencies and the nationalists and liberals. Haykal's other aim, therefore, was to stress the special national characteristics of Arab socialism as practiced in Egypt in order to achieve a common viewpoint among the intellectuals.

My aim is to analyze the contents of Arab socialism and of Communism, in order to compare these two doctrines and highlight their differences. As preamble, however, I wish to indicate that my intention is neither to disparage Communism nor to vilify Communists, for several reasons:

The first is that our experience in socialism rose from nothing, but from now on is open to debate and confrontation. . . .

The second is that we believe in the right of the people to choose their own system. If the American people choose capitalism, it is their right, and if the people of the Soviet Union choose Communism, that is also their right.

The third is that no one can deny that Communism as experienced in the Soviet Union has achieved great results for the people of that country, even though the price they paid under the terror of Stalinism was tremendous. In fact, the Soviet Union has taken a great leap forward in the course of the last forty-three years, and together with the U.S.A. it has become one of the two great world powers as regards scientific progress and production.

Finally, the fourth reason is that the existence of a Communist world opposite the capitalist world has created an extremely important international balance, which has allowed many colonized and conquered people to rise up against their masters.

1. The first difference between Arab socialism and Communism lies in the conception of class by each. The existence of classes and their conflicting interests and the class struggle from which the movement for social progress stems are accepted facts. It is here that the first difference appears between Arab socialism and Communism; it lies in the solution proposed by each of the two systems to the problem of conflicting contradictory class interests.

The solution proposed by Communism is proletarian dictatorship represented by the Communist Party, whereas Arab socialism proposes the fusion of the differences that exist between the classes. Communism asks the dispossessed to revolt and transform all the possessors into dispossessed. It also asks them to get rid of all property owners, by any means, if necessary by massacre—all such owners being in its eyes exploiters.

The Communist solution is therefore the final elimination of all classes by a single class. Arab socialism asks the dispossessed to revolt so that they may have access to property and take their rightful share of the national wealth. For Arabs, it is a question of eliminating the contradictions between the classes within a framework of national unity and revolutionary plotting, while society evolves to form only one class in which each member occupies a place commensurate with his work, without the impediment of any class barrier.

Thus punishment and vengeance mark the first steps of Communism, the class struggle inevitably assuming, in the eyes of the Communists a bloody character. As to Arab socialism, its origins are in justice and equality. Revolutionary intrigue is carried out in a peaceful manner, unsoiled by bloodshed, and without the specter of the gallows in the background.

2. The second difference, which derives from the first, concerns the ideas of the two systems regarding private property. As far as Communism is concerned, every property owner is also an exploiter; hence, it is necessary to eliminate him in order to eliminate exploitation itself.

For Arab socialism, with its different point of view, property is of two kinds—that which exploits and that which results from work. Communism affirms: Whoever possesses exploits; he must be eliminated. Arab socialism says: There are proprietors and proprietors. In fact, there is a kind of property that represents the result of work and that cannot be used by the owner to exploit or dominate others. This property is an essential right. It is a right that should be extended so that as many as possible can share in it and benefit equally from it. As for the exploiting proprietor, Arab socialism continues: Do not kill him. Take from him rather the means that make him an exploiter, then allow him to live in the new society. It does not matter if he enters with anger and bitterness the society that is capable of educating him, since it is capable of educating its children and initiating them into a new way of life.

3. The third difference emerges from this logical chain of thought. Communism says: It is necessary to expropriate. Arab socialism says: It is necessary to compensate. This difference is the inevitable consequence of the two former differences. Arab socialism has as its aims justice and equality, not punishment and vengeance. Private property is a right—even an aim, one may say—on condition it does not end in exploitation. The system of nationalization with compensation, as was practiced by Arab socialism in its attempt to increase the people's share in the national wealth and its revenues, is not only a guillotine that operates automatically, rising and falling to cut up and destroy. On the contrary, nationalization is carried out in a responsible, patriotic manner. This explains the apparent difference in the procedure employed with regard to certain firms affected by these measures. Total nationalization has struck first at all the international monopolies, starting with the Suez Canal Company, which was dominated by Britain and France. Then came the Company of New Egypt, a simple façade behind which lay Belgian interests, followed by banks and insurance companies, so as to prevent money's becoming the weapon of exploitation. Nationalization was then extended to public services closely linked to the public interest, such as the Tramway Company, for example, and the Lebon Company, and took in the heavy industry that exercised a direct influence on the national economy.

In other cases—altogether ninety-one cases affected by the revolutionary measures—nationalization has not been total but partial (50 per cent). Such is the case, for example, with the works of Yasin the glass manufacturers. Muhammad Sayyid Yasin, their founder, has made a real effort in a new productive bid. He has succeeded, and in his success lies a whole history of struggle and experience. . . .

4. Let us turn now to the role of the individual in society. In the Communist society, the state possesses everything. The individual is a tool; he receives what is necessary for his essential needs. . . . In Arab socialism, the state is an instrument of the people for achieving justice and guaranteeing its application.

While the individual in the Communist society feels he is only a small cog in a huge machine, the individual in the Arab socialist society feels that his capacities for invention are not subject to limitation or hindrance, so long as he does not indulge in exploitation.

In Arab socialism, the individual is the very basis of the social structure. There is nothing in it that fetters ambition. . . . Arab socialism desires that workers in the factories shall be coproprietors, concerned with profit not only from the viewpoint of production but also from a personal point of view. . . .

[*In the passage omitted, Haykal alludes to his visit to the U.S.S.R. and to the talks he had with various Soviet citizens.*]

One, for example, named Stephanovsky, was an employee in one of the government services. I asked him this question: "What is your ambition?" Perplexed, he replied, "Ambition . . . ambition . . . I don't understand you." I asked him, "For example, do you want to have a car some day?" He replied sharply, "No, no. I am too ordinary to own a car. I dream only of owning a motorbike." Even dreams have limits that must not be exceeded. . . .

The underground stations [in the Moscow subway system] were very elegant and luxurious. The contrast was particularly striking between the clothes of the travelers in the trains and the imposing marble walls and sparkling lights suspended from the ceiling. . . . The real tragedy, however, was the enormous contradiction between the different aspects of present-day life. The difference between the trains and the travelers is hard to imagine.

In short, the difference and the points of conflict between the Communist point of view and the point of view of Arab socialism on this question are as follows: Communism says that the present does not interest us; we look only toward the future. Arab socialism says, on the contrary, that the present does interest us. . . . If the present loses all love of life, the future cannot be created from nothing.

Communism says: It is important to sacrifice everything now in order to gain everything tomorrow. Arab socialism says the sacrifice must not exceed its limits, otherwise it will kill the sense of liberty and humanity in the individual.

> We proclaim the necessity for work . . . but we refuse slavery. We aim for production . . . but we want a society where well-being reigns. We are working to produce . . . but we do not forget the necessity of providing employment for all. We build factories . . . but we build houses as well. We are building dams and power stations . . . but we have a special budget for hospitals and schools.

It is because of this, for example, that, at the outset, Communism had no fixed working hours. On the contrary, these hours grew longer and longer, in the sole interest of production, with no increases in wages. Even to this day, the workers in Communist China have no annual holiday.

Arab socialism reduced the number of working hours right from the start. There is no doubt that present circumstances help Arab socialism to follow this line of action. First of all, there has been enormous progress in the means of production. The Soviet Union, for example, at the outset, did not have the same success as we have had. We start with the most up-to-date achievements of modern science. Our factories and tools are the most modern yet produced. Progress in the means of production permits us to decrease working hours, and consequently helps us to insure the welfare of the individual, without this being at the expense of production as regards quality and quantity.

The basis of the disagreement concerning the individual in Communism and Arab socialism is that Communism regards the individual as a simple historical result. . . . Arab socialism considers that the cycle is complete and that there is a balanced relationship between the individual and history. Man is a result of history, but at the same time he is one of the causes of history. Man is molded by history, but he also molds history.

5. Thus another difference appears between Communism and Arab socialism. Communism was founded on the sacrifice of several generations of men in order to arrive at a growth of production. Especially during the Stalinist period, it put these ideas into practice by confiscating all national resources and mobilizing the total work force toward production. The extreme cruelty of the conditions in factories and on collective farms, the coercion and oppression, could only be justified to the generation of that time by looking toward the future.

Arab socialism has another view on this question. To achieve an increase in production and eventually the highest level of production necessitates a general national mobilization of all resources, but the present generations have the right to live. . . .

6. We come to a sixth difference between Communism and Arab socialism. It is the difference between abject servility and free initiative. Above all, it is the difference between immobility and dynamism, or rather between blind fanaticism and free thought. Even though it undertakes to conform to Marxist dialetic, Communism cannot depart from the well-defined paths without being accused of deviationism, as was the case with Tito, who was attacked when he tried to transform, modernize, and free himself and to become independent.

The Arab socialist feels that all the richness of thought throughout the world is available to him. He can benefit from it and explore its possibilities. Above all, he feels that he is capable of adding something to it and sharing in its growth. He adds to it his own national experience, and he helps it grow by his historical heritage.

In his speech made on the eve of the celebration of the revolution, Gamal

Abdel Nasser expressed this idea in these words: "We do not open books to find all the answers, but we open the book of our reality [time] and try to find the solution of its problems."

That is the difference between the Communist and the Arab socialist. The Communist is a pupil who remains faithful to the words of Marx, Lenin, Stalin, Khrushchev, and Mao Tse-tung crammed into his head. Even though these words are in many cases divergent and remote . . . different and contradictory . . . , the Communist must listen and obey. The Arab socialist is a pupil who remains faithful to the history of his nation, to his national heritage, to the problems of his people, and to their hopes.

It is possible that this is the reason for the failure of Arab Communists to achieve the least following among the people, particularly in the United Arab Republic. The Arab masses have heard nothing from the Communists but stiff foreign slogans. They see in the Communists only puppets, worked by string from behind their frontiers.

7. Communism believes that political organizations should be confined to the Communist Party alone. For this reason, that supreme and unchallenged authority is exclusively in the hands of the Party. No revolution can be lawful unless the Communist Party is the instigator and the master. Arab socialism considers that the organization encompassing political activity must extend to the whole nation.

To achieve democracy, Communism sees no way other than the dictatorship of one party, the Communist Party, which permits the existence of no other party. Arab socialism proclaims the idea of national union to organize political action on the basis of the whole nation so that the meaning and foundation of democracy may extend to all the people.

National union, it is true, still needs to be more clearly defined and developed, so that it may achieve all that is expected of it. However, these are only details, although they have a very great importance.

But what is important is that Arab socialism has succeeded in finding a means of organizing political action in accordance with its now national circumstances—and even international circumstances. In effect, the powers that face each other on the international scene [i.e., the United States and the U.S.S.R.] are ready to penetrate the country by manipulations and to divide it so that each can secure the support of a group or interest and use it for its own designs.

26. OUR SOCIALISM IN RELATION TO CAPITALISM AND COMMUNISM*

Fathi Ghanim

Fathi Ghanim belongs to the Egyptian leftist group (whose members range from Fabian socialists to Marxists) that publishes the influential ideological review Ruz al-Yusuf (Rose of Joseph) *in Cairo. Basically, this group supports Nasser's economic policy, and many of its members, after oscillating between Egyptian nationalism and Arab nationalism, now solidly support the latter. (The Marxists seem more interested in Egypt's pre-Islamic past.) The publishers of* Ruz al-Yusuf *and* Sabah al-Qahira *(a more popular type of publication) have studied and publicized the writings and ideas of the Arab nationalists. They have also tried to propagate the ideas of a democratic, cooperative socialism based on the idea of consumer interest. But because of their weak ideological foundations, they have been forced to lean more and more on Marxism, especially after the increase in influence of a group who were released from prison as a consequence of Khrushchev's visit to Egypt in 1964. This article, one of the many that tried to define the ideological tenets of Egypt's cooperative socialism, is critical of both capitalism and Communism. See also Fathi Ghanim, "Dimuqratiyyat al-ishtirakiyya" (The Democracy of Socialism"),* Ruz al-Yusuf (Rose of Joseph), *Cairo, October 26, 1959, p. 1.*

There are two well-defined but completely opposed methods of ensuring the progress and development of a nation—one in the West, especially in America, the other in the East, particularly in the Communist countries. It is worth while to examine the inherent characteristics of these two methods before reviewing the characteristics of our own regime.

In the West, economic progress results from the activities of individual businessmen, heads of industry and commercial establishments, etc. These businessmen do not plan their projects with public interest in mind; profit is the prime motive behind their activities. When he builds a factory, forms a company, or constructs a block of flats, a businessman is not thinking of the needs of the community. He has only one aim: to sell to whoever has the money to buy, and to make a profit on the deal. . . . The industrialist does not select his industry with regard to the over-all interest of the nation; he

* Extract from Fathi Ghanim, "Ayn ishtirakiyyatuna min al-ra'smaliyya wal-shuyu-'iyya" ("Our [Superior] Socialism in Relation to Capitalism and Communism"), *Ruz al-Yusuf (Rose of Joseph)*, Cairo, February 13, 1961, pp. 8–9.

prefers to manufacture spirits rather than set up a foundry or a steelworks. The same goes for the capitalist who may prefer to invest his money in a night club rather than use it to prospect in the desert. . . . In effect, for the businessmen as for the capitalist, what counts is profit, by whatever means. . . .

On the other hand, flooding the market with consumer goods creates a special mentality among buyers—the selfish mentality of the individual who thinks only of himself and of his own welfare.

The individual who is used to devoting the whole day to the choice of an elegant tie . . . is likely to be highly selfish; by his very nature, he rejects all efforts to persuade him to sacrifice a little of his well-being for the sake of the general good. He is not concerned about the "general good" and ignores the millions whose standard of living is very low. He regards them as foreigners, treats them as though they were a different kind of creature, unconnected with himself, as though they were living in a different world and not in the same country. . . .

All this is reflected in the political regime of this individualistic society; businessmen claim absolute political freedom and refuse to admit that they can be restricted in any way. They have only one aim: to prevent any state intervention that might restrain the activities by which they hope to enrich themselves and exploit the other classes of society.

Western economists believe that private enterprise, despite many imperfections, does not completely suppress the freedom of the individual, ensures economic development, and raises the standard of living without resorting to compulsion; economic growth develops naturally and finally expands to cover all the needs of the people.

But what is this freedom of which the West is so proud? It is that of the businessmen and the monopolies, whose influence dominates the press and the radio, and who take pains to hide the reality of a situation that is contrary to the interests of the majority. Besides, this individualistic philosophy is of no advantage to a nation that desires rapid progress and improvement and is impatient at the thought that its standard of living might remain very low for many generations or for many long centuries.

We find in the Communist countries the second method of ensuring development and progress. The exact opposite of Western methods, it suppresses private enterprise and private control, and aims to carry out only projects that are in the general interest. Heavy industry has priority over consumer goods. Individuals live as if they were in a huge factory, with no prospect except work. They have sacrificed their well-being and cannot choose their own living accommodations or clothes. Sometimes the family lives in one or two rooms; the wife has only one kind of shoes; the materials from which she makes her dresses are available only in certain qualities or colors. The superfluous is unknown. The import of perfumes, spirits, and automobiles is absolutely forbidden.

Individuals are swallowed up in the mass. Their productive work is supervised by a group of directors and technicians linked to political chiefs, whose aims—for the interest of all—are well understood.

This means that one generation or more is sacrificed completely for the sake of future generations. Consequently, those in political power must maintain a strong regime extending its control to every sector of life to ensure that the wheel of productivity turns without hindrance and that no negligence prevents the carrying out of schedules as planned.

Experience has shown that, in the Communist countries, the political power group can keep all the reins well in hand. It is helped by the clarity of its line of conduct, despite its tight hold over the individual. It is helped also by the individuals themselves, who in the heat of work forget their egoism, which in any event receives little or no encouragement in their current way of life. They do not have the leisure to choose ties, gaze in shop windows, and ponder over a restaurant menu . . . Everything is prepared and clearly defined in advance, and their minds are geared to productivity and work.

This kind of life runs into a crisis as soon as the state, with the majority of its projects achieved, begins to expand the consumer market. From this moment, men begin to acquire the consciousness of their personality. . . . In actual fact, the average man in the cities of Russia then sees opening before him the possibility of choosing goods—a situation that changes his mentality and consequently the political regime itself.

Consumers represent an enormous force. They run into millions, and their numerical force has an influence on the directors, technicians, and politicians, who judge it wise to be in harmony with the feelings of the force which the consumers represent.

We in the U.A.R. adopt neither private control nor collective control which totally paralyzes private initiative. We favor a midway solution which does not merely try to maintain a balance between the two regimes. It is in fact a unique system, whose essential characteristics are as follows:

a desire to hasten economic development with the least possible delay;

a determination not to sacrifice the special interests of the individual, except within reasonable limits, and not to destroy man's feeling of individuality.

On the first point—i.e., our wish to catch up as rapidly as possible in our economic development—there can be no dispute; this desire is solidly anchored in the minds of the whole Arab nation.

The second point—where private interest stops and general interest begins—is far from clear to the majority of the middle class. This confusion results from our desire to foster both individuality and a sense of the general good in the individual. That is a difficult ideal to achieve. Although man can easily accept that which emphasizes his individuality, he finds it difficult to accept the idea of toil for the general good.

In the towns today, the average person is always in a position to choose what he intends to buy, and all the efforts of the state to limit his choice—or to suppress it—come up against solid opposition. It is enough for the state to forbid the importation of English wool, silk ties, perfumes from Paris, or records and record players, and it clashes immediately with the frantic desire of the individual to buy these objects and get them for himself by any possible means. Every day the U.A.R. Customs continue to intercept travelers arriving from abroad laden with these goods; their joy at having procured them is such as to vere on madness.

The important thing here is not to find means of forbidding the entry of goods, but rather to understand the mentality of the buyers of these goods; their individualism and their own particular interests always take precedent over their consideration for the general interest. . . . We are expected at the same time to concentrate on work and the application of the five-year plan so as to raise the standard of living of the poor majority.

Today we come up against a sharp contradiction when we ask consumers to be both consumers and producers and demand that they consume the least while producing the maximum. The Communists tell us that in order to resolve this contradiction it is necessary to establish an authoritarian regime and accustom people to privation and sacrifice in the interests of future generations. . . . We reject this opinion, which in effect does not coincide with the nature of our people. . . .

We cannot forget that the Arab nation had an ancient civilization and that it is deeply ingrained in the souls of the people. Although he may be poor and illiterate, the ordinary man retains the pride and the glory of belonging to an ancient race. That is why he refuses completely to sacrifice his individuality, and why he refuses also to merge himself totally with the mass.

That is why it is wise constantly to try to reconcile the pressing need to hasten development in the interests of society with the no less pressing need to preserve man's individuality, in spite of the contradiction that this effort entails. The way to achieve this is to consider the contradiction not as shameful but rather as a fact of our life. It follows from this that rather than suppress the contradiction we must try to overcome it by being conscious of it and understanding it in its reality. We must take it into account when, as ordinary citizens, we consider our political regime. We must take it into account when we prepare our final constitution. . . .

By persuading the individual that his interests and those of the nation can coincide, we can assure the success of our democratic, socialist, and cooperative regime. It is not a difficult thing to achieve, for each of us, no matter what our particular interests, is a noble, good hearted citizen, capable of limiting his individuality.

27. THE CRISIS OF THE ARAB LEFT*

Clovis Maqsud

Clovis Maqsud (see p. 59 above) *was a member of the Lebanese Phalanx and subsequently joined the Arab National Bloc, a group that wanted to maintain a democratic, independent Lebanon rather than to support the interests of a specific group. Ideologically, Maqsud was for a time the principal theorist for Kamal Jumblat's Popular Socialist Party. In 1956, however, he opposed Jumblat because of the latter's pro-American attitudes and drifted closer to association with the Ba'th.*

Maqsud is one of the most original Arab thinkers. He has expressed himself searchingly, with clarity and force, on all major problems confronting the Arab world. In Ma'na al-hiyad al-ijabi (The Meaning of Positive Neutrality) *(Beirut: Dar al-'ilm lil-malayin, 1960), he defined the nonalignment of the Arab world as a consequence of international forces rather than as an organic growth of Arab nationalism. (See Leonard Binder,* The Ideological Revolution in the Middle East *[New York: John Wiley and Sons, 1964], pp. 242 ff.) However, the main problems dealt with by Maqsud have been ideological. In 1960–61, he was a member of the Arab Socialist Association presided over by Colonel Kamal Rifa'a of Egypt's Revolutionary Council, who had been active in various Marxist organizations in 1947–51. The history of this association (whose members came from several Arab countries) is basic to understanding not only Maqsud's views but also the ideological problems confronting the Arab world generally. The key issue was to determine the role of the intellectual in the new revolutionary national and socialist framework of the Arab republics.*

Ideology in the Arab world, from the turn of the century to World War II, had developed relatively freely within a broad spectrum of ideas that ranged from extreme Marxism to Islamism. There were no national states whose political philosophies relied exclusively on one of the existing ideologies. Even if certain ideologies seemed stronger than others, the lack of national independence prevented a full ideological confrontation, since none of the ideologies could determine the final form of a regime. The period before the 1950's, therefore, could be called relatively liberal.

The Egyptian revolution of 1952 produced new conditions. The revolution had certain goals but no ideology, except broad but vague democratic social attitudes. The ensuing permissive atmosphere in Egypt in 1952–58 stimulated an intensive intellectual activity whose depth and scope are still to be deter-

* Extract from Clovis Maqsud, *Azmat al-yasar al-'arabi* (*The Crisis of the Arab Left*) (Beirut: Dar al-'ilm lil-malayin, 1960), pp. 9–21.

mined. Leftist or socialist currents mushroomed, and the Marxist groups occupied an important place among them. Meanwhile, the military regime had secured full national independence and acquired authority, prestige, and influence, both internally and internationally. A state with a sustaining bureaucratic structure had fully emerged. The crucial problem faced by the Egyptian regime was to define its base of political power and to make it harmonize with the changing social structure, with the underlying currents of thought, and with the country's future social and cultural goals. The key issue, therefore, was to define ideologically the relationship of the existing military leadership with the emerging socio-economic structure and the new philosophy of life stemming from it.

The Marxists posed the strongest ideological challenge to Nasser's ruling group. They regarded the military's role in the transformation of Egypt as short and transitional. The rise of Marxist thought had been greatly aided by the fact that Egypt's anti-imperialist and anti-Western "neutralist" policy had undermined the force of sociodemocratic ideas of the West and of their intellectual representatives. The Marxists critically questioned the social bases of the military regime. They felt that the military was socially and ideologically unqualified to carry out the full modernization of Egypt. For them, the military was a power group whose range of thought and action would be confined, in the long run, to the concepts of the anti-imperialist, nationalist bourgeois class to which they belonged. True, the struggle against imperialism and the urgent need for development had engendered in the military a certain revolutionary dynamism, but this would exhaust itself soon after independence and national statehood were firmly secured. Consequently, the Marxists felt that they alone were eminently qualified to bring Egypt into the new age.

The clash between the organized political power and the leftists occurred in 1958–59. Many intellectuals were dismissed from universities and government positions, and the militant Marxists were imprisoned. These measures were hailed in the West as proof of Nasser's anti-Communism. (There was truth in this belief.) But the measures also betrayed a certain intellectual insecurity on the part of Nasser's group and marked the beginning of a severe intellectual crisis. Nasser followed up the anti-Communist measures with efforts to devise a new social philosophy that would incorporate the main currents of thought in the Arab world. A variety of institutes and associations were formed, consisting of intellectuals and professionals, and even al-Azhar was subjected to reform in order to bring it into the twentieth century, according to the dreams that Muhammad 'Abduh had formulated at the end of the nineteenth century. Yet, all these measures, and the socialism they engendered in Egypt, suffered from a basic contradiction, which defeated their purpose. The Marxists were silenced chiefly as enemies of democracy and as agents of a foreign power, just as the Muslim Brotherhood had been disposed of as the enemy of progress. (Some members of the Brotherhood were rehabilitated.) The revolutionary government had, therefore, disposed of Marxists in order to protect democracy and freedom, which in this case meant simply freedom from being forced to accept a certain ideology.

But in initiating his subsequent ideological measures, Nasser did not scruple to violate the same democracy and freedom in reorganizing and directing from the top the intellectual life of Egypt in a manner decided by his own group.

The result was intellectual apathy, servility, and forced formal political loyalty. There burst into the open a struggle between the organized authority, conscious of its identity and purpose, and the society at large, which refused to be regimented into a preconceived scheme. This "intellectual crisis" was discussed in a series of articles in al-Ahram *in March, 1961, and in two debates in June of that year. The articles were published in a volume by Muhammad Hasanayn Haykal,* Azmat al-muthaqqafín (Crisis of Intellectuals) (*Cairo: al-Shirka al-'arabiyya al-muttahida lil tawziyya, 1961*). *The discussion, largely stimulated and controlled by the government, explained the background of intellectuals in Egypt and in the Arab world generally but did not diagnose the real cause of the intellectual crisis. Yet, the cause was obvious: Directed from the top, the discussion had been aimed ultimately at enlisting the support of the intelligentsia for Nasser's socialism generally and for the forthcoming nationalization decrees of July-September, 1961, specifically. The Arab Socialist Association, to which Clovis Maqsud belonged, was part of the Egyptian Government's endeavor to combine socialist ideas with the ideas of Arab nationalism and to use them to prepare the ideological ground for Arab unity. This was to be the* Arab ideology, *a unique blend of progressive ideas, human freedom, and national aspirations, opposed to both Communism and capitalism. As indicated by his previous writings on the subjects of socialism and nationalism, Maqsud was uniquely qualified for the task. See, for example,* al-Mahiyya al-ishtirakiyya al-'arabiyya (The Nature of Arab Socialism) (*Baghdad: Maktabat al-nahda, 1959*), *and* Nahw ishtirakiyya 'arabiyya (Toward Arab Socialism) (*Beirut: Dar Munaymina, 1957*). *The formulation of general socialist principles did not, however, attract unanimous consent, especially since the Marxists continued to pursue their own policy. Maqsud, therefore, was forced to answer some basic and difficult questions—how to preserve freedom and democratic values—the very spirit that made social thoughts attractive, without destroying them in the web of the organization established to implement them; and how to distinguish the humanist philosopher Marx from pragmatic masters of power such as Lenin.*

The extract is taken from a book in which Maqsud tries to find an answer to the foregoing questions.

The left in the Arab world is undergoing a severe crisis—a crisis with roots that are implicit, on the one hand, in the historical circumstances that created the Arab left itself and, on the other, in the crisis of the left in general.

What do we mean by the left? The "left" is a political term that denotes those classes who work for an ever-widening participation of the masses in the various economic, political, and cultural fields, on the basis of ever-decreasing class differences. The left includes all the elements who are determined to liberate man from all conditions that cause him to live on the periphery of life and events and who are determined to make him an active agent in determining his future and achieving his dignity and prosperity. The various ideologies that have attempted or are attempting to translate these wishes and endeavors into practical programs have not faced the same problems. Furthermore, the motives that led some ideologies to work within the general framework of the left have not been the same. Therefore, diverse ideological and political schools of thought inevitably arose within the left, and it has become necessary to reappraise the criteria for determining whether or not a group of people belong to the left.

Despite these obvious or latent differences in the currents of the left, certain ideological presuppositions act as a common denominator in determining belongingness to the left. In addition to the brief definition cited above (which constitutes the practical foundations of the left), certain ideological commitments must be satisfied if we desire the left to keep to its progressive path. Several groups can work together for temporary or short-term objectives that are of the essence of leftist planning and strategy, but such groups cannot continue to work indefinitely to strengthen the means for safeguarding the progressive participation of the masses in national life.

In order to follow a progressive path and to clarify and foresee its results, we must accept certain basic philosophical theories. We must admit, for example, that mind emanates from matter and that evolution is the genuine expression of the inner spirit of our existence. The conjunction of theory and practice is a basic prerequisite for finding a method of dealing with affairs that conform both with the requirements of our modern age and with the objectives whose achievement would solve the problem of man and lay the foundation for human and social happiness.

In view of these definitions, which, as a whole, constitute the ideological and practical legacy of the left, diverse socialist groups, with their diverse policies, and certain progressive elements were all termed "leftist." Although some radicals have denied that certain progressive elements were leftist, the term "left" covers anyone who works for reform (being convinced of its value), but not one who accepts partial reform as a barrier to prevent the completion of the social revolution. Some conservatives submit to partial reforms which are carried out either under pressure from the left or as a result of the dire need to protect capitalism and exploitation. In such cases, their reforms act as an opiate on the increasing consciousness of the people, and as an attempt to keep the initiative for directing economic progress with those classes who believe in, and work for, the preservation of class differences and the denial of the ownership of the means of production to the people and their representatives.

Is Communism within or outside the pale of the left? The over-all impression is that Communism and the Communists are of the core of the left. The capitalist bourgeoisie in its propaganda has attempted to isolate the left and to picture Communism as the "extreme" left. This being so, the remaining left would appear to be ranged under this "extreme." In this manner, spokesmen for capitalism would place Communism within the left and make of it the logical end of the road for any leftist movement. In this manner, capitalism aims at striking a blow at the left and at creating a polarity between itself on the one hand and Communism on the other. When this polarity is achieved, discontent and antagonism within the capitalist camp would be limited, since, in accepting this polarity, one would have to admit that Communism is the only alternative to capitalism. But so that it should not fall into a severe crisis of conscience because of the cessation of ideological development, capitalism resorts to partial concessions calculated to reduce the tension in its structure and the struggle against its very foundations. A psychological atmosphere is created wherein revolutionary secession from capitalism would be rendered impossible, since a revolutionary drive would become the mere tool of Communism. The net result is that Communism and its leaders would see in this distorted logic a perfect proof of the contradictions inherent in capitalism and, in such contradictions, the perfect tool to serve their own purposes. For capitalist mentality regards any secession from capitalism as a deliberate move toward Communism. If this revolution against capitalist exploitation and the tradition of dissent against the ideological and psychological atmosphere created by capitalism gives birth to a deep-rooted revolutionary challenge independent of Communism, the dualistic structure of capitalism is quick to impeach and to suffocate this challenge. Therefore, the basic problem facing such a genuine challenge is that the left should persevere in the face of this capitalist siege and attack its dualistic structure by clarifying its own independence and the basic revolutionary impulses that gave rise to it. The crisis of the left in general lies in the fact that the left is unable to rise to the occasion and to its responsibilities in our modern age.

This crisis, which has resulted from the dichotomy between what exists and what is required, has led to two erroneous attitudes among leftists vis-à-vis the Communists. (1) The men of the left feel inferior to the Communists and submit to the logic that maintains that Communism is the highest form of socialism. (2) These men often react negatively to Communism. Let me now explain these attitudes in detail.

1. There is no doubt that the efficiency of Communist organization, its apparent ideological wholeness, and the fact that certain Communist parties have assumed power in certain countries, doubtless have led socialism to feel inferior to Communism. Socialism appears to lack unity and has no ideal model that socialists can point to. Almost all states that have achieved a socialist program have been small, like Sweden, where socialism was no more than a logical development of a certain historical and social evolution. Since such socialist systems were not exposed to internal or external setbacks, they have not invented methods and means that can be applied at various times and circumstances. Thus, socialism, without an international, self-sufficient status, becomes a mere movement, parts of whose socialist program may be adopted by capitalist regimes without thereby endangering any of the basic existing nonsocialist systems. Because of socialism's lack of appeal—which has resulted from the absence of ideological, philosophical, and practical homogeneity—various men of the left have been attracted to Communist political strategy

(without necessarily joining the Party), although they can plainly recognize the failings and irrationality of Communism and the Communist parties. Among them are such groups as the Peace Partisans, the Women's Rights societies, the groups for Democratic Rights, and the Democratic Youth movements. These people are not necessarily Communists but they feel somewhat inferior to them. Grasping the situation, the Communists often conceal their true intentions by coining slogans calculated to draw to them elements of public opinion that are ordinarily far removed from Communism. Even when these elements discover the truth about such slogans as "Peace and Democracy," which denote something that the Communists themselves do not accept, the leftists continue to work within these Communist-organized fronts. They believe that Communists must not be denied access to public life and that the non-Communist left, because of its weakness, must obtain the support of what is even more to the left and is more efficacious, both politically and internationally. Despite their dangerous policy, such leftist elements are potentially the supporters of a clear and positive leftist movement. Thus, one must not ignore or refuse to deal with them but must constantly work to draw them back to their natural sphere of action. These men have erroneously drifted toward Communism not because they are unaware of Communist violations of man's rights at various times and places but because they feel an urgent desire to quicken the transition to the socialist society and man's liberation from the exploitation of both men and machines. This sense of urgency masks a revolutionary spirit of which the Arab left stands greatly in need.

2. Another danger to the left resides in a negative reaction to Communism and Communists. Much Communist activity at various levels doubtless constitutes a provocation and a threat to man's dignity, liberty, and prosperity. At various periods in the history of the relations between the left and the Communists, the latter concentrated on the destruction, not so much of the forces of reaction and capitalism, as of the forces of socialism and progressive liberalism. The history of Communist parties contains many instances where the forces of reaction were placated and even strengthened so that the Communists could strike at the left. To the Party's rank and file, Communism justifies such contradictions on the basis that these leftist, non-Communist movements are attempts to waylay the "labor movement" or that they are "an extension of capitalism." Such false charges leveled at the left, especially after the left has offered the popular movements all it had by way of sacrifices, inevitably create a negative reaction, often akin to a sense of emotional outrage. When the Communists plan to make themselves the only active revolutionary and progressive agents (even to the extent of suppressing leftist movements that are more sincere and radical than they are), and when their plans become manifest, a natural reaction to this great lie sets in. It soon becomes apparent that Communism pursues objectives that are diametrically opposed to the slogans the Communists bandy about. The Communist Party, it is seen, seeks to usurp power.

This strategy, which becomes progressively more obvious as the Party increases its power, is coupled with the Communists' other stratagem in time of weakness. They lie low when they are not influential and when they are trying to organize their ranks. Members of the left inevitably recall how, with a view to infiltrating the basic social scene, the Communists exploited the left's adherence to freedom and its consequent readiness to support the Communists' individual, social, and labor problems. The left then recognizes such a strategy of exploitation for what it really is and knows that, according to Communism, adherence to absolute freedom is a mere throwback from the traditional bourgeoisie and a sign of the vacillation and weakness of the non-Communist left. The left then discovers that Communism treats it on two different, contradictory levels. At certain times, and on the public level, Communism uses the left as a façade and as a mere tool for its activities. At other times, Communism treats the left as including "all honest citizens"; at still other times, it describes the left as the only enemy of the people's national and class struggles. What is important to the Communists is that the left should remain ideologically fragmented and incapable of independent revolutionary control.

When it discovers these facts, the left reacts either violently and rashly or by attempting to strengthen and clarify its own revolutionary message. In the first case, a gap appears in the left through which various nonrational elements penetrate and lead the left away from its objectives, hinder its unity, and pervert its essence. The result is that the left comes to ignore or pardon certain [conservative] policies and tendencies which are diametrically opposed to the values and the ideals for which it is working.

Owing to this often shameful acquiescence on the part of the left, traditional modes of thought have restored vitality to the forces of reaction, after the left had already challenged them vigorously and had, at various times, become capable of destroying them. It [refrained] and was set back because of emotional attitudes. This attitude also causes the left to stray from its revolutionary path and to yoke itself to a reactionary policy which tolerates it only as long as it needs to regain the energy of which the left had once deprived it. This attitude also implies that the left comes to acquiesce in Communism as the product of the socialist revolutionary tradition, despite Communism's deliberate perversion of this tradition. It also implies that the left must concentrate its energy on rectifying and combating this perversion.

This is what we meant by the left's straying from its revolutionary path. The left's reason for existence is that it should combat reaction, protect evolution, and define its nature. What is needed to protect the left from perversion is a deeper, more comprehensive commitment to the values and ideals for which it is striving, not a total preoccupation with rectifying errors and fighting Communism. This means that the left should concern itself not only with consolidating its independence, but also with strengthening its own ideological foundations. It presupposes that Communism must not be combated except in order to protect and ensure progress, i.e., to protect socialism and the advancement of the masses. It is futile to fight Communism as such if the power that is fighting it is neither positive nor revolutionary. We can go even further and maintain that persistent opposition to Communism is in fact wrong, even if it proceeds from conviction that such opposition would protect the gains of the left, since this persistence would eventually rob the left of its effective humanistic outlook and would disfigure the left precisely as the Communists are attempting to do.

It appears, therefore, that a comprehensive ideology and a total commitment to socialism are of paramount importance so that no gap may be created in the left and so that no emotionalism develops toward Communism. This emotionalism in the left breeds exhaustion and a lack of self-confidence, so that no new ideas to deal with new problems and requirements are forthcoming. It is possible that it will not lead to the ignorance of the major issues facing man, but it will certainly render the left incapable of solving these issues in a radical manner for fear that such solutions might be similar to Communist or non-Communist [i.e., rightist] solutions. At certain moments in history, this timidity has been responsible for the vacillation of the left. The left has often lost the initiative or has placed itself in a general political framework created by the reactionary regimes or has accepted liberal capitalistic standards for determining the propriety of its own revolutionary path. With the loss of the ideological and practical initiative, the masses have lost confidence in the leadership of the left. The result is that Communism has now become the punishment [the alternative solution] for the left's timidity and vacillation.

This analysis leads us to a fundamental question the answer to which may clarify the nature of the crisis in the left. The question is: Is Communism a part, or does it lies outside, of the left? The answer, very frankly, cannot be either a categorical yes or a categorical no. This is not because one is afraid of committing himself to a certain viewpoint or because it is difficult to define the left, but because, over the past few years, a certain confusion has arisen. In answering this question, we must, to begin with, clearly distinguish between Communism and Communists and, again, between Communists and Communists. To do so is sometimes rather difficult, and this is why the answer to the question cannot be categorical. Thus, the left must now define the criteria according to which certain Communists might be accepted or rejected as clearly belonging to the left. This, again, means that the left must define its own standards, which it can only do if it attains a deeper understanding of what it wants and how it can achieve it.

Communism as a philosophical doctrine and as a comprehensive outlook on life and existence emerged as a fundamental challenge in the modern world when Marx and Engels laid down its scientific foundations. To a considerable extent, therefore, the left and Communism hold common theoretical and philosophical positions. To that extent, Marxism may be considered a living part of the left. Inasmuch as Communism directly adopts fundamental Marxist theories, by that much can it be asserted that Communism is of the core of the left. But is modern Communism known to be merely Marxist or is it more? If Marxist Communism were to stand still, it would thereby be doing violence to Marxism itself. It would be closed in upon itself and would lose its vitality and its ability to develop in accordance with modern progress. Therefore, modern Communism is not merely Marxist, but is Marxist-Leninist, as the Communists themselves admit. Therefore, it is not purely Marxist but embraces the Leninist interpretation of Marxism. (Many major socialist schools of thought regard Marxism as a starting point without considering it as the end of the road.)

Thus, modern Communism has confined itself, and adhered, to the Leninist interpretation of Marxism, thereby excluding from its ideological development any other interpretations of Marxism, of some of which the left might approve. It has rejected all liberal and progressive tendencies that were not Marxist but were complementary to Marxist doctrine. This deliberate exclusion has introduced another element into Communism, namely, its wilful isolation, which has become part of Communist dogma. In confining Marxist interpretation to Lenin, despite Lenin's considerable revolutionary and ideological contribution to the development of Marxism, in excluding all other interpretations, and in making of this the measure of loyalty through strict party organization, modern Communism has been led to adopt a limited outlook on life and to become incapable of absorbing man's complex problems. Communism has now become a certain program of action whose characteristics are seclusion, blind discipline, and a separation between means and ends, both ethically and philosophically. This is a philosophical part of Communism that is influenced by Stalinism. Therefore, we find that modern Communism is the narrow Stalinist program for the implementation of Lenin's interpretation of Marx. The resolutions of the Twentieth Party Congress [of the Communist Party of the U.S.S.R.] constitute a departure from Stalinism and a step beyond the monistic interpretation of Lenin. There are certain signs pointing in that direction, but they are not sufficiently clear to allow us to assert that the present Soviet regime is a leftist society, simply because of this new urge for freedom.

Furthermore, the break with Stalinism has thrown wide open the possibility that Communism may become a vast potential of the left. Thus, we can assert that Communism in Yugoslavia has, in our view, become a part of the international left, as a result of laying itself open to progressive tendencies in the world. But Communism is, by and large, still in the grip of an ideological restlessness that places it at a crossroad. It can either revert to Stalinism or continue to open itself out. If the first path is chosen, as has recently happened in China, then Communism is outside the pale of the left. If it chooses the second path of liberation, it can become a part of the left, and then the conflicts within the left will become secondary and concerned only with side issues. This tremendous development, whose results will be very important to the future and the evolution of humanity, must be treated by the left in a manner that would enable it continuously to attract Communism to the path of liberation, despite the psychological difficulties within the ranks of both parties. It is possible that Communism will change. The manner in which this change is accomplished will determine whether or not Communism is to belong to the left.

We conclude, then, that there is a conflict raging in the international Communist movement and within the regional Communist parties. Those Communists who work from conviction to develop this freedom drive are potential members of the left. Others, who follow the Stalinist line, i.e., who assume that it is futile to interact with leftist tendencies, are decided enemies of the left and may be considered to be a part of the reactionary and nonrational elements who want to arrest the movement of history and of evolution. It may well be that political life will, in the future, consist of a struggle between a stagnant reaction and a stagnant Communism on the one hand pitted against the vital forces that work for progress. Events have proved that certain Communists are potential members of the left and that certain others are, potentially, the left's most bitter and most dedicated enemies.

If we decide that the left embraces all those who work for an ever-increasing participation of the masses in all walks of life, we shall find that the left's axis is socialism. This does not mean that modern socialism embraces the whole of the left. Furthermore, the crisis in the left in general is caused either by an absence of mature consciousness among the masses that renders them incapable of supporting leftist policies, or by an absence of cohesion and harmony among the various parties of the left.

However, our view that socialism is the axis of the left may not meet with unqualified support, even from certain quarters in the left. Some leftists claim that Communism, by being the "extreme" left and the most comprehensive and influential of the doctrines of the left, has a better title than socialism to be considered the axis of the left. But for Communism to belong to the core of the left, it must meet the basic requirements of the left. Thus, while some Communists do meet these requirements and others do not, discussion of Communism on our part will not be in the traditional manner of political commentators, which treats international Communism as a homogeneous whole.

It appears, therefore, that the basic problem facing the left is to define the relations between Communism and socialism in general. We have maintained above that the leftist, and especially the socialist, attitude must rid itself of two complexes as regards Communism. The first is the inferiority complex and the second is emotionalism. But freeing the left from these complexes is not sufficient: It is far more important to clarify, in a comprehensive manner, the left's theoretical and practical position as regards Communism. This is not to deny that there are other problems concerning the relations between socialism and the progressive and national freedom movements that still need clarification and settlement, but, compared to the major problem, such issues are secondary. In addition, the problem of the relationship between socialism and the liberals and radicals, in general, is to some extent determined by the problem of the relationship between socialism and Communism.

28. LITERARY SCHOOLS AND SOCIALIST LITERATURE*

Louis 'Awad

Louis 'Awad (b. 1915), a leading Egyptian intellectual, is codirector of the Arab Encyclopaedia, *literary critic of* al-Ahram, *and professor at the Institute of Advanced Arab Studies. He studied at Oxford and received a Ph.D. degree from Princeton University. He was professor of English literature at the University of Cairo and served in the United Nations. He is the author of about a dozen works, in both English and Arabic, dealing primarily with literature. 'Awad has participated intensively in Egyptian ideological movements, chiefly as a socialist. Although he cannot be considered a Communist or even a dogmatist of the left, he has been jailed for subversive activities. He was one of the victims of the 1959 purge, but he was soon released and rehabilitated. 'Awad's views on literature, many of which were disseminated for years in the literary sections of two Cairo newspapers,* al-Jumhuriyya *and* al-Ahram, *were of considerable importance in molding the literary skill and taste of the new generation of writers in Egypt and even in the rest of the Arab world. If one considers the vital role played by literature in shaping the political and social attitudes of the Middle Eastern intelligentsia, then the political role of literature becomes self-evident.*

Eight years have now passed since *al-Jumhuriyya* first asked me to take charge of its literary section. The motto that I chose for this section, "Literature in the Service of Life," continued to appear for six months. When my university teaching took me away from the literary section, this motto was removed and the section drifted in a direction that I cannot really describe, since it was unlike any school of thought or any literary genre I know of. The removal of this motto was not unexpected, since the idea of linking literature to life was damaging to certain people, some of whom were very honest and others not. Some men openly declared, while others murmured under their breath, that the literary section of *al-Jumhuriyya* was pressing culture and literature into the service of socialism.

And here we are, eight years later, marching forward into socialism and asking ourselves the same old questions: What is the role of literature in a socialist society, and what are its relation to life and its objectives? Then, again, we ask ourselves a no less important question, namely, what are the constituent

* Extract from Louis 'Awad, *al-Ishtirakiyya wa-al-adab wa-maqalat ukhra* (*Socialism and Literature and Other Articles*) (Beirut: Dar al-Adab, 1963), pp. 7–15, 21, 55–60.

elements of this literature and how do we protect socialist literature from both friend and foe, since an ignorant friend may prove more dangerous than a rational foe? Thus, we find ourselves compelled to reopen the controversy centering around two schools of art, literature, and thought commonly summarized in the two phrases, "art for art's sake" and "art for the sake of life." Accordingly, there will also be a conflict between "literature for its own sake" and "literature for the sake of life," between "knowledge for its own sake" and "knowledge for the sake of life," and between "thought for its own sake" and "thought for the sake of life." We shall also find ourselves compelled to study literature and socialism in the light both of human experience and of our own. For I maintain that we must study literature and socialism in the light of the experience of other human societies before we turn to study our own literature and society, for the simple reason that this experience has been more profound and more challenging in certain other countries than in our own. Ours is a society that has recently adopted socialism, both in theory and in practice. It would therefore be valuable to study how and why other societies faced the problems of "art for art's sake" and "art for the sake of life," etc. We can then profit from the results they achieved and avoid the pitfalls.

I myself have always preferred that literature be for the sake of life rather than for the sake of society, not because I despised society or because I sought obscurity in some abstract notion like "life," but because I felt life to be an altogether more comprehensive term than society. Life embraces both society and the individual, and it would be wrong to discard the individual from any social philosophy we might construct, either theoretically or in practice. Whereas it would be most beneficial to allot to human thought its natural place in society in such a way that the individual would not forsake his individuality, the part would not leave the whole, and his legitimate sphere would not be forsaken, causing damage to society.

It would be preferable to hold literature, art, knowledge, and culture to be in the service of life rather than of society, since society is normally understood to be a palpable entity, possessing certain palpable material relations and values, whereas life implies the whole of existence, both soul and spirit, matter and thought, members and functions. Finally, it would be preferable to hold this view of art and literature because the term "society" usually implies a certain society limited in time and place, whereas life is boundless and is a flowing stream that takes one into past, present, and future. The term "life," therefore, embraces all societies, both national societies in particular and human society in general.

Thus, in calling for literature to be for the sake of life, we are advocating something that is both national and human, both material and spiritual (since literature becomes a function of both material and spiritual life), both social and individual (since literature becomes a function of both society and the individual).

This, in my opinion, is the core of our socialism, which can and must be broad enough to embrace all these values and fields. Had our socialism been a merely national one, lacking in humanity, it would have been Fascist or Nazi. Again, had our socialism been an international one, lacking in nationalism, it would have been one of those anarchist illusions brilliantly contrived by Jewish thinkers, who, perhaps, deliberately fabricate them in order to destroy nationalisms. Had our socialism been materialist in means and ends, lacking in thought and idealism, our society would have been distorted. Had our socialism been a mere spiritual vision, incapable of facing the demands of material life, it would have been like a sumptuous palace built upon sand. Again, had our socialism been a comprehensive, tightly knit system that is collective and hostile to individuality, we would have reverted to the life of bees and ants. Had our socialism been mere ink on paper and an empty slogan to drug the populace but permitting the individual to do exactly what he wants, it would have been impossible for the public sector, i.e., public ownership and services, to stand as a barrier against the re-emergence of individual exploitation.

Our socialism, then, does and must embrace all these meanings. From amid these contradictions, harmony must be established so that life can become richer. The economy has been stabilized upon the principle of public ownership, where individuality is not done away with and where private ownership is respected so long as it does not harm society. This is what makes our socialism a humanist creed that serves the individual and the society, spiritual and material life—past, present, and future.

Socialism as we understand it, then, is a humanist creed, and socialist literature is humanist literature. "Literature for the sake of life" and "literature for the sake of humanity" are synonymous.

This socialist humanist literature is threatened by two dangers: the danger of the worship of the individual and of the worship of the group. If we permit ourselves to benefit from the experiences of others, we would know that the worship of the individual in the cultural sphere is represented by the school of thought that upholds art, knowledge, literature, and even religion "for their own sake." The worship of the group is represented in the various materialist and idealist schools of thought which view literature, art, and knowledge as mere tools for the service of spiritual life alone.

The danger in these schools of thought is that they oversimplify life and sever the genuine bond between spirit and matter, the perfect and the existent, form and content, the ideal and the real in life.

World literature experienced this disjunction at its most acute in the nineteenth century with the appearance of the theory of art for art's sake. When Oscar Wilde, for example, wrote in *The Picture of Dorian Gray* that "the artist is the creator of beautiful things," he made beauty the sole criterion of art, thus depriving art of its content and rendering it a mere form. If we carry this to its logical conclusion, we shall have to assert that if an author has an elegant style, there will be no need for us to examine what he has written or to determine whether it is genuine or false, honest or corrupt, progressive or reactionary, civilized or degraded, human or bestial—so long as what he has written gives us pleasure. That is precisely the view of the famous critic

Walter Pater, who writes in his book *The Renaissance,* that to regard all things and principles of things as inconstant modes or fashions has more and more become the tendency of modern thought . . . , and that the service of philosophy, of speculative culture, toward the human spirit is to rouse, to startle it into sharp and eager observation. Every moment some form grows perfect in hand or face; some tone on the hills or the sea is choicer than the rest; some mood of passion or insight or intellectual excitement is irresistibly real and attractive for us—for that moment only. Not the fruit of experience, but experience itself is the end. . . .

Such a view of art and literature makes of them something akin to the sexual thrill that is sought for its own sake. It is tantamount to our saying that the end of love or marriage is not their product but their thrill. In this way, artistic experience, whether in the artist or in the person who receives his art, becomes merely a beautiful excitement, desired for its own sake and caused either by the beauty of the picture or the enjoyment of the experience. This is, in fact, an advanced form of hedonism or the apprehension of beauty through the senses. Indeed, the term "hedonism" aptly fits those worshipers of beauty. Oscar Wilde's theory that beauty is art's only justification is manifest in the following: "Those who perceive ugliness in beautiful things are degenerate. But their degeneration has no magic, and this is shameful. Those who perceive beauty in beautiful things are cultured and full of promise. They are the pure ones who see only beauty in beautiful things," or in another saying, "There is no such thing as a moral or an immoral book. Books are well written or badly written," or in his statement that "All art is useless."

The "art for art's sake" school began in the nineteenth century as an outspoken and somewhat pompous attack against the predominance of "art for the sake of morals" school, and of the "literature of a message" movement, or what we now call the literature of commitment. The trouble with all these literary schools is that they simplify the meaning of art to the point of naïveté, making the content of art take precedence over its form. Some schools went so far as to exploit art quite openly for the purpose of preaching or of instructing the workers in religion, in their struggle to win their rights. This we find in the novels of Charles Kingsley and others, commonly called the Christian Socialist school, which flourished around the middle of the last century.

But the art for art's sake school went too far in the opposite direction in calling for the worship of beauty. It did not merely divest art of all ethical and social content but divested it also of all that did not arouse a feeling for beauty in man. In so doing, it created a new tyranny, the tyranny of form with which to combat the obsession with content or make-up. The basic error of this school is precisely the error of any school of art that simplifies art to the point of naïveté by separating the picture from the content. Thus, the art for art's sake school isolated literature from society, morality, and all the sublime, deep, and permanent constituents of life. It claimed that art was a sovereign territory where beauty formed the only authority—a territory with no boundaries and no laws except what is framed by beauty. In such a territory, the final end was pleasure or happiness, which are of course certain goals in life. But to maintain that they are the only or the final objectives of life is to make of life something vapid that does not deserve to be lived.

This "expressionist" school, as it is sometimes called, was followed by the "impressionists" toward the end of the last and the beginning of the present century. We gain an insight into the views of this school by paraphrasing the words of one of its leading exponents, the eminent American critic Joel Spingarn, in his book *Creative Criticism and Other Essays:* that the function of criticism as regards the impressionist critic is to feel certain sensations when receiving a work of art and to express these sensations and his own point of view. . . .

In the same context, Spingarn claims that the critic, in reviewing the life of a poet or discussing his social environment, is exceeding his mandate as a critic and would be considered an historian or sociologist. These views of Spingarn, the apostle of the impressionist school, effectively isolate art from the essential features of individual and social life, that is, the most basic elements of human life. Nothing of value would remain from a work of art save the sensations aroused in reader or spectator. As for the deep significance of human life, the consciousness, the contemplation, the ethical insight, the knowledge, the purification of emotions, the power of faith—all these things find no place in the impressionist doctrine. Impressionist criticism prevents us from explaining artistic creation in the light of the lives of its creators or of the age in which they were created, as if a work of art is born in total vacuum or as if it is the product of a mere moment's sensation experienced by the artist. Furthermore, the art for art's sake school worships beauty. The impressionist school worships sensations. If the first school is hedonistic because it puts beauty before any other artistic value, the second school is doubly so, because it places sensations before any other value. Even beauty itself would become, not an absolute value as it was in the past, but something which cannot be measured except through sensation. This latter is a supremely individual state, which often differs from one person to another, depending upon the environment, the culture, and the preparation of each person and, even, the moment when the work of art is received. After a heavy meal or during a hangover either from alcohol or from love, a man may feel suffocated by a poem, a story, or a picture created by a great artist and may be more receptive to something that suits his own condition. The art for art's sake school can, in searching for beauty, conform to certain objective definitions, norms, and criteria distilled from the experience of humanity throughout the ages. When Oscar Wilde wrote, "The aim of art is to reveal the art and conceal the artist," he had in mind the objectivity of art and of its laws. He was indeed warning against personal art which reveals and expresses the artist's personality, views, sensations, and aims. In impressionist art, the whole emphasis is upon the image of the world as impressed on the consciousness and sensations of the artist. It describes the world as the artist, not as other people, sees it. This, in fact, amounts to an outright rejection of all norms and laws coming from without. Reality exists only as perceived by the artist, or, rather, as apprehended by his sensations. Everything is molded and colored in accordance with the artist's apprehension. Nothing remains except the self, each separate from the others, which provides the only window upon the world. According to this impressionist philosophy, the individual is the center of the universe and the measure of all things. Everything, including human existence itself, is only a field for the experiments of the impressionist artist.

These, then, are two examples of schools of literature and art that are hostile to socialism. The art for art's sake school is hostile to socialism because it isolates the artist from life and society, separates the content of art from its form, and erects above human society a sovereign territory which is the absolute territory of beauty.

The impressionist school is hostile to socialism because it is an excessively individualistic school, which makes of a man's sensations the measure of all things in art, life, and society, rejecting in the process all values and all norms that do not proceed from the artist's own self.

These schools are antisocialist because the starting point of any socialist literature, art, science, culture, and even religion is the acceptance of the "objectivity" of humanity. It must be admitted that the pursuit of literature, art, science, culture, and religion for their own sakes is a myth that may sometimes be useful but is in fact the product of a disjunction in life, and of the genius of the human mind whenever it wishes to disclaim its responsibilities toward life and humanity. . . .

The humanist school is opposed to socialism. It supports the cause of science, industry, democracy, and freedom, while holding the people's rights in contempt under the pretext of protecting the human heritage and the stable values of society. The solution proposed by the humanist school to surmount the crisis of bourgeois civilization, which first appeared toward the end of the last century, is one that is opposed to a socialist philosophy with human roots. This is because humanism calls for the unconditional acceptance of [certain] social, ideological, and artistic bonds, defining will as the will . . . to submit to these bonds. On the other hand, socialist philosophy, humanly interpreted, far from attacking knowledge, asks for more. It does not despair of knowledge because of its tyranny or its abuses but requires knowledge to serve humanity and be a boundless field used by man for the exploration of himself and the universe, to the end that humanity might progress, both materially and morally. Far from attacking freedom and democracy, socialist philosophy desires their increase throughout the world and for all classes of men. It is not content with theoretical freedom and democracy or the purely legalistic and formal rights of man, which were all introduced by the bourgeoisie in their revolt against absolute monarchies and feudalism. Rather, it considers them to be certain gains made by humanity on its long path to achieve complete equality and brotherhood among men. Socialism seeks to attain a more profound sense of freedom, democracy, and the rights of man by providing the masses with the material and economic guarantees necesary for the safeguarding of these values. Far from denying individualism and the independent existence, behavior, and will of each person, socialist philosophy seeks to spread this individualism and this independence among the masses, where previously they were confined to a small segment of society. In placing the rights and independence of the group before those of the individual, humanitarian socialism is not deprecating the rights and independence of the individual but is doing so merely on a temporary basis, until the masses have rid themselves of the whims of individual men and until individualism has been diffused among all members of society. . . .

We have reviewed the attitudes of the various postsocialist schools of art and literature in order to determine where they stand vis-à-vis socialism and how they might fit into the socialist society. We have found that these schools are of two kinds: idealist and materialist. The most important of the first type are the art for art's sake school, the impressionists, the new humanists or literary humanists, the neoclassical or Catholic revivalists, the various schools of the unconscious, and the existentialists. The most important of the second type are the literature of commitment school, the social realists, and the material or economic determinists. We have seen that the idealists and the materialists are either openly opposed to socialism or are antisocialists by reason of their limited appeal.

We shall now attempt to determine the attitude of socialism toward all these schools and shall try to answer the following questions: Is there a socialist literature? What are the boundaries of this literature? Do all these various schools have a place in socialist society? What is the attitude of socialism and socialist society to these schools?

I do not pretend that my answers will be definitive and conclusive, precluding any further discussion of the relationship between socialism and literature. Nor do I claim that it would be a good thing for socialism or literature to try and discover such a conclusive and definitive answer, since any answer that pretends to be definitive would, in reality, be naïve and may impose a kind of ideological dogmatism on art and life.

Therefore, I maintain that:

1. The starting point in any discussion about the nature, role, and aim of literature in a healthy socialist society is that socialism is, first and foremost, a human ideal. Its most important characteristics, therefore, are a tolerant spirit and a comprehensive outlook. Genuine socialism is free from dogmatism and from doctrinaire policies. It accepts any advancement of man's humanity, even if this is achieved in a manner different from its own. As an enlightened and human message, socialism believes that the strengthening of man's humanity is its prime objective and recognizes that this is to be achieved in stages. It disclaims for itself what others have claimed, namely, that theirs is the perfect and final word on human ideology and organization. It sees itself as a mere advance of humanity toward its sublime ideal.

2. Given this starting point, the attitude of socialism toward the heritage of humanity, past, present, and future, has been revealed. True socialism is based upon "the great recognition" and not upon "the great refusal." This recognition does not mean blind adoption. Socialism recognizes the heritage of the past, the present, and the future, and all that satisfies man's thirst for justice, virtue, and beauty. It accepts everything that underlines man's right to these ideals and that translates these ideals into the realm of practical life on

the widest possible scale. True socialism recognizes every serious contribution of art, thought, and literature, irrespective of the contradicting positions of the schools concerned. It recognizes the philosophies of idealism, materialism, individualism, and collectivism; the classical and the Augustan, the romantic and the symbolist, the realist and the surrealist, the rationalist and the imaginative. It recognizes the great human heritage with all its contradictions, because it considers that progress can be effected only by resolving these contradictions and merging them into a harmonious synthesis which is superior to its constituent elements. It believes the starting point for resolving life's contradictions to be, first, their acceptance and, then, their merger. It feels that the nonacceptance of these contradictions would be tantamount to a "great refusal," which can lead only to a suicidal and antihuman mentality. Genuine socialism is an enemy of death and a friend of life—not the life of one particular generation, class, or civilization, but of man whenever and wherever he exists.

3. Genuine socialist philosophy is based upon the great recognition, and not upon the great refusal. It views every school of thought, art, and literature as a positive and creative aspect of the heritage of humanity—this positive aspect being the criticism of life. It regards idealism as a critique of materialism and vice versa, individualism as a critique of collectivism and vice versa. Form is seen as a warning against the danger of content, and content is seen as a warning against the danger of form. True socialism, therefore, considers every serious school of art, literature, and thought to be a valid criticism of life and regards the criticism of life as a prerequisite for its growth and development. Progress can be achieved only through criticism, which separates the seeds of life from the seeds of death.

4. The great recognition does not mean acceptance and the great refusal does not imply mere rejection. If genuine socialism is based upon the "great recognition" of the whole heritage of humanity, this does not entail the acceptance of the whole heritage. Socialism realizes that many schools of thought, art, and literature are in the grip of a crisis so that they see nothing but themselves and build themselves upon the destruction of others. Socialism recognizes the value of these schools insofar as they constitute a critique of life, but it rejects them of necessity insofar they are a way of life. Socialism recognizes idealism as a critique of materialism but rejects it as the key to existence. The same is true with respect to materialism, classicism, romanticism, symbolism, realism, surrealism, and transcendentalism; to individualism, collectivism, rationalism, irrationalism, subjectivism, objectivism, formalism, commitment, noncommitment, existentialism, and nihilism. This is true of any "ism" or any narrow doctrinaire movement that claims to be the magical remedy for the ills of humanity. The truth is that the real source of the ills of humanity is that chronic dogmatism which impedes the growth of life, and the "great refusal" of anything which does not serve the self. True socialism rejects nothing except this great refusal. It may indeed reject all these schools of thought insofar as they constitute partial solutions to the human condition, but it accepts them insofar as they are a critique of life.

5. Genuine socialism feels that the main danger of these schools of thought,

art, and literature lies in this separation between subject and object, form and content, thought and mind, principle and practice, function and functionary, means and ends. It considers thought, art, literature, and everything in life to be at its best whenever a total synthesis of these elements is made, so that no distinction can be drawn between ideal and material. This perfection of thought, art, and literature which baffles critics has no other explanation except this perfect homogeneity of these incomplete elements or, rather, this synthesis of the ideal and the material. The words "evil" and "imperfection" were coined by men to describe this gulf between subject and object. Death denotes a total and irrevocable disjunction of spirit and matter.

True socialism accepts the thought, art, literature, and ethics where perfection can be attained through a synthesis. Thereafter, no discussion of schools and ideologies would be possible, since these would form only parts of life. Discussion would then revolve around human thought, art, literature, society, and civilization.

Thus, socialism, recognizing that "evil" and "imperfection" are manifestations of this disjunction, emphasizes every value that seeks to dissolve life's contradictions into a greater whole.

6. Socialism as a social doctrine, clearly defined in time and place, may adopt certain currents of thought, art, and literature that may serve its direct purposes and be relevant to its own circumstances. In this manner, socialist thought, art, and literature may come into existence. As a human ideal, however, socialism recognizes the dangers of a narrow doctrinaire outlook or of what we have termed the great refusal. It considers its art, literature, and thought, insofar as they are partial and are the product of the contradictions of life, to be dependent upon its own victory and fulfillment. When socialism is triumphant, humanity will draw nearer to unity and cohesion. Thereafter, there will be no aristocratic, bourgeois, or proletarian thought, art, or literature. One thing will remain: the human.

7. Art for art's sake, literature, knowledge, justice, and virtue for their own sakes—all these are myths created by idealists to protect themselves from the onslaught of the materialists. Similarly, art for the sake of society, the literature and the art of commitment—these are all myths created by the materialists to protect themselves from the onslaught of the idealists. Both myths are born out of a deep sense of cleavage between spirit and matter, subject and object, the whole and the part, the permanent and the temporary, i.e., they originate from a disregard of the unity of existence. No thought and no deed on earth has ever been done solely for its own sake. No thought and no action has ever been done with itself as it own end. Everything on earth, all thought and all action, must be done for the sake of man and of humanity as a whole. True socialism believes that any art, thought, or literature that does not emanate from and end in man is sterile. But it also believes that the real man from whom they emanate, and the perfect man to whom they aspire, is a man who represents the unity of existence.

VII. *Socialism in the Doctrine of the Ba'th*

29. THE SOCIALIST IDEOLOGY OF THE BA'TH*

Michel 'Aflaq

Michel 'Aflaq is a co-founder (with Salah al-Din Bitar) of the Ba'th al-'arabi al-ishtiraki *(Arab Socialist Resurrection) movement. As both a theory and a political organization, the Ba'th has played a crucial part in the contemporary history of the Arab world, particularly in Syria, Lebanon, and Iraq.*

'Aflaq was born in Damascus in 1912, to a Greek Orthodox Arab family that dealt in grain. He studied in Paris, where he became a Communist, but after he returned to Syria and became a secondary school teacher he turned against Communism. Unlike most other Arab politicians, 'Aflaq was an ineffective public speaker, yet he early achieved great popularity among Arab intellectuals. He was almost ascetic in his living habits, and he generally refused to accept high office. 'Aflaq's early success, and that of the Ba'th generally, stemmed chiefly from the timing of the movement and its ability to place within an ideological framework the major problems facing Syria and the Arab world.

The Ba'th was launched in 1940. It emerged into the open in 1943, when Syria gained formal independence, began publishing the journal al-Ba'th *in 1946, and held its first congress in 1947. Those years corresponded to Syria's gaining of independence and its attempts to devise for itself a new role and a new identity within the Arab world. The nationalist currents that had developed in Syria since the turn of the century made it clear that Syria would become a fountainhead of the Arab renaissance and a natural leader in future developments.*

Syria's economy—a fairly balanced one—was dominated by an urban commercial middle class in which Christian groups occupied a large place, although they made up only 14 per cent of the total population. This trade-oriented economy seemed unsuited, by both mentality and organization, to meet the immediate problems of mass economic development and extended

* The first excerpt in this work dealing with a general definition of Ba'th's socialist ideology and its differences from other types of leftist and rightist socialisms is taken from Michel 'Aflaq, *Fi sabil al-ba'th* (*For the Sake of the Ba'th*) (Beirut: Dar al-tali'a li al-tiba'a wa-al-nashr, 1959), pp. 96–100. The sections dealing with Islam, capitalism, and class struggle are taken (titles slightly altered) from a new edition of the same work (2d ed.; Beirut: Dar al-tali'a li al-tiba'a wa-al-nashr, 1963), pp. 122–24, 135–36, 219–23.

social welfare posed by conditions after World War II. Divided into various religious groups, subgroups, and national minorities, and without well-defined natural boundaries, Syria lacked the conditions necessary for establishing strong internal unity. The large investment in land undertaken by business groups after the war was initially successful in increasing agricultural production, but socially and politically it proved to be a liability because it led to sharper differences in wealth. These conditions provided fertile ground for the emergence of socialist ideas in the form of reformist measures as early as March, 1949, when Colonel Husni Za'im led a coup and took over the government. The next dictator, Adib Shishakly, opposed Syria's union with Iraq in a kingdom, launched a series of development measures and worked closely for a time with Akram Hawrani and his Socialist Party, which was founded in 1950. Private enterprise was still recognized as the chief element of the economy. Deteriorating relations with the West and the struggle within Syria between small but dynamic leftist and rightist groups striving to dominate a large but unorganized conservative center led to economic stagnation and, at the same time, increased demands for economic reorganization. The rapprochement *with the U.S.S.R., which was greatly accelerated by the French-British-Israeli attack on Egypt in 1956, led to the public expression of pro-leftist sentiments.*

Alongside these developments was the political mobilization of the lower classes, as well as an increased sense of economic and social expectation, which seemingly could be fulfilled more easily by a revolutionary regime. The Ba'th's fortunes and ideology closely followed these developments. The nationalism preached by 'Aflaq adopted social goals, which were generally defined as socialism.

Meanwhile, 'Aflaq had overcome the most difficult ideological hurdle—the definition of Islam's place and role in his nationalist theory. Almost from their very beginnings in the 1920's, the nationalist movements in Syria and Lebanon had two major aspects that were in fact contradictory. One nationalist current, backed somewhat by popular groups, envisaged nationalism mainly in Islamic terms, but many intellectuals seemed to lean toward a secular nationalism and thus were able to soothe the fears of the Christian Arabs, who were afraid of being absorbed in a state that had a huge Muslim majority. Another nationalist current, promoted chiefly by Lebanese Christians, defended the idea of an independent state protected by European powers.

As early as 1943, 'Aflaq had described Islam as part of the foundation of Arabism and a response to the Arab soul's permanent search for noble and higher spiritual pursuits. True, 'Aflaq had taken religion out of the narrow limits of orthodoxy, but at the same time he indicated that Muhammad and Islam expressed the best of Arabism and helped recast the Arab society into a new form. Consequently, the relation of Arab nationalism to Islam was unique, and Islam could be considered, even by Christian Arabs, a national culture. This interesting view was in part a preparation for further identifying Islam with Arab nationalism and thus removing the popular distrust shown by the masses toward secular nationalism and secular socialism. The distrust naturally was toward socialist theory itself and not toward its fruits. In expressing his views on socialism, however, 'Aflaq seemed to be far more secularist than he might have intended. The constitution of the Ba'th Party, after introducing sweeping nationalist principles (one Arab nation forming an indivisible political-economic-cultural entity with an eternal misson of renewing human values and increasing progress and harmony), defines its economic and social policy. This policy aims at achieving social justice through redistribution of wealth and nationalization of industries, participation by workers in management of industries, limitation of land and industrial ownership, and economic development. The Ba'th constitution unequivocally proposes measures to control the economy through state intervention, but it is too general in its plans for development. Yet, the great service rendered by Islam to Arabism in the past could not be repeated in the twentieth century since the problems challenging Syria were not essentially religious but political and social. The measures in the social and political fields were envisaged strictly in secular terms and this in practice was a radical departure from the spirit of Islam and its socio-economic concepts. Thus, in the last few years—that is to say, since the Ba'th's coming to power—'Aflaq and the Ba'th in general have often been described as godless and as enemies of religion. The Ba'th's nationalism gave a dominant place to the state, which, by necessity, was to be limited to a small ruling group backed chiefly by the military. This became an elite group without popular roots.

In the political field, 'Aflaq's ideal of Arab unity made the Ba'th appear as its natural instrument and Syria as its center. The union with Egypt in 1958 collapsed in 1961, and the second union undertaken with Iraq and Egypt in 1963 remains so far on paper. The chief cause for the failure of the union was Ba'th's insistence on preserving its organization and freedom of activity and its implicit refusal to surrender completely to Egypt Syria's potential leadership of the Arab world, even though Egypt seemed to be politically more capable of achieving unity.

Moreover, the activities of 'Aflaq and of the Ba'th Party in Syria, leading to the latter's accession to power in 1958 and 1963, did not appear as a process of assimilation of other groups but as a twisted maneuver to subdue and eliminate parties and groups that disagreed with the Ba'th.

In the elections of 1949, the Ba'th had suffered a heavy defeat, and in 1953 it had united with Akram Hawrani's Arab Socialist Party; in 1954–55, it had begun to collaborate with the army and had entered the government by assuming some ministerial positions. The Ba'th finally succeeded in eliminating Antun Saadeh's Syrian Social Nationalist Party, and then collaborated with the Communists, spreading its control over the press and the government. After it had eliminated the conservatives, the Ba'th was threatened by the Communists, whose well-knit organization and ideology proved to be far stronger than anything the Ba'th had to offer. Having destroyed the regime's democratic, constitutional bases, despite lip service to a democratic system in its constitution, the Ba'th appeared unable to control the government or to find popular support. Consequently, it engineered the union with Egypt in

1958, lest the Communists take over. But the party then did its best to undermine the union. The zenith of the Ba'th's and of 'Aflaq's popularity came in 1963, when the Ba'thist wing of the military in Iraq acquired power. But the Ba'thist National Command, established over parties in both Syria and Iraq, was torn apart by successive coups led by officers in each country. The records of union talks with Egypt in 1963 reflect a rather dismal picture of 'Aflaq's and of the Ba'th's intellectual theories. (Sections of the minutes are reproduced on pp. 275–94, below.) The popularity of both 'Aflaq and the Ba'th seem to be declining rapidly. Their ideas have failed to meet the test of time and of practicality. 'Aflaq is no longer consulted on all important matters, and although the group in power in Syria calls itself Ba'thist, in reality it has come to be confined to the military. It may be that the Ba'th era is over.

'Aflaq and his party have helped speed up the social and political synthesis in the Fertile Crescent. They have mobilized the masses for nationalism, socialism, and unity. They have removed the barriers that outwardly seemed opposed to the materialization of these goals, but they were unable to create a new system based on these theories. The middle classes were destroyed in Syria, and the country's economic development came to a standstill; in international politics Syria's role was minimal. Thus, the ground was prepared for a regime that could offer a clear, practical, enforceable socialism and nationalism. Since the Communists had failed to achieve power, the field was wide open for Nasser's pragmatic, eclectic socialism and, hence, for unity on Egyptian terms. Many intellectuals who supported 'Aflaq and the Ba'th Party in general seem to have come to the conclusion that Nasser and his brand of socialism were the immediate and only alternatives for achieving rapidly the present ideals of the Arab intelligentsia.

The Harakat al-qawm al-'arabi (Arab Nationalist Movement) operating in all Arab countries of the Fertile Crescent is gaining the support of former Ba'thist intellectuals and is struggling to achieve a socialist Arabism based on the model of Egypt and possibly under Nasser's leadership.

'Aflaq and the Ba'th in general have received great attention in the West. An extensive treatment within the general framework of politics is Gordon H. Torrey, Syrian Politics and the Military, 1945–1958 (Columbus, Ohio: Ohio State University Press, 1964). Partial treatment is given in Leonard Binder, The Ideological Revolution in the Middle East (New York: John Wiley & Sons, 1964), pp. 156–92; in Nicola A. Ziadeh (Ziyada), Syria and Lebanon (London: Ernest Benn; New York: Frederick A. Praeger, 1957); and in Muhammad Shafi' Agawni, "The Ba'th: A Study in Contemporary Arab Politics," International Studies, III (1961–62), 6–24 (reprinted in Benjamin Rivlin and Joseph S. Szyliowicz [eds.], The Contemporary Middle East: Tradition and Innovation [New York: Random House, 1964], pp. 452–60). The constitution of the Ba'th Party is printed in Middle East Journal, XIII (Spring, 1959), 195–200, with corrections in Middle East Journal, XIII (Autumn, 1959), 487–89. It also appears in Sylvia G. Haim (ed.), Arab Nationalism: An Anthology (Berkeley, Calif.: University of California Press, 1962), pp. 233–41. The latter *includes a passage from 'Aflaq's writings. See also Jubran Majdalani, "The Arab Socialist Movement," in Walter Z. Laqueur (ed.),* The Middle East in Transition *(London: Routledge & Kegan Paul; New York: Frederick A. Praeger, 1958), pp. 337–50; and Kamel S. Abu Jaber,* The Arab Ba'th Socialist Party: History, Ideology, and Organization *(Syracuse, N.Y.: Syracuse University Press, 1966). The latter is a comprehensive study with relevant bibliography.*

After a period of internal strife in which the military acquired power, the Ba'th issued a provisional constitution in 1964. Syria was proclaimed a democratic people's socialist republic as part of the Arab fatherland. The head of state was to be a Muslim. All means of production were to be collectively owned. See Hisham B. Sharabi, Nationalism and Revolution in the Arab World *(Princeton, N.J.: D. Van Nostrand Company, 1966), p. 161. Extracts from Ba'th ideology may be found on pp. 111–12, 135–39. See also Gordon H. Torrey, "Arab Socialism," in J. H. Thompson and R. D. Reischauer (eds.),* Modernization of the Arab World *(Princeton, N.J.: D. Van Nostrand Company, 1966), pp. 178–96.*

'Aflaq's chief writings have been published under the title Fi sabil al-Ba'th. *A general statement on Ba'th ideology and socialism may be found in a joint work by Michel 'Aflaq, Akram Hawrani, Munif al-Razzaz, and Jamal al-Atasi,* Hawl al-qawmiyya wa-al-ishtirakiyya (On Nationalism and Socialism) *(Cairo: al-Matba'a al-'alamiyya, 1957). Seven volumes published in Beirut by the Syrian Government—*Nidal al-Ba'th fi sabil al-wahda al-huriyya wa-al-ishtirakiyya (The Struggle of the Ba'th for the Sake of Unity, Freedom, and Socialism) *(Beirut: Dar al-tali'a, 1963–65)—cover the period from 1943 onward. These books contain party communications and declarations and speeches by leaders and are excellent primary sources.*

1. The Philosophy of the Ba'th and Its Differences from Communism and National Socialism

The Arab Ba'th is a unique movement that undertakes neither to disguise problems nor to treat them superficially; it sees itself as reflecting the soul of the nation and her various needs. When we say that this revolutionary movement must first of all forge the essence of the nation and rekindle in the Arab personality its strength to fight and to shoulder the responsibilities of life, we also have in mind the recovery by Arab thought of its aptitude for seeing things directly, freely, without artifice or imitation. Arab thought will then be in line with the laws of nature and of life; it will be able to understand problems in their true perspective and organize its work in a creative manner. In saying this, we have in view our great mission which is to lead the Arabs, individually and collectively, toward this healthy state of thought and mind.

To philosophize on the society of tomorrow is contrary to our ideas. What we are trying to do is to forge a society that will find within itself its means of existence and elements of survival. It is hardly necessary to be a great prophet to predict that certain unchanging and tangible facts such as socialism compel our attention. The Arab nation is socialist and one cannot conceive of a healthy society within this nation without socialism. Ba'th socialism is in perfect accord with present Arab society, a society whose past, present, and future are linked to the soil. This uncompromising and courageous socialism differs from the socialist name and label behind which the leaders and politicians shelter.

Theoretical Differences Between Our Socialism and That of the Communists

Socialism in the Communist system is not limited only to the organization of the economy; it must obey the ends and aims of the Communist system. Communism, as a universal doctrine, aims in effect at world-wide revolution and can only henceforth be applied if this revolution is an entire success. On the other hand, as long as the revolution is not at an end, the economic system of a Communist country will remain subject to the aims and directives of the policy of the Communist movement, including preparation for war and competition with other countries. It is for this reason that Tito was considered a defector from objective Communism because he did not agree that Yugoslavia should be made to serve the general aim of world revolution. Tito refused to submit the production and resources of his country to a Communist general policy under the direction of Moscow.

Arab Ba'th socialism, on the contrary, limits itself to organizing the economy so as to redistribute the wealth of the Arab world and to establish a basis for an economy guaranteeing justice and equality among all citizens, and also to promote a revolution in production and the means of production.

Communist socialism is impregnated with Communist philosophy. This philosophy emanates from a specific group with its own particular requirements, characteristics, and conditions. Our socialism is impregnated with our philosophy. This philosophy emanates from an Arab group with its own special needs, its own historical conditions and characteristics.

Communist philosophy is based on belief and materialism. It explains historical and social evolution solely and wholly by economic factors, which results in its changing its philosophy and spiritual beliefs. The philosophy of the Arab Ba'th does not agree with this materialistic conception. On the contrary, it considers that the "spiritual" factor plays a very important part in the evolution of history and human progress. Consequently, it considers that the spiritual influences that have appeared in the Arab world, such as Islam, are in no way strange.

Being materialistic, Communist philosophy accords only little importance to the individual; it does not respect him and it scorns his freedom. It is concerned only with the mass. This conception leads to dictatorship and the creation of a materialistic society completely lacking in spirit. This philosophy similarly results in a lack of balance between the individual and society and between Arab societies and others. Our socialism, on the contrary, is based on the individual and his personal freedom; it does not allow his individual liberties to be scorned and considers all individuals as equal and a tyrannical dictatorship unnecessary.

Practical Differences Between Our Socialism and That of the Communists

Communist socialism has gone too far in the direction of nationalization; it has abolished property rights and consequently has killed all individual initiative. Ba'th socialism, on the contrary, believes that the main strength of a nation resides in individual initiative which encourages action; it is careful not to abolish private property, therefore limiting itself to the creation of strong impediments to abuse.

Communism does not recognize the right of succession. Our socialism, on the contrary, recognizes it and believes that a citizen cannot be deprived of it. Nevertheless, to prevent the wrongful use of the national wealth and the exploitation of labor, we have imposed certain changes that make this right in certain cases almost theoretical and that reduce it in other cases to a simple moral right.

Criticisms of Communism

Communist socialism is limited. It is based, in effect, on an economic philosophy, Marxism, whose economic and historical conceptions nowadays cannot stand up to true scientific criticism. In addition, we observe that this Communist socialism is difficult to achieve and does not correspond to the reality we know. In fact, it can only succeed through world revolution. Ba'th socialism is flexible and is not tied by artificial economic laws. In addition, it can be easily achieved and corresponds to reality, for it consists simply in a fair and healthy economic reorganization of Arab society. This socialism will be achieved when Arabs take charge of their own destiny and free themselves from imperialism and feudalism.

Russia may not have broken with Communism as her first leaders saw it, but she has nevertheless abandoned the theory of world-wide revolution. She has restricted herself to aiding expansion of revolution and the propagation of a Communism conforming to the interests and aims of Russia.

Theoretically, Communism is a universal party without geographical limits and does not constitute a state. Nevertheless, we observe that Russia, like the other great powers, has it own civilization, aims, and relations, and tries to be a center from which her strength and civilization may radiate. This is a contradiction of Communism as it was conceived by the first philosophers.

We consider that the Communist Party is a destructive force, for two reasons. The first resides in its deceptive socialism which promises the Arab people all they direly need, at the same time trying to drag it into the clutches of another state, Russia. The second reason is its internationalism.

When Our Socialism Succeeds . . .

If we come to power in Syria, we will abolish the differences between the privileged classes and the others; we will ensure justice, at the same time preparing ourselves to perfect our work. Perhaps we shall not be able to give the people all they desire; perhaps even we shall take a part of what they need, in order to equip the army and ensure the success of the *coups d'état* in all the Arab countries. Socialism cannot be achieved in Syria alone, for Syria is a small state with limited resources. It cannot be achieved, because imperialism and the pressure exerted by all the other Arab countries make the total success of socialism just as difficult there. That is why our socialism will only be able to gain definite recognition in the framework of a single Arab united state—that is to say, when the Arab people are freed, and when the impediments that oppose the success of socialism, such as imperialism, feudalism, and the geographical frontiers created by politics, are removed. This does not prevent certain Arab countries from putting this doctrine into practice before others, although perhaps only in part.

Differences Between Our Socialism and National Socialism

Theoretical differences. The National Socialism of Germany and of Italy is linked to Nazi and fascist philosophy, based on the idea of racial superiority and on the difference between peoples, i.e., on the superiority of one kind over another and their right to dominate the world. These philosophies likewise establish differences between nationals of the same nation, which leads to the dictatorship of an individual or of a class. True socialism cannot succeed in such a system.

Ba'th socialism is inspired by its own philosophy, does not despise other nations, and does not aim at domination. It is an end in itself, to procure economic and social benefits that are easily achieved. It does not cloak political or denominational ambitions.

Practical differences. Subjected to Nazi and fascist regimes, National Socialism in Germany and in Italy is closely linked to their aims: expansion and colonialism. These aims can only be achieved, therefore, by territorial expansion. Thus, National Socialism is only a means to imperialism. Ba'th socialism, on the other hand, does not aim at expansion. Its sole aim is to create a fair economic system in the Arab world. It supports all that tends toward the liberation of peoples still under colonial rule. It desires that other peoples may practice socialism and follow an economic policy that gives justice to all and a higher standard of living for all peoples, at the same time conserving the individuality of each.

2. The Ba'th Attitude Toward Religion

Before we discuss the policy of the future Arab state and the place of religion in the life of nations in general and of the Arab nation in particular, I would urge you, at this stage of liberation and reawakening, to acquire a solid culture and always to make use of it. Without freedom of thought, you will never arrive at the truth or be able to formulate the correct solutions for your own and your nation's problems.

Religion Is a Basic Factor in Human Life

From the earliest times to the present, religion has been a basic factor in human life. We would like, at the outset, to reject the callous, contemptuous attitude to religion prevalent among certain superficial young men. Religion is a serious subject and it cannot be dismissed with a few superficial comments. But we must distinguish between the essence of religion and its objectives, and religion as it becomes manifest under certain circumstances.

The problem, then, is to distinguish between the genuine and the apparent character of religion, because religion encompasses both. The problem arises when a wide gulf separating the genuine from the apparent content of religion creates a contradiction. When appearances are diametrically opposed to the genuine character and objectives of religions, crises arise among men. Such crises assume various forms in accordance with the intellectual level of men and the extent of their interest or lack of interest. The issue is a complicated one, involving science, thought in general, passions, and private interests. Arab youth must take a calm view of the situation and must pronounce a dispassionate judgment. They must come to recognize the part played by emotions and private interest in this issue, and only in this manner can the matter be settled with approximate accuracy and to the public advantage.

Islam Is a Revolution That Can Only Be Understood by Revolutionaries

A momentous event occurred in our national life, an event of both national and human significance, namely, the rise of Islam. I do not believe that the Arab youth give it enough importance and I do not find them concerned to study it in depth. I believe that Islam possesses a magnificent moral experience and a tremendous human experience which can enrich them and their culture, in both theory and practice.

Does our youth consider the fact that, when it arose, Islam was a revolutionary movement that rebelled against a whole system of beliefs, customs, and interests? Can they not perceive that Islam can only be properly understood by revolutionaries? After all, this is only natural, since all revolutions are identical and eternally unchangeable. All revolutions, past, present, and future, have the same psychological conditions and, to a great extent, the same objective circumstances. It is very strange, therefore—and this you must ponder—that those who seem to be the staunchest defenders of Islam are themselves the most unrevolutionary elements. It is inconceivable that such men really understand Islam and, at the same time, very natural that those who are closest to Islam in sentiment and spirit are the revolutionary generation who are presently rebelling against the old and the corrupt. Nevertheless, we find that not all, and not even most, of this revolutionary generation acknowledge this link with Islam, while those who pretend to maintain this link are themselves the enemies of revolution and the upholders of a corruption that must be overcome before the Arab nation can progress.

You undoubtedly know certain elementary things about Islam, and I hope that you will come to know everything. The first thing you know about Islam is that it was first preached by one individual, who was able gradually to attract a few, mostly uninfluential, converts. Those men suffered a great deal of harm and persecution for thirteen years in Mecca before the *Hijra* [to Medina, A.D. 622]. After the *Hijra,* Muslims became relatively more powerful. They were no longer a limited number surrounded by a sea of enemies but a band of faithful and dedicated men.

Does anyone who has not known persecution and has never fought in the ranks of the few who have right on their side against the deluded majority—does such a person have the right to speak in the name of Islam? Does he have an exclusive title to Islam? I personally do not think so, nor do I believe that anyone has this right except those who are persecuted, who have principles and courage, and who preach their faith to all since it is of benefit to all—even when the majority of men and the circumstances are against them and work to destroy them. Such men have this right because all messages and calls, whether social or religious, should be judged by action and not by talk. It is always easy to talk or to write since the energy expended is minimal, but the value of principles can be assessed only by the test of action. If we accept this standard, we shall be able to see our path more clearly and shall discover much falsehood and deception, ignorance and vanity among those who fancy themselves as, or claim to be, men of principles. We shall find that these men have chosen the easy way out and decided to back the winner. They have contrived to acquire all means of comfort and protection in society and to safeguard their private interests, their comfort, and their vanity. We shall discover that these men are not those who are best suited to fight for their principles. . . .

The Ba'th Party member must satisfy very rigorous conditions which are almost contradictory. He must fight all deception and all attempts to prevent progress and liberation that are made in the name of religion for the purpose of preserving corruption and social regression. But at the same time, he should be able to understand the true religion and the genuine human spirit which is, in essence, positive, possessed of faith, and intolerant of recusancy and stagnation. He must recognize the people as friends, whose confidence must be won, and not as enemies. It is true that the people are deluded, but we cannot show them how they are deluded unless we understand them, react with them, and share their life, their emotions, and their mentality. Every step we take in their direction gives us hope that they will move closer to us. Thus, the Ba'thist is always exposed to danger: If he follows this path, there is danger that he will reacquire the reactionary mentality against which he had formerly rebelled. If he follows an opposite path and declares an open war against erroneous beliefs, he is in danger of becoming a negative person, of losing the positive aspect of Ba'thist teachings, and of moving closer to the negative Communism which we have rejected. He may also find himself allied to one form or another of a sham liberalism which is mere show and empty boast. In fighting reaction and resisting its challenge, its slander, and its provocations, the Ba'thist must constantly bear these positive, spiritual principles in mind and must remember that he is fighting not the ideals themselves but their perversion by reaction. He must not forget that, in guiding the people to the proper level of consciousness without hurting their feelings, he is a revolutionary who does not accept, either for himself or for his nation, a cheap and reactionary interpretation of beliefs and spiritual ideals. He must bear in mind that he defers to the people only temporarily and only for the sake of preparing them to understand more difficult matters. The faith of the Ba'thist in man generally and in the Arab man in particular must constantly compel him to be more audacious in combating erroneous and outdated beliefs. Since the Arab nation is fertile and holds within it the experience of centuries of misery, regression, and injustice, he must not suppose that it cannot support so much revolution and liberation. Thus, it is ready to surge forth and to attain a spiritual level of great intensity. . . .

3. Ba'th Views on Capitalism and the Class Struggle

I do not suppose it would be necessary to explain in detail that the party's views and its publications over the years have stated that we have, from the beginning, categorically rejected the capitalist outlook. Nor need I emphasize our rejection of any creed that gives the object more importance than the man, since our party believes that man is himself the highest value, while capitalism believes the contrary.

Capitalism is not a philosophy but an existing situation: It represents man's submission to the objects that he has created or produced. If by capitalism we understand unlimited individual freedom of possession with all its consequences, if it is said that such a freedom is sacrosanct and that neither society nor the state has the right to interfere with it, then we say that no one, not even in the capitalist countries, would be found ready to defend such a view. For these capitalist countries and societies have recently come round to the view that unlimited individual ownership is not sacred, does not always yield the desired results, does not always conform to the public interest and that the state must interfere to safeguard this latter. But if capitalism is understood by some people to mean a system which opposes all others that do not recognize man's absolute freedom, then we might here recognize a certain positive element. But in reality, this is not capitalism but the socialism that we and many other nations advocate: a socialism that is vital, that is genuine and not artificial, and that does not seek to substitute one disease for another or to destroy the idol of capitalism in order to erect the idol of a society which enslaves men and represses their healthy initiative. Our socialism is one which, as we stated, considers man to be the highest value and to be a master of all that he creates. Therefore, we believe that a genuine, far-sighted, and wise creed must evolve in order to destroy exploitation in all its forms without suppressing individual freedom. This, in turn, leads me to ask whether our party believes in class structure and struggles.

There is no theory of class structure in the Marxist sense in our ideology but we do recognize class structures without accepting their Marxist interpretation. Marxism was right in stating that the great struggle of our age was between classes, thus making the class struggle a law of historical evolution. The Marxist analysis of the characteristic features of our age is accurate. Therefore, we cannot possibly ignore the class struggle.

But Marxism greatly exaggerated its importance, erected it into an international conflict, and almost completely ignored the vital historical development of nationalism. Marxism falsely believes that the links between exploiters and exploited throughout the world are much closer than those linking one particular class to its nationalism. Events have proved the falsity of this view since international proletarian solidarity did not evolve in the manner and to the same powerful extent that Marxism predicted.

There is no doubt that within the same nation there is a struggle between those who own the means of production and those who do not. But even within the same nation, it is not possible to view this struggle in the literal and arbitrary manner proposed by Marxism. To begin with, we have rejected internationalism in the Marxist sense and have advocated a free cooperation among independent socialist countries. Hence we accept the links binding us Arabs to other nations and we admit the possibility of meeting together on equal terms, not under the orders of an organization like Communism. This latter course has led, as you know, to the subjection of all the working classes to the Soviet Union, where they act as mere agents of Soviet policy.

Hence, our advocacy of free cooperation among independent socialist countries is more realistic and appropriate. Within the Arab world, we have tackled the problem in a manner that differs from Marxism: We have postulated the national problem as an indivisible whole and have not, like the Marxists, merely isolated the economic aspect, namely, the conflict between the owners and those who do not own. Our problem is much more extensive than this: It is a problem of a nation that is fragmented and partly colonized. Fragmentation is the major obstacle in its path of progress. It is also a problem of a backward nation—in mentality, in its economy, in politics, and in everything. We must build everything anew. Thus, we have placed the Arab nation to one side and all who attempt to retard its progress, to another. The capitalists and feudalists are not the only enemies of the Arabs; there are also the politicians who cling to this state of fragmentation because it serves their own interests; there are, in addition, those who submit to the imperialists, in one form or another, and, finally, those who fight ideas, education, evolution, enlightenment, toleration, and the independence of our homeland. All these men we have placed on one side and the Arab nation on another. Therefore, we do not claim to have divided our nation into two or more classes, on the Marxist pattern. We maintain that a man of religion, for example, who sows the seeds of religious fanaticism and is poor, is as detrimental to society as the capitalists and feudalists who exploit workers and peasants.

Nevertheless, our comprehensive national outlook which elevates our problem and transcends the purely economic must not make us forget that the economic problem is essential. If we are to justify our lenience toward exploiters and reactionaries by using nationality as an excuse, we would deprive our struggle of its vital nerve. This conflict between the masses who are deprived of ownership and the exploiting class, which hinders all development and is deaf to all appeals to the national interest, is in fact beneficial and should not frighten us, since it will lead to national resurgence. From the liberation of the poor masses will issue forth the virtuous Arab citizen who is capable of understanding his nationalism and of achieving its ideals, since nationalism loses all its significance if it exists alongside injustice, poverty, and privation.

The matter is not as easy as you might suppose. We must preserve this tension between the two aspects of the problem and must constantly warn against the loss of the nationalist idea or its identification with criminal class interests. We must guard against the deceptive boasts of interested men who falsely advocate the national interest and merely wish to protect their skins when, in attempting to influence us, they ask: "Are we not all of one nation?" The Ba'thists must be on their guard against such guile. Nationalism as currently understood in our homeland or in the West is, for the most part, a negative and illusory concept permeated with reactionary and exploitationist beliefs. It is our duty to strip away this mask of negativism and deception. Nor need we be afraid of this, because a core will always remain after we have purified the nationalist ideal. This core may be something very simple and insubstantial but it is nevertheless essential. Nationalism, in truth, is not vanity, is not fanaticism vis-à-vis other nations, is foreign to all material interests of a certain class, and is, in fact, humanism itself manifested and realized in one living reality: the nation.

Therefore, we accept only the positive aspects of nationalism, having cast aside all fanaticism and superficialities. Nationalism is the spiritual and historical bond between members of a nation, whom history has stamped in a special manner and has not isolated from the rest of humanity. History gave those members of a nation a distinctive character and a distinctive personification of humanity so that they might become active parts of this latter, creating and interacting with the whole. This, then, is our nationalism. It is not built upon malice toward other nations or toward our fellow-citizens. The struggle we have created within our nation is not vicious but beneficial. Love, in reality, is a hard thing. For when we love our nation and our fellow-Arabs and wish them a prosperous future and a dignified life, we do not shrink from the use of force against all who attempt to hinder our progress and our evolution.

Those rulers and others with vested material or moral interests who obstruct the nation's unity must be fought decisively by the people. But they must be combatted in a spirit of love, since the struggle of the people against them does not issue from greed or envy or spite but from the love of life itself, which these men are trying to suffocate and retard.

VIII. *Nasserism*

30. THE PRINCIPLES THAT GUIDE EGYPT'S POLITICAL LIFE*

Gamal Abdel Nasser

The political and social ideas of Gamel Abdel Nasser (Jamal 'Abd al-Nasir), derived basically from the practical needs of a changing society, have had a strong impact on the entire Arab world. Nasser's social origins and background help explain his ability to understand the spirit of the Arab masses, to identify himself with them, and to manipulate them for his political purposes.

Nasser was born in Alexandria on January 15, 1918, the son of Abdel Nasser Husein ('Abd al-Nasir Husayn), a postal clerk, and Fahima, a coal merchant's daughter. He attended primary school in Cairo, and secondary school in Helwan and Alexandria, studied law for six months, and received a lieutenant's commission from the Military Academy in Cairo in 1937. He served in the Sudan, was an instructor in the Military Academy, and participated in the Arab-Israeli war of 1948. The defeat of the Arabs crystallized his thoughts about the need to remedy the corruption in the Egyptian Government and to restore Egypt's pride and self-confidence. His revolutionary activity, which began after 1948, brought him into contact with the Muslim Brotherhood and various other groups that were likely to support the overthrow of King Faruq's regime. He formed a Free Officers' Committee, out of which grew the Council of Revolutionary Command, which overthrew Faruq in July, 1952; and in 1954, Nasser emerged as the leader of the revolution after General Muhammad Naguib, its nominal leader, was ousted. He was elected president of Egypt in 1956 and he has been re-elected twice, in uncontested elections, most recently in 1965. After the Israeli forces defeated those of the U.A.R. in June, 1967, Nasser resigned the presidency but, on popular demand, reassumed office the following day.

Friendly to the West and not quite certain of his policy at the beginning, Nasser gradually adopted a radical foreign policy, which was soon reflected in his internal rule. The arms deal with Czechoslovakia, the Bandung conference, the final departure of the British from Egypt, the seizure and nationalization of the Suez Canal, and the abortive British-French-Israeli attack on

* Extract from *Address by President Gamal Abdel Nasser at the Meeting of the National Assembly's Ordinary Session, Cairo, March 26, 1964* (Cairo: Information Department, [1964]), pp. 3–47, *passim.*

Egypt—all in 1955–56—made Nasser a world personality and a champion of nationalism, nonalignment, and anticolonialism.

Although Nasser originally was not against political parties, eventually he banned them as representing only minority views and strove to create an organization that would embrace the entire nation. The Liberation Rally (1953–56), the National Union (1958–62), and the Socialist Union (1962) derived from his efforts to create a mass party. Nasser, as leader (ra'is), has dominated them, but the idea that the leader must be able to interpret the people's wishes remains a cardinal principle in his thought. The union of Egypt and Syria in the United Arab Republic in 1958 was a great victory for him, and the collapse of the union when Syria withdrew was a severe defeat. This experience enabled Nasser to estimate better the practical obstacles to unity, as well as the different views of other Arabs about political parties and government.

Nasser's political thought was determined on the one hand by the very nature of Egyptian society, which he described in *The Philosophy of the Revolution* as "not yet crystallized, which continues to ferment and be agitated, which has not yet settled down and taken on its final shape, which, in its development, has not yet caught up with the nations that have preceded [it] on the path." On the other hand, it was determined by the potential role Egypt could play in international relations. This was described in terms of three circles or zones: Arab, African, and Islamic. The Islamic and African circles eventually coalesced and shrank considerably, while Arabism, composed of nationalism and Islam, became the core of Nasser's thought.

The political and social ideas included in Nasserism, it has been said, were suggested by his own countrymen and by intellectuals elsewhere in the Arab world. But it was Nasser who assembled disparate ideas into cohesive plans of action and translated them into concrete realities. Aware of the political role of ideologies, as the extract from the unity talks in 1963 indicate (see pp. 275–94, below), he has used them to justify and legitimize his policies.

A composite ideology whose content varies considerably, Nasserism may be divided into three closely related segments: foreign policy, nationalism, and socialism. Nasser's foreign policy toward the other Arab countries can be regarded as born out of protest against the artificial division of Arab lands into several states and against their backward economic, social, and political systems which consist of both monarchies and socialist republics. The ultimate goal of this view is a Pan-Arabism that would lead eventually to unification and integration in the form of one Arab state. To a large extent, nationalism and socialism have become the means for fulfilling this unity. The main conditions for unity are free choice by people seeking union, consolidation of internal unity by each Arab state, willingness of a majority in a country to live in a union, and adoption of socialism. In its global foreign policy, Nasserism opposes colonialism, neocolonialism, imperialism, spheres of influence, foreign military bases, and alignment with the Great Powers, despite the fact that Nasser's own policy in Yemen contradicts these principles. One may, in fact, refer to the Arab world as Nasserism's sphere of influence, even though in many cases this influence is perpetuated by domestic groups sympathetic *to Nasser's views on unity, nationalism, and socialism. The outcome of Nasserism as an ideology may indeed be determined by the course of the U.A.R.'s foreign policy.*

Aside from its manifestations in foreign policy, nationalism is described by Nasser as love and solidarity among Arabs, as a movement and philosophy for political, social, and economic mobilization, and as a struggle for the unity, freedom, integrity, and dignity of Arabs. The bases of Arab nationalism are unity of language, culture, and hope, and strategic necessity. These are manifest in unity of thought, conscience, and feelings, community of future goals, and the need to oppose foreign powers who want to control the oil and strategic areas of Arab lands.

Nasser's early socialist views—especially those on equality—were sentimental yearnings rather than rationally conceived plans. He visualized the middle classes—professionals, small shopkeepers, and middlemen—as nonexploiters, and regarded capitalists and feudalists—whom he usually identified with building and landowning—as economically harmful. Instead of changing his basic orientation, Nasser gradually altered his social views according to the need for economic development and unity. First, about 1955, he spoke about closing the gap between classes and referred to this measure as socialism; later, he set up a series of planning organizations.

In 1961, he adopted a series of laws to nationalize large enterprises according to the six principles of the revolution. This was part of his attack on imperialism, feudalism, monopolies, and the domination of capitalism. It aimed also at establishing social justice, a truly democratic system, and a powerful army to guarantee the achievements of the U.A.R. Despite Nasser's professed wish to make the workers and peasants its social foundation, this socialism came to rest on the bureaucracy and the intelligentsia. Nasser's nationalist and socialist views acquired their final form in the National Charter of 1962, which is a cogent analysis of the U.A.R.'s political and social revolution and an ideological appeal to Arab intellectuals. It describes revolution as "the only way that enables the Arab struggle to abandon the past and orient itself toward the future" and move out of the regression that was the natural consequence of oppression and exploitation. The Arab revolution, according to the Charter, would arm itself with three values: a scientific and free conscience (thought), a rapid adaptation to circumstances in line with the final objectives and moral principles of the struggle, and a perfect understanding of these objectives or goals—freedom, socialism, and unity. Freedom, both individual and national, meant liberation from feudal domination and colonialism. Socialism was a means and a goal—that is, both sufficiency and justice. Unity was the restoration to its natural state of "the same and unique nation torn apart by its enemies against its own wishes and interests." The Charter analyzed the situation of the Arab world generally, political democracy (a natural part of social democracy based on freedom from exploitation, on equality of opportunity, and on security for the future), and ways to reach the ultimate goals. The Charter remains the foundation of Nasser's internal and external policy, but its fulfillment will depend more on the outcome of relations among Arab states than on its ideological force. The speech reproduced here was addressed to the Assembly elected according to the Charter.

For additional information on Nasserism, see Gamel Abdel Nasser, The Philosophy of the Revolution *(Cairo: Information Department, 1964);* President Gamal Abdel Nasser's Speeches and Press Interviews *(issued regularly by the Information Department, Cairo); Jean and Simonne Lacouture,* Egypt in Transition *(London: Methuen; New York: Criterion, 1958); Wilton Wynn,* Nasser of Egypt: The Search for Dignity *(Cambridge Mass.: Arlington Books, 1959); Keith Wheelock,* Nasser's New Egypt *(New York: Frederick A. Praeger; London: Stevens & Sons, 1960); Charles D. Cremeans,* The Arabs and the World *(New York: Frederick A. Praeger, 1963); Benjamin Rivlin and J. S. Szyliowicz (eds.),* The Contemporary Middle East *(New York: Random House, 1965); Tom Little,* Modern Egypt *(London: Ernest Benn; New York: Frederick A. Praeger, 1967);* Middle East Forum, *April, 1959 (special issue on Nasserism); Fayez Sayegh, "The Theoretical Structure of Nasser's Socialism," in Albert Hourani (ed.),* Middle Eastern Affairs Number Four *(St. Antony's Papers, No. 17) (London and New York: Oxford University Press, 1965); and George Lenczowski, "The Objects and Methods of Nasserism,"* Journal of International Affairs, *XIX, No. 1 (1965), 63–76. On the impact of the Israeli-Arab war of 1948, see Constantin K. Zurayk (Qustantin Zuraik),* Ma'na al-nakba *(Beirut: Kasnaf Press, 1948), translated into English by R. Bayly Winder as* The Meaning of the Disaster *(Beirut: Khayat's College Book Cooperative, 1956).*

The elected popular Assembly is a serious and decisive event in the life of the Arab nation. The revolutionary popular will has opened the road and prepared for it this major role. The will of the popular revolution has paved the way for what it was able to achieve with God's help, namely, the defeat of imperialism, the overthrow of reaction and exploitative capitalism [which are] partners [in an] unholy alliance against the people, [and which] wish to terrorize and subjugate the people so that they may be able to proceed in the spoliation of their wealth and labor and ensure their own luxury and wealth at the expense of the blood and sweat which flow unlimited from millions of workers. . . .

This Assembly which stems from the will of the masses must always stay with them. It cannot afford to raise itself pompously above their demands; nor can it forgetfully drop behind their aspirations. It must always keep abreast of the masses and must never forget to light up their life. This Assembly has . . . grown out of a revolution and it must march along the path toward the revolution to the end. It has grown out of hope and it must carry this hope all the way [to] fruition. It has grown out of the will for drastic change and it must attain the broad objectives of change, the objectives of unbounded sufficiency and justice, of unrestricted social and political democracy, of a society with equal opportunities for all and no class differences, and of new vistas in which the Arab individual can do honor to life and life can do honor to the Arab individual. . . .

The six principles [that guided Egypt's political life in 1952–64] . . . were as follows: the elimination of imperialism and its traitorous Egyptian agents; the eradication of feudalism; the destruction of monopoly and of the domination of capital over the government; the establishment of social justice; the establishment of strong national Army and the establishment of a sound [democracy]. . . .

What happened to each of these six principles? How did each one of them turn into a weapon bringing victory and sovereignty to the Egyptians over the few years which have elapsed since then?

First: the first principle—the elimination of imperialism. I do not think we need much effort to prove that this nation today is foremost among the independent countries of the world after having been a foreign-occupied base firmly gripped for more than 70 years and terrorized by 80,000 armed British soldiers on the banks of the Suez Canal. . . .

Second: the second principle—eradication of feudalism. The ownership of the greater and more fertile part of the agricultural land was in the hands of a small number of big landlords, besides other vast areas held by agricultural companies that were owned by foreigners, though they tried to conceal their real identity behind Egyptian façades. In accordance with the socialist laws, including the Agrarian Reform Law, the area of lands that has been expropriated for distribution to farmers amounted to 944,457 feddans. . . .

Through [regulation] of the rental of agricultural land, which was a part of the Agrarian Reform [Law]; through the consolidation of cooperation and [availability] of interest-free financing, as well as [reorganization] of agricultural land on the largest scale, there came about a transformation in the conditions governing the productivity of the agricultural land, besides the transformation which took place in connection with its ownership. . . .

Third: the third principle is the abolition of monopoly and the domination of capital over the government. . . . the public sector . . . consolidated itself through the complete domination of capital . . . in banks, insurance companies, foreign and internal trade companies which were nationalized and which became public property. It [i.e., the consolidation of the public sector] was followed by the socialist decrees of July, 1961, which ensured the public ownership of the larger part of the means of production, particularly in the industrial field. Clear limits for public ownership were then drawn so as to include the main skeleton of production, such as railways, roads, ports, airports, motor power, the means for land, sea, and air transport, then the heavy, medium, mining, and [the] building materials industries, the effective part of the consumer industries, in a manner which would leave no room for exploitation. This was connected with the realization of complete popular supervision over foreign trade, the breaking of any monopoly in internal trade which was thrown open to private activity. . . .

Fourth: the fourth principle—the establishment of social justice. Experience has proven that social justice cannot be attained except upon the two bases of sufficiency and justice, neither of which could attain the objective without the other. Indeed, each of them without the other would take a course contradictory to the objective.

Sufficiency—that is, increased production—without justice means a further monopolization of wealth. Justice—that is, the distribution of national income without increasing its potentiality—ends only in the distribution of poverty and misery. But both together—that is, sufficiency and justice—hand in hand [they] reach their objective. . . .

In the field of internal action: The final step lay in the liquidation of the ruling alliance between reaction and imperialism as well as the liquidation of their inherited privileges. There was no enmity toward any individual or family. . . .

Although I consider that this class has been liquidated, I find it important here to make two remarks:

First: To see with tolerance that we were not against individuals. We were opposed to class distinction. It was our right to eliminate its effect but it was not our right to destroy the dignity and humanity of individuals. Therefore, a new page should be opened in front of all without distinction.

Second: We should not, at any cost, permit the emergence of a new class which would believe that it is entitled to inherit privileges from the old class. . . .

We moved from the domination of one class which monopolized all privileges, to a position which, for the first time in our country, allows for the establishment of a social democracy on the basis of sufficiency and justice and social democracy.

The old picture of a state of princes, pashas, and foreigners has disappeared and [has been] replaced by a state of farmers, workers, intellectuals, soldiers, and national capital—the working popular powers and its leading alliance. . . .

In the stage of the great upsurge which followed the stage of the great conversion, there are three major objectives which we have unlimited capacity to achieve if we arm ourselves with sincerity to both the experience and to the hope.

First: There is the objective of continuous development, a comprehensive plan preparing for another comprehensive plan, a doubling of the national income followed by another doubling based on the result of the first doubling. . . .

Second: There comes after development the objective of democracy and the continuous expansion of its framework and deepening of its concept. In the next stage, there are interactions which we should allow to have full effect on life in our society.

We have to complete the structure of the political organization of the Socialist Union. Though the general structure of this Union is now perceptible before us, this structure should be full of effective and creative life . . .

But we should not allow ourselves to get entangled in lengthy philosophical discussions on the role of the Socialist Union.

The Socialist Union, in short, is the political organization of the working popular powers through which they work to ensure that authority shall, at all times, remain in their hands and shall not move into other hands.

This is the aim of all political organizations, including parties. But whereas a party represents a certain interest in any country or class, the Socialist Union does not represent a group or a class but expresses the political will of the active popular powers allied within its framework. . . .

Third: There follows the stage of upsurge with development and democracy, the objective of realizing over-all Arab unity.

Although we cannot, as yet, give this inevitable unity its final shape, the success in realizing the aim of development and the aim of democracy in this country, which we consider to be the base and vanguard of the Arab nation, will bring nearer the day of unity, define its final form, and mold it in accordance with the will and requirements of national conscience. . . .

31. STATUTE OF THE ARAB SOCIALIST UNION*

Since the July 23, 1952, Revolution committed itself to its six principles and the struggle of people was transferred by the socialist conversion of the July, 1961, laws, the stages of the struggle [have] dictated establishing a popular formation, that is, the Arab Socialist Union. This would be capable of safeguarding the six principles of the Revolution and would give the Revolution impetus toward its greater goals defined in the National Charter.

The Arab Socialist Union represents the socialist vanguard which leads the people, expresses their will, directs national action, and undertakes effective control of the progress of such action, within the framework of the principles of the National Charter. The Arab Socialist Union is the meeting place of the demands and requirements of the people.

The Arab Socialist Union, as a strong popular formation, includes the active powers of the people. The alliance of such powers is represented in the Arab Socialist Union.

Objectives

—To realize sound democracy represented by the people and for the people,

* Extract from *Statute of the Arab Socialist Union* [December 7, 1962] (Cairo: Information Department, n.d.), pp. 3–12.

so that the Revolution will be by the people insofar as its methods are concerned, and for the people in its objectives.

—To realize a socialist revolution, that is, a revolution of the working people.

—To give revolutionary impetus to the potentialities for advancement in the interests of the people.

—To safeguard the guarantees embodied in the National Charter, which are:

—To safeguard the minimum representation for workers and farmers in all popular and political formations at all levels, thus guaranteeing that at least 50 per cent of the membership of the Arab Socialist Union itself is made up of workers and farmers, as they are the overwhelming majority of the people deprived for a long time of their fundamental rights.

—To safeguard the right of criticism and self-criticism.

—To realize the principle of collective leadership.

—To strengthen cooperative and labor union formations.

—To transfer the authority of the state gradually to elected councils.

Duties

—To become a positive power behind the revolutionary action.

—To protect the principles and objectives of the Revolution.

—To liquidate the effects of capitalism and feudalism.

—To fight against infiltration of foreign influence.

—To fight against the return of reactionism which was eliminated.

—To fight against infiltration of opportunism.

—To resist passivity and deviation.

—To prevent haphazard work in the national action.

Work Principles

The Arab Socialist Union is the comprehensive political structure of national action. Its formation embraces all powers of the people—farmers, workers, soldiers, intellectuals, and holders of national capital—with the understanding that they bind themselves to national action in close solidarity at all levels, from the base of the organization to its collective leadership.

To ensure that this popular organization attains its objectives, relations between the members themselves, and between them and their formations, must be based on values and principles ensuring positive momentum for the ASU in the direction of its revolutionary goals.

Most important of these principles are:

—Respect by the minority of the will of the majority, so that there may be no scope for the emergence of dictatorship within the . . . Union.

Gaining the confidence of the people through conviction. This confidence, which is the means for the people's obedience of their leaders, is not the product of fear but of conviction, and does not impart to leaders at any level acquired rights, leading to the creation of dictatorships within the formations of the Union.

—Observance of order and obedience in relations between the leaders and the socialist vanguard. There must be readiness to give and to sacrifice. The people must be convinced.

—Striving to establish sound relations between the Union and the working people.

—Striving to solve the problems of the people.

—Striving to maintain the revolutionary drive among the people.

—Facts must be revealed to the people.

—Overbearance, or any form of haughtiness, must not be shown toward the working people.

—Mistakes must be acknowledged and quickly corrected.

—The Arab Socialist Union, the authority of the people, assumes the action of leadership, guidance, and control in the name of the people. The labor unions and popular councils, on the other hand, implement the policy drawn up by the ASU while the National Assembly, which is the supreme authority in the state, implements, conjointly with the syndical and popular councils, the policy laid down by the ASU.

The ASU does not replace labor unions, cooperatives, or youth formations, but strives to discharge its mission and realize its objectives with the help of these formations in the manner set in the Charter.

In the light of the ASU formations at all levels, the Charter becomes the proper theory of our Revolution and the revolutionary ideology for the application of our socialism.

In assuming its role of leadership, carrying the responsibilities of the vanguard, guarding the guarantees safeguarded by the Charter, practicing its functions in a democratic manner [and] its upsurge from within the population and representation of their aspirations and expression of their will, the ASU establishes the principle of sovereignty of the people and a fundamental concept of political and democratic organization—that sound democracy becomes, in socialist logic, a means and an end for national struggle.

32. ARAB SOCIALISM IN THE MAKING*

Muhsin Ibrahim

Muhsin Ibrahim, the chief editor of al-Hurriya (Liberty), *a magazine published in Beirut, has written several books on contemporary Arab ideology. He is a spokesman for the Arab Nationalist Movement, which follows Nasser's policy and philosophy in seeking Arab unity.*

The Arab Nationalist Movement (Harakat qawmini al-'arabi) *came into*

* Extract from Muhsin Ibrahim, "Arab Socialism in the Making," *Arab Journal,* Vol. I, Nos. 2–3 (Spring–Summer, 1964), 15–25; the article appeared originally in Arabic. Reproduced by permission.

being after Nasser denounced the Ba'th on July 22, 1963, for its alleged failure to live up to the unity agreements. Convinced that the Ba'th was unwilling, or perhaps incapable, of working for Arab unity, many Arab intellectuals in Syria, Lebanon, Jordan, Kuwait, and Iraq decided to organize and strive to achieve the goal by themselves. The movement received U.A.R. support but was banned elsewhere. In 1964, it became part of the Arab Socialist Union, which embodied the ideas of nationalism, socialism, and unity as expounded by Nasser. Adopting the principles of the mother revolution in the U.A.R., the Union intended to link nationalism and socialism and to consolidate the individual revolutions in each Arab country into one that would represent the main stream of Arab thought. It attracted many former Ba'thists as well as Marxists, who saw an opportunity to turn the Arab revolution into a leftist victory. It also had secularist features, but these were not openly acknowledged. The following resolution gives a good idea of the aims of the Arab Socialist Union. It was adopted at a congress of Syrian unionists held July 14–18, 1964, in Beirut and was published in the Egyptian Gazette, *July 20, 1964:*

"Inspired by the experience of the Arab revolution, the conference of unionist organizations in Syria passed the following resolutions:

- *The Arab revolution is a revolution for liberation, socialism, and national union, and any attempt to separate the last two objectives represents a deviation from the Arab revolution.*
- *The Arab revolution is an integral revolution despite the different origins of its constituent revolutionary movements.*
- *The workers, farmers, revolutionary educated people, and soldiers are the basic forces of the Arab revolution.*
- *The requirement of political, economic, and social affinity for union is but a sly pretext for avoiding union.*
- *The United Arab Republic is the main base of Arab revolution and Arab union, and every attempt at union away from the United Arab Republic is a new form of secession.*
- *The integrity of the Arab revolution requires an Arab revolutionary organization, and all revolutionary organizations are invited to merge into one Arab revolutionary organization.*
- *The revolutionary leadership, which has proved its efficiency throughout the battles it fought, belongs to the command of the July 23 Revolution under President Gamal Abdel Nasser's heroic and enlightened leadership.*
- *As proved by its experience in Iraq and Syria, in which it resorted to fascist methods, the Ba'th Party has isolated itself from the Arab revolution and placed itself in an adverse position to it.*
- *The unionist organizations and groups in Syria represented in this conference have decided to dissolve themselves and merge into the Arab Socialist Union in the Syrian Region.*
- *The Arab Socialist Union in the Syrian Region assumes as its first task the restoration of the United Arab Republic by removing the secessionist Ba'thist regime and every other secessionist obstacle. . . .*

– The Political Bureau elected by the constituent conference will undertake political work, ideological guidance, and revolutionary organization during the transition period and will be responsible to the constituent conference. . . ."

Muhsin Ibrahim has been one of the active members of this group. The following article analyzes the evolution of Arab socialism and links it to its fountainhead, the Egyptian Revolution and Marxism.

The Main Characteristics of the Present Phase in the Development of Arab Socialism

Chief among the issues of today's Arab socialism is that which relates to the emergence of the "scientific approach." This looming phenomenon seems to be the major contribution of the present phase. Confronted with a number of problems, Arab socialism, in ideology and practice, is now re-examining its theoretical foundation. The problems that have prompted this self-appraisal are the following:

1. *The problem of "transition" into socialism.* Up until the beginning of the present phase, the question of "transition" had been submerged in vague notions and obscure concepts of socialism which predominated in the debate. Basically, the "transition" was thought of to be one of developing the "national struggle" into a "socialist struggle"; that from the latter, a progressive economic and social transformation will then evolve.

On the other hand, this theory of transformation of the "Arab national struggle" into a "socialist struggle" had, for a long period of time, been stated with a premise that ruled out the necessary recourse to class struggle. The relatively long life this theory enjoyed had been due mainly to its having adopted a type of analysis that drew its power by appealing to notions such as the "special circumstances of Arab society" and to political objectives such as "national unity." The analysis goes like this: The "special circumstances" of Arab society will enable it to "transform itself into socialism within the framework of national unity and the eventual peaceful reconciliation of existing contradictions." In other words, the experiences of European societies where capitalism could not be defeated without a class struggle are due mainly to the peculiar nature of European society; Arab society is shaped in such a way that neither the existence nor the emergence of such a struggle will be permitted.

These vague conceptions of "transition" into socialism in Arab society have now given way to the development of a more mature approach which emphasizes the real issues involved in the "transition." Class struggle is now recognized as inevitable if Arab society is ever to achieve a successful "transition" into socialism.

In the past, as we have seen, analysis of Arab society ruled out the need for class struggle because of the "special circumstances" of this society. Present analysis emphasizes that these "special circumstances," different though they are, give us a society with merely a different balance of power structure. For an effective "transition," the potentialities of this structure should be fully realized; this can be done by a thorough exploration of this structure and an accurate determination of the alternatives it offers.

But the fact remains that transition into an Arab socialist society cannot be achieved without first defeating exploitative capitalism and feudalism; that only by revolution can these institutions be defeated; and this would consequently allow the productive members of society to assume full power. These members unmistakably are neither the feudalists nor the capitalists. They are the peasants, the workers, the educated, and the soldiers.

Only this way can the avenues for a socialist revolutionary transformation be opened. And this, clearly, is a class struggle.

2. *The objectives of transformation into socialism.* Previous phases in the development of Arab socialist thought were characterized by vagueness and contradictions. Into this conglomeration of uncertainty the so-called "reformist" elements were allowed to infiltrate under the banner of "Arab socialism." These elements were in fact neither socialist nor revolutionary.

Even these elements in Arab socialist thought varied in their definition of "socialism." Some said, "Socialism is not necessarily nationalization, for the latter is a means not an end. The end is 'economic growth' and 'social justice.' As long as these are possible to achieve by recourse to other means, it follows that nationalization is not inevitable."

Others saw the realization of "socialism" through "progressive taxation," "social security," and the assurance of an "adequate standard of living." These ideas stemmed from the concept of the "welfare state," which, this group alleged, was "the same as the modern concept of socialism."

Another group claimed that one could draw a line between economic development and the reconsideration of wealth distribution and the ownership of the means of production. From this assumption they concluded that "socialism" at this stage in the development of Arab society was exemplified by economic development; and, therefore, it was too early to consider the question of ownership and distribution!

Finally, there were those who advocated the concept of a "mixed (socialist) economy." For it, they envisaged a public sector with a limited ownership of some basic public utilities and some of the large means of production. On the other hand, they envisaged a private sector which would assume various types of important patterns of growth. In other words, "socialism," as seen by this group, was "based on the co-existence of the principles of individual and public ownership."

But these obscured concepts of objectives, with which Arab socialism was flooded, have also given way to a new understanding that rejects the concept of a "welfare state," the concept of a "mixed economy," etc. In this new concept of socialism one can see a precise definition of objectives. It clearly states that socialist transformation has the objective of establishing the material foundation for a progressive society and the setting up of public ownership for the means of production. It further states that the latter is fundamental for the emergence of a socialist society.

Fundamental though it be, public ownership does not deny the existence of small private businesses, crafts, and a limited private agricultural land. These forms of private enterprise will, however, remain partial and limited in a socialist society. Furthermore, development in the transformation process will inevitably accelerate the shrinkage of these forms of private enterprise.

3. *The socialist revolution in the realm of social relations and political institutions.* In this area too, lack of perception was evident in previous phases of Arab socialist thought. What seemed to have been missed was no less than the very essence of socialist approach whether in analysis or in thought. At times, "Arab socialism" was conceived of as an "economic revolution" whose sole objective was to organize the economic life of society. At other times, "Arab socialism" was conceived of as the "economic aspect of Arab nationalism," etc.

These conceptions cleared the way for ideas such as a "socialist remedy for an economic problem" and a "democratic remedy for a political problem." This erroneous way of thinking made it possible for some to consider the revolutionary transformation of society as two distinctly separate processes: an economic process through socialism, and a political process through democracy.

This line of reasoning was clearly an attempt to retain the capitalist tools of analysis and apply them to the so-called "political problem" i.e., the question of political rights and political institutions. This was unmistakably "liberal capitalism" disguised under "socialism."

The advocates of this approach must have had one thing in mind, i.e., the artificial separation between the political and the economic aspects of society where it would not be permissible in the process of change to advance "socialism" at the expense of "democracy," and vice versa. Put in a different way, the entire revolutionary process of change was reduced to "ingredients of reconciliation whose ultimate success lay in mixing the proper measurements of democracy and socialism."

These shaky concepts (envisaging a revolutionary process with separate components partially advancing) have now retreated in the face of an advancing ideological force. The position of this new force on matters of ideology is clear. It rejects the concept of an amputated "economic revolution." It also rejects the concept of social life as one made up of two distinctly separate fields of endeavor. It further rejects the artificial separation of the question of socialism and democracy.

The emerging concept of socialism sees in the socialist process not merely a material change in the economic life of society, but (by virute of public ownership of the means of production) also the elimination of exploitation and contradictions in social relations. Only by freeing these relations from undue pressure can true democracy flourish, where democracy means the emergence of political institutions that represent the real productive members of society, on the one hand, and their ability to exercise their political rights, on the other.

4. *Transferring state-owned means of production into direct social ownership.* One of the most pressing issues facing contemporary socialism is the question of state vs. direct—ownership of the means of production. Arab socialism in its turn and in line with its dynamic nature has also begun to consider this important question.

Arab socialism views this problem by first stressing that socialism is not fully achieved by mere nationalization and state control of the productive means. Nationalization is only a step in the direction of socialism. For exploitation to be removed, for social relations to be freed, and for democracy to be reinforced, the foundation of socialism must be completely established. This, Arab socialism asserts, can be achieved by transferring the productive means from state into direct social ownership, thus transferring the actual control into the hands of the real producers. This, by definition, means "self-management." By supporting self-management, the necessary guarantees against the problems of bureaucracy have been provided and the freedom in social relations has consequently been furthered. This then is the favorable environment for the true exercise of democracy.

5. *The question of unifying the Arab socialist movement in the Arab homeland.* In the process of their growth, the Arab socialist revolutionary movements have acquired new dimensions and their achievements have focussed the debate on the question of "one Arab socialist movement."

The debate has actually revolved around a number of issues that have a direct relationship to the Arab socialist revolution. These issues are the following:

(*a*) Given that the socialist revolutionary movements in the Arab homeland are independent of one another, could we conclude that that is conducive to Arab unity simply because the [separate] socialist program of each revolution is assumed to be oriented toward this unity?

(*b*) Or, if we are to await a total Arab revolution which would then provide the true basis for Arab unity, how could we then expect the fulfillment of this revolution without the emergence of a united Arab movement in all parts of the Arab homeland?

(*c*) If the latter is true, i.e., if a united Arab socialist movement should emerge, *how* could it emerge? What are its possibilities and what form shall it take? And finally, what avenues are open to it?

These, then, are five major problems that we had to become acquainted with in order to perceive the main characteristics of contemporary Arab socialism. Evidently, Arab socialist growth stands at the threshold of a significantly major development. It remains for us to show, however, what constitutes the "Arab socialist camp" and who is responsible for the theoretical and practical development of Arab socialist growth.

Who Is Responsible for the Development of Arab Socialism in the Arab Homeland: The Role of the July 23 Revolution

The objective historian who sets out to trace back the historical development of Arab socialism will inevitably find that this development was carried out by three major pioneering forces: the July 23 [1961] Revolution in the U.A.R., the Algerian Revolution, as well as the Arab unionist forces and popular movements who were determined on marching forward and interacting with this progressive trend. To verify this statement, let us subject it to some historical analysis.

In the preceding discussion of the major issues that have confronted "Arab socialism," we discovered that at the outset this concept was very vaguely defined. The revolution of July 23, being the first of its kind, had, therefore, the task of subjecting the concept to its first practical test.

To carry this responsibility, the revolution of July 23 had two circumstances in its favor: First, it had already completed the political liberation and economic independence and, second, it was endowed with a specific type of leadership which, by virtue of its dynamic nature, had the capacity to perceive the real historical meaning of the step, to rise to the level of the event, and to foresee the successive stages involved in the struggle.

This revolution was, therefore, partly a natural outcome of an already completed preparatory stage (between 1952 and 1961) that involved, besides political liberation and economic independence, the initiation of a "guided" economic set-up. It was these steps that had set the stage for the July, 1961, socialist revolution which was conceived to be the only process capable of transforming society.

The union of Syria and Egypt placed the July 23 Revolution at the helm of a new historical force. New horizons opened; but also new requirements emerged. We should, therefore, ask: "What fruits did the union bear?"

In the first three years of the union and those which preceded the July Revolution of 1961, a major question was longing for an answer: "Should the building of the new state be confined to an agrarian reform, a guided economy, and social security? Or does it require the search for far more promising horizons through the socialist approach?"

Not before the middle of the fourth year (July, 1961) was the answer found. It was symbolized by the socialist resolutions of July, 1961. Not only did it put the revolution on the right track of socialist growth, but [it] also brought about an era of clarity for the objectives of Arab socialism. The nature and meaning of the socialist process also gained clarity.

From this, the idea of public ownership grew and began to crystallize. Consequently, public ownership came to be understood as the fundamental principle for the emergence of a socialist society and the establishment of its progressive material foundation.

Though marking a major turning point in the history of Arab socialist growth, the July resolutions were far from being a complete answer. To be sure, they were merely partially socialist. They were also very dangerously obscure. And in this area of obscurity the following theoretical and practical questions remained unanswered:

1. To have understood the July resolutions in their true context, it was essential to have provided full verification of the objectives of the socialist process. While, for example, the principle of public ownership may have been understood from the said resolutions, other vital questions remained unanswered. Such is the question of "private ownership." Could the socialist process accommodate the co-existence of two such basic principles?

2. It is to be conceded that the enactment of the July laws was a step in the direction of socialist transformation. But what is the underlying theoretical basis for such a step? It was clear that the July resolutions were based on the assumption that transformation was possible without recourse to class struggle; that class differences could be eliminated peacefully within the framework of "national unity" represented in a political organization (National Union) encompassing all classes. But this deprived the leading revolutionary movement of the alliance of the productive popular classes who, alone, were capable of guarding the revolution against subversion by the forces of exploitation.

3. Furthermore, the July resolutions lacked the clear conception of what was really involved in the process regarding social relations and political rights and institutions.

In themselves, these resolutions did constitute a tangible basis for the liberation of social relations from exploitation, pressure, and contradiction. They did also aim at enabling the struggling masses to control society's political institutions and exercise their political rights. Nevertheless, they fell short of bringing this about to its fullest extent. Why? Because instead of taking a clear and positive form, the change in social and political institutions was made to depend on passive forms of criticism directed against the evils of the bourgeois system. It was essential also to have provided the necessary tools that could bring about transformation. Such a tool would be an organized revolutionary movement which would lead the allied productive classes of society in the direction of democracy and ultimate control of political institutions.

It has become clear from the preceding why the July resolutions were considered only partially socialist and that this type of socialism remained vague and dangerous. It is to be stressed, however, that this objective appraisal is in no way intended to underestimate the historical value of these resolutions. On the contrary, what took place in July, 1961, will remain a significant turning point in the history of Arab socialism. It is to be recalled that these resolutions were the first serious action Arab socialism ever achieved.

Furthermore, the vagueness and obscurity that accompanied these resolutions were justifiable on the ground that Arab socialism itself, in theory and in practice, was still in its infancy. And this partially socialist approach to social transformation did ultimately lead, being correctly oriented, to the inevitable confrontation with the basic issues involved. But before these issues became discernible to the revolutionary forces, the reactionary forces were faster to recognize their implications. They thus moved faster and made their surprise attack by breaking the union of Syria and Egypt.

The secessionist movement in Syria was, therefore, an attempt at burying the July socialist resolutions before they could fully materialize as a completed socialist program capable of bringing about the full revolutionary change in the economic, social, and political structure.

The Second Major Development as a Reply to Secession

The secessionist blow which was dealt at the U.A.R. was definitely a setback in the struggle for Arab unity. There was, nevertheless, a positive aspect to this setback: It alerted the unionist forces in the Arab homeland to the reality of class differences and brought to light the difference between the nut and the shell in political slogans. Consequently, two distinctly opposite Arab camps emerged.

On the ideological level, the developments instigated a dialogue in which the U.A.R. revolutionists and other Arab unionist forces became fully involved. The dialogue centered on the meanings offered by the union and those which evolved from secession. It actually led to new frontiers in Arab thought and was, in the final analysis, a second major achievement in the development of Arab socialism. To be sure, the "National Declaration" of the U.A.R. embodied the results of this specific dialogue which opened new horizons in Arab socialist thought and revolutionary struggle.

Chief among the achievements of this development in Arab socialism was that it provided what the July resolutions had left out. Instead of avoiding the issue of a class struggle, the new development recognized its inevitability and equipped itself in order to face it. This realistic approach strengthened Arab socialism and gave it the power to plough deep into the heart of existing problems instead of pretending their nonexistence, or, at best, skimming over their surface.

When the question of transformation into socialism was now raised, all its fundamental elements were spelled out. It became evident that class struggle in Arab society was an unavoidable element in the transformation process. Objectively analyzed, class differences were seen as a phenomenon that actually existed. It came to be recognized as a serious stumbling block obstructing the Arab revolutionary movement. To overcome it was to face it and to crush it, not to avoid it by deviating from the main path and following a detour.

Transformation into socialism, therefore, was seen to hinge on the defeat of the feudalist-bourgeois alliance through a revolutionary process. It was also seen to hinge on the complete assumption of power by the productive classes of society. It thus became clear that the responsibility for transformation could not be carried through a political structure whose theoretical foundation was based on the concept of "peaceful dissolution" of basic social contradictions (between the forces of exploitation and the real productive classes).

From that, it followed that only by allying the real productive sectors of society together and by defeating the forces of exploitation can transformation into socialism be achieved.

It was this clarity in the revolutionary concept of transformation that gave this phase of Arab socialism a special significance. It was this clarity also which enabled the nationalist revolutionary struggle to transform itself successfully into a socialist revolutionary struggle.

Besides this clarity in the nature of Arab socialist revolution there was also clarity in the objectives of socialist transformation. This made it possible for the "National Declaration" of the U.A.R. to embody both the methodology for the achievement and the precise definition of objectives of its socialist revolution, whether in the field of "national product," industry, trade, capital, or real estate. The definition of objectives in these areas strongly emphasized the fundamentality of public ownership of the means of production as the only basis for a truly socialist society.

Having started from a correct premise and having equipped itself with the right tools of analysis, the new ideological force arrived at similarly sound conclusions regarding socialist change in the realm of social relations and political rights and institutions. The original negative criticism of the bourgeois social structure and its [products of] forged political rights and political institutions now developed into positive socialist thought. This was necessary for the understanding of democracy in its revolutionary context. We thus saw "liberal bourgeois concepts" (which artificially separate between democracy and socialism) give way to a concept which states forcefully that "democracy and socialism are one inseparable extension to the revolutionary struggle." In other words, socialist transformation was conceived to be the only gate that leads to the liberation of social relations and political rights and institutions—that is, to liberate them from undue pressure, exploitation, and forgery.

If negative criticism was to develop into a positive attitude, it was not sufficient to merely speak of the organic unity of democracy and socialism and their relationship to the revolutionary struggle. It was essential to come up with a positive formulation for a process of achieving democracy and for a method of reinforcing it within the framework of socialist transformation.

The debate actually led the U.A.R. to adopt some basic principles in its "National Declaration." The most significant of these principles were that the "Arab Socialist Union," which emerges from the alliance of society's productive classes, is the representative authority of the people and that which enhances the capabilities of the revolution; that the political organizations of the people which are based on direct free elections shall inevitably represent the forces of the majority; that authority of elected assemblies over the executive branches of the state shall be continuously emphasized; that it is of the utmost necessity that, within the framework of the "Arab Socialist Union," a new political organ be created to mobilize and embrace the benevolent elements of leadership and organize their efforts; that it is essential for group leadership to be guaranteed; that popular organizations are capable of playing an influential and effective role in preserving the elements of true democracy; and that criticism and self-criticism are some of the most important guarantees of freedom, etc.

From the point of view of ideological thought, the greatest value these general principles carry lay in that they put the search for democratic reinforcements on the right track. As we said earlier, public ownership of the productive means, considered objectively, became a fundamental principle for the socialist transformation in both the social and political realms. Public ownership became, therefore, a clear objective for the revolution.

The search for democratic reinforcements went even further. It manifested itself in more sophisticated arguments such as that which relates to the question of state vs. direct social ownership of the means of production. It revolved around the meaning of this transference and the process it should follow. In other words, Arab socialism, in its search for democratic guarantees started to examine such progressive socialist theories which favor the placing of the productive means under the direct control of producers, and the achievement of self-management.

In practice, the effects of this ideological trend appeared in the U.A.R. when workers were actually allotted a share in profits and representation on the boards of directors. Of course, it would have been meaningless to have taken these measures if they had not been based on a clear understanding of the issues—that is, to have had a clear differentiation between "state ownership," which does not completely preclude exploitation and contradiction, and "direct ownership," which is the true corrective device in social relations and reinforcement of political democracy.

There has been still another development after the secessionist setback of September, 1961. Earlier in the discussion a statement was made to the effect that a new outlook is now being sought regarding relations between the various Arab revolutionary movements. This became a necessity because one of the major contributing factors to secession was the partial contradictions in the relations of these movements. To be sure, it was the deepening of these differences that provided the reactionary forces with an appropriate climate to reactivate their power and consequently subvert the unity of Syria and Egypt.

It was, therefore, natural for the postsecession period to have been witnessing numerous attempts which aimed at laying down the groundwork for the establishment and solidification of ideological and practical relationships between these movements. These trends found expression in the slogan which called for "the meeting of all Arab revolutionary forces" in a single front. As to the development of this "front," two alternatives were seen: Either it would remain a "front" which will continue to embrace numerous revolutionary forces, or it would evolve into a united revolutionary movement.

In the United Arab Republic, this development found expression in the "National Declaration" of July 23. The "Declaration" stressed the belief in the "inevitability of a unified progressive popular movement in the Arab world which would assert itself in the subsequent stages of Arab struggle."

To conclude this section, let us reiterate the main points: Besides familiarizing ourselves with the main characteristics of this stage, we discovered that it was the second most important in the postsecession period. It has been made clear that this stage was held in reverence because it offered constructive and brave criticism, perceptive debate, and genuine interaction that won it a unique historical significance. These elements entered the ideological bloodstream of Arab revolutionary movements who were able to perceive the meaning of unity and discover new horizons which secession uncovered.

But again it was an open debate because a number of basic questions remained without definite answers. These questions and the debate that grew around them will be the subject matter of the following final section.

Features of the Third Major Development in Arab Socialism

It is evident from the preceding discussion that the achievements of Arab socialism after secession marked a fundamental turning point in the history of this movement. Divided into two phases, the July, 1961, resolutions were the backbone of the first phase; in the second phase, or in "postsecession socialism," the achievement was mainly in the area of crystallizing the concept of socialism. The latter, significant and historically important though it was, left a number of questions without definite answers.

First, the question of a leading socialist revolutionary movement. This question was closely related to the meaning of transformation into socialism, the implications and workability of the process itself. In other words, it was not sufficient to state that the productive class was the only qualified revolutionary force which is capable of overthrowing the feudalist-bourgeois alliance and consequently effecting socialist transformation. People's capacity to revolt hinged on the emergence of a leading revolutionary movement which was capable of crystallizing their motivations and helping to launch them in the direction of socialist struggle.

It was also insufficient to state general principles which emphasize the importance of a socialist economic structure as the fundamental principle for socialist transformation in the realm of social relations and political rights and institutions. The instrument which could translate these general principles into action should have been specified and provided as well.

From this, we could discern a fundamental difference between popular organizations, which were set up by election, and leading socialist revolutionary movements which "mobilize and organize the efforts of benevolent elements that are capable of leadership." Organizations that come by popular vote are unquestionably important if society's productive classes are to be represented in a political body that reinforces their alliance and if they are to become the source of power for the state. However, before these organizations become truly "representative authorities which enhance the capacities of their revolution and safeguard democratic values," it is imperative that a leading socialist revolutionary movement emerge to embrace and organize the efforts of selective "benevolent elements that are capable of leadership." This movement would then inspire elected popular organizations and inject in their bloodstream the ability to exercise their authority. This movement is, therefore, the backbone of socialist revolution.

This fundamental question did not escape the dialogue which revolved around socialist growth in the postsecession period. As a matter of fact, some results of this dialogue were actually presented in the "National Declaration." It emphasized "that there is a (clear) need for the creation of a new political body within the framework of the Arab Socialist Union which will mobilize and organize the efforts of benevolent elements that are capable of leadership. It will also crystallize the revolutionary motivations for the public, feel their needs, and help find right answers for these needs."

On the other hand, the dialogue did not reach its fullest extent regarding the question of a leading socialist revolutionary movement. Nor was an answer found to the question as to whether one or a multiplicity of such movements should lead the revolution.

The second fundamental question which remained unanswered was that concerning individual (private) ownership. In postsecession socialist growth, transformation was clearly working on the principle of public ownership for the means of production. However, obscurity continued to engulf the question of individual ownership. This allowed rightist elements to exploit this issue for the purpose of distortion.

It was clear that the idea of permitting "unexploiting individual ownership" did not mean that a socialist society could be established on two equally fundamental principles: Public ownership for some means of production, on the one hand, and individual ownership, on the other. In fact, the idea of allowing "unexploiting individual ownership" was put forward originally in the general context of public ownership of the means of production; the latter was by far the more fundamental principle for transformation in a socialist society, and objectively and ideologically, the process of transformation will carry with it an accelerated growth in the weight and extent of public ownership. Correspondingly, an accelerated shrinkage in the extent of individual ownership will take place. Ultimately, this "unexploiting individual ownership" would be transformed into small and limited forms within a general basic framework called the "public ownership of the means of production."

As we said earlier, some rightist elements took advantage of this obscurity and began to speak a language quite foreign to socialism. The need thus arose for Arab socialist growth (after secession) to acquire greater clarity. It should do that if it were to silence the rightist elements and if it were to bring to an end their ability to capitalize on this issue on the ideological level.

Thirdly, there was the question of transferring the means of production from public to "direct social ownership." It is to be conceded that postsecession socialism was not far from grasping this matter. Allotting to workers a share of profits and a representation on the boards of directors were themselves indications of awareness in the U.A.R. Yet the matter did not gain enough clarity in conception or regarding methodology to enable the transformation in this area to be carried to its fullest extent. Instead, this lack of clarity led to greatly confused meanings of expressions such as nationalization, state ownership, and public ownership.

Fourthly, there was the question of unifying the Arab socialist movement. Here, too, clarity in postsecession socialist thought was not sufficient. This insufficiency led to incomplete formulation of the structure of relationships between various elements and forces in Arab socialist struggle.

It is obvious, therefore, why the debate remained unclosed. It is precisely this lack of answers which set the stage for the third major development in Arab socialist thought. On the practical level, the events of the year 1963 paved the way and provided the proper circumstances for the execution of the third stage in the development of Arab socialism. . . .

The year 1963 witnessed the fall of a separatist regime in Syria and a dictatorship in Iraq. The collapse of these two regimes made it possible for the initiation of a historical dialogue over the tripartite unity of Egypt, Syria, and Iraq. To be sure, unity was not the only subject matter of that dialogue. Unity was merely the proper gate. Having entered this specific gate, the parties concerned then stood in a spot in which they came face to face with fundamental Arab socialist problems, whether in ideology, in struggle, or in application.

It turned out that the same forces that crystallized "postsecession socialism" have now carried out the third step: The socialist revolution of July 23 and the unionist popular movements were able to extract full conclusions from current events.

33. THE PHILOSOPHY OF THE UNIFIED ARAB STATE*

Muta Safadi

The Syrian writer Muta Safadi is better known for his novels and poems than for his political thought, yet he often injects political themes into his novels. Many of his heroes are protagonists of current ideas.

In the following essay, Safadi presents a picture of the conditions that confront the new Arab state. His views reflect the conditions that prevailed in 1959, when the creation of the United Arab Republic gave some Arabs the hope that all Arab lands could be quickly unified. Safadi sees the state as the creator of an Arab nation with a sociopolitical life that corresponds to the requirements of modern nationhood.

* Extract from "Fi Falsafat al-dawla al-'arabiyya al-nahdawiyya" ("Of the Philosophy of the Unified Arab State"), *al-Thaqafa al-'arabiyya* (*Arab Culture*), Beirut, April–June, 1959, pp. 11–14.

What Is the Arab State

The new Arab state emerges today to face the past and the present heritage of Western political systems that embody a particular theory of politics. This new state also confronts a vast body of shattered traditions dating from the age of regression, imperialism, and feudalism.

We do not propose to deal here with the broad philosophical outlines of this state. Now that our unified state has come into existence, however, we must search for ways and means by which the revitalized philosophy of Arab nationalism may be translated from the realm of theory to that of practice. In other words, we seek to discover ways of developing dynamic, homogeneous institutions that would constitute the basic structure of the modern Arab state.

Let us first ask ourselves, What is the unified Arab state? Is it merely the sum total of government departments, the civil service, ministers, and leaders, or is it something that transcends these? Is it a dictatorship or a democracy? What are its objectives and what is its mission?

As a matter of fact, we cannot, within the context of this treatment, offer anything other than general answers that may lead to more detailed planning in other, more exhaustive studies. In the first place, we must establish the basic character of the Arab state and the peculiar national and historical circumstances that caused it to emerge. Its character is not that of a government ruling and operating under normal circumstances. It is a revolutionary state.

Secondly, this state has not evolved from ancient governmental practices and traditions. Rather, it has created itself with no ancient political roots.

Thirdly, this state, in relation to the social, moral, and spiritual conditions prevalent and to the economic and human opportunities offered therein, is a radical state. In relation to the Arab world around it, it is a store-house of a nationalist and liberated heritage embracing the whole future of the Arabs and their new revolutionary potentiality. It is the core of the Pan-Arab state. In relation to the enemy, whether it be the Jewish or imperialist enclaves or the other tyrannical or opportunistic regimes, it constitutes a front that marshals the strength to liberate all the Arabs and that possesses all the potentialities for free and strong development. The more this state develops in a positive manner, the more these enclaves are threatened with extinction until the time comes for them to disappear altogether.

In relation to the world in general, this state represents the entry of a new force—with its own peculiar ideas about man, life, and international relations—on the stage of history. It pursues a middle path between the two ill-fated and aggressive paths of Western civilization, Communism and capitalism. This path would attempt to put an end to the stalemate that is imposed upon the whole of humanity as a result of deviations committed by a certain diseased part of the whole.

In relation, therefore, to the anxious and threatened human race, it is a state that desires genuine freedom and represents the power of sublime ideals in its policy of positive neutrality. These ideals would offer history a new path of progress by which its worn-out and age-old problems can be overcome.

They would offer man the chance to reacquire spontaneity, freedom, and peace.

As to the question of whether the state is to be democratic or dictatorial, we cannot define its character in this regard in accordance with the common meaning the West attaches to these two terms. Given the peculiar structure of this state, its form of government will also be a particular one in harmony with the freedom emanating from the depths of the Arab spirit during its various historical manifestations.

The true democracy in which the Arabs believe is the democracy of free individuals, not of public opinion or of the mass which has no particular character. At the time the Arab state emerged, Arab society was not actually composed of these free individuals. The vast majority were living in total isolation from, and ignorance of, the historical times in which they were living, and were unable to exert any real influence upon the course of events. Hence, the emergence of the Arab state was characterized by its revolutionary nature and was understood only by the *avant garde,* who were, historically speaking, the dynamic element in Arab society. The Arab state was brought into being by this element, which had made use of, and consciously activated, the national revolutionary potential. Thus, the creation of the Arab state of Egypt and Syria was a comprehensive Arab effort in the sense that all the Arabs helped indirectly to create this state, as a result of the tremendous drive for freedom unleashed by this *avant garde* throughout Arab society.

This spirit of free individualism, then, began to appear among members of the *avant garde* who represented the historically active element of the nation. This individualism did not appear through elections or ballots but through the movement of heroic selectivity which is a national symptom of the general revolutionary situation prevailing in the Arab world.

As this movement led to the emergence of leaders among this *avant garde,* so the Arab state, which is the administrative personification of this *avant garde,* selects its own leaders as a result of this spontaneous movement of heroic selectivity. Those men who possessed the greatest measure of freedom—i.e., the ability to liberate others, to revolutionize them, and to inspire their free creativity—were themselves the fruits of heroic selectivity and the ones who were destined to guide and lead. The meaning of leadership, as far as the *avant garde* and the Arab states are concerned, is not personal domination that is out of touch with the masses. The value of any Arab leadership is to be measured by its ability to create autonomous leadership in every individual under its authority—that is to say, by its capacity to put an end to the bondage of the masses to itself and to substitute a relationship of interaction between a leadership that unleashes individual freedom and free individuals who furnish this leadership with a creative and constructive spirit of endeavor.

The government of this Arab state is in the hands of this revolutionary *avant garde,* who led this movement of rebellion and were triumphant throughout this great region of the Arab homeland.

The roles of the *avant garde* and of the state are not radically different.

Their activity was always one of providing the impulse for proper consciousness and for a revolutionary spirit at the same time. However, this impulse, in the first place, was also generating basic negative forces that were directed toward the destruction of the impediments to Arab revolution, such as feudalism, imperialism, and political fragmentation. In the second place, the role of the state is still, on the one hand, based on the removal of the legacy of these impediments like the social, psychological, and metaphysical diseases that cling to the Arab personality from within, and, on the other, the activity of the state is directed toward the creation of institutions capable both of organization and of reconstruction, for the ultimate purpose of producing the comprehensive structure of the Arab state.

This spontaneous movement of selectivity was the one responsible for producing both the *avant garde* and the leaders of the Arab state and is currently operating within the state to create leaders who are both heroes and scholars. Indeed, the present leadership of the United Arab Republic is, to a large extent, composed of heroes and scholars.

The State and the Nation

It is evident that the Arab nation, in its state of fragmentation prior to the creation of the unified state, was always isolated, in varying degrees, from its various governments. No Arab state could continue to exist except by working constantly to maintain this fragmented condition. Hence, the state stood apart from the nation it led and opposed the natural urge of the nation to unite. Having lost all its popular support, the state resorted to alliances with other anti-unionist forces, e.g., imperialism, Zionism, feudalism, and Communism.

Once it had lost its Arab leadership at the time of the 'Abbasids, our Arab nation preserved its total isolation from the various states that came into being, whether they were imperialist-dominated or assumed a falsely Arab guise. The policy that the nation pursued was one of noncooperation, to the extent that the word "state" became, for the Arabs, a synonym for enmity, persecution, and malice. In return, the state made use of all laws, methods, and regulations in order to detract from the people's dignity, oppose their vital national interests, exploit their weakness for the purposes of lording it over them, and arrest their potentialities or pervert their objectives.

In brief, the fragmented Arab states were alien to the nation, personified all its corruption, terrorized it, prevented its progress, suppressed its potentialities, and paralyzed its will to contribute to the age in which it lived.

Plainly, then, the unified Arab state represents the absolute negation of the earlier fragmented states. The first task of the new state, then, is to restore the spiritual link between itself and the nation. By spiritual link, I mean this inherent organic bond between state and nation that causes the state to be a natural organic extension of the nation, as the head is to the body, and renders this part complementary to the body politic as a whole.

Historically, the Arabs always took care to maintain their existence as a nation amid the upheavals of their governments and states, amid unity and then fragmentation, internal growth, and external domination. Throughout their long history, they were never able to reconcile their unified nationality in a unified state. The pre-Islamic Arab states, for example, held sway over a part only, but not the whole, of the nation. When Islam had unified them, an Arab state came into being only in the early years, but was later to incorporate both Arabs and other nations in a state that lost its distinctive national character. Thus, this state became a very thin masking of intense national rivalries within it. The nations that had forcefully been brought under subjection soon threatened the state with extinction and put an end to the flourishing civilization of its various nationalities, especially the Arabs.

Thus, for the first time in Arab history, a state is born which is based upon Arab nationalism. The first characteristic of the United Arab Republic is that it is the state of the unified Arab nation. It has achieved the deepest historical urge of the Arab nation, since its very origins. This state, then, is not merely the hope of the present nor is it just the solution of current political and national problems. It has actualized an age-old Arab dream and has restored the lost core of the Arab nation. The Arab nation had always lacked this core in its attempt to create its own independent entity, like all other nations.

The Arab state—and herein resides its momentous significance in relation to the nation—is the Arab nation as it has actualized itself. Prior to the state, the nation is a mere potentiality whereas, with the creation of the state, it attains actuality. Therefore, the state personifies the nation, gives it its temporal character, places it in the stream of history, and works to actualize the national potentiality through the realm of civilization and social and scientific creativity.

This means that the relationship between state and nation is not one of quantity, by being the state of *all* Arabs. This word "all" does not solely imply a numerical total. The state is the nation when this latter has been transferred from the abstract to the concrete. Thus, the term "state" carries a wider meaning than does the word "government." The state is not merely the sum total of public administrative offices and institutions. It comprises not only the judicial, legislative, and executive functions. This is merely its outward appearance. In reality, it represents the general, active, and creative force emanating from the nation as a whole. It controls and unleashes the national potential, it consummates all practical activity and all values, it offers a rich source of guidance to all work, within a civilized harmony that possesses a distinctive character, that of Arab nationalism.

In other words, the relationship of the state to the nation may be compared to the relation between life and the sources of energy in the organism. It touches these sources, reveals them, encourages them, and moves them to grow and develop within its own comprehensive policy. Throughout their long history, the Arabs have never felt, as they do today, the need for this sort of existence, which is self-conscious, plans its movement, and unifies the potentialities of the organism to which it gives life.

This relationship, then, is qualitative, humanistic, and distinctive. It is not bound to the nation as a living and featureless whole but seeks to find free individuals. It is the state of a nation that has become one of free individuals.

Thus, in our Arab state, we cannot separate between the conceptual and the practical aspects of the state vis-à-vis the people, since all that the state requires is drawn from national values and not from the practical necessities of life. These latter may or may not be in harmony with our values since, by nature, they are detailed and limited to routine relations which do not tally with the revolutionary standards that the state must work to preserve in all its planning and under all circumstances.

The distinctive relationship between state and nation means that the state must establish equality among all individuals and must also distinguish between them as independent entities possessing varied potentialities. Thus, the law prescribes the limits of good and evil but becomes pernicious when it tries to prescribe an ideal personality for all the citizens. The state must view the individual, not as a means to further its own powers, but as an end in himself; an end, moreover, that is implied in the end of the state itself. This entails a socialist relationship between state and individual, a relationship that evolves individual from collective liberty. This is not the liberty that is based upon harmony in the protection and the exchange of interests, as advocated by the English school, nor is it a merely formal liberty, which is in reality the performance of a certain role, implicit in the national spirit, as Hegel would have it. Rather, it is a freedom that is manifested in the individual response to the public interest which carries with it all the distinctive potentialities and features of that individuality. Inasmuch as this is a genuine voice of admonition, which emanates from the heart of national creativity, by that much will these various responses be enriched and more comprehensive. When these responses are finally actualized within each individual, they will then ascend and unite with the liberty of the state, as a larger and distinct individuality.

IX. *Arab Thought and Contemporary Western Civilization: Interpretations*

34. THE INDIVIDUAL AND SOCIETY*

'Atif Ahmad

This article represents an effort by Professor 'Atif Ahmad of Cairo University to explain the relations between society and the individual in a rational manner by taking man's environment as the conditioning basis of his social behavior. Inspired by Marxist theories, Ahmad's approach contrasts sharply with Islamic traditions of thought, and his arguments are intended to justify Egyptian socialism.

The relation between the individual and society is a contemporary question that has attained special importance in the conditions of the present world civilization of capitalism and socialism. It has become a major problem facing thinkers everywhere, and the traditional question they now ask is this: The individual or society?

From the replies given, three distinct trends can be observed; the advocates of each are convinced of having discovered the secret of human happiness.

The first consider society as superior to the individual, the value inherited from our forebears tipping the balance; they believe that conduct regulated by particular individual values is at the bottom of the human misery here on earth.

The second group sees things quite differently. According to them, the self is the true reality. The individual represents the authentic being, and a predominance of social values would only have one result—slavery. That is why individual liberty, as they understand it, is the most precious thing man possesses.

The third group, the moderates, consider that neither the individual nor society should have an advantage over the other, and that a compromise is preferable.

Thus, the question is posed and the possible solutions outlined. According to the ideas of the theorists, all we have to do is to choose one of the solutions.

* Extract from 'Atif Ahmad, "Bayn al-fard wa-al-mujtama'" ("Between Individual and Society"), *al-'Ulum (The Sciences)*, Beirut, September, 1960, pp. 56–58.

Nevertheless, if one goes deeper into the matter, one quickly rejects the replies given on realizing their deficiencies. These deficiencies relate to a philosophy of a unique nature concerning the understanding of society, which wins over the doctrinaires by pretending to forget—through ignorance—that they are forever harping on the same wrong idea, namely, that there is a division between the individual and society and that it is their faith in this division that dictates the question: The individual or society?

The first thing to be done is to put the problem in its proper place, to verify the facts, and, finally, to discover the right way of solving it. And in this case, what is the actual bond, therefore, between the individual and society? One feels that, in the history of humanity, man never has lived without society, and never will do so. In the dawn of history, in the most distant times, when the human species was still in its primitive stage, the first men lived in the forest in separate groups. They did not live alone. . . . When the group evolved into a primitive community, the individuals grouped together in a society and became associated collectively in work. The individual did not feel himself imprisoned by the others—quite the contrary. He considered being separated from the others as a kind of death sentence. After this came slavery, feudalism, and exploitation . . . represented at various stages in the evolution of human society. Despite the savage brutality of those systems, no member of a society withdrew from it and went off to live on his own in the forest or in the desert. Why?

The conclusion is quite simple: It is that man is a social being, and can live only among others. . . . The aim of life is life itself, i.e., the satisfaction of human needs. These cannot be supplied completely by natural and spontaneous manifestations. Thus, man who lives by nature must, by a kind of human obligation, inescapably engage in production, i.e., struggle against the natural order of things, conquer it, and exploit nature to satisfy his needs.

From the very first, his life is crystallized in his mode of production, which is the direct expression of his way of life. Of necessity, life is fashioned according to the laws of production that govern it, and production cannot be an individual operation. In their struggle against nature, which they exploit to meet their needs, individuals are not in the least isolated or cut off from one another. They participate socially in production as amalgamated groups or committees. Thus, production is always and in all circumstances a social matter. . . .[1]

Consequently, society constitutes a human necessity, imposed by the laws of production as well as by those of biology. Does the symbiosis between the individual and society mean that no individual or private existence is any longer possible? . . .

The reality of today acknowledges productive, creative hands and their part in the great scientific achievements, and sees the question of personal existence in a different light. . . . The integration of each man into a specific society has two sides—a general and a particular one. The first comprises the

1. The author refers to his source, Jean Baby, *Les Lois fondamentales de l'economie capitaliste*.

general conditions that surround man, whose specific possibilities are influenced according to the very nature of these conditions, linking his individual existence to that of others to constitute a unique entity—society. The second comprises the biological conditions, the personal potentiality of each individual as such, even though he has not yet reacted to contact with society.

However, as soon as the inescapable confrontation of the individual and society occurs, the two aspects combine in each individual to constitute a straightforward manifestation of his social existence, since he lives in society.

What are the general conditions that relate the individual existence of each human being to others? Once again, these relate to production, by which I mean the laws governing the relationship of production to men and to society, for through production a well-defined relationship grows between people —a relationship defined by the nature of the productive force and by other natural conditions. This relationship to production shows the degree of response among men and determines the value they derive from their experience. I mean by this that it determines their way of life and, consequently, their position in society.

If we were to question the validity of this statement in the light of past history, the answer would be in the affirmative. In primitive communities, the concept of production was based in effect on collective ownership of the means of production—in this case land for the purpose of hunting—and the conditions of those barbarous times compelled men to work together in large communities. Thus, one finds in primitive communities that everything—including sexual relations—was shared, and that all values reflected this form of ownership; food, shelter, and all the necessities of life were shared in a spirit of mutual aid. The individual, therefore, perceived his own existence only through his relations with the group.

In a slave society, where relationship to production was based on ownership of the available means of production (i.e., slaves), this gave rise to two contradictory points of view, one for the free man and the other for the slaves. The individual was either a master of slaves or a slave himself.

The slaves—the majority of the people—were treated as tools of production and deprived of all humanity, for no other reason than the enslaving nature of the production, which enlisted human existence in the service of profit for the individual and made slaves of men.

In a feudal society, where the relations of production were based on ownership of land and on the products of nature which were monopolized by the feudatories, individuals were similarly divided into different groups—that is to say, opposing groups. . . .

In all human societies, the individual's way of life was determined by the relations of production. The decisive factor conditioning the life of the individual certainly did not come from his individual existence, even though specific circumstances played an important part in establishing the final characteristics of this existence. This indicates that members of a specific society were the products of particular social conditions determined by specific factors. These factors were distinctly reflected by individuals and their particular characteristics.

Every individual constitutes a shade or a definite color in the total picture that we call society. An organic unity exists between the two—the individuals being the various features of society. Perhaps each nuance has its own particular significance, but in the long run the human face emerges as a type of its own. . . . If we examine carefully the face of socialist society, the charm of symmetry dazzles us and begins to give us a sense of human perfection, while if we endeavor to do likewise with regard to capitalist society we are soon overwhelmed by the tragedy of the exploitation of man by man. . . . [This is] the tragedy of a savage struggle, of intellectual poison, [promoted] always with the purpose of glorifying exploitation and surrounding it with bright colors, so as to capture forever the life of all productive individuals. . . .

In a class society where a capitalist regime holds the upper hand, there is a contradictory relationship in individual existence; i.e., all realization of individual existence is at the expense of another human being. Whenever the capitalist's profits increase, the wages of the workers decrease; and whenever the workers' wages rise, the capitalist's gains decrease.

Each rise in the profits of a capitalist diminishes the gains of another. Whenever new workers are engaged in a factory, the level of wages for the old workers in endangered; and whenever an individual rises in importance, others fall.

There is a conflict in the capitalist society because unity and exploitation exist at the same time. The class system is based on the exploitation of labor by a handful of individuals, and from this results the sharp contradiction between the different needs of individuals. Hence is also born the contradiction between the individual and society which takes a specific intellectual form in individualistic philosophies, the natural outcome being self-centeredness and feelings of hostility toward others.

At their height, the individualistic philosophies result in existentialism, and they are a true expression of the crisis of man in a capitalist society and the expression of man's inability to resolve this contradiction scientifically.

Whenever the individual feels the hostility of others toward himself, he withdraws into himself. But he cannot resign himself to living alone, and thereafter he is caught in a vicious circle, with himself as the center, eventually losing contact with others as well as with himself. His whole life becomes loneliness, anxiety, violent internal disturbance. . . . If he had been aware of the reality of the link between the individual and society, he would have understood that his individualistic philosophy is nothing but a social phenomenon stemming from an internal bleeding at the heart of organized class society.

The situation is entirely different in socialist society, where production is oriented not toward attaining the maximum individual profit but, on the contrary, toward guaranteeing the lives and future of men and satisfying their physical and cultural needs. We find here—but not in capitalist society—

a unity of view regarding improvement and close coordination in the existence of individuals. Each improvement in the life of an individual corresponds, at the same time, to an improvement in the lives of others; and each time production increases, general prosperity increases also. No more exploitation, no more interest at the expense of the work of others, but a close and conscious cooperation toward a worth-while human life. Socialist society is simply the realization of the existence of individuals, the expression of their lives both on social and human levels.

35. EAST AND WEST—SHALL THEY MEET?*

Anwar al-Sa'dat

Anwar al-Sa'dat (b. 1918), a close collaborator of President Nasser since their years of secret revolutionary activity, is one of the most versatile members of the Revolutionary Command Council. He was president of the Egyptian National Union, a political organization, in 1957-61, and chairman of the Afro-Asian Conference held in Cairo in 1958. His record also includes membership in the rightist, pro-German al-Fata' al-misri *(Egyptian Youth Organization) in 1940-41. He had close relations with Hasan al-Banna, and acted as liaison between the Muslim Brotherhood and the officers' secret associations. From 1954 to 1961, al-Sa'dat was secretary general of the Islamic Congress, which aimed to replace the disbanded Muslim Brotherhood and proposed to create close relations between Egypt and the Muslim countries of Asia and Africa through three committees in the cultural, economic, and administrative and financial fields.*

Anwar al-Sa'dat is a prolific writer. Among his books are Revolt on the Nile *(London: Allan Wingate; New York: John Day, 1957), which provides excellent information on the revolutionary officers' relations with religious and rightist groups, and* Qissat al-wahda al-'arabiyya (Story of Arab Unity), *from which the following material was extracted. In it, al-Sa'dat totally rejects Western civilization as being geared to the domination of weaker nations by the powerful through the exploitation of religion, science, and ethics. This is the view of the politician and not of the intellectual. He views the evacuation of Egypt in 1956 by French, British, and Israeli forces as a victory of the East over the West, and he ignores the crucial role of the United States in this evacuation.*

* Extract from Anwar al-Sa'dat, *Qissat al-wahda al-'arabiyya* (*Story of Arab Unity*) (Cairo: Dar al-Hilal, 1957). It appeared as "Orient et Occident" in *Orient,* No. 6 (1958), 145–54.

The decision to nationalize the Suez Canal [1956] is a turning point in the history of humanity, and heralds a new era, with a new evolution and a new history.

Today—or to be more exact, since the nationalization of the Suez Canal—whoever reads the English, French, or American press, or that of other Western powers, realizes that in each line there is some hesitation over the words West and East; the reader remarks differing trends: Sometimes the West is afraid of the East, and sometimes it provokes it. Now, through this distrust or provocation, there shines a glaring, obvious truth—namely, that in the West, all the ideas about understanding the East and associating with it have flourished only under the harsh light of distrust and watchfulness, hostility, and provocation.

For my part, I do not use the terms West and East in the sense in which they are normally used today—as referring to the two big blocs that divide the world—East meaning Russia and her allies, and West meaning America and her allies. On the contrary, when I use these terms, I revert to their original meaning, in keeping with the times and with history, and the nearest interpretation to my own is that of Kipling, the poet of colonialism, in his famous poem: "East is East, and West is West, and never the twain shall meet."

As soon as we try to define boundaries between East and West—which are precise enough to allow us to classify the countries by study and analysis consistent with history and reality—we come up against numerous difficulties.

For example, are the frontiers in question geographical in origin, or are they a fact of civilization, in the sense that the characteristics of this or that civilization, taken in the light of its history, permanent features, and common origin with various peoples, represent the true boundary—as in the case for what we include under the name East on the one side and West on the other?

Or, again, are the boundaries determined by race, so that we may say that, race being the specific factor, certain races constitute essentially the West and others the East?

If, by adhering to geography, we were to repeat, as did the scholars of the nineteenth century, that the dividing line between West and East roughly follows a line from north to south touching the eastern shores of the Mediterranean—the countries situated to the east of the line constituting the East and the countries to the West the West—we would be committing a grave error, indeed; in effect, Egypt, Palestine, Libya, Tunisia, Algeria, and Morocco would all be ranged in the West, although they are linked to the East by the ancient bonds of history and civilization. The same goes for all institutions involving purely Eastern peoples, who would find it impossible to assimilate with the West, from which they remain as far removed as possible.

An error of the same kind might be made with regard to Australia and New Zealand, which, on the lines of the division in question, form part of the East, although their history, civilization, and institutions do not bind them to the East, from which they are separated to a maximum degree both in spirit and by natural inclination. We shall no longer take race as a criterion, for China unites in a single people innumerable races, as do also America and Russia.

The only sound criterion that remains to us, therefore, is civilization, defined as a common spirit and inscribed in the institutions that provide the very basis on which we can distinguish between East and West. We can thus define as Eastern the group of peoples whose civilization and history belong to the East, a similar definition being likewise applied to the West.

We shall thus avoid mistakes: Tunisia, Algeria, and Morocco form part of the West according to the map, but in reality they are bound by their civilization and their history to the East. The same reasoning applies, in reverse, to Australia and New Zealand, which, according to the map, are situated in the heart of the East, while in reality, by civilization and history, they are attached to the West. . . . As I have already said, and as the present world situation proves, we are engaged in a battle that concerns not only Egypt but that began many long centuries ago between East and West, and the fate of which was definitely sealed by the nationalization of the Suez Canal. That is why we see the Western press and governments since the proclamation of today immersed in a fear and terror that strongly resembles mass hysteria, to the point where the Western powers assemble their fleets, equip their troops, and proclaim to the whole world that they are preparing for hostilities, and thus provoke the opinion of the free world. The Western press can no longer disguise the truth; it proclaims its fear of the East, at the same time provoking it; it weeps and laments over the fate of the West, since the East can no longer be humiliated.

The Western view of the East springs from two sources: Either it is mistrust, giving rise inevitably to precautionary measures and incessant preparations against an Eastern plot, or it is provocation aimed at humiliating the East and thwarting its aspirations. In both cases, what the West has in view is the acquisition of the resources of the rich East, for the enrichment of the Western community and its sons, and the suppression of all progress, instruction, and power, so that this same East may be reduced to weakness and ignorance, and kept underdeveloped under the yoke of the Western protectorate.

How can we define the role of the nationalization of the Suez Canal in the progress of this struggle? That is what we shall now examine.

The Facts of the Struggle

Let us go back to what I just said about the Western view of the East. What is this struggle, in fact?

In order to uncover this truth, we must treat as historical events all the signs that came from the West during the Battle of Suez. We are going to dig into the facts of this struggle, which marks, in a way no less real, the end of the tragedy of the domination of East by West.

[The following] is a symptom whose appearance is of exceptional importance: In an unguarded moment, the French Premier declared that Muslims should have confidence in the help of France, which would look after the common good of Islam and the Muslims. The responsible English did not waste their time.

The Western press, however, proclaimed with more frankness that the struggle was between Islam and the Arabs on the one hand and the West and the Christians on the other. A certain section of the press went so far as to declare that the Muslim East wanted to annihilate the Christian West. It is here, in this premeditated confusion, that the heart of the problem lies.

The East, which today confronts the West in the battle for the Suez Canal, extends from China to the Atlantic Ocean. China has a population of 600 million, and the Chinese of all stations are rising to brave the West. . . . In India, 380 million men likewise are rising to brave the West. . . .

The problem, therefore, is not that of a Muslim East; it is that of an East deceived, an East colonized by a West that has sucked its blood. That East wishes to avenge itself, but not in the Western manner by hostility and usurpation. All it wishes is to live freely and independently, that each nation shall make her own destiny, exploit the riches of her soil for the benefit of her own children, and respect the independence of other nations, whether they be Eastern or Western.

Thus, Egypt can be aided by 1,500 million men, of all stations in life, of different religions and instruction, but all united in the same resolution and the same faith.

Western propaganda, according to which the Islamic East is seeking to destroy the Christian West, sows confusion and flagrantly contradicts the facts. But it constitutes a symptom of the struggle that is destined to continue between East and West before one story ends and another begins. For if the conflict for the Suez Canal had involved India and the West, we would have heard similarly, from the voice of the Western press, that the Hindu East was seeking to destroy the Christian West. If the conflict for the Suez Canal had involved Burma and the West, we would have heard similarly, from the voice of the Western press, that the Buddhist East was seeking to destroy the Christian West.

What I want to say in conclusion is that the West-East struggle is as real and as old as the civilization of the East and the designs of the West. This struggle will last as long as the East is rich in resources and treasures brought from the depths of its soil, from the goodness of its earth, and the abundance of its various products; this struggle will carry on as long as the West persists in its present view of the East, founded on entirely mistaken and unjust principles which are in total contradiction with earthly and divine principles.

What are these mistaken principles? How have they been able to develop and assume enough importance to menace, by the Suez affair, the security of humanity and inspire the repulsion of all that is just, true, and generous? How has the West sought to involve, in these demonstrations of hostility and hatred, religions that counsel only love and peace? That is what we are now going to examine.

Mistaken Principles

The West sees in the East only swarming millions of starving, naked, and ignorant people, toward whom it has the duty to assume the role of tutor according to the principles of humanity, the Christian religion, and European civilization!

There again, the West runs counter to truth, to history, and to human values. Has it, in effect, the prerogative of carrying the Christian message? Has it the right to interpret it in a manner contradictory to its fundamental principles, to enlist it in the colonial adventure founded on hate and discord between the sons of humanity? No, that is one thing we do not accept, we in the East, for we know Christianity and its principles: The Christians are people like ourselves; our land is the cradle of this religion; it is from our soil that the new message went forth to conquer pagan Europe!

The diversity of our beliefs and our laws does not prevent us in the East from recognizing Christianity, from respecting it and separating it from all the West would add to it. The Buddhists, the Hindus, the Muslims, the Confucians, the Christians of the East, and the Copts know Christianity better than the West knows it or claims to know it.

In pronouncing the puerilities about Christianity, the West forgets that the millions of orientals, whom it sees naked and starving, knew civilization, religion, and wisdom while Europe was still wandering in the blackness of ignorance and living under the influence of witchcraft and myth. The East, the cradle of Christianity, knows that it is founded on the two principles of faith and charity. Do these figure in what the West calls Christianity?

The East, the cradle of Christianity, knows that the basis of its message is not to separate men, but to urge them to love one another for all time. If, then, a man of black or yellow race should approach a Christian to ask him to cure him, the Christian will treat him exactly as if he were white. Does the West really understand Christianity as we understand it in the East?

No, for the West wallows in the materialism that penetrates all its principles and shames the letter and the spirit of Christianity. It is the West that has created the myth of the white man and his superiority over the "colored"; it is the West that undertakes the killing of the innocent, assuming the right to determine the destiny of their countries; it is the West that calls piracy courage, for whom the stripping and subjugation of man are established rights.

That is the fundamental point of conflict between East and West. For us orientals, religions are a spiritual refuge where our souls find peace from the cares of this world. The West, on the other hand, enlists religion in its plans for domination.

For us orientals, Christianity has a universal message of mercy which in principle does not differ from other religions and beliefs that we practice, for they all teach love, brotherhood, and peace. The Westerners, on the other hand, consider themselves as the privileged guardians of Christianity, and those who are not Christians as illiterates, sorcerers, and barbarians.

It is thus that the West has gone astray, that Christianity and its principles are mixed with the acts of this sinful world, forgetting that the East is the cradle of Christianity and the source of all religions. [Al-Sa'dat describes the battle for the Suez Canal as the encounter of the forces of East and West and mentions again that some Europeans asked that Western civilization be safeguarded.] . . .

But Western civilization and its heritage, for which Europe and America fear so much, live only on the debris of the East and would not flourish if they had not sucked its blood. That is the astonishing truth.

Western civilization is not today a civilization [*hadara*] as the term is understood by science and theory, but only a way of life [*madaniyya*], and there is a big difference between a civilization and a way of life. A civilization, in fact, is characterized, above all, by its ideals and spirtual principles, and material institutions come only in second place; we see, therefore, that it is not concerned with appearances but is above all founded on the spirit.

A way of life, on the other hand, is not concerned with ideals or spiritual principles, and in the life of the individual or of the group, it presents only a purely material and readily artificial face, as if life itself were as mechanical as machines or pushbuttons. There is no value in a way of life that ignores the very essence of human life.

Civilization, therefore, is defined and will always be defined by the highest human values, while a way of life interprets human values in terms of material progress. By virtue of this argument and what we see all around us, we can appreciate the distance that extends between a civilization and a way of life, and can identify the so-called civilization of the West as the Western way of life. And there, as I see it, is another conflict between West and East: The West claims the right to impose its present way of life; it claims that the basis of the new message is to make the Eastern peoples receive only some examples of this Western "civilization" in well defined and restricted form—for example, when the West introduces a democratic system to an Eastern people it is not in the same form as in the West. Westerners content themselves with imposing on the people [of the East] a system designed to ensure Western authority and domination, finally baptizing it democracy and calling it the outcome of modern Western civilization.

When the West introduces modern science to an Eastern country under the yoke of colonialism, this knowledge is not transmitted by natural stages, for the Western concept of civilization is that the East should not have more than the outer shell of Western science, the preservation and usages of knowledge being reserved for the white man.

Hence many peoples, victims of colonialism, have thus far been suffering and have been incapable of growth, since they have neither medicine nor geometry—these skills being reserved, in the Western theory of civilization, for the white man, the chosen man. That is how the West ensures its domination. One last illustration of this state of affairs: England invites military missions to come to England from various Western and Eastern states. It happened that in 1950 some Egyptian officers formed part of one of these missions. On their return, they told how the main meetings were barred to them and to other delegations from Eastern countries, because those meetings dealt with military secrets reserved for the English and the Europeans. . . . These examples illustrate what is understood in the West by civilization, or, rather, way of life.

The Eastern idea of civilization differs radically. The East is proud of the fact that the greatest civilizations known to man were nurtured on its soil: the Chinese civilization, which discovered wisdom and light; the Pharaonic civilization, which astonished and continues to astonish the world by its brilliant past in science and the arts; the Indian civilization, which, since antiquity, has plumbed the secrets of the spirit and of matter and presented to humanity a philosophy and science whose glorious heritage will remain until the end of time.

The East, therefore, interprets civilization as founded on spiritual rather than material values. We believe that the Chinese, Egyptian, or Indian civilizations invented ethics and humanities and arts, honored the family, organized the relationships of individuals with one another, and the relationships of individuals to society or to the government—the Chinese civilization remaining unsurpassed in its theory of power and the applications of power, on the one hand, and of subjects and their essential politeness, on the other.

But the sole result of these civilizations has not been the establishment of human values. Science, art, mathematics, and architecture remain as testimonials to the permanence of the superiority of these civilizations over thousands of years. The East conceives civilization as an edifice where coexistence reigns for the good of all, and that is why it is proud of its civilization, which it deems superior to the Western way of life.

Everything was therefore abundantly clear to the East when it threw off the vestiges of colonialism and Western domination. It now desires to make up for lost time. It feels an ardent desire for the civilization which is part of its lifeblood and which will devour it like a fire; and the civilization engrained in it burns with a flame which cannot be extinguished.

The West finds itself—with its "civilization" built by the sword, by fire, by piracy, and by violence—faced with people who possess a pure and genuine civilization, faced with people who would live honorably and rescue their spiritual strength from the grip of Western "civilization."

The struggle will continue until the true civilization triumphs over the false—in other words, until supreme values replace base methods of force.

36. THE ARABS AND THE CIVILIZATION OF THE CENTURY*

Muhammad Wahbi

Muhammad Wahbi is a Lebanese whose writings on Arab intellectual and philosophical problems are both critical and detached. In his first book, Azmat al-tamaddun al-'arabi (The Crisis of Arab Progress) (*Beirut: Dar al-'ilm lil-*

* Extract from Muhammad Wahbi, *'Uruba wa-insaniyya (Arabism and Humanism)* (Beirut: Mansharat 'Uwaydat, 1958), pp. 13–20.

malayin, 1956), Wahbi argued for a more basic revolution within Arab society to absorb modern civilization in all its aspects, instead of concentrating solely on gaining independence. In a later book, he discusses, among other ideas, the clash between conservative and revolutionary tendencies and stresses a basic problem of the Middle East: Is there one civilization, or is the Middle East divided into Western and Eastern civilizations? Is the first materialistic and the latter spiritualistic, as claimed by Anwar al-Sa'dat in Egypt (see pp. 229–35, above) and many others in the East? Or is there just one civilization with many cultural aspects? Wahbi claims that there is one civilization—the contemporary one to which all mankind belongs. (A similar idea was put forth by Dr. Abdullah Cevdet, a Turkish thinker, at the turn of the century. "If you speak about civilization," he said, "there is just one, and that is in the West. Consequently, one is either in it or out of it. There is no other alternative to being civilized." Abdullah Cevdet's thoughts exercized a profound influence on Atatürk and were expressed in his reforms.)

Today there are two opposing currents of ideas in the Arab East. In fact, since Western civilization overwhelmed this region, two main trends have come to light; one is conservative in character, the other revolutionary. The first is the color-bearer of the opposition to that civilization; it stands against it. Its supporters [the conservatives] are convinced that this civilization is purely materialistic and that material things are all that matter to it; it is the source of all aggression in the peoples who are influenced by it. The East, on the other hand, is spiritual in nature, and must in no way renounce its spirituality.

To justify this extreme thesis, some go so far as to say that this [Western] civilization carries within it the germ of all wars, which, in their eyes, is proof of its extreme materialism. . . . They also maintain that this civilization came to us via colonialism, which it embodies and which it serves; we must therefore reject it and avoid it. They affirm that it is in great part the work of Zionism, which penetrates its web and directs it; we must therefore beware of its misdeeds and its depravity. It is clear that these arguments are fallacious, and have no logical connection.

The supporters of the second trend [i.e., the revolutionaries] nourish such admiration for this civilization that they launch an appeal in favor of its complete adoption. They also believe in the materialism of the West and the spirituality of the East, and this influences their attitude, although their admiration does not prevent them from proclaiming their great disappointment in spiritualism and their blind attachment to materialism. There is another so-called intermediate trend between these two extreme, exclusive, and opposing trends, and this invites comparison. The supporters of this consider it appropriate to adopt only one part of Western civilization—that which refers to science, which is indispensable to progress, the rest being discarded, especially as regards morals. This theory is also founded on the belief that Western civilization is materialistic, while the East is spiritualist.

Thus, if we examine the ideas of the supporters of these three trends, we note they agree in affirming the materialism of the West and the spirituality of Eastern thought. Frankly, I do not see how such a "consensus" has been achieved and on what logical foundation it is based. Is it because Western civilization abounds in achievements of a material nature, although these are but the expressions of a spiritual force? And what is spirituality, then, if not the close relationship of all absolute values within the sole aim of dominating nature and utilizing it, rather than fleeing from it in order to shelter in a sterile world of sentiment and fancy? And what do Eastern morality and spirituality represent with regard to the behavior of the really civilized man, whose behavior is so full of love for truth and fulfillment of duty, so rich also in profound respect for the liberty of others?

None of these theories is right; all are constructed on false bases. There is no spirituality today in the East. It is in the West that one must look for spirituality, which is the prime cause of all evolution.

Although these three concepts are completely valueless, there is nevertheless one that we should qualify as dangerous, and that is one called "intermediate." In appearance moderate, it is hypocrisy itself. More than the other two, it exercises an evil influence on the mind, for it is more convincing by its moderation, although it is founded on a basic contradiction. In fact, in Western civilization, no knowledge is born or developed except on a moral basis, and it would be nonsense to wish to adopt scientific progress while rejecting its foundations. This proves that this civilization is one and indivisible, that its different branches are nourished by the same spirit, and to dismember it would lead to its losing all value and usefulness. Such a conception can only be qualified, in effect, as cowardice and weakness; it derives from an inability to discover truth, which leads to fear and hesitation.

In fact, it matters little whether we align ourselves with one or the other camp. Whatever we do, the course of things will not be changed. In fact, the influence exercised by Western civilization is effective and spontaneous because of the constant contact of modern life and the multiplicity of the means of communication. There is nevertheless another important fact that is indisputable: Not only do we derive no value from this influence, but it threatens to endanger Arab thought if it remains linked to a wrong conception of the spirit of this civilization. In fact, if we stick to this conception, we will derive absolutely no profit from this influence, but, on the contrary, will suffer its ill effects and serious consequences.

Consequently, if we wish to keep ourselves as much in the background as possible regarding the essence of the things we are ourselves adopting, then we are working toward our own ruin by isolating ourselves and shutting ourselves up in the poor sphere in which we circle today with our false ideas and opinions.

It is of prime importance to us to revise the conception we have built up about Western civilization; to convince ourselves, subsequently, that it is necessary to adopt this civilization as a whole, voluntarily and openly! It is, in fact, the civilization of the century for the whole world. There is no other alternative for a people who wish to live and do not desire to become fixed in a past which is over, but to accept it and assimilate it in its totality.

The expression "Western civilization" is nevertheless somewhat exaggerated; it is important now to examine its meaning and define it. It seems to indicate that this civilization is uniquely that of the West; in reality, it is the civilization of the whole of mankind.

In fact, one of the characteristics of the present time is that it cannot allow the existence of several separate civilizations, man's situation being far different from what it once was. In the past, a particular civilization appeared, then crumbled or disappeared under the influence of political events or as a result of the appearance of another civilization and its contact with it. It sometimes happened that different civilizations existed in widely separated regions of the world. But man's life today is no longer what it was yesterday.

Humanity has profoundly changed. Having once lived isolated from one another, as in sealed vases, the nations of today lead the same collective existence. This is the result of the growth of all forms of communication and their extraordinary rapidity. These communications have facilitated the diffusion of ideas and news. Geographical frontiers and great distances no longer play any role, with the result that humanity as a whole lives as one single family under the same roof. As a result of this evolution, humanity has been entrusted with a unique mission—that of carrying the torch of a civilization that cannot but be unique. It is difficult for this civilization not to be the synthesis of what the human spirit has produced in the course of time. It cannot, in fact, forget the past even in part, because it is the path that led to the present, and do not all people today collaborate in this common effort which bears the mark of each? Similarly, this civilization cannot remain fixed on all or part of the past; the law of evolution does not allow it.

The present civilization is that of all humanity, and although Europeans have played a considerable role in its creation and have stamped it with their seal, that does not imply that it can be considered basically as European.

This civilization, in fact, is only the result of a convergence. It was formed in the melting pot of former civilizations and what they engendered—the essential contributions of the human spirit in the course of its evolution, the transformations and improvements demanded by progress.

To carry the torch of modern civilization is today the mission of all nations that are to participate in its expansion, each according to its possibilities. It is no longer possible today to make a distinction between the mission of one nation and that of another. It carries with it responsibilities of which each nation bears a part. The value of a nation is measured according to the importance of the responsibility it assumes and carries out effectively. It is measured also according to the importance of these responsibilities with regard to the common good. We note, when we consider the spirit of this civilization, that it represents the highest degree of civilization in man, as such. Among its various elements, we must note the scientific spirit, with all the intelligence it implies; the result of a wide culture; the constant and disinterested search after knowledge.

This scientific spirit has allowed industry to develop, and has transformed the conditions of life. It is distinguished also by a social spirit, which includes a growth in cooperative movements, and the birth of a large number of practices that have helped in the development and progress of social life. Finally, it is distinguished by the existence of international public opinion, which is now a powerful force in politics.

Nevertheless, when we examine all these elements more closely, we can see that they all stem from one source—freedom. Freedom is, in fact, the soul of all endeavor, whether scientific or social. That is why the manifestations of national liberation are the most important consequences of this civilization in the political sphere.

As to the aggressive colonialist tendencies that still exist, they are not important and only survive in a minority of politicians who are not the representatives of the will of their people, as events prove.

That freedom should be considered the soul of present-day civilization is a fact that proves that we are at the summit of human evolution, for freedom is the essence of man. Civilization has allowed him to discover this, and to identify himself closely with it, but not without meeting many obstacles on the way. That is why we can say that the destiny of each nation depends on the way in which it fulfills its mission in the service of this civilization.

37. THE CAUSES OF THE CRISIS IN ARAB THOUGHT*

Ishaq Musa al-Husayni

Dr. Ishaq Musa al-Husayni, a Palestinian living in Cairo, is the author of The Moslem Brethren: The Greatest of Modern Islamic Movements *(Beirut: Khayat's, 1956) published originally in Arabic as* al-Ikhwan al-muslimun: kubra al-haraka al-islamiyya al-haditha *(Beirut: Dar Bairut, 1952). In the book from which the following excerpts are taken, he deals with the broader cultural problems that confront the Arab world.*

The crisis is, in origin and essence, a crisis in thought from which proceed all the other crises that arose from time to time. This crisis has five manifestations.

The first is uncertainty. We are uncertain where we are going, like a man

* Extract from Ishaq Musa al-Husayni, *Azmat al-fikr al-'arabi* (*The Crisis in Arab Thought*) (Beirut: Dar Bairut, 1954), pp. 15–24. (A review appeared in *Middle East Journal,* XIII [Winter, 1959], 97–98.)

leaving his house in the morning with no clear idea of what he intends to do. He sees many paths before him and dashes into one of them without knowing where he will end up. He may achieve something or he may not. It might take a short time or a long one, and he may find what he wants or he may not. In other words, we inhabit cities with nameless streets and numberless houses. If we had clear foresight, we would have planned our cities so that, before leaving our houses, we can specify the street and the destination we seek. Because of the widespread faith in destiny, in the over-all ordering of the universe, and in the total foreordination of all our comings and goings, it may be that this has led to our complete reliance on God and to the absence of planning which would do away with uncertainty. A poet has expressed this sentiment by saying: "To seek your fortune when your fortunes have already been allotted is a crime that would lead to ruin." Another poet has written: "Our destiny is foreordained. Thus activity and inactivity are both futile. It is sheer madness to seek your fortune, since the fortune even of the unborn child is determined in advance." I need not emphasize, however, that Muslim thinkers have drawn the real moral from this belief. They have distinguished it from true submission to God and have defended the Almighty from charges of injustice, often quoting the words of the poet: "He is bound and thrown into the sea and is told, 'Don't get soaked!' "

The second manifestation is extemporization. Where there is uncertainty and absence of planning, there will always be extemporization. Our literature defines rhetoric as speech consonant with the requirements of the situation. An Arab proverb says, "The proper words for the proper occasion," and another says, "The best oratory is extemporaneous." But it often happens that we are faced with situations for which we are not prepared. We view the problems of life so closely that they become blurred. When these problems arise suddenly, we improvise solutions that are often wrong.

The third manifestation of this crisis of thought is the absence of reason: correct and logical thinking based on study and meditation. The men of thought have not participated effectively in building our modern society, and have not been given the chance to do so. We do not possess institutions that include scholars working each in his own specialized field. We have no writers researching and studying our various problems, recording their opinions, and transmitting their knowledge to successors in order to evolve a scholarly heritage embracing all walks of life. We have no specialized books in such fields as economics, sociology, agriculture, etc. If we are forced to do some research, we borrow, quote, and make a show of approximating what is written by foreign authors. We have no conferences to discuss and debate various problems that would require the knowledge of experts and scholars. We have no intellectual societies that expound and uphold various ideas. We have given our whole attention to politics, and have emptied it of all its real content, so that now politics is merely tinkering with words. True political thought, which embraces economic, social, industrial, and other questions, has not been sufficiently studied.

The fourth manifestation of the crisis is the absence of courage, ideological freedom, and self-criticism. Our sense of collective responsibility is not strong enough to lead to the disinterested expression of truth, for the sake of God and the fatherland. The thinking man among us is suspect. If he departs from the ordinary, he is accused of hypocrisy or unbelief. Thus, freedom of thought is imprisoned within us, where it tortures our conscience, and the crisis becomes worse from one generation to the next. The modern life enjoyed by other men is an object of envy for us when we visit the West. This modern life, in both its spiritual and material aspects, did not descend from on high, nor was it evolved suddenly, but it was made possible by the participation of scholars and men of thought. In this context, I would like to draw attention to the work of the Fabian Society, founded in England in 1883, which prepared the ground for the creation of the democracy we presently witness in England and elsewhere in the West. The activity of this society was purely rational. It tackled social problems individually and, in its successive pamphlets, enlightened the public and the various governments. Its studies were based on freedom of thought, pure science, and specialization, with the ultimate aim of service to society. The members of this society refused to join the government, since their aim was not to get into power but to lay the scientific foundations for good government and to support the government by offering sensible opinions. They were afraid that if they were to join the government they would be distracted from the original aim for which they labored.

The fifth manifestation is our obsession with the past and the respect, bordering on worship, for ancient laws, repeating all the while this vague and magical incantation, "We can remedy the present only with the remedies of the past." This in effect means that we must go back to live in deserts and caves, ride on camels, wear our traditional baggy robes, treat diseases by cauterization, allow epidemics to decimate us, content ourselves by reading incantations, and suffer the resources of the earth to remain buried.

It is undeniable that Arab history witnessed periods of great power and dominion, intellectual eminence and concern for experimental knowledge that was of great service to humanity. The Arabs may be justly proud of this heritage. But all this has passed away. Neither regret nor negative adulation nor imitation can bring it back. Two things only can do so: One is to seek for the true causes of that intellectual eminence and material prosperity, in order that we may benefit therefrom in building our modern society and restore our waning morale by recalling past glory. Nations possess peculiar characteristics which render them susceptible to grafts that are taken from their own stem, so to speak.

The second requirement must be our determination to link the ancient with the modern. Of modernity we have nothing at all at present, so we must adopt it unhesitatingly wherever we find it. It is wrong to suppose that modernity begins where antiquity has left off. Between ancient and modern there is a vast chasm that we cannot bridge, whatever our might or resources. We must therefore begin at the stage reached by civilized nations. This entails the adoption of a different attitude than the one we adopt today, or at least that some of us wish to adopt, toward modern civilization in general. This latter, with its experimental science, its industry, its studies that are based on statistics, its attitude toward the value of the individual in society, its application of modern methods of government, and its social justice—this civilization is the only bridge that can link our past with our present.

These, then, are the manifestations of the crisis in thought that we experience today. Other and similar manifestations do undoubtedly exist, and my own treatment has naturally been too generalized. I must now turn to some detailed examples. I shall cite three basic problems: (1) the form of the state that has not yet crystallized; (2) our turbulent material life; and (3) our moral or spiritual life, which contains many flaws.

The Form of the State

Writing about governments and their influence on shaping the minds of the peoples, Bertrand Russell said: "Give me a well-equipped army backed by an authority which would provide it with a higher salary and more food than most people can obtain and I will guarantee that within thirty years, I will get most of the citizens to believe that two and two makes three, that water freezes when boiled and boils when frozen or any other absurd notion that may be of service to the state."

In point of fact, however odd in form, the state is capable of directing the people in any way it desires. A proverb that is born of experience says, "The people follow the religion of their kings." And yet, Arabs still differ as to which form of state should exercise power. There are three conflicting schools of thought: The first calls for a religious state that derives its authority from canonical legislation. The second calls for a sectarian state that derives its authority from the wishes of the various sects. The third calls for a secular state that derives its authority from the public interest which in turn follows the development of the people and renders all the citizens equal in rights and obligations. This last is the form chosen by most nations, both Eastern and Western, after having undergone severe trials and painful calamities.

In our part of the world, people have misunderstood the term secular state, supposing it to mean a nonreligious state that works to undermine religion. That is a false notion. Linguistically and historically, the term implies a modern state that pursues two aims: (1) absolute justice and complete equality among individuals, irrespective of their creed, and (2) civic legislation that is based on the discoveries of modern knowledge about material and moral problems in society, and that develops so as to suit the changing circumstances of the various nations. These two aims, far from negating religion or battling against religious creeds, are, in fact, derived from the sublime ideals advocated by all religions. There is a difference between separating religion from the state and separating religion from society. Religion can no more be severed from society than the soul from the body. Religion, in its own ways, treats of the life of the soul, while the social, political, and economic sciences treat of the life of the body in accordance with their various and developing methods. After a long period of unity, psychic and physiological medicine have finally drawn apart. This is because life is of more value to man than anything else and, in order to preserve it, man has had to sacrifice some of his religious vanity. But there are some who still live in an era when the two medicines have not yet parted and are thus exposed to grave danger.

Thus, to link religious and secular remedies would result in rival inclinations, diversity in the distribution of authority, and the conflict of sects and classes at the expense of the state itself. Throughout the course of history, we have seen that whenever secular and religious authority were combined, one would suffer at the expense of the other. Therefore, and after long experience, men in most countries of the world have come to agree that the two authorities should be separated so that each can proceed along its natural course and each can develop for the benefit of both and of humanity at large.

I must here mention that Islam, which has been unjustly accused of stagnation, has prepared the ground, through such doctrines as analogy *[qiyas]*, individual interpretation *[ijtihad]*, consensus *[ijma]*, and public interest *[al-masalih al-mursala]*, for this development of secular and religious affairs. Had it been otherwise, Islam, at its early stages, would never have contributed so generously to human civilization, both materially and spiritually. In the age of decadence, and to some extent even today, the Muslims blocked all these avenues to progress for fear of their consequences. But such suppression was worse in its effects than the emancipation of thought. Indeed, one has only to look at most of the Islamic world today, and to compare it with the past or with the conditions prevalent elsewhere in the modern world, in order to perceive this truth.

Moreover, secular legislation has been adopted by most Islamic countries. Modern jurists have been able to reconcile this with Islamic law, despite opposition varying in intensity in various countries. I would like to quote here a respected modern jurist, ʻAbd al-Rahman Badawi, a judge at the International Court at The Hague. While addressing a committee entrusted with the drawing up of a constitution for independent Egypt in 1922, he said: "Whereas the minorities tend to remember the past with its record of persecutions, it is a fact that both the majority and the minority lived under an authoritarian regime where both were equally persecuted. We do not wish or contemplate the revival of the past within our modern system. Religious differences, even with us, are beginning to fade away and it will not be long before they totally disappear from our social relations. We must not therefore allow this spectre to overshadow us. Indeed, I greatly fear this problem, especially in an age where religious differences have weakened and where the factor of common interest, irrespective of creed, has become the binding link among men in society. I hope to see the day when all our activities, even marriage, divorce, etc. are unified under one well-organized civic system of life. We want a purely nationalist policy, which pays no regard to religions and sects but works always for the interest of the nation."

Turning now to some Arab countries that live under a sectarian system, we find that there is much complaint therefrom. If my guess is correct, such a system is inevitably on its way out, since divided loyalties and conflicting hopes weaken the structure of the state. . . .

It is high time that the Arabs must take account of three considerations: The first is that constructive nationalism is founded upon complete justice among the citizens and works to unite them by all means, especially through legislation. The absence of justice breeds grievances and, in the end, allows the enemy to break through our lives. The second is that constructive nationalism inevitably entails the adoption of the ways of modern civilization. This latter has arrived at a scientific solution for the various economic, social, and political questions of state. We must adopt, understand, and use these solutions. The third is that the adaptation to world civilization is a matter made imperative by modern developments in the various means of transport and communication. Such adaptation demands unification, cooperation, and the rejection of all forces pleading for isolation and individual action. If this is necessary internationally, it is much more so on the home front and among the various groups that make up a nation.

X. *Arab Unity and Ideology*

38. GREATER SYRIA AND ARAB UNITY*

The question of unity in the Arab Middle East was alive as early as 1941. In that year, Anthony Eden declared that the British Government would support closer ties among Arab countries. Soon afterward, in 1942, Nuri al-Sa'id of Iraq published a Blue Book proposing a federal union in the Fertile Crescent linking Syria, Lebanon, Palestine, and Transjordan to Iraq. In reaction, the Jordanians proposed a Greater Syria under the monarchy of Jordan. The unity scheme displeased the Sa'udi dynasty, which did not want its rival Hashimite crowns of Jordan and Iraq to be strengthened. Syria and Lebanon, in turn, rejected the proposal since, as independent democratic republics, they could not be united under an absolute monarch. The Syrian answer, in the form of a book supposedly written by a group of educated Syrians—Kalimat al-suriyya wal-'arab fi mashru'at surriyya al-kubra (Views of the Syrians and the Arabs on the Greater Syria Plan) *(Damascus, 1947)—apparently emanated from the government. Meanwhile, the Egyptian Government had submitted to a General Arab Conference, in 1944, its own scheme of unity—a loose organization in which each of the seven participating states would preserve its independence and political regime. The League of Arab States was subsequently formed on March 22, 1945. In any case, from the very beginning, political differences constituted a major obstacle to unity. The controversy over unity continued, largely as a reaction to the idea of a Greater Syria under a monarchy.* *(See the speeches and letter of King 'Abdallah on pp. 250–54.)* *The extracts indicate that, even before independence was achieved, there were tensions between monarchies and republics.*

THE APPEAL OF H. R. H. PRINCE 'ABDALLAH TO THE SYRIAN PEOPLE AND THE ARAB WORLD

People of Syria, both city and country dwellers, from the Gulf of 'Aqaba to the Mediterranean and the Euphrates.

All men have come to know that the Arabs, during their great revolt,[1] did not sow civil discord or attempt to usurp power, but were champions of justice, freedom, and national sovereignty who believed in their right to a free life. They rose up in arms to defend Arabism and Islam. Their leaders defined the borders of their homeland as stretching from the Arabian Peninsula in the

* Extracts from *Kitab al-urdunn al-abyad: al-watha'iq al-qawmiyya fi wahdat suriyya al-tabi'iyya* (*Jordanian White Book: The National Documents Concerning Natural Syrian Unity*) (Amman: al-Matba'a al-wataniyya, 1947), pp. 75–77, 104–8.

1. In 1916.

south to Syria and Iraq in the north. This was the objective of their revolt and of their national aspirations. In this, they manifested their belief in their glorious heritage and their faith in the promises made to them by the Allies, especially Great Britain, who undertook to support their claims, respect their desires, and guarantee their independence.

The Great War ended, and the rights of the Arabs were sealed with the blood of their heroic martyrs.

The military and political leaders of the Allies were fully cognizant of the importance of the Arab revolt to the outcome of the war. They lavished praises on the Arab leaders. As a result, Iraq, the Hijaz, Najd, and Yemen all obtained their independence.

Only the Syrian lands were kept fragmented and anxious to reunite within their natural borders, in one land united by nationality, geography, and history and irrigated by the water of the Euphrates, the Orontes, and the Jordan. If the conflicting foreign interests had led to the fragmentation of its unity, the principles of international justice, the natural rights of life, and the promises made to Syrians in particular and Arabs in general were all factors acting against the disruption and fragmentation of the same land and the same family.

People of Syria!

Now that the call for Arab unity has become definite, it is essential to this blessed call that we openly advocate the necessity of uniting the Syrian regions, basing this upon the express will of the nation ever since the last war and upon the vital, natural, and legitimate interests of the people.

Today, we attempt, through political channels and trusting in certain rays of hope contained in the promises of the Allies and in our past endeavor and our present position of authority in southern Syria, to defend your will as expressed in the resolution of the General Syrian Congress of March 8, 1920, which, together with the McMahon correspondence, placed its faith in the Hashimite house.

The charter of the Syrian Arab nation and its call for total unity have always been our charter and our call. Although circumstances have made us tarry for a while in a certain region of Greater Syria, we work today in the light of a new democratic charter, supported by past and future promises to implement the national will for union with the rest of Syria. We firmly believe in our country's rights and our nation's support, drawing, in all this, upon our past history, our past struggle, and our sacrifices. We do not forget the friendship of the Allies, and the prominent role played by Great Britain in supporting the Arab cause. We are also grateful to the Free French representative, who, with characteristic French magnanimity, declared last year the termination of the French mandate over Syria and Lebanon and the proclamation of their sovereign independence, as guaranteed by the British and other governments.

People of Syria!

Our sister state Egypt has responded to the principles enunciated by the great Arab revolt. Its Prime Minister has called for an official Arab conference that would attempt to remove the obstacles and make a *rapprochement* easier. We must thank Egypt for this gesture. We call upon Iraq also to respond to this invitation by Egypt, which we ourselves welcome. We hope that this conference will support the charter for a united Syria so that Greater Syria can occupy its proper place alongside a Pan-Arab union.

At the same time, we call upon the leaders of public opinion [*ahl al-hall wal-'aqd;* literally, men who bind and deliver] to rally to this project for a total Syrian union. Let them debate the issue at a special Syrian conference, which we would welcome here in our capital whenever they choose. Or let all classes, sects, leaders, and scholars examine the implications of this project carefully and give it their support.

The truth is clear as daylight, and now is the time for serious endeavor. The future beckons the Arabs to retrieve past glory and achieve unity. God helps those who help themselves, and in Him we trust.

Amman, April 8, 1943

The Project of Greater Syria as It Figured in the Discussions of Arab Unity [Conference of Alexandria, 1943] and in the Charter of the Arab League [Cairo Conference, 1944]

During the discussion of Arab unity [the Alexandria Conference], the subject of Greater Syria was reviewed. Both the Syrian and the Jordanian delegations concurred in the necessity of creating a natural Syrian unity. However, the form of government in this state was left undecided. Jordan expressed its adherence to the original plan of a constitutional monarchy, in accordance with the resolution of March 8, 1920. This resolution was framed by representatives of Greater Syria and was considered by all the Syrian regions to be their common national charter at that time. No Syrian region had the right to abrogate it unilaterally.

The Syrian delegate, however, expressed his attachment to recent developments in northern Syria, the emergence of the Republic, and the desire to impose the republican system upon Greater Syria as well. It was the opinion of Jordan that the only natural and legitimate solution of the problem would be to hold a free plebiscite throughout the Syrian regions and to acquiesce in the over-all will of the nation.

Reference was later made to the possibility of a federation between the governments of the independent Syrian regions. This federation would be created by a special charter and would possess its own council, without disturbing the form of the regional governments. It was intended to hold a special conference for regional Syrian governments in order that this problem could be tackled naturally and within a legal framework. But this was not to be, and the questions of both union and federation have been suspended without justification, although such suspension is detrimental to the national interests of this one Arab country.

In order to clarify the facts, we shall quote the observations made by the delegate of northern Syria concerning natural Syrian unity, together with other remarks made by the delegates of Egypt and Iraq. These words prove that the strengthening of relations between two or more states of the Arab League, far from constituting a breach of the League Charter as was rumored, is in fact an affirmation of the aims of the Charter itself. Here are some random remarks, recorded in the official minutes, made by H.E. Sa'd Allah al-Jabri, the delegate from northern Syria:

> The fragmentation of Syria went against its political and geographical nature. It was the result of certain foreign agreements and interests, both open and secret, which were imposed on the people by force.
>
> Syrians, like all sincere Arabs, desire unity, especially in this era, which witnesses the gradual dissolution of small nations.
>
> The Syrian problem is the concern of four regions: Syria, Lebanon, Palestine, and Transjordan.
>
> There are basic factors that make for unity in these regions, irrespective of the nature or form of this unity. This unity is the objective we have sought in the past and have worked to achieve unconditionally and in the face of all obstacles. But, twenty years later, each country has become used to its own particular manner of life and its own character, and this development has necessitated a change in our policy. We must now attempt to compromise with and to persuade each other. With Damascus as the capital and the republican system as a basis, we insist upon unity but leave the choice of the particular form of unity to the citizens.
>
> The inhabitants of Lebanon, including many Christians and all Muslims, especially in the parts added to Lebanon after the Great War, desire to join Syria unconditionally.
>
> We are therefore anxious to create Greater Syria and do away with the fragmentation imposed on us by force, foreign interests, and political rivalries. We want to arrive at this objective by any means chosen by the countries that were carved out from Syria. We do not deny that there are many obstacles to be overcome. This program of cooperation between us and Lebanon may be taken as an example of how the affairs of regions cut off from their mother country may be handled, until the union is achieved and this unjust fragmentation of Syria is ended. Indeed, this fragmentation has retarded Syria's growth and removed it from its rightful place. While desiring that this unity should be effected through peaceful persuasion and mutual understanding, we wish to reaffirm the necessity of retaining Damascus as capital and the Syrian republic with all its republican institutions.

The Opinion of the Jordanian Delegate

THE CHAIRMAN (EGYPT): What form will this unity between Syria and Jordan assume?

H.E. ABU L-HUDA PASHA (THE JORDANIAN DELEGATE): The form of this unity will be determined by majority opinion.

THE CHAIRMAN: But what is your own opinion?

ABU L-HUDA PASHA: I believe it should be a monarchy.

THE CHAIRMAN: But Syria is a republic.

ABU L-HUDA PASHA: A republican system may be replaced by a royalist regime. I say this because I know that many Syrians prefer a royalist regime. I also believe that the present leaders of Syria are genuine patriots who will not allow this question of monarchy vs. republic to stand in the way of their country's prosperity. If they find that it is to the interest of their country, I am certain they will change their form of government.

The Possibility of Syrian Unity or Federation as Discussed in Debates Centering on Article 9 of the Charter of the Arab League

Following is the text:

"ARTICLE 9. Member states of the Arab League desiring to strengthen their common ties and cooperation among them in this Charter may enter upon any agreements they like in order to achieve this purpose. Treaties and agreements, both past and future, between one member state of the League and any other state shall not be considered binding upon the other members."

'ABD AL-HAMID BADAWI PASHA: "I would like to stress that closer ties between two or more member states would by no means be considered contrary to the Charter. Indeed, they would underline the basic aims of the Charter itself."

'ABD AL-RAHMAN 'AZZAM PASHA: "I do not consider this article to be framed in a negative sense. I believe it was put in in order to emphasize the rights of member states to conclude whatever agreements they like that are broader in scope than this Charter."

The Attitude and Reservations of the Iraqi Government

H.E. The chairman of the subcommittee in charge of the projected Charter of the Arab League,

Dear Sir,

I have the honor of informing your excellency that due to the delay in the signature of the minutes of the sessions of the political subcommittee of the Preparatory Committee of the Arab Conference, caused by a motion to add to and amend the projected Charter of the Arab League, certain League states had not yet consulted their governments. Therefore, to remove any possible misunderstanding and to inform my government accordingly, I would like to present to your excellency the Iraqi Government's view that the following points should be made clear:

One—Article 12. League states must not, either collectively or individually, interfere in any quarrel of any kind arising between Iraq and any state or states within or outside the League, except at the request of Iraq and the other state or states.

Two—Article 14. This article gives the League the right to establish a more extensive cooperation among League states than is specified in the Charter, providing such states agree to this. It is obvious that this mandate is really a confirmation of the right at present enjoyed by League states. Therefore, it must be made clear that no state of the League can object for any reason at all if other League states decide to increase cooperation between them.

Three—Article 15. It is the right of the citizens of each state of the League to choose their own form of government. Since Article 15 does not make this principle clear, it is necessary to explain that Iraq cannot possibly forsake a principle that has been adopted throughout the civilized world.

I would be grateful if your excellency would acknowledge receipt of this letter so that I can inform my government before March 15.

[Signed] Tahsin 'Askari
Minister-Delegate of Iraq.

39. ISLAM AND ARABISM AND THE UNITY PLAN OF KING 'ABDALLAH OF JORDAN*

King 'Abdallah of Jordan

The drive for unity or a Greater Syria was renewed after Transjordan attained independence from the British in 1946 and the proclamation of the ruler (amir) *as king seemed assured. Actually, the title Hashimite Kingdom of Jordan was not conferred until 1948 or recognized internationally until 1949. From the start, the incumbent King 'Abdallah faced the opposition of Egypt and especially of his bitter enemies, the followers of Hajj Amin al-Husayni, the former Mufti of Jerusalem. The latter was supported by Egypt, Sa'udi Arabia, and Syria, all of which were opposed to the expansion of Jordan. Deprived of an economic basis (it added the eastern section of Palestine in 1948–49), Jordan sought to increase its influence—possibly through a merger with Syria. King 'Abdallah therefore revived the idea of a Greater Syria. He regarded Jordan as part of Syria, and described unity as a necessary measure for assuring national security. He justified his own claim to the throne of Greater Syria as a natural consequence of his royal family's contribution to the Arab cause. It is interesting to note that, despite the Pan-Islamic, Pan-Arabic aims of his movement, Hasan al-Banna, the leader of the Muslim Brotherhood, opposed the idea of a Greater Syria under the Jordanian monarchy.*

Some insights into the background of these developments may be found in Philip Graves (ed.), Memoirs of King 'Abdallah of Trans-Jordan, *trans. G. Khuri (London: Jonathan Cape; New York: Philosophical Library, 1950).*

The first extract is a speech delivered by King 'Abdallah at the opening of the Islamic Cultural College in Amman on September 19, 1947. The second extract is an answer to Shaykh Hasan al-Banna's request to King 'Abdallah to end his call for a Greater Syria. *(For al-Banna's views, see pp. 115–22.)*

* Extract from al-Maktab al-da'im lil-mu'tamar al-qawmi al-urdunni (Permanent Secretariat of the Jordanian National Conference), *Suriyya al-kubra aw al-wahdat al-suriyya al-tabi'iyya: haqiqa qawmiyya azaliyya. Radd 'ala kitab "kalimat al-suriyya wa-al-'arab fi mashru'at suriyya al-kubra" (Greater Syria or Syrian Natural Unity: An Eternal National Truth. Answer [Rejection] of the Book "Views of Syria and the Arabs on the Greater Syria Plan")* (Damascus: al-Manshur fi Dimashq, 1948), pp. 61–65 (King's speech), 36–38 (letter to Hasan al-Banna).

Speech of King 'Abdallah

It gives me pleasure to announce the opening of the Islamic Cultural College, which has been founded on national and Islamic bases in order to disseminate true knowledge and faith. I have also noted with appreciation the sentiments expressed by the various speakers, and it is my dearest wish to see my beloved people striving for the right causes, endeavoring to be constructive, and calling for unity rather than fragmentation. I hope and pray that our religious and educational institutions will continue to preach this message and to create a new, vigorous Arab generation which is possessed of all virtues and ideals that give it mastery over the earth and make it fit to receive God's light and the divine messages of justice, freedom, and human dignity.

However, with reference to what certain speakers have said about Islam and Arabism, and to the resolutions of our national congress held last week as regards unity—I would like to comment on the speech of the President of Syria, broadcast two days ago from Damascus, in the course of which he made some unfounded allegations about this faithful Syrian Arab land. Let me first say, May God forgive him! In paying homage to Islam and to Arabism within the precincts of this College, I send my best wishes to the Syrian nation throughout its homeland and greetings to the Syrian President in the northern region of our beloved homeland. I pray that God will help me to bear with patience and to forgive and forget. But we must continue to work for our national rights and to try to make those who bitterly oppose us see the truth. The Syrian President has seen fit to perpetuate national fragmentation and intensify this animosity among brothers. We, however, can do no more than bow to the nation's free and unified will, without either forcing its decision or doubting its judgment. This is why I call for a general plebiscite of the Syrian nation, in order that a common decision be taken regarding its unity or its federation. No honest man can possibly take us to task for such a view. No honest man can conceivably see in this policy any ground for alarm or for declaring it to be detrimental to Arab problems or the unity of Arab ranks—provided there is good faith. But I believe that prevarication in such a problem is far worse and far more dangerous, especially as our call genuinely serves our countries' common interests, has always been honest and fraternal, and has never violated the nation's charter and the unanimous national resolutions. Our nation shall never forsake its natural right to unity or federation, no matter what lies are propagated or what charges are made against its national charter, as, for example, that it is inspired by Zionism and imperialism. The truth is that the nation has framed this charter in defiance of Zionism and imperialism and of the attempt to fragment our homeland. Furthermore, the nation shall implement its own charter of its own free will after it shall have framed it in a way that would guarantee the national rights specified in the Charter of the United Nations.

Therefore, our call is no mere desire on our part for an increase of royal power, but is rather the task entrusted to us by the nation. We thank God that our family has never pursued power for its own sake. Our struggles for our country and people are of greater value than any royal power.

Al-Daylami in the *Masnad* of Firdawsi records the following saying of 'Ali ibn Abi Tallib: "Whoever does not, by knowing more of this world, grow more abstemious, draws further away from God." As for the President's claim that my recent message to him entails his having to break the oath he took to be loyal to the constitution, I have really no comment to make.

Our message to him was in reality a cordial invitation freely to come to an agreement. It could not possibly be interpreted as implying the breaking of the oath that he took on two occasions, namely, on March 8, when Syria's independence was declared together with its natural borders; and when the regional Syrian republican constitution was proclaimed. This latter calls, in any case, for comprehensive unity.

However, the President still works to preserve this state of fragmentation. He and his friends have gone so far as to invent a quarrel among Arabs of the same region. He has perverted the Arab League Charter by interpreting it as antagonistic to any free unity of our countries, although he knows very well that that Charter has, both explicitly and implicitly, called for stronger bonds between League states and for the encouragement of national aspirations. "Syrian unity" is very much a national aspiration, not solely because of natural and national rights, but also by reason of common regional interests. It is strange that the President should feel it is his right to impose a republican regime upon our kingdom—a regime which arose accidentally—and should deny to us the right to ask for a united national plebiscite where the nation's will can be determined. Is he not really advocating a dictatorship in the guise of a republic? It is very strange that he should justify this fragmentation indefinitely by arguing that there can be no unity between a free man and an unfree man, although he knows perfectly well that Jordan is fully independent and has treaties and alliances with major powers. He also knows that the present world situation does not allow for isolation and that a federation where each party retains its rights would create a unified power which would benefit all parties concerned. There can be no room for denial that Jordan is a part of the Syrian entity and that to abandon or renounce this entity is to renounce the national charter and to submit to the solution imposed by foreign imperialism and the consequent fragmentation of the same land. It is indeed regrettable that a fighter for Arab causes [i.e., the Syrian President] should consider this call for Syrian unity or federation a violation of international law and of the U.N. Charter. This charge is unjustifiable, not only from the national but also from the international point of view, since the U.N. Charter has explicitly recognized the right of self-determination. Furthermore, common geographical, historical, and national considerations are recognized in international law. With all due respect to the present regimes in the regional Syrian states and to their independence, we do not see that this state of affairs necessarily precludes any free call for the restitution of our natural right to unite or federate. Nor can this call be considered as an intervention in the regional

Syrian state since the Syrian people in all the regions have already accepted the principle of natural Syrian unity in its general charter of 1920. Besides, the constitution of the regional Syrian Republic does not admit accidental national fragmentation and, indeed, stipulates that Jordan should be united or federated to Syria. The constitution in fact states that any other course of action would be tantamount to a denial of the will of the one nation and of its rights and interests. Non-Syrian states do not, of course, have the right to defy the will of the Syrian people within their own homeland as a whole or to interfere in their internal affairs. The safeguarding of independence and the repulsion of the Zionist menace are not grounds for bombastic talk within the one nation. In any case, Jordan is closer to Palestine, and any threat to the latter is a direct threat to the former as well. Jordan has always been the first to answer the call of duty in Palestine. Indeed, the father of the Arab revolution [i.e., King Husayn of Hijaz], who is the dearest man to our hearts, lies buried in the Aqsa Mosque in Jerusalem, ever present in our hearts and a symbol of the vow we have taken to God.

Although Syria does not belong to any ruling family, as the Syrian President has said, it does owe something, without the need for gratitude, to a family that, in two world wars, has answered its call. This family is in duty bound to oppose Syrian fragmentation or the renunciation of its common charter. Syria, in its natural borders, and not just in one of its regions, belongs to all of itself and is the legacy handed down by its martyrs and heroes. Those who fought for it are its own sons, whose rights and obligations are those of the nation itself. Its will shall remain entire and unfragmented. Peace be upon this land of freedom and dignity, from the Gulf of ʻAqaba to the Mediterranean and the Euphrates.

Reply to H.E. Shaykh Hasan al-Banna, Director-General of the Muslim Brotherhood, Egypt

Greetings. I received your letter on August 30 [1947], delivered by your messenger, Mr. ʻAbidin. My answer will be as one Muslim brother would address another, neither shunning the truth nor avoiding blame.

Our call for the unity of the Syrian countries has itself been expressed by the first Syrian National Convention. It is also the call that was pronounced by our now legislative assembly, whose decisions we are bound to accept. We cannot possibly betray the trust of our people whom certain dissenters are endeavoring to isolate from our one homeland. Such a betrayal would be detrimental to their national rights and their moral and material welfare. No Muslim and no Arab would want to inflict this upon another Muslim or Arab.

Therefore, we mean to achieve a common Syrian charter by freely advocating it. We have no desire for personal glory or private gain, but look solely to the interests, the prosperity, and the future of the Arabs. We advocate the unity of the Syrian region in a manner that would safeguard the national interests of the Syrians and be brought about by their own free will and choice.

In our latest statement and in our message to H.E. the Syrian President may be found ample proof of this. There is no justification for this hostility against us. Rather, it is those who brought upon us the enmity of brothers and strangers alike that stand most in need of good advice. What is so reprehensible in our call for a preparatory national congress that would include representatives of the peoples and governments of a single nation, so that they can, of their own free will, create a union or a federation? Is this sufficient reason for antagonizing a fellow-Arab who has not forced them to do his bidding but simply asked for an open deliberation [*shawra*] of national leaders and who is prepared to abide by whatever decision they think fitting?

This hostility, if it has been the work of some sowers of discord who have succeeded in deceiving our coreligionists and in disseminating their false propaganda in the Arab world, is truly reminiscent of the schemers of the Quraysh tribe who failed to exhaust the Prophet's patience or to make him abandon his mission. It grieves me that Your Excellency seems to have been taken in by those liars who distort an innocent call for a common national charter into alleged "treason." These men aim to keep our one homeland fragmented, implementing in this a certain policy of which you yourself are aware. In this, they are also at one with certain fanatics in Lebanon. Their purpose is ultimately to undermine Arabism and Islam. It also grieves me that Your Excellency should make a distinction between Syrian unity and the call for the unity of Egypt and Syria. This one homeland cannot survive in its present state of national, political, and economic fragmentation.

If truth is truth at all times and places, then why can we not debate the issue on the basis of open deliberation and the common interests of an unfortunate Arab country? Why should this be detrimental to the Egyptian problem? Our Egyptian brethren are the Arabs who care most for their country's unity. No honest Egyptian would accept the fragmentation of his country into governments and states in the north and south without rising up in arms to safeguard the unity of his homeland.

Our attitude to the Egyptian problem, which we sincerely regard as our own, is no mere propaganda. We consider this to be our duty. As for your objections against Syrian unity, we believe that our general statement and our cordial message to the Syrian President contain an ample refutation. We need only add that a federation and a union, where some regions would enjoy a certain measure of autonomy, are not really open to the sort of objections you have cited. Thus, we hope that the Muslim Brotherhood will come round to our point of view, namely, an exchange of opinions among governments instead of the present campaign of slander. We believe that this is the most equitable solution of the problem. Our call for an open deliberation among Muslims, as is commanded by God, is not in defiance of the Arab League. Indeed, the reverse is true. We have pledged ourselves and all we own for the Arab cause. Having been turned out of our country, we have not been humiliated or brought low, and God Almighty can grant us the victory.

40. THE CHARACTERISTIC FEATURES OF UNION AND FEDERATION*

'Abd al-Rahman al-Bazzaz

'Abd al-Rahman al-Bazzaz, a former teacher and ambassador, became prime minister of Iraq in 1965 (see pp. 52–54). In the book from which this extract is quoted, al-Bazzaz proposes a union of Arab states under a federal form of government, which he considers the most suitable system for the Arab world.

Having reached this stage in our discussion, we should mention briefly the most important characteristics of these two types of states. Each, undoubtedly, possesses distinctive features and advantages.

In a union, complete harmony is achieved between the members of society, and all differences are, as much as possible, removed. Authority is concentrated in a single body wielding power over all the affairs of state—over questions of higher policy, of sovereignty, of peace and war, or those concerned with internal affairs and ordinary everyday problems, such as public health, culture, the arts, entertainment, municipal affairs, supply, and reconstruction. In a unified state it is highly unlikely, although not impossible, for one region to secede and become independent. This type of government is usually suited to small or medium-sized states where a particular form of organization has been traditionally handed down through the course of many centuries. In some states it might conceivably be the final stage of a long evolution toward total unification.

The federal system, on the other hand, is more suited to vast countries that have different geographical regions, that possess varying political systems, and where the social classes are not in total harmony. Furthermore, the federalism comes nearer to the spirit of our modern age, since it implies specialization. In other words, the federal state concerns itself with the major problems relating to its over-all structure, its foreign policy, its defense, its finance, and its economy in general. Regional governments are left to deal with local or regional problems, such as health, culture, city planning, roads, and other problems that have become increasingly important in modern life. The functions of the present-day state have multiplied in a way that no nineteenth-century thinker would have thought possible. The federal system, too, is appropriate for large nations that have lived under different forms of govern-

* Extract from 'Abd al-Rahman al-Bazzaz, *al-Dawla al-muwahhada wa-al-dawla al-ittihadiyya* (*The Federal State and the Unitary State*) (2d ed.; Cairo: Dar al-'ilm, 1960), pp. 89–94, 99–102.

ment and diverse social and economic conditions. It provides a practical solution midway between submission to fragmentation and the idealism calling for "complete fusion and total union."

This was perhaps the intention of the men who framed the national charter in Iraq after World War II. In discussing the political system of the future Arab state, they wrote, "Arab unity is a national necessity, required by their [the Arabs'] very existence, imposed by their will to life, which is the natural right of the Arabs. Arab nationalism considers unity a national objective to be attained through all possible means, such as a federal system which seems a practical step toward this unity."

The Ideal System for the Arab Countries

One might now ask: Which of these two systems is better for the Arab countries? Before giving an answer, we must first define these countries or, rather, think about them realistically.

They stretch across a vast land mass between two great continents. They are made up of regions with very different climates. Some are Mediterranean by location and climate, others are tropical. Some are among the world's mildest and most beautiful spots and resorts. The population, too, of this Arab world varies greatly in culture, economy, and lineage. The inhabitants of seaports like Alexandria, Beirut, and Latakia live differently from those of San'a', Riyadh, Mecca, or Rabat, while the city dwellers of Damascus, Aleppo, and Mosul, with their inherited culture, differ greatly from the Bedouin and the lake [*Hor*] dwellers in southern Iraq. Among the Arabs there are some who have attained high academic distinction in the greatest universities of the world, while millions of others cannot even write their own names.

Have we carefully considered the actual area of this one homeland in order to judge the best form of government suited to us in this age? Perhaps the following geographical facts may be helpful in elucidating the problem.

The area of the Arab world is more than 4 million square miles, greater than the whole of Europe, including Russia. The area of Switzerland, which is a federation, is less than 16,000 square miles, and the Arab world is 250 times larger.

India, often referred to as a subcontinent, has an area of only 1.25 million square miles; that is, the Arab world is three and a half times larger. In fact, the whole of the United States is a little more than 3 million square miles, about one-third less than the Arab countries.

These figures, I believe, suffice to give us a clear idea of the vast domain of the Arab world. We must, therefore, give serious thought to the question of choosing the right form of government for this great territory.

The countries of the Arab world are, politically speaking, a most curious amalgam. Some are completely independent, others are semi-independent. Some are inferior to colonies in status, others are still protectorates of one state or another. Some are monarchies, others are republics, and some monarchies are absolute, while others are, at least theoretically, constitutional. There are also shaykhdoms, principalities, and so forth.

Our homeland, then, is vast in area, with diverse regions, political systems, and social standards. All this leads us to declare that a federation would be the best form of government for this one people, which still possesses, despite all divergences, the basic constituents of a single nation.

There are also other factors that we must neither ignore nor overemphasize —as, for example, the presence of ethnic and religious minorities. Therefore, a federal system appears to be the most suited to our needs, especially at the present time. If we add to these considerations the fact that a total union of the whole Arab world would necessitate the destruction of all monarchies and that certain countries, because of their present situation or of the services rendered them by their kings, do not wish to change their status, it becomes perfectly obvious that a federal system is the most practicable solution under the circumstances.

General Principles

I suppose it would be valuable if, at the end of my discussion, I attempt to lay down some general principles to be seriously considered when the federal constitution is drawn up.

1. Emphasis must be placed upon the one Arab nation. This fact is the cornerstone of any general Arab entity to be created. The attempt by certain groups to weaken nationalist sentiment by strengthening local and regional tendencies is the greatest threat to our future entity. It should be clear that when we call for a federation, we are not renouncing faith in our one nation but merely choosing the best governmental system for it under the present circumstances.

2. It must be stressed that choosing any one of the many systems of government is only a means to an end, not the end itself. Our real end is to "achieve the greatest possible measure of prosperity and happiness for the greatest number of Arabs." This prosperity and happiness can be properly and finally achieved only if "a general political entity" is created that unites the Arabs in their various countries, protects them from all internal and external aggression, and seeks to establish social justice. In pursuit of these goals, we must not be led astray by phraseology and other technicalities of this sort.

3. The world is constantly progressing. It behooves us to choose a system of government which would be capable of renewal and progress. Our laws and institutions must be flexible and must allow for development, avoiding the extremes of rigidity or impetuous change, the latter being resorted to only by men to whom a gradual and reasonable evolutionary progress is denied.

4. When, on the other hand, we call for a comprehensive Arab federation, we do not mean to deny the possibility of the creation of stronger bonds between some regions of the Arab world.

We are here concerned with the whole rather than with the parts. In other words, total union is a very natural and reasonable demand in the case of certain regions of the Arab world. Jordan, for example, is a part of southern Syria that was carved out for well-known purposes, under well-known circumstances. Jordan does not possess the constituent elements either of a state or of a region, in the strict geographical sense. No sensible person can dispute this fact. Indeed, many Western writers have confirmed it. Similarly, Aden and the other protectorates form, undoubtedly, a natural complement to the Yemen. Other principalities of the Arabian Gulf are parts of bordering Arab states, and it would be perfectly natural and reasonable if such regions were to unite.

However, some Arab regions differ very much from others. The Yemen is different from the Najd, while al-Sha'm (Greater Syria) differs from Arab North Africa, even though all these regions are parts of the great Arab homeland, complementing each other and constituting through their conjunction a "complete entity" from the geographical, historical, economic-mercantile, and political points of view.

Furthermore, social or political circumstances may, at a certain period, necessitate the creation of ties between two Arab regions that are stronger than those of a federation. Such a case would be considered an exception to the general rule itself.

5. Our federal system must be a mixture of "idealism" and "realism." Idealism is valuable insofar as it helps us to frame higher principles, which emanate from our existence as a single nation, and to support our view concerning the sublime goals of life. But when idealism is either neglected or overemphasized, it can blind us to reality, turning the good that we desired into an evil, whose consequences are felt, without exception, by everyone.

It may be advantageous to explain these ideas further. When we stress the unifying forces in the Arab nation and their antecedents, we must also not forget the forces making for disunity and their antecedents. To attempt, at the present time, with all the factors making for disunity, to attain complete union, a total merger, would be a rash undertaking. It would be tantamount to denying certain palpable facts, which no reasonable person can possibly do.

6. It is futile to tackle our problems emotionally. A certain measure of rationality is necessary, but our rationality must not be so predominant as to render us overcautious and, perhaps, cowardly. We must remember that for many centuries we have lived in subjection to several foreign powers: the Turks, the Persians, the British, the French, the Italians, the Spanish, and the Portuguese. These nations have, at different times, occupied various parts of our homeland. They have handed down to us, willy-nilly, particular conditions and have created among us dissensions and differences.

We have living among us today ethnic and religious minorities, with some of whom no merger is possible, while with others we are linked by national or religious ties. Some time must elapse before we can succeed in proving our good faith to them and consolidating our own power. Evolution is the *sine qua non* of politics.

Therefore, despite the fact that federation seems to be the final and ultimate answer for some of us, according to others, it is only a reasonable step forward in our progress.

41. A VIEW OF ARAB UNITY*

Nabih Amin Faris

Nabih Amin Faris (b. 1906), a former curator of Arabic manuscripts at Princeton University (1937–42) and head of the Arab Desk, U.S. Office of War Information (1942–45), returned to Lebanon to become professor of Arab history in the American University of Beirut. He has written more than a dozen books on various aspects of Arab culture and history, including al-'Arab al-ahya (The Living Arabs) *(Beirut: Dar al-'ilm lil-malayin, 1947) and* Min al-zawiya al-'arabiyya (From the Arab Viewpoint) *(Beirut: Dar Bairut lil-tab', 1953). His careful examination in these works of the historical, political, and cultural foundations of Arab nationalism has gained for him a leading position in the movement for Arab unity.*

In the following extract, Faris presents the background of the Arab nationalist movement and, on the basis of its history, proposes a federation as the best way to secure Arab unity. (See also the interpretation of the birth of Arab nationalism, pp. 8–10.)

Arab unity is a dream long pursued by the Arab elite, which has striven with enthusiasm and conviction to achieve it. But the pursuit has met with many obstacles, some of which were the work of imperialists, while others are believed to be the responsibility of the Arabs themselves, with their social, economic, and political circumstances. Still others were caused by a combination of all these factors.

The origins of Arab nationalism have deep historical roots. Nationalism itself appeared as an effective force during the caliphate of 'Umar and, to a certain extent, during the Umayyad caliphate, especially in the period preceding what are called the "reforms of 'Umar ibn 'Abd al-'Aziz," which attempted to reconcile the Arab and Islamic ideas. As a result of these "reforms," the emphasis shifted to Islam, and the Arab element no longer had the upper hand in running the affairs of state. Islamic and non-Arab elements began to affect administration. Thereafter, the Islamic idea dominated the affairs of the caliphate and was exploited by princes and sultans for purposes of domination in the name of religion. Were it not for this religious element, the Arabs would not have acquiesced, as they did in most cases, in the rule of the Buwayhids, the Seljuqs, the Mamluks, and, finally, in four centuries of Ottoman hegemony.

In fact, despite its ancient origins and its appearance in various social, po-

* Extract from Nabih Amin Faris, *Dirasat 'arabiyya* (*Arab Studies*) (Beirut: Dar al-'ilm lil-malayin, 1957), pp. 104–11.

litical, and ideological forms at various periods, Arab nationalism did not crystallize until after the proclamation of the Ottoman constitution of 1908 and the emergence and activities of the Eurasian movement, represented in the Society for Union and Progress [*Jam'iyyat al-ittihad wal-taraqqi*]. To a great extent, therefore, the Arab idea was a reaction against Turanianism, which attempted to "Turkify" all national groups within the Ottoman Empire. To a lesser extent, the Arab idea attempted to underline nationalistic elements and to withhold its support of the Islamic idea as expounded by the advocates of the Islamic League [*al-Jam'iyya al-islamiyya*]. The various secret societies fostered an Arab spirit and called for a renaissance that would restore Arab glory and the right of the Arabs to the caliphate, which was usurped by the Ottomans. Nevertheless, certain secret societies and quite a number of those working for the Arab cause were, even at that time, toying with the idea of a dualistic Ottoman state, including both Arabs and Turks.

World War I broke out, and the great Arab revolt began. This revolt did not possess the necessary prerequisites for success and did not win the support and adherence of a strong and conscious Arab public opinion. It was weak and soon became even weaker as a result of the rivalries of Arab families, the plots of imperialists, and the weakness of its popular base. But in recent Arab nationalist history, it remains the great Arab revolt not because of the success it achieved, but because it was a symbol: It was the first revolt against the caliph that aimed at Arab unity and in which the sharif of Mecca, the descendant of the Arab Prophet, rose up in arms against a foreign caliph for the sake of Arab nationalism.

Before this Arab movement had time to achieved liberation and unity, or even to grow stronger and organize the countries of the Fertile Crescent, it was stricken with the loss of a number of its ablest supporters, who were executed by the Turks. Later on, it was faced with a rival created by the imperialist powers in the settlements that followed the war, by which the countries supporting the Arab movement were divided into artificial states and principalities. This fragmentation led, as a matter of course, to the emergence of regional movements directed against liberation from imperialism. The Pan-Arab movement was thus reduced to narrow regional ideologies, and the sentiment for unity was shattered. The imperialists had totally isolated the Arab countries from each other, creating artificial frontiers, entities, and governments. Each Arab region was thereafter politically isolated, and economic and cultural life was diversified. In each area, a ruling class arose whose interest it was to preserve this regionalism and independence in order to continue its authority and influence. Consciously or otherwise, these ruling classes fostered regional consciousness. This tendency was strengthened and supported by elements that were concerned with keeping the Arab countries fragmented and by others that sincerely believed that such regionalism was in fact realistic and truly reflected the historical nature of each region and its inhabitants. Thus, the process of "Balkanizing" the Arab world was completed and consummated in the Charter of the Arab League.

But the ideal of Arab unity still enjoys the allegiance of an elite, which sees it not solely as the realization of a dream but as the best means for coping with the turbulent Arab scene, for making the Arabs freely contribute to history, and for securing them a place in the progress of civilization. And this, in spite of the fact that the obstacles in the path of unity are far more formidable at present than they were at the turn of the century. At that time, the ideal of unity was at least comprehensive, despite its opacity. Today, it is no longer comprehensive and must, in addition to facing the imperialists and Israel, meet opposition from the interested parties entrenched in every Arab political entity: kingdoms, republics, shaykhdoms, and so on. These obstacles render the realization of Pan-Arab unity a remote prospect. There can be no way out except by violence or by federation. An Arab country may be able to play a role similar to the one played by Prussia in forging German unity, if international circumstances are favorable. But a unity forged by violence can also be dissolved by violence, and this may lead to consequences that can turn the Arab problem back to where it was a hundred years ago.

The only avenue open to the Arabs now, if they wish to overcome most of the practical difficulties in the way of unity, is a federal union. Federation may, in the end, prove to be the best means for unity.

In order to secure as successful a federation as possible, we must take into account the present Arab scene with all its drawbacks and must bear in mind and work to strengthen the very important underlying cultural and economic influences upon unity or federation.

The Arab world is made up of two groups of lands, in Asia and in Africa. The Asian Arab lands are divided into three main regions: the valley of the Tigris and Euphrates, natural Syria, and the Arabian Peninsula. The African Arab lands are divided into two main regions: the Nile Valley and the countries of the Maghrib. All these regions constitute natural geographical and economic units, and the social conditions prevalent in these regions are very similar. Their historical legacy is, to a great extent, a common one. It is not, therefore, unreasonable if we advocate a political union of the regions of each of these lands to complement their geographical, economic, and historical unity. A federal union can thereafter be created from among these smaller units, and a United Arab States could emerge.

As regards these smaller political unities, I would suggest the following:

1. The Fertile Crescent. This would include the first and second regions, that is, the Tigris and Euphrates valleys (including Kuwait) plus natural Syria. The geographical, economic, and historical links binding them, together with their almost identical social and cultural levels, necessitate such a division. This unit would include Iraq, Syria, Jordan, and Palestine, after the last has been liberated. It is advisable that Lebanon should be excluded for reasons that I shall later expound.

2. The Arabian Peninsula. This would include Sa'udi Arabia, the Yemen, and those forgotten shaykhdoms, known as protectorates, like Bahrain, Qatar, the Trucial Coast shaykhdoms, the sultanates of Muscat and Oman, the Aden Protectorate, and the Crown Colony of Aden.

3. The Nile Valley. This would include Egypt, Sudan, and Libya, which

is only an extension of the western Egyptian Desert on the one side and of Tunisia on the other. But the requirements of the present situation oblige us to treat this area on the basis of the present political setup.

4. The Maghrib. This would include Morocco, Algeria, and Tunisia.

The Arab world stands at the threshold of events of momentous importance. The centuries-old imperialist sway has begun to wane while the responsibilities engendered by independence are many in number and of grave importance. The Arabs will not be able to meet the challenge of the modern world of progress unless they stand united politically and economically. Reason dictates solidarity and unity.

Before I bring my arguments to a close, I would like to turn to Lebanon and to my reasons for wishing to exclude it at present from unity. I do this not because Lebanon has been tardy in working for the Arab cause; indeed, since the dawn of the modern Arab awakening, Lebanon has worked in the forefront of those who struggled for Arabism. Its contribution to the revival of Arabic poetry, literature, science, and the Arab spirit has been of major importance. Lebanon is of the very core of Arabism geographically, economically, and culturally. When national consciousness is firmly established among the Arabs, we shall find Lebanon to be the cornerstone of the Arab structure. Therefore, one must not impose upon Lebanon any solution that it does not wish to accept of its own free will.

On July 9, 1946, I openly advocated the creation of a United Arab States. Today, ten years later, I believe that the setbacks suffered by the Arab world would not have taken place if it had been united. Calamities will cease only with federation. A United Arab States is the ideal means toward achieving Arab unity, which has been and still is the Arabs' ultimate hope.

42. COMMUNISM AND THE PROBLEMS OF THE ARAB WORLD*

This article expresses the viewpoints of Arab Marxists from Algeria, Jordan, Iraq, Lebanon, Syria, and Sudan on the question of unity and on the social groups and the political regimes striving to achieve it. Only the working class is considered capable of leading the Arab countries to union. The U.S.S.R. has generally opposed the nationalist plan of unity.

The Problem of Unity of the Arab Peoples

The movement for Arab unity is aimed at reuniting the Arab peoples and reflects the historical situation of the Arab countries. It results not from chang-

* Extract from "L'Étape actuelle du mouvement de libération nationale des peuples arabes," *La Nouvelle Revue Internationale,* October, 1963, pp. 120–25, 128. It also appeared as "Le Communisme et les problèmes du monde arabe," *Orient,* No. 27 (1963), 195–203.

ing circumstances nor from the desire of one class or one party. The symbol of Arab unity was born at the end of the struggle against colonialism and imperialism to achieve national independence.

Up to World War II, the idea of Arab unity was expressed in abstract terms circulating in limited intellectual circles. Sometimes the imperialists themselves spoke of what they termed "Arab unity." Thus, in the first years following the war, they undertook the creation of a plan for a "Greater Syria," a union of the countries of the Fertile Crescent which was to embrace Lebanon, Syria, and Jordan, the setting up of an Iraqi-Jordanian federation, and the like.

The progressive aspect of Arab unity is directed against imperialism and feudalism. It is this which is supported and developed by all the democratic forces of the Arab nations. It has the sympathy and approval of the vast masses of the population. The reactionary aspect is apparent in the wish of the Arab bourgeoisie to subject the liberation movement to their selfish class interests. The bourgeoisie does not struggle hard for the complete suppression of colonialism and the eradication of the vestiges of feudalism. The conquest of power is their final aim.

The Arab peoples consider this unity as essential for reinforcing their solidarity in the struggle against imperialism and for counteracting dictatorial regimes in order to achieve radical social reform. The Communists have always supported and continue to support the democratic aspect of Arab unity, and they criticize its reactionary side. The movement toward unity has not achieved, in all countries, the same over-all intensity among the masses. But the Communists look to the future. They cannot remain indifferent to the question of unity.

The struggle between the two conceptions of Arab unity, the bourgeois and the proletarian, became particularly acute from 1957 onward, although the potentialities of the two parties involved in this struggle were unequal. The bourgeoisie is in power, and the progressive forces very often cannot openly express their views. But, in spite of this, the concepts and the ideas of the working class concerning unity have acquired an immense popularity.

The union of Syria and Egypt provided a touchstone for the bourgeois method of solving the problem of Arab unity. Certain groups of the Arab bourgeoisie, which had welcomed with enthusiasm the idea of uniting the two states, have begun to change their position. Today, the Ba'thists, who are in power in Syria and in Iraq, emphasize more and more clearly the local characteristics of each Arab country.

The Communists, however, cannot consider the question of Arab unity apart from the final aim of their struggle—the elimination of the exploitation of man by man and the building of a classless socialist society. But the bourgeois class in certain Arab countries strives to demonstrate that the liberation movement that has developed under the concept of Arab unity has already a socialist character.

The Egyptian bourgeoisie retains for itself a special place in the achievement of Arab unity, owing to the fact that Egypt is the strongest and most industrially developed country in the Arab East. She sees the problem of Arab unity from the angle of her domination over her "younger sisters." The imperialists support the aspirations of the reactionary party of the Egyptian bourgeoisie. They are ever ready to encourage the constitution of any union whatsoever of Arab states, provided such a union has no democratic or anti-imperialist foundation. If the envisaged union of Egypt, Syria, and Iraq would injure imperialist interests, it is hardly likely they would support this project. They do not wish to see a strong Arab empire, with immense oil riches, under the unlimited power of Abdel Nasser. So they endeavor to encourage a rival force to head such a federation. Recent events show that certain Arab nationalists and Ba'thist partisans of 'Aflaq form just such a force. It is not by chance that the Ba'thists speak of the collective control of the proposed federation. It is clear that by "collective control" they mean the limitation of the power of President Nasser.

It has been emphasized in debate that the idea of Arab unity occupies the minds of numerous intellectuals, army officers, and students, who see in it the means of realizing their dream of a powerful Arab state. The feudalists, the proimperialist bourgeoisie, and other reactionary secessionist forces are avowed enemies of unity. They fear to lose the control of the state machinery that defends their interests. After the union of Syria and Egypt, these elements began to dread that the more influential Egyptian bourgeoisie might dominate them and deprive them of local and foreign markets. Recently, they have become alarmed by the changes occurring in Egypt.

The idea of Arab unity is widespread among the peasants, particularly since the adoption of the laws of agrarian reform in Egypt, then in Syria. The working class, by nature an internationalist force, is in favor of a democratically achieved form of Arab unity that is prepared to struggle against imperialism and colonialism for the raising of the workers' standard of living, for friendly relations with socialist countries, especially the Soviet Union, and for the establishment of a steady progression toward socialism.

According to the historical background of the different Arab countries, one can see among the classes a tendency toward either unity or secession. In 1958, the Syrian bourgeoisie favored union with Egypt, since it considered itself menaced by the "Communist threat." It was for separation when the more powerful Egyptian bourgeoisie began to take over its markets and endanger its interests.

In the matter of Arab unity, two trends must be distinguished, the nationalist-bourgeois trend and the democratic-revolutionary one. The first, whose slogans may well be very different from its aims, considers that Arab unity can only be achieved by observing four conditions: anti-Communism and anti-democracy, reinforcement of nationalist and chauvinistic ideology, isolation of the Arab peoples from the socialist camp, and coming to terms with imperialism. Its supporters wish to collaborate with imperialism but are afraid of falling under its direct control. At the same time, they do not wish to break off relations completely with the socialist countries, insofar as they are rewarding. But when they see that this collaboration strengthens the popular movement, they endeavor to reduce it. They are constantly maneuvering between imperialism and socialism.

Several different trends can be seen in the bourgeois-nationalist line. One is represented by the Egyptian bourgeoisie, which, because of its will to expand and dominate, tends toward total unity of Arab states, to the point of destroying the autonomy of the other countries. The Ba'thists, for their part, desire a federal union in which Nasserism would not extend beyond Egypt and they would dominate in Syria and in Iraq.

For the representatives of the democratic-revolutionary line, Arab unity must be based on democracy and take into account the objective conditions of each country. This idea of unity permits the formation of a strong alliance between sister Arab countries that allows for the interests of each; great opportunities for economic, social, and political progress are open to a federal state of this kind. The democratic-revolutionary conception binds together the Communists, the national democrats, and the independent socialists.

The main lesson to be learned from the union of Syria and Egypt, declared a Syrian comrade, is that Arab unity is not viable if one country is in an inferior position vis-à-vis a more powerful one. In September, 1961, when Syria broke away from the U.A.R., the Communist Party declared that this did not indicate the collapse of the idea of Arab unity but of the anti-democratic policy of dictatorship and of the domination of one country over another.

The plan of a new federal union between Egypt, Syria, and Iraq, as formulated in the Cairo declaration of April 17, 1963, takes account of the objective conditions of each Arab country and upholds their independence in a number of areas. In particular, it forecasts national parliaments. The lesson of the union of Syria and Egypt has brought about these modifications. But we must not delude ourselves, for the basic principle of democracy is not respected. As events in Iraq have shown, this federation is directed against democracy and, in particular, against Communism—not against imperialism. One point deserves attention. It concerns "national security," which, according to the Cairo declaration, is taken over by the central government. Consequently, if a popular movement develops in one of the countries of the federation, troops from another may be sent to ensure "national security" and repress it, even though the local parliament does not agree. Already at this preliminary stage, the federation is torn by profound contradictions. Certain Syrian and Iraqi Ba'thists would like to create an Iraqi-Syrian federation.

A Lebanese comrade dwelt on the history of the idea of Arab nationalism. It was launched for the first time, he said, by the Arab national liberation movement at the beginning of the twentieth century. Its centers at that time were Damascus, Beirut, and Baghdad. It urged the Arabs to struggle for national sovereignty against the Turkish occupation. It was of a democratic character and took into consideration the distinct characteristics of each country. It culminated in the Arab Congress held in Paris in 1913. Arab hopes, however, clashed both with Turkish greed and with the interests of the French and English colonialists who wished to seize the wealth of the Arab countries.

In spite of their differences of opinion, the Turkish and Franco-English colonialists conspired to crush the liberation movement of the Arab peoples.

There was a period in Arab history when the ruler of Egypt, Muhammad 'Ali, took possession of Syria and the Lebanon. The population of these countries and several others welcomed him joyfully, for they were hostile to the occupying Turks. But once he had unified and occupied these countries, Muhammad 'Ali took to pillaging their national wealth, caring solely for the interests of Egypt. Finally, the peoples of Syria, Lebanon, and other Arab countries took up arms against Muhammad 'Ali and his son, Ibrahim Pasha. Thus collapsed an Arab state founded on the domination of one nation over others.

The present situation of the Arab countries, in particular Iraq, Syria, and Lebanon, is such that the national bourgeoisie could not till now ensure unity by its own means. More and more, therefore, it had recourse to imperialism. It is important that each Arab country develop economically and socially on a democratic basis in close cooperation with the socialist camp. When this is accomplished, unity will result.

A comrade from the Sudan emphasized that for thirteen years the bourgeoisie of his country has supported the idea of unity with Egypt. He described the weakness of the national bourgeoisie and its willingness to be helped by the Egyptian bourgeoisie to struggle against imperialism. However, a mass movement against colonialism has grown and developed within the country, in which the working class has played a major role. After independence, a bourgeois party came to power. Although it had obtained a majority in parliament, it could not change the democratic character of the mass movement and impose unity with Egypt. The working class launched the idea of the right of the Sudanese people to self-determination, which was approved unanimously by parliament.

In looking into the possibilities of Arab unity, we must take into account the role of the working class, for without radical transformation in the nature of political power, the experience of the union between Egypt and Syria will be repeated, perhaps in a different form, and no true democratic unity will be achieved. The basic question is that the possibility of uniting must not be thought of only in the light of the contradictions between the different strata of the Arab bourgeoisie. It must be founded on a scientific base, and the possibility of achieving union must be considered by relying on the main forces of the national liberation movement: the working class, the peasants, the nonproletarian social strata of town and country.

We also believe, declared an Iraqi comrade, that the Arab bourgeoisie is incapable of ensuring the unity of the Arab peoples on a democratic basis. But in the sphere of national democratic revolution, and until socialism succeeds in the Arab countries, some form of federation or confederation of two or three countries or more may appear. The bourgeoisie certainly cannot bring about a really democratic union. But the achievement of Arab unity is possible in the course of the development and deepening of the national democratic revolution and the formation of a national democratic state in which the working class, in conjunction with the peasants and all workers, will play the principal role. But even in these circumstances, there will certainly be no question of automatic integration of all the countries in the alliance, for there will still remain economic and political differences between countries for some time.

The problem is not one of a choice between Arab unity within the framework of the victory of socialism and unity within the bourgeois dictatorship, which exists today in the greater number of Arab countries. At the present stage of the struggle for liberation, the choice is between the democratic-revolutionary solution and the nationalist-bourgeois solution. Against the bourgeois solution stands the solution of the proletariat and its party. It is based on four conditions: democracy and support of the masses; resolute struggle against imperialism; reinforcement and widening of relations with socialist countries, and in particular with the Soviet Union; respect for the interests and equality of the Arab peoples in all domains and countries. This proletarian solution could be the foundation of a mass movement in the Arab countries.

The problem of Arab unity, a Jordanian comrade has stated, is tightly bound to the general acceleration of the national liberation movement and to the change in the balance of power on the international scene. It cannot be considered independently of changes in the balance of world power at the expense of peace and socialism. Experience shows that the bourgeoisie desires unity of the Arab countries because it wants to acquire new markets. For example, the Egyptian bourgeoisie wishes to absorb the whole Arab market, the Syrian bourgeoisie wants to have the Iraqi and Jordanian markets, and so on.

The slogan of Arab unity has helped the national liberation movement. Historically, the development of the liberation movement, in particular after the political independence of several countries, has shown the inability to establish an Arab bourgeois regime along classical lines. This demonstrates that the aims of unity cannot be confined to the widening of markets. The problem of trade is not a basic problem for the masses. The will to create a market—that is, union founded on the idea of a single market—conflicts not only with the interests of the masses but also with those of certain groups of the national bourgeoisie. Unity, like agrarian reform, industrialization, and other great problems of the Arab peoples, cannot be assured by capitalism.

We have seen that the Syrian bourgeoisie on the whole did not support the union of Syria and Egypt, as it existed from 1958 to 1961. Perhaps the workers and peasants were more enthusiastic than the bourgeoisie in this respect. The Ba'th Party was the only one to desire and to support the union with Egypt. This party is led principally by petit-bourgeois anti-Communist elements that represent all that is most reactionary both in Arab history and in the Western right-wing socialist movement. The Ba'th Party was formed after World War II as a counter to the Communist movement.

Recently, it has adopted the slogan of Arab unity on the basis of an anti-colonialist struggle. The bloody events in Iraq [the reprisals against Communists], however, showed the worth of the speeches of these leaders regarding democracy. But this does not mean that in the future a split may not occur in this party, as when, after the union of Syria and Egypt, the Hawrani group broke away from 'Aflaq's.[1]

Arab unity, stated those present at the meeting, must be founded on liberty, democracy, and equality of all the countries. It must also be explained to the masses that union of the Arab peoples is possible by means of noncapitalist development; that the formation of a national democratic state allows workers and their organizations to participate directly and actively in the political and economic life of the country; and that it accords them full democratic rights.

43. ARAB REVOLUTIONS AND UNITY: A CONSERVATIVE APPRAISAL*

The influential Beirut daily al-Hayat (Life) *was published by Kamal Muruwwa, a liberal, democratic-minded intellectual, who was, however, regarded by some Arabs as right of center. Muruwwa believed that the social and political aims of the Arab nations could be attained best through democratic parliamentary governments that respect local differences and pursue moderate foreign policy lines. These views placed him in opposition to President Nasser of the U.A.R., whose agents bombed the office of* al-Hayat, *and it was there that Muruwwa was assassinated in 1965.*

In an interview with Kemal H. Karpat on July 30, 1964, Muruwwa claimed that a proper application of Islamic laws would prevent disparities of wealth. The inheritance law in particular, he felt, could dissolve big fortunes within three generations. Muruwwa believed that the bourgeoisie would triumph in the Middle East since socialist experiments—especially that of the Ba'th—had been unsuccessful. Muruwwa expected that an antisocialist revolution would take place among Eastern Arabs. However, Egyptians, according to Muruwwa, could not revolt because of geographical conditions, which prevent aid from outside as well as escape. The West, he believed, supported socialism because it would ultimately help solve the problems of Israel by weakening Islam, which, in turn, provides the chief resistance to the acceptance of Israel. Consequently, Muruwwa believed that Nasser's policies were ultimately detrimental to Islam as a whole. Muruwwa, however, greatly admired Turkey, which he regarded as a truly Muslim country. He believed that Turkish reforms, rather than destroying Islam, actually strengthened it by separating its spiritual aspects from politics.

1. The Ba'th united with Akram Hawrani's Arab Socialist Party in 1953 and separated in 1958. See section on the Ba'th, pp. 185–97, above.

* Extract from "Ya 'uqala' al-arab ittahidu" ("O Arabs of Sound Minds, Unite!"), *al-Hayat* (*Life*), Beirut, September 22, 1963.

The article from which the following extract has been taken appeared anonymously in al-Hayat. *It was credited to a "Former Arab Politician," and may have been written either by Jibran Shamiyya or by Muruwwa himself. It represents the judgment of some Arabs regarding the U.A.R. and regarding the internal rivalries that are undermining Arab unity.*

During the summer of 1960, I was talking with some friends, who like myself were in their forties, about the necessity of creating a party representing moderate Arab opinion linked to the values of democracy and freedom. In the framework of such a party, we would struggle against the political and intellectual oppression imposed on us by Arab socialist and revolutionary movements, certain that the majority of Arabs would support common sense, moderation, and wisdom. For political and social extremism hides its weaknesses under verbal excess and intimidation.

At that time, Syria and Egypt were still in a union, and only a minority discerned failure. Qasim was still a national hero [in Iraq], and the wave of Arabism that issued from Cairo excited the majority of the population. My friends thought then that any action in the political and intellectual sphere opposed to this current was veritable suicide. They considered that this generation had had its time and was finished. For them, the future belonged to the young people under forty, and power to the bold and not to the wise.

Three years have passed since that meeting. Let us now draw up a balance sheet of the situation in the "liberated" countries under the control of young revolutionaries of all degrees.

Syria

The most outstanding event marking Arab political life during recent years was the shattering of the union of Syria and Egypt; not that the Ba'thists were necessarily secessionists, as Cairo claims today, nor that the Egyptian regime was personal, dictatorial, and dynamic, as the Ba'thists affirm, but for a reason far removed from all this and inherent in the union itself since 1958.

In effect, this union was decided upon more or less by revolutionaries quite ignorant of government, politics, and the situation of the Arab countries. They made up for deep and careful consideration with slogans, campaigns for agitation, and street demonstrations. But far-sighted Syrians realized that a union that purely and simply attached Syria to Egypt carried within it the seeds of failure. In vain, they tried to stem the flood of propaganda, which cost Egypt enormous sums and which finally overwhelmed the country.

Is there any need to recall that that union was preceded and prepared by an alliance between Ba'thists and Syrian Communists who governed the country in 1957 and 1958? The conviction of patriots, such as Michel Liyan, 'Adnan al-Atasi, and Munir al-Ajlani, appalled the moderates, and no one any longer dared express any opinion.

Have we forgotten that a group of officers led by the Communist Colonel

'Afif al-Bizri concluded this union?[1] They made their way to Cairo and deposited Syria at the feet of Nasser. They were joined by the Ba'thist minister for foreign affairs, Salah al-Din Bitar, who gave his blessings to the operation and urged Cairo to accept the gift. Back in Damascus, they forced parliament to make this generous gift official.

Still, there were people like Shukri al-Quwatli, Khalid al-'Azm, Sabri al-'Asali, Leon Zamaria, who proposed a federation instead of a union that was contrary to the interests of Syria and destined to failure. Their proposal was ignored, and they were obliged to adopt the union in its sterile form.

The Egyptian party was no more realistic or far-sighted than the Syrian. Perhaps it was more ignorant of the situation in Syria. Complete and centralized government, the division of Syria into provinces, total Egyptian domination—such were the conditions that President Nasser imposed on the Ba'thist and Communist negotiators. Secession was the fatal consequence.

Syrian revolutionaries took control again after the *coup d'état* [the Ba'th take-over] of February 8, 1963, and immediately reverted to their old methods, drowning the idea of union under a wave of agitation and street demonstrations. They then hastened to Cairo once more to throw themselves into the arms of Nasser.

On April 17, 1963, the Egyptian, Syrian, and Iraqi revolutionaries published their famous declaration.[2] Once denounced by Cairo,[3] it appeared as the greatest betrayal, the most abject delusion of the Arab peoples in the course of the last few years. For they proclaimed publicly their adherence to the union, although in fact each had agreed to retain total independence in all essential domains for a period of at least five years.

Then they did not waste any time in launching a campaign of accusation and slander against one another, thus proving their insincerity regarding "the indispensable meeting of three revolutions."

The internal politics of the revolutionaries in Syria consisted only in plunder and theft under cover of agrarian reform and nationalization. For all confiscation of land and nationalization of public services or factories not immediately accompanied by fair indemnity payments are no more than plunder and theft, no matter what the principles may be in which they are disguised. Their socialism, such as it appears till now, is only a shabby form of municipal Communism founded on their envy and hate of the landowner class, which prefers the country to the town; it favors minorities over the majority.

One of the successes of Syrian socialism was the monopoly it established of the corn market, which the government took over as a matter of course. During the time of independence, it cut the cost to the buyer by 30 per cent of the previous year's price, thus gaining the hatred of the peasants. Finally, the government came into conflict with businessmen and heads of industry by refusing to specify its economic policy. So, confidence disappeared and eco-

1. This view is contrary to the generally held opinion that the Ba'thists asked for union in order to prevent the Communists from taking over the government in Syria.
2. See pp. 275 ff. The agreement was never carried out.
3. A reference to Egypt's refusal to agree with the Ba'th on terms of unity.

nomic activity was at a standstill. Workers and tradesmen were idle, and it could be said that not since World War II had Syria experienced a more serious economic crisis than the one she has had since she has been in the hands of the revolutionaries of last February 8.

Their speeches on the subject of economic union with Iraq have had a strong resemblance to the declaration of April 17. In effect, the promoters of the two *coups d'état,* Syrian and Iraqi, could not agree on a single article when the talks on the sharing of the waters of the Euphrates took place, although this was one of the easiest questions they had to negotiate. It leads one to suppose the same result for the coming economic negotiations.

Iraq

The situation of the Iraqi revolutionaries is not any better. Perhaps they are meeting greater and more urgent difficulties. Yet, although they have not dubbed their socialism Ba'thist or disorganized the economy by similar steps as those taken in Syria, the lack of confidence that they inspire and the danger of the policy that they may adopt are likely to land Iraq in a crisis as serious as that of Syria.

Under the monarchy, Iraq enjoyed religious and social peace. Royalty was a symbol around which different opinions met and fraternized. All were amicable. It was Iraq's means of existence and its guarantee of national unity. The royal power preserved 70 per cent of the oil revenues, which represented 70 million dinars, for a development fund that originated all its achievements, such as dams, the pride of present-day Iraq, and which, if it had pursued its course, would have made Iraq the paradise of the region. When, by ill luck, the government arrested a Communist or a plotter, a wave of protest spread across the world.

Then came the [Qasim] *coup d'état* of July 14, 1958, which was marked by a cruelty and savagery that the world had not seen since the Communist revolution in Russia. The 70 million dinars allocated to the development fund excited the greed of the revolutionaries. The fund was suppressed, and with it the development projects. The money went into the revolutionaries' pockets. Afterward, faithful to tradition, they began to kill each other in a series of massacres that covered the country from Mosul to Basra.

With the collapse of the state and the disappearance of the symbol that unified them, the Kurds judged the occasion ripe for a rising and proclaimed their autonomy. For two years, Qasim tried in vain to subdue them.

The Ba'thists seized power by another coup in February, 1963, and were to share with their brother Syrians in the betrayal of April 17. Then they applied themselves to the solution of their internal difficulties, and first and foremost the Kurdish question.

Although we may wish to see the government bulletins announcing final victory proved true, the information furnished by neutrals indicates that the Kurdish war will drain the strength and resources of the state for a long time, and that the present government is ill qualified to arrive at a peaceable and acceptable agreement with the Kurds.

Moreover, once the Kurdish question is settled, the problem of religious denominations will arise, as indicated by Talib Shabib during the Cairo talks. For when the Kurds have obtained self-government, the Shi'ites will form the great majority of the Iraqi Arab element. At the present time, this majority is claiming its share of power and is far from accepting the present policy of the government. Another difficulty is added to all of these. After five years of revolutionary government, the Iraqi state finds itself with a budgetary deficit despite the enormous oil revenues, although before the *coup d'état* of 1958, it enjoyed assets and prosperity seldom achieved.

The balance sheet for this government since 1958, therefore, shows the dislocation of the machinery of state, the birth of racial and denominational movements, and let us not forget the massacres and butchery that are likely to flair up again at any moment.

The Yemen

Even the contented Yemen was promoted by the revolutionaries to the ranks of the "liberated" countries.

On his accession, Imam al-Badr showed his willingness to surrender the absolute power of former times and install a parliamentary system corresponding to the degree of evolution achieved by the Yemeni people. As far as we knew, the Imam was a "liberal." President Nasser had taken him under his wing and had assured him of his support on several occasions.

But, in secret, the revolutionaries were finalizing a plan that hardly matched their lavish assurances. They urged al-Sallal to revolt. The attempt was unfortunate, for once in power, al-Sallal sought the help of his Zaydi sect. This was the signal for civil war, thanks to the revolutionaries and the accuracy of their policy.

Still, if the situation had not gone further than civil war, perhaps the Yemenis would have been able to put an end to it by their own means. But Egypt wanted to enter the conflict. She sent 30,000 soldiers to support the revolution. Yet after a year, victory is still as uncertain as on the first day, and the war would have exhausted the Egyptian treasury and mortgaged it had it not been for constant and massive American aid.

As for the Yemeni revolutionaries, as usual they are turning on each other; al-Sallal eliminates Baydani and accuses him of treason, then he in turn incurs the anger of his protectors. As previously in Iraq, denominationalism makes its appearance through the errors of the revolutionaries. The Shafi'is of the Yemen claim their rights from the Zaydis, through Baydani. Rumors circulate on the possibility of partitioning the country between Zaydis and Shafi'is. And so the Arab revolutionaries, who received the Yemen united under the power of the Imam, will leave it in the name of their socialism and their own particular conception of Arabism, divided forever among warring sects.

Should the Arabs rejoice at this general revolutionary policy in Iraq and the Yemen and value the fidelity to the principles of Arabism? To crown it all, have the revolutionaries not established denominational divisions in these two countries and class hatred in Syria as well?

Algeria

We must treat Algeria—the apple of our eye—with great circumspection, for this country has fully paid its debt in suffering and sacrifice. We hoped to see the Algerian leaders agreeing on a democratic regime that would guarantee the unity of the country and ensure the representation of all shades of opinion. Our hope is that the present situation, in which a single leader dominates and appropriates all the power, is only a transitory phase and that the country will revert without too much damage to truly democratic ways. Otherwise, Algeria risks exposing herself to the same scourge that ravished the countries of the East. Already there is rumor of the existence of an Arab-Berber conflict, provoked by selfishness and personal power. May Algeria be preserved from the misfortunes of Iraq, the Yemen, Syria, and Egypt!

Egypt

Egypt is the fifth of the "liberated" countries and the last we shall deal with in the course of this study. She is the brain behind the *coups d'état* in the Arab world; she incites them, encourages them, supports them, then denounces them, makes difficulties for them, and does not stop until they fail.

Each time a *coup d'état* occurs in an Arab country, one is sure of finding the hand of Egypt there, either stirring it up, sustaining it, or lending it support. But as soon as it succeeds, she comes out against it and is bent on demolishing it, inciting another rebellion to balance it. This is what happened with Qasim and the Ba'thists in Iraq and in Syria, and apparently she is following the same policy in the Yemen. For she demands that the promoters of the *coups d'état* obey her blindly, act according to her will, and comply with her instruction. This is how she acted during the union with Syria in 1958, and today she still does not seem to have changed her policy or profited from past experience.

At home, the Egyptian Revolution is far from realizing its objectives. The annual birth rate exceeds the progress it has made, so that the standard of living is steadily going down.

All she has done is to generalize the poverty and impose it equally on all. Then, to prevent the people from realizing their situation, she keeps them busy with adventures in Syria, Iraq, and the Yemen and with attempted *coups d'état* in Jordan and Sa'udi Arabia.

The Egyptian Government has suffered defeat after defeat since it made itself the champion of a certain kind of Arab unity, which it wishes to impose by methods peculiar to itself. Worse still, it cannot be credited with a single success in any of its Arab enterprises. The union with Syria was a failure, also its intervention in Lebanon in 1958. It could not agree with Qasim. It was disappointed equally in its repeated intrigues against the Sa'udi and Jordanian regimes, as the two monarchs proved their capacities to stand up to it. It was no more fortunate in its attempts to come to an agreement with the Ba'thists of Iraq and Syria. Its military escapade in the Yemen was a total and irreparable failure.

Several questions arise here:

Do the Egyptian people not have great need of the resources and men purposelessly sacrificed in the Yemen?

Did the Egyptian Government consult its people before dragging them into this adventure?

If it has been able to transport a whole army with its equipment to the Yemen, thousands of miles away, is it not surprising that it has been unable to transport them a few dozen miles across the Sinai Desert as far as the Negev?

And if it has such a military force at its disposal, why is the Gulf of 'Aqaba still open to Israel, and why does the international force still continue to be stationed on its soil?

Must the perpetual failures of Egypt always be imputed to the mistakes of others, or is it not rather a stigma peculiar to its leaders, which prevents them from agreeing with any Arab regime of any form whatsoever?

There are two reasons for the ease with which the Egyptian regime manages to interfere in the internal affairs of other Arab countries.

On the one hand, the very nature of the Egyptian people, accustomed to obeying any master, gives the illusion that the reigning power is solidly established and can concentrate all its efforts on inciting subversion among its neighbors. On the other hand, there is the fact that the United States depends upon Egypt in her Middle East policy. Her aid, exceeding several million dollars, allows the Egyptian Government to pay its agents in the Arab countries well.

But this internal stability, obtained by police methods and fear, will not last, no matter how docile and submissive the Egyptian people may be, especially since Arab networks operate in Egypt, as those of the Egyptians work in other countries. The Ba'thists proclaim their intention of infiltrating the Egyptian people to help them get rid of the Nasser dictatorship.

That is a summary of the revolutionary policy of the young generation during the past seven years: imposture and delusion that disfigures the idea of Arab unity; disorganization and ruin of the national economy; hate and villainy toward one class; accusation, invective, and abuse poured from the propaganda agencies; the dictatorship of municipal Communism disguised as socialism and supported by an intolerable police oppression; and massacres and racial and denominational divisions in more than one country.

I take up again my talk with my friends who abandoned politics to the revolutionaries, and I ask them:

Do you still believe that our generation has passed its day and that the present one is more worth-while?

Do you resign yourself to leaving the country in the clutches of a band of snarling, malicious profiteers and adventurers?

Do you not feel responsible for the fate of your countries, for the sake of your children and grandchildren?

Are you so much dominated by fear that you have become incapable of taking up a simple position or expressing an opinion?

You still represent the majority in your countries, no matter what the revolutionaries say. Is there not one among you to proclaim the truth? And to show the way to your fellow citizens?

"When God wishes to humble a people, He gives precedence to the young over the old."

In effect, in several Arab countries, the young have taken over power. They maintain themselves from one country to another by using intimidation and bluff. They make war, giving the impression of being millions, although they are only a handful. Come! Stir yourselves from Morocco to Kuwait so that reason, probity, and honesty may reign among Arabs instead of unrest, betrayal, and stagnation!

44. IDEOLOGICAL PROBLEMS IN THE ARAB WORLD AS SEEN BY ITS LEADERS*

All Arab leaders have issued ideological declarations at one time or another. Some were intended for domestic consumption, some were designed to stress or reject a particular viewpoint. Seldom were ideological positions stated frankly and confronted with the views held by others. A unique opportunity to look into the actual beliefs of Arab leaders was provided by the unity talks held in Cairo in March, 1963. The discussions continued in April, after the Iraqi delegation joined the talks. The result was a tripartite declaration issued on April 17, 1963.

The participants in the discussion included some of the leaders and chief ideologists of the Arab world, such as Egyptian President Nasser; Michel 'Aflaq and Salah al-Din Bitar, the founders and philosophers of the Ba'th; Luai Atasi, a general and chairman of the Revolutionary Council of Syria; Hani Hindi, then minister of planning and later leader of the pro-Nasser Syrian Arab Nationalist Movement; 'Abd al-Rahman al-Bazzaz, then the Iraqi ambassador in Cairo and later premier, well-known writer on Arab nationalism; several members of the Egyptian Presidential Council, notably Premier 'Ali Sabri, Marshal 'Amir, and Col. Kamal Rifa'at; and other political personalities. Membership in the discussion committee alternated considerably.

The discussions were held in secret, but when the Ba'thists repressed the Nasserites in Syria and Iraq several months later, the Egyptian Government

* Extracts from Walid Khalidi and Yusuf Ibish (eds.), *Arab Political Documents, 1963* (Beirut: Slim Press, 1964), pp. 120–23, 136–38, 143–45, 147–56. The spelling of names in the original text has been adapted. Reproduced by permission.

published the minutes first in al-Ahram *and then in a special volume,* Mahadir jalsat mubahathat al-wahda (Minutes of Discussions on Unity) (*Cairo: Dar al-qawmiyya lil-tab'a wal-nashr, 1963*). *A selected English translation of the minutes appears in* Arab Political Documents, 1963 (*Beirut: Slim Press, 1964*). *For the Ba'th view on the talks, see Riad Taha,* Mahadir muhadathat al-wahda (Records of Unity Talks) (*Beirut: Dar al-kifah, 1963*). *For a lengthy analysis of Arab foreign policy, based on unity talk records, see Malcolm H. Kerr,* The Arab Cold War, 1958–1964: A Study of Ideology in Politics (*London: Oxford University Press, 1965*).

'AFLAQ: . . . By freedom, do you mean democracy or liberation?

NASSER: As we understand it and as it is found in the [National] Charter [of Egypt], freedom means a free country and a free citizen. The Charter explains this in great detail and perfectly clearly. Socialism, again, implies sufficiency and justice and the Charter also defines these two terms very fully. Unity is a popular, historical, and actual will, and the Charter devotes a whole chapter to constitutional unity in all its forms. The socialist path is defined, beginning with internal trade and ending with the popular control over the means of production, passing through agriculture, the private sector, and the public sector. All national activity is fully defined in the Charter.

'AFLAQ: The slogan of the Arab Nationalist Movement is Unity, Liberation, and Socialism. There, freedom means liberation.

NASSER: Naturally, for we have to liberate ourselves from the domination of feudalism and capital.

'AFLAQ: Not quite. Liberation there implies liberation from imperialism.

NASSER: When the revolution broke out in 1952, we had our six well-known principles: the destruction of feudalism, and of exploitation and the domination of capital, and the creation of a strong army, social justice, and a proper democratic life. We began to implement these principles from the very first day. Last year, we promulgated our Charter, in which is contained a detailed exposé of all these principles. What is implied there by the freedom of the individual? We maintained that this freedom entails total freedom for the people and its denial to enemies of the people. In order to buttress this freedom, we spoke of self-criticism, of the freedom of the press, and of all popular organizations. We linked the election ticket to the loaf of bread; in other words, socialism is a prerequisite of freedom. We also advocated that democracy, socialism, and freedom are interdependent. Now then, how does the Ba'th define democracy?

'AFLAQ: In fact, I believe that you do not lack a definition of democracy and socialism but I have observed that, sometimes, socialism has taken the place of democracy.

NASSER: Have you read the Charter?

'AFLAQ: Yes.

NASSER: Then it appears that you were reading one line and skipping the next. It is not at all what you imagine. Our revolution was the first to call for social democracy, meaning that political [democracy] was inconceivable without social democracy. This fact led us to socialism and to the inevitability of socialism as a prerequisite for true democracy. Otherwise, democracy would have become the dictatorship of capitalism and feudalism. This is what is generally termed bourgeois democracy. But there was never any mention of socialism taking the place of democracy. What I said was that socialism was necessary for democracy, in order to avoid exploitation. . . .

We got rid of feudalism and capitalism and all foreign concerns were nationalized. In this, we acted as the vanguard of the working people, who now rule in Egypt. We do not govern in the interest of a class but of the coalition of workers, peasants, and intellectuals and, indeed, of the whole working people. In this way, our policy is other than what you imagine. France, for example, which is a capitalist country, might institute nationalization but this would only be in the interests of the capitalist government. Here, however, it is the working people who rule the land and its task is to abolish class differences. In the public sector, we have implemented democracy by specifying that a certain ratio of workers should be present on the boards of management of the companies. Now, the ratio is two workers out of seven board members and we plan to increase this proportion until only one member will be an appointment.

Then, we come to face the eternal problem of all socialist countries: bureaucracy. This goes hand in hand with socialism. We have already proffered a solution: association of the workers in the board of management and a share of the profits. For example, when the workers are getting 25 per cent of the profits, their representative on the board may, let us say, object to the unnecessary purchase of a car for the board since this might directly affect the profits. This has actually happened in some companies.

Then again, we have organized trade unions and the Socialist Union[1] within a factory. If any flaw is detected, the union in question will inform the General Union of Labor whose duty it will be to inform the minister of labor. The Committee of the Socialist Union will similarly inform the Higher Council and in this manner the people's wealth will not be squandered. This procedure is entirely democratic and, as a result, there has been a rise in production and the worker now feels that he is his own master and that he owns the factory.

SABRI: Workers nowadays are more careful about their factory's machines than was the owner in the old days.

NASSER: The next point, which complements the socialist setup, is the fixing of wages. Our law states that £5,000 is the maximum wage—not, by the way, the maximum income. Hence, the rest is all profit. We also fixed a minimum wage for workers. In the past, this was 15 piasters a day. Now it is 25. We also fixed the wages for overtime and the social relations within the factory. Now, certain workers are receiving very substantial wages. We also specified bonuses. What all this adds up to is that all the people now share in production. Our experiment is not really the same as the Yugoslav one. We

1. The U.A.R. government-supported political organization.

have studied this latter, together with the Russian, the Chinese, and the Indian practice. We also invite certain experts in socialist economy and discuss matters with them. The last one was here two weeks, Professor Petelheim, professor of planning at the Sorbonne. He is regularly consulted by the Russians, the Yugoslavs, the Indians, and the Algerians. Baghdadi, Sabri, and I met him and he told us about what he saw here and there. Petelheim's view, for example, was that our own experiment was unique and very advanced.

It seems that your [i.e., 'Aflaq's] impression of our experiment is very sketchy. One of you said yesterday that our experiment "could be termed" socialist. It is not that at all. It is in fact socialist and built upon a revolution which has destroyed the alliance of feudalism and capitalism and has given all power to the working people. It has also radically altered social relationships and has ended all foreign exploitation by nationalization. We were not content simply to drive the British out and "Arabize" our economy; we also obtained complete control of it. For your information, Mr. 'Aflaq, the consensus of opinion among world economists was that such a process of socialist transformation was inconceivable within ten years, especially as we had begun this only in 1956. In 1952, we were simply army officers, who knew nothing more than military strategy. Our meetings then with traditional economists only made things more complicated, since they could not discover a solution. But after that we launched into this process, having honestly and conscientiously attempted to learn. Please don't forget that your present slogan, "No Socialism without Socialists," was the one we launched in 1961, prior to the July, 1961, socialist decrees.

BITAR: Socialism is to be protected by socialists. What we want to arrive at is government by the people.

NASSER: Fine. We are prepared to have immediate elections and let the people govern. But we should like to know what you mean by "the people."

'AFLAQ: The workers, of course.

NASSER: Who else?

'AFLAQ: The working people, i.e., the peasants and workers, who are in the [Ba'th] Party.

NASSER: But do you fancy that government by the people, even though you have elections, is merely a few people sitting in a room and deciding affairs? You are mistaken, for then you would have isolated the whole people and ruled as a tiny minority. . . . Political stability can never come about in Syria unless all banks and insurance companies are nationalized. Otherwise, capitalism will be ruling Syria and your government will be a façade.

'AMIR: We believe that Syria is ruled by big business.

NASSER: If we ask ourselves how we can achieve political stability, we soon realize that this can only be through making the banks run the country, especially in Syria. They can give loans to, say, Khalid al-'Azm and deny them to a small merchant in the market [*suq al-hamidiyya*]. The banks, being the wealth of the country, must not be controlled by Reaction—otherwise your socialism will be meaningless. Banks, and thus the nation's wealth, must pass into the hands of the people.

ATASI: Quite right, Your Excellency. But it seems to me that a hasty measure like the one you are proposing would not be very wise, seeing that we have certain obligations, etc. I think this problem must be carefully studied. . . .

BITAR: I think, Mr. Atasi, that political stability cannot be divorced, as the President maintains, from the power of capitalists. Their power must be very gradually curtailed. As for the banks, I do not think this measure is possible.

ATASI: I meant that Decree No. 117 would be immediately implemented.

'AFLAQ: There is no immediacy about it.

ATASI: True. But how long do you think it will be before Decree No. 117 is implemented?

BITAR: There is first the stage of "Arabization" of banks.

ATASI: You mean nationalization.

BITAR: No, I mean Arabization first.

'AMIR: This stage of Arabization has already been reached.

BITAR: We went back on Arabization. We made progress only in one case, namely, the Syrian Bank, whose head office was in Paris. Only this bank was Arabized or nationalized. As for other banks, such as Intra and the Bank of the Arab Nation, through which Nazim Qudsi and the others made their entry on the scene—all these are Arab in name only. Their head offices are not in Damascus, so we cannot call them Arab.

ATASI: Then how would you Arabize them?

BITAR: There are two stages, first Arabization and then nationalization.

NASSER: This is what we did in Syria during the Union.

BITAR: Yes, indeed. These decrees are well known.

ATASI: We know them, as they all came at a certain period.

NASSER: I do not see the need for two stages.

BITAR: I agree.

NASSER: Arabization inevitably leads to nationalization. . . .

[*The Syrian delegation departed to seek new instructions at home. After March 21, the Syrian newspaper* al-Ba'th *attacked the old union between Egypt and Syria. This was an indirect attack on the Egyptian influence and domination as well as an attempt to undermine Nasser's effort to establish a centralized union in which the Egyptians would have the upper hand. The conflict was voiced in* al-Ba'th *and in the Cairo* al-Ahram. *The following extracts are taken from the minutes of talks held on April 6, 1963. Although they contain little ideological substance, they do illustrate attitudes and tactics as well as the sources of ideological inspiration of some Arab theoreticians.*]

NASSER: I will answer your remarks. You departed on Thursday [March 21]. The principle that we had all agreed upon was to shelve our doubts. But we cannot be naive about this: We must wait and observe.

I read *al-Ba'th* every day, issue after issue—I now have a whole stack of them. However, I never interfere with what Haykal writes in *al-Ahram*.[2] The

2. Muhammad Hasanayn Haykal, the editor of *al-Ahram,* usually expressed the viewpoint of the Egyptian Government.

first time I asked him what he was writing about was when you were here last time and, being a Thursday, you wondered what Haykal was going to write about on Friday. I asked to see him to discover whether he had written anything that might annoy you.

BITAR: Yes, I remember the incident.

NASSER: Well, even after your article "More Royalist than the King," I asked him what he was proposing to write about and he said that he was going to reply to this. I then asked him to wait and be patient. That day, he changed his subject and wrote about his meeting with Maisky, the editor of *Pravda*. On Wednesday, I saw the issue of *al-Ba'th* which claimed that the people in the Union were put in "cold storage" and that our meetings in Egypt consisted of a "hodgepodge" of peasants, etc. All this, added together, made one pause and think. I could neither control my patience nor the patience of others. I saw Haykal's Sunday article entitled "I Protest" but I never imagined that it was either aimed at or could lead to deposing a government. Haykal had written a series of three articles all dealing with these matters raised by *al-Ba'th*. After the first article had had its effect, I asked him, once again, to be patient.

BITAR: His article was broadcast, Your Excellency.

NASSER: So were the articles in *al-Ba'th* on Damascus Radio. You once said that *al-Ba'th*'s articles were not broadcast but, in point of fact, the article "More Royalist than the King" was broadcast by both Damascus and Baghdad Radios.

BITAR: I am talking about Syria, Your Excellency. Was it broadcast on the Syrian Radio?

NASSER: Yes.

BITAR: Was the whole text of it broadcast?

NASSER: I will get you a duplicate of *al-Ba'th*'s articles picked up from Damascus Radio. In any case, it was *al-Ba'th* that attacked the Egyptian regime even after the secession. . . . I never said that the criticism of *al-Ba'th* revealed a methodological difference. My view is that there is no such difference for the very simple reason that I still do not know what Ba'thist ideology is. I have read the constitution of your party plus the two books issued by the party and an anthology of Ba'th articles in *al-Ba'th* (one of which, I think, deals with socialism and is by Mr. Zuhur [Syrian minister of economy]). All these I have read in detail but I have not been able to discover any ideology. Our differences are entirely personal.

BITAR: You are being very unfair to us, Your Excellency.

NASSER: Let me say a few more words on this subject. Let us take *al-Ba'th*. Recently, I sat down to read some of its editorials but, while reading, I remembered having read all this before somewhere. My memory, thank God, is good, and I soon discovered the source of these editorials—Stalin's book *Leninism*. These editorials were copied word for word from that book and I invite you all to compare the two! Lenin maintains that the popular base leads and is the vanguard [of] the thinking enlightened mind. All this is copied verbatim from Stalin's book, with, however, a great deal of confusion and misconstruction. Because Lenin says something, you take from it what you want and add other things to it. You then say that we have no popular organization. . . . The article published in *al Ba'th* on the people and the later article on popular organization are taken practically verbatim. If this is ideology . . . I say this is a matter that demands another type of thinking. This is not ideology, my dear Salah [Bitar], this is plagiarism . . . plagiarism from a specific book with the object of giving the impression that there is no popular organization [in Egypt], that popular organization was in cold storage and the people were in cold storage and that today popular organization is the Ba'th Party itself.

In point of fact, Lenin quite definitely distinguishes between the party and popular organization and says that the party is the leader while the popular organization is the councils of soviets which are the popular councils. You, on the other hand, say that since the party is the popular organization, its disappearance from the scene at the time of the Union led to putting the people in cold storage, and you call this ideology.

What I am trying to say is that there are no ideological or methodological differences between us. I do not remember any such ideological conflict during the Union except that, during the Union, you asked that all newspapers should be suppressed in Syria and I refused. However, our sole conflict arose over one issue, which you then called partnership. You asked that a committee be formed of three Syrians and three Egyptians which would run the Union. These three Syrians were to be Bitar, 'Aflaq, and [Akram] Hawrani. But what about all the other nationalist groups in Syria? This, I maintain, was our main difference by reason of which you all tendered your resignation—a resignation which, I repeat, amounted to not merely a withdrawal from the government but to a conscious blow against the Union. I have already stated that this step helped the cause of secession. No genuine unionist could have tendered a collective resignation and engaged in such party maneuvers. Now, then, on what basis are we going to cooperate in the future? If party tactics are to be the order of the day, then, I regretfully decline!

BITAR: But I have told Your Excellency that we only resigned a year after you yourself had, to all intents and purposes, dismissed us.

NASSER: That is a matter of opinion. . . .

[*The following excerpt from the meeting that took place on the afternoon of April 7, 1963—a meeting at which only the Egyptian and Syrian delegations were present—relates to the basic point of disagreement between Nasser and the Ba'thists—a disagreement about the structure of the proposed union and the role of political organizations—and to Nasser's criticism of Ba'thist philosophy, expressed in the slogan Unity, Freedom, and Socialism.*]

NASSER: . . . I fully agree with Mr. Atasi that genuine national unity in each country must precede the creation of a federal union. Otherwise, we should be leaving ourselves to deal with endless problems and headaches within a union. Furthermore, I believe that political unity must subsist concurrently with or precede a constitutional union. Otherwise, we should have, in each country, various antagonistic political groups. These groups would not be able to meet together without such a political unity. The business of government would then become one of coalition. In such circumstances, it would be better to have contractual government or confederation. Such a contractual government is of course a simple and clear state of affairs. But if we create a federation, with one organization here, two or more in Syria, two or more in Iraq, we should all add up to a collection of six or seven diametrically opposed groups. Each one would then plan its own programs and we should therefore meet with two obstacles: The first would be regionalism. We simply must take this into account in our union, for one of our mistakes in 1958 was our attempt to do away with regionalism. We repeated the slogan of "No Regionalism" which we had, in fact, taken over from you without pondering it too long. In point of fact, this regionalism exists and will make itself felt when we come to create the union. If we take it into account, we can then proceed to solve the problems it creates, but this takes some degree of patient work.

The second obstacle or danger in the union would be the conflict or the clash and competition between parties or groups. Each would attempt to win over the maximum numbers of people to its side and this might make party officials oblivious of the interests of the union as a whole. They might consider that their aim would be to win support for their party to assume office. The solution of this problem lies, to my mind, in the national unity of the regions and then in the union itself. This implies the unity of political action on two levels. How, then, are we to achieve this national unity? For this to come about, there must be a unity of aims, and this, I think, generally speaking, exists. On broad matters of principle I see no differences but there will be in matters of implementation. It follows that there must be something, call it a charter or program, that will embody our common notions concerning the principles upon which we are agreed. For instance, what do we mean by freedom? Or socialism? If these are empty slogans, they will lead to opportunism. The worst fault of political parties is slogans. Their implementation is often left vague. This *laisser-faire* attitude could lead to the assumption of power by a small minority, usually those with financial interests. Thus, before we sign the constitution of the union, we must draft a charter in which we lay down the broad outlines of our joint political endeavor. This is a safeguard to the union. . . . What do we mean when we say "Unity, Freedom, and Socialism"? How does unity relate to the Arab world, for instance? President al-Sallal [of the Yemen] sent me a telegram proposing to come last Friday and I replied by saying that his arrival would embarrass me a great deal since we still had problems to solve and his arrival might therefore be interpreted as an attempt to create a sort of Cairo-San'a' axis within the union to face a Baghdad-Damascus axis. Had he come last Friday, this possibility would obviously have occurred to some of you. Thus, I asked him to delay his arrival until after an agreement on union had been reached. He could then act freely in any manner he pleased. What, then, do we mean by unity? Perhaps our answer to this question will be the simplest of all. What do we mean by socialism and freedom? In a future union, I could not possibly claim that our own eleven-year-old socialism should be put into effect in Syria in so many hours. However, it is well known that socialism aims to do such and such and must therefore progress along certain lines.

Then again, what do we mean by freedom? Are we simply to be satisfied with current definitions throughout the world or should we not rather specify in a written charter what this implies, how it is to be practiced, and who is entitled to it?

Having done this, the rest—and I mean here the constitution—will be easy. This latter we can then agree upon, provided, of course, that mutual trust exists. Do you agree to all this? . . .

ZUHUR: There are, in fact, two stages. The first will be to create a Unionist Front in Syria and the second the merger of popular organizations within one charter and one internal organization. But, meanwhile, where do we stand? In other words, how are we, as separate states, to coordinate our efforts?

NASSER: I believe that, as states, we must also begin to create a front. In other words, one common front will then link our front here, yours in Syria, and also the one in Iraq.

ZUHUR: Fine. This will be at the level of popular organizations. But as governments or states, how shall we proceed?

NASSER: I think that such popular organizations are what affect states. Have I understood your question properly?

ZUHUR: But during this transitional stage, there must be some kind of union between the various states, as states.

ATASI: This would be laid down in the charter.

'AMIR: Popular organization determines the bases of the union. . . .

BITAR: Your Excellency, we seem to agree that drafting the political framework of the union is our simplest task, seeing that we have interpreted the unity of these three states to mean a federal union. Your Excellency's recognition of regionalism, not necessarily as an anti-Arab sentiment, but as the legacy of long historical separation, is a valid one. Federal union, in my opinion, is to be based on the fact that we are one nation and that one day we shall all constitute one state. But within this single state, we must not refuse to recognize the existence of various regions, a situation which, I repeat, is not antithetical to Arab nationalism. Other federal unions throughout the world have clearly shown that such a setup is both constructive and useful. The most important difference between our union and others, such as the Indian or West German or Italian, is that ours is revolutionary, not evolutionary. If left to themselves, Egypt and Syria would remain separate. But circumstances have bred national revolutions which seem to render their merger inevitable. The proof of the revolutionary spirit of any Arab revolution lies in its unfolding, day by day, the genuine Arab character of each country. . . . Constructive criticism cannot destroy unionist forces within each of the three countries; any political union between them would be a mere formality. I can therefore say that when we departed, on March 21, our intentions were of the best. The article "More Royalist than the King" in no way justifies such a campaign against our party. *Al-Ahram* claims that our intent was malicious. Very well, then, let us talk about this. Good and bad intentions are very personal and psychological concerns. How, then, can we objectively plan away such subjective legacies of the past? Our newspaper may perhaps tomorrow publish an article which we may or may not have scanned beforehand and which produces an adverse reaction here. Let us also suppose that this article is erroneous. The reaction to it should be in the form of constructive criticism. In any case, such errors can never be said to be the result of malice or of good intentions unless we constantly meet together and form some kind of body to deal with such problems. As far as the [Ba'th] Party is concerned, *al-Ahram*'s interpretation of the incident has been false and illusory. The fact that *Le Figaro,* for example, prints someone's statement does not make that statement true. We all know what journalists are like. It is said that our article was never disaffirmed, but I say that we have never seen it in the first place.

NASSER: Don't you read the Lebanese press? It was also published in Lebanon.

BITAR: We have not seen it so as to refute it.

NASSER: Don't you read the Lebanese press?

BITAR: No, we don't.

NASSER: Neither the French nor the Lebanese press?

BITAR: No, we don't. They do not enter Syria, so . . .

NASSER: But this is incredible! What kind of talk is that?

BITAR: Your Excellency, when you read them, please contact us.

NASSER: You don't read the Syrian, Lebanese, or French press! How on earth do you govern your country?

BITAR: Well, then, let someone get in touch with us and inform us. We don't have the time to read.

NASSER: Before I go to sleep, for example, I read all the Lebanese, French, British, and Syrian press. Yesterday, I asked for the monitoring reports of Syria and discovered that *al-Ba'th*'s articles, which Mr. Bitar had said were not broadcast in Syria, were in fact broadcast every day at 10:30. One must constantly be in touch with current events for his work to be of any value. . . .

[*The following lengthy extract deals almost exclusively with ideological questions as related to practical politics.*]

ATASI: Your Excellency was talking about a merger of political leaderships which is also what Mr. Bitar was referring to, irrespective of what we have already discussed. Now, we seem to agree that political leadership must be unified, whether on the regional or the federal level. It is from this point that we ought to continue our discussion.

NASSER: Before uniting the political leadership, the question of unity of aims is vital. How can we discuss a political framework without first agreeing on common aims and without solving this ideological conflict? The problem is, does this unity of aims exist or does it not? Hence, I believe that this question of ideological differences, which was raised both yesterday and today, is of paramount importance. . . .

ZUHUR: . . . If these differences in ideology exist, then they must be thrashed out, for they can occasion violent clashes. It would be tantamount to a clash between faith and heresy, for, if I have my own way of thinking, another man's views may be heretical as far as I am concerned. I think it would be practical to have our Iraqi colleagues here with us the day after tomorrow when such differences could be discussed. If we finally come to an agreement, then we can proceed accordingly and, if not, then no meeting is possible. This is the only practical way in which to organize our coming together, for it seems that our present discussions will not prove to be enough.

NASSER: Could you please tell us what these ideological differences are, for we maintain that our differences are personal in character.

ZUHUR: We can discuss them later, when the Iraqis are present.

ATASI: Excuse me. I suggest that we form a tripartite committee, representing the three countries, for this purpose. If we leave this discussion general, it will not be ensured.

NASSER: How many of us are there? . . . this is a subject which interests everybody, not merely the Ba'th.

SUWAYDAN [Syrian Minister of Agriculture]: Yes, it is of interest to the Arab Nationalists and to other groups as well.

ATASI: In order for this to occur, may I suggest that, as far as the past is concerned . . .

ZUHUR: We close this chapter.

'AYSAMI [Syrian Minister of Agricultural Reform]: I agree.

SHA'IR [a member of the Syrian Revolutionary Council]: Me, too.

ZUHUR: I also agree. In fact . . .

'AYSAMI: We have agreed to this and it must be so.

ATASI: Correct.

SHA'IR: And if Haykal says something in *al-Ahram,* we will close down his newspaper. [Laughter.]

NASSER: These are ideological differences, dear Mr. Sha'ir. [Laughter.]

[*During the meeting that took place on the evening of April 7, 1963, Egyptian, Syrian, and Iraqi delegations were present.*]

SHABIB [Foreign Minister of Iraq]: . . . What I want to emphasize is that differences of interpretation regarding these slogans are possible, not solely as between one revolution and another, but also within the same revolution. Within the same party or movement or federation, several points of view are possible. Final agreement is achieved through a text which ensures that such differences do not lead to conflict. Within the same movement, for instance, a majority opinion is binding, and similarly within a front.

Thus, it would be very difficult to say that there are ideological differences. There may perhaps be differences in method or in interpreting the content of these slogans, but such differences are in fact signs of vitality and are necessary both now and in the future. Any movement that does not allow for free discussion and conflicting viewpoints is indeed stagnant. But there must be a bond that can tie up such differences and ensure that the movement reaches in its totality the same conclusion. I speak for the Iraqi delegation when I say that the three revolutions in the U.A.R., Syria, and Iraq meet in the same common aim and the same basic policies and that this meeting of the mind past and present, and this determination to establish a union between the three revolutions and the three regions, conclusively proves that ideological differences are absolutely nonexistent. As a member of the Iraqi delegation and as a Ba'thist, I affirm that there are no differences in ideology. Hence, I think our discussion ought now to proceed to essentials.

NASSER: In yesterday's and today's session, I took the view that there were no ideological differences between us, but Mr. Bitar and Mr. Zuhur said that ideological differences do in fact exist. This was the point we reached yesterday.

SHABIB: This is correct, Your Excellency, there may perhaps be differences in method . . .

NASSER: We must be perfectly clear on this point. Between us and the Syrian Ba'th there have been dealings in the past, and thus we must thoroughly examine such statements, on the assumption that people might misunderstand if words or slogans are thrown at them indiscriminately. There is a difference between our saying that there are ideological differences and that there are differences in method. Yesterday's and today's discussion mentioned ideological differences—we were all present—and it was for this reason that we decided to devote this session to such differences. Hence, we felt that Iraq should participate in this discussion because this subject is important to us all since it relates to the future of our federal state.

ZUHUR: The question has to do with defining the scope of theory. Hence, if we include the method of implementation in the meaning of "theory," we can say that there are ideological differences. Otherwise, if we do not include the method in defining any theory, then we cannot say that ideological differences exist between us. Thus, a misunderstanding has arisen over the definition of the word itself. We have agreed that our aims are common but that there are differences over the way in which these aims are to be implemented. In point of fact, and taking what Mr. Shabib has said into consideration, we seem to be agreed that there are no basic differences and, by implication, no ideological differences.

BITAR: As others have pointed out, I do not believe that there are ideological differences. Indeed, the three revolutions have common aims: We are agreed about socialism and capitalism and about the nature of our future regime. Again, we are agreed about forming a union and about freedom and the people's participation in its country's affairs and its liberation from feudalism and capitalism. All this we seem to agree upon. But how to implement all this?

Have these revolutions sprung from different sources? Our very regional separation from one another has rendered your revolution Egyptian, ours Syrian, etc., but we all have the same aims. All these revolutions are proceeding toward unity, and the road to this lies in the coming together of these revolutions. It is therefore our task to ensure their mutual interaction so as to produce homogeneity. The varying backgrounds of these revolutions may have produced a variety of interpretations, and thus their meeting together is vital so that such interpretations can be clarified and synthesized. We must know, for instance, what we mean by "the people," or by "unity."

Another important point is that the various methods must be unified. You have here both theory and practice, and the practices themselves can be modified only in the process of implementation. . . .

SHABIB: We cannot in this discussion go into the various socialist steps that we might adopt in Iraq, Syria, or Egypt because these can only be determined in practice. However, agreement over the content of theory seems assured. Freedom, in general, seems to imply that such movements as have led these revolutions, have contributed to them, and can enrich the new Arab experiment and belief in unity and freedom—such movements deserve to be associated and be allowed freely to associate in building the new Arab federal state. Other movements must be denied this freedom but such denial and the method of political exclusion may indeed be done differently in the different regions. The clarification of the content of theory has in fact been accomplished during our past sessions. We have discussed the question of parties and fronts and the problem of freedom. Moreover, the opinion of the U.A.R. on such matters is clear in the charter, which preceded the revolutions of Iraq and Syria. . . .

NASSER: . . . We ask, will new parties be allowed to function? If you ask me this question, my answer is "No," because the charter has delineated the nature of our regime and how its base is a coalition of the popular working forces of workers, peasants, soldiers, intellectuals, and national capitalism. What is democracy? We answer that the charter says such and such. What is freedom? It is the freedom of country and individual. All these are very clearly defined and such definitions are vital for us if we are not to contradict ourselves in the future.

We are to form a federal state and, indeed, a single one, but we must be perfectly clear about the varying interpretations of each of these slogans. There must be a thorough synthesis of all such interpretations.

When we come to draft a constitution, we must be perfectly clear in our minds about the basic foundations of our society and its liberties, which we should, in turn, define lucidly and be agreed upon. Agreement about basic social principles does not imply immediate implementation. We should not, for instance, insist that your socialist implementation must tally at every point with ours. If 80 per cent or 90 per cent of your economy is in the public sector, then your socialism will be a very advanced one. Socialism does not at all mean 100 per cent nationalization. We, for example, take it to mean the people's control over the means of production and we say this may be anything from 40 to 80 per cent. We do not maintain that socialism implies immediate nationalization. I believe that this discussion is useful and facilitates our agreement concerning a constitution.

ATASI: In order to understand this discussion, we ought, I believe, to hear what the Socialist Union [the political organization of Egypt] has to say and discuss matters accordingly. Such conceptual discussions need some preparation.

SA'DI [Vice Premier of Iraq]: We cannot today begin to discuss what we understand by freedom or parties or the various stages required, for the simplest of such topics would need weeks of debate. In a session such as this, we cannot define what we mean by freedom. We can only hope to agree about the general connotation of such words as socialism, freedom, and unity. To discuss the freedom of the individual, of society, of their mutual cooperation, of parties, and of one-party systems would be to involve ourselves in subjects that are still debated all over the world. As a party, we may perhaps not be in a position to answer such questions. I cannot say whether we, as the government, shall proceed in a one- or multi-party system. If there are several parties, what principle are we to adopt in allowing them to function? These are all matters that cannot be answered at present. . . .

ZUHUR: . . . The problem is basically one of experience, Your Excellency. In Egypt, you have now an experiment which is eleven years old and has passed through many stages. At the beginning, the Army's revolutionary vanguard felt the need for popular organization to stop the gap between the governing and the governed. Various attempts were made, beginning with the Liberation Committee, then the National Union, and now a third attempt is in progress, based on the charter and following most important developments: in agrarian reform, in nationalization, and, specially, in postsecession experiences. This third attempt, the Socialist Union, rose out of two previous ones which were unsuccessful or not successful enough. They were therefore replaced. Thus did the revolution proceed in Egypt. All the while, the revolutionaries had taken it upon themselves to carry through certain measures so as not to lose touch with the purport of the revolution.

What about the experience of other countries? In Iraq, there were popular revolutionary movements which passed through exceedingly difficult periods. In Syria, too, such movements existed, although the circumstances were not so excessively difficult as in Iraq. These movements, then, were in existence prior to the assumption of government by the revolutionaries and before they had themselves been able to benefit the people. When one is not in government but belongs to a popular organization, he carries no responsibility. He can bandy slogans about and is not responsible for their implementation or for their consequences. Hence, the revolutionary movements of Syria and Iraq have not been through the very difficult times that the Egyptian revolutionary experiment has had to undergo.

It is only their two ways that diverged but it seems that they have now met. In my opinion, their aims are identical, and in most policies of implementation I think they will also meet. There was nothing at all wrong with nationalization in Syria. The only error was that it should have been more firmly proposed. In other words, reactionary elements should have been isolated and prevented from exploiting the spirit of regionalism, for their class interest propels them to strike against nationalization. I mean to say that nationalization should have been followed by a final process of isolation of the forces of reaction. But the measures adopted in Syria were, I think, extemporaneous.

The basic question is that these revolutionary movements must afford each other a total recognition of status and must know also how to interact properly so as to march in step. One might, for instance, wonder about the question of democracy and might ask, when he witnesses such gigantic strides being accomplished by the men of the Egyptian Revolution, where are the popular organizations that must implement such measures? In fact, such vast progress is carried through by the state and any other Arab revolutionary movement might, in their place, be forced to follow the same path. For a popular organization is not the creature of a day and the revolutionary cannot afford to wait until a proper popular organization takes charge of these measures.

Indeed, when revolutionary movements find themselves in power, they discover that many of their previous views must be discarded or reappraised. For, while such movements are operating on the level of national struggle, they ask for a bourgeois type of democracy so as to obtain for themselves the best possible conditions, but, when in government, such movements maintain that such a bourgeois democracy is a great danger to the revolution for, in elections, these revolutions would be swept away. . . .

HINDI: Mr. Zuhur has dealt comprehensively with popular movements and, in doing so, has almost destroyed the value of theory as a working program with specific ends. Thus, he has assumed that when popular movements are not in power they advocate a bourgeois democracy but when in power they discover that parliamentary democracy is unsuitable and therefore undesirable.

I feel, on the other hand, that such an ideological volte-face is very grave indeed. One gets the feeling that we are discussing a topic which, in Syria at least, plays a very important ideological role. We must create a studied, not an improvised, union and, thus, many of these points that were raised need to be clarified. . . .

I agree with Mr. Sa'di that we cannot settle all the details. However, underlying each of these slogans, it is imperative that we frame certain basic principles which would then form the basis for discussion.

In deciding upon a federal union as the form of our state, this implies that we spring from various regions with varying social and economic backgrounds. But in insisting upon unity within this federal regime, we implicitly recognize our regional status with a view to developing and merging it into one Arab society. Accordingly, we must define our slogans, since we cannot build this union nor can the citizen of this new state live his daily life under the aegis of wide generalities like unity, freedom, and socialism [the slogans of Ba'th socialism]. . . .

SA'DI: I would like Mr. Hindi to tell us exactly what he means.

HINDI: You may remember that there are three basic slogans about which there seems to be general agreement, whether in the Maghrib, the Yemen, Iraq, or anywhere in the Arab world. The battle is raging around these slogans. This is all from the theoretical point of view.

Now in practice and in government, we find that these slogans need an almost daily interpretation, from the political, economic, social, and even military points of view. If one asks about the role of the military in this conflict, our Algerian brethren would supply the answer. If we talk of freedom, we find that there are two basic schools of thought; the one is Western, democratic, and bourgeois and the other subordinates the individual's freedom to that of the group, as in Communism or Nazism. When we come to discuss this question in the context of our own tripartite union, we must underline the word freedom with certain points. For instance, we must agree about the form of government, the duties of citizens and their rights, and the role of trade unions and political movements. Again, in socialism, the process must be repeated. Mr. Shabib says that the Iraqi public sector owns 9 per cent, which is excellent. But what about the agricultural and other sectors? We cannot build a state in which the Syrian economy is almost capitalist while the Iraqi and Egyptian economies move firmly toward socialism.

SHABIB: I think that we acknowledge the fact that differences do indeed exist and that regionalism is present at all levels. That is why we say that there are both regional and federal problems. I do not suppose that we have decided that the role of trade unions is to be the same in all the regions, for their nature varies from one region to another. In Iraq prior to the revolution, trade union leaders were pressed into the service of the regime. The peasant movements, for example, were set up to serve the needs either of 'Abd al-Karim Qasim or the Communist Party. The circumstances of each region must determine the reorganization of trade unions. We accept the principle that the people are the source of authority, since popular association is basic and necessary for true popular government. But the role of each class of people—of intellectuals or of the military, for example—varies in degree and in kind from one country to another. The starting point is to associate all popular forces in rule, but the degree and the timing differ from one region to another.

NASSER: . . . When a revolution assumes power, it must know how to keep it and has therefore to deprive its social enemies of their essential weapons. The enemy, it must be assumed, would be fighting a battle to the death and Reaction is, to begin with, stronger than the revolution, especially if this latter's aims are vague. We discovered this fact in Egypt, for in 1952 Reaction lay low and we said then that coexistence was possible. But even from their point of view, this was out of the question. In 1954, we found out that Reaction exploited the crisis and was almost successful in assuming power. Again, in 1956, Reaction closed its ranks against us. The people for whose sake you carry through your socialist measures are very difficult to assemble, but reactionaries can be collected together at a minute's notice at al-Sharq Club in Damascus. In any crisis, they rapidly gather themselves together and form a cabinet. Therefore, Reaction is stronger than you are and will continue to be so.

On September 28, 1961, Reaction engineered the secession. We had thought that its power was broken by the nationalization decrees where we nationalized to the value of £600 million, but it was then that Reaction entered the battle for power.

Hence, the primary factor that ensures the continuation of revolution is to make clear the aims of the revolution and to deprive its enemies of all their weapons. The second factor is to organize the popular working forces. A single-party dictatorship can never take the place of popular organization. If the working people are not brought together and made to feel that the Revolution exists in fact to serve their aims and aspirations, then Reaction and capitalism would be able to draw to themselves and to deceive a large segment of the working people, and especially of the bourgeoisie, by making them understand that their interests are in jeopardy. . . .

'AYSAMI: I think it has now become perfectly obvious that a merger of the popular forces is necessary for insuring the continuation of political union and for its development. But how are we to accomplish such a merger? Should we discuss this now? Or should we plan to create interaction in the future or to form committees representing unionist forces that will debate the points at issue which, in turn, seem to be methodological rather than basic? No doubt, the experiences of the Arab world have forced the nationalist groups and organizations to develop as, for example, in the field of political organization, where we started with the Liberation Rally, then the National Union, and finally the Socialist Union. This last experiment has undoubtedly benefited from past experience by discarding, for instance, any notion of *rapprochement* between classes and by relying in the first place on the popular classes, since the bourgeoisie cannot be relied upon to take their interests to heart.

Similarly, we find that the Ba'th has been forced to develop its initial ideology. It seems to me that the conception of democracy was initially affected by the mood of the times and hence was perhaps Western in color. The nature of this early struggle may have dictated the conception of a democracy for all classes. But now, with a legacy of bitter experience and of conflicts with Reaction, capitalism, and imperialism, the Ba'th is tending to view freedom as properly belonging to the working classes and to other socialist-minded bodies. It may, therefore, be finally forced to adopt a single-party system as its policy.

What I mean to say is that it would be a mistake to lay down a general and comprehensive theory of society that would attempt to explain all the problems of life—similar, for example, to the Marxist—for such a closed system is unsuitable for our developing age. . . .

NASSER: . . . Have you publicized the fact that your conception of democracy has changed? No, and hence ambiguity exists. We must be completely aboveboard with each other so as to avoid any misunderstanding. You mention something today that is news to me. I have here the constitution of the Ba'th Party and my impression is that its democracy is bourgeois. This also accords with your own slogans and writings. Now you tell me that this has changed. Have the people or your popular base been acquainted with this change? I do not suppose so, for I know all your party circulars. It would be very easy, then, for us to frame these definitions, for the constitution must include such definitions—and I believe we could easily agree. But we cannot leave every region full freedom to organize its political activity, for we should then begin to feel a widening chasm inside the republic which would ultimately destroy it. Thus, we must agree that political activity must be organized on the federal level.

SA'DI: Different viewpoints certainly exist, Your Excellency. But at the same time, such differences cannot be completely obliterated. Our path, then, lies through constructive interaction which alone can do away with such differences. There must be some sort of framework within which such differences can be brought together and finally synthesized. This synthesis may be complete within a short or a long period but progress and synthesis are inevitable.

The scope of freedom and of socialism will become apparent in the nature of things. . . .

NASSER: . . . I hear Mr. 'Aysami saying that their point of view has changed. Well, what is your new point of view?

'AYSAMI: I say there has evolved . . .

NASSER: There is an evolution. What is this new evolution?

'AYSAMI: Change is one thing and evolution is another. I meant that the [Ba'th] Party's conception has evolved, not changed, since 1943. In other words, the nature of the struggle at that time may have necessitated that freedom should be enjoyed by all forces of opposition to a regime which collaborated with imperialism. This was a conception dictated by the nature of that struggle. But now, when revolutionary movements have proved themselves capable of assuming power, we can proceed to discuss whether freedom is to be granted to all groups. Can Reaction, capitalism, and racialism be allowed to enjoy their freedom? That is the question.

The tendency now is to deny freedom to the enemies of revolutionary socialist organizations. This is what I meant by development. The nature of present struggles and the progress attained by Arab revolutionary movements are all leading toward a *rapprochement,* which may not at present be total, but which we hope will be attained by interaction, constructive discussion, and the will to realize our major aims. It is then that differences even in method will vanish.

ATASI: I conclude, Your Excellency, that a detailed or specific definition of freedom is now difficult to arrive at.

NASSER: Well, then, what about democracy?

ATASI: Or a definition of democracy, for that matter. If you ask me personally, I will say that this is not quite clear to me, either. I think that the same applies to my colleagues. We have not yet arrived at a specific or exhaustive definition.

'AMIR: Clarity is very necessary in this regard. We need not specify an absolute mode of socialist implementation for each region. But certain standards must exist. I might perhaps maintain that socialist implementation implies total nationalization of the means of production. Indeed, we may differ over this point and socialism may mean other than what I have said.

NASSER: But the charter does not call for total nationalization of the means of production but only that the people must control the means of production.

'AMIR: I was only stating my personal views, not quoting the charter.

NASSER: There is a difference between control and nationalization.

'AMIR: I was only making assumptions and instead of saying one party I said I might say so and so. There are several viewpoints concerning socialist implementation, but a basic pattern should here be evolved.

ATASI: If you, Marshal 'Amir, were to ask how we define socialism in Syria, I believe that none of my colleagues would be in a position to answer this question. Before March 8, the conception of freedom was different from what it is now. In order to crystallize in our minds, such a conception must be thrashed out within the group.

'AMIR: Mr. Atasi, a new state is about to arise and every citizen of this state has the right to know what his role is to be in this society. As a future ordinary citizen of this state, and irrespective of my being at present in power, I have the right to know how I am to be treated, and whether my freedom will be restricted, and, if so, to what extent? In other words, the individual's role in society must be made clear. When I say his role, I do not mean that all the details of this should be clarified, but I mean that the essential principles of society must be clear to all. . . .

SHA'IR: The three revolutions are essentially similar. It follows that the specification and implementation of the basic constituents of the state need not be at all foreign to us. There was once a union between Syria and Egypt and together we began to implement nationalization. If we now attempt to define socialism, there will be nothing new in it as far as Syria is concerned. This also would apply to Iraq. Thus, I believe that we must specify this from the very beginning, because if we leave such conceptions vague, generalized, and admitting of various interpretations, the future before us will be dark, indeed, as our discussions may then be fruitless and inimical to the interests of a strong and healthy union. . . .

'UMRAN [member of the Syrian Revolutionary Council]: I believe, Your Excellency, that an almost unanimous agreement can be perceived concerning general principles, but differences may arise about the various stages or about implementation in the various regions. I believe the content of freedom and democracy is clear—namely, that the people must effectively exercise full authority. But at what point can they in fact do so? Here is a point at issue. But in reality, the conception of freedom and democracy is clear: a people exercising its authority. When, however, is another question. Some maintain that this comes about through party organization so that the whole people would constitute the base. Here, one might maintain that we ought to begin from the foundations. As long as our aims are identical, we may agree to form a federal union and then coordinate efforts in the various regions so as to attain specific ends within a specific time. . . .

NASSER: We must view the party as the revolutionary vanguard or leadership. But popular organizations are something else. I have noticed that some of you have affirmed that the two are identical. Indeed, Ba'th has done that already. [Laughter.] But this is a false notion, because if we maintain that the two are identical, we shall soon find that the party will be isolated from the people. How are popular organizations to be formed? They must consist of trade unions and cooperative societies. Such organizations need not be party members. It is the responsibility of the Front to lead and guide and at the same time organize the people in popular assemblies. Such assemblies are the only way by which popular organizations can be consolidated and by which a conflict can be avoided with bureaucracy. This is the proper path before us. . . .

PART TWO

Political and Social Thought in Turkey

I. *Introduction to Political and Social Thought in Turkey*

The first two and one-half decades after the establishment of the republic in Turkey (1923) were chiefly a period of political and cultural consolidation. The Turkish national state had been established in opposition to the universalist doctrines of Islam and of Ottoman tradition, both of which had rejected the idea of a national state. In an effort to instill in the Turkish people a sense of national identity, the ruling elite—that is, the modernist, secularist group—adopted radical nationalist views. It relied heavily on Turkey's past, and at times it even created theories to bolster the Turkish national ego—as, for example, the sun-language theory, according to which all languages were said to have originated in Turkish and that Turks were among the original creators of world civilization.

Two social forces—the ruling elite and the rural elite—combined to create the unity and stability that were essential to root the idea of belonging to a nation and to a national state. The former—intellectuals, military and civilian bureaucracy, and segments of the urban population—controlled the main urban centers and enjoyed relatively free access to political power if it conformed to the nationalist, secularist principles of the republic. The latter—notables, landowners, and the newly rising commercial class—dominated mainly the rural areas. The first group was oriented toward cultural and political modernism; the second was motivated chiefly by economic and social considerations. Both groups enjoyed relatively high social status. The urban intelligentsia controlled the government but had limited economic means at its disposal. The rural elite had limited political power but owned land, shops, and other forms of wealth. This sharing of power by two sections of public life had profound social and economic drawbacks, but it also created an atmosphere of political quiet, in which the Turkish national state could be firmly established and a sense of national unity could be fostered.[1]

A Turkish national identity came into being after 1920. The new nation's internal cohesion was built around the idea of the territorial integrity of a modern state that rose above religious differences and a vague promise of future welfare and prosperity. Traditional influences certainly went into the new concept of nation and nationhood, but they seemed to be, in the main, the cement rather than the foundation blocks of the new nation. Minority nationalism and regional allegiances gradually lost their dynamic appeal. The Kurdish elites and the elites of other Muslim groups were accepted by the ruling Turkish political and social circles and, in fact, were assimilated into the Turkish nation. Islam was removed from politics and the importance of

1. See Kemal H. Karpat, "Society, Economics, and Politics in Contemporary Turkey," *World Politics,* XVII (October, 1964), 50–74.

religious differences was minimized. The modern concept of nation was in fact superimposed on religious allegiances and created new loyalties to the national state.

Nationalism became the ideology of the new Turkish Republic. Republicanism, populism, secularism, statism, and reformism—officially proclaimed as additional principles in 1931 and incorporated in the constitution of 1937—were merely corollaries of nationalism.[2] Nationalism aimed at creating an integrated Turkish national state or a modern political system that superseded all religious, regional, and group identities and loyalties. In fact, the reforms undertaken in 1923–35 were practical measures designed to consolidate the modern national state and to create a political community sharing its ideals, a feeling of identity that was purely Turkish. In other words, the republican state tried to assure its own survival by creating a self-confident Turkish nation proud of its past and its achievements. In the latter context, history was reinterpreted and rewritten, often arbitrarily.[3] The Ottoman failures were attributed to men who were alien to the national spirit, while its achievements were hailed as the result of Turkish genius. The lack of clearly defined concepts of modern statehood and nationhood, and especially the tendency to regard the latter in the light of communal feelings inherited from the *umma* (the Muslim community), led to contradictions. These were solved, however, by political decisions that asserted the supremacy of the state and its sustaining social order, the ruling bureaucracy-intelligentsia.[4]

Atatürk, although less of a believer in the absolute power of ideology, did not hesitate to use ideological appeals in order to enhance the feeling of Turkish national identity and solidarity. Atatürkism[5]—that is to say, the six principles of the Turkish Republic—became in fact an ideology attributed to Atatürk. Much of this ideology, born from the demands of a rising national state, has become outdated by economic and social pressures that I shall discuss later. Yet Atatürkism still survives as the chief foundation of Turkish national statehood and appears as a predominantly political ideology.

Economic development, a preoccupation of the contemporary emerging states, did not become a major issue in Turkey until the late 1920's. The civil code of 1926, adopted almost intact from Switzerland, regulated in detail the acquisition, transfer, and inheritance of every kind of property, including land;

2. Note the fact that Egypt also had six principles but of a different kind. See pp. 202–4.

3. Bernard Lewis, "History-writing and National Revival in Turkey," *Middle Eastern Affairs,* IV (June–July, 1953), 218-27.

4. These issues have been treated at great length in Kemal H. Karpat, *Turkey's Politics* (Princeton, N.J.: Princeton University Press, 1959), and in various articles in which I have tried to point out that nationalism, although serving initially the integrative purposes of the national state, expressed also a variety of thoughts and values inherited from the past and was also a means of easing the effects of rapid social change. See, for example, "Recent Political Developments in Turkey and Their Social Background," *International Affairs,* XXXVIII (July, 1962), 304–23, and "Society, Economics, and Politics in Contemporary Turkey," *World Politics,* XVII (October, 1964), 50–74.

5. Also referred to as Kemalism.

the Obligations Code regulated all forms of transactions. The enforcement of these codes depended on sound, modern administrative and judicial systems, which, in turn, more than ever needed a rational economic basis.

As in the past, the economy had a capitalist orientation in the sense that it permitted a degree of freedom of enterprise and accumulation of private capital, diversification of occupations, and social stratification. The integrated political system and the relatively rational, uniform economic relations had a generalizing impact on the social structure, unifying various social groups with similar interests into larger classes that gradually acquired, under the impact of expanding education and political liberalization, a rational understanding of their respective group positions and interests.

In the context of economic development and the reconciliation of social conflicts, the government backed *Kadro* (1932–34), a review that attempted to formulate an ideology of economic development by borrowing ideas from Marxism, Italian corporatism, and socialism, but without accepting any one as its main source. *Kadro* claimed that Turkey's problem was not class conflict but the need for capital, increased production, and economic self-sufficiency.[6] It was shut down in 1934 primarily because of its increasing reference to social classes and their conflicts and its efforts to give a new economic orientation to the program of the ruling Republican Party. These attitudes threatened a small group in that party, which claimed to represent the ideas of an integrated modern state, but which had become, in fact, the spokesman for the new ruling elite.

The social balance in Turkey was upset by the introduction of a multi-party system in 1945. This political experiment offered the rural groups an opportunity to acquire political initiative and to gain office influence in government and it enabled the masses, hitherto deprived of a political role, to participate in public life through direct vote.

The main concern of Turkish leaders at the beginning of the experiment (see Inönü's speech, pp. 314–17, below) was that the reforms were not sufficiently rooted to permit the evolution of politics within the generally accepted principles of a modern republic. The question defined in general as "acceptance of Atatürk's reforms" referred actually to a more basic question—whether or not the republican regime and the national state, together with all the loyalties they entailed, were firmly rooted. The first year of the multi-party system proved that the modern national state and the republican regime were generally accepted and could provide the basic framework in which politics could follow their natural course.

The ideologies that emerged in the 1940's reflected to a large extent the conflicts created by social restratification. Liberalism was the first major ideology to emerge after the political liberalization and the replacement of one-party rule with a multi-party system in 1945–46. Though disjointedly formulated, the liberal ideology represented the grievances of the agrarian, commercial, and working classes against the ruling bureaucracy and its statist

6. See Karpat, *Turkey's Politics*, pp. 70–73.

philosophy. The bureaucracy was supported and relied upon by the Republican Party, which had incorporated in its organization most of the upper intellectual groups. It was obvious that the elites, after achieving their main purpose—the establishment of a national state—had little justification for their political supremacy, especially since the republican regime was hardly challenged by any group, however conservative.

The drive against the ruling order was eventually organized and led by the Democratic Party with the support of many intellectuals, including military men from the lower urban classes. This broad base of support brought the Democratic Party to power through elections in 1950.

During the multi-party period, and especially after 1950, the approach to economic development followed a rather different course. The state continued to play a major part in establishing cement and sugar factories and other major industries, but it also provided extensive credits to agriculture, which was almost entirely privately owned, and to private industry. Moreover, departing from past practices, the government refrained from entering into direct competition with private enterprises, at least in some fields. In other cases, often guided by political motives, it provided tax exemptions, crop subsidies, and other economic inducements and opportunities to landowners, contractors, and commercial groups, to enable them to accumulate capital and participate in economic development on their own initiative. As a consequence of the additional activity in the private sector, a new entrepreneurial and managerial group developed rapidly in a relatively competitive atmosphere. This group also acquired political power in the ruling Democratic Party. Members of this group, using government power for their own advantage, made up much of the membership of the Vatan Cephesi (Fatherland Front), which was created by the Democrats in 1958 to crush the opposition.

Under the guise of economic liberalism, however, the Democrats soon espoused the demands of the major agrarian and commercial groups and threatened to convert their rule into an oligarchy of wealth and power, without the participation of the old intellectual bureaucratic elites. Nationalism became a conservative ideology incorporating a body of ideas based on the Ottoman-Islamic cultural heritage, which the Democrats used to muzzle social criticism. Many pressing social and economic problems could not be aired, lest they be considered subversive. Thus, a new ruling group used nationalism to prevent other groups from expressing their demands. Liberal intellectuals demanded the establishment of parties divided on ideological lines to clarify the political position of each social group.

The rise of this new type of middle class oriented toward economic activity occurred without compensatory developments elsewhere in society. The inflationary policies the government used as a means of development caused a sharp decline in the living standards and social status of the salaried class, which had already lost political power to the agrarian and commercial groups. Meanwhile, the peasantry and the workers, who benefited initially from the abolition of political restrictions and economic measures designed to win them over to the ruling Democratic Party, began to voice new demands. These demands could no longer be satisfied by the give-away policy the government had practiced in 1950–57.

Thus, in 1955–59, the social structure of Turkey had become further differentiated and diversified into a variety of social groups, each conscious of and interested in its own economic and political destiny. These were the new social foundations on which a new ideology could develop. The intelligentsia and the military and civilian bureaucracies, which were apathetic to true social reform and to the economic plight of the lower classes in 1920–45, gradually emerged in the late 1950's as the champions of social justice, economic development, and general welfare for the masses. They attacked the faulty tax system, the government's unplanned policy, and especially the groups that benefited from economic liberalism in 1950–58. The entrepreneurial groups answered by pointing to the increase (more than twofold) in national income, and to the participation in economic and political life of the lower classes, not as exploited groups, as the statists and socialists claimed, but as dignified, free citizens. They claimed the citizens realized that the existing democratic political and social regime had enabled them to liberate themselves from bureaucratic rule and that they would not accept the domination of the new "socialist" elites.

All these discussions took place in 1955–60, in newspapers and reviews such as *Forum, Pazar Postası (Sunday Mail)*, *Varlık (Existence)*, *Dost (Friend)*, and a variety of smaller publications, especially those published by schoolteachers. Among these reviews, *Forum* deserves special mention. It began to publish in 1954 and gradually assembled in its list of contributors Turkey's leading intellectuals, and especially those who were social-minded. *Forum* adopted an evolutionary democratic viewpoint and provided an objective, balanced analysis of Turkey's major problems. It was, indeed, the main source of learning for democratic-minded Turkish intellectuals.

In 1958–59, Turkey seemed ripe for a basic social and political change from within, since the Democratic Party government proved dangerously blind to the new forces developing in society. The government's repressive measures against opposition in 1959–60—that is, against the Republican Party, which included all dissatisfied groups—were desperate efforts to stem the rising tide of demands for change. The Democrats had already had a warning in the elections of 1957, when, contrary to their expectations, they failed to win an absolute majority vote but stayed in power because the opposition votes were split among three parties. What Turkey needed was a government that would recognize the various social groups, accept as legitimate their claims for sharing economic and political power, and establish the constitutional system accordingly. The basic task was to harmonize the political regime and the social structure by establishing a new balance among the existing social groups on the basis of their power in society.

This situation provided the social and political bases for the ideological reorientation of the intelligentsia, chiefly the secularist, modernist, and nationalist groups. Deeply attached to their authoritarian, statist, and elitist philosophy, this group began gradually to embrace social justice and economic development. Soon socialism became their new ideology. The revolution of 1960 destroyed the ideological shields of the upper economic groups and permitted free discussion. As a consequence, socialism—ranging from Marxism to Fabianism, and justifying itself primarily on economic and social grounds—became a major ideological current. Nationalism, in turn, notwithstanding its various subdivisions, espoused economic liberalism, traditionalism, and religion, and became the ideology of the economic and social *status quo*.[7]

Turkey thus entered the age of modern ideology at the level the West had attained in the nineteenth and early twentieth centuries. All this was possible thanks to a modern political structure—the national state—which generated a new pattern of ideological development.

The revolution of May 27, 1960, removed the social and political barriers to reform that had been embodied in the Democratic Party government. The revolution began as a *coup d'état* directed against the oppressive policy initiated by the Menderes Government; it soon became a social and political movement in which all groups participated.

The military could hardly anticipate the ideological struggle that followed their coup. The old regime was accused of having destroyed the bases of Kemalism through its reactionary, regressive policies. But the return to Kemalism (*Atatürkçülük*) urged by the intelligentsia had little in common with the meaning attached to the concept in 1923–45. Nationalism had been the dominant feature of Kemalism in the past; now, social and economic questions acquired priority. In fact, Kemalism was described as a progressive social and economic ideology that had been perverted by privileged groups into a narrow political dogma. Consequently, it was necessary to engage Turkey on the right path of modernization by achieving rapid economic development and social justice. This modernization was often referred to as Westernization, but no longer in the same context as in 1930–60. This was to be an economic and social Westernization to create material advance and comforts, but not by the methods used in the West. The apologists for rapid economic and social development rejected the democratic political means of the West as totally inadequate and proposed a system of executive supremacy to carry out their plans most efficiently.

The key ideological problem in Turkey after 1960, therefore, concerned the method of achieving economic and social development. There was unanimous agreement about the need for development and the fact that the state had to have some role in it. There was disagreement about the extent and nature of the authority the government should be granted. In other words, the question was whether economic development and social justice should be imposed by a group from the top or should be carried out by terms of a consensus of all

7. Discussed in Kemal H. Karpat, "Ideological Developments in Turkey Since the Revolution of 1960," in *Turkish Yearbook of International Relations 1966* (Ankara: The School of Political Science); a revised version will appear in Malcolm H. Kerr (ed.), *Radical Ideologies in the Middle East,* to be published by the University of California Press, Berkeley, Calif., in 1968. This forthcoming study will cover most of the relevant bibliography.

social groups capable of contributing to but also sharing in economic development. Development presented as an economic problem was in reality a political and ideological question that could determine the very characteristics of Turkish democracy.

The ideas about executive supremacy or statism and socialism were expressed in newspaper and magazine articles throughout 1960–61. Toward the end of 1961, a group of intellectuals, many of whom had been associated with *Forum* (and some with the Republican Party), decided to publish a new periodical, *Yön* (*Direction*), to express more cohesively their ideas about socialism, statism, and social justice. Many of these intellectuals had been associated with the State Planning Organization (SPO) established in 1960, and their plans for economic development were based on a rather extensive statism. Political parties were banned from activity during the SPO's initial activities, and therefore could not express their viewpoints. After the elections of October, 1961, however, a popularly elected parliament convened. The Justice Party, the main opposition group representing free enterprise, was associated with the Republicans in a coalition government. It began to object violently to the expanded statism proposed by the SPO. Clearly, the statism proposed by intellectuals and accepted initially by the Republican Party had to be modified if the coalition was to survive at all. The Republicans seemed willing to compromise. They thus dashed the hopes of the new elite group, which sought to consolidate itself in power as the agent of social justice and economic development. The publication of *Yön* on December 20, 1961, therefore, must be viewed as the intellectuals' reaction to the abandonment of their brand of statism. They described the rejection of statism as a direct blow to social justice, democracy, and modernization, and blamed the political parties and parliamentary democracy for its rejection.[8]

The socialist intellectuals' strong attacks on parliamentary democracy were coupled with even stronger condemnation of private enterprise. The new middle classes in entrepreneurial positions, whose number and power increased considerably after 1950, reacted to these attacks by defending private enterprise as being capable of achieving economic development and as providing the foundations necessary for political democracy. Economic and social issues thus became the main forces determining Turkey's ideological orientation. Political institutions were considered determined by the economic and social structure. The socialists regarded the elimination of the last vestiges of the traditional social organization as an essential condition of Turkey's rapid modernization. They proposed the virtual elimination of landowners, capitalists, and all major enterprises forming the upper layer of the existing system based on private property. The apologists for free enterprise advocated the imposition of restrictions on state enterprises, full parliamentary control of the civilian and military bureaucracies, and subordination of government functions to the needs and traditions of society. The policies of all the coalition

8. See Kemal H. Karpat, "The Turkish Left," *Journal of Contemporary History*, I, No. 2 (1966), 169–86.

governments in 1961–65 reflected, to a very great extent, the thoughts prevailing among various social groups, indicating the emergence of a process of mutual social interaction that could lead to a natural relationship between politics and social structure.

The new ideological outlook in Turkey drastically changed the orientation of nationalism and Islamism, the two other major currents of thought. Nationalism was officially accepted as the regime's ideology, although it included a great variety of other tendencies, and it was incorporated in the constitution in 1937. But this nationalism was devised and implemented chiefly with an eye to political purposes intimately connected with the establishment and consolidation of the national state. By 1960, a sense of national identity and allegiance to the national state prevailed among all major social groups. Having achieved its major political mission, therefore, nationalism was bound to acquire a new form and to conform to the new social and economic currents. Representatives of conservative nationalism—racists, Turanists, Islamists, and Ottomanists—appeared as apologists for free enterprise, parliamentary democracy, and liberalism, not because they held firm convictions but because they hoped that these concepts offered the best means of maintaining the *status quo*. As usual, all the nationalists presented their views as outgrowths of Atatürk's ideas. But taking courage from the developing social consciousness, the moderate social-minded groups and the leftists offered their own interpretation of nationalism. This new nationalism was to be no longer the monopoly of a self-designated group but was to become a country-wide community of feeling. One would attempt to raise the cultural and material standard of the lower classes out of a sense of duty.

The struggle over nationalism was concluded with the adoption of the constitution of 1961. After intensive debate, the drafters agreed to mention nationalism in the preamble only. Article 2 of the constitution defined the Turkish state as a *national*, secular, social republic. The old brand of nationalism, however, maintained its vigor among the small-town intelligentsia and middle-school students and teachers. But as the following translations indicate, even they were influenced, to some extent, by the current thinking about human rights, economic development, social organization, and modernization.

The question of Islam in Turkey is not dealt with here, since religion is no longer a major ideological force that is capable of affecting the political regime and the social and economic organization of Turkey. Religion still has a part in the day-to-day conduct of Turkish politics, but its role is far less significant than it was ten years ago. Through the force of events rather than through the efforts of an enlightened body of religious men, Islam in Turkey is gradually acquiring purely spiritual features as it becomes an inner regulatory force.

Turkey's Islamic characteristics will continue to survive indefinitely in a variety of forms, in family and individual attitudes, and in social relations. Islam in Turkey today is a source of cultural rather than political influence, interwoven with other forces that shape the personality of the Turkish people. Henceforth, Islam in Turkey must be approached much as religion is studied in the West. Turkey, moreover, may soon witness a revival of religious studies.

Such a revival should not be viewed as a form of reaction to modernism but as the very product of modernization itself, as the Turks search for a spiritual fountainhead in their own culture, and as they try to accept the dualist philosophical foundations of Western civilization.

The following extracts provide a general picture of ideological developments following the Turkish revolution of May 27, 1960. Since the emphasis is on the main trends of thought, the most representative writing—even that of little-known authors—is included rather than the work of those who are better known. Turkish public opinion is not guided by a small group of writers who, as in most Arab countries, reflect chiefly the government viewpoint, but by an aggregate of ideas and opinions that are identifiable with various social groups.

Consequently, the material included comes mainly from the daily press of the postrevolutionary period. Indeed, a new phase of ideological development has begun since 1960, and this must be distinctly separated from that of previous periods. As noted in the general introduction, Turkey's level of development differs from that of the Arab countries and Iran.

The following selections indicate basically that current Turkish political and social thought is still evolving and thus has not fully acquired its permanent features. One may venture to predict that, for the next few decades at least, Turkish ideology will not be determined by a single group, but will be a composite body of democratic beliefs, reflecting the views, interests, and aspirations of all the social groups that make up modern Turkey.

II. *For a New Democratic Order*

45. THE CAUSES OF THE REVOLUTION OF MAY 27, 1960, AND THE NEW CONSTITUTIONAL REGIME*

The social motives of the Turkish revolution of 1960, the emerging political struggle between political parties and the military, and, finally, the features of the new Turkish constitutional regime may be discerned in the following documents. The first extract, a military communiqué, was issued following the take-over and was printed in all Turkish newspapers on May 28, 1960. It stressed national unity and claimed that the take-over was not directed against any particular group, although in reality it was aimed at the Democratic Party. The second extract, the report of the constitutional committee, which was composed of university professors, provides an insight into the intellectuals' views of the revolution. The third extract is a message from Ismet Inönü to his party in which he stressed the need for a return to civilian rule.

Ankara Communication of the Committee of National Unity

Owing to the crisis into which our democracy has fallen and to the recent, sad incidents and in order to prevent fratricide, the Turkish armed forces have taken over the administration of the country.

Our armed forces have taken this initiative for the purpose of extricating the [political] parties from the irreconcilable situation into which they have fallen and for the purpose of having just and free elections, to be held as soon as possible under the supervision and arbitration of an above-party and impartial administration, and for the purpose of handing over the administration to whichever party wins the elections.

The action is not directed against any person or class. Our administration will not resort to any aggressive act against personalities, nor will it allow others to do so.

* The first extract appeared, in an English translation, as "Communique Issued by the Turkish Armed Forces," in *Middle Eastern Affairs,* XI (June–July, 1960), 189.

The second and third extracts appeared in *News from Turkey,* May 30, 1960. I have altered and condensed these English texts after comparing them with the original Turkish texts.

The Turkish texts of all three extracts appear in Sabahat Erdemir (ed.), *Milli Birliğe Doğru* (*Toward National Unity*) (Istanbul: Bakanoğlu Matbaası, 1961), I, 293, 318–21, 317–18.

All fellow-countrymen, irrespective of the parties to which they may belong, will be treated in accordance with the laws and all the principles of law.

For the elimination of all our hardships and for the safety of our national existence, it is imperative that we remember that all our fellow-countrymen belong to the same nation and race, above all party considerations, and that, therefore, they should treat one another with respect and understanding, without bearing any grudge.

All personalities of the [Democratic Party] cabinet are requested to take refuge with [i.e., surrender to] the Turkish armed forces. Their personal safety is guaranteed by the law.

We are addressing ourselves to our allies, friends, neighbors, and the entire world. Our aim is to remain completely loyal to the United Nations Charter and to the principles of human rights; the principles of peace at home and in the world set by the great Atatürk are our flag.

We are loyal to all our alliances and undertakings. We believe in NATO and CENTO, and we are faithful to them.

We repeat: Our ideal is peace at home, peace in the world.

Preliminary Report of the Professors' Committee Charged with Preparing the Draft of the New Constitution

It would be wrong to view the situation [i.e., the military take-over] in which we find ourselves today as an ordinary political coup.

It is regrettable that, for many months and even years now, the political power that should have been the guardian of civil rights and that symbolized the principles of state, law, justice, ethics, public interest, and public service has lost this quality; it has become instead a materialistic force representative of personal influence and ambition and class privilege.

Whereas the power wielded by the state should represent a social capacity that derives its vigor from the law to which it is attached, this power was transformed into the means of achieving personal influence and ambition. That is why political power ended up by losing all spiritual bonds with the true sources of state power, which reside in its army, its courts of justice and bar associations, its civil servants desirous of demonstrating attachment to their duties, and in its universities; it descended into a position of virtual enmity toward the basic and essential institutions of a true state and also toward Atatürk's reforms, which are of vital importance and value in making it possible for Turkey to retain the position that she merits in the world community of civilized states.

The pressure and oppression that the state brought to bear on citizens in general and on the political opposition, then on civil servants and the press, was extended also to the youth in our universities and even to their experienced instructors with thirty and forty years of service to their credit, then to the many other educators and their aides and students who demonstrated or indicated great promise for the future. This was done to such an extent, in fact, that the state let loose against the universities a mob of persons in authority and their underlings on the police force [or unknown persons dressed up to impersonate the police], each so blinded by the desire to further his own interests as to forget all about professional integrity and its sacred prerequisites; it caused these persons to use firearms and kill or cripple innocent students in surroundings that no rule of law or regime with the slightest attachment to such concepts would have dared to defile. . . .

No clique that caused acts so totally devoid of any connection with the true concepts of right, law, and state could continue to be looked upon as a social institution; this group, in the guise of a government, had lost every semblance of a social or national institution. This particular deed stripped every semblance of a social or national institution from the government and showed it up for what it had become, namely, a means and a tool for the realization of personal power and ambitions.

The situation was the same from the viewpoint of legitimacy. The legitimacy of a government is not derived solely from the manner of [its] acquisition of power, but also from the manner in which it respects, while in office, the constitution that brought it to that elevated position; by the manner in which it cooperates with public opinion and the army, with the legislature and the judiciary, and with institutions of learning; and by its ability to continue to exist as a rule of law.

Instead, the government and political power kept formulating new laws totally contrary to the constitution, and then proceeded to utilize these laws to violate the constitution. It also engaged in activities without the benefit of any law.

Then, again, it behooves the government to be a factor of peace and tranquillity, but this one forfeited any claim to legitimacy by the manner in which it set political and state institutions and their staffs at each other's throats, by the manner in which it vilified each of them at home and abroad and transformed each into a factor of anarchy.

The political power also caused the Grand National Assembly (whose function is to represent the nation) to lose its attributes as a legislative organ; by transforming the assembly into a partisan group serving personal and group interests, it brought it to a state of actual and effective disintegration.

These are the reasons why we are faced today with the necessity to reorganize and re-establish our state and social institutions, political power, and a legitimate government.

We look upon the action of the Committee of National Unity [i.e., the military government] in arranging for the administration to be taken over by state forces and institutions as a measure dictated by the imperative need to re-establish a legitimate rule so as to redress a situation in which social institutions had been rendered virtually inoperative, in which the people were led to anarchy by being set at each other's throats, and in which there was being exerted a conscious effort to destroy all the ethical and moral foundations required to support such institutions.

Two initial measures are required to remedy such a situation:

(1) to set up a functioning and provisional government to provide at the outset the type of democratic administration desired by the nation, to safeguard human rights and liberties, and to look after public interests;

(2) to draw up a new constitution, since the present constitution has been violated and rendered inoperative, to ensure the establishment of a state based on the rule of law, to reorganize state bodies, and to provide for all social institutions firm support based on the principles of democratic rights and justice.

Furthermore, there is the need to formulate a new electoral law calculated to ensure the manifestation of the people's true will to prevent oppression by a political majority, and thereby to forestall the degeneration of political power.

Once these preparatory measures are completed, in a short time elections will be held, institutions will be created, and a state truly based on the rule of law will have been re-created. . . .

It is essential that the proposed constitution should contain every necessary provision to realize the true ideology of a state based on the rule of law. It must safeguard human honor and dignity, and personal rights and freedoms no less than all social rights. It must be in the nature of a factor of equilibrium for the establishment and preservation of social institutions; it must make provision for institutions to ensure that an incumbent parliamentary majority shall not be able to paralyze political activity, that is, the mainstay of democracy, by exceeding its legitimate rights in order to crush and oppress a parliamentary minority that may develop and become tomorrow's administration in power.

Not only are the members of this commission in complete agreement on these principles, but they are in complete accord also with the chairman of the Committee of National Unity and the esteemed commander [Cemal Gürsel] of Turkey's armed forces.

The Message Sent by the Chairman of the People's Republican Party Ismet Inönü to the People's Republican Party Branches

The glorious Turkish Army has taken the destiny of the nation into its hands and put an end to the manifestly anticonstitutional regime of oppression that was leading the country to material and spiritual collapse.

In an address to our beloved nation, General Cemal Gürsel, chairman of the Committee of National Unity and commander-in-chief of Turkey's armed forces, declared that the Committee of National Unity was determined to establish a decent, fair, honest, and democratic rule and quickly turn over the administration of the state to the national will.

In the interim, it is of paramount importance that you should preserve peace and tranquillity among citizens. The PRP [People's Republican Party] organizations must be seriously on guard against sentiments of revenge and the venting of personal grudges that tend to become contagious at such critical moments; they must also endeavor to protect citizens from such sentiments and tendencies.

The firm decision of the Committee of National Unity to establish a rule of fair and honest democracy constitutes the best guarantee of present and future confidence and tranquillity in our country. It behooves our citizens to await the fair, free, and honest elections with calmness, and with full confidence in the unsullied traditions of the Turkish Army.

I salute you one and all with affection and esteem, and extend all best wishes for success in the realm of service to the nation.

46. THE MEANING OF MAY 27*

Kemal Uygur

Kemal Uygur is a major or kurumay, *a staff officer reresenting the elite of the military who is charged with planning and assumes the highest responsibilities in the Turkish armed forces. He was one of many participants in an annual essay competition initiated by the newspaper* Cumhuriyet (Republic) *in honor of its founder, Yunus Nadi. The article expressed simply but emotionally the general view of the causes of the revolution and the army's role in it. The competition title for 1960 was* 27 Mayısın manasını anlatın (Explain the Meaning of May 27).

Revolutions are born of needs. But they are legitimate only if they manifest the needs of an entire nation, not the needs only of an individual or specific group. A revolution that is not supported by the masses without a doubt assumes the character of an opportunist movement undertaken for the promotion of selfish interests. In such a situation, there is no unity of thought in the society. Consequently, revolution occurring in such conditions manifests itself as a bloody clash between groups mutually opposed in interest and conviction. The result is that such a country is dragged into a dark chasm, from which it is able to extricate itself only with difficulty. The best example of this is the series of *coups d'état* that have recently occurred in Syria.

After this simple introduction, let me focus on the following point:

The needs that the Turkish nation accumulated over the past ten years were manifested in the form of the "great revolution and national reform movement of May 27, 1960." This movement drew all its strength from the entire nation. As a result, it was bloodless and achieved success within a few hours, thus stirring the admiration of the world and earning the title "Model Revolution."

* Extract from Kemal Uygur, "27 Mayıs" ("May 27"), *Cumhuriyet* (*Republic*), Istanbul, Novembr 18, 1960, Essay No. 19.

The Atatürk reforms were suppressed in favor of the special interests of the reactionary regime of recent years, and the natural rights of the nation were violated. The national reform movement was a reaction against this. The result of the restoration of these violated values in the name of the nation may be stated briefly: It may be described as the *beginning* of the process of resuscitating in every field a *Turkey* that had been moving backward, of bringing it to a point from which it may move to achieve the level of modern nations.

Now, what are the causes and factors that drove the nation to such a revolution? Let us list them in order.

Economic causes. The inflationary policy that they followed was like a nightmare for the country and left it no room to breathe. Investments were sacrificed to an unjust, unplanned, and partisan policy and resulted in an extremely burdensome public debt. The treasury was completely drained. In order to meet its internal needs, the government ceaselessly printed paper money. This printing operation, undertaken without any basis in value, caused a decline in the value of the currency, both internally and externally. Commerce degenerated. There was no hesitation in using influential persons, not only to secure personal interests, but even to undertake various illegal actions.

Governmental and political causes. Within the public service, corruption, bribery, and intrigue were spreading. Members of the ruling party had assumed complete dominance of the machinery of the state. Foreign policy was unproductive and humiliating. As a result, the external prestige of the state had fallen sharply. Moreover, there was no such thing as stability in policy. Only a face-saving policy was attempted, and the maintenance of such a system was accepted as the only solution. Is not the Cyprus policy the best example of this? Its form changed from annexation to partition and finally to independence, whereby the Greeks gained the main influence.

Social causes. The ties of mutual love, tenderness, and affection among citizens were shattered as a result of degenerate partisanship. In place of sincerity, there was a feeling of doubt and suspicion. The people were divided into two opposing groups that regarded one another as enemies. Prosperity and happiness gave way to uneasiness.

Poverty was resurrected and was not slow to undermine the morals of the innocent children of the country. Particularly deplorable was the fact that state officials operated houses of prostitution as private sources of income.[1]

Exploitation of religion. Religion became a fearsome weapon in the hands of men of state. Fanaticism was fanned. As a result, the bigots who had been lying in wait stepped fearlessly onto the scene. Nor was it long before the bigots' tongues, like the tongue of the snake, poured poison into pure, clean spirits.

1. This was not proven.

Violation of right and freedom. There was no room for freedom of thought and expression in the country. The press had been silenced. There was an attempt to cover improprieties by means of press censorship. Rights and the rule of law were denied to those who belonged to any party other than that in power.

Abandonment of knowledge and learning. In everything he did, Atatürk always relied on the teachings of science, saying "the truest guide in life is science." And this is also one of the most important elements influencing others. But the fallen regime was so blind that it could not see this well-lighted way. With every step, it sank deeper into a pit. Such important national causes as education were being abandoned as a result.

Oppression and violence. All the measures and arrangements that were made served no purpose other than to drag the country ever closer to the precipice. Leadership sold out in the face of increasing blunders and abuses. These opportunist manipulators had lost confidence in the bureaucracy, the judiciary, and the military, because they themselves had undermined the procedures for maintaining confidence in these fundamental elements of the state machinery. But what had happened was irrevocable. In order to make the regime permanent, they even took the path of oppression and violence. They wanted to employ murder against those who resisted their designs. For this purpose, they were actively trying to use the security organization and a number of innocent and deceived people whom they were actively trying to arm.

Arbitrary government. The country was lost in confusion because of legal disorder and a haphazard form of administration. Laws and regulations followed no standard but were adapted to suit personal circumstances. There was no room for planning in [government] action. The basic controlling factor in all types of activity was the eagerness to secure votes.

Terrible ambitions. But even all this was not enough for them. The aroused personal interests and ambitions, which had now assumed a fearful form, with everything that had come to pass, had become insatiable. They said to themselves: "Let us arrange matters in such a way that the people's eyes will not see, their ears will not hear, their minds will cease functioning, and we can assume complete supremacy in all our actions. Thus, we can easily perpetrate our crimes, fill our personal coffers, control the havens of debauchery, and ultimately secure the permanent endurance of our regime." And what else could one expect from Celal Bey [Bayar], the Balkan guerrilla [*komitacı*] and unlucky clerk of the Young Turks, or of Adnan Bey [Menderes], who administered the government as though it were a farm, since he had no other experience.

Suppression of the constitutions. The fearful effort was soon transformed from intention into action. Those who established the "Investigation Commission" did not hear the cries of their own consciences, weak as they were. Personal greed had blinded their eyes, darkened their hearts, and deadened their minds to feelings of virtue and conscience. The law that established the Investigation Commission [with absolute powers to investigate the opposition] and determined its activities was passed by the Grand National Assembly, which manifests the national will. But the commission was given absolute powers superior to those of the Assembly. This law was the death warrant of the fallen regime. It violated the constitution and transformed the parliament into a party caucus, thus depriving it of its legitimacy. Social conscience and national will were completely crushed. The rights and freedoms of the citizen could no longer be discussed. The Investigation Commission had assumed a position superior to the national will and had the power to perpetrate all sorts of evils. Let us pause here and consider for a moment.

The eternal leader Kemal Atatürk says:

> To make matters in the country even more deplorable and critical, those in power are not above negligence, corruption, and even treason. They are even capable of tying their personal interests to the political goals of the invaders. The nation might suffer ruin and exhaustion in its utter poverty.
>
> Oh, son of the Turkish future! Even under these circumstances it is your duty to preserve the independence of the Turkish Republic.[2]

Yes, it was past time to save Turkish independence and the republic from this oppressive internal enemy. The spirit of the Father [Atatürk] again addressed the youth and reminded them of their duty. The enlightened youth [i.e., the student demonstrations] on April 28 [1960] placed the first black seal on the accursed government. Its mouth frothing with hatred and rage, fearing for its very existence, the government struck out and shot down the country's youths with the bullets of the police. These noble martyrs painted crescents [i.e., the national emblem] on the golden pages of history with their blood. The full terror of the tragedy that reigned fell over the country like a black cloud. The presses had been brought to a stop. Censorship stretched like a black veil over the truth.

Love of duty and patriotism. The time had finally come to break the evil and oppressive hold of this ten-year-old government, which had become tyrannical and illegitimate. Where was the power that would break this hold? It was [to be found in] an organization that was nothing but the personification of the youth: the army.

Was it not the most natural and legitimate duty of the army? Did not the law order it so? Of course it did. All the citizens, with tearful eyes, said to the army, "Do your duty."

2. The call to youth charging them with the defense of the regime was the concluding paragraph of Atatürk's six-day speech. See *A Speech Delivered by Ghazi Mustapha Kemal, President of the Turkish Republic, October, 1927,* trans. Hans Kohn (Leipzig: K. F. Koehler, 1929), pp. 723–24. An earlier version was delivered by Atatürk at the war memorial of Dumlupınar, near the Dardanelles, on August 30, 1924.

It was May 27. The army undertook its duty and, within a few hours, without bloodshed, completed the job and broke the back and arm of the tyrant. The sun, when it rose that day, shone more brightly. With golden hair and a sweet smile, it spread across the fatherland, spreading the good news of the birth of right, justice, and freedom.

Long live the dear and sacred Turkish fatherland! Long live the Turkish nation, to eternity, with its army, its rights, justice, and freedom. . . .

47. DEMOCRACY AND REVOLUTION IN TURKEY*

Ismet Inönü

Ismet Inönü (b. 1884) has been belittled by his enemies and described as a great statesman by his supporters. He commanded the armies that defeated the invading Greek forces in 1921, became prime minister in 1923, and was Atatürk's chief collaborator. After Atatürk's death in 1938, Inönü became president of Turkey and assumed dictatorial powers as head of state and permanent chairman of the only political group, the People's Republican Party. In 1945, at the peak of his power and prestige, Inönü decided that the time was ripe to initiate Turkey's transition to a democratic, multi-party system. He silenced opposition in his own party and gradually created the legal and political conditions necessary for a multi-party system. See Kemal H. Karpat, Turkey's Politics *(Princeton, N.J.: Princeton University Press, 1959).*

Inönü's party lost power to the Democratic Party in the first truly democratic national elections, held in 1950. For the following ten years, he was in the opposition and fought staunchly to preserve democracy. In 1959–60, the ruling Democratic Party tried to silence all opposition, but its efforts met violent resistance from the press, the intellectuals, and, especially, the Republican Party. The Democrats finally attempted to use the army against Inönü's party. At this point, the army intervened (May 27, 1960), ousted the Democrats, and installed itself in power.

Three months after the revolution, a group among the junta, backed by some intellectuals and newspapers, began a campaign against political parties and democracy. They described the party system as the cause of regression and internal dissension and advocated a strong government headed by an elite.

* Extract from Ismet Inönü, *Ulus* (*Nation*), Ankara, September 9, 1960. The speech also appeared in *Cumhuriyet* (*Republic*), Istanbul, on September 9, 1960, and it is reproduced in S. Toktamış (ed.), *Ihtilalden Sonra Ismet Inönü* (*Ismet Inönü After the Revolution*) (Istanbul, 1962), pp. 22–27.

The attacks on democracy brought forth a strong statement from Inönü, who had retired temporarily from public life after the coup. Inönü asserted that the ultimate purpose of Turkish reforms was to create and consolidate democracy based on a multi-party system. On balance, he felt, the free political system had resulted in more good than evil since its inception in 1945. He rejected the view that military intervention was necessary to resolve the struggle among the parties, and he emphatically reminded the army that it should relinquish power to a civilian government elected by the people. This speech, clearly defining Turkey's major political issues, had profound significance in mobilizing the forces of democracy and paving the way for the return to a multi-party system.

Inönü's speech is also essential for an understanding of the philosophy of and the approach to democracy in Turkey. The speech, slightly shortened in translation, was addressed to Turkish youth on the fortieth anniversary of Izmir's liberation from the Greek occupation.

During Atatürk's time (1920–38), there were serious attempts to establish a multi-party system. The Progressive Republican Party was established on its own and included the members of the Second Group [of the First National Assembly, 1920–22]. This party did not last because of reactionary uprisings in the East [i.e., the Kurdish revolt] and the newness of the reforms [republic, secularism]. The establishment of the Free Party [by Fethi Okyar] in 1930 was due to Atatürk's initiative and desire. The leaders of this party decided to end their activity, since the party could not continue to work during a period in which the reforms were barely striking roots. Thus, the two parties could not survive. Their closure, regardless of the importance of the causes and motives that necessitated it, was a regrettable experience, and [can be described] as a reason for the delay in our democratic evolution. The multi-party life began afterward, in 1945.

I [Inönü] had a position [president] during that period. I must stress the fact that my role was markedly different from Atatürk's. I opened the way to democracy but did not choose the people [who engaged in politics]. I gave everybody an equal chance. The multi-party experiment was met with hesitation not only by those accustomed to rule under a one-party system but also by honest patriots who feared, on the basis of past experience, that the reactionary forces would prevent the country's progress. I, the spokesman for those supporting the new experiment, was encouraged to initiate the democratic experiment, which was the purpose of [Atatürk's] reforms, by the following consideration: the belief that our nation had achieved an inner [structural] strength based on the [lessons] drawn from the democratic experiments in the past twenty-five years.

In my estimation, the time was ripe for trusting the safeguarding of the republican regime and the reforms to the nation through a free political life. This new [democratic] way of life would strengthen the Turkish nation internally and gain it the respect of the outside world for being a civilized [*medeni*] society.[1] New generations were brought up in twenty-five years. The majority of the nation consisted of men of twenty-five years of age who could not give up the use of the Latin alphabet. This generation was going to defend the reforms for the sake of its own life and its own interests. The forward-looking group among women, who formed half of the nation, was used to the new way of life to such a degree as to find it impossible to bear the return to the old life. The other reforms also had been tried through long experience in the past years. In short, a mass of people, powerful enough to resist the reactionary forces, had come into being. If the methods of civilization [i.e., democracy] could resist the old attitudes long enough, they were bound to create useful influences in the national structure. Finally, in comparison with the time of the first attempt to introduce a regime of freedom and democracy, we were [in 1945], as a nation, in a more consolidated and mature state. Difficulties were bound to arise any time we entered the democratic regime. The importance attached to difficulties is bound to be forgotten soon after the initial experiments. The national life, thereafter similar to the life of advanced nations, would assume a natural course.

We entered the experiment of democracy when we [Inönü] had extensive power and wide reputation. Now, fifteen years afterward, we can consider our gains, that is, the foresight in our decision [to adopt democracy], as well as our losses, or the evil resulting therefrom, and balance one against the other. We have registered more gains than losses during the last fifteen years. True, certain reactionary forces evolved more rapidly than our estimations in 1945. . . . The reactionary currents left no impact on the national structure. The youth, the idealists, the political parties, and the politicians upholding the republic and the reforms were supported by the people as a whole. This protection turned into victory. The fear, thanks to the nation's backing, did not materialize that the reactionary forces . . . , through evil-minded politicians, would become masters of the country, would destroy the bases of the Turkish Republic, and return to the Middle Ages. . . .

[*After condemning the Democratic Party rule in 1950–60, Inönü continues:*]

I am not at all apprehensive of the final result. It means that certain forces in human nature will resist [ill efforts] until the regime of freedom and civilization is assimilated by the nation. It is a law of nature that such a regime will be established at a high price and through sacrifices. If one views past events with such an attitude, then these events must be considered as constituting the natural phases of an evolution. The future, therefore, must be viewed with the enthusiasm felt for an ideal cause, which shall be victorious. . . . The nation's firm intervention [i.e., the military revolution] occurred as the reform of May 27. It ended the unfortunate, lost period [1950–60] and opened a new, progressive, and enlightened era.

Three months after the revolution, we seem not to recall the social and political life that prevailed in the period before it. . . . It is a very wrong and

1. Inönü equates civilization and democracy.

dangerous diagnosis to view the revolution of May 27 as a military intervention caused by the struggle among political parties and as aiming at ending such struggle. Such a diagnosis views as equals the minority [i.e., the Democrats] who wanted to enslave the nation by force . . . and the majority [i.e., the opposition] who fought . . . to safeguard the nation's rights. The old government was a minority that had lost its legitimacy. It was forced out not by one or two political parties, but by a front of national resistance and opposition composed of the nation's majority. This struggle forced the ruling [Democrats] to resort to the last means, that is, to use this great, honest, and enlightened army, established to defend this country, as an oppressive tool against the people. The army . . . refused to become a tool for oppressing the people. . . .

It is, therefore, wrong to look upon the revolution of May 27 as an intervention aimed at ending the inter-party struggle, instead of seeing it as an action directed against men who tried to install oppression despite the nation's resistance. A correct diagnosis is the first step in the cure of an illness or the repair of a wrong. Actions based on wrong diagnosis are either effectless or harmful to the main goal. This point must be properly instilled into the nation's conscience. What is the future? One wrong aspect of the diagnosis is the belief that the People's Republican Party is anxious and impatient to assume power as soon as possible, and the main role is attributed to my own power ambition. I have achieved in the past all the political positions that a man may aspire to in his lifetime. The impact of such positions on me are less important than the events of daily life. The only important problem for all of us is to convince the citizen that the main safe way for the country is to see that the work undertaken by the revolutionary regime is finished in success and honor. The revolutionary period will end in October, 1961, when responsibilities are to be transferred to the Grand National Assembly. Who will come to power? This has no importance for me. There is going to be a free, honest election, and the nation will establish its own rule. The PRP certainly will strive to perform its duties . . . in opposition or in power, it will fulfill its duties with dignity and enthusiasm. The forthcoming government may be formed by one of the existing parties or by those to be established anew. I am not concerned or apprehensive about these alternatives. Regardless of who assumes power, a progressive era will begin for the nation. The power [i.e., government] thus established will continue to rule until the nation decides the opposite. . . . I am viewing the future with peace and faith in bright, progressive achievements.

48. LABOR—A NEW FORCE IN TURKISH SOCIETY*

Bülent Ecevit

Bülent Ecevit (b. 1929) is a well-known Turkish journalist and a deputy from Ankara in the Grand National Assembly. As a member of the People's Republican Party, he was minister of labor in the coalition governments in 1961–65. It was largely because of his efforts that labor legislation was enacted and workers as a group were incorporated into the social and constitutional system that emerged after the revolution of 1960. Workers now form a main pillar of Turkey's democratic regime. Ecevit is presently secretary general of his party and spokesman for the group advocating a left-of-center policy.

One of the important developments since May 27, 1960, is the fact that a new force in Turkish society has begun to make its presence known. This force is labor. When political, social, or economic decisions with potentially broad effects are made, it will, henceforth, be necessary to give prominent consideration to the views, tendencies, and reactions of labor.

Such a need was not felt prior to May 27, 1960. Before that date, defense of the rights and interests of the workers in public administration and policy depended on the social awareness of those in power. Such early measures as the first steps on the road to humane and lawful working conditions, taken during the years of the liberation struggle, the promulgation of progressive and broad-minded labor legislation after the proclamation of the republic, the establishment of worker's insurance, or the efforts to support unionism–none of these resulted from the pressure of the workers themselves, who were still weak and few in number. Rather, these achievements were due to the social awareness that motivated the government.

Likewise, during the period after 1950, anti-labor efforts were easily–and, in large measure, successfully–undertaken. Such measures included an end to progress toward workers' rights; deception and numbing of workers and union leaders by offers of minor and temporary benefits; and use of political and economic pressure to persecute or eliminate those who refused to submit to such deception.

Thus, for example, the worker is today able to put pressure on the parliament to speed up its deliberation on the law granting the right to strike, and effectively to demonstrate his impatience with a delay of a few months. [By

* Extract from Bülent Ecevit, "Işçi–Türk Toplumunda yeni bir kuvvet" ("Labor–A New Force in Turkish Society"), *Milliyet*, Istanbul, January 10, 1963.

contrast], during the ten years between 1950 and 1960, when, in spite of earlier promises to the contrary, the right to strike was not granted—indeed, even preparatory steps were not taken—the workers as a group were unable to show the slightest reaction, nor were they able to support the few unionists who did react.

It is only since the revolution of May 27, 1960, that Turkish workers have been able to pursue their own rights and interests and to assert themselves as a significant factor in society in the determination of important political, social, and economic matters.

The causes of this development are not to be found in any sudden increase in the number of workers.

An End to Feudalism

One of the main reasons for this development is that the system established by the pre-May 27 regime for the purpose of deceiving and numbing the workers in order to dominate them was brought to an end. This was a sort of *ağalık,*[1] [or at least] an adaptation to industry, particularly in the public sector, of the system of *ağalık* prevailing in some economically backward areas. In place of the landlord [*ağa*[2]], there were in the factories and some other key places, partisan administrators, such as personnel or administrative directors, foremen, gang chiefs, and [even] labor representatives and union leaders. The fate of the worker was largely in their hands. Perhaps the institution of *ağalık* fills a void in places where it has not yet been possible to establish certain institutions peculiar to advanced societies or where the power of the state has not yet been sufficiently developed. But the adaptation of this primitive system to industry was not born of the necessity to fill a void. Rather, it was undertaken because of the desire to dominate the workers and prevent them from achieving a position of strength in the society.

Thus, the major change brought about in the field of industry by the action of May 27 was to destroy that primitive system at its roots. It was only after the destruction of that system that the labor movement in Turkey was able, after ten years of stagnation, to move ahead on the road of material evolution.

Freedom

Moreover, this evolution has been facilitated by the greater freedom of expression and debate in social and economic matters that has prevailed since May 27, as well as the constitutional guarantees of a number of social and economic rights.

The present government is facilitating this evolution even more. It has taken steps to establish a fruitful system of consultation and joint action with the unions in the solution of social problems. Without waiting for pressure from below, it has recognized the right of the workers and unions to a respected position in a democratic society undergoing industrialization.

1. Originally it referred to leadership in local, rural communities; now, to abusive control of villagers.

2. The communal leader. Now used as a pejorative for feudal-minded (mainly rural) proprietors.

In the near future, with legislation granting the right to strike and engage in collective bargaining [granted in 1963], the unions will be able to fulfill their real responsibility of protecting the rights and interests of the workers. Then the workers in Turkey will constitute an even more effective force than today.

When the Turkish worker gains this type of power, when he achieves sufficient power to require that his views, tendencies, and reactions be considered in the formulation of important political, social, and economic policies—then he will be able to affect our social life and structure in various ways.

Support of the Worker

The workers wish to utilize fully their newly gained rights and weapons of self-defense. In order to do so, they will find it necessary to acquaint themselves more closely and more intelligently with social and particularly economic problems. This will benefit not only the workers but the entire society, because the workers, in order to raise their wages and to benefit from the opportunities afforded by the right to strike and bargain collectively, will want to strengthen their employers and the national economy in general. Thus, the voluntary support of the employed in increasing the rate of development will be secured. In order not to lose this very valuable voluntary support, those in power must be careful to adhere to [the principle of] social justice in directing [national] development.

Labor has already begun to play a most constructive role in utilizing idle capacity in our industry and in resisting importation of certain commodities that hamper local industries. The warning of labor in this connection has been very valuable to the government.

Democracy's Search for the Citizen

Although a large majority of them have no [formal] education, the workers feel a greater inclination to concern themselves with social and economic problems than do those who have had much education. These workers will cast their votes in an increasingly intelligent manner. In thus becoming [full-fledged] citizens, they will ensure the more effective functioning of democracy in our country. In fact, the legalization of strikes and collective bargaining, the securing of profit-sharing, and the participation of workers in the administration of the state sector, will complement political democracy. These will lead to [the establishment of] industrial democracy, and the workers will spend their working life in a democratic environment. The worker will then be able to fulfill the ideal of the democratic citizen. Hopefully, the workers will establish a tradition of disciplined and productive labor within a democratic framework in Turkey.

Thus, labor will participate more energetically and effectively among those who are called "the energetic forces" [*zinde kuvvetler*], i.e., those who defend democracy.

By the same token, labor's proud voice is raised in a reassuring manner even now, at a time when democracy is under threat.

Civilized Man

Another very important effect of labor's increased weight in Turkish society will be the consolidation of reform. It must be admitted that the gap between the intellectuals and the people, an inheritance from Ottoman times, has continued even since the proclamation of the republic. Despite all the well-intentioned efforts, despite democracy itself, it has been impossible to forge sturdy links between the intellectuals and the people. As a result, the intellectuals, who formed the vanguard of Atatürk's reforms, have failed to establish the roots of these reforms among the masses. Henceforth, the workers will be able to forge such firm links between the intellectuals and the people.

In a sense, the standard of living the Atatürk reforms are expected to bring to Turkey is inseparable from the technology of Western civilization. The vast majority of the workers are persons for whom Western technology has become a way of life and a source of livelihood. Consequently, while the intellectuals had to make a deliberate effort to adopt the Western way of life, the industrial laborer finds it a most natural thing. As his earnings and capacities increase, he will adapt to it even more quickly. While visiting a factory in an Anatolian town, I learned that the books most read by the workers were the world classics. This does not mean that the development and awakening occurring among the workers will necessarily end the leadership of the intellectuals in Turkish society. But it will, in all likelihood, require those intellectuals who do not wish to lose their position of leadership to exert greater efforts to adapt themselves to Western culture. It will, in all likelihood, require them to read more extensively and, especially in economic and social matters, to go beyond formal learning and long obsolete dogmas and clichés. It will require them to follow developments in the West more closely, and it will require them to become sufficiently knowledgeable and aware of the economic and social problems of our society so that they may understand them at least at the level of a well-trained Turkish union leader.

In short, the new development in the Turkish labor movement, if properly understood, can become one of the most influential forces working to enhance economic development, fruitfully to administer democracy, and firmly to implant Atatürk's reforms among the people.

III. *Atatürkism*

49. ATATÜRKISM IS SECULARISM*

Yaşar Nabi Nayir

Yaşar Nabi Nayir was born in the old Turkish town of Üsküp-Skoplje in Macedonia (now Yugoslavia) in 1908, and he emigrated to Turkey when he was quite young. Even as a youth he was identified with Atatürk's nationalist, secularist, modernist, republican policies. He purposely avoided involvement in practical politics, but through his writing he fought vigorously to uphold the principles of the modernist regime, and his interest in literature was a consequence of and complementary to his political views. For about thirty years, Nayir has published the weekly review Varlık (Existence)*. Through it, and through his books, he has succeeded in generating a modern way of thinking in Turkey. Several literary schools have been formed around* Varlık*, some that have imitated the West and some that have been genuinely Turkish. The thousands of books published by the Varlık publishing house under Nayir's direction provide a splendid source for studying the development of Turkish thought.*

After the revolution of 1960, both rightists and leftists newly interpreted Atatürk's ideas, and some of them perverted his original meaning. Consequently, Nayir assembled a collection of thirty-five articles on Atatürk and his ideas by some of Turkey's best-known intellectuals. The following extract summarizes some of these articles, but stresses secularism as the foundation of Atatürk's thought and presents a general picture of the modernization reforms. It should be noted that Nayir's views on secularism have remained rather orthodox and that he regards the society at large as still unaffected by modernization.

The new system of thought and the new path [of life] brought about by Atatürk's words and reforms constitute Atatürkism. If the great leader's words and deeds were studied as a whole, on would come to the conclusion that this system of thought was founded on secularism and on orientation toward the West. Let's consider the main reforms. The foundation stone of Atatürk's reforms was the abolition of the sultanate [1922], followed shortly by the abolition of the caliphate [1924]. There are kings in the West, and there are also

* Extract from Yaşar Nabi Nayir, *Atatürkçülük Nedir?* (*What Is Atatürkism?*) (Istanbul: Varlık Basımevi, 1963), pp. 283–92.

internationally accepted religious offices. But the concepts and attributes of those cannot be compared in any way with the divine authority of the Ottoman rulers. The Ottoman sultans were for centuries the representatives of a rigid tradition, whereby the ruler was considered the sole master of the country and God's representative and shadow on earth. . . . Despite the constitution that deprived them of authority and power, the sultans could still nurture the hopes of those who had an interest in the maintenance of the old order. The annihilation of scholarship, which was the main fortress of opposition to secularism, could not be accomplished as long as the foundations [of the sultanate-caliphate] remained intact.

The weekly holiday law seems insignificant among other reforms. Actually, it had a profound meaning because . . . it tested in a masterful way the resistance potential of conservatism. The weekly holiday was changed from Friday to Sunday, that is to say, to the holiday of the West. Thus, it removed one of the main obstacles to orientation toward the West and assimilation into it. . . .

The educational reform law that closed the old traditional school [*medrese*] was the chief blow directed at scholasticism and backwardness [traditionalism]. The secular education directed by the state was the only type permitted, and this forestalled reactionary attacks. The *medreses* had prevented all associations with the West as well as every step forward and had been the standard-bearers of opposition to modernization. The subsequent closing of religious courts [*seriat*] proved that logically there could not be two different court systems in a country. . . . This was a natural consequence of the first reform and completed the total, categorical liberation of state affairs from theocratic pressure. The law concerning dress reform, besides changing the primitive oriental look of our people, ended the domination of those who used [the traditional headdress] as a symbol to achieve authority over the ignorant people. The law closing the convents and mausoleums abolished the last nests of backwardness and inertia. The civil code [introduced in 1926] abolished the provisions that derived from Islam and were not compatible with modern legal understanding. It was one of the most decisive steps taken toward adapting the way of life to Western rules.

The script reform broke the last ties to Islamic Eastern civilization and culture. Indeed, in order to establish our national culture within Western civilization and in order to evolve from the *umma* system into national statehood, it was essential to liberate ourselves from the influence of Arab religious philosophy. We could not achieve this liberation as long as we used Arabic in writing and reading. We could not achieve language reform with this writing and could not liberate our language from the stringent rules of Arabic and Persian grammar. The fundamental change in language occurred only after new generations, unaware of Arabic, graduated from our universities. . . . Today, the new generations find it easy to understand the West in various branches of science and fine arts and equally difficult to understand and assimilate the East. This difference opened a gap in understanding between the new and old generations, but this gap will disappear by itself as the old generations grow smaller and the new ones increase in size. Then the Western way of thinking and understanding will be greatly accelerated. . . .

[*After mentioning the university reform, the emancipation of women, the introduction of surnames, and the abolition of titles, Nayir concludes by stating that these were steps in the transition from theocracy to secular democracy.*]

The foundation of Atatürk's reforms is secularism. Consequently, it is more appropriate to talk not about *reforms* but about *one reform* by Atatürk. What was the justification for this great reform achieved by Atatürk in the short span of fifteen years between the proclamation of the republic [1923] and his death [1938]? Atatürk diagnosed the sickness of the Ottoman Empire while he was still a student at the war college. . . . In order to save the state, there was no other solution but to destroy everything ranging from the government apparatus to the citizens' mentality and to build them anew. Nobody had the immense power necessary for such an undertaking, and there were only a handful of people who believed in the necessity of total change. . . .

[*After mentioning various reform attempts that had, in the past, been opposed and eventually destroyed by religious reactionaries, Nayir continues:*]

What did the continuous regression and decadence in the Islamic world mean while the Christian, Western world living in welfare and happiness advanced at an incredible speed? Did it indicate that one of the religions was stimulating progress, while the other was its enemy? One cannot accept this hurried [superficial] view. History shows that Christianity, which is 600 years older [than Islam], kept the Western world under heavy oppression in the Middle Ages and opposed all innovation. Islamic countries, on the other hand, achieved brilliant progress, were opened to science, and for long kept Europe in fright. This means that religions are what men interpret them to be. Consequently, the fault lies not with religion but with the so-called men of religious learning [*ulema*], who changed religion as they pleased and, taking gifts from the bigots, permitted them to exploit the people as they wished. Traditions, as we call them, are a centuries-old, superstratified accumulation of these opinions and superstitions . . . imbedded in the people's minds.

Atatürk was very fond of democracy. He admired the French Revolution. He had such a belief while preparing the War of Liberation [1919–22] and made reliance on the people a habit from the very beginning. . . .

[*Atatürk, according to Nayir, met with the opposition of a conservative majority in the First National Assembly (1920–22) and fought desperately to persuade the majority and to prevent it from crushing the enlightened minority.*]

He [Atatürk] realized that a Western type of democracy could benefit only the reaction . . . as long as people were not enlightened and not delivered from ignorance and bigotry. This man [Atatürk], who was so fond of democracy, realized that real democracy could not be established before delivering the nation from the oppressive influences of the theocratic order. . . . Atatürk never interfered with the faith and worship of people, but stood fast with unyielding will before the clergy [*hojas*] and men who had gone to Mecca on pilgrimage [*hajis*], when they tried, on behalf of religion, to interfere in worldly affairs. Expressing his views on religion, Atatürk stated: "A natural religion must be compatible with reason, technology, science, and logic." He differed from false men of religion on this point. These men wanted reason and logic, science and technology to follow unconditionally religious commands and opinions expressed on behalf of religion. They defended the view that the worldly order should be directed by men who spoke on behalf of God. Atatürk said the following in order to warn the people about the empty words of these ignoramuses:

> There is a yardstick for our religion available to everybody. If you use this yardstick, you will realize immediately what conforms and what does not conform to religion. If something satisfies reason, logic, the interest of the nation, the interest of Islam, do not ask anyone and accept it, for that thing is religion. If our religion [Islam] was not compatible with reason and logic it could not have been perfect and the last of religions. . . .

It is for these reasons that Atatürk was firm against all reactionary movements, regardless of how unimportant these might have been. . . . Atatürk's declarations on religious bigotry have the value of a testament for the Turkish nation. Atatürk said:

> You must know that the evil men who guided us along wrong paths covered themselves often in religious garb. They deceived our pure and innocent people with the words of the *şeriat*.[1] Read our history and see that all the evils that destroyed and enslaved our nation came out of the curse and evils that acted in the guise of religion. . . . The reactionaries believed that they could be backed by a certain class. This is definitely a misconception. We shall smash all the opponents and march on our way toward progress. We shall not hesitate on the path of progress. The world is progressing at a tremendous speed. Can we remain outside this stream?

Atatürk, who loved democracy and placed great value on national will, never permitted the reactionaries to enjoy the tolerance necessitated by national will [respect for elected reactionaries]. He knew that the slightest weakness in this field would lead to the destruction of democracy and open the way to the re-establishment of the sultanate and the caliphate and to their natural intellectual consequence, which is the darkness of the Middle Ages. Democracy was acceptable, but in order to establish the real democracy based on

1. Islamic religious law (the equivalent of the Arab *shari'a*), which became a general type of common law under the Ottoman Empire. It was abolished in 1923–26.

the people . . . it was essential to remain alert so as not to be defeated by the admirers of the autocratic ages and be sabotaged by those who were accustomed to seek personal interest by deceiving the people. . . . It was necessary to enlighten the nation and enable it to differentiate the good from the evil. . . .

Atatürk's basic ideal was a great, emancipated Turkey, even more developed than contemporary civilization; it was to be a country that lived according to the Western yardstick and was an inseparable part of the West. But Atatürk knew that this ideal could be reached only by secularization in every field. His understanding of history and his own observations indicated clearly that the West reached this high level of living only after the entire social order was secularized. The period between the Renaissance and the French Revolution in the West was a struggle between theocracy and secularism. Almost two hundred years later, we are still waging the same battle. We have incessantly lost time with occasional advances and regressions. Consequently, twenty-five years after Atatürk's death, we are far from having achieved his dream of Westernization. . . . This is the reason for which I regard secularization, and insist upon it, as the foundation stone of Atatürk's reforms.

50. ATATÜRKISM IS ECONOMIC LIBERATION AND ANTICOLONIALISM*

Şevket Süreyya Aydemir

The publishers of Kadro (Cadre), *a review published in 1932–34 and initially with Turkish Government support, tried to develop a socialist, statist, nationalist philosophy for republican Turkey. They took their direction from Marxist and corporatist views. Şevket Süreyya Aydemir (b. 1897) was the leading ideologist among the five intellectuals who published* Kadro. *Around 1960, he again became prominent in Turkish affairs, and he associated himself with the socialist groups that emerged in 1960–65. His economic outlook is authoritarian but not extremely leftist. His publications include an autobiography,* Suyu Arayan Adam (Man in Search of Water) *(Istanbul: Remzi Kitapevi, 1959) and a three-volume biography of Atatürk,* Tek Adam (Unique Man) *(Istanbul: Remzi Kitapevi, 1963–65).*

What is Atatürk's ideology? This is a topic whose thesis, antithesis, and synthesis were not developed systematically by Mustafa Kemal, who was above

* Extract from a speech given at Robert College in Istanbul, "Atatürk ve Atatürk Ideolojisi" ("Atatürk and the Atatürk Ideology"), in Nusret Kurosman (ed.), *Çeşitli Cepheleriyle Atatürk* (*Atatürk in His Various Aspects*) (Istanbul: Istanbul Matbaası, 1964), pp. 26–40.

all a realistic man of action. Nevertheless, there is a movement [of national liberation] led by Mustafa Kemal, and this movement has an axis made up of ideas and principles. These ideas, when put together, form one of our era's currents of thought. This current opened and determined the fate of an epoch, not only for us, but for all countries resembling our own. The name of this current is Atatürkism and its pioneer is Atatürk. . . .

The movement of national liberation is not an event limited only to Turkey. It left its mark on the course of contemporary events. . . . The struggle for liberation and for national freedom was the pioneering and leading movement aimed at the liquidation of colonialism. It also provided the principles of thought and action for an underdeveloped country seeking, through free, civilized, and peaceful means, a place among the nations of the progressive world. . . .

The Turkish movement of national liberation, which began in 1919 and developed under Mustafa Kemal's leadership, was the consequence [of economic colonialism] and had the following basic characteristics: unconditional national independence, unconditional popular sovereignty, unconditional economic and financial freedom. . . . Mustafa Kemal's principles . . . embodied the following ideas:

1. Anti-imperialism [means] national independence.
2. Anti-capitalism [means] a free national economy and opposition to foreign capital and privileges.
3. Unconditional popular sovereignty [means] the return of everything to the true masters of the country.

These three principles are the concrete expressions of Atatürk's ideology, and we must be ready to struggle for them today. . . .

51. ATATÜRK AND HIS ECONOMIC POLICY*

Kenan Bulutoğlu

Kenan Bulutoğlu is a member of the Faculty of Economics, Istanbul University. He belongs to a group of young Turkish economists who advocate land reform and increased government intervention in the economy and who define their program as socialism. This article stresses that a certain legacy in the economic field—namely statism—has been inherited from Atatürk and that, consequently, contemporary Turkish governments must take into consideration Atatürk's economic policies as well as his cultural and social legacy. There is an obvious ideological bias in the article, and the quotations are chosen accordingly.

* Extract from Kenan Bulutoğlu, "Atatürk ve Iktisadi Siyaseti" ("Atatürk and His Economic Policy"), *Cumhuriyet*, Istanbul, November 13, 1963.

It is difficult to reach precise conclusions regarding the nature of Atatürk's economic policy and its swings to the left or right throughout his lifetime. First of all, since Atatürk was not an economist, it would be irrelevant to attempt to find a set of coherent decisions derived from a clear, well-defined economic doctrine. But as a statesman, as the founder of a modern state, he followed an original, noteworthy economic policy. It would be even more difficult to distinguish these policies, which can be ascribed directly to his own ideological inclination, from those that stemmed from the advice of politicians who participated directly in the exercise of power. Moreover, the fact that economic concepts were often applied by changing somewhat their original Western meaning also helped somewhat to render uncertain his economic policy.

Economic subjects virtually were not dealt with in the Great Speech.[1] This indicates that, during the War of Independence and the first years of the republic, problems of economic policy were not a major preoccupation of the government. In any case, for Mustafa Kemal, economic problems were secondary to political independence and, therefore, could be solved after the latter was achieved. In an interview with the tradesmen and artisans of Konya in 1923, he candidly declared that, apart from economic independence, he did not have a well-defined program of action in the field of economics:

> I can formulate my ideas in two categories: those concerning the present and those concerning the future. For the time being, the only things I am preoccupied with are the capitulations [i.e., the special privileges granted to the Western Powers]. With regard to what must be done in the future, especially in order to make Turkish trade competitive with world trade, I am confident that you know better than I what measures are necessary.

Even at that time, however, Atatürk had realized the importance of economic issues:

> The new Turkish state will lay its foundations not on the bayonet but on economic power, upon which the bayonet also is based. The new Turkish state will be an economic state.[2]

Not until after World War II was the term "economic state" introduced into books of political science or used commonly together with the term "economic democracy." Atatürk, who grasped very well the importance of economics, influenced also by the pressure of subsequent events, initiated a constructive economic policy. I shall try to outline the features of this economic policy in the three special fields where it was most noticeable: economic inde-

1. Atatürk's six-day speech, *A Speech Delivered by Ghazi Mustapha Kemal, President of the Turkish Republic, October, 1927,* trans. Hans Kohn (Leipzig: K. F. Koehler, 1929).

2. Most of the quotations in this article are taken from Korkut Boratav, *Türkiye'de Devletçilik, 1923–1950* (*Statism in Turkey, 1923–50*); Bilsay Kuruç, *Iktisat Politikasinin Resmi Belgeleri, Türk Iktisadi Gelişmesi Araştırma Projesi serisi No. 16, 17* (*Official Documents of Economic Policy. Project series 16, 17 of Turkish Economic Development*) (Ankara: School of Political Science, 1962). The references are given by the author and have been preserved intact.

pendence and anticolonialism, industrialization and statism, and feudal conditions and agrarian reform.

1. *Economic Independence and Anticolonialism*

As I pointed out above, the most clear economic credo of the participants in the War of National Liberation, and of Mustafa Kemal himself, was their uncompromising, hostile attitude toward the exploitation of the economy by foreign capital under the privileges and protection accorded by the capitulations. The speeches of Mustafa Kemal on this subject are unreserved, violent, and bitter:

> We are men decidedly devoted to the doctrine that teaches us to fight, nationally united, the imperialism that wants to ruin us and the capitalism that wants to swallow us. (Speech in the Grand National Assembly, January 1, 1920.)

Capitalism here means exploitative foreign capitalism, i.e., colonialism with all its political aspects.

After the abolition of the capitulations, the foreign companies and utility monopolies established in key sectors of the economy—such as mines, railways, utilities, and so on—under the privilege of concessions were nationalized. Atatürk's suspicious attitude toward foreign private capital was only too clear. Nevertheless, he pointed out that he would welcome the kind of foreign capital that would work for the interests of the country:

> It would be erroneous to think that we are against foreign capital. We are always ready to grant necessary guarantees to foreign capital and it is desirable for foreign capital to add to our labor and to our wealth, and to bring about good results—but not as before. (Inaugural speech at the Congress of Economy, İzmir, 1923.)

The kind of foreign capital he was most cautious about consisted mainly of private companies that aimed to use the Turkish economy as a reservoir of raw materials and, hence, as an open market. He admitted, however, that the capital borrowed from foreign powers could be helpful in economic development, provided that it was used for good purposes. During Atatürk's lifetime, in fact, Turkey received credit from various foreign powers, but the amount did not exceed that of the old debts, which were being repaid at the same time. It must also be noted that Atatürk thought that foreign capital could not be the main force behind economic development and that the main support had to come from internal resources:

> In order to preserve the structure of the state, it is necessary and possible to govern with the revenues and resources of this country and without having recourse to foreign countries.

This cautious attitude of the young republic toward foreign debt is understandable. Public finance was still under the heavy burden of Ottoman debts, contracted during the period of [the empire's] decline.

During the period of the Ottoman Empire, the Turkish economy had all the characteristics of a dependent, semicolonial economy. The capitulations prevented the adoption of a protective tariff and thus hindered the development of a national industry. Modern capitalist technology was introduced in the country to produce only those goods that could not be imported from abroad and had to be produced in Turkey. This was a dichotomic type of economy, which still prevails in many underdeveloped countries; an enclave sector made up mainly of foreign companies confined to the port cities or a series of companies scattered throughout the country exploiting natural resources [such as] mines or plantations. It is noteworthy that the impact of this sector on national development decreased even more because of the fact that the foreign companies used to take out of the country a large part of their production in the form of profits. Except for this small modern sector, the entire economy was feudal. A large majority of the Turkish statesmen in the years of decline were aware of the fact that the development of a national manufacturing industry was dependent on the abolition of the capitulations and the introduction of a protective tariff system.

According to the Treaty of Lausanne [1923], a full protective tariff policy could be adopted only by 1927. Republican Turkey had long looked forward to the day when it could enact a protective tariff as the date for completing its economic independence. Flags were hoisted on the anniversary of the Treaty of Lausanne partly to hail this event. Today, forty years later, the flags are again hoisted. But now the purpose is to greet the admission of Turkey into the Common Market, the abandonment of the freedom to impose tariffs, which was secured in the past as the yardstick of sovereignty. This participation could have been hailed as a success if, during the past forty years, Turkey had established an industrial capacity capable of competing fully with the industries of the Common Market countries. Would these countries then accept Turkey in the Common Market?[3] The answer can perhaps be found in their refusal to admit the United Kingdom into the Market.

2. *Desire for Rapid Industrialization and Statism*

During the first years of the republic—starting with the Economic Congress of Izmir in 1923—the policy followed was to place trust in private entrepreneurship and in its ability to achieve economic development. In spite of these encouraging measures, the actual result cannot be considered satisfactory. Furthermore, the outbreak of the Great Depression, the increasing foreign trade deficit, and, consequently, the pressure on the value of the Turkish lira contributed to the government's turning to a new and more interventionist policy. After Inönü's speech in Sivas, statism was enforced [beginning in 1930–31] as the government's official economic policy.

Atatürk defined statism as follows:

> The statism that we are implementing is a system peculiar to Turkey, engendered by its own needs. It means that while recognizing private entrepreneurship as the main basis, but realizing that many activities are not undertaken,

3. Turkey was accepted as an associate member.

the state must be given the control of the economy to face all the needs of a large country and of a great nation. . . . The state wanted to perform certain economic activities that had not been undertaken by private enterprise in the shortest possible time and it succeeded in doing so. . . . The way we have chosen to follow is a system different from economic liberalism. (Inaugural speech at the Izmir Fair, 1935.)

He also pointed out that statism was not in any way the same as collectivism or Communism, which aimed at removing all instruments of production and distribution from the ownership and control of private enterprise. This definition—doubtless like many other similar definitions proposed by official and nonofficial interpreters of statism—is not clear. Furthermore, since statism was the government's official economic policy, no one dared speak against it. Instead, everyone tried to interpret it according to his own tendencies and interests.[4]

The economic functions of the state, beginning with limited intervention and going toward fuller intervention, can be ranked as follows: (1) to provide public services; to undertake activities that by their nature can be undertaken only by a central body using public finance [i.e., taxes], such as defense, justice, police protection, and so on; (2) the construction of a basic infrastructural network, such as highways, railways, harbors, dams, and so on; (3) utility and resource monopolies, i.e., those activities that by their nature can be operated efficiently only in monopoly conditions: utilities, mines, etc.; (4) production for market demand.

Those with conservative tendencies would define statism in such a way as to cover only the first two groups of activities. Those with leftist leanings would include in this concept all natural resources and those activities that were not undertaken by private entrepreneurs, either because of high degrees of risk or simply for lack of capital. The group supporting the view that large sectors of the economy should be left to private business were headed by Celal Bayar, then minister of economy. Those advocating bold government initiative in erecting new plants and accelerated industrialization were seeking support from Ismet Inönü, then prime minister.

Atatürk himself favored the doctrine defending accelerated industrialization according to which the government would set up new public enterprises to

4. Serbest Fırka (the Liberal or, more correctly, Laissez-Faire Party of 1930) opposed statism from its very inception, but it directed its criticism more against state capitalism than against popular statism, arguing that statism enriched a few with the taxpayers' money. After the party was disbanded (in the latter part of 1930) at the government's request, no one dared speak openly against statism. When the principle of statism was inserted into the constitution in 1937, a member of the Grand National Assembly asked the government: "If a citizen speaks and advocates laissez-faire, will he be brought before the criminal court and charged with attempting to change the state regime?" A member representing the views of the government answered: "An action against the principles of statism, like any action against the constitution, will be prosecuted as a crime." Another member answered: "No activity in favor of laissez-faire which contradicts the doctrine of statism will be allowed." Fortunately, this narrowmindedness has never been enforced. To the best of our knowledge, no one was taken before the court on the charge of advocating laissez-faire, even in the period when statism was at its peak, but many were imprisoned on charges of socialism or Marxism.

meet the market demand. Furthermore, Atatürk pointed out that statism was a policy that conformed basically to the wishes of the Turkish people:

> The policy that our party follows is on the one hand entirely democratic and popular, and on the other hand it is, from the economic standpoint, statist. By their temperament, our people are genuinely statist, for they feel that they have the right to ask the state for all that they absolutely need. Consequently, there is a fundamental similarity between the program of our party and the aspirations of our people. (Speech at Izmir, January, 1931.)

Significantly, the policy makers who implemented statism tried to present it as an economic system above and beyond the controversy concerning capitalism versus socialism. Doubtless, as an economic system, statism represented a movement toward collectivism rather than toward capitalism and was, therefore, a kind of leftist radicalism. But the political philosophy supporting this view on economics was not clearly determined. The government claimed that its policy was neither socialistic nor capitalistic. The collectivist structure in industry did not stem from a prior labor movement; it was generated by the governing elite's desire for rapid industrialization. The intellectual movement led by *Kadro*[5] tried to define the philosophy of this shift toward collectivism. Statism, *Kadro* explained, was a movement to achieve the synthesis between the need for industrialization and the goal of a classless society.

As in every mixed economy that lacked strong ties with the masses, statism ran the risk of becoming state capitalism. This, indeed, became a reality and, due to a series of developments, gained momentum. After 1946, strong tendencies toward Trujilloism transformed state economic enterprises into an outright [economic] instrument in the hands of the private interest groups that controlled the government. The fact remains, however, that Turkey, as an underdeveloped country, was the first to use statism as a means for industrialization.

In our time, many underdeveloped countries (India, Egypt, Algeria) have adopted more or less the same policy and are openly declaring that socialism as a political philosophy underlies their policy of industrialization.

3. *Policy Against Feudal Institutions*

Atatürk tried to eliminate the feudal institutions through some more or less formal legal reforms. But the emancipation of landless peasants from serfdom by way of radical land reforms was one of his most cherished goals. He frequently declared that agrarian reforms were necessary and that it would be advisable to limit the size of private land ownership in order to achieve them:

> First of all, it is necessary that no peasant be left landless in our country. More important than that is to provide for a statute to prevent the parcelling of land and keep it large enough to provide a living for the peasant's family. It is necessary to limit the size of land ownership according to the fertility of land and the density of population in the region. (Inaugural speech in the Grand National Assembly, November, 1937.)

5. See p. 299.

Despite Atatürk's statement about the necessity of an agrarian reform in almost every one of his inaugural speeches in the Grand National Assembly,[6] the government failed to implement an extensive agrarian reform in his lifetime or thereafter. Even during Atatürk's lifetime, in fact, the big landowners exercised an important influence in the People's Republican Party, then the party in power and the only one legally in existence. Pretexts such as the lack of regular land surveys and the priority of settling first the immigrants [exchanged populations] led to the repeated postponement of land reform. Finally, even when reform was voted in 1945, its enforcement was effectively blocked and it was considerably watered down with later amendments.

The agrarian reform was the only one of Atatürk's economic programs that was not implemented. After his time, the increasing number of landless peasants came to look upon land reform as a matter of life or death. Today, many countries recently liberated from colonial rule are trying to undertake the first steps in an economic policy that was pioneered by Atatürk. With his remarkable reforms, which broke the vicious circle of traditionalism in Turkey, Atatürk—this magnificent radical from a semicolonial feudal society—is still leading his own country, and countries in similar situations, toward progress.

6. Especially the inaugural speeches of 1929, 1936, and 1937.

IV. *Socialism and Statism*

52. FOR SOCIAL JUSTICE AND DEVELOPMENT*

In its first issue, the review Yön (Direction) *published an ideological statement proposing statism as a means of providing social justice and stimulating economic development. The statement brought together ideas that had been more or less floating around and proposed them as guideposts for concerted action. It was framed to appeal mainly to intellectuals and, despite its claims to democratic order, it lacked that populist democratic spirit so dear to the Turkish masses. At first, the declaration was signed by more than 160 people —more than half of whom were junior academicians, journalists, or writers— and later by about 500. The publication of the statement had a brief impact:* Yön's *circulation went up to 30,000, but soon dropped back to about half that number. Some of the original signatories eventually came to disagree with the revolutionary, antiparliamentary views subsequently adopted by* Yön. *Others, dissatisfied with* Yön's *"bourgeois statism," supported more radical leftist reviews such as* Sosyal Adalet (Social Justice) *and* Eylem (Planned Action); *the latter expressed the viewpoint of a Marxist group that was associated with the Türkiye Işçi Partisi (Labor Party of Turkey). Some of* Yön's *contributors—Doğan Avcıoğlu, Mumtaz Soysal, and Sadun Aren, for example—eventually deviated to the left, but the review continued to publish many articles on social problems.*

The undersigned, holding responsible positions in various segments of Turkish society, consider it appropriate to publish this statement embodying their common views at this time, when the Turkish people, in the midst of very grave economic, political, and social problems, is searching for a course that will lead to the realization of all its aspirations. We believe that such a statement will open the way for significant debates that will prove helpful in the solution of our problems.

1. We believe that the aims assumed by the Atatürk reforms, such as attainment of the level of modern civilization, the final solution of the problem of education, the enlivening of Turkish democracy, the realization of social justice, and the establishment of a democratic regime on firm foundations depend

* Extract from "Bildiri" ("Declaration"), *Yön (Direction)*, Istanbul, No. 1 (December 20, 1961), 12–13. This English version has been adapted from Frank Tachau's translation, which appeared in *Middle Eastern Affairs* (March, 1963), pp. 75–78.

upon the success we will achieve in rapid economic development, that is, in the rapid increase in the level of national productivity.

(*a*) In the broadest sense, Westernization—the aim of the Atatürk reforms—can be realized by approaching the level of productivity of the West. As the level of productivity in Turkey rises, the country's social structure will change, the dichotomy between city and village will disappear, opportunities will increase, and rationalism, the basis of Western civilization, will spread among the masses.

(*b*) Given a low level of productivity, the hope for a basic rise in the cultural level of the masses is a sheer delusion, no matter how much effort is put forth. Unemployment, starvation, nakedness, cold, and misery will impede the orientation of the masses toward education; the struggle for existence will assume greater importance than the urge to learn.

(*c*) Democracy is, above all, a regime based on human dignity and the supreme value of the individual. A government that cannot eliminate hunger, unemployment, and homelessness, no matter how much we may favor it, will inevitably cease to be democratic and ultimately will collapse. . . .

(*d*) A policy of social justice that fails to emphasize the rapid increase in national income will be unable to do more than share the poverty. On the other hand, a development policy that does not recognize social justice is doomed to failure. Consequently, one of the chief means of [achieving] a policy of social justice must be an increase in the level of productivity.

2. We consider it essential that such persons as teachers, writers, politicians, labor leaders, businessmen, and administrators, who are in a position to give direction to Turkish society, reach agreement on the main tenets of a clear philosophy of development.

(*a*) In the twentieth century, as the result of developments in the means of communication, the masses have learned of the high standard of living prevailing in other countries or among other social classes; more important, they realize that the achievement of this standard is possible for them. As a result, our poverty is even more painfully obvious. The situation is further aggravated by the rapid population increase and the failure to deal with our problems in a manner consonant with this increase.

Turkey is today in a serious economic and social crisis. The social crisis has emerged as a natural consequence of the economic crisis. A backward agriculture, quite apart from failing to secure the resources needed to match our increasing imports, is not even capable of meeting the basic needs of the increasing population. Landlessness, which pushes increasing numbers into the cities, results in difficulties in the way of employment and housing for this flood of new urbanites. If basic measures are not taken, then the problems of shanty towns and unemployment will become dangerous sores in the national life and may [even] prepare the way for social and political upheaval.

Because of the rapid increase in population, half of the Turkish population consists of children under the age of eighteen. As recent events have clearly shown, a large segment of this avalanche of children will be deprived of education and a secure future.

(*b*) The most deplorable fact is that, among those who have control over Turkey's future, there is as yet no realization of the serious problems that confront us. They have not as yet adopted an applicable philosophy of development. The concept of development has not yet been understood in all its ramifications. What is overlooked is that development cannot succeed without basic reforms and, by the same token, that one of the results of development will be changes in the social order and in individual behavior. Consequently, it is idle to wish for development, while at the same time opposing fundamental reforms and new methods. The upshot of this situation is that many of those in positions of authority in the society sincerely believe that the solution to the development problem lies in a slight increase in foreign aid, the development of tourism, and increased exports of agricultural products.

(*c*) The task of directing the development of Turkey toward a clearly defined goal is beyond the competence of the State Planning Organization, which is responsible to the political authorities. It is true that the State Planning Organization, which has brought the country's leading experts together, has drawn up a strategy of development and indicated the first steps to be taken in this direction. But this cannot be considered adequate. The prospective plan will merit consideration and attain success only when those who are in a position to give direction to Turkish society arrive at some agreement on a clear philosophy of development.

3. As starting points for our philosophy of development, we consider it essential to utilize all our capabilities, rapidly to increase investments, to plan the entire economy, to bring about social justice for the masses, to put an end to exploitation, and to make the masses masters of democracy.

We believe these goals are attainable through a new concept of statism.

(*a*) The Turkish economy will continue as a mixture of private and state enterprise. However, we do not believe that an economic system based primarily on private enterprise can bring Turkey, given its present social structure, to the level of contemporary civilization quickly and with social justice. In the light of history and economics, we believe that development based on private enterprise is slow, painful, wasteful, and impossible for an underdeveloped country dedicated to the principle of social justice. Such a development process, moreover, is not democratic, because, in a broad sense, political power depends upon economic power.

(*b*) Private enterprise depends on profits. If the motive power of an economic system consists of the profit incentive, the inevitable result will be a very slow rate of development, increasing inequities in the distribution of income, the adoption of a philosophy of a "millionaire in every district," the wasteful diversion of national wealth from the most useful to the most profitable projects, and the frequent occurrence of stagnation and unemployment. Nowadays, no underdeveloped country can afford these features.

The process of development in the Western countries, in spite of colonization and [other] favorable conditions, took place slowly, wastefully, and with difficulty, and was realized under liberal regimes that were not subject to popular vote. It is only in the twentieth century, with the basic rise in the level of productivity, that the economic systems of the Western countries have been brought to a satisfactory level of operation. In spite of this, the socialist parties, thinkers, and even liberal politicians of the West are pointing out that the economic systems of their own countries are wasteful, that they neglect basic necessities, and that they are inadequate from the point of view of rapid development and establishment of social justice.

(*c*) This is why we consider it necessary for Turkey to adopt a new concept of statism adequate to the needs of our day. Furthermore, we think it important to point out that the popular notion that private enterprise is inevitably profitable and state enterprise inevitably unprofitable has been fostered by extensive propaganda and is not based on sound arguments. We wish to recall that, in places like England and France, some industries have been nationalized for the purpose of realizing greater productive potential.

We believe the reasons why some state enterprises remain unprofitable are not to be sought in the policy of statism itself; on the contrary, the causes lie in our failure to apply a systematic and sufficiently extensive policy of statism.

4. We realize that the new statism, in order to attain the goals we have outlined above, must necessarily assume the form of judicious state intervention.

(*a*) In order to speed up development, it is necessary to increase national savings and to direct a significant portion of increased national income into savings; this can be accomplished only through broad and skillful state intervention.

Through statism, it is possible to increase the yield of taxation, one of the chief sources of savings. In our day, equity in taxation is a necessity. But the most important objection nowadays to taxation of high incomes, with the object of securing justice in taxation, is that this will result in a decline in investment by these funds. Statism, because it directs national savings into investment, counters this objection. Furthermore, statism brings about an equilibrium between the blessings and the pains of development and facilitates the adoption of the concept of saving by the masses. Additionally, the profits of state enterprises may, without deviations from the policy of taxation, become an important source of savings.

The goal of increasing savings potential by rechanneling unproductive forces into productive uses should become attainable by means of democratic but planned organization by the state.

(*b*) We believe that, with our present capabilities, it is possible, through better organization and administration, to create much greater and more productive savings than at present. Accordingly, total planning of economic life is necessary. Planning must bring with it the authority and the means to direct economic activity toward the desired goals in due time and in their entirety. One of the main conditions for securing this is that the key industries dominating various sectors of the economy be placed unconditionally under state control. We consider statism an indispensable element in any serious planning.

(*c*) Planning requires a transition to large economic units. The Turkish economy, however, is based upon very small enterprises in the fields of agriculture, industry, and commerce. Accordingly, it is necessary to develop productive cooperatives in order to organize farming, to spread cooperativism among small crafts, and to establish large units insofar as possible in agriculture and commerce, just as in industry, by reducing the number of retail sales outlets and shortening the process of transferring commodities from producer to consumer.

The foundations of the Turkish economic system must be built upon the organization of a broad cooperative sector side by side with the state sector.

(*d*) Statism is also the most suitable system for avoiding inequities in the distribution of income, realizing social security, countering the pressure of a class of middlemen on producers and consumers, and eliminating the imbalances among various districts.

The basic goals of statism are to bring the working class to a high level of merit and to raise wages derived from labor to a high level. A system that permits the oppression of those who must live from the sale of their mental and physical capabilities, a system that closes its eyes to the unjust profits earned by the land speculators and the middlemen who exploit the field of commerce, a system that fails to protest the fact that such as these enjoy incomes in excess of those earned by higher civil servants, intellectuals, professionals, and scientists—such a system cannot continue to operate in the twentieth century.

(*e*) Statism is a weapon in the struggle to resist the monopolization of the democratic regime by one element alone; it serves to secure control of democracy by the masses. The inauguration of a planned educational mobilization, widening the road opened by the village institutes, enabling millions of the peasants' and laborers' children to achieve equality in the field of education and in the national administration, preparation of the masses for improvement by means of adult education—all this can be accomplished only by means of a sensible policy of statism.

It is the function of statism to strengthen the labor unions and to achieve a fundamental land reform that will replace the rural landlords with farmers' organizations and cooperatives. Moreover, these measures can be accomplished only by means of state intervention.

The goals we wish to achieve may be subject to debate on this or that individual point. It is the purpose of this statement to open the way for such debates.

We believe that the first necessity for the resolution of the crisis in which we find ourselves today is for those who represent the various segments of Turkish society, as well as those who have attained positions of responsibility for the nation's future, to proclaim openly their ideas and to agree on a fundamental philosophy of development.

53. FOR FREEDOM AND PRIVATE ENTERPRISE*

Ahmet Hamdi Başar

Yön's *statement calling for socialism aimed clearly at limiting the freedom of private enterprise and eventually restricting party activities. The coalition government, composed of the Republican Party, which supported statism, and the Justice Party, which supported private enterprise, was deadlocked in passivity. It failed to back officially any specific ideology. The ideological discussions, therefore, were carried on freely by individuals and private organizations.*

A statement opposing Yön's *statism-socialism appeared in* Barış Dünyası (World of Peace), *a review edited by Ahmet Hamdi Başar (b. 1897). An advocate of rational economic development based on private enterprise, Başar considered classical socialism and capitalism obsolete and recommended first national consolidation and then economic methods suitable to conditions in developing countries. Başar, who had written a dozen books on various Turkish economic and political problems, believed that both socialists and liberals had a wrong conception of the material world and its relation to social values. The statement of* Barış Dünyası *was submitted to, and received the endorsement of, the trade and industrial chambers, which, in all Turkish cities and towns, represent entrepreneurs, trade and craft organizations, and other sections of the middle classes engaged in economic occupations.*

The main solution to our problems is work. Article 1. Our main problem is the need to increase our working capacity to the maximum, to use our resources in the most rational fashion, to raise our production well above the present level, and to achieve national development in the shortest possible time. We believe that large investments will increase work capacity and productivity, and we shall thus solve all our problems.

Statism is a commonly acceptable regime. Article 2. Our development depends on our consolidation as a modern nation and on acquisition of technology. We are faced with endless needs in the social, economic, political, and cultural fields. These could be solved through the regulatory, protectionist, constructive intervention and assistance of the state. We consider such statism as a doctrine and a regime acceptable to all.

* Extract from Ahmet Hamdi Başar, "Kalkınma Prensiplerimiz" ("Our Principles of Development") *Barış Dünyası (World of Peace)*, Istanbul, April, 1962, pp. 18–22.

It is dangerous for the state to become capitalist and investor. Article 3. The national development duties of the state must rely on a philosophy accepted by the majority. The political regime in charge of the administration must also conform to this view. The underdeveloped countries are deprived of the benefits of freedom and individualism under which the West developed. The development philosophy of a new country is faced by two problems totally different from each other; namely, whether the state should intervene in economic life as investor and administrator or should help establish a regime based on private property and initiative.

We believe that the state should assume the responsibility of establishing a regime of private property and private initiative and of assuring economic freedom for citizens. If the state assumed the role of a capitalist and employer and made the citizen a hired hand, this would create great dangers in underdeveloped societies. Those societies did not mature through a historical process and did not develop a middle class with enough consciousness to assume power over the administration. The political power [group] representing the state could deprive the citizen not only of his economic freedom but also of his political rights by expanding its authority in the economic field, regardless of whether it came to power through elections or other means.

The natural form to be taken eventually by such a regime would be an open or disguised dictatorship. One may think that a free political life will prevent the establishment of such a dictatorship. In reality, political parties in underdeveloped countries are not mature and are not based on classes with social consciousness as in the West. These parties are unable to play a peace-making role among social classes, and consequently society is surrendered to a partisan class. We, as a nation, ought to realize today from experience what it means to have the power in the hands of such a class, and that dictatorship can be established through partisanship even in a multi-party system. . . . State capitalism cannot be defended under any conditions in societies in which the ruling class consists of partisans [members of a party]. Consequently, we must face the state development policy in our country . . . with the demand that it achieve economic freedom for the citizen through a regime of private property and initiative and bring about social justice.

Our regime is a statism that should develop private enterprise and achieve social justice. Article 4. We believe that private initiative and acquisitive ambitions derive from natural human instincts that should not be destroyed but stimulated. The purpose is not to use these instincts as means for selfish, materialistic, unlawful, and immoral purposes. This can be prevented by giving proper form and spirit to the moral and legal regulatory order of society.

The liberal ideas of the eighteenth and nineteenth centuries cannot be accepted in any society today. The contemporary principle is social security and justice. The great differences in wealth and living standards can cause the destruction of both the poor and the rich. But the rights of capital, initiative, and labor should not be ignored, and a certain degree of social differentiation must be accepted. The modern, progressive societies can avoid disintegration if they accept the spirit of mutual understanding and assistance among social classes and consider events not from the viewpoint of class interests but from that of national interest. . . . A nonpartisan state can become an institution that would guarantee social peace and mutual assistance among classes. The state would lose its impartiality if it became a capitalist and employer . . . and the representative of a social class. The worker would naturally be deprived of his rights, chiefly the right to strike, in a system of state enterprise. Strikes would appear as rebellions against the state. . . .

Our middle class must be improved. Article 5. We cannot accept the idea that state capitalism is necessary in our country, because we do not yet possess a strong middle class. . . . In the republic, many people belonging to the middle class were trained . . . in trade, industry, banking, and other fields of activity. Private enterprise dominates in totality our trade and more than half of our industry, . . . and the overwhelming majority of agriculture is privately owned and managed. But the qualitative and quantitative development of our middle class was not accompanied by a similar evolution in the field of social responsibility, and this is most upsetting. Our middle class did not fight for economic freedom, as in the West. On the contrary, it was attached to the state to a very large extent, and consequently, despite its growth in strength, it avoided, to a shameful degree, becoming involved in or working for the solution of national problems and thus left itself open to dangers. We hope these people realize that they would not be able to go along forever with all those who would hold power. . . .

It is possible to achieve rapid economic development and social justice based on private enterprise. Article 6. We believe that, in view of the present conditions, Turkey could neither reach rapidly the level of contemporary civilization nor achieve social justice without an economic system based on private enterprise. We believe, in the light of history and economic sciences, that economic development not based on private enterprise is faulty, costly . . . and unable to prevent in developing countries the annihilation of opposition by those who hold state power in their hands. . . . Private enterprise is based on profit, which is the driving power of the economic system. The state can take measures to enlarge profit opportunities and thus strengthen the enterprises and increase the speed of development. . . . In our country, the state enterprises operate in many fields in a manner far costlier than private enterprises. The state enterprises, despite long term credits given at 1.5 per cent interest, foreign loans, and many privileges, . . . cannot compete with private enterprises, . . . which operate with great difficulty and still make profits. . . . We want to point out that the claim that state enterprises could be profitable and productive is deprived of sound foundations and rests on propaganda. The fact that the state and its enterprises are transferring some of their operations to [private] contractors in order to become more effective proves this point. . . . We find it possible and useful that the state should retire in a planned and programed manner from the operation of economic enterprises. It can encourage the establishment of cooperatives and joint companies by entrepreneurs and capitalists, . . . producers, managers, and workers, and urge the people to invest in them.

We are totally opposed to state capitalism. Article 7. We find dangerous the state investment of funds secured through taxation and the subjection of high incomes to heavy taxes. Such a policy would destroy the sources of income. . . .

Our greatest problem is the establishment of a modern state. Article 8. The state structure, organization, and mentality . . . are, to a large degree, incapable of achieving the nation's material and moral development and consolidation and [its] democratic administration. . . . Despite many successful reforms, we have not been able to engage in building a modern, populist state because of our inability to reform [economic] statism. The modern state [should be] in the hands of capable people, experts and elites with morality and integrity. . . . In addition, there is a need for planning bodies to regulate the society's life as a whole by cooperating in a democratic fashion with professional and popular organizations and by defining state responsibilities and authority in conformity with popular sovereignty. . . .

It is possible to solve all problems in peace and mutual understanding. Article 9. We are firmly against all movements that create animosity among classes, groups, and nations. We want to work for embodying in our life a moral mentality nourished by love, a feeling of mutual assistance, sacrifice, and tolerance, . . . which we find in the noble character of our nation. . . . National solidarity based on brotherly feelings, mutual sacrifice, assistance, and tolerance is the only road to development.

54. ON YÖN AND STATISM*

Kemal H. Karpat

Yön's *proposal for adopting statism was criticized on social, political, and historical grounds by Kemal H. Karpat, a Turkish political scientist who has taught at Montana State University and at New York University and who is now Professor of Middle East Studies at the University of Wisconsin. The article appeared in* Forum, *a liberal, social-oriented review published in Ankara,*

* Extract from Kemal H. Karpat, "Yön ve Devletçilik Üzerine" ("On Yön and Statism"), *Forum,* Ankara, December 1, 1962, pp. 8–9; December 15, 1962, pp. 13–15; January 1, 1963, pp. 11–13.

only after it had been read and rejected in advance by both socialists and defenders of free enterprise, who found that it expressed an unfamiliar viewpoint and represented a new approach.

I have carefully read the declaration and the articles published in *Yön*. To express concisely the scattered ideas floating around is to render a service to the intellectual life of the country. I appreciate this and hope that these ideas will be given additional elaboration. It is impossible not to agree with the general purposes expressed at the beginning of *Yön*'s declaration. However, the idea of total statism, through which these aims are to be attained, does not correspond either to Turkey's realities or to her economic and social history.

The main struggle in our country today is, to put it generally, a struggle between the state bureaucracy and productive groups. This bureaucracy and the intellectual groups formed within it have hitherto decided their role in society and their relations with the people according to their interests and views and by having control of power. Thus, from a position above the people, they have made modernization and progress a cultural problem and have refused to recognize the economic and social problems that are to give depth, significance, and form to modernization. In reality, theirs was an elitist attitude; the intelligentsia was an aristocratic group that lived above society, it was supported by the state, and derived its power justification from diplomas.

The habits dating from the Ottoman Empire have had a great effect upon the birth of such a state of affairs. But the principal reason is that the bureaucracy, in other words, the intelligentsia, has held absolute control over the power of the state. The new intelligentsia formed after the Tanzimat [1839] took the place of the old ulema (one can rightly call the new intellectual elite the modern ulema) and found in the sultan the only obstacle to its own power. Previously, the sultan had abolished the Janissaries [the footsoldiers who checked the throne's power] and had thus infinitely increased his own power. But in the period of the *Ittihad ve Terakki* [Union and Progress Party of Young Turks] (1908–18), the sultan's authority was greatly reduced and there was no power left to check the intelligentsia. This situation might have been a step forward toward a kind of preparation leading to popular sovereignty or democracy. The next logical step was to set up democracy, and this was the main purpose of the republican regime. The full implementation of this idea of democracy, which manifests itself in the shape of a constitution and laws, is a long and difficult process, which we are facing now.

It is unnecessary to dwell further upon these background matters. The main point is this: The intelligentsia, in which the bureaucracy is included, has emerged as a distinct social group. It has its own philosophy, point of view, interests, means of communications, schools, etc. It has regarded each event and every other social group and its activities from its own point of view and has determined its interest position accordingly by using the state power, which it has held in its own hands. For instance, during the Union and Progress era, the state (I regard the government as an institution that functions in accordance with the philosophy and interests of those who command it) attempted to create an entrepreneurial group. Such an action had a nationalistic goal, but was also dictated by the need to create a supporting social and economic basis for the state—that is to say, for the intelligentsia. The bureaucracy and the intelligentsia emerged as distinct social groups and viewed themselves as superior to other social groups. They took upon themselves the duty of guiding other groups, not through free discussion, but through the force of state power. This situation is the greatest disaster that can befall a society. Every society is managed by leaders—a kind of elite—and there is probably no other solution to this situation. But there is one condition; the elite and the intellectuals must come out of society without severing their contacts with it. They must maintain their ties with the community, represent the views of various groups in the community, and live in harmony with them.

The separation of the intellectual from society and the assumption of a materially and spiritually superior position for himself will prevent him from being a true leader. People believe only in those men who have come from their own ranks, in those who understand and respect them and who secure their material and cultural development. But people will believe in the intellectual who secures the free development of all people through their own participation. No one will submit to being taken by the hand and led like a child. Everyone would prefer to develop freely his own personality. The main problem is to provide everyone with equal opportunity for development in every sense, and this is something that has never been achieved in our history.

In Turkish social history, the intellectuals and the people have been separated. The power of the state has passed in absolute fashion into the hands of the intellectual. This situation has tragically resulted in breeding suspicion and distrust between the two sides. In order to bridge this gap, Ziya Gökalp and Atatürk (through the principle of populism) exerted certain efforts, but these efforts have been perverted by the intelligentsia, which has applied populism in an erroneous and incomplete fashion. If the history of the War of Independence [1919–22] is objectively studied, it will show that, besides indignation at the invading forces [the Allies and Greeks], the masses followed Atatürk, hoping to be rid of the oppression of the intellectual bureaucratic group. The popular program prepared by the government in September, 1920, and the discussions around it are enough to give an outline of the basic ideas of the Turkish Republic concerning the wishes of the lower groups. The people will recognize the intellectual's value, not according to his diploma, but according to his practical social, economic, and cultural contribution to their own betterment. In order to understand the relations of a person with other people, it is necessary to look first at that person's place in society and to consider whether he has more political, social, and cultural privileges than others. To find out this relationship, one must look not at the existing laws but at reality, at facts. If the intelligentsia separates itself from society and gives itself the air of a superior being by relying on diplomas [this is the remainder of a habit dating from the *Icazetname,* diplomas given to graduates of religious schools of the ulema], then the people will be estranged from it. Just as the people opposed the old ulema in various ways, now they oppose the "modern" intellectual, whose social position is not different from the ulema's. The old ulema were supposedly concerned only with abstract religious matters, which were considered above everything else. The modern intellectual has treated science in a similar fashion. He has separated science from the human being and society and has idealized it like a divine revelation. Thus, science is separated from the concept of utility, and, on top of it all, the intellectual has declared himself the protector of science and has ceased being scientific. On the other hand, the intellectual has abundantly made use of the social position and the economic gain provided by this role of protector of science.

The evolution of our social history has another aspect. The disintegration of the old organization of the Ottoman state left the productive groups utterly unprotected and with no means to deal with the new groups emerging as a result of the new social and economic conditions. For instance, the land regime began to change rapidly. The *miri,* or state lands, started to become private property, and this development took place within the framework of economic and social conditions that were different from those of the past. New social groups and a clash of interests appeared on the scene. Therefore, in order to understand the social situation in Turkey, one must study comparatively the developments in the bureaucratic structure of the Ottoman state and the developments in the social body and to ascertain thoroughly their mutual relations. As developments in both bodies progressed in different directions, the clash between state and society became unavoidable.

During the republic, this dichotomy in development continued and finally gave rise to the multi-party system and to the present situation. The transition to the multi-party system (1945) is the most important event in Turkish social history. It is the first concrete evidence indicating the two different types of social and political developments occurring in two hundred years of Turkish history. It is an event that provides the most ample opportunities for future development. The multi-party system (not the Democratic Party) has led to the mobilization of social groups and has provided the opportunity for them to exercise pressure on the state and on its bureaucracy with the ultimate purpose of defining for them a new role conforming to the needs of a modern society. It was very natural that this political movement, which led to a complete civilian administration, should give rise to deep reactions and to conflicts. The main problem was to change the role of the government as an institution with absolute control over society and its destiny in such a way as to place it in the service, and under the control, of society. In other words, it was necessary for the government to become empirical in its judgment and functional in its role in order to meet man's daily needs. These were events that took place in Western Europe in the seventeenth and eighteenth centuries. They marked the end of state domination over the individual and its acquisition of new roles. This event at last is taking place in Turkey. It has been achieved not by any single party but by the multi-party system itself. I, personally, do not think that the multi-party system is opposed to Kemalism; it is its natural result. The real problem is to complete the transition to the multi-party system and democracy.

The relations between state and individual are being changed. The political and social attitudes inherited from the autocratic past have been profoundly shaken. These developments in turn have created profound repercussions in our traditionalist thoughts and attitudes. If we detach ourselves today from hate and passion and look clearly at the progress registered during the last fifteen years of multi-party life, we will perceive that the democratic way we have chosen is a very sound one. We will then see more clearly that the troubles and crises we have gone through have not been in vain.

Atatürk's reforms aim ultimately at bringing freedom to the individual. To give these reforms fascist meanings and to identify them with coercion is to deny completely their spirit and the lessons of history. That the multi-party life has led to politically motivated reactionary concessions and has destroyed many useful institutions and debilitated some of Atatürk's basic principles is a known fact. But if we compare what we have lost with what remains, we see that the system set up by Atatürk is standing firmly on its feet.

The greatest mistake of the Democratic Party was its failure to understand the relations between state and society. It regarded the state as an institution existing for the sake of the party and used it as such instead of transforming it into an impartial institution without damaging its prestige. The state needed to develop the technique of modern administration, while using impartially the authority granted to it by law. After the limits of state authority had been properly determined, the enforcement of this authority and the respect and obedience due to those who enforce the law would have been accepted voluntarily. Such a relationship is the foundation of modern society. But if the state is not impartial, the groups that take control of the government (the intellectuals and the bureaucracy under one-party rule, certain interests under Democratic Party rule) will use it for their own advantage and, in the end, degenerate it. In spite of all this, many problems have been aired during the multi-party era, and the relations between the state and society and social groups have been better understood. This alone is great progress. Today, we are making efforts to create a progressive order, and we will sooner or later achieve this. But to look upon compulsion and force, that is to say, upon an authoritarian regime, as the only way to achieve such an order amounts to denying human rights and freedom, which are the very basis of a progressive order. Let us not forget that, in all our history, authoritarianism, dictatorship, and compulsion have been the dominant methods and have sapped almost to the extinguishing point the creative strength of the people. We should extricate ourselves from such habits and accept the whole range of human freedoms, this being the main condition for creating a progressive society.

The most important result of the social evolution we have undergone recently has been the change in the meaning attached to the state and in the function of the intelligentsia, which had achieved social position and economic power through control of the state. Slowly, the intellectual is entering into the service of society; he is using his energy for this purpose and is being forced to comply with a new system of modern, democratic values. This transformation creates profound psychological problems that are not quite accessible to objective analysis. I am not going to take up these questions *in extenso*.

The economic difficulties that have resulted from inflation since 1953 and the justified complaints of state employees who face decreasing living standards have given rise to a negative attitude toward the multi-party system and the political parties. But there is also the reaction of the intelligentsia against the new functions and roles imposed upon the state and society by the requirements of democratic life. Perhaps the greatest reaction and frustration in a person is caused by failure to reach the position of power and social prestige he expected. Our intellectual, prior to the establishment of the multi-party system, had prepared himself for important positions and had been brought up to look upon a diploma from an institution of higher learning as sufficient to secure him a high position. If, in addition, one could get a degree from an institution abroad and stammer a foreign language, there was no impediment to the easy attainment of top positions. The multi-party system has upset all such calculations. In the new system, income and position come either as a result of work and achievement or else by joining a political party. Whether joining a party is evil or good is not important. The important thing is the fact itself. The intellectual who did not join the winning party, who joined it but failed to achieve a position, or who made the mistake of joining the wrong party felt that he had missed his due reward. Then he went to join the group of passive malconents sitting on the side and began to nourish a grudge, not against the party that failed his expectations, but against the system as a whole. This intellectual became a victim of the multi-party system and started to criticize it. In order to justify himself, he supposedly judged everything from the viewpoint of Atatürk's reforms. In other words, he used Atatürk as a shield and, disregarding facts, stigmatized every move he disapproved of as contrary to Atatürk's reforms. But the leaders of the political parties were also members of the intelligentsia, the difference being that the critical intellectuals were not in power, whereas the intellectuals being criticized were in power. Undoubtedly, there are Kemalist intellectuals who see events as they are, but these are few.

The unfortunate aspect of these developments is the fact that neither those who are critical nor those who are being criticized have been able to understand the true nature of the impasse in which they find themselves. Both groups are used to treating all national events in a personal manner and thus are unable to understand the intellectual deficiencies of the old system, which has made them what they are. Should the critical party come to power, it will do exactly what its predecessor did. The way out of the impasse calls for a new point of view, for a new human philosophy, which would enable the intelligentsia to look upon and analyze men and human events objectively. To look upon human beings with respect, to love them, and to act in order to develop them mentally and physically is the foundation of this new philosophy. The first thing to do to acquire this philosophy is to get rid of ideas proposing to use human beings as lifeless tools to achieve this or that aim.

The reactionary policies of certain parties seemed to justify the intelligentsia's anti-democratic attitude, but this is not enough to condemn the multi-party system *in toto*. If the opinion of workers and peasants—in other words, of those citizens who are truly productive—were to be asked, it is certain that they would heartily support the multi-party system. For this system has given them a chance to gain dignity and the right to enjoy life. Let there be no mistake. People will not become fanatically attached to this or that party. They will behave according to their own interests, and this is a completely natural attitude. If a leader in the past went beyond all bounds of moderation in using power, there is no reason to blame the people and make them pay for the leader's errors by abolishing a system in which people have a potential say. But the intelligentsia, not being used to attaching any importance to the feelings and ideas of the common people, has brushed aside the people's opinion about the multi-party system with an old attitude: "What do the ignorant people know?"

Now let us turn to our main subject, to the statism that *Yön* defends. My opinion is that many of the intellectuals who defend the idea of statism are merely revealing their negative reaction against the multi-party system and democracy. Under the present circumstances in Turkey, the creation of a statist system is only an effort to restore to the intellectual the privileged social position he had lost. There is no doubt that economic and social problems have, in our era, come into the foreground and exercised a profound impact on political life. But such a situation does not necessitate the intrusion of the state in every economic activity and its regulation of all social life. One cannot decide in advance that various voluntary, private organizations are unable to cope with and solve at least part of the economic and social problems. Such a thought is dangerous and directly opposed to human nature. If one believes that free individuals in a society cannot solve, through free discussion, the problems of that society, then it is difficult to believe that the intelligentsia of that society, which is principally to blame for social backwardness, should be able to solve such problems. How can one say that the intelligentsia, which for fifteen years has not produced any noteworthy economic, political, or social work (a small group of capable men excepted), should, after taking over state power, become capable of solving all the society's problem? Instead of advancing total solutions, would it not be more practical to take specific problems one by one and give to every individual the opportunity of participating in the discussion and eventual solution of such problems?

To what extent would it be right to expand infinitely the powers of the State Planning Organization? The latter has only recently been set up, has put forth only a few statistics, and has not yet accumulated even the necessary data or experience for economic planning. One should not jeopardize the vital role to be played by the State Planning Organization in preparing objective plans for economic development by turning it into an instrument of political power. This attitude will be detrimental to the very existence of the institution itself. There is no doubt that, under present conditions in Turkey, the state is bound to take over many public duties. But to assign to the state by arbitrary decision all kinds of new responsibilities without taking into account the individuals and organizations that have the means to meet such responsibilities is to give to statism a political, authoritarian, and monopolistic meaning.

Yön sees large-scale investment by the government and the resulting increase in production as the only way out of Turkey's present economic *impasse*. . . . But the extreme statism proposed as the chief means of realizing this aim is no solution. To try to regulate all investments under the state's strict authority would cause the flight of private capital from the market and even from the country. It seems to me that *Yön* talks of economics, production, and related problems in a mechanical, abstract fashion. *Yön* thinks that a few economic theories, a few decisions, and an organization to administer these decisions—all these being decided on a theoretical basis without proper attention being given to the individuals and society—will cure every social and economic evil. The success of economic policy in an underdeveloped country such as Turkey is determined by a variety of "meta-economic" factors that have to be carefully taken into account. I recall the words of a famous Harvard professor, who said that he spent thirty years studying investment, production, and economic development problems, but in the end realized that all these problems were ultimately related to the social structure of a community and to the conflicting ideas and interests therein. The problems defined as economic were in reality social and cultural.

Yön is not concerned with objective economic forces. It is concerned with the effects created by economic forces, i.e., not with the facts of economy, but with its repercussions. *Yön* regards social justice as the justification for statism. In order to secure social justice, it recommends, first of all, heavy taxation for persons with high incomes. The fundamental point of departure for *Yön*, therefore, is the desire to create a kind of equality in income. In order to prove the existence of social injustice, it compares the incomes of real estate speculators with those of high government officials and university professors. It is obvious that this is done in order to appeal to emotions. Those who understand economics just a little realize very well that such comparisons do not properly reflect reality. To compare better the income distribution and to arrive at more correct results, one must compare various sectors of the economy and keep in mind also their contribution to the national economy. One should not capitalize on extreme profits made during brief periods of crisis. Moreover, wherever private property and free enterprise exist, there is bound to be a difference of income between various groups.

However, all these do not imply that there is no problem of social justice in Turkey. Without doubt, the need to secure social justice is one of Turkey's great problems and it definitely must be solved. But personally, I should like to see talks of an objective nature between those who complain of the lack of social justice and those who are in a position to do something about it. For instance, why not confront businesses and employers with trade union representatives or with organizations of craftsmen and shopkeepers and with cooperatives, instead of expecting state intervention from the top? Anyway, the greatest grievances of the working class are directed against state enterprises. The state has not been able to secure social justice within its own enterprises; I doubt if it can achieve it on a country-wide basis. (Of course, social justice should be determined according to the individual's contribution to national income. I must state that the demands for economic freedom of certain groups in private enterprise, which have made huge profits without contributing to national income and which are presently attacking *Yön* and want it prosecuted, are baseless, antidemocratic, and reactionary.)

I don't believe that a group (intelligentsia) that defends social justice in an abstract fashion and styles itself as its representative and enforcer will achieve success. I have never seen, in any part of the world, true happiness created by a group that adopted abstract principles and acted arbitrarily in enforcing them to create happiness for others. Social justice can be achieved only by objectively looking at the reality of human life and by considering its problems one by one in the light of free thought. We cannot separate social justice from social responsibility. If we try to give each individual and organized body a sense of responsibility toward other individuals and toward society as a whole, we can then achieve social justice.

The spread of social responsibility can and is being undertaken by organizations, schools, the press, and literature. The intellectual can assume a creative function in society by imbuing himself with a sense of social responsibility. The first and most important reform must take place in the field of education, for our education is still immersed in vagueness, in cultural scholasticism with tinges of feudal romanticism. Our present educational system is turning out men trained in the concepts of the sixteenth century. The state can accomplish a reform in education and should help to educate men with a sense of social responsibility.

Yön defends statism as the only solution to economic problems. But if the state gains absolute authority in the economic field, it is bound to spread its power into other fields of activity. In a country such as ours, where the state is used to regulate all the material and spiritual aspects of the individual's life (only in the multi-party era did we begin to free ourselves from this), it is obvious that the state will eventually control all activity.

Yön points to the widening scope of state activity in the West and uses it as another reason for expanding statism. There are great differences, however, between the meaning attached to the state in the West and *Yön*'s conception of the state. In the West, the state is a body performing public duties under the control and administration of the people. If some private enterprises have in time been taken over by the state, this is because the services performed by them have become public. Besides, these organizations passed under state control as a result of mutual agreement (and with compensation), without giving rise to any crises. Western man regards the state as a body born within society, not above it, and as working to meet the people's needs and changing its functions according to such needs. He does not recognize the state as a divine being with absolute powers over the individual. The state (rather, the Eastern concept of the state, with which *Yön* would tackle economic development) has always dominated our society and used its authority to give to the social body whatever form it deemed necessary. Above everything else, the state has regarded itself as the protector of morality. Instead of being preoccupied with the individual's practical needs and conditions of life, it has tried to give man lessons in idealism. It has taken truth, ideals, and morality out of the people's conscience, has defined them legally according to its own philosophy, and has forced individuals to accept them.

Turks have attributed the decay of the state to the weakening of morality since the time Koçübey issued his memorandum in 1630 on the causes of disintegration of the Ottoman government. But we have not learned to think about the factors that can make people moral or immoral. If we could connect matters of morality to events in economic and political life and to organizations, then we could arrive at more valid results. One cannot study the factors influencing people's inner life by separating them from social conditions, especially state philosophy and policy. To ignore all these forces is nothing but a medieval thought. Personally, I think that the greatest reform in Turkey would occur if a radical change in the meaning of the state took place. Naturally, the state will continue to exist as an organization, but its philosophy and function will change.

If there is unrest in our society today, the principal reason lies in the disharmony between state and society. While the latter is struggling to conform to the requirements of the twentieth century, the state is still tied to an Ottoman conception of authority. . . .

The statism proposed by *Yön* is also described as socialism. In fact, statism is described as an inescapable result and means of socialism. *Yön* greatly confuses issues. Socialism did not develop in the West out of the sheer imagination of an intellectual group. It came out of the working masses and developed in connection with their lives. Socialism originally was a free, voluntary movement, which strove to achieve respect for human liberties and made great contributions to human culture. It came about as the result of a natural social evolution. Western socialism tried to avoid those opportunistic intellectuals who joined the movement out of whim and caused the greatest damage to its cause. One must not insist on comparing the problems of socialism and statism in the underdeveloped countries with the situation in the West and expect that the two will develop in similar and parallel fashion.

I believe that it is necessary to take into account the conditions of each country when analyzing movements that appear similar in name only. That is why conditions in Turkey must be studied objectively and free from doctrinal bias. I believe that to look at Turkish conditions today from the viewpoint of certain doctrines—namely, socialism or capitalism—is to ignore the country's realities. Turkey's main problem is to free state and society from the effects of surviving Ottoman concepts of society, government, and authority. The first thing to do today is to complete the transition to a modern concept of the state.

It can be said that the statism proposed by *Yön* may enhance these efforts and even give society a modern aspect. I believe, however, that what *Yön* wants to accomplish by using authority was already accomplished by Atatürk, who underlined the future direction of development—a democratic country with a sense of national identity. There is no need to turn back. The thing to do is to build upon the existing foundations, and the way to do this is not extreme statism. The way out is to study objectively the new social groups that have already emerged along with their interests, desires, and organizational progress. The greatest progress achieved so far by various social groups has been the emergence of group identity, interest, consciousness, and the formulation of demands for a respectable place in the new social structure.

Turkey is now at a turning point. There is a great awakening all over the nation. We are confronted with a social awakening. For the first time in our history, there is an awakening from below. This is a constructive awakening, as long as it is correctly understood and correctly channeled. Masses of people, yearning for civilization and freedom, are forcing the state and society to conform to the necessities of this age. At various times in our recent history, we have seen examples of this yearning by people for a new form of life. But every single manifestation has been repressed under various pretexts. The forward movement of people for freedom has been repressed, sometimes because of religion and sometimes for reasons of order and security. Those asked to provide the justification for such repressions have usually created an absolute structure within which they assumed position and fame and ignored responsibility. In all these repressive actions, the main role has been played by the state or rather by those who, one way or the other, got hold of state power. They have destroyed progressive efforts and have coerced society to accept might as right. Thus, though the rulers have not been able completely to eradicate the creative force of man and society, they have succeeded in retarding their revival. After every forward attempt in the direction of progress and freedom, society has been forced into conservative molds and has been frozen in its *status quo* in order to prevent further efforts. Here, too, the state, relying on its absolute powers, has been able, through indoctrination and the creation of new values, to prevent the free development of man and society. Our social history has been dominated by conservative concepts and frozen social rules.

Our present social values and social philosophy are inherited, in good measure, from the period of decline of the Ottoman Empire. Though we are deprived of any dependable knowledge of history, still our affection for history is great. This is a result of a conservatism for which the main responsibility falls upon the state. (Certain progressive accomplishments in the cultural field are exceptions.) But all these conservative attitudes have begun to disappear, thanks to the changes that have come about in the last fifteen years. The old forms are breaking down. People are being freed from the tutelage of the state and are seeking and demanding their freedoms as individuals and social groups.

Our social order—which also means our political order—rests on two levels—upper and lower group structures. The huge masses in the lower group have for centuries been forcibly persuaded that they have no governing abilities or talents and have been accustomed to obey their leaders without asking any questions. It is obvious that this is not a civilized order of things. It is the result of the *Kul* philosophy[1] of the Ottoman state.

Formerly, in the traditionalist era, there was a suitable society and a political order upon which the Kul state could rest. Both the ruler and the ruled believed that their destinies were preordained and lived their lives without establishing connections with each other and without calling the upper groups to account for their actions. But today, the foundations upon which the old dualism was based have disappeared. The political education provided by the multi-party life on the one hand and the effects of economic development on the other have radically shaken society's old structure. This change, in turn, has forced upon man the need to find a new identity for himself as a free individual and to create a new society accordingly. Since people cannot create immediately new rules and new values to replace those belonging to the old order, there results a certain vacuum of regulatory rules, and a certain pessimism pervades society. Certainly, there is an atmosphere of pessimism in Turkey today. Hesitation, aimlessness, bewilderment, and lack of confidence are apparent. These must be regarded as normal. Those who act with such feelings are those who look backward, whereas those who look into the future know that the events taking place in Turkey today are preparing the way for a progressive and modern life.

One must be optimistic. For my part, I am very, very optimistic, for some of the objectives proposed earlier, during the founding of the republic, are today, at last, on their way toward materialization, even though through different means. Foremost among these objectives is the establishment of a truly free order. In such an order, people would express themselves, work, and live freely—without a tutor at their heads. They would learn how to govern themselves by themselves and create a political order that would contribute to their development. Today, this is happening in Turkey. Slowly, with great difficulty, a free order is being born. In these trying circumstances, people are discussing, fighting to find the best solutions for the future. If looked at from the viewpoint of the developments described above, *Yön*'s position—in spite of certain progressive ideas—is reactionary in spirit and in its general philosophy. It may seem progressive culturally, but from the point of view of political authority it is reactionary. *Yön* would raise the state above society and the individual and would remold men against their wishes. *Yön* is afraid of the awakening coming from below. Trusting the superiority of a few people, it has decided arbitrarily that the destiny of society should be entrusted to those few. The justification is supplied in the form of high-sounding slogans, such as progress, economic development, education, etc. . . . Actually, none of

1. The term is derived from the *Kapıkulu,* servants of the Ottoman Government or of the bureaucracy, who were trained to serve only the government without regard to the interests or opinions of social groups.

these can be accomplished without the willful participation of society. But *Yön* is not interested in people. It wants to force society to accept some abstract thoughts created by speculative reasoning. Though it claims all the time that it is socialistic and pro-labor, it is well known that *Yön* has little support in labor circles. The worker has suffered much from those who claimed to be "superior intellectuals" and who tried to solve everything by sitting at their desks. Labor knows this very well and does not come anywhere near accepting abstract, doctrinaire views.

In spite of its defense of freedom, *Yön* is really afraid of the essence of freedom. By entrusting freedom, or rather the freedom of action, to a small elite group, it wants to place the freedom, the desires, and the lives of other people under the "superior" custody of this enlightened group. In spite of its progressive claims, the fact that *Yön* wants a hierarchical order based on upper and lower strata means nothing but a return to the Ottoman state structure.

But under the conditions prevailing today in Turkey, such views, even if forced upon society, would not take root. We cannot engage any longer in an action that does not take into account the views and desires of individuals and social groups and does not involve them in making decisions in the economic and social fields. If we are to give a new form to our society and our state—and I think this is an absolute necessity—we can succeed only by conforming to the wishes of individuals and social groups. The first people to be consulted would be the manual and white-collar workers in villages and towns. If the leaders of our present political parties had reflected correctly the true needs and desires of the people, we should have been able to see how valid and mature is the thinking of our people.

Today, the leaders of most of the political parties can manipulate the votes of the people thanks to old loyalties and to their own privileges that stem from family prestige and property. Even this situation, which was more widespread several years ago, is now slowly disappearing, because the people have been awakened through political education. People are expecting to support and would support the persons and parties that would earnestly try to understand their problems and solve them. Should the intelligentsia give up its preoccupation with its own status and abstract theories and decide to mix with the people, it would then understand that the existing situation in Turkey is very different from what the intelligentsia assumes it to be.

The crux of the problem is to reform the structure of today's parties, something which the people can succeed in bringing about by putting pressure on the parties. The first condition for this is the abolition of the limitations imposed on party activities (through a law passed by the military government). Next comes the respect due to the elected authority, the Grand National Assembly, which has been elected by free vote. Today, there is a calculated and planned campaign against the Grand National Assembly, against democracy, and even against the main civil liberties. In a democracy, the actions of members of parliament, ministers, and officials can and should be made subject to question and criticism. But criticism should not shake the very foundations of the institutions that represent the popular will. Once the moral foundations of such institutions are undermined, it is very easy to destroy the institutions entirely and replace them with an extremist regime.

Perhaps without wishing to do so, and perhaps as a reaction to its political opponents, *Yön* has taken a stand against democratic institutions. It is very natural for our party life, which is only twenty years old, not to function in an ideal fashion. It is also natural that political life be upset by all kinds of difficulties. But, through trial and error, society will take its natural course and, with the pressure of forces from within, it will establish its true social and political identity. This has been the case everywhere, and it will be the case in Turkey.

Yön proposes to introduce the masses to democracy through statism. Today in Turkey, the masses are on the way to attaining democracy by themselves through political parties. The state could abolish the obstacles that prevent the people from achieving full political education. With this aim in view, it can help the social groups to reach mutual understanding while learning to remain neutral. *Yön* recognizes no place for political parties.

It is difficult to understand the kind of democracy *Yön* and its new statism would bring about. A real democracy today does not reject political parties. Consequently, *Yön*'s "democracy" is not the usual kind of democracy, *Yön* deals also with the problems of materializing "democracy." Since political parties are rejected, this "democracy" would use forced short cuts or revolutions. Consequently, the statism proposed by *Yön* is nothing but the coming to power without elections of a small intellectual group and the establishment of an authoritarian system. Such a system is not different from a fascist or semifascist regime. No kind of statism can survive in today's Turkey without recourse to some sort of fascist regime.

Let me sum up my thoughts. It is impossible not to agree with some of the factual views and objectives proposed by *Yön*. But the authoritarian, statist methods recommended in order to reach these objectives are dangerous and may lead Turkey to disaster. Though an authoritarian regime appears to be a short cut, still I believe that in reality it is long, hard, and full of dangers. The alternative is to widen the base of the present political system and strengthen it by taking into account public opinion, facts, and history. Thus, we may succeed in becoming a really progressive society. Today, a new social order is being created. Certain social groups that formerly wielded power and had special privileges are now forced to abandon their places to others. Meanwhile, the intellectuals must establish working relations with other groups and harmonize with the needs of society. Instead of giving orders from above, they must learn how to take their place in society according to their abilities and practical potentialities. It is natural that they will not easily abandon their old superior social status. They will defend their privileged positions in various ways by advancing all kinds of ideas. Viewed within the framework of the general social change occurring in Turkey, *Yön*'s ideas are in reality a defense of the old privileged position of the intellectuals. *Yön*'s arguments about economic development are in reality a justification for the power position sought by the intelligentsia in the new order. It is obvious that society needs economic development. Using this as a pretext, *Yön* wants to give power on behalf of statism to a small group and thus ignore other alternatives that are capable of securing real economic development. *Yön* ignores empirical approaches and instead adopts doctrines. It belittles the social groups, such as workers, small artisans, and tradesmen, that are the foundations of the new social order and of democracy by refusing to consult them.

Yön's philosophy is elitist. For this reason, if *Yön* does not revise its ideas, it will soon find itself the spokesman for an extreme rightist regime. This, like every other extremist regime, will be a source of disaster for Turkey. I think this is the result and meaning of statism as propounded by *Yön*.

55. STATISM—THE QUESTION OF LIMITS*

Sadun Aren

Until he was elected to the Grand National Assembly on the Labor Party ticket in 1965, Sadun Aren (b. 1922) was a professor of economics in the Faculty of Political Science, University of Ankara. Aren has been a staunch advocate of expanded government authority and statism—which in Turkey is regarded basically as a form of socialism. He has drifted gradually to the political left and has become an open advocate of complete socialism. The following article is an example of the rather strange reasoning Aren uses to enhance the prestige of state enterprise and to dismiss the private sector as insignificant.

Since statism emerged as a political means, the problem of its limits has become a basic question in some minds and a subject of debate. The question of setting limits to statism is also becoming an even more important topic of heated debate since the new statist viewpoint was issued in the last few days. According to this viewpoint, the public sector will have priority in our economic development, whereas the private sector will be used as its complement. . . . It is necessary to determine precisely the [economic] areas left to the public sector and those left to private enterprise. Otherwise, private enterprise, fearing that its operations will be taken over one day [by the government], may remain hesitant and fail to work with full enthusiasm. . . . This contention, if studied closely, is not as reasonable as it appears at first sight. Indeed, drawing a line between the private and public sectors may be feasible under two

* Extract from Sadun Aren, "Devletçilik, Sınır Meselesi" ("Statism—The Question of Limits"), *Yön* (*Direction*), Istanbul, January 17, 1962, p. 16.

forms. First, one may list one by one the areas [of economic activity] reserved or forbidden to public enterprises. This can be called a legal boundary, since it can be established by law. The second way of determining the boundary can be devised by relying on economic considerations. Consequently, the limits of public enterprises will be determined by studying the facts and reasons that necessitated the introduction of statism. . . .

[The author points out the practical difficulties encountered in determining by legal measures the limits of statism, reminding us that private and public enterprises functioned side by side and that no private enterprise was nationalized during the previous thirty years.]

Consequently, one might think that those who demand the limitation of state enterprises are afraid more of the competition of such enterprises than of nationalization. One cannot ask that boundaries be drawn based on such reasoning. The entrepreneur investing in a certain field is bound to think of other entrepreneurs investing in the same area and be prepared to meet their competition. Equally, he must think of the competition of public enterprises. The only valid reservation in this field may concern the state's intervention to alter competitive conditions in favor of public enterprise. Such an objection cannot be sustained in a serious statist system, because the state will take into consideration only the economic rationale in the administration of public enterprises. . . .

Those who desire to limit the scope of public enterprises by taking into consideration the type of enterprises [to be left to the state] aim basically at limiting the volume of the public economic sector. If the areas open to public enterprise were limited, it would be very natural, then, that these enterprises would be prevented from expanding, and their relative place in the national economy would be limited. . . . We must point out, first of all, that a country that has decided to achieve economic development through public enterprise cannot establish in advance a limit to the activities of such enterprises. . . . The boundary between the private and public enterprise will be determined by two actual factors; first, the nature of enterprise, and second, the financing power and the enterprising ability available to both the private and public sectors. The nature of the enterprise implies whether or not there is need of a special effort and care—that is to say, whether the personal profit motive functions effectively. The personal profit motive operates, as is known, in agriculture, small manufacturing, commerce, transportation, and repair jobs. . . .

On the other hand, in big industry and trade there cannot be a question of special effort. The personal profit motive therefore loses its efficiency, since the work is carried out by officials and workers. . . . Financing—that is to say, the [monetary] means available to private and public sectors—is determined by the tax and credit policy adopted by the political power [government] and cannot form a natural boundary. If the government imposes heavy taxes, the investment ability of the private sector is restricted, and vice versa. If the new concept of statism is preserved, and even if taxation is carried on to an advanced point, still the individuals will have an income that they can use freely or save. If the private sector shows entrepreneurial ability, it can amass private savings and enter into major dealing and the private sector may thus expand. If the private sector acts with reticence and the public sector is more enterprising, then the latter will expand.

56. THE PHILOSOPHY AND PURPOSE OF THE LABOR PARTY OF TURKEY*

The Labor Party of Turkey was established by a small group of trade unionists in 1961. One year later, its leadership was assumed by Mehmet Ali Aybar (b. 1910), a Turk who was educated in France, where he became a Marxist. Despite its efforts, the Labor Party has failed to attract many workers, and its membership is composed mainly by the urban intelligentsia. Yet the party's propagandists, although hindered by an internal struggle between "dogmatists" and "revisionists," have fought energetically to spread their views in towns and even villages. For tactical reasons, the party has accepted outwardly the idea of free parliamentary elections. An extensive party program was adopted at the party convention on February 11, 1964. These excerpts are taken from a pamphlet expressing the party's basic viewpoint, which was preserved in the new program. (See also Kemal H. Karpat, "Socialism and the Labor Party of Turkey," Middle East Journal, *XXI [Spring, 1967], 157–72.)*

In Articles 2 and 3 of its bylaws, the Labor Party of Turkey [Türkiye Işçi Partisi—TIP] has indicated the people to whom it belongs, the people whose rights, freedom, and interests it defends, and the means to be used in attaining these goals. The Labor Party of Turkey is the party of our poor people, who depend on their labor for their livelihood. The two articles describing the characteristics and purposes of the party are as follows:

Article 2: The characteristics of the party. TIP is the political organization of the Turkish labor class and of the working classes and groups (farm hands, small farmers, salary and wage earners, craftsmen, artisans, low-income professionals, progressive youth, and socialist intellectuals) gathered around it and following its [labor class] democratic leadership for attaining power through

* Extract from *Türkiye Işçi Partisi Kimlerin Partisidir? (To Whom Does the Labor Party Belong?*) Istanbul: Sıralar Matbaası, 1962), pp. 1–4.

legal means. TIP evaluates events at home and abroad from the viewpoint of the labor class and of the toiling popular masses; it defends their rights and struggles to materialize their rights and freedoms.

The toiling masses of people constitute the majority of the nation and are the real source of all riches and values and the only driving force for social progress. They bear the heavy burden of this progress. Consequently, the struggle for the rights, freedoms, and interests of the masses of people is a struggle for the rights, freedoms, and high interests of the Turkish nation as a whole.

TIP ranks are open to all citizens who accept the party program and bylaws and side with labor, regardless of their race, faith, sect, color of skin, sex, and class [social] origin.

Article 3: The purpose of the party. The purpose of TIP is to materialize the principles indicated in its program through the rights and freedoms recognized by the constitution and the laws. The question of making Turkey an advanced society and the question of placing the toiling masses of people in a position to decide about the affairs of the country (and of enabling them to live in human conditions) are two interrelated aspects of the same problem. One cannot be achieved without the other. If the toiling masses of people cannot be made to display enthusiasm and confidence for work through the achievement of [decent] human living conditions, Turkey cannot develop herself and cannot reach the level of contemporary civilization. TIP has understood this truth and made it a goal in its program as is presented below in résumé:

To educate and enlighten the working class and all the toiling masses and to transform them into the driving, enlightened force behind the nation's development and progress; to make the labor class and the toiling masses of people the deciding force in the country's affairs, through the full use of their rights and freedoms guaranteed by the constitution; to suppress the dangerous influence and domination of big landowners and big capitalists in cities, who jeopardize the democratic regime, delay economic development and cultural progress, and oppose social justice and security; and to give priority to industrialization and make a planned statism working for labor and through the participation of the toiling masses of people the basic force organizing and directing the national economy and social and cultural life.

The private sector shall be made a useful section of the national economy to be tied to a plan and thus provide the political democracy with an economic and social core and prepare the conditions for transition to a more advanced social order through democratic means. For this purpose, (*a*) all means of production and exchange shall be nationalized, beginning with those in key positions in the national economy and following these with [the nationalization of other enterprises] necessary for economic development and social progress; (*b*) the branches of basic [heavy] industry shall be established and operated by the state as state property. . . .

[*The program states further the party's goal of distributing land to landless peasants, of training personnel needed for development, of achieving economic and cultural progress simultaneously, of finding employment opportunities and distributing income according to one's effort, all through a general plan. It concludes on the following high note:*]

The purpose is to end the system of exploitation of man by man and to make Turkey a country where people rely on each other as brothers, cooperate in freedom and equality, and live in an advanced civilization and culture, in full independence in the service of humanity, peace, and democracy.

V. *Nationalism*

57. NATIONALISM-RACISM-TURANISM IN TURKEY*

A. N. Kirmaci

The extremely egocentric, isolationist wing of the nationalist movement, advocating a conservative, antisocial, elitist nationalism, prevailed in Turkey until the end of World War II. (The moderate and liberal groups remained a minority and, despite their better intellectual preparation, their views had limited impact.) This extreme, antisocial nationalism, which had strong traces of racism, survived well into the 1950's. The Democratic Party government (1950–60) modified considerably the anti-Ottoman, anti-Islamic, and materialist features of the old nationalist ideas, emphasizing instead Turkey's historic spiritual heritage, including Islam. Consequently, racism lost its primacy. The racists, nevertheless, were free to spread their ideas by adjusting them to the new spirit. Türk Yurdu (Turkish Homeland) *expressed a highly refined and sophisticated view concerning Turkey's Ottoman Islamic heritage, while reviews such as* Hür Adam (Free Man) *and* Serdengeçti (Volunteer) *represented the lowbrow aspect of racist, extremist nationalism.*

Meanwhile, social tension rose steadily because of uneven economic development and inequitable distribution of national income. Consequently, the Democratic Party government indiscriminately supported all rightist currents appearing under the name of nationalism and used them to silence groups clamoring for social justice. Many of the "nationalist" publications were subsidized from secret state funds.

The revolution of May 27, 1960, uncovered all these dealings and inflicted a crushing blow on the prestige of the so-called nationalist groups. Those who had identified themselves with the ousted Democratic Party government were wide open to the criticism and attacks of groups they had accused of being "leftist" in the past. After a few months of uneasy silence, however, the extreme nationalist and racist groups attempted to resume their activities, apparently encouraged by a group of officers in the ruling junta, headed by Colonel Alparslan Türkeş, which wanted to use these nationalist groups for its own power purposes. At this point, the intellectuals and the liberal press reacted.

* Extract from A. N. Kirmaci, "Türkiyede aşırı cereyanlar: Milliyetçilik-Irkçılık-Turancılık" ("Radical Currents in Turkey: Nationalism-Racism-Turanism"), *Vatan* (*Fatherland*), Istanbul, November 24–27, 1960.

They advanced the view that the old type of nationalism, open to racist and Turanist interpretations, was obsolete and utterly unsuited to the spirit and needs of the century. They ridiculed the concepts, myths, and beliefs of the extreme nationalists, and attempted to replace the old type of nationalism with patriotism. Many of the ideological bases of the old nationalism, including Ziya Gökalp's ideas, were consequently reinterpreted in the light of new concepts.

On nationalism in Turkey and on Ziya Gökalp, see Niyazi Berkes, Turkish Nationalism and Western Civilization *(New York: Columbia University Press, 1959), and Uriel Heyd,* Foundations of Turkish Nationalism *(London: Luzac-Harvill, 1950).*

The following article appeared in four installments in the daily Vatan (Fatherland). *Although it is a rather balanced piece of writing, occasional phrases and ideas can be construed as damaging to the nationalists' reputation.* Vatan, *originally a liberal daily, began to support leftist causes after Ahmet Emin Yalman was ousted as its editor in 1960. A. N. Kirmaci is apparently a pen name for one of* Vatan's *writers.*

Before considering the history and nature of nationalism in Turkey and the world, we must stress emphatically the differences between nationalism and patriotism and the need for keeping the two well separated. Patriotism, or love for one's country, is a natural feeling. It is instinctive, inborn in man. This feeling has been present everywhere since the beginnings of social life. It has not been created by history, indoctrination, propaganda, and has not been forcefully and artificially imposed on human societies. This inner and ever-present feeling is rooted in nature, in the land on which one lives, in the air one breathes, in the water one drinks. There are no abstract or ideological aspects of this feeling. . . .

Nationalism, and especially extreme nationalism as applied after World War I, is a confused, abstract, and vague feeling that originated in the not-too-remote history of feudalism and the age of empires. Nationalism, when moderate, has some good and constructive aspects, such as defense of national interest, solidarity, and the recognition of the right of self-determination. But it can have extremes and abnormal aspects, such as the refusal to recognize the right of existence to other nations, the desire to revive the glories of the past, to expand everywhere, and to create new forms of empires. The nationalism of the Kemalist regime—that is to say, nationalism in its moderate form—is a normal principle worthy of respect both for us and for others. Nationalism in its extreme, exaggerated, abnormal form is a dangerous and harmful feeling.

The dangers and harm created by [extreme nationalism] are external and internal. Externally, one can no longer [expand] wherever and whenever one wants to.[1] . . . In such a case, God forbid, one may be deprived [of his own territory]. . . . Internally, the danger is also worth considering. The danger lies first in the fact that the sympathizers and promoters of extremism are

1. An allusion to Turanism.

everywhere—weak and pitiful men who lack ideas, understanding, and integrity. They are enemies of true patriots, of men of thought, and of free intellectuals. . . . They display the darkest form of bigotry toward freedom of thought by branding those who do not hold similar thoughts as leftist, Communist traitor, atheist, Masonic, Zionist, and at least [foreign] agents. But [these extreme nationalists] are the first to fall victim to the trap of real leftists, Communists, and atheists. These nationalists, advancing exaggerated ideas, have not produced one great man, an internationally known thinker, philosopher, artist, sociologist, etc. . . . They ignore the true patriots and free intellectuals. Although they are unaware of the ethics of science, religion, civilization, individual, and society, they propose to give lessons to others in national ethics, values, and education. Still worse, these people often do not believe in their own contentions . . . but strive to build for themselves the reputation of heroes, of models of integrity and morality . . . through soapbox oratory, demagogy, and exploitation of citizens' noble and pure feelings. . . .

[*After giving examples of the damage caused by extreme nationalism to Turkey and the world in general, the author continues his discussion:*]

The nationalism in today's republic—that is to say, Kemalist nationalism—is based above all on liberal, free, and democratic foundations. It recognizes equality in the rights of the individual and society and holds them as sacred and inalienable. It respects the rights and interests of other nations as equal to its own. This is the human and modern understanding of nationalism. Nationalism is different from national bigotry. . . . Kemalist nationalism . . . is an effort to take an honorable place in the family of nations, it strives to work for the ideals of humanity on the path of culture, civilization, and progress as a country and as a nation having the full mastery of its rights and interests within the boundaries of the National Pact.[2] This nationalism has nothing in common with mysticism and chauvinism. In other words, Kemalist nationalism means a free, independent, healthy, and indivisible country and a nation [that strives] in every field of culture and civilization—political, social, economic, financial, and legal. It is the reality of freedom and independence and the ideal of culture and civilization.

Kemalist nationalism is not aristocratic, either. It rejects categorically, in every sense of the word, the supremacy of a class or a group. It does not accept the rule of ideology [*fikir*] and terminology. It is populist. It is, therefore, opposed to the aristocracy of sultanate, caliphate, religion, and even of capital. . . . Kemalist nationalism relies on the sound foundations of reality and national interest and works on the path of right and truth. . . . It is warm love and sincerity, an honest wish and aspiration. In order to be a Turk, it

2. The pact of 1919, which laid the political and territorial foundations of modern Turkey.

suffices to want to be a Turk and cherish the idea of being one.[3] Thus, this nationalism is not aggressive, belligerent, and adventurous. It is peace loving and humanist and has the motto: "Peace at home, peace abroad."

[*The author analyzes and rejects racialism as being deprived of sound foundations and concludes that it can lead only to dictatorship and eventually prepare the ground for leftism. He then analyzes the historical causes that gave birth to racialism in Turkey and finds that racialism, Turanism, and the mystical concept of "red apple"* [kızıl elma] *were related and were born basically from the fact that the Turks were deprived of a true concept of national identity. The concept of* kızıl elma,[4] *found in early Turkish writings, was often referred to by Ziya Gökalp. Kirmaci, apparently quoting Gökalp's ideas about* kızıl elma, *agrees that the concept expressed the yearning for a country with a true Turkish national culture.*]

> Son, this is our desire on earth: a country with a pure Turkish culture. For centuries, Turks have covered themselves with the glory of heroic deeds. . . . They have invaded India, China, Egypt, Byzantium, the East, and the West . . . but never fulfilled the *kızıl elma,* their wish on earth. Many times, Turks conquered continents. But in reality, they were the ones who were invaded, because their spirit and soul were subject to the environment they conquered. They became Hindus, Arabs, Persians, or Europeans according to the country conquered. A Turkish law and philosophy were not born. . . . We have produced hundreds of famous poets, scientists, philosophers, but they produced their works in Arabic, Persian, Russian, and Chinese. . . . These [thinkers] gave to each of these nations a glorious history. The Turk always sacrificed himself for the others, and his own being remains incomplete. . . . Thus, son, you will find the *kızil elma* in national unity, national existence, and there the culture and social conscience of the Turkish community will develop. . . .

Ziya Gökalp has insisted upon *hars,* or national culture, as having the basic meaning of that indestructible quality of national identity [i.e., national personality]. It was not a culture that rested exclusively on unity of flesh, blood, bones, form, color, or origin. That culture was to be the product of nature, of the place and time, and, if one may say, also in part of the land on which one lives, of the fatherland, and the climate. . . . The source of culture is in the people [*halk*]—indeed, the large masses of people. Consequently, the nationalism of Ziya Gökalp is democratic in the truest sense of the term. Extreme nationalism and racialism, as they are understood today, have no relationship whatsoever to this democratic attitude. . . . The utterly dangerous psychology created by extreme nationalism and racialism in men, and especially in the

3. Inönü's expression.

4. According to Osman Turan, the *kızıl elma* was a myth that "symbolized the ideal of world domination." The idea derived from a brilliant metal ball on Justinian's monument in the church of St. Sophia. The Turks believed that possession of that ball would help them achieve world domination. Osman Turan, "The Ideal of World Domination Among the Medieval Turks," *Studia Islamica,* IV (1955), 77–90.

leaders of this movement, is the same everywhere. This psychology manifests itself in megalomania; . . . once in power, such men begin to think that mankind did not produce and will never produce men similar to themselves. . . .

[*After bitterly criticizing Hitler and Mussolini and the great harm they caused to mankind, the author concludes:*]

One cannot ignore the fact that the sympathizers of these extreme movements still exist in Turkey as they do elsewhere in the world and that, at times, they try furtively, behind the scenes, to play effective roles. But we cannot and will never accept these men as the masters of our destiny. Those days . . . are past for Turkey. After the struggle for national liberation and the movements for establishing a republic and reforms, Turkey has become a country that looks forward not backward. Blessed and many times [blessed] be Atatürk.

58. THE PROGRESSIVES AND THE REACTIONARIES*

Halil Tideli

The review Toprak (Earth), *the spokesman for a rightist nationalist group, has tacitly rejected the revolution of May 27, 1960, and has consistently opposed the leftist intellectuals. The following article refers to a number of symbols and issues, the attitude toward which determines one's ideological position. The rightist groups usually court the masses by appealing to their attachments to tradition, religion, and homeland. The leftist groups, unable to appeal directly to mass sentiments—except in terms of social and economic welfare—have defended the rule of an elite, to which the article refers.*

These days, whenever I become engaged in informal conversation or in discussions of the country's problems, two words immediately strike my ears: "progressive" and "reactionary." What are progressivism and reaction?

Since we are asking ourselves this question, let us examine the connotations of these words. First, let us take up the "progressives."

* Extract from Halil Tideli, "Ilerici ve Gerici" ("The Progressives and the Reactionaries"), *Toprak (Earth)*, Istanbul, April 1, 1962, p. 14.

There are numerous wretches among the people who are called quasi-intellectuals [*yarı münevver*]. Their heads are devoid of ideas, and by the same token their hearts are bereft of belief or ideals. They have nothing to offer but idle chit-chat. They are great admirers of chatter. They merely repeat superficial bits of knowledge they have gathered here and there or a few academic terms they have learned in parrot fashion. How deplorable it is that they often manage to find some who are naive enough to listen to them! Such as these are among the first to label themselves as progressive.

There is still another type of progressive! This type accuses all those who disagree with them of reaction and backwardness. They hold a monopoly on love for Atatürk. They alone recognize the supreme national interest. In their view, nationalism is an outmoded sophism. To believe in and value holiness—religion—is fanaticism. They conceive of democracy as a type of oligarchy formed by the dictatorship of the intellectuals. Or, rather, such a conception serves their purposes more effectively. The man without ideas who said, "The vote of one intellectual must be made equal to those of four villagers," came out of this group. Those who categorize people by saying, "Those in this party are progressives; all the others are reactionary," come from this group. Those who say, "Nationalism is a vestige of the Middle Ages," belong to this group. The idea of changing the national [independence] anthem, the prayer of Turkish freedom, comes from this group.[1] Those who wish to resurrect the village institutes, every one of which became a hotbed of Communism, belong to this group.[2] And finally, those who revile and insult our nation as "tail [*kuyruk*],[3] reactionary, racist, fanatic, chauvinist, charlatan" belong to this group.

The people we have just briefly described are those who represent themselves as progressive. Now let us examine those who are labeled "reactionary" by these standard-bearers of rare ideas. . . . Most, if not all, of these are devoted to their religion and nation. They are conservative to the necessary extent. They are always opposed to quasi- and extreme leftism, to deviant ideologies, and especially to such thoroughly dangerous and harmful movements as Communism and Zionism. They are uplifted by and take pride in their past. They always defend the sanctity of the family and private property. Their national consciousness is constantly awake and alert. They resist those who regard their past with contempt or who try to erase it from their memories. They violently reproach those who wish to destroy, either directly or by stealth, their morals, family, religion, virtue, and nationhood.

There we have a description of those who are called reactionary by those who pass themselves off as progressives.

1. The Turkish national anthem has a somewhat religious nationalist spirit. Its words were written by Mehmet Akif, an Islamist nationalist poet of the War of National Liberation (1919–22) who is the idol of the conservatives.

2. The village institutes, educational institutions established in the early 1940's, were changed into teacher-training schools by the Democrats. After the 1960 revolution, the socialists tried unsuccessfully to revive them.

3. A term coined after the 1960 revolution to designate followers of the ousted Adnan Menderes and his Democratic Party.

These descriptions should render the identity of the real progressives and reactionaries as clear as the light of day. And this truth is known by all the "progressives" who support themselves with slander. They know it, but when they see good moral character in others, which they themselves lack, they are constantly driven toward an inferiority complex. As a result, they seek an escape through slander. They have even adapted themselves to the [Turkish] proverb: "Defame, smear so that a trace may remain," which has come like a command to slaves who have sold their souls for the money of the red dictators sitting in the Kremlin in Moscow.

Such is the present-day condition of us who live on this portion of paradise, our dear Turkey, kneaded with the blood of millions of martyrs. It is true that the fools among us who portray themselves as progressives are in a minority. But as we are children of the same country, this split saddens and sorrows all true sons of Turkey. But we also have a consolation: The establishment of a progressive Turkey is no longer an illusion. The realization of the distant ideal is close at hand. The "Sick Man" has recovered and stands on his feet like a block of granite, a column of steel. The final victory belongs to the nationalists, who have followed the path opened by the late great thinker Ziya Gökalp. Progressive Turkey will rise from the strong arms and noble shoulders of those who belong to the Turkish race, the Muslim community, and Western civilization.[4] The grand Turkish state will very soon assume its rightful place on the map of the world.

59. THE IDEAL TURKISH YOUTH*

Aytuğ Kaplan

The old type of nationalism is influential in the middle schools, where most teachers were brought up with the nationalist ideas that prevailed during the 1920's and 1930's. The essence of this nationalism is Islamic, traditional, and moral; it is anti-Communist. It rejects the moral values of the West, but accepts Western technology and science. Lately, many reservations raised against the West have been abandoned, especially since political debate began to be concerned chiefly with economic problems.

The following essay, by a middle-school student who was probably not older than sixteen, shows the state of mind prevalent among some groups of Turkish youth. Submitted to a competition entitled "Türk Gençliği Nasıl Olmalıdır?" ("What Should Turkish Youth Be?"), it was subsequently published in the nationalist daily Yeni Istanbul (New Istanbul) *and won a prize.*

* Extract from *Yeni Istanbul (New Istanbul)*, November 16, 1962.

4. Three slogans attributed to Gökalp.

The youth of a nation is the most effective force in determining the power and the civilized place of that nation. An alert and determined youth, with high morale and sound morality, is the nation's source of confidence and strength. A nation based on such sound foundations certainly will make great strides forward into the future. . . . Our nation, therefore, is in dire need of an ideal youth.

Turkish youth must assimilate the steel-like quality of its ancestors and try to be worthy of them by drawing inspiration from their soul. . . . This youth must be a whole, united around an ideal, and, as a Muslim group, deeply attached to the principles of Islam and to its own national character and personality. Our ancestors drew their divine force from love of Turkism and of the Muslim faith. They fought with this love in their hearts and spread our glory everywhere. They spread fear and terror among our enemies and gave pride and security to our friends. They left to us a glorious history, which the youth of no other nation possesses. The great duty of Turkish youth is to show respect for the sacred memory of its ancestors and to take inspiration from their exceptional, inherent qualities. . . .

Turkish youth must be conservative by remaining loyal to its traditions and honoring moral existence. It must be attached to the moral values that made us what we are. It must not accept the traditions of the Western world. It ought to bring to their senses the disoriented ones who have embarked on this path.[1] It must be extremely sensitive in safeguarding our national traditions. . . . The nation that rejects moral values cannot escape from Communism. It is true that, in order to progress in the field of modernity, we must Westernize. But this does not mean that we must abandon our own traditions and embrace the customs and mores of the West. The eyes of Turkish youth should not see the ordinary dealings of the West but its science and technology. . . .

Turkish youth must be self-sacrificing and patriotic and must dedicate itself to the fatherland and the nation. It must be careful of the "acrobats" of politics who work for their own interest. It must know how to silence them. . . . Turkish youth must rid itself of laziness, and destroy the mentality of *nemelazımcılık*.[2] It must know the value of time and give to science the time lost at poker games, at *tavla*,[3] in coffee shops, and in rock-and-roll indignities. Turkish youth must not accept ideas aimed at destroying our national unity . . . . It must keep alive national feelings and teach [i.e., remind] their true identity to those who err toward Communism. Turkish youth must follow the path of Atatürk, who said, "Rise, Turk. There is no boundary to your loftiness." Turkish youth must not depart from the path of faith illuminated by the rays of Islam. . . .

1. That is, those who have embarked on the path of taking up Western habits.
2. An "I don't care" attitude; the *Ma-fish* of the Arabs.
3. Backgammon, a Mediterranean game resembling checkers or draughts.

60. THE QUESTION OF "OUTSIDE" TURKS*

Necdet Sancar

Necdet Sancar is an exponent of nationalism and Pan-Turkism in its new form. In the past, Pan-Turkism was a theory of territorial expansion known as Pan-Turanism. Unity of race and language was its basis, and its purpose was to unite all Turkic groups in one country, the Turan. Most Turkic groups outside Turkey (totaling some 30–40 million people) live in the Central Asian republics of the Soviet Union and in China's northern provinces. Pan-Turanism and Pan-Turkism (there are some differences of emphasis between the two) were, therefore, movements that threatened the internal security and unity of the Soviet Union.

After World War II, following the emergence of new concepts of human rights and freedoms, Pan-Turkism changed its content considerably. The apologists for Pan-Turkism advocated the liberation of Turkic groups from Soviet rule (some even discussed the fate of Turks under Chinese rule) as a consequence of the right of self-determination and independence as granted to the former Western colonies in Asia and Africa. The idea of uniting all these Turkic groups in one single state, Greater Turkey, was abandoned. Governments in Turkey have rejected the idea of dealing with the Turkic groups in the U.S.S.R. The following article presents the arguments of Pan-Turkists concerning the Turkic groups living in the Soviet Union.

Turkey is the only independent area of the [Turkic] lands stretching from the Aegean Sea to beyond the Altai Mountains. Turks inhabit these lands in a scattered fashion. A small group of Turks who do not possess their freedom live in the Balkans, some on the [Mediterranean] islands, and some in the Arab countries, our southern neighbors. But the great mass live in Asian lands, which begin east of Turkey and extend to the Sea of Japan. We call these enslaved men, who have the same origin [*soydaş*] as us, the "outside" Turks. This is one of the most important problems of Turkey and of the Turks of Turkey. This problem is important for several reasons.

The outside Turks present a problem of national honor. We must think of a nation whose members are enslaved and held prisoner by others, although they are perhaps twice as many as its sons who enjoy liberty. Does not this painful situation hurt and wound, in fact trample under foot, national honor? This is the reality faced by Turks today. Only about 25 million people have

* Extract from Necdet Sancar, "Dış Türkler Meselesi" ("The Question of 'Outside' Turks"), *Son Havadis (Last News)*, Istanbul, October 11, 1961.

their freedom on these lands created by God as the Turk's own domain, whereas twice as many are slaves and prisoners. No other nation in the world faces such a tragic situation. . . .

This painful reality is not encountered by any other modern nation in the world and cannot be borne by the high feeling of human honor. . . .

The outside Turks constitute for Turkey a question of state security. States with a population of 25 or 30 million people surrounded by enemy nations cannot regard their future with confidence. Turkey is one of these states. Consequently, the independence gained by outside Turks, in addition to [satisfying] our national honor, will constitute a guarantee for Turkey. . . . If the Eastern Turks can establish their independent states on their own fatherland, then Turkey will have on its side a trustworthy brother power and, in case of war, will receive great help from it. . . .

Finally, the outside Turks constitute for the Turks of Turkey a humanitarian problem: Is not the principle of self-determination a humanitarian principle of our age? Those who do not accept this principle are the inhumane regimes and states. In this era of freedom, how can one forget millions of Turks living on their own lands as the slaves of others? Are the descendants of the Turks who lived for 1800 years as the most advanced and superior nation on earth inferior to the Negroes of Africa so as to leave the [outside Turks] under the yoke of tyranny? The civilized world is obliged to think about these unfortunate enslaved people. Indeed, lately, America [the United States] has begun to deal with the question of Turks enslaved by Moscow. . . .

It is indeed painful that the Turks of Turkey are apparently unaware of this problem, which is so important for them. . . . For years, these national problems, vital to Turkey's future, have been covered with a veil. Governments deprived of a national policy have not included in their program the problem of outside Turks. The people who are considered intellectuals . . . prefer to remain silent when faced with the policy of their governments and of high politicians, who avoid the problem of outside Turks. Common people, on the other hand, deprived of the enlightened guidance of intellectuals, are unaware of this national and human problem. . . . Propaganda has made the question of outside Turks appear not as the problem of the freedom of enslaved millions but as a dangerous adventure likely to push Turkey into tragedy. The heroes promoting this negative propaganda based on lies and calumnies are the enemies of Turkey's national problems. The local reds are the leaders and the most fierce exponents of this viewpoint.

It would be a great blow to Russia if the Turks living in their homeland in Asia were to gain their freedom. This is the reason why the native reds are the greatest enemies of the outside Turks. If the Turks living in the eastern Turkic lands were to won their independence, Russia, which is the real fatherland of our own reds, would be shattered, the best lands it exploits would be taken away, and the Kremlin's plans for world domination would go bankrupt. . . . But neither the thick veil thrown upon national problems, nor the sneaky foreign propaganda . . . can obscure the great importance that outside Turks have for the life of Turkey. Those Turkish intellectuals who understand the significance of national problems . . . have defended the cause of freedom for the outside Turks despite everything.

Patriotic Turkish intellectuals, whose number is increasing every day, will continue to defend this problem as a national cause. This problem will come to an end when the entire Turkic world is independent. . . . The liberation of outside Turks is not a question of armed intervention, as foreign propaganda tries to insinuate. . . . It is a national problem and, therefore, must rest upon ideas, national consciousness, and nationalism. National consciousness and nationalist ideas can never accept any action that may endanger the national life or existence of Turkey. Still, there are a considerable number of things to be done without endangering Turkey. First of all, the Turks of Turkey must be made aware of the importance of the problem of outside Turks. . . . The second question is to make the outside world aware of this problem. . . .

PART THREE

Political and Social Thought in Iran

Introduction to Political and Social Thought in Iran

Iran's social structure is probably the most complex both in the Middle East and in the Muslim world. Its complexity arises, first, from a set of historical and cultural conditions unique to Iran and, second, from the nation's still unfinished political and social modernization. Historically and culturally, Iran differs from other Middle Eastern countries in that it was able to preserve its national identity throughout the Islamic era. Men of Persian origin or those educated in Persian culture contributed vitally to the broadening of Islam into a universal religion. A visitor to Iran today cannot fail to perceive, through the maze of modern imports ranging from dress to mechanical gadgets, certain characteristics that belong distinctively to the country and its history. One cannot claim that Iran has fully assimilated modern foreign influences into its own culture. But it would be equally wrong to claim that Iran has lost its native characteristics under the onslaught of foreign influences. The attachment to the past and the desire for innovation stand side by side; neither has sufficient stamina fully to suppress the other and to emerge as the country's leading idea. Reform and change in Iran have not profoundly affected the constitutional structure, as they have in Turkey and the Arab republics. They have been used to reassert the power of the ruling political institutions—the monarchy, in particular—and to legitimize them as part of Iran's national existence. Shiʿism, transformed in the course of centuries into a kind of national religion, is an instrument of power in the hands of the clergy and landlords, but is incapable of stimulating new thoughts for change from inside. Bahaʿism was born in Iran and the hard core of its followers, whose numbers are estimated variously at from 500,000 to 2 million, still practice one of the most liberal, humanitarian religions in the world.

Iran's distinctive personality becomes more evident when one comes to know better its leaders and intellectuals. Social and civic responsibility, interest in public service, respect for authority, and other qualities necessary in a modern community may, at times, be conspicuously absent in some of them. But in intellect, artistic finesse, and discriminating taste, the Iranian as a person offers promise of achievement far above other Middle Easterners. Richard N. Frye has written of a "Persian mystique,"[1] an intangible sentiment akin to religious belief. "It is the sum total of the cultural experience of the Iranian people with the same continuity of tradition which may be observed in ancient Egypt and elsewhere. It is not easily defined, and has symbolic elements such as the institution of Shahinshah 'the king of Kings' and a sentiment regarding the ruler like . . . 'the kingly glory' of the ancient Persians which descended on them from heaven."[2] This sense of identity, which is reflected in Iranian

1. Richard N. Frye, "Iran and the Unity of the Muslim World," in Richard N. Frye (ed.), *Islam and the West* (The Hague: Mouton & Co., 1957), pp. 179–93.
2. *Ibid.*, p. 186.

nationalism, and the country's natural resources are assets and sound bases for rapid modernization.

The questions of minorities and of tribal organization have often been mentioned as hindrances to Iran's national unity. Experience has shown, however, that no minority group, unless subject to outside instigation, is articulate enough to engage in divisive struggle. The Persians have been able to dominate the minorities through skillful use of their cultural superiority, political craft, and religious policy. The Azerbaijanis, despite linguistic and racial affinities with the Turks, have remained loyal to Iran.

In terms of actual achievements, Iran's rate of material and cultural progress is disappointing. The nation's internal development has been delayed largely by the throne's very inability to adapt itself to the requirements of the twentieth century. The throne, supported by a large segment of the body public and assisted by the intellectuals, has perpetuated the belief that the Persian personality and culture are rooted in dynastic traditions and that the downfall of the dynasty would cause social disintegration. It is true that the throne is still the chief institution rallying the average Iranian and commanding the loyalty of the masses, but the exalted, almost mystical popular image of the throne that is perpetuated through all available media does not satisfy the educated. Few intellectuals would agree to an outright abolition of the monarchy, yet very few will accept indefinitely the throne's present policy, which seems modern and reformist to the outside world but is traditionalist and autocratic to its own people. Ideological and political developments in Iran, therefore, seem to be conditioned on the one hand by a monarchy that clings stubbornly to its traditional, archaic prerogatives and on the other hand by a growing body of intellectuals who demand change and progress without being able to advocate (like the Communists) the removal of the chief obstacle to change, a social-political structure based on the monarchy. The proposal that the monarchy be replaced by a republic appears too radical and is likely to be rejected by even the most progressive intellectuals.

An Iranian king threatened with loss of his powers might argue that a diminution of royal prerogatives would violate national traditions and weaken the very foundations of society. This argument would be valid for many conservative Iranians and would turn them into rabid nationalists dedicated to preserving their national identity by preserving the throne. Even some of the radical reformists would often succumb to its background of indoctrination and eulogize the past greatness of Persia in the often-used slogan, "Twenty-five hundred years of uninterrupted dynastic rule."

The beginnings of political modernization in Iran were encouraging. The first truly democratic movement for constitutional monarchy in the Middle East took place in Iran in 1905–6. Because its leaders were middle-class elements—merchants, religious men, and intellectuals—it differed from the Ottoman constitutional experiment of 1876, which was promoted by the bureaucrats. The Iranian constitution of 1906 has been preserved, with some amendments, to date. The power of the throne has not substantially decreased, although the use of power is more moderate and refined. The Shah's prerogatives in directing the council of ministers, convening the parliament, and establishing political parties are almost supreme. Hence, popular participation in making or executing decisions is greatly reduced, despite the deceptive façade of a parliament and political parties.

The throne's social role largely conditions its political function. Throughout its existence, the throne has been the foundation and the apex of a social organization buttressed by a traditional philosophy. The emerging upper social groups, created by modern economic conditions, have been incorporated into this traditional social structure dominated by the throne and compelled to espouse its values. One may say that the throne, through its overwhelming control of the army, the bureaucracy, and the secret police, has successfully prevented the challenge of new groups. It has been aided by special ideological conditions that do no exist elsewhere. The army and intellectual groups in the Ottoman Empire and in some of the Arab monarchies could rise against the throne after constitutional and administrative reforms had considerably weakened the monarchy's religious foundations. The fact that the Iranian monarchy's ideological foundations were rooted chiefly in national traditions and national history jeopardized the possible secular impact of constitutional reform.

The caliphate doctrine of Shi'ism, the religion of Iran, was tailored to provide useful arguments in support of the hereditary monarchy. During the reign of Reza Shah (1925–41), however, Zoroastrianism, the religion of ancient Persia, was officially restored in order to curtail not only the influence of the Shi'ite clergy but also to bolster the position of the monarchy by reviving Persian national dynastic traditions. The political philosophy of Zoroastrianism, the official religion of the Sassanians, upheld the king's supremacy; this feature was transferred, with some modifications, to Shi'ism. The Iranvij society surviving from the days of Reza Shah still claims that Shi'ism is just an Islamicized form of Zoroastrianism.

If the Persian monarchy had been closer to the spirit of orthodox Islam and had drawn its *raison d'être* solely from Islam rather than from non-Islamic, national sources, constitutionalism and secularism would have greatly undermined its strength. The strength of the Iranian monarchy lies in its own history and national traditions. One may say that political power and the present upper social organization in Iran, interwoven as they are around the throne, cannot exist without each other. The lower classes—peasants, workers, and service groups—are outwardly incorporated into the existing social system. In reality, however, the intensification of economic growth and various other modernizing influences, the much advertised reforms initiated by the Shah himself, and sporadic outbursts of economic nationalism, especially during Muhammad Musaddiq's premiership (1951–53), have created patterns of stratification and interests that differ from and often conflict with the archaic structure at the top. Traditional loyalties and allegiances to national values prevail among the lower groups.

The question remains unresolved, however, whether the archaic social and political structure at the top can coexist indefinitely with the lower levels of society, whose consciousness derives its force from modern economic and social forces. The problems besetting Iran's lower classes are predominantly economic. The success of the Tudeh Party, before it became discredited because of its open support of the Soviet Union, cannot be explained merely in terms of its anti-imperialism and anti-Westernism, since no major problem (except the oil question) divided Iran and the West. Tudeh's success can be attributed to its program which, by promising social and economic reforms, appealed directly to the common man. The party's Marxist ideology did not awaken much suspicion until its leaders began to quote Lenin and Stalin and awakened the Russophobia of the average Iranian.

Most political efforts in Iran today are directed at establishing a true constitutional monarch and a free political life and carrying out social reforms. All parties, despite their widely divergent ideologies, are united in their desire to achieve the goal of a constitutional regime. The constitutionalists may be described as liberal nationalists and anti-imperialists. Among these, the influence of the late Ahmad Kasravi (1890–1946), the advocate of modernism and a return to Zoroastrianism, is strongly felt.

The conservative branch of Iranian politics is represented by the traditionalists, some of whom are also known as Pan-Iranians; and the religious conservatives, who are also nationalists. They are opposed to foreigners, leftists, secular nationalists, and, at times, even the Shah. The *Fedayan-e-Islam* (Volunteers of Islam, or Islam's Sacrifices) led by Mulla Kashani was the main group, but it was banned. Most Iranian intellectuals belong to liberal constitutionalist or secularist organizations.

The extreme left is represented by the Tudeh (Masses) Party, which operates chiefly underground. It tries to appeal to all classes, promising welfare to the poor, moral satisfaction to the intellectual, liberty to the constitutionalist, and repentance to the rich. All these goals are to be attained in a socialist Iran. The party's anti-Western and anti-imperialist propaganda has acquired nationalist tones designed to counteract the accusations that Tudeh has ignored the national interests of Iran. Other leftist groups include the Toilers Party, the Socialist League, and some of Musaddiq's followers in the National Front.

The New Iran Party—the party in power—follows basically the Shah's plans for reform.

The ideological situation in Iran is inadequately reflected by the limited number of translations presented in this work. Difficulties of a technical nature have confined our selection to the throne's directives on reforms, the reaction of the constitutionalists, and the views of the Tudeh Party.

The following books contain information about Iranian ideology: I'raj Afsher, *Index Iranicus,* Vol. I (1910–58) (Tehran: University of Tehran, 1961), a bibliography containing some 6,000 titles, which was compiled by the editor of *Rahnama-ye-Kitab* (*Guide to Books*), a periodical review of Iranian publications; Richard W. Cottam, *Nationalism in Iran* (Pittsburgh, Pa.: University of Pittsburgh Press, 1964); Donald N. Wilber, *Contemporary*

Iran (New York: Frederick A. Praeger, 1963); Amin Banani, *The Modernization of Iran, 1921–1941* (Stanford, Calif.: Stanford University Press, 1961); Leonard Binder, *Iran: Political Development in a Changing Society* (Berkeley, Calif.: University of California Press, 1962); and Sepehr Zabih, *The Communist Movement in Iran* (Berkeley, Calif.: University of California Press, 1966).

The following articles, and especially the first, are very useful: F. Kazemzadeh, "Ideological Crisis in Iran," in Walter Z. Laqueur (ed.), *The Middle East in Transition: Studies in Contemporary History* (London: Routledge & Kegan Paul; New York: Frederick A. Praeger, 1958), pp. 196–203; James A. Bill, "The Social and Economic Foundations of Power in Contemporary Iran," *Middle East Journal,* XVII (Autumn, 1963), 400–413; Richard N. Frye, "Iran and the Unity of the Muslim World," in Richard N. Frye (ed.), *Islam and the West* (The Hague: Mouton & Co., 1957), pp. 179–93; and A. K. S. Lambton, "A Reconsideration of the Position of the Marja' al-Taqlid and the Religious Institution," *Studia Islamica,* Paris, XX (1964), 114–35.

61. THE SHAH'S PROCLAMATION ON REFORM AND STATEMENT OF THE NATIONAL FRONT*

The Shah has taken the lead in initiating reforms in Iran, notably in distributing about 750,000 acres of crown land to landless peasants. At his urging, reformist measures also have been undertaken in government and administration. These reforms, however, have been opposed by landed groups as well as by intellectuals, who have asked for more basic measures, including a faithful observance of the fundamental law, or constitution. The first of the following extracts contains the main directives proposed by the Shah in 1961. The second, issued by the National Front, a coalition of constitutionalist, nationalist, and religious political parties, called upon the government of Dr. 'Ali Amini to respect the constitution. Dr. Amini had formed a government in May, 1961, after two contested elections had been held in 1960–61 and two governments had resigned because of pressure from the Shah.

The Shah's Proclamation on Reform

[To] His Excellency Doctor 'Ali Amini, Prime Minister:

The statement of His Majesty the Shah at the meeting of the Council of

* Extracts from *Ettela'at* (Air Mail Edition), Tehran, November 15, 1961. These English versions have been adapted from Peter W. Avery's translation, which appeared in *Middle East Journal,* XVI (Winter, 1962), 86–90. Reproduced by permission.

Ministers on 20th Aban in the year 1340 [November 11, 1961] in the Marble Palace is forwarded herewith:

"Our concern for this country and its people has made us determine that steps in preparing the ground for achieving the social, material, and intellectual advancement of the realm should be taken without delay, for the attainment of the basis of a developing society in a rapidly progressing world. These steps include the possibility of achieving sound government of the people by the people, which is at the root of democratic principles. Every minute we lose in seizing this valuable opportunity is tantamount to a grave crime on our, the government's, and the nation's part. We have always put the lofty interests of nation and country above all else. Thus, for the comfort and well-being of the people, for the establishment of social justice, and for the progressive development of individual members of the community toward a life in keeping with the standards of the modern world, we decree that the necessary steps be taken. No difficulty or hindrance can be admitted in this process as an obstacle to the implementation of the required measures. Accordingly, acting on the right given us by the Fundamental Law, we being recognized as one of the originators of law, we commission the government, until the convening of a parliament (based, we hope, on valid elections without the need again ensuing for annulment of elections due to their improper conduct), to put into execution the laws required for convening village councils and, in respect of the laws governing city, provincial, and district councils also, to bring about the necessary modifications in the existing laws, after careful scrutiny with regard to the circumstances and the needs of the day. These may be put temporarily into execution with our Royal Assent so that, with a period of practical experiment and removal of obvious defects, they may be submitted to the legislature to gain legal validity and affirmation after the opening of both houses of parliament.

"The meaning of democratic government is this, that the people's affairs be assigned to the people themselves as they gradually obtain the right degree of maturity; that they possess authority to act in the administration of all local matters; that they participate and take action with respect to price regulation of foodstuffs, public health, education, municipal affairs, local road construction, with the joining of branch roads to main trunk routes, without tampering with or damaging the bases of the country's central domestic and foreign policy.

"For essential reforms the government must:

"1. In the administration and recruitment of civil servants, expediting the drafting of a new civil service law with attention to essential minutiae, put into effect rules of service in a uniform manner equally applicable to every ministry, taking the special duties of each ministry into consideration, but obviating all forms of discrimination. . . . In laying the foundations of each ministry's organization on the basis of present and future needs, the conditions of permanence and promotion in the state service will be merit, honesty, and personal ability. Above the level of director general, the Council of Ministers will carry out the necessary investigations.

"2. Guaranteeing civil servants' livelihood to cover their own and their dependents' welfare and to free them from apprehension about their future is an aim whose achievement must, of course, begin with giving employees living accommodations under a special scheme. Then, gradually, provision must be made for other amenities, such as cooperative societies, etc., to meet the officials' needs. Accomplishment of this duty on the government's part will begin with rigorous application of the principle of first things first. The most important categories of civil servants must be given priority, and these include army, police and gendarmerie employees, schoolteachers, and Ministry of Justice officials, all of whom have a specially important standing. Houses assigned to these categories must, as far as possible, be close to their place of work to economize in transport and obviate waste of time in travel.

"3. The government must not relax vigilance in the sphere of agriculture and its mechanization. The law for land reform and limitation of proprietorship should be put into effect; if the land reform law proves impracticable, the government must, with utmost dispatch, embark on its revision in whatever way is deemed necessary to assure its proper and complete execution; and meanwhile, regulations must be instituted to guarantee the welfare and well-being of those cultivators left under landowners. For the benefit of the cultivators, advantage must be taken of the results accruing from the attraction of experts and commissioning of various cooperative establishments.

"The government must especially strive to achieve an extraordinary increase in production. For local road construction between villages and joining branch feeder roads to main trunk routes and other development projects, development and construction battalions of young people must be set up and the means of mechanizing agriculture furnished, including familiarization with cultivators, the use of chemical fertilizers, and modern agricultural methods, the digging of irrigation channels, construction of rural houses, and exploitation of the land.

"The development and construction battalions, losing no time joining forces with municipal authorities in towns, will assist in building factories and workers' housing.

"4. Under the present law, the condition of labor is relatively satisfactory. However, employers must be persuaded to build houses for workers; and this can be arranged so that it is reckoned as a portion of the insurance employers are legally bound to pay.

"The government must give special attention to the protection of home industries and promotion of the country's own factory products. This must be done in such a way that, when local products have as far as possible matched the same products abroad, improvements will continue and consumers' desire for home goods be increased, which will be in their best economic interests.

"The government must guide and aid factory owners in renewal of plants and also training of technical personnel and management for the proper maintenance of industrial installations. It will protect every type of production unit and domestic industry against foreign markets. In the factories, after assessments have been made, workers, should they be willing, may have 25 per cent of the stock sold to them on a suitable installment basis. Thus, the workers themselves may be participants in the factory's profits and, becoming concerned in the proper running of the business and quality of the products, not spare their best efforts.

"5. In the matter of taxes, which are still not received in a proper or equitable manner from the wealthy, the minister of finance has the duty, after close study and anticipation of sound and just collection of revenues, to make proposals that will ensure that the wealthy pay dues relative to their capacity. Illegal impositions on the impecunious will be avoided, while dealings between payer and revenue collector will be based on a feeling of mutual confidence and understanding. Thus, gradually, the routine of rendering taxes due will become general, with an ethical relationship established between taxpayers and collectors.

"Special attention should be paid to the stabilization of a revenue system so that the people's and investors' confidence will be attracted.

"6. As regards education, which is essentially important, our future being to a large extent dependent upon it, there must be a revision of educational programs. This will ensure that our education system possesses the practical and useful aspect that is consonant with the state of a society and country in the process of maturing and developing. You must leave no stone unturned to extend and broaden free elementary education and intermediate vocational training, while taking steps for general secondary education at the intermediate and higher levels according to what obtains all over the world. So that no talent may be deprived on the grounds of lack of means, the Ministry of Education must watch pupils from the very first day they enter primary school, keeping records of all those with outstanding ability. Thus, at the right time, either directly or through city, provincial, or district councils, study scholarships will be made available to these youngsters of ability. The utmost care must also be exercised in sending students to foreign countries, so that, while the country's finances are not wasted, intelligent individuals, of value for their country's needs, may be trained for service under the supervision of conscientious people.

"In conclusion, as we have said, all regulations are secondary to the survival of the country and its people. If we wanted merely to follow anachronistic and outmoded rules, neglecting the present world situation and taking advantage of existing opportunities, we would be guilty of a major crime toward our people. The country's advancement and its people's welfare will take precedence over the observance of regulation-bound views and personal predilections. Without loss of time, the government must, trusting in our special support and gracious favor, devote itself to eradicating the roots of corruption with complete sincerity and the utmost speed. In achieving this great task, it must fear no obstacle or hindrance. We are convinced that every individual of the noble and sensible Iranian nation will take part in this process, based as it is on social justice, with one mind and one voice with all their strength, and so increase the glory of this historic land."

Hirad,
Head of the Imperial Bureau

Statement of the National Front

The establishment of legal government is the aim of the Iranian National Front [so as to avoid] the return to despotism fifty-five years after the constitution was inaugurated.

Fellow-countrymen: The Fundamental Law clearly lays down the rights and spheres of responsibility of the nation, the constitutional monarchy, and responsible government. On the strength of this Fundamental Law, the Iranian nation was not and is not in a position to infringe upon the real rights of the constitutional monarchy. Therefore, justice and expediency decree that the Throne should, on its part, preserve the rights of the nation—particularly as, in accordance with Article 39 of the Supplement to the Fundamental Law, the Throne is bound by oath to do this and because, whenever the Fundamental Law, which defines the relationship between the nation and the Throne, is not respected, irreparable harm to the state results.

With these facts in mind, the National Front, on the basis of the Fundamental Law and of constitutional conventions, strongly protests against the statements Dr. Amini made as prime minister to the Association of Press Correspondents. Warning is given that the instructions issued from His Imperial Majesty's bureau concerning the enactment and modification of laws without parliamentary approval cannot be considered in the best interests of the Throne and must be deemed contrary to the clear purport of the Fundamental Law because:

In the instruction issued from the Throne to Dr. Amini, in spite of the fine words in the preamble about the desire for securing social justice and reform, the following statement occurs: "According to the right given us by the Fundamental Law, we being recognized as one of those with the right to initiate law, we charge the government, until the convening of parliament, with putting into execution laws required for forming village councils; and in respect of the laws governing city, provincial, and district councils also, with bringing about necessary modifications in existing laws, after careful scrutiny with regard to circumstances and the needs of the day. These may be put temporarily into execution upon receipt of our Royal Assent so that, with a period of practical experiment and removal of obvious difficulties, they may be submitted to the legislature to gain legal validity and authorization after the opening of both houses of parliament." After this, the throne confers on the government the right of lawmaking, which is parliament's prerogative, in respect of enacting, modifying, revising, and abrogating civil service, land reform, tax, and education laws, although this is contrary to the Fundamental Law in both letter and spirit, as will be shown below. Abrogating the rights of parliament, which are in fact the rights of the nation, is in no way consonant with the essential substance of the Fundamental Law, the guarantee of the country's stability, independence, and constitutional sovereignty.

The Throne's statements given above are expressly contrary to the Fundamental Law and against the interests of the realm and the people because:

In the above instruction, it has been asserted that the Throne is one of the initiators of law; apparently, Article 27 of the Supplement to the Fundamental Law, defining the separation of powers, is the basis of this interpretation. But the primary purpose of drawing this article was to separate the duties of the three powers so that one power should not interfere in the functioning of the other. The above interpretation, however, whereby the government is deemed to have the right to enact laws, one of the special rights of parliament, goes contrary to what is intended by the word "lawmaking" in the drawing of the above-mentioned article.

Initiation of law means the preparation of bills and the drafting of a law. What lawmaking is intended to mean, with mention of the fact that each of these two houses of parliament and His Imperial Majesty have the right to initiate law, is that both houses or His Majesty through the government have the right of preparing drafts or bills. Confirmation of this opinion lies in the fact that, in this article and others, the promulgators of the Fundamental Law upheld a difference between the *initiation* and the *enactment* of law. In the Fundamental Law, it has been made clear that laws are valid and can be executed only after parliament has passed them and they have received the Royal Assent. . . .

For the reasons given, the Throne and the executive power do not have the right of enacting laws, and the enactment of law is among the special rights of parliament. If the case were other than this, certainly reference or indication would have been given on this matter. Lack of reference to the right of enacting law, in the section dealing with the rights of the Throne, confirms that the matter of *initiating* is not the right of *enacting*.

The Supreme Court, in giving a guiding opinion, has clearly stated that enactment, modification, and recision of laws is one of the special duties of parliament, and no other body has the right of enacting law.

Now you, Dr. Amini, and your respected colleagues should realize that, according to the clear purport of Article 64 in the Supplement to the Fundamental Law, where it is laid down that "ministers cannot, by using verbal or written orders from the sovereign, relieve themselves of responsibility," you do not have the right to take steps to modify or abrogate laws.

The National Front gives notification to the leaders of Iran, who have attained their high places through the blessings of this same Fundamental Law and constitution, that it will concentrate its efforts on reviving the constitution and, by preventing infringement of the Fundamental Law, [will] seek to insure the safety of the country.

The National Front cannot tolerate any infringement on the rights of parliament, which is the representative of the whole nation; neither can it tolerate violation of the Fundamental Law, because it considers embarking on such a dangerous course injurious to the state, nation, and constitution, and, in this connection, it proclaims to all classes of the people, whose Fundamental Law was obtained by the sacrifice of the lives of their gallant forebears, that, for the preservation of the Fundamental Law and the nation's rights and for the protection of the constitution, the utmost vigilance will be shown and the followers of individual rule [will] not [be] permitted to deprive the people of their rights.

Tehran, Wednesday, 24 Aban 1340/
15th November 1961
Executive Committee of the National Front

62. REACTION OR REVOLUTIONARY CHANGE IN IRAN*

Ehsan Tabari

The Tudeh (Masses) Party emerged in Iran in the early 1940's as a radical leftist organization with a pro-Soviet attitude. It became increasingly active in Iran's internal politics, first by adopting a liberal façade and thus receiving support from leading intellectuals and from the trade unions. Although the party was outlawed in 1949, its members continued to be active. Some of the militants went abroad to engage in systematic leftist propaganda, directed chiefly at the many Iranian students in Europe and the United States. Donya (World), *a periodical published somewhere in Europe, and pamphlets and books published abroad are smuggled into Iran and distributed among Iranian intellectuals. The following article presents a leftist view of the Shah's reform attempts and of the political situation in Iran generally.*

The Persian administration, headed by the Shah, is scrambling to confirm and perpetuate the existing social and economic conditions in order to preserve its power. After the successful *coup d'état* of August 19, 1953, the Shah and the reactionary administration turned all their attention to revenge. The regaining of power enabled them to crush savagely those vast social forces that had been fighting the people's enemies, the imperialists, the courtiers, etc. The American and English imperialists helped the Shah to create a regime of terror

* Extract from Ehsan Tabari, "Tasbit-e erteja'i ya tahawul-e enqelabi" ("Confirmation of Reaction or Revolutionary Change"), *Donya: Organ-e Te'orik va Siyasi-ye Komite-ye Markazi-ye Hezb-e Tude-ye Iran (The World: The Theoretical and Political Organ of the Central Committee of the Iranian Tudeh Party)*, Second Series, III (Summer, 1341 [1962]), 3–9.

and oppression. He concentrated despotic powers in his hands, committed unprecedented treasons openly and daringly, gave the nationalized oil back to the colonialists, violated neutrality, and opened the country's doors to the imperialists' goods and capital. And to carry out these aims, he chose violence and terror as the only effective method. The security organization[1] was thus created along with military courts, secret trials, terror on the streets, physical tortures, destruction of home and properties belonging to liberals and true patriots. . . . The blackest strata of the ruling class put at the Shah's disposal the most bloodthirsty individuals, such as Azmudeh and Bakhtiar, in order to have their revenge on the revolutionary elements.

With the passing of time, however, the ruling class realized that shooting alone could not guarantee power perpetually in a land where people were stirred to defend their national interests.

Consequently, while not abandoning terror, another method came to be used along with it, beginning with the premiership of Manuchehr Eqbal [Manichir Iqbal]. This second method consisted of political maneuvering designed to deceive public opinion. At the order of the Shah, two political parties—*Melliyun* and *Mardum*—were set up.[2] The Shah promised "100 per cent free elections." In his monthly press conference, he claimed that, in the course of the following ten years, the living standard of every Persian would be raised to "ten times" the current level. This machinery of deceit became even more colorful under 'Ali Amini, who declared himself the champion of "revolution from the top." . . . It took Amini only a year, however, to flee from the arena he had entered so noisily.[3] Once more, the initiative rested with the Shah, with little change in the tactics used for the past ten years in manipulating public opinion.

Why did the Shah and his imperialist masters find this so-called gradual change advisable? Here are the reasons:

The method of terror and intimidation did not work because:

1. Intelligent public opinion, created by the vast propaganda activity of the Tudeh Party and other patriotic and progressive groups, proved to be very different from the public opinion of Reza Shah's time. Surely, the Shah aspires to the absolute rule of his father and would like very much to lean on a throne on the backs of a silent and obedient mass. He recently said to the reporter of *Le Monde*, the French newspaper, "My father's dictatorship was a necessity, so is my power." He also declared to a reporter of the *Deutsche Zeitung*, "The prime ministers are responsible to my person; whoever is not able to carry out his duties must go."

The expectations of the father and son may be identical, but the social milieu is radically different. Muhammad Reza Shah rules an Iran where

1. The Iranian secret police and intelligence service.

2. The Melliyun (National) Party, generally the majority party in Iran, was established in 1958. The Mardum (People's) Party, established in 1957, has advocated a progam of social welfare and land reform.

3. Amini resigned in 1962, when his proposal to cut government expenditures by 15 per cent was rejected.

social and national consciousness have reached proportions that were unimaginable during his father's time. The people's legitimate demands can be heard, muffled but steady as the roar of an approaching storm. Thus, he is trying to postpone the fatal hour by reconciliation, retreat, [and] maneuvering. . . .

2. Another reason must be sought in the daily change of balance of power in favor of the forces of peace, democracy, and socialism and against those of war, reaction, and imperialism. The period prior to World War II, when British imperialism imposed dictatorships on the world's nations, is past history. Even the postwar period, when this role was transferred to the new leader of capitalism [the United States], has run its course. In today's world, progressive forces have gained enough strength to be able to influence the people's destinies.

Furthermore, the internal conflict within the imperialist camp has become stronger. John Foster Dulles' power structure is threatened by frightening splits; this is, indeed, different from those times in which the *coup d'état* of 1953 was carried out under the leadership of [U.S.] General Norman H. Schwarzkopf and [U.S. Ambassador] Loy Henderson. In many Asian, African, and Latin American countries, basic changes are taking place. The Iranian people, who were among the first to rise against imperialism after World War II, hear of popular uprisings in Cuba, Algeria, other Middle Eastern countries, Indonesia, India, etc. To prop up the crumbling structure of feudalism is impossible in an Iran where both the forces of production and the capitalist system of production have grown [to be contradictory]. The Shah is trying to find new bases of social support by shifting [the emphasis] from the feudalists to the capitalists.

What Is the Content of the Shah's Reformist Claims?

These reforms do not aim at basic changes in the structure and order of the society, i.e., they do not aim at transferring political leadership from the procolonialists to the anticolonialists and at eradicating feudalism and introducing a dynamic and progressive economic system. On the contrary, these claims are designed to perpetuate the privileges of the court, landowners, and capitalists, and to continue an antinational foreign and domestic policy. In other words, these insignificant pseudo-reforms are affected in order to leave intact what is basic and essential [in the old system]. Under the pretext of land reform, for instance, the Shah is trying to sell out the undesirable villages to the peasants, while leaving whole villages of superior quality in the hands of the landowners. He hopes to create by this an antirevolutionary stratum and thus save the large estates from the pending blows of revolution. He further hopes to transform landowners into capitalists by encouraging the former to buy state-owned factories and guaranteeing them 6 per cent profit. Again, the Shah wants to "improve the situation of the worker" by having him share in the profits of the industries. This scheme, which is a mechanical imitation of the [methods of] some Western capitalist countries, is designed to dull the workers' class-consciousness by creating in them a fanciful image of participation in ownership.

The insincerity of such a promise is all too obvious in a country where labor laws and workers' insurance are not enforced, where working hours sometimes reach 10-12 hours; where medieval methods of labor hiring, especially in rug weaving, are prevalent; where the workers do not belong to labor unions and have no right to strike. . . .

The *coup d'état* regime claims to decentralize the administration, allegedly so that the different provinces may develop their own economies more efficiently. But, in practice, the Shah is trying to revive the ancient satrapy system, by giving vast powers to governors who are chosen by him in the first place and who are obedient to him in every way. The purpose of a truly sincere, genuine decentralization, however, should be to give the essential rights to different peoples [i.e., ethnic groups] of the land, within the framework of an undivided and independent Iran. The *coup d'état* regime claims that it is fighting corruption and bribery, but the "great trials" of Amini's rule were designed primarily to settle political accounts among the rival groups in the ruling class. Our courts of justice, moreover, acted as legal bathhouses, out of which the dirtiest thieves of public funds emerged forever cleansed. The Shah is talking about strengthening democracy by introducing city and village councils, while at the same time he deems it within his own right to set up or dissolve not only cabinets but the two [legislative] chambers, to direct legislation, to invest powers, to command the army, to represent the government. The claims to create a modern industry and technology by means of long-term economic plans are also insincere. His five-year or seven-year plans serve the strategic goals of the imperialists by providing them with markets. These plans are not concerned with the orderly development of our own economy. Even as such, these plans are either never carried out or carried out very badly. As an example, one may indicate the dams that were built at exorbitant cost; because of major technical defects, they proved useless.[4]

These pseudo-reforms are intended to deceive the backward and gullible elements by offering them a mirage of reforms and to create hope among those people who are favorably disposed toward "quiet, gradual, and peaceful progress" without the need for an organized, active, and revolutionary struggle.

The Shah's Reformist Promises Will Not Satisfy True National Aspirations

1. The people want the government to follow a positive neutral policy by leaving CENTO, by annulling the mutual agreement with the United States, and by expelling the American advisors. The people want a radical land reform: Crown lands, state lands, and privately owned lands should be distributed among the peasants without compensation and in the shortest possible time.

The people want to industrialize the country and to introduce metallurgy but, since the colonial allies do not want this, everything ranging from needles

4. The first two plans favored large projects that needed considerable foreign currency. The third plan, introduced in 1963, tried to avoid the errors of the first two. It paid closer attention to the private sector, and its investment quota was raised almost to the level of that of the state sector.

to tractors is imported. The people want protection of customs and the domestic market, promotion of domestic products and of exports. They are acting for economizing in the export of currency, for the nationalization of oil industries, the ousting of the international oil consortium, and the establishment of chemical and petrochemical industries. The people want free activity for various political parties, truly free elections, and a chance for activity for those who have been forced by the present regime to exile themselves. . . .

2. The present administration lacks both sincerity and ability, even for the realization of these superficial reforms. The planned reforms are often superficial, erroneous, and amateurish. The present administration is not capable even of coping effectively and speedily with such small matters as earthquake and flood damages, let alone the daily increase in the cost of living, inflation, the bankruptcy of domestic industries, chronic deficits in the budget, and lack of balance between exports and imports.

3. The governmental machinery is corrupt and fully engaged in the embezzlement of public funds. It is unable to enforce laws, it discriminates in the allocation of funds to privileged individuals, and it falsifies reports and statistics. Even if the ruling class wanted, it would not be able to control this labyrinth of useless bureaucracy through the thick walls of its palaces.

4. For speedy and profound reforms, a coordinated, continuing, and useful activity is needed. And for this, the participation and productivity of the whole nation are necessary. City-dwellers and villagers alike must be inspired by enthusiasm for work and with respect and confidence in their leaders. The Shah and his administration are not forces capable of stimulating physically and psychologically the people who, in the last analysis, constitute the gold backing of any reform.

5. The ruling class and its imperialist masters are torn between their internal conflicts and intergroup rivalries, thus paralyzing each other's activities. In spite of repeated attempts by the Shah to reconcile them, intergroup provocations explode at times so intensely that they threaten the very existence of the regime itself.

6. The administration lacks the necessary financial resources. There is no doubt that Iran is potentially very rich, but actually it has grown very poor because of the age-old colonialist exploitation and social and economic retardation. In order to remedy this situation, the present regime knows only two ways: to give the oil riches to the colonialists and to contract heavy loans. The country is so poor that the government has had to spend the funds earmarked for the five-year plan to meet its budgetary deficit. Furthermore, the government has had to resort to auctioning the state factories in order to pay the compensation due to the rich landowners.

7. The speedy progress of the socialistic nations and the increasing weakness of the capitalistic ones will not allow these painfully slow changes to bear fruit. . . . The Shah said on his last trip to America, "This kingship business is only a headache for me." One must say that this "kingship business" will generate more dangerous headaches, because it is an outdated and condemned institution.

However, the present regime will not collapse by itself. The two above-mentioned methods, i.e., terror and reform, promise to help it live longer than one might expect. The only sure way of attaining our national aspirations is to overthrow the regime by a persistent and definite revolutionary struggle. The Tudeh Party of Iran and other progressive elements in the country offer "revolutionary change" as the only alternative to the Shah's "reactionary perpetuation." The urgency of our alternative becomes more evident when we realize that our country is lamentably underdeveloped due to centuries of social and technical stagnation. We are at least 100 years behind the developed societies. This situation places before the present generation of Iran a weighty and grave historical duty: to achieve the historical greatness of Iran in the shortest possible time through organized, untiring activity based on scientific and exact planning. Some of the representatives of the ruling class offer alternatives to our proposal. Mr. Matin Daftary, the leader of *Ettefaq-e-Melli* [the National Union Association], suggested that the way to reform was to bring "retiring [literally, secluded or withdrawn], competent men" to hold responsible positions. Mr. Kaviani expressed the same idea in different words in one of the recent issues of [the weekly] *Khandaniha*. Mr. Amirani [then editor of *Khandaniha*] maintained that affairs would fall into their proper courses if they were entrusted to onlookers with insight, who had gained perspective owing to their distance. The present leaders cannot see, because they are too close to the source of affairs. Some of the right-wing members of the National Front maintain that reform must be sought in an overt manner through militancy, while remaining within the limits of law, and through individuals who are not affiliated with Communism.

We believe that all these schemes for leadership are misleading and that they originate in the politically satisfied minds of those who are in no hurry and who, furthermore, do not concern themselves with the thousands of hungry, sick, and homeless people of Iran, who want the most expedient and definite change. There is only one way to basic reform in our society: concentrated fighting by the genuine aspirants for change who dare to use any means of struggle to oust imperialism, to secure political and economic independence and democracy, to defend neutralism and peace, to eradicate feudalism, and to adopt noncapitalist means of development. Our party knows both the direction and the method for such reforms. It has been appealing for a long time to the progressive elements in the country to consolidate their forces in a united front. Nevertheless, we realize that our duty extends well beyond the attempts to recruit followers for action from the existing progressive groups. Our ultimate aim is the mobilization of the absolute majority of people in cities [especially the workers] and in villages by taking utmost advantage of the revolutionary atmosphere prevailing in the society. Our party can fulfill its crucial historical tasks only by attaining the level necessary to become ideologically and structurally a "workers' party," in the fullest sense of the expression.

Index of Names

Index of Names